Political Languages

Studies of the German
Historical Institute London

GENERAL EDITOR: Andreas Gestrich

The Voice of the Citizen Consumer
A History of Market Research,
Consumer Movements, and the Political
Public Sphere
Edited by Kerstin Brückweh

The Holy Roman Empire 1495–1806
Edited by R. J. W. Evans, Michael
Schaich, and Peter H. Wilson

Unemployment and Protest
New Perspectives on Two Centuries of
Contention
Edited by Matthias Reiss and Matt Perry

Removing Peoples
Forced Removal in the Modern World
Edited by Richard Bessel and
Claudia B. Haake

**Wilhelmine Germany and
Edwardian Britain**
Essays on Cultural Affinity
Edited by Dominik Geppert and Robert
Gerwarth

The Diplomats' World
A Cultural History of Diplomacy,
1815–1914
Edited by Markus Mösslang and Torsten
Riotte

**European Aristocracies and the
Radical Right 1918–1939**
Edited by Karina Urbach

The Street as Stage
Protest Marches and Public Rallies since
the Nineteenth Century
Edited by Matthias Reiss

Monarchy and Religion
The Transformation of Royal Culture
in Eighteenth-Century Europe
Edited by Michael Schaich

**Science across the European
Empires, 1800–1950**
Edited by Benedikt Stuchtey

The Postwar Challenge
Cultural, Social, and Political Change in
Western Europe, 1945–1958
Edited by Dominik Geppert

Writing World History, 1800–2000
Edited by Benedikt Stuchtey and
Eckhardt Fuchs

**Britain and Germany in Europe,
1949–1990**
Edited by Jeremy Noakes, Peter Wende,
and Jonathan Wright

The Mechanics of Internationalism
Culture, Society, and Politics from the
1840s to the First World War
Edited by Martin H. Geyer and
Johannes Paulmann

**Private Law and Social Inequality
in the Industrial Age**
Comparing Legal Cultures in Britain,
France, Germany, and the United States
Edited by Willibald Steinmetz

**British and German Historiography,
1750–1950**
Traditions, Perceptions, and Transfers
Edited by Benedikt Stuchtey and
Peter Wende

Rethinking Leviathan
The Eighteenth-Century State in Britain
and Germany
Edited by John Brewer and
Eckhart Hellmuth

**England and Germany in the High
Middle Ages**
Edited by Alfred Haverkamp and
Hanna Vollrath

Political Languages in the Age of Extremes

EDITED BY

WILLIBALD STEINMETZ

GERMAN HISTORICAL INSTITUTE LONDON

OXFORD
UNIVERSITY PRESS

OXFORD
UNIVERSITY PRESS

Great Clarendon Street, Oxford OX2 6DP

Oxford University Press is a department of the University of Oxford.
It furthers the University's objective of excellence in research, scholarship,
and education by publishing worldwide in

Oxford New York

Auckland Cape Town Dar es Salaam Hong Kong Karachi
Kuala Lumpur Madrid Melbourne Mexico City Nairobi
New Delhi Shanghai Taipei Toronto

With offices in

Argentina Austria Brazil Chile Czech Republic France Greece
Guatemala Hungary Italy Japan Poland Portugal Singapore
South Korea Switzerland Thailand Turkey Ukraine Vietnam

Oxford is a registered trade mark of Oxford University Press
in the UK and in certain other countries

Published in the United States
by Oxford University Press Inc., New York

British Library Cataloguing in Publication Data
Data available

Library of Congress Cataloging in Publication Data
Data available

Typeset by John Saunders Design & Production
Printed in Great Britain
on acid-free paper by the
MPG Books Group, Bodmin and King's Lynn

ISBN 978–0–19–960296–4

1 3 5 7 9 10 8 6 4 2

Foreword

The idea for the present volume originated in a conference held at the German Historical Institute London in March 2004. The aim of the conference was to initiate an interdisciplinary and transnational dialogue on the complex relationship between language and politics in the short twentieth century. This period may be called an 'Age of Extremes' (Hobsbawm) in many respects, not least in the sense that fierce ideological confrontations prompted an acute awareness of the power-wielding function of words, narratives, and images. Strangely enough, historians are only just beginning to pay more attention to the political uses of language during the twentieth century, with propaganda still at the heart of their interests, whereas linguists engaged in the critical analysis of discourses and communicative practices have contributed very important work, most notably on official and private language use under National Socialism and in the postwar German-speaking societies. Bringing eminent scholars of the two disciplines together was therefore an occasion to move ahead towards a more comprehensive approach to this field of research.

One means of achieving this end has been to assemble and confront up-to-date work on totalitarian regimes (fascist Italy, Nazi Germany, the Soviet Union, the German Democratic Republic) and pluralist Western regimes (Britain, West Germany, Austria, the USA). The resulting collection of essays thus invites us to compare the ways in which leadership was presented, enemies were depicted, power was challenged, and identities were sustained through the use of language in both dictatorships and democracies.

Another step towards a comprehensive perspective has been to extend our understanding of language. Although most essays in this volume focus primarily on spoken or written language, the term 'political languages' as used in the book's title has a wider significance. Much needed attention is given here to the interplay between verbal, visual, and acoustic signs, to the narratives in which these were embedded, and to the mass media and ritualized communicative practices by which the words, images, sounds, and narratives acquired their particular meaning in a given political situation.

Finally, the comparative study of political languages in the sense described is part of a broader agenda to renew the writing of political history, an agenda which is now being pursued at various places in Germany as well as in Britain, not least at the German Historical Institute London. An essential prerequisite for this renewal of political history is to stretch the notion of the 'political' itself. The authors of this volume have agreed that the political as an object of study should no longer be limited to the spheres of government and the state, but conceived of as a continuously contested communicative space whose boundaries are constantly being redrawn. The authors' enquiries into the semantics of inclusion and exclusion, the religious dimensions of leadership, the definitions of the self and the private, and the linguistic strategies of survival in conditions of extreme oppression are only some of the most important fields in which the new, comprehensive approach to the study of language in the political sphere is being put to the test.

The German Historical Institute owes thanks to many individuals and institutions. First of all, thanks must go to the former director of the German Historical Institute, Professor Hagen Schulze, whose generous support and enthusiasm for the topic made the conference possible. Dr Matthias Reiss gave useful advice during the planning phase and helped to establish contacts. We are also grateful to those who, like Professor Ingrid Gilcher-Holtey, Professor Raphael Gross, Dr Jochen Hellbeck, Professor Lucian Hölscher, Dr Nick Stargardt, and Professor Melvin Richter, stimulated debate and chaired sessions during the conference. The difficult task of carefully revising the texts of the non-anglophone contributors was undertaken by Dr Angela Davies. In addition, Angela Davies greatly helped in editing the volume. Many thanks go to her for her untiring efforts. Critical comments by Professor Terence Ball, Professor Kathleen Canning, Professor Michael Freeden, Professor Jörn Leonhard, Dr Sandra Maß, Dr Oliver Müller, Professor Stefan Plaggenborg, and Dr Nick Stargardt were very helpful. The main credit, however, for conceiving and organizing the conference, as well as for editing the present volume, should go to Professor Willibald

Steinmetz, and I should like to take this opportunity to express my thanks to him.

Andreas Gestrich

London
February 2010

Acknowledgements

The editor would like to thank the following for permission to reproduce copyright material:

Plate 8.1 'Captain America Captures Spy Ring!' From the first issue of the Captain America series, published by Marvel Comics, March 1941. Reproduced by permission of Marvel Entertainment.

Plate 8.2 'Hang Around Girls, We Like It!' Poster designed for Walter Kidde & Co. in 1942. Division of Political History, National Museum of American History, Smithsonian Institution.

Plate 8.3 'Bugs Every Marine Should Know', by Sgt. Fred Lasswell, published in *Leatherneck* Magazine, March 1945. Courtesy of *Leatherneck Magazine*. Also reproduced in Edmund P. Russell, '"Speaking of Annihilation": Mobilizing for War against Human and Insect Enemies, 1914–1945', *Journal of American History*, 82 (1996), 1505–29.

Plate 8.4 'Who is This Man??', back cover of an anonymous pamphlet, *Hitler Doomed to Madness* (Greenwich, Conn., 1940). Image courtesy of the Holocaust Center of Northern California, San Francisco, California. Also reproduced in Francis MacDonnell, *Insidious Foes: The Axis Fifth Column and the American Home Front* (Oxford University Press: New York, 1995), 90.

Plate 8.5 'Wanted! For Murder' by Victor Keppler, 1944. US National Archives and Record Administration, Still Picture Branch (NWDNS–208–PMP–91); <http://www.archives.gov/exhibit_hall/powers_of_persuasion/hes_watching_you/images_html/wanted_for_murder.html>, accessed 12 Dec. 2004.

Plate 8.6 '… Because Somebody Talked!' by Wesley, 1943. Printed by the Government Printing Office for the US Office of War Information. US National Archives and Record Administration, Still Picture Branch (NWDNS-44-PA-227A); <http://www.archives.gov/exhibits/powers_of_persuasion/hes_watching_you/images_html/somebody_talked.html>, accessed 12 Dec. 2004.

Plate 8.7 'The Sound that Kills', US Office of War Information, 1942. From the collections of the Division of Political History, National Museum of American History, Smithsonian Institution.

Table 14.1 'Types of presupposition', reproduced by permission of Oxford University Press. From *Oxford Introduction to Language Studies: Pragmatics* by George Yule © Oxford University Press, 1996.

Fig. 14.1 'The discourse about the Waldheim Affair', reproduced by permission of Routledge. From Martin Reisigl and Ruth Wodak, *Discourse and Discrimination: The Rhetoric of Racism and Antisemitism* (London, 2001), 100.

All reasonable effort has been made to contact the holders of copyright in materials reproduced in this book. Any omissions will be rectified in future printings if notice is given to the German Historical Institute London.

Contents

List of Figures   xiii

List of Plates   xiii

List of Tables   xiii

Part I. Introduction

1. New Perspectives on the Study of Language and
   Power in the Short Twentieth Century   3
   WILLIBALD STEINMETZ

2. Politics as Linguistic Performance: Function and
   'Magic' of Communicative Practices   53
   ANGELIKA LINKE

**Part II. The Rise of the Dictators and the
Semantics of Leadership**

3. *Fascistese*: The Religious Dimensions of Political
   Language in Fascist Italy   69
   EMILIO GENTILE

4. Visualizing Political Language in the Stalin Cult:
   The Georgian Art Exhibition at the Tretyakov Gallery   83
   JUDITH DEVLIN

**Part III. Mind Your Words! Policing Linguistic
Boundaries (1920s–1940s)**

5. Revolutionary Selves: The Russian Intelligentsia
   from Old to New   105
   IGAL HALFIN

6. Faced with Death: Gestapo Interrogations and
   Clemency Pleas in High Treason Trials by the
   National Socialist *Volksgerichtshof*   151
   ISABEL RICHTER

7. Policing Tonal Boundaries: Constructing the
   Nazi/German Enemy on the Wartime BBC   169
   SIÂN NICHOLAS

8. Keep Quiet . . . But Tell!! Political Language and
   the 'Alert Citizen' in Second World War America   195
   OLAF STIEGLITZ

9. Telling the Truth: Counter-Discourses in Diaries
   under Totalitarian Regimes (Nazi Germany and
   Early GDR)   215
   HEIDRUN KÄMPER

**Part IV. The Growth of Linguistic Awareness in
the Cold War Era**

10. The Unknown and the Familiar Enemy:
    The Semantics of Anti-Communism in the USA
    and Germany, 1945–1975   245
    THOMAS MERGEL

11. Semantic Strategies of Inclusion and Exclusion in
    the German Democratic Republic (1949–1989)   275
    RALPH JESSEN

12. War over Words: The Search for a Public Language
    in West Germany   293
    MARTIN H. GEYER

13. The Return of Language: Radicalism and the British
    Historians 1960–1990   331
    GARETH STEDMAN JONES

14. Suppression of the Nazi Past, Coded Languages,
    and Discourses of Silence: Applying the
    Discourse-Historical Approach to Post-War
    Anti-Semitism in Austria   351
    RUTH WODAK

Notes on Contributors   381
Index   387

List of Figures

14.1 The discourse about the Waldheim Affair   363

List of Plates

Plates appear between pages 210 and 211

8.1 'Captain America Captures Spy Ring!'

8.2 'Hang Around Girls, We Like It!'

8.3 'Bugs Every Marine Should Know'

8.4 'Who is This Man??'

8.5 'Wanted! For Murder'

8.6 '. . . Because Somebody Talked!'

8.7 'The Sound that Kills'

List of Tables

5.1 Social position of Bolsheviks enrolled in Tomsk
academic institutions (1923)   127

5.2 Social position of Bolsheviks at Tomsk State
University (1925/6)   128

5.3 Social composition of the Leningrad State
University Party organization in 1927   133

5.4 Alterations in the social positions of Tomsk
students (1928)   135

14.1 Types of presupposition   367

PART I

Introduction

1

New Perspectives on the Study of Language and Power in the Short Twentieth Century

WILLIBALD STEINMETZ

For intellectuals who lived through all or part of the period which Eric Hobsbawm aptly called the 'Age of Extremes', or the 'Short Twentieth Century',[1] one of the most formative experiences was the realization that the political significance of certain vocabularies and communicative practices could change rapidly. Words could wield political power, but at another moment even a whisper could endanger one's life. In the Age of Extremes this was a common experience, not limited to intellectuals, and so the essays in this volume are mostly about ordinary citizens, state functionaries, propagandists, and politicians who either initiated, or tried to make sense of, marked changes in the political uses of language. Intellectuals, however, unable to get along without words, had to be even more sensitive to shifts in their meaning. Hence intellectuals will figure prominently in this book and in the following introductory remarks. While reflecting on language in its relation to political power, intellectuals not only commented upon but actually intervened in situations of verbal political warfare, sometimes directly, sometimes indirectly or in hindsight. In any case, there is much to be said for the argument that the twentieth century saw a growing reflexivity in the theory and practice of contending with language politically. Literary and academic writings on political language were instrumental to this increasing reflexivity. They informed the linguistic performances of politicians, propagandists, and citizens whose strategic uses of language, in turn, contributed to a growing linguistic awareness among intellectuals and the public at large.

[1] Eric Hobsbawm, *Age of Extremes: The Short Twentieth Century, 1914–1991* (1994; repr. London, 1995). As in Hobsbawm's book, both expressions will be used interchangeably here.

There were other trends in the Short Twentieth Century which played a more profound role than they had in earlier periods and will therefore be addressed in this book. It is important to clarify, for instance, to what extent the successive mass media revolutions actually transformed the mechanisms of political communication and to what extent the overlapping of old and new mass media altered the spoken and written language itself. Has politics really, as has been claimed, become divided into two almost separate spheres, a show business side dominated by the formats of mass media, and a secret backstage side where the important decisions are made?[2] And if so, is this a phenomenon of the post-1945 period only, supported above all by television, or is it typical of the entire twentieth century? This volume's focus on political languages, that is, various modes of using spoken, written, visual, corporeal, or other signs in political communication, leads to a sceptical view of the alleged power of mass media to 'colonize' public politics and force 'real' decisions back into some arcane space. The essays in this book suggest that politics, rather than breaking into two separate spheres, is better understood as a continuum of verbal, visual, and other communicative performances by all kinds of political actors, ruling elites, media professionals, party organizations, and individual citizens.[3] Within this continuum of symbolic utterances it is by no means predetermined that language used in a face-to-face communication may not be suitable for use in the mass media, and vice versa. Also, the notion that political decisions can somehow be isolated from the continuous flow of communication preparing them, lending words to

---

[2] The classical statement of this position is Murray Edelman, *Politics as Symbolic Action: Mass Arousal and Quiescence* (Chicago, 1971). Following this line of thought some authors argue that politics is 'colonized' by the media, especially television. See Thomas Meyer, *Mediokratie: Die Kolonisierung der Politik durch das Mediensystem* (Frankfurt, 2001). For a more differentiated view which stresses the ambivalent results of the 'interpenetration' between the media system and politics, see Werner Holly, 'Tabloidisation of Political Communication in the Public Sphere', in Ruth Wodak and Veronika Koller (eds.), *Handbook of Communication in the Public Sphere* (Berlin, 2008), 317–41, at 320.

[3] This conception of politics takes up ongoing German research on the history of the political as a communicative space; for this see Thomas Mergel, 'Überlegungen zu einer Kulturgeschichte der Politik', *Geschichte und Gesellschaft*, 28 (2002), 574–606; Ute Frevert and Heinz-Gerhard Haupt (eds.), *Neue Politikgeschichte: Perspektiven einer historischen Politikforschung* (Frankfurt, 2005); Willibald Steinmetz, 'Neue Wege einer historischen Semantik des Politischen', in id. (ed.), *'Politik': Situationen eines Wortgebrauchs im Europa der Neuzeit* (Frankfurt, 2007), 9–40. Angelika Linke argues in a similar way from a linguistic perspective in her essay in the present volume.

them, symbolizing, legitimizing, and interpreting them seems to be questionable. Decisions are subject to articulation in language and, in order to be effective, must refer to modes of communicating and means of verbalization or visualization which are familiar, or at least understandable, to those who are supposed to execute or abide by these decisions.

Another issue open to debate and central to the book's concerns is the relationship between public control of language use and the stability of political systems. At first sight, it seems obvious that the stability of twentieth-century political regimes—totalitarian or liberal, right or left—has depended to a considerable degree on their ability to set boundaries to what may be said for their citizens. Despite much evidence in favour of this notion, however, one could equally argue for the opposite view, namely, that strict policies to enforce certain usages of language resulted in ritualized forms of communication which, in the long run, impaired the regimes' capacity to learn and to handle crises. The collapse of the Soviet Union and its satellite states may in part be attributed to such a lack of communicative openness.[4] Thus pronounced governmental attempts to police the boundaries of what may be said by citizens could, sometimes, result in instability rather than stability. Shifting our perspective from governments to individuals, we come across a similar dialectical movement. There is no doubt that even under the most repressive conditions in twentieth-century dictatorships, opportunities did exist for individuals to evade or subvert the linguistic boundaries imposed upon them by censorship, the guidelines of ruling parties, or physical violence. On the other hand, when these dissenting individuals sought to evade the prescribed rules, they were forced time and again to resort to the very terms and concepts they abhorred. Hence their challenges to the dominant modes of language use were often only partially successful. The Age of Extremes provides countless examples of struggles over what could be said and done between individuals and state or party officials. Several examples of such struggles will appear in this volume, which will help to identify patterns that were typical for the respective political regimes, periods, and situations.

[4] With regard to the GDR this argument has been put most forcefully by Ralph Jessen, 'Diktatorische Herrschaft als kommunikative Praxis: Überlegungen zum Zusammenhang von "Bürokratie" und Sprachnormierung in der DDR-Geschichte', in Alf Lüdtke and Peter Becker (eds.), *Akten. Eingaben. Schaufenster. Die DDR und ihre Texte: Erkundungen zu Herrschaft und Alltag* (Berlin, 1997), 57–75.

Even at the level of purely descriptive historical semantics, the twentieth century is still under-researched compared to earlier periods. So far, the field has been dominated by studies on the history of political ideas. This book, by contrast, presents case studies that are based on source materials referring to concrete political interactions. Thus a good many of the book's essays, for example, those on the depiction of enemies, on verbal and visual modes of inclusion and exclusion, and on elements of religious rhetoric, will substantiate the claim of contemporary intellectuals that mutually exclusive 'binary opposites',[5] and quests for 'entities, absolutes, finalities',[6] were indeed typical elements of socio-political discourse in the Age of Extremes. A second volume would be necessary, one that expanded its scope beyond the time limits of this one, in order to analyse how the binary rhetoric, so prevalent in the Age of Extremes, was supplanted by another rhetoric that for lack of a better label we provisionally term a rhetoric of difference. Attentive newspaper readers can easily find evidence for the idea that the aftermath of our period has been marked by widespread demands for a 'multifarious politicization of difference'[7] and ever more intense, albeit increasingly paradoxical, struggles over the recognition of the 'other' in all kinds of social and political relations.[8] There is, however, a consecutive relationship between that new, 'postmodern' language of ubiquitous difference and the previous binary and exterminatory rhetoric of the Age of Extremes: many of those who now demand recognition as 'other' (different) do so precisely because they themselves, or their ancestors or communities, were stigmatized and victimized at some point during the Short Twentieth Century. On the other hand, the discursive strategies of the stigmatizers and victimizers from

---

[5] Hobsbawm, *Age of Extremes*, 4. For further thoughts on the use of binary opposites in history see Reinhart Koselleck, 'The Historical-Political Semantics of Asymmetric Counterconcepts', in id., *Futures Past: On the Semantics of Historical Time* (Cambridge, Mass., 1985), 159–97.

[6] Jeffrey C. Isaac, 'Critics of Totalitarianism', in Terence Ball and Richard Bellamy (eds.), *The Cambridge History of Twentieth-Century Political Thought* (Cambridge, 2003), 181–201, at 182, quoting Simone Weil, 'Words and War', *Politics*, 70 (1946).

[7] Peter Dews, 'Postmodernism: Pathologies of Modernity from Nietzsche to the Post-Structuralists', in Ball and Bellamy (eds.), *Twentieth-Century Political Thought*, 343–67, at 359, quoting William E. Connolly, *Identity/Difference: Democratic Negotiations of Political Paradox* (Ithaca, NY, 1991), at 87.

[8] Dews, 'Postmodernism', at 359–60, referring to Judith Butler and Jean Baudrillard. See also James Tully, 'Identity Politics', in Ball and Bellamy (eds.), *Twentieth-Century Political Thought*, 517–33.

the Age of Extremes are still capable of revival. This volume's final essay by Ruth Wodak on hardly concealed anti-Semitic language in the 1990s gives disquieting examples of the re-enactment of linguistic patterns which one would prefer had disappeared.

The present volume is unusual in juxtaposing studies of political languages in dictatorial and liberal regimes, Communist, National Socialist, and fascist variants of totalitarianism, and different kinds of democracies. So far, collective or single-authored works on our topic have largely remained within the boundaries of one ideological tradition or have sought to undertake comparisons between different totalitarian regimes or between different kinds of democracies.[9] This volume's structure reflects our intention to test the hypothesis that, at a certain level of abstraction, comparable patterns of political argument may be identified even across the divide between the democratic and dictatorial regimes in the Short Twentieth Century. Of course, this is not to say that the practical 'meanings', in Wittgenstein's sense, and moral results of similarly constructed arguments have not been widely different. Comparisons aim to establish differences as well as similarities. Democratic political institutions and constitutional guarantees for oppositional rights, free speech, and human dignity do, indeed, make a difference, even if authorities or groups in society are tempted to violate them. But, unless these constitutional rights are actively asserted, the differences may dwindle to nothing within a short time.

Research on the above-mentioned issues has been fairly uneven. For some areas, and especially for the comparative dimension, there is not much to begin with. The time has not yet come for a work of synthesis on political languages in the Age of Extremes, and given the amount of linguistic competence such a project would require, it is doubtful whether one single author will ever be able to produce it. That is why the contributions to this collective volume represent attempts to explore the field. Though they can present no more than case studies based on evidence from one or two countries, each of them provides new insights on

[9] An exception is Igal Halfin (ed.), *Language and Revolution: The Making of Modern Political Identities* (London, 2002), which compares constructions of Soviet subjectivity, identity, and memories with the cases not only of Nazi Germany and fascist Italy, but also republican France and post-war West Germany. See also the collection by Kirill Postoutenko (ed.), *Totalitarian Communication: Hierarchies, Codes and Messages* (Bielefeld, 2010), which also contains comparative essays including democratic regimes.

one or several of the broad questions just outlined. Taken
together, they allow for comparisons and bring us closer to formulating general hypotheses. Whether it will be possible to define
enough unifying features to render the 'Age of Extremes' a meaningful temporal unit for the historical study of language and power
may be the ultimate point on the list of unresolved questions.

Despite our fragmentary knowledge so far, the volume can
build on what earlier generations of twentieth-century intellectuals
found out about political languages. These generations were in
the advantageous, though sometimes uncomfortable, position of
learning and feeling physically what it was like when sudden shifts
and ruptures in the uses of words or modes of speech altered their
individual lives. As a first step, then, it may be illuminating to
follow a handful of exemplary European intellectuals—academics,
novelists, playwrights—in their endeavours to advance our knowledge by recalling their personal experiences of language use in
the Short Twentieth Century.

Five Testimonies on Language and Power in the Age of Extremes

References to linguistic change are easy to find in autobiographical texts, book prefaces, and literary or academic works. Most of
these references remain at the level of scattered remarks on the
contested meanings of certain lexical items in particular situations.
Some authors, however, made the analysis of entire vocabularies
over long periods of time a major concern. A case in point is
Raymond Williams (1921–88), one of the founders of cultural
studies in post-war Britain. In the introduction to his book
Keywords, he gives a lively account of how he came to develop
casual observations on linguistic change into an object of extensive
studies in historical semantics.[10] Williams begins by telling his
readers that in 1945, when he returned to Cambridge University
after being released from service in an artillery regiment, he
encountered feelings of estrangement. Things somehow were no
longer as they had been before he had had to leave Cambridge at
the end of the 1930s. Soon he found that he shared these feelings
with other academics who had just come from the war. Speaking

---

[10] Raymond Williams, *Keywords: A Vocabulary of Culture and Society* (2nd edn. London,
1983), 11–15.

to one of them, they both said, as he remembers, simultaneously: 'the fact is, they just don't speak the same language.'[11] Williams then goes on to explain how, starting from this observation, he began to explore the shifting usages of one particular English word that interested him: 'culture'. He did so, he says, from a historical as well as class-conscious and generation-conscious point of view, and he gradually extended his search to include ever larger clusters of words connected to 'culture': terms such as 'art' and 'industry', 'class' and 'democracy', 'the masses', 'society', and 'community'. These enquiries resulted in his first major book, *Culture and Society* (1956), to which his later work *Keywords*, first published in 1976, was originally conceived as an appendix.[12]

In the British academic community of the late 1950s and 1960s, when he completed most of the research for *Keywords*, a historical-semantic approach like that practised by Williams was exceptional. He had little material to rely on except the *Oxford English Dictionary*, which was weak on twentieth-century usages and disregarded spoken language, and whose tendency to favour 'orthodox' meanings, especially for 'certain sensitive social and political terms', he found unhelpful.[13] Williams, by contrast, was interested in showing how contests over meaning were always 'embedded in actual relationships' and how both meanings and relationships varied in the 'processes of social and historical change'.[14] By the standards of his time this was a fairly advanced approach, though in the practice of his lexical work Williams fell a little short of the expectations raised. He neither specified the actual relationships that he examined, nor did he provide details concerning the source materials for the contemporary usages presented in *Keywords*.[15] It is obvious that the twentieth-century parts of his dictionary articles were mainly based on what he himself had read, heard, or simply felt to be the case. In other words, he relied on his own experience without caring too much about documenting

[11] Ibid. 11. The person referred to may well have been Eric Hobsbawm. In an interview with the *New Left Review*, dating from 1977 and entitled 'Cambridge Again', Williams said: 'The first person I met again whom I knew was Eric Hobsbawm. We agreed that we were in a different world.' See Raymond Williams, *Politics and Letters: Interviews with the New Left Review* (London, 1979), at 61.   [12] Williams, *Keywords*, 14.
[13] Ibid. 18.   [14] Ibid. 22.
[15] Cf. Williams's own assessment of the shortcomings of *Keywords* in another interview with the *New Left Review*. Williams, *Politics and Letters*, 176–8. For a more thorough critique of the dictionary's epistemological failures, see Quentin Skinner, 'The Idea of a Cultural Lexicon', *Essays in Criticism*, 29/3 (July 1979), 205–24.

his evidence and elucidating its context. From the choice of entries as well as their content, it is fair to assume that for Williams, the experience which counted most and which provided the background knowledge for his semantic findings was the long tradition of class struggle in Britain. Williams was born into a Welsh working-class family and had early become a Communist. Although he began to distance himself from the Communist Party during the war years, he still considered himself to be left of the Labour party after 1945.[16] Perhaps this firm ideological conviction was why the physical experience of violence in the European wars of the mid-twentieth century was less disturbing for him than for other young academics of his generation.

It was different with the German historian Reinhart Koselleck (1923–2006) who, in the late 1950s and 1960s, laid the foundations of the discipline known as history of concepts (*Begriffsgeschichte*) in Germany and later became a leading figure in historical semantics worldwide.[17] For Koselleck, although he did not speak openly about it before the 1980s, the decisive experience which gave the impetus to his scholarly work was exposure to being killed, and the capacity to kill others, in the name of mutually exclusive ideologies during the Second World War. Only two years younger than Raymond Williams and not yet 17 when Hitler began the war, Koselleck had no chance to go to university after school, but volunteered in 1941, like his class-mates, for the *Wehrmacht*. Serving, like Williams, in an artillery regiment, he fought on the Eastern Front and was wounded shortly before his division moved into Stalingrad, thus escaping the German army's worst catastrophe of the war, only to be captured by the Red Army in May 1945 and transported via Auschwitz, then used by the Russians as an interim camp for German captives and displaced persons, to a prisoner of war camp in Kazakhstan. Koselleck was luckily released from there earlier than most of his comrades, and was

---

[16] See Williams's own account of his early years up to the 1950s. Williams, *Politics and Letters*, 21–93. For a more thorough investigation of Williams's positioning in the formation of the New Left and how this was linked to his own research agenda and British intellectual debates generally, see Gareth Stedman Jones's essay in this volume.

[17] The most comprehensive study of Koselleck's intellectual biography is Niklas Olsen, 'Beyond Utopianism and Relativism: History in the Plural in the Work of Reinhart Koselleck' (Ph.D. thesis, European University Institute Florence, 2009). For the following biographical account see in more detail ibid. at 20–3. Cf. also my obituary of Koselleck: Willibald Steinmetz, 'Nachruf auf Reinhart Koselleck (1923–2006)', *Geschichte und Gesellschaft*, 32 (2006), 412–32.

finally able to take up his studies at Heidelberg University in 1947. In the same year he went through a re-education procedure in Lower Saxony, led by a British 'democratizing' team of which no other than Eric Hobsbawm, six years his elder, of Austrian-Jewish origin and, in 1947, still a convinced Communist, was a member.[18] By that time Koselleck, not least as a result of his experiences in Russian captivity, had become a firm anti-Communist, but he had also developed a solid scepticism about extreme nationalism and, in general, all ideologies which purported to sacrifice human beings' present lives and social relations for a far removed, but allegedly better, utopian future.

His first academic work, *Kritik und Krise*, accepted as a doctoral thesis in 1954 and published in 1959,[19] was devoted to uncovering the 'pathogenesis', as he called it, of this mental habit of subjecting present political structures to a permanent moral critique by an appeal to history conceived of as a unified, teleological process. He was not the only post-war author to trace the roots of this utopian vision of history back to the eighteenth century, thereby establishing a link between twentieth-century totalitarian attitudes and the Enlightenment.[20] In doing so, he was certainly more radical than others in placing totalitarian and Western liberal ideologies on the same footing with respect to that particular point, and he has been heavily criticized for this. His personal experience of re-education in 1947 and his relationship with Carl Schmitt seem to have played a part in this overly negative view of Anglo-American liberalism.[21] More important in our context is

[18] For Hobsbawm's view of this episode see Eric Hobsbawm, *Interesting Times: A Twentieth-Century Life* (London, 2002), 179.

[19] Reinhart Koselleck, *Kritik und Krise: Ein Beitrag zur Pathogenese der bürgerlichen Welt* (Freiburg, 1959); published in English translation as *Critique and Crisis: Enlightenment and the Pathogenesis of Modern Society* (Oxford, 1988).

[20] Olsen, 'Beyond Utopianism', 46–103, provides a good interpretation of Koselleck's dissertation in its intellectual and biographical context; cf. also Jason Edwards, '*Critique and Crisis* Today: Koselleck, Enlightenment and the Concept of Politics', *Contemporary Political Theory*, 5 (2006), 428–46.

[21] Koselleck's former resentment of re-education can still be sensed in his retrospective account given on the occasion of the fiftieth anniversary of the granting of his doctorate: 'In my childhood I experienced—physically in the brawls at school—the collapse of the Weimar Republic. The liberals had disappeared. What followed in my youth was the awakening of the National Socialist movement . . . ; then, while I was a soldier, war, total bombing, multiple death; then radicalization going along with the erosion of the totalitarian system; finally collapse and Russian captivity. In the East I experienced the brutal hypocrisy of the socialist system, when I at last reached the West the hard-won success of liberal re-education which I had to work through and digest. Thus, in the condensed suc-

Koselleck's special sensitivity to the language in which the modern, teleological concept of history has been couched since the Enlightenment. While in *Kritik und Krise* he still buried his short remarks on the history of concepts such as 'history', 'revolution', 'progress', or 'crisis' in the footnotes, he elaborated on these and related concepts at book length in his own contributions to the multi-volume dictionary *Geschichtliche Grundbegriffe*, of which, from 1972 to 1997, he was the principal editor.[22] Koselleck's war experiences and his political stance against utopianism were no longer directly discernible in the research agenda which he drew up for the authors of the dictionary in the late 1960s. By this time, methodological considerations inspired by linguistics had become more prominent.[23] As the collective work on the dictionary advanced through the 1970s and 1980s, and as the debate on historical semantics and the 'linguistic turn' became increasingly internationalized during the 1990s, Koselleck developed more subtle theoretical views on the mutual dependency and co-evolution of socio-political structures on the one hand, and the semantics describing and re-enacting them on the other.[24] Still, his original interest was preserved in the structure of the dictionary *Geschichtliche Grundbegriffe* itself. By focusing on the transitional period from the late Enlightenment to the era of revolutions, reforms, and restorations up to 1850, the work as a whole lends support to Koselleck's hypothesis that the decisive semantic shifts which inaugurated our own modern age took place in the so-called *Sattelzeit*, at least in the German-speaking countries. That is why we read relatively little about how twentieth-century polit-

cession of four political regimes, there lurked each time a new utopia which, complacently interpreted the course of history as a realization of its own ideas. Utopias were concealed behind manifold masks whose common origin in the Age of Enlightenment I tried to uncover . . .' Reinhart Koselleck, 'Dankrede', in Stefan Weinfurter (ed.), *Reinhart Koselleck (1923–2006): Reden zum 50. Jahrestag seiner Promotion in Heidelberg* (Heidelberg, 2006), 33–60, at 58–9 (my own translation).

[22] Otto Brunner, Werner Conze, and Reinhart Koselleck (eds.), *Geschichtliche Grundbegriffe: Historisches Lexikon zur politischen Sprache in Deutschland*, 8 vols. (Stuttgart, 1972–97).

[23] The best summary of Koselleck's programmatic conceptual-historical approach, its advantages and shortcomings compared to Quentin Skinner's history of ideas 'in context', is Kari Palonen, *Die Entzauberung der Begriffe: Das Umschreiben der politischen Begriffe bei Quentin Skinner und Reinhart Koselleck* (Münster, 2004); for an introduction to Koselleck's conceptual history in English see Melvin Richter, *The History of Political and Social Concepts: A Critical Introduction* (New York, 1995).

[24] As can be seen e.g. in his articles collected in Reinhart Koselleck, *The Practice of Conceptual History: Timing History, Spacing Concepts* (Stanford, Calif., 2002).

ical communication actually functioned in this huge dictionary, conceived by a scholar whose initial aim had been to explain the dynamics which ultimately produced the crises and horrors of the Age of Extremes.

Both, Raymond Williams and Reinhart Koselleck, turned their attention primarily to the lexical side of language. They were interested in the histories of clusters of key terms and, in Koselleck's case, the long-term transformations of concepts evoked in people's minds by the use of such terms. Theoretically, they both knew about the importance of social and communicative 'embeddedness' for the explanation of shifts in meaning, but in practice they confined most of their studies to the diachronic level. Thus their works are instructive on the outward appearance and general direction of semantic change over long time spans, but much less so on the mechanisms that brought about, consolidated, or upset specific meanings in concrete interactions, whether in politics, philosophical discourse, or everyday communication. It is perhaps no accident that literary works—novels and plays—as well as more or less fictionalized diaries, letters, and autobiographies bring us closer to understanding the synchronic occurrence and functioning of linguistic change. Literary works and ego-documents do not need to provide general conclusions based on systematically gathered evidence, as do academic works. Novels or autobiographies by definition present the situations they describe as unique, individual cases. However, the very process of fictionalizing also implies a generalization of previous experience—first-hand or second-hand, close or remote. Although, in principle, extreme caution must be exercised when locating situations described in fictional texts to specific historical periods and interpreting these fictional situations as reformulations of what authors had themselves lived through, there are passages in literary works where readers have good reason to do just that: to attribute what is narrated to the authors' own, or their relatives' and acquaintances', personal 'spaces of experience' and 'horizons of expectation'.[25]

This is the case with one of the most extraordinary literary testimonies ever written on the Second World War, the Holocaust,

---

[25] On these concepts as categories of historical analysis see Reinhart Koselleck, '"Space of Experience" and "Horizon of Expectation": Two Historical Categories', in id., *Futures Past*, 267–88.

and life under Stalinism, the novel *Life and Fate* by the Russian author Vasily Grossman (1905–64).[26] Born in the city of Berdichev (Ukraine) into a family of intellectuals of Jewish descent, Grossman started his career as a writer in the second half of the 1930s. When war broke out he volunteered, and from August 1941 worked as a war correspondent for the army journal *Kraznaya Zvezda* (Red Star). In that capacity he took part in all stages of the Eastern war, often on the front line, from the precipitate early retreats of 1941 to the battles of Moscow and Stalingrad, the recapture of his homeland Ukraine by the Red Army, the liberation of Treblinka in 1944, and, finally, the capture of Berlin in April and May 1945. His reportages were very popular with readers and later served, with his notes, as material for *Life and Fate*.[27] By the time he started working as a war correspondent, his mother Ekaterina, who still lived in Berdichev, had already been put in a ghetto by the Germans. She was killed in September 1941, along with thousands of other Jewish women, children, and men, by the Einsatzgruppe C.[28] Grossman was only certain of this when he entered Berdichev with the Red Army.[29] The brutal death of his mother haunted him for the rest of his life. It was to her that he dedicated his novel.[30] And it was also because of his

[26] Vasily Grossman, *Life and Fate*, trans. and with an introd. by Robert Chandler (London, 1985). This English edition, unfortunately, omits a few philosophical passages which the translator deemed to be too 'sententious'. The Russian original was first published in 1980, sixteen years after the author's death, by Éditions l'Âge d'Homme in Lausanne. A new German edition (the first appeared in 1984), containing postfaces by Jochen Hellbeck and Wladimir Woinowitsch, was published in 2007 as Wassili Grossman, *Leben und Schicksal* (Berlin, 2007). For Grossman's biography see John Garrard and Carol Garrard, *The Bones of Berdichev: The Life and Fate of Vasily Grossman* (New York, 1996); see also Jürgen Zarusky, '"Freiheitliche Erinnerung": Vasilij Grossman und die europäische Erinnerung an Totalitarismus und Zweiten Weltkrieg', *Forum für osteuropäische Ideen- und Zeitgeschichte*, 10/2 (2006), 81–110. My account of Grossman's biography and the genesis of his novel is based on these publications.

[27] A selection is available in a new English edition, Antony Beevor and Luba Vinogradova (eds.), *A Writer at War: Vasily Grossman with the Red Army 1941–1945* (London, 2005).

[28] For the mass killings at Berdichev and other Ukrainian places in the autumn of 1941 see Peter Longerich, *Politik der Vernichtung: Eine Gesamtdarstellung der nationalsozialistischen Judenverfolgung* (Munich, 1998), 376–86.

[29] See Grossman's reports about the killing ground of Berdichev, in Beevor and Vinogradova (eds.), *Writer at War*, 247–61.

[30] Twenty years after her death, in 1961, he wrote her a letter in which he identified his own fate and that of his book with hers: 'I am you, dear Mama, and as long as I live, then you are alive also. When I die, you will continue to live in this book [*Life and Fate*], which I have dedicated to you and whose fate is closely tied with your fate.' Quoted from the English translation in Garrard and Garrard, *Bones of Berdichev*, 353. In the novel itself the

familial involvement in the Holocaust that after the war, Grossman, along with Ilya Ehrenburg and on behalf of the Jewish Anti-fascist Committee, set to work on the *Black Book*, which documented the murder of the Russian Jews by the Germans and their collaborators. In the climate of growing anti-Semitism and verbal obliteration of the Holocaust in post-war Stalinist Russia (in official language, the politically correct formula was to speak of 'persecutions of peaceful Soviet citizens', thereby omitting the special ordeal of the Jews), the *Black Book* was not allowed to be published, and the Committee on whose behalf it had been prepared was dissolved in 1948.[31] Grossman thus found himself silenced and pushed into an oppositional position.

To regain recognition as an author he chose the Great War of the Fatherland as the theme for an epic novel, the first part of which, *Za Pravoe Delo* (For a Just Cause), was published with some cuts in a literary journal in 1952. He soon earned serious criticism in *Pravda*, however, for not depicting the heroes of Stalingrad with due veneration and for making the physician Viktor Shtrum, a Jew, living far from the front in Kazan, the central figure instead.[32] These criticisms must be seen in the context of an anti-Jewish campaign of early 1953, aimed against Jewish doctors who were accused of plotting against Stalin. Grossman was even made to sign a letter condemning these doctors. Stalin's death on 5 March 1953 saved him from further persecution, and in the less repressive atmosphere after 1956 he became more daring while composing the second part of his book, *Life and Fate*. His hopes of publishing it were futile, however, as the KGB, informed by anxious journal editors, seized the completed manuscript in February 1961.[33] The KGB censors immediately sensed the

figure of Anna Shtrum, mother of the central figure Viktor Pavlovich Shtrum, is easily recognizable as a literary personification of the author's mother.

[31] Cf. Zarusky, 'Freiheitliche Erinnerung', 48–9. In Russia, the *Black Book* could only be published under Gorbachev. For a new English translation, see Ilya Ehrenburg and Vasily Grossman, *The Complete Black Book of Russian Jewry*, trans. and ed. David Patterson, foreword Irving Louis Horowitz, introd. Helen Segall (London, 2002); the report on the massacres at Berdichev, ibid. 12–20.

[32] No English translation of the book is available, but a German one was published in 1958, after Grossman's temporary rehabilitation, in the GDR. Vasilij Grossman, *Wende an der Wolga* (Berlin, 1958).

[33] In fact, they did not seize two manuscripts which Grossmann, with foresight, had deposited with friends, thus enabling them to have the novel published abroad many years after his death.

danger, because Grossman vividly described not only the denunciations and interrogations which put people into the Gulags, but
also Nazi concentration camps and methods of terror, including
the gas chambers. Although the differences between the two
systems come out clearly and are the topic of explicit reasoning
by characters in the novel and the author himself as narrator,[34]
even the implicit suggestion that comparisons of certain aspects
might be possible was unbearable to Soviet officials, despite
ongoing liberalization under Khrushchev. In addition, the censors
feared a repetition of the case of Boris Pasternak, whose novel
Doctor Zhivago had been a tremendous success in the West shortly
before.[35] Moreover, and most dangerously perhaps, Grossman's
style was extremely realistic, but not in the sense of Socialist
Realism. His figures were not ideal types, but appeared as individual characters who had doubts, displayed inconsistent behaviour, and moved back and forth depending on social relations and
the varying situations they had to master. Thus life under Stalin
was not painted in black and white, but in shades of grey as far as
political attitudes were concerned, and in many colours for
human characters, emotions, living conditions, and, of special
interest to us here, communicative practices.

Long passages of *Life and Fate* can be read as analyses of typical
communicative situations in Stalinist Russia and, to a lesser extent,
in the orbits of the German army, the SS, and the Gestapo.
Frequent changes of scene and switches in perspective within the
networks of figures connected by family, love, work, or the war
give the book an almost film-like quality. This allows Grossman
to avoid a one-dimensional interpretation. At key moments of the
story the author himself intervenes as commentator, but most of
the time he speaks indirectly through the utterances or inner
monologues of his figures. Slipping into their roles, he points to
the slightest details carrying political meanings: the lengthened

---

[34] See e.g. the author's quasi-academic reflections on variants of anti-Semitism.
Grossman, *Life and Fate*, 484–7. The architecture of the novel itself, the centrality of the
chapters on the gas chambers (ibid. 532–54), and the explicit statement that with the battle
of Stalingrad 'the death sentence was passed on Auschwitz, Buchenwald and the nine
hundred other German labour camps and concentration camps' (ibid. 646) are proof that
Grossman regarded the Soviet position as morally superior to that of Nazi Germany, even
though on the same pages he also stated that this was the moment at which the fate of all
those later persecuted and repressed by Stalin, including the Jews of the Anti-fascist
Committee, was decided (ibid. 646–7).

[35] Cf. Garrard and Garrard, *Bones of Berdichev*, 257–9.

pronunciation of a phrase, a sudden pause in conversation, the gentle scorn in the glance of an interlocutor who would, perhaps, turn out to be a denouncer tomorrow. Grossman thus makes clear that it was not just the choice of words, the lexical side of language, that decided one's fate, but at least as much *how* things were uttered and how they were understood by those who were present or were told about the situation later. For instance, a trivial conversation over a drink with an army commissar could take a critical turn when it came to making a toast and the person asked to do so was either too slow or overzealous in raising a glass to the health of father Stalin.[36] Everyone had to be alert all the time; army commissars themselves felt uneasy in the presence of others who gave the impression of knowing more about dealings and sayings in the inner circles of power.[37] Those who were naive enough inadvertently to touch upon a taboo topic—Stalin's son who had been captured by the Germans, for example—could make things worse by skipping to another topic even more unspeakable, such as German propaganda leaflets. Still, the mood of the interlocutors dictated whether they sank their teeth in or let the perpetrator off the hook—for that particular moment.[38] The important point, however, was that one could never be sure. Time and again Grossman allows his figures to be confronted with some sloppy remarks they had made years ago and which were brought up against them when they least expected it.[39]

One of Grossman's major themes is the yearning for unreserved, confidential communication—and the repeated destruction of its tender beginnings. The physician Viktor Shtrum, the novel's central figure, deludes himself into thinking that in the seclusion of Kazan, where he and some colleagues from his Moscow research institute have been evacuated with their families, open communication of this sort would be possible. And indeed, Shtrum and his circle of friends at Kazan are shown engaging in unheard-of conversations which reveal their disbelief in Trotsky's and Bukharin's guilt,[40] their dreams of a free press

---

[36] Grossman, *Life and Fate*, 218–19.   [37] Ibid. 105.   [38] Ibid. 107–8.

[39] The most drastic example is during the interrogation of former army commissar Krymov in the Lubyanka: 'Wherever he had been, he had left footprints behind him: a whole retinue had followed on his heels, committing his life to memory.' Ibid. 771–88, at 774.

[40] Ibid. 274–5. The English edition has an omission here; cf. the complete text in the German edition, Grossman, *Leben und Schicksal*, 336–7.

providing real 'information',[41] and their disdain for Socialist
Realism in literature.[42] One of the friends, Karimov, a Tartar,
goes so far as to say that the Soviets of the 1920s had not only
murdered many of his people, as elsewhere, but annihilated the
Tartars' entire national culture. Although he is contradicted on
this point by his Russian interlocutors (except Shtrum, the Jew),
the dispute ends peacefully.[43] Signs of anxiety, distrust, and future
mischief, however, pervade the supposedly confidential conversations in Kazan. The figure who embodies the wish to remain
faithful to the party line is Sokolov, one of Shtrum's colleagues,
who repeatedly calls for an end to such loose talk. Once the
members of the institute resume their work in Moscow, the
moments of freedom are over. Sokolov makes it unmistakeably
clear that there is no more room for confidentialities. He brushes
aside Shtrum's whispered question as to whether he had had any
news from the Kazan friends by saying loudly that he had heard
nothing. By raising his voice, he was signalling that any special
and personal relationship, independent of the state, was now out
of place.[44]

In the central parts of his novel Grossman depicts the peak of
the battle of Stalingrad as a brief flaring up of a spirit of freedom
in the people. The latter part of the novel, by contrast, is characterized by a backsliding movement. The state, its apparatus, and
its ritualized exercises of enforced conformity gradually regain
their power over the people. Grossman exemplifies this most dras-
tically in the figure of the former army commissar Krymov, lover
of Shtrum's sister-in-law Zhenya. A committed Bolshevik,
Krymov, to his great surprise, is arrested from the front line in
Stalingrad and taken to the Lubyanka in Moscow, where he is
confronted with all kinds of allegations about his past, most of
which, he has to admit, are true. He ends up physically broken
by endless interrogations and torture in the Lubyanka, where he
himself had committed ruthless acts of denunciation in the years
of the Great Terror. Compared to Krymov, Shtrum's fate is less
brutal, but he, too, ends up a broken man. Back in Moscow,
Shtrum is asked to join in the public accusations against other
members of the institute and, when he refuses, is made a scapegoat by politically more reliable colleagues. He has to fill in ques-

---

[41] Grossman, *Life and Fate*, 276.   [42] Ibid. 281–3.
[43] Ibid. 285   [44] Ibid. 569–70.

tionnaires about his past ('the same as before the war'[45]), is indirectly attacked in a wall newspaper, and is finally dismissed after
refusing to write a letter of repentance ('you know what's
expected'),[46] and to appear personally before the academic
council to perform an act of self-criticism.[47] After a while, in a
sudden reversal of fortune, he is reinstated by a mysterious phone
call from the almighty Stalin himself. But he pays for his luck by
suffering feelings of shame. Moreover, he betrays his former ideals
by signing an open letter condemning an Anglo-American campaign to rehabilitate the alleged murderers of Maxim Gorky, one
of them a Jewish doctor named Lewin. Grossman thus lets
Shtrum's story end with a rehearsal of his own experience of submission, which had consisted in signing a similar letter in 1953.

These are only a few examples showing how Grossman repre-
sents the complexity and variety of patterns of communication
under Stalin. As a novelist Grossman had greater freedom than
Williams or Koselleck to dwell on non-lexical elements, which are
hardly traceable in the sources available to historians: the body
language of facial expression and gestures; the emotions signalled
by tone, voice, pauses, or silence; the influence of the reactions
expected from interlocutors to what people said or suppressed. It
remains Grossman's achievement to have anticipated in a grand
narrative, composed in the 1950s, much of what historians of
Stalinist Russia have been able to describe in more detailed work
only since the 1990s.[48] On the other hand, we should remember
that his perspective may be atypical. Grossman was apparently
better at understanding the self-perception of free-thinking figures
like himself than that of those who aspired to be faithful to the
party line. In his novel the latter are depicted as hypocrites or
opportunists betraying their true selves. But it would certainly be
wrong to assume that ordinary Soviet citizens always clearly distinguished between a 'private' self which they cherished secretly and
their public persona which they allowed to pay lip service to what
was required from above. On the contrary, there is evidence, at

---

[45] Ibid. 576.   [46] Ibid. 671.

[47] On the rituals of repentance and self-criticism see Lorenz Erren, *'Selbstkritik' und
Schuldbekenntnis: Kommunikation und Herrschaft unter Stalin (1917–1953)* (Munich, 2008).

[48] See e.g. Orlando Figes, *The Whisperers: Private Life in Stalin's Russia* (London, 2007);
Sheila Fitzpatrick, *Everyday Stalinism. Ordinary Life in Extraordinary Times: Soviet Russia in the
1930s* (Oxford, 1999); ead., *Tear off the Masks: Identity and Imposture in Twentieth-Century Russia*
(Princeton, 2005).

least for the period up to the war, that many citizens voluntarily applied to themselves languages supplied by the regime to describe a specific form of Soviet subjectivity in which the private/public dichotomy, typical of bourgeois liberal thinking, was toned down.[49]

Although it gives voice to multiple perspectives, Grossman's epic novel has blind spots. One of them is gender related. The novel's central figures are all male. Most of what happens is described from their point of view, and almost all the communication that takes place is between males. There are only a few scenes in which female figures move to centre stage and offer the reader any potential for identification, but what they do and say is related to children, husbands, or lovers and reflects a position of vulnerability. Anna Shtrum writing her last letter from the Ukrainian ghetto to her son Viktor;[50] the army surgeon Sofia Levinton adopting a small boy, David, and protecting him while they are both taken to the gas chambers;[51] Zhenya, Shtrum's sister-in-law, trying to get through the visitors' office to her lover Krymov in the Lubyanka and experiencing the humiliation of imploring petty officials;[52] Marya Ivanovna, Sokolov's wife, who feels attracted to Shtrum and yet stays with her husband:[53] none of them is described as attaining a position powerful enough to challenge male superiority—physical, institutionalized, or discursive. It could be argued that this is an adequate reflection of what public and private communication was like for women under the conditions prevalent in an age of war, civil war, and genocide. The Age of Extremes—a male-dominated discursive universe?

More differentiated views on this issue are possible. They are provided, for example, by the literary scholar Ruth Klüger in her autobiographical account of her youth. The German edition was first published in 1992 under the title *weiter leben*.[54] The account

---

[49] Most pronounced in this direction is Jochen Hellbeck, *Revolution on my Mind: Writing a Diary under Stalin* (Cambridge, Mass., 2006); see also Igal Halfin, *Terror in my Soul: Communist Autobiographies on Trial* (Cambridge, Mass., 2003).

[50] Grossman, *Life and Fate*, 80–93.   [51] Ibid. 541–54.

[52] Ibid. 746–52.   [53] Ibid. 706–8.

[54] Ruth Klüger, *weiter leben: Eine Jugend* (Göttingen, 1992). I use the eleventh edition (Munich, 2003). Literally translated, the main title means 'staying alive', or 'living on'. The first English-language edition is *Still Alive: A Holocaust Girlhood Remembered*, foreword by Lore Segal (New York, 2001). In the UK this translation was published under a different title: Ruth Kluger, *Landscapes of Memory: A Holocaust Girlhood Remembered* (London, 2003). The English-language editions differ from the German in many respects. I have used (and when necessary translated) the German version where this is the case.

encompasses the period from her Vienna childhood in the 1930s to her difficult acclimatization in America of the late 1940s and early 1950s. The book is replete with observations on language use in gendered power relations. Assuming a decidedly feminist stance, Klüger describes how she developed communicative competence and asserted a language of her own in adverse surroundings where the boundaries of what could be said were almost always set by men, though often enforced by women, in Klüger's youth above all by her mother. The very first episodes depict the young girl's desire to know; her tenacity in asking forbidden questions about relatives who had disappeared in concentration camps; her obstinate habit of openly reciting ballads by the German poets Schiller and Uhland in the street against the wish of her great-aunt, who expected a Jewish girl to take care not to make herself conspicuous and provoke 'rishes' (anti-Semitism);[55] and her contempt for her teacher in the Jewish school who, although himself a Jew, had rebuked unruly children by saying that they were behaving as if they were in a 'Judenschule'.[56] From early childhood, then, Klüger's rebellion, as she presents it retrospectively, was directed against female as well as Jewish self-stereotyping and self-abasement. She views these typical forms of communicative behaviour as having stiffened the hostile attitudes they were meant to soften. If the book has a political message, it is the insight that an exclusionary or derogatory ideology can never be countered unless one avoids reproducing its key concepts and manners of speech.

Klüger's autobiographical narrative is frequently interspersed with reflections on her efforts to find effective counter-discourses against misogynistic and anti-Semitic attitudes. In the first of these reflections she interprets the very act of publishing her life story as an act of resistance to the occupation of her own past, and that of all other women, by male memories: 'Wars, and hence the memories of wars, are owned by the male of the species. And fascism is a decidedly male property, whether you were for or against it. Besides, women have no past, or aren't supposed to have one. A man can have an interesting past, a woman only an indecent one. And my stories aren't even sexy.'[57] In another reflection Klüger

---

[55] Kluger, *Landscapes*, 10. The English edition does not mention the names of the poets whose works she recited; cf. Klüger, *weiter leben*, 13.

[56] Kluger, *Landscapes*, 14.   [57] Ibid. 7.

deplores that the Jewish religion still does not permit her, a woman, to say the traditional kaddish, the prayer for the dead, and thus deprives her of coping in a religious way with her father's death in the gas chambers.[58] Hence she defends her writing of poems as a kind of substitute. For her, the poems she has composed in remembrance of her father are a 'home-made kaddish', that is, a self-invented communicative practice to mourn her father. At the same time she concedes that poems with their rhythms and rhymes are a way of veiling the 'crunching rage' that should be felt and expressed when dealing with Nazi ghettos and extermination camps.[59] Already as a child, Klüger tells us, she resented that her male relatives prevented her from expressing Jewish religiosity. Her cousin insisting on the youngest male's privilege of asking the ritual question at the seder evening;[60] her great-uncle taking away the Bible as she was about to read the story of Ruth:[61] experiences like these forced her early on to look for non-religious languages as an alternative means for forming her own personality. At a young age it was above all the literary language of Goethe and Schiller that served this purpose. But even the propaganda of the Nazi paper *Der Stürmer* and anti-Semitic films such as *Jud Süß* helped her, she says, to fortify herself in her attempts to resist the ruling ideology.[62]

She continued her education in Theresienstadt, where she was detained from September 1942 to May 1944. Of course, she hated Theresienstadt, which she compares to an 'ant heap under destructive feet', 'a mudhole, a cesspool, a sty where you couldn't stretch without touching someone'.[63] But on the other hand, she 'in a way' loved it too for what, despite the chaos produced by the Germans, the thousands of sharp-minded, ever (self-)critical, and well-organized Jews had made out of it—a place where she could do what the Germans wanted Jews not to do: read books, discuss literature, listen to lectures by Leo Baeck, and enthusiastically applaud the freedom-loving verses in Schiller's plays performed

---

[58] Kluger, *Landscapes*, 24.

[59] Klüger, *weiter leben*, 38. Here the German edition differs from the English text. In the latter she speaks only of 'a kind of exorcism'; her 'rage' is not mentioned, and the poems themselves are not quoted; see Kluger, *Landscapes*, 35–6. Moreover, between the publication of the first German text (1992) and the English translation she learned that her father had most probably not died in the gas chambers, but in a different, 'and perhaps a slightly lesser, nightmare' (ibid. 37).

[60] Ibid. 43–4.
[61] Ibid. 50–1.
[62] Ibid. 51–2.
[63] Ibid. 98–9.

by Jewish actors and actresses.[64] She also kept her habit of reciting poems, a habit which she continued while at Auschwitz-Birkenau. There, reciting ballads was one strategy for standing through the endless roll calls, musters, and inspections. The rhythm of the ballads helped her to structure and, literally, kill the time.[65] Klüger admits, however, that only a lucky coincidence, and neither poems nor her own quick-wittedness, saved her from the systematic dehumanization and denial of the right to live which began with the 'bullying noise' with which the SS men shouted their 'raus, raus' on the ramp,[66] and ended by being burnt in the chimney overlooking the whole place. She was saved from this by a well-meaning young clerk, herself a prisoner, who whispered the decisive words in her ear while she stood in the queue, waiting to be 'selected' for a work camp by an SS man: 'Tell him you are fifteen.'[67] Once in the work camp of Christianstadt, poems again played a part in her survival strategy, but this time they were composed by herself: two poems on a morning in Auschwitz, one ending with a sunrise symbolizing hope, the other with the chimney symbolizing complete annihilation.[68] Interpreting her own poems in one of her interspersed reflections, Klüger strongly rejects the notion, popularized by Adorno and others, that one should (or could) not write poems after and about Auschwitz. In her situation as a child in the camps, she claims, the act of composing and reciting these poems was a first 'therapeutic effort' to counter absurdity and destruction by creating a whole, at least in metrical language. And she also rejects the opposite position, popular among literary critics, that only hermetic lyrics in the style of Paul Celan's *Todesfuge* were appropriate when contending with the Holocaust.[69]

Generally, Klüger adopts a critical position towards all those who, after the war, wanted to prescribe, in one way or the other, how she should come to terms with her memories. Here again,

---

[64] Ibid. 94–8. The Schiller episode is not mentioned in the English edition; for this cf. Klüger, *weiter leben*, 102.

[65] Ibid. 123–4. The English edition does not mention ballads specifically and describes the use of poetry in much more general terms: 'Poetry wasn't connected with the outside, the real, world. Its value lay in the comfort it provided, in that profound consolation that could fill the mind when a malevolent environment tried to suck it dry.' Kluger, *Landscapes*, 116–17.   [66] Ibid. 108.   [67] Ibid. 125–6.

[68] Klüger, *weiter leben*, 124–6. Only the poem called 'The Chimney' is briefly mentioned in the English edition; Kluger, *Landscapes*, 152.

[69] Klüger, *weiter leben*, 126–8. This reflection has been omitted in the English edition.

Klüger presents herself as someone who struggled consistently against conventional phraseologies and always insisted on her right to find languages of her own. Against the Germans she was in contact with while staying in Bavaria immediately after the war, or met later on, she insisted on her right to speak openly and in unmistakable terms about her experiences. She neither let them get away with attempts to suppress their own past and that of the victims, nor did she tolerate euphemisms or comparisons setting off the calamities endured by German civilians or soldiers against the fate of the Jews; nor did she give in to silencing herself just out of politeness to spare them uneasy feelings.[70] She was equally critical of her elderly Austrian-Jewish relatives whom she met when she arrived in New York in 1947. Their habit of unconditionally approving everything American appeared to her, at that time still only a 16-year-old girl, like a repetition of the Jewish self-abasement she had known from her Vienna childhood. And when her aunt told her that she had to 'erase' from her memory 'everything that happened in Europe' and wipe it off 'like chalk from a blackboard', she protested vehemently and broke off contact.[71] A psychotherapist whom she consulted several times during her first year in New York evoked a similar response because he wanted to persuade her that her problems had nothing at all to do with what she had gone through in the concentration camps. She wanted to speak about her episodes of feeling worthless compared to those victims who had died, but this man ignored everything which, for her, made up her identity and thus denied her the right to exist.[72]

Finally, Klüger also criticizes, though with more sympathy, certain fixed ideas she found among the mostly younger Germans she had discussions with while staying in Göttingen in the early 1990s. Here it was the idea that the uniqueness of the Holocaust makes any kind of comparison impossible and illegitimate which

---

[70] Ibid. 72, 85–6, 89, 110–11, 142, 158–9, 215–20. As Klüger addressed these remarks to her German readers in particular, most have been either omitted or changed significantly in the English edition. Remarks similar to those in *weiter leben* can be found at Kluger, *Landscapes*, 69–70 (on German students who denounce today's Jews for their dealings with the Arabs); 80–1 (on Gisela who claimed that Theresienstadt wasn't that bad); 88 (on Gisela comparing her mother's fate with that of Ruth's mother); 149 (on Germans who had 'employed' Polish forced labourers); 191–2 (on Germans unwilling to acknowledge their crimes); 197–8 (on her German teachers in Bavaria and their 'Nazi-bred contempt for women'); 203–7 (on her complicated discussions with the German writer Martin Walser, whom she befriended while at school in Bavaria).

[71] Ibid. 215–19, quotations at 219.   [72] Ibid. 229–38.

raised her concerns. If that were really the case, she argued, we would end up as 'isolated monads', no longer able to communicate at all or to build 'bridges' of understanding between personal experiences which are, by definition, unique.[73] According to Klüger, not the act of comparison as such is illegitimate, but only comparing with the intention to equalize everything, to wipe out differences, to deflect attention from one's own guilt, to deny others their unique experiences, to silence them.

The course of Klüger's life during the worst decades of the Short Twentieth Century was certainly unique, as was her way of verbalizing what had happened to her and how she reacted to it. On the other hand, she also describes patterns of communication which are repeatable. With respect to our interest in political languages, her most important insights concern the limits, but also the opportunities, of the powerless—children, women, minorities, oppositions—to challenge the concepts and phraseologies imposed by the powerful and validated by the opportunists. In her case there were those who did not dare to cross the linguistic boundaries, or even confirmed them by self-abasement and self-stereotyping. But she also has many stories to tell about successful emancipation, her own in the first place, from those boundaries of the speakable. The words and ideologies she opposed were specific, namely, German anti-Semitism combined with misogyny in various shapes, as were her methods of countering both, for instance, by composing and reciting poems. But there is no reason to assume that the communicative mechanisms as such, the movement either to strengthen prescribed languages by repeating them, or to upset them by inventing new ones, are specific to Klüger's particular space of experience, or to the Age of Extremes in general.

What may be typical of the Age of Extremes is a growing awareness of these communicative mechanisms in political thought and practice. At a theoretical level, we might turn to Antonio Gramsci's *Prison Notebooks*, written between 1929 and

[73] Ibid. 69: 'We would be condemned to be isolated monads if we didn't compare and generalize, for comparisons are the bridges from one unique life to another.' Cf. also ibid. 70: 'Don't I often insist that I learned something in the camps about what happens to us in extreme situations, which was good to know later on and was usable precisely because I don't reject all comparisons?' Further reflections on comparisons along similar lines, ibid. 106–7 ('fear of death in cramped quarters' offering a 'bridge to understanding the kind of transport I have been describing'); 163–4 (experience of famine in common with Germans of her generation: 'Comparisons arise spontaneously when we remember those last months of the war, and they are not only differences').

1935, for an early and as yet incoherent conceptualization of the ways in which language was involved in movements upholding or upsetting 'hegemony'.[74] However, it is only in the second half of the twentieth century that more explicit examples can be found of this line of thought being put into practice beyond individual cases, that is, at the level of the political. The main reason for this is probably that to challenge ruling ideologies by verbal means was simply not enough to topple the brutal force of the fascist, National Socialist, or Stalinist regimes of the 1930s and 1940s. Only their eradication in 1944–5, or softening after 1956, made it possible to think of overthrowing an entire political regime by a conscious strategy of redefining the rulers' concepts or replacing them with new ones.

A public intellectual whose writings and career demonstrate this opening-up of opportunities in 'post-totalitarian' societies is the Czech playwright and civil rights activist Václav Havel who, in the course of the 1989 revolution, became president of the Czechoslovak Republic. The term 'post-totalitarian' was coined by Havel himself in the dismal decade after the crushing of the Prague Spring of 1968. He used the term to define a system which no longer relied on crude terror, mass executions, concentration camps, or Gulags, but primarily on the compliance of its own cit-izens.[75] The citizens complied, he argued, out of a mixture of res-ignation, fear of informers who would get them into trouble, and a certain indolence caused by their wish to protect the little com-forts they had secured in their 'foxhole of purely material exis-tence'.[76] In public, he said, they adopted a 'principle of outward adaptation' and 'dissimulation' resulting in the 'routine perform-ance' of ideological slogans and 'hypocrisy as the main form of communication with society'.[77] No doubt, outward order and

---

[74] The connections between Gramsci's reflections on language and political change are explored by Peter Ives, *Language and Hegemony in Gramsci* (London, 2004). According to Ives, Gramsci used reflections on linguistic change primarily as a metaphor for what happened, or should happen, in the political terrain, rather than explicitly theorizing on contests over words and concepts as a determining factor in power relations. Nonetheless, the impor-tance of the workers' 'verbal conception' of the world for the outcome of their political struggles is stressed by Gramsci in the context of his 'philosophy of praxis'. Cf. Quintin Hoare and Geoffey Nowell Smith (eds.), *Selections from the Prison Notebooks of Antonio Gramsci* (London, 1971), 333.

[75] Václav Havel, 'The Power of the Powerless' (1978–9), in id., *Open Letters: Selected Writings 1965–1990*, sel. and ed. Paul Wilson (New York, 1991), 125–214, at 131–45.

[76] Václav Havel, '"Dear Dr. Husák"' (1975), in id., *Open Letters*, 50–83, at 62.

[77] Ibid. 57–8, 62.

quiet were thus established, but individuals paid for it by a 'permanent humiliation of their human dignity',[78] and the system as a whole was brought close to 'entropy' because of the ensuing 'distrust of all variety' and 'aversion to everything unknown'.[79]

Havel had reached this diagnosis as early as the mid-1960s when, in the somewhat more liberal atmosphere, he worked as a dramatic adviser at the Theatre on the Balustrade in Prague. In a speech delivered to the Union of Czechoslovak Writers in 1965 he stringently dissected the communicative patterns which had caused the system's intellectual immobility and made it incapable of coping with reality effectively. Three mechanisms in particular, he suggested, brought about what he then called 'evasive thinking', that is, 'a way of thinking that turns away from the core of the matter to something else'.[80] The first was the use of 'magic words' which either deflected criticism of bad conditions, as when a fallen window sill in a housing estate was called a 'local matter', or seemed to suggest that the means to handle such negative conditions, in this case 'socialist maintenance by the tenants', were a necessary stage in the development of socialism.[81] The second was what he called 'false contextualization', which placed specific grievances, such as rotting buildings, into ever wider contexts until one was made to believe that the buildings have to rot because otherwise 'we would have long ago been involved in World War Three' and the 'prospects of mankind' would be endangered.[82] The third was 'dialectical metaphysics', a form of reasoning which dissolved concrete realities in 'vacuous verbal balancing acts' such as 'in a certain sense yes, but in another sense no', 'we must not, on the one hand, overestimate, nor, on the other hand, should we underestimate', and so on.[83] Anyone who has had any experience of language use in the Eastern bloc countries, whether Czechoslovakia, the German Democratic Republic, or the Soviet Union itself, could cite many similar examples of these typical phraseologies. As early as the mid-1960s, Havel had warned that their conventionalized use would result in a 'ritualization of language', and that language itself would thereby be deprived of its 'most essential importance'.[84]

---

[78] Ibid. 78.　　　　　　　　　　　　　　　　　[79] Ibid. 71.
[80] Václav Havel, 'On Evasive Thinking' (1965), in id., *Open Letters*, 10–24, at 15.
[81] Ibid. 12.　　　　　　　　　　　　　　　　　[82] Ibid. 13.
[83] Ibid. 14.　　　　　　　　　　　　　　　　　[84] Ibid. 12.

In the 1965 speech to his fellow writers Havel was still optimistic that literature, if conceived as an 'autonomous form of knowledge', could serve as an antidote to ritualization within the political system.[85] His attitude became bitter in 1978–9, ten years after the end of the Prague Spring, when he wrote his famous manifesto *The Power of the Powerless* for a Polish–Czechoslovak collective volume on freedom and power. The ossification of the regime and the language mechanisms which upheld it were now such that change through official politics seemed hopeless. Ritualized communication had resulted in an anonymization of power and created a 'social auto-totality'.[86] The only way to challenge it was to deploy linguistic and symbolic counter-strategies in the pre-political sphere of civil society, speech acts such as Charter 77, which would then act as a 'bacteriological weapon'.[87] Havel encouraged his Polish and Czechoslovak friends to think of such seemingly minimal matters as 'real politics', in contradistinction to 'political work in the traditional sense'.[88] His manifesto thus not only advocated a change in oppositional strategies, but also aimed to redefine key political concepts, in this case the concept of the 'political' itself. For him, the redefinition of old terms and the search for unconventional ones was an essential part of the new strategy. The opposition movements had to learn not to reproduce and thereby stabilize any of the regime's phraseology. Havel extended his self-critical remarks on the uncritical use of concepts to Western journalists who, like the Eastern opposition movements themselves, routinely spoke of 'dissidents'. This was a term which, in his view, created false associations in suggesting that the opposition consisted of merely a handful of prominent troublemakers, eager to promote their own publicity, isolated from the bulk of the citizens, and therefore rightly ignored by the regime.[89] Alternative terms such as 'small-scale work', 'citizens' initiatives', 'dissent', or 'defense' were much more likely, he said, to render what the opposition was actually doing, and better expressed public support for, and the legitimacy, of its acts.[90] By

---

[85] Ibid. 24. A similar view on the political function of literature can be found in Hans Magnus Enzensberger's writings in West Germany around 1968; see Henning Marmulla, 'Poesie, Politik und das Politische in der literarischen Sprache der 1960er Jahre: Das Beispiel Hans Magnus Enzensberger', in Steinmetz (ed.), *'Politik'*, 479–97.

[86] Havel, 'Power of the Powerless', 143.

[87] Ibid. 149.

[88] Ibid. 152 and 159.

[89] Ibid. 167–71 and 174–5.

[90] Ibid. 175–7 and 180.

such attempts to redefine things and build up corresponding 'parallel structures', Havel hoped to initiate a 'creeping process' that would, in the end, erode the post-totalitarian systems.[91]

It is remarkable to what extent Havel's ideas on how to fight established regimes resembled similar aspirations articulated at almost the same time by West European and American 'new' social movements and emerging 'green' political parties. Like Havel they favoured bottom-up symbolic actions and created alternative political terms. Could this similarity be interpreted as a sign of convergence between Eastern and Western civil societies in the late 1970s and 1980s, despite persistent ideological confrontations and Cold War attitudes on the surface of official power politics? Havel himself obviously believed in such a convergence, even at the level of official politics. He warned his Western readers that parliamentary democracies were not immune to the kind of acquiescent ritualism in language and behaviour that he had described for the Eastern bloc. According to him, post-totalitarianism was 'merely an extreme version of the global automatism of technological civilization'.[92] These statements read like an echo of what leftist Western prophets such as Herbert Marcuse had claimed more than a decade earlier. As early as 1964 Marcuse, in his *One-Dimensional Man*, had lamented the 'authoritarian ritualization of discourse' and its spread across 'democratic and non-democratic, capitalist and non-capitalist countries'.[93] He also blamed technological rationality for this one-dimensionality. And, like Havel in the 1960s, Marcuse worried about the inability of the 'libertarian communist opposition' to escape that ritualization.[94]

Although the two critics, Marcuse and Havel, may not have had much in common, they described the ways in which ritualized speech on both sides of the ideological divide blocked the articulation of truth in almost identical terms. For the same reason they also shared a deep distrust of the magic of abstract words, even if apparently well intentioned. When Havel was awarded the prestigious Peace Prize of the German Booksellers Association, only weeks before the 'velvet revolution' of December 1989 in Czechoslovakia brought him to power, he made his distrust of

---

[91] Ibid. 192 ('parallel structures', an expression quoted here from Václav Benda) and 201 ('creeping process').   [92] Ibid. 207.

[93] Herbert Marcuse, *One-Dimensional Man: Studies in the Ideology of Advanced Industrial Society* (London, 1964), 101–2.   [94] Ibid. 102.

promising words the keynote of his acceptance speech. 'Reform', 'peace', Willy Brandt's 'Ostpolitik', even Gorbachev's 'perestroika' were all, in his view, in danger of becoming 'arrogant words' and should be rejected.[95] Perhaps in this case Havel's scepticism about magic words was leading him a step too far. There was probably no other single word which did more to end the Age of Extremes, and, along with it, the post-totalitarian systems Havel had fought against for decades, than 'perestroika'. He was right to point to his experience that the use of abstract magic words may end up in delusions, but in this case he missed the fact that such words may also be invested with hopes that make them instrumental in overcoming repressive regimes.

Analysing Political Language Historically: Conception of the Volume

Our survey of five intellectuals' testimonies on language and power in the Age of Extremes has brought to light a wealth of observations, hardly reducible to a coherent narrative and even more difficult to condense into a single research agenda. A few conclusions, however, may be drawn. Most importantly, there are good arguments suggesting that to compare patterns of language use and how they functioned in the antagonistic political systems of the twentieth century, fascist or Communist, democratic or post-totalitarian, is a sensible way of approaching our subject and should not be rejected out of hand as illegitimate. The experiences and reflections of our five witnesses have shown that, in this respect, the Age of Extremes is indeed a meaningful unit of analysis. Of course, as Ruth Klüger has stressed, such comparisons are not about playing down the essential differences in the regimes' ideologies, institutions, or propensity to violence.[96] But what they can do is to draw attention to the repetitive features of certain communicative practices which occur when people interact in situations of extreme power differentials. Probably none of these repetitive features is unique to the twentieth century. It could be

---

[95] Václav Havel, 'A Word about Words' (1989), in id., *Open Letters*, 377–89, at 389. The German version of this speech was read, *in absentia*, at the Frankfurt Book Fair on 15 Oct. 1989.

[96] See also Ruth Wodak's critical remarks on comparisons which use false generalizations, equalize victimhood, de-historicize or de-contextualize the objects compared, and thereby serve to deny one's own guilt or shift it onto others, in her essay in this volume.

argued, however, that the political upheavals of this century have done much to make people more aware of their incisiveness. Raymond Williams's realization that the meanings of keywords are contestable and dependent on social class; Reinhart Koselleck's insight that the basic concepts of our modern political and intellectual life not only indicate underlying structural changes in history, but have also been powerful agents within processes of structure formation; Vasily Grossman's numerous examples of the importance of body language, subtle undertones, and sudden silences in creating an oppressive atmosphere in which nobody dares to speak out; Ruth Klüger's insistence that racial or gender stereotypes can only be counteracted by finding a language of one's own; and, finally, Václav Havel's informed comments on how to avoid 'evasive thinking', ritualized phraseologies, and abstract magic words: none of these findings could have been formulated so strikingly without their author's very personal, and often physical experiences in the Age of Extremes. Yet it is the repeatability of the situations referred to, and their comparability across national and ideological borders, which enables us to transform our authors' insights, and the terminologies they used to describe them, into valuable tools of analysis.

Moreover, the works of at least two of our exemplary intellectuals, Williams and Koselleck, demonstrate that in the course of the twentieth century, and increasingly so since the 1960s, the political significance of language has become a subject of wide-ranging academic studies. These late twentieth- and early twenty-first-century enquiries into political language are no longer confined to the domains of classical rhetoric and lexical semantics which dominated the field almost exclusively into the early twentieth century.[97] Equal attention is now being paid to the political relevance of patterns of argument, narratives, images, metaphors, rituals, symbols, and other discursive forms. Like classical rhetoric, however, these more recent enquiries into political language often have repercussions for, or are adaptable to, practical purposes.

---

[97] Recent scholars of rhetoric extend the scope of their enquiries beyond the classical figures and genres of rhetoric into modern and contemporary forms of language use which other scholars would deal with under different labels, such as discourse analysis or historical semantics. For a pronounced statement in favour of new directions in the study of rhetoric see Nancy S. Struever, *Rhetoric, Modality, Modernity* (Chicago, 2009). Impressive outcomes of this broadening of scope are the following massive volumes: Gert Ueding (ed.), *Historisches Wörterbuch der Rhetorik*, 9 vols. (Tübingen, 1992–2009).

Hence they cannot be seen in isolation from the phenomena they observe, but feed back into them in a circular movement. The scientization and politicization of language studies is itself a distinctive feature of the Age of Extremes.[98]

Within this field there is probably no better example of the co-evolution and mutual reinforcing of research and practice than propaganda studies.[99] Triggered by the First World War and becoming more systematic in the following decades, the scientific analysis of propaganda uncovered a broad range of mass-persuasion techniques which had been used by the belligerent powers to support the war effort.[100] There was a consensus, particularly in defeated Germany, but much less so in Britain, that propaganda had a decisive role in the Allied victory by destroying the morale of the German home front.[101] Hence propaganda was mystified as a most powerful weapon, particularly by leading propagandists of extremist movements of the left and the right, who vied for control over mass audiences.[102] In Britain, by contrast, during the

[98] The interplay between academic language studies and practical politics is an important though somewhat neglected aspect of the general twentieth-century process of the 'scientization of the social' described by Lutz Raphael in 'Die Verwissenschaftlichung des Sozialen als methodische und konzeptionelle Herausforderung für eine Sozialgeschichte des 20. Jahrhunderts', *Geschichte und Gesellschaft*, 22 (1996), 165–93.

[99] An excellent historical overview of propaganda techniques which includes outlooks on their scientization in the twentieth century is Philip M. Taylor, *Munitions of the Mind: A History of Propaganda from the Ancient World to the Present Day* (3rd edn. Manchester, 2003). Also useful are Bertrand Taithe and Tim Thornton (eds.), *Propaganda: Political Rhetoric and Identity 1300–2000* (London, 1999); and Ute Daniel and Wolfram Siemann (eds.), *Propaganda: Meinungskampf, Verführung und politische Sinnstiftung 1789–1989* (Frankfurt, 1994).

[100] For the impact of the war generally see Taylor, *Munitions*, at 190–7. A pioneering study was Harold D. Lasswell, *Propaganda Techniques in World War* (London, 1927); on Lasswell and the development of British and American propaganda studies from the 1920s to the 1940s see James Farr, 'The New Science of Politics', in Ball and Bellamy (eds.), *Twentieth-Century Political Thought*, 431–45, at 432–41. Attempts by the British government to improve propaganda during the war itself are discussed in Philip M. Taylor, *British Propaganda in the Twentieth Century: Selling Democracy* (Edinburgh, 1999), at 1–62; see also M. L. Sanders and Philip M. Taylor, *British Propaganda during the First World War* (Manchester, 1982). French scholars and authorities tended to construct an antinomy between propaganda and democracy; see Didier Georgakakis, *La République contre la propagande: aux origines perdues de la communication d'État en France, 1917–1940* (Paris, 2004), at 105–53. On the other hand, the Bolsheviks were quite effective in observing their own propaganda efforts and learning from early mistakes; see Peter Kenez, *The Birth of the Propaganda State: Soviet Methods and Mass Mobilization, 1917–29* (Cambridge, 1985).

[101] Hitler's own views on this issue reflect mainstream German (right-wing) opinion in the 1920s and 1930s. See Adolf Hitler, *Mein Kampf* (563rd edn. Munich, 1941), at 193, 198–9, 533–4; id., *My Struggle* (Cheap edn. London, 1935; repr. London, 1987), at 80–4, 88, 190–1.

[102] A Communist answer, written in exile, to Hitler's and Goebbels's glorification of their own propaganda was Willi Münzenberg, *Propaganda als Waffe* (Paris, 1937).

1920s and 1930s, original pride gave way to critical voices and even shame because the 'atrocity propaganda' of the First World War was increasingly believed to have gone too far.[103] As the term 'propaganda' was often associated with political extremism, Western liberals in general became more reluctant during the inter-war period to adopt it for their own public communication policies; they preferred the term 'information'. Thus in France, what had been the Ministry of Propaganda under Léon Blum's popular front government was renamed 'commissariat de l'information' under Daladier; Franklin D. Roosevelt chose to call the agency which coordinated US propaganda efforts the Office of War Information;[104] and the British, too, called their authority responsible for supervising and instructing the BBC and other propaganda agencies the Ministry of Information.[105]

From the early 1930s on, the radio, as a new medium, held a particular fascination for scholars and practitioners of propaganda. Unlike any other medium, it was capable of reaching listeners collectively as well as individually in their homes. At the same time, the radio could create communities of simultaneous experience within nations and even across national borders. Moreover, as an oral medium, its appeal went beyond the literate classes to include the whole population, even children. These features made broadcasting particularly attractive for totalitarian regimes.[106] Goebbels's apparent success in using broadcasts to mobilize German public

Münzenberg, chief propagandist of the KPD and a member of the Reichstag until 1933, had been the leading figure of a media empire comprising several Communist newspapers and two 'proletarian' film production companies during the Weimar Republic. Another important figure in this context was Serge Chakotin. His attempts in the early 1930s to deconstruct Nazi propaganda in order to organize an effective Social Democratic response came too late to stop Hitler's accession to power and were first published in Danish exile: Sergei Tschachotin, *Dreipfeil gegen Hakenkreuz* (Copenhagen, 1933). An extended French version, partly censored by a French government then still afraid of offending Hitler, was published in 1939: Serge Tchakhotine, *Le Viol des foules par la propaganda politique* (Paris, 1939); and finally, an English translation appeared one year later in the United States: Serge Chakotin, *The Rape of the Masses: The Psychology of Totalitarian Political Propaganda* (New York, 1940).

[103] See Siân Nicholas in this volume.
[104] See Olaf Stieglitz in this volume.   [105] See Nicholas in this volume.
[106] Early National Socialist experiences with the new medium are reviewed in Eugen Hadamowsky, *Der Rundfunk im Dienste der Volksführung* (Leipzig, 1934). The extension of the political sphere through the radio and its specific advantage, orality, in the Soviet Union during the same period is explored by Jurij Murašov, 'Sowjetisches Ethos und radiofizierte Schrift: Radio, Literatur und die Entgrenzung des Politischen in den frühen dreißiger Jahren der sowjetischen Kultur', in Ute Frevert and Wolfgang Braungart (eds.), *Sprachen des Politischen: Medien und Medialität in der Geschichte* (Göttingen, 2004), 217–45.

opinion in favour of Hitler's war policies accelerated efforts in Western democracies to explore the possibilities offered by the wireless. However, as Siân Nicholas has shown, it was some time before the BBC, in a process of trial and error rather than guided by research results, found effective ways of countering German radio propaganda.[107] The same can be said of French public and private radio stations during the 'phoney' phase of the war.[108] It was only from the middle years of the Second World War that radio research became more systematic, particularly in the USA.[109] From then on and all through the Cold War, scientific propaganda research in general and subsequent activity in the USA, Britain, and other Western countries, was increasingly initiated by non-governmental or quasi-governmental organizations. They were supported by national governments who sought to improve their own capacity to persuade, and aimed to educate their citizens to be alert to the secret tricks of their enemies.[110] As a side effect, propaganda research contributed to developing theories and methods of textual analysis, for instance quantitative semantics and content analysis, whose relevance now extends far beyond their original purpose of explaining the functioning of home or enemy propaganda.[111] Thus the more refined versions of content analysis are now practically indistinguishable from corpus-based approaches to discourse analysis, despite their different origins and theoretical foundations.[112]

[107] Siân Nicholas, *The Echo of War: Home Front Propaganda and the Wartime BBC 1939–1945* (Manchester, 1996), the quotation ibid. at 8. See also Nicholas's contribution in this volume.

[108] See Jean-Louis Crémieux-Brilhac, *Les Français de l'an 40*, 2 vols. (Paris, 1990), i. 297–312 and 274–6.

[109] First results were published in Paul F. Lazarsfeld, *Radio Research 1942–43* (New York, 1944); Ernst Kris and Hans Speier, *German Radio Propaganda: Report on Home Broadcasting during the War* (New York, 1944).

[110] For the 'de-centred' organization of wartime propaganda in the USA see Stieglitz in this volume. See also the comparison between American and West German anti-Communist propaganda activities by Thomas Mergel, in this volume.

[111] Alexander L. George, *Propaganda Analysis: A Study of Inferences Made from Nazi Propaganda in World War II* (Evanston, Ill., 1959) focuses strongly on methods, especially content analysis; Harold D. Lasswell and Nathan C. Leites, *The Language of Politics: Studies in Quantitative Semantics* (Cambridge, Mass., 1949; 2nd edn. 1965) looks at quantitative approaches; and Elke Blumenauer, 'Die Erforschung der NS-Propaganda und die Entwicklung der Inhaltsanalyse in den Vereinigten Staaten', in Jürgen Wilke (ed.), *Pressepolitik und Propaganda: Historische Studien vom Vormärz bis zum Kalten Krieg* (Cologne, 1997), 257–83, concentrates on content analysis.

[112] For an introduction to corpus-based discourse analysis see Tony McEnery and Andrew Wilson, *Corpus Linguistics: An Introduction* (2nd edn. Edinburgh, 2008).

Research and practice do not always appear as closely inter-twined as in propaganda studies during the era of the world wars and the early Cold War. But even the historical enquiries of the 1960s and 1970s into early modern or nineteenth-century uses of political terms, as in the case of Williams's *Keywords* and Koselleck's *Geschichtliche Grundbegriffe*, were not completely separated from con-temporary concerns and regularly had some repercussions, if only theoretical or methodological, on ongoing political debates. This connection between scholarly work and practical politics is explored in two essays towards the end of this book, one on post-war West Germany, the other on post-war Britain. Martin Geyer looks at how research on political language in West Germany was sparked off in the 1950s and early 1960s by the persistent use of Nazi vocabulary in the public sphere. This research on Nazi lan-guage contributed to an increasing sensitivity to the mobilizing power of socio-political terms in general.[113] Geyer goes on to explain how, in the late 1960s and early 1970s, academic studies on concepts and terms were driven by, and fed back into, the intense party-political strife of that time between German Christian Democrats, Social Democrats, and extra-parliamentary opposition movements. The emergence of conceptual history as a method is thus situated and explained as occupying a particular place in the intellectual and party-political context of West Germany after 1945. Similarly, in his essay on social historians of post-war Britain, Gareth Stedman Jones retraces how the work of scholars such as Raymond Williams and E. P. Thompson, who accepted the pre-discursive primacy of 'class' for the formation of experience, was shaped not only by a Marxist, but even more by a peculiarly English vision of history, articulated above all by Carlyle. In his vision of history spoken words were only a 'superficial film', whereas 'real' history could only be discerned in the inarticulate doings of the people.[114] From the 1970s, this Anglo-Marxist view of

---

[113] This point is also made by Thomas Mergel in this volume. For a thorough linguistic analysis of the ongoing contests about 'guilt' between perpetrators and victims in the first decade after the war see Heidrun Kämper, *Der Schulddiskurs in der frühen Nachkriegszeit: Ein Beitrag zur Geschichte des sprachlichen Umbruchs nach 1945* (Berlin, 2005). See also her dictionary of the relevant terms and strategies of argument in this debate, *Opfer—Täter—Nichttäter: Ein Wörterbuch zum Schulddiskurs 1945–1955* (Berlin, 2007). The importance of the Western Allies' attempts to regulate and de-Nazify public language use in their occupation zones is explored by Dirk Deissler, *Die entnazifizierte Sprache: Sprachpolitik und Sprachregelung in der Besatzungszeit* (Frankfurt, 2006).

[114] Gareth Stedman Jones, in this volume; the quotation of Carlyle at p. 342.

history was challenged, Jones continues, on the one hand by the slow disintegration followed by the sudden destruction of traditional English working-class life in the Thatcher years. It was challenged on the other hand by a new generation of historians who adopted the 'linguistic turn' precisely because 'class', as conceived by Thompson or Williams, no longer seemed to work as an explanatory variable for contemporary and earlier historical processes.

Similar points concerning the repercussions of political ideologies and events on the academic study of political language, and vice versa, could be made with regard to other individual researchers or schools, regardless of whether their disciplinary backgrounds are in political theory, history, linguistics, cultural anthropology, or the social sciences. More or less explicit thoughts on contemporary politics and its analysis are discernible, quite obviously, in Michel Foucault's entire work on the repressive force of discourses. But they are also present, for instance, in the history of liberal and republican ideas 'in context' as conceived by Quentin Skinner and J. G. A. Pocock,[115] in Michael Freeden's studies of competing ideologies such as liberalism, conservatism, and socialism,[116] in the enquiries into 'languages of class' as practised by Gareth Stedman Jones,[117] or in Critical Discourse Analysis as demonstrated in this volume's final chapter by Ruth Wodak's trenchant analysis of racist and anti-Semitic stereotyping in the Austrian 'liberal' party's election campaigns of the 1990s.[118]

---

[115] Both authors have published collections of their most important theoretical, methodological, and political essays: Quentin Skinner, *Visions of Politics*, 3 vols. (Cambridge, 2002); J. G. A. Pocock, *Political Thought and History: Essays on Theory and Method* (Cambridge, 2009). An excellent introduction to Skinner's work and its political implications is Kari Palonen, *Quentin Skinner: History, Politics, Rhetoric* (Cambridge, 2003).

[116] Michael Freeden, *Ideologies and Political Theory: A Conceptual Approach* (Oxford, 1996); see also his collection of essays, *Liberal Languages: Ideological Imaginations and Twentieth-Century Progressive Thought* (Princeton, 2005), and id., *Ideology: A Very Short Introduction* (Oxford, 2003), at 51 for his analytical definition of 'ideologies' as 'complex combinations and clusters of political concepts in sustained patterns'. Freeden goes on to state that ideologies attempt 'to end the inevitable contention over concepts by *decontesting* them, by removing their meaning from contest' (ibid. 54), and also that ideologies 'compete over the control of political language as well as competing over plans for public policy' (ibid. 55). In this introduction the term 'ideology' is used in Freeden's sense.

[117] Gareth Stedman Jones, *Languages of Class: Studies in English Working-Class History* (Cambridge, 1983). This book, and especially the essay on Chartism (ibid. 90–178), set off an unusually polemical debate which was not only about methods, but also about the relevance of Marxism in contemporary Britain.

[118] On Critical Discourse Analysis in general see Ruth Wodak (ed.), *Methods of Critical Discourse Analysis* (2nd edn. Los Angeles, 2009).

These preoccupations of academic research with practical or normative concerns are in no sense regrettable. There is no such thing as absolutely value-free scholarship with a subject like political language, even if one examines historical periods far more distant than the Short Twentieth Century, the ideological conflicts of which are still, to an extent, our own.

This is not the place to discuss these various, and different, approaches to the study of past and present political languages.[119] For this book is not dedicated primarily to exploring the advantages of one special set of theories and methods over others. Rather, the book's research agenda is, above all, object centred. At the core of the volume are empirical studies of the political uses of language in a particular historical period, the Age of Extremes. Its overall aim is to develop a better understanding of this period's distinctiveness with regard to the functions and purposes of language use under conditions of extreme ideological confrontation, terror, and violence. Within this framework most of the book's case studies assume the perspectives of one or several individuals, or groups, who were either subjected to these conditions or sought to uphold their positions of power through more or less conscious linguistic moves. Agents might undertake such moves for a variety of purposes: preserving spheres of private expression; extending unrestrained public speech; creating boundaries of the speakable for others; forging new communities and excluding supposed aliens, to name but a few.

Thus in addition to being object centred, the book's essays are also agent centred in their approach. In this respect, they differ from the stricter variants of discourse analysis in the tradition of the early Foucault's *Archaeology of Knowledge*,[120] even if some essays are clearly inspired by the later Foucault's theories of governmentality, normalization, and techniques of regulating the self. This theoretical framework plays a part in Olaf Stieglitz's essay on the discursive and pictorial construction of enemies, spies, traitors, and

---

[119] A useful introduction to various shades of discourse analysis applied to contemporary problems is Ruth Wodak and Michał Krzyżanowski (eds.), *Qualitative Discourse Analysis in the Social Sciences* (Basingstoke, 2008). For recent debates on historical semantics and conceptual history see Willibald Steinmetz, 'Vierzig Jahre Begriffsgeschichte: The State of the Art', in Heidrun Kämper and Ludwig M. Eichinger (eds.), *Sprache—Kognition—Kultur: Sprache zwischen mentaler Struktur und kultureller Prägung* (Berlin, 2008), 174–97.

[120] Michel Foucault, *The Archaeology of Knowledge* (London, 1972; first published in French, 1969).

the figure of the 'alert citizen' in the USA during the Second World War. It is also significant in Igal Halfin's contribution on the ways in which members of the Russian 'intelligentsia' tried to re-fashion themselves as faithful party members in the course of Bolshevik party purges and admissions procedures during the 1920s. But here, too, as in all other essays, there is a desire to describe the speech acts of identifiable actors. Their individual names may be of secondary importance; their utterances may be cited as examples of patterns of speech rather than for any unique-ness in personal style or content, as is the case in Halfin's piece or in Isabel Richter's essay on prisoners' defence strategies in Nazi Germany. Yet individual agency, not only of 'subalterns' or victims, but also of those in power—state prosecutors, judges, high party officials, chief ideologues, propagandists—is an important explanatory variable in these as well as all other contributions.

Another important characteristic of this volume is that 'lan-guage', our prime object of interest, is understood here in a broad sense. Hence the book includes essays focusing on verbal, as well as visual and audible signs. Examples are Judith Devlin's inter-pretation of an exhibition of paintings of Stalin in the Moscow Tretyakov Gallery, Stieglitz's essay on the US popular print media's depiction of the Japanese and German enemies during the Second World War, and Siân Nicholas's essay on the special 'tone' of BBC radio broadcasts against Hitler. Along with an analysis of the sounds and images themselves, these contributions deal with the respective communicative spaces and mass media—picture galleries, posters, cartoon series, radio transmissions—the specific 'material' qualities of which had an impact on what the signs might mean in the respective situations. In the case of the wartime BBC, for example, Nicholas shows that the success of broadcasts with listeners depended not only on the vocabulary used and the 'tone' of the speakers' voices, but also on the correct choice of format: news, serious documentary series, light talks, comedy, or music programmes. Making too much fun of Nazi leaders was banned from the BBC soon after the war broke out, and vulgar sarcasm or comic songs about Nazis repeatedly caused angry reactions within the BBC and from listeners. The specific-ities of the radio itself as a medium, the fact that the BBC was seen as the 'guest in the home' and therefore expected to maintain a certain standard of decorum, was responsible for a certain restraint from satire and a much toned-down aggressiveness against the Germans compared to other media such as the popular press, cheap popular literature, cartoons, material objects like playing cards, and films.

While some essays concentrate on the impact of the mass media and the propaganda effects brought about by the interplay between texts, images, and sounds, others emphasize the ambiguous messages made possible by the propagandists' more or less conscious borrowings from traditional languages. Among these, religious myths, symbols, and narratives receive particular attention in this volume. An exemplary case is provided by the paintings of Stalin displayed in the 1937 exhibition in the Tretyakov Gallery. In her analysis Judith Devlin shows how these paintings recalled religious iconography and implicitly drew on religious legends of martyrdom and salvation which, despite official suppression of the Orthodox Church, were still present in people's minds. In the 1930s, open references to religious feelings were of course taboo. Hence, on a more superficial level, the paintings presented themselves as visualizations of another mythical language, the language of romantic adventure tales and folklore. This emotional, popular language was tolerated, Devlin argues, even encouraged by the regime to enhance its appeal. Elements of religious language were contained in this popular language as a subtext. Thus, by means of these paintings, Stalin's propagandists, perhaps unknowingly, managed to effect an unobtrusive transfer of legitimacy from a traditional, religious belief system to the new cult of Stalin's leadership. By comparison, the fascist leadership cult of Mussolini, as interpreted in Emilio Gentile's essay, made a much more pronounced use of emotional appeals to religious concepts and symbols; so much so that for some proponents of the regime the fascist language, or *fascistese*, as Gentile terms it, became a religious belief system in and of itself.

In addition to religious language, family narratives and imagery form another reservoir traditionally exploited in political struggles. While religious messages were apparently well suited to twentieth-century dictators such as Mussolini, Stalin, and Hitler, who wanted to build up or sustain an image as the long-awaited saviours of their peoples, family narratives could be put to broader use and serve a great variety of political purposes, legitimizing as well as polemical or destructive ones. Rulers, whether dictators, kings, or democratically elected leaders, could be represented as benevolent patriarchs, but also accused of being bad fathers or husbands, who had betrayed their 'families', that is, their peoples. A twentieth-century example of applied family narratives is the propaganda duel, fought out via radio broadcasts, symbolic actions, printed and pictorial media, between Marshal Pétain and General de Gaulle in the months and years following the French defeat of June 1940. Both leaders enacted their struggle for the soul of France, conceived of as a female figure, and the hearts of Frenchmen and Frenchwomen, as a family drama with varying scenes.[121] In doing so, Pétain and de Gaulle continued traditions of politicized family narratives already in place during the old French monarchy and the French Revolution.[122] Family rhetoric was also prominent in Stalinist Russia. Not only was Stalin himself praised as a foresighted father, the Russian country imagined as a mother, and the Soviet citizens belittled as children, but loyalty to this grand Soviet family was vigorously promoted against the upholding of confidential ties and privacy within smaller, natural families.[123] Thus the strategy of projecting family narratives and metaphors onto the political game seems to be as widely used as the application of religious imagery and language to political leaders.

Yet, there appears to be a difference between these strategies. Whereas the establishment of a political religion centred on a secular charismatic ruler or a particular regime requires the demise

---

[121] See the analysis of this duel in Freudian terms by Jean-Pierre Guichard, *De Gaulle et les mass-média: l'image du Général* (Paris, 1985), at 341–63.

[122] On 'family narratives' as a category for analysing eighteenth-century disputes between supporters of the French monarchy and the revolutionaries, see Lynn Hunt, *The Family Romance of the French Revolution* (Berkeley, 1992). More generally on the family metaphor in political contexts, see Francesca Rigotti, *Die Macht und ihre Metaphern* (Frankfurt, 1994), at 77–114.

[123] On the 'familiarization of the political' in the visual language of Soviet films see Sabine Haensgen, 'Die Familiarisierung des Politischen im Kino der Stalinzeit: Zur Filmkomödie als Genre sowjetischer Populärkultur', in Frevert and Haupt (eds.), *Neue Politikgeschichte*, 115–39. How children were made 'familiar' with Lenin and Stalin is explained by Catriona Kelly, 'Grandpa Lenin and Uncle Stalin: Soviet Leader Cults for Little Children', in Balázs Apor et al. (eds.), *The Leader Cult in Communist Dictatorships: Stalin and the Eastern Bloc* (Basingstoke, 2004), 102–22; rival family narratives depending on the ethnic background of addressees are explored by Jan Plamper, 'Georgian Koba or Soviet "Father of Peoples"? The Stalin Cult and Ethnicity', ibid. 123–40; see also Klaus Gestwa, '*Social* und *soul engineering* unter Stalin und Chruschtschow, 1928–1964', in Thomas Etzemüller (ed.), *Die Ordnung der Moderne: Social Engineering im 20. Jahrhundert* (Bielefeld, 2009), 241–77, at 258–64.

of traditional, church-bound religion, at least among significant segments within a society, no comparable process of emancipation is necessary for the transfer of family imagery to the political sphere. The very concept of a 'political religion' reacts to an environment which has already undergone a certain degree of secularization, understood here in the sense of a widespread acceptance that religion should be separate from other spheres of life, such as politics or the economy.[124] Convinced Christians or Muslims in the twenty-first century would probably reject this idea of separation, an idea which a majority of Europeans seem to have embraced during the Short Twentieth Century. For firm believers, religious language *is* political and political language *is* religious; in their view, the very concept of a 'political religion' is a tautology. Whether the speakers of *fascistese* in Mussolini's Italy belonged to the category of firm believers and genuinely accepted fascism as a religion *tout court*, or whether they were merely hypocrites or cynics who adopted religious vocabularies and imagery for propaganda purposes, may be difficult to decide. A close reading of the relevant texts may well reveal evidence to support both hypotheses. Yet ambiguous cases like this seem to be the exception rather than the rule in twentieth-century European political discourse.

As far as Europe is concerned, it can be regarded as a distinctive feature of twentieth-century political struggles that politicians and peoples were, in general, disposed to draw a clear line, only to be crossed in exceptional circumstances, between 'religious' and genuinely 'political' vocabularies, images, or narratives. On the other hand, Ronald Reagan's rhetoric of the empire of 'evil' during the final phase of the Cold War and President Bush's extension of this rhetoric to global culture wars after the events of 9/11 remind us that in the USA, and even more so in other parts of the world, the blurring of the distinction between 'religious' and 'political' linguistic repertoires has always been an option, if not the norm.[125] That there is a European–American divide on this issue is confirmed by Thomas Mergel's finding that early Cold

---

[124] This is also stressed by Emilio Gentile, *Politics as Religion* (Princeton, 2006), at pp. xiv–xvii. In addition to the separation of a religious from a worldly sphere, 'secularization' may have at least two other meanings: first, a general decline in religious belief; and secondly a 'privatization' of religious practice. For these conceptual distinctions see José Casanova, *Public Religions in the Modern World* (Chicago, 1994).

[125] See Sandra Silberstein, *War of Words: Language, Politics and 9/11* (London, 2004), at 40–2 and 46–55.

War anti-Communism in the USA inscribed itself into a world view which conceived of Communism as a false political religion as opposed to the true one, which was supposed to have been realized by 'God's own people' in America itself and the Western world. By contrast, Mergel explains, West German post-war anti-Communism, although no less vigorous, was devoid of such theological overtones when describing West Germany's democratic position, not least because of the deliberate desire of post-war West Germans to distance themselves from the religious self-descriptions of the Hitler regime. In West Germany, the label of a—secularized—political religion was attached only to the opposite side, the Soviet Communists, who in this respect too were declared to resemble the Nazis.

Whether couched in religious terms or not, demonizing alien powers, internal enemies, or unwanted categories of people, such as migrants or Jews, has been a feature common to all political systems and all periods of history, especially at times of real or imagined threat from outside. Many exclusionary discursive strategies have a very long shelf-life. Christian anti-Judaism is one of them. Thus, to quote Mergel once more, US Senator Joseph McCarthy found the 'un-American' Communists who betrayed America even worse than Judas who had betrayed Jesus Christ. And Ruth Wodak points out that even at the turn of the twenty-first century, the same age-old Christian anti-Semitic stereotypes of the 'traitorous' and 'vengeful' Jew are still sufficiently present in collective awareness that politicians allude to them and audiences understand them in European countries with strong anti-Semitic traditions, such as in her case Austria.

However, languages other than the politico-theological are available for achieving the verbal exclusion of alien enemies on the one hand, and the inclusion of those supposed to belong to imagined communities on the other. Thus metaphors of space and inside–outside relations, for example the metaphor of 'containment', played a prominent part in the Cold War.[126] Several essays in this book address the issue of how political actors tried to forge communities while excluding or annihilating others by verbal means. In this context, the use of metaphors derived from gardening, medicine, and personal hygiene, particularly images

[126] See Paul A. Chilton, *Security Metaphors: Cold War Discourse from Containment to Common House* (New York, 1996).

of eradicating weeds, parasites, or bacteria by chemical, surgical, or biotechnical means, had been increasing since the late nineteenth century and reached a peak in the middle decades of the twentieth.[127] The most brutal example, and one in which the murderous deeds surpassed the brutality of words and images, was, of course, National Socialist anti-Semitic discourse.[128] Metaphors of pests to be weeded out were also applied to the kulaks during the years of Stalinist terror, while at the same time the valuable bodies of Socialist workers had to be cultivated like garden plants.[129] At the height of the Second World War even semi-official propagandists in democratic countries did not hesitate to use dehumanizing images, as when the Japanese were depicted as insects in an American Marine Corps magazine.[130] Similar metaphors that equated Communists with diseases such as cancer or tuberculosis which supposedly infected the political corpus of the American nation lived on into the Cold War.[131] In post-war West Germany, however, this 'language of hygiene' (Mergel) as applied to Communists was restrained or even explicitly rejected, again because of its close association with National Socialism. Older ethnicizing and racist stereotypes of the Russians, threatening to 'flood' West Germany and its new Western allies with 'Asiatic', violent hordes, assumed the function of drawing a line between 'us' and 'them'. Moreover, during the 1950s and 1960s, West German media and politicians not infrequently tried to discredit the policies of Soviet Communism and its satellites in the East German government by equating them with National Socialist methods.

On the other side of the Berlin Wall as well, the ideological opponent was equated with Nazism. Ralph Jessen's analysis of official languages of inclusion and exclusion in the German Democratic Republic underlines the fact that Ulbricht's and

[127] See Sarah Jansen, '*Schädlinge': Geschichte eines wissenschaftlichen und politischen Konstrukts* (Frankfurt, 2003); Philipp Sarasin, 'Die Visualisierung des Feindes: Über metaphorische Technologien der frühen Bakteriologie', *Geschichte und Gesellschaft*, 30 (2004), 250–76; Christoph Gradmann, 'Invisible Enemies: Bacteriology and the Language of Politics in Imperial Germany', *Science in Context*, 13 (2000), 9–30.

[128] An example is the propaganda film *Der ewige Jude* (The Eternal Jew) by Fritz Hippler, released in 1940. This film's sources are explored by Stig Hornsøj-Møller and David Culbert, '"Der ewige Jude" (1940): Joseph Goebbels' Unequalled Monument to Anti-Semitism', *Historical Journal of Film, Radio and Television*, 12 (1992), 41–69.

[129] See Gestwa, '*Social* und *soul engineering*', 265–7.

[130] See Stieglitz in this volume.   [131] See Mergel in this volume.

Honecker's propagandists tried to establish a specific GDR identity by dissociating its history from the National Socialist past and emphasizing instead the East German people's orientation towards a common future in the great family of Socialist countries. Responsibility for National Socialism was shifted onto the old elites and capitalists who continued to dominate West Germany, which was thus portrayed as the sole representative of the negative strands in the German past. This version of history was made plausible by carefully orchestrated scandals exposing the real or alleged Nazi past of prominent West German politicians. Jessen discusses several other rhetorical strategies that were designed to strengthen the ever precarious inner cohesion of the GDR. According to his analysis, none of them ever gained broad acceptance below the level of ritualized public communication; the exception was a specific 'GDR language of community', a harmonizing language which suggested that all 'classes' of the GDR were united in their efforts to work for the benefit of the whole. Vestiges of that language, Jessen claims, still live on in the discourses of nostalgia for the GDR perpetuated by some segments of the East German population within reunified Germany. Jessen's most important finding, however, and one which continues Václav Havel's reflections, concerns the value of ritualized language use as a symbol of unity and a practice which actually reinforced integration as long as GDR citizens paid at least lip service to the prescribed formula. Towards the end of the Age of Extremes, then, the radical ideology which had marked its beginnings, Soviet Communism, had become a standardized language, and not only in the GDR.

It was clearly different in the early stages of Soviet Communism, the decade after the October Revolution of 1917. The rituals of soul-searching, narrating one's own autobiography, and questioning those who aspired to become, or wanted to remain, good Bolshevik revolutionaries were then only in the making. Igal Halfin's close reading of documents of local party proceedings in the 1920s reveals that categorizations of class-affiliation and narrative strategies to describe ideal life-trajectories of true Bolsheviks were still in flux and could not be directed fully from the centre. During the 1920s, candidates for party membership experimented with different models of telling their own life stories. Members of local purge and admissions committees possessed considerable leeway in interpreting the signs of whole-hearted belief or of adhering to old habits, while local statisticians were active in reconfiguring the class profiles of applicants and in defining new categories, such as the 'toiling intelligentsia'. In the early Soviet Union then, paying lip service to some standardized formula, as in Czechoslovakia or in the GDR from the 1960s to the 1980s, was not sufficient. True, as Halfin makes clear, there were limits to what could be said, if a life story was to be credible, but within these limits variation was possible—and even necessary. The question remains, when and why did the kind of ritualized language described by Havel and Jessen become normality in the realm of Soviet Communism?

A possible answer worth pursuing might be that ritualization set in as a response to the extreme unpredictability of what was deemed politically correct speech and behaviour. If it is true that Soviet citizens exposed to purges or interrogations had no clear guidelines for how to tell their story or state their case, then the outcome of such proceedings was unpredictable. As long as expulsion from the party was the only consequence of choosing the wrong words, people could live with this unpredictability. But from the moment when the outcome almost routinely became a matter of life and death, that is, from the beginning of the Stalinist terror waves, knowing how to speak and behave politically correctly was essential for survival. The problem during the terror years was that nobody except Stalin himself, and, perhaps, a few mysterious individuals around him, could know beforehand what kind of utterance was required, or might be tolerated, by the 'party line' valid at that moment. For the rank-and-file party members, and even for the highest party leaders, not to mention opponents of the regime, this was an unbearable situation.[132] Establishing rituals of linguistic performance was an escape from that situation, an escape which was necessary above all in order to re-stabilize the ruling parties themselves. After some relapses, that escape finally became possible in the years after 1953/6. Whether we should imagine the establishment of these rituals as the outcome of deliberate choices or as a creeping process remains an

---

[132] Vivid contemporary descriptions of this dilemma by an ex-Communist can be found in Wolfgang Leonhard, *Die Revolution entläßt ihre Kinder* (Cologne, 1955), at 39–40, 222, 226–7, and 240–5; cf. the (abridged) English trans. *Child of the Revolution* (Chicago, 1958), at 45–6, 243, and 248–9.

open question.[133] The paradox is that the linguistic routines which were meant to re-stabilize the ruling parties in the end contributed to destabilizing their regimes.

Compared to these long waves of shifting relations between language use and power in the realm of Soviet Communism, those within the National Socialist, fascist, and authoritarian regimes of central and southern Europe were relatively brief, with the possible exception of Franco's Spain and Salazar's Portugal,[134] so their rulers and subjects could scarcely develop similarly routinized uses of ideologized language. This might at least be viewed as a hypothesis worth testing. Its tacit acceptance may be the reason why scholars of fascist and National Socialist languages have long tended to separate the official fascist or Nazi idioms and propaganda from the ordinary use of language by individuals under Mussolini's or Hitler's regimes, and to treat them, in fact, as two distinct fields of enquiry. The assumption underlying this distinction was that Italians under fascism and Germans under Nazism were themselves able to draw a clear line between the official ideology and their own ordinary language. This, however, is anything but self-evident. In Germany, doubts about its validity have increased since there has been a marked shift of focus from studying the (public, propagandistic) language use of National Socialism to investigating (private, everyday) language use during the Third Reich.[135]

The reach of official ideology into ordinary people's writings and conversations has thus become more obvious. But what needs

---

[133] The creeping-process hypothesis is more plausible; a good example, again referring to the GDR, is provided by Sandrine Kott's analysis of growing linguistic conformity and its depoliticizing effects on the oral and written documents produced by socialist work teams (*Brigaden*). See Sandrine Kott, 'Entpolitisierung des Politischen: Formen und Grenzen der Kommunikation zwischen Personen in der DDR', in Moritz Föllmer (ed.), *Sehnsucht nach Nähe: Interpersonale Kommunikation in Deutschland seit dem 19. Jahrhundert* (Stuttgart, 2004), 215–28. See also Mary Fulbrook, *The People's State: East German Society from Hitler to Honecker* (New Haven, 2005), at 257–60 (on 'channelled discussions') and 271–86 (on ambivalences between standardized phrases and individual ways of playing the system in citizens' communications, the so-called *Eingaben*).

[134] Studies of twentieth-century political language in the Iberian peninsula are rare, but see now as a starting point for Spain the magnificent historical dictionary of concepts by Javier Fernández Sébastián and Juan Francisco Fuentes (eds.), *Diccionario político y social del siglo XX español* (Madrid, 2008). See also Michael Scotti-Rosin, *Die Sprache der Falange und des Salazarismus: Eine vergleichende Untersuchung zur politischen Lexikologie des Spanischen und Portugiesischen* (Frankfurt, 1982).

[135] For further discussion of this shift and the relevant literature see the contributions by Linke and Geyer, both in this volume.

to be explored more thoroughly is the precise interconnection, or the continuous flows back and forth, between the two communicative spheres. To what degree, when, and for what purposes did ordinary Germans—civilians and soldiers—adopt the terms and phrases that Goebbels's propaganda apparatus offered them? How selective were their appropriations of official Nazi idioms? And, conversely, were there instances when the Nazi authorities themselves adapted their own public language to what was said in the streets or written in private letters? In recent years, some progress has been made in approaching these questions. The German armed forces postal service, the *Feldpost*, has received particular attention. Millions of letters were exchanged every week between soldiers at the various fronts and their families and friends at home. Careful semantic analyses of significant samples have shown that ordinary Germans, in general, were much more ready than had been assumed to adopt National Socialist phraseologies and terms.[136] This inclination was not solely an outcome of censorship. In fact, no one was forced to express a firm belief in the *Führer* in private letters, as there were enough 'harmless' topics like food, health, or family matters to discuss. Silence was always an option here. An even more important finding, however, does not concern the explicit adoptions of Nazi propaganda messages or ideological terms, but points to a deeper level of agreement between National Socialists and ordinary Germans brought about by the ubiquitous use of certain basic, inconspicuous metaphors or axioms such as, for example, expressions of a desire for purity.[137] Writing about purity on the Eastern Front could apply to personal hygiene and, at the same time, to fears for the health of the imagined collective body of the German people that had to be 'cleansed' of 'parasites'; the metaphors of 'purity' and 'cleansing' served as a kind of bridge between everyday concerns about dirt and the readiness of soldiers and civilians to collude with mass killings of Jews, Red Army commissars, and so-called 'partisans'.

A very different communicative space in which official National Socialist language was, in part adopted and transformed, in part

---

[136] The best study so far is Sven Oliver Müller, *Deutsche Soldaten und ihre Feinde: Nationalismus an Front und Heimatfront im Zweiten Weltkrieg* (Frankfurt, 2007).

[137] On the purity topos in *Feldpost* letters see Michaela Kipp, '"Großreinemachen im Osten": Sauberkeitsvorstellungen und Feindbilder im NS-Vernichtungskrieg in Osteuropa 1939–1944/45' (Ph.D. thesis, University of Bielefeld, 2008).

rejected, by individuals is examined in this volume by Isabel Richter. The individuals she examines were definitely not followers, but opponents of the regime who had been accused of acts of high treason before the National Socialist People's Court, the *Volksgerichtshof*.[138] Richter analyses pre-trial Gestapo interrogations on the one hand, and post-trial clemency pleas by the convicted prisoners on the other. Not surprisingly, in the latter case prisoners regularly distanced themselves from their past left-wing ideas, expressed their unreserved wish to be part of the *Volksgemeinschaft*, and promised to work for the war effort. To this extent they conformed to what they believed were the expected catchwords of the National Socialist idiom. But Richter also finds 'verbal fragments' of resistance in the interrogation transcripts, utterances of allegiance to Socialist or Communist values which helped the prisoners to stabilize an alternative vision of the self and of political belonging, even in the face of impending death sentences.

Defiance of National Socialist ideology and phraseology could go much further in the most secret form of (written) communication, diaries. In her essay looking at a number of examples of dissidents' diaries under the Third Reich, Heidrun Kämper focuses on the linguistic techniques which allowed the diarists to develop private languages of their own in an environment of denunciation and imminent danger of arrest. She finds that techniques varied considerably, ranging from complete camouflage by using apparently empty phrases, code names, and private terms to an almost careless, only haphazardly concealed documentation of the writer's and his circle's resistance activities. The most famous diary she analyses is that of Victor Klemperer (1881–1960), whose book *LTI* (*Lingua Tertii Imperii* = Language of the Third Reich) is one of the earliest, and still one of the best, accounts of language use in Nazi propaganda and in everyday communication.[139] For Klemperer, the very practice of noting down his observations on language use on an almost daily basis, a practice which he continued into the periods of the Soviet occupation of Eastern Germany

---

[138] For the larger context see Isabel Richter, *Hochverratsprozesse als Herrschaftspraxis im Nationalsozialismus: Männer und Frauen vor dem Volksgerichtshof 1934–1939* (Münster, 2001).

[139] Victor Klemperer, *LTI: Notizbuch eines Philologen* (Leipzig, 1946). An English translation is available: *The Language of the Third Reich: LTI—Lingua Tertii Imperii, A Philologist's Notebook*, trans. Martin Brady (London, 1999). Also available is *An Annotated Edition of Victor Klemperer's LTI: Notizbuch eines Philologen*, with English notes and commentary by Roderick H. Watt (Lampeter, 1997).

and the early GDR, served as a distancing device. Klemperer himself called it a 'balancing pole': commenting on the language of others in his diaries allowed him to manage the balancing act between preserving his inner self, including his own language, and the necessity of concealing his inner thoughts while conforming to what was required in public.[140]

Kämper's linguistic examination of diary-writing under National Socialism, Richter's analysis of prisoners' responses to Gestapo interrogations, and Halfin's enquiries into negotiations in Bolshevik party purges are good illustrations of this volume's contention that to study political languages in the Age of Extremes amounts to more than just looking at propaganda or other forms of public communication, such as parliamentary debates or protest marches. Analysing transcripts of oral face-to-face inter-actions, reading documents produced in trials before courts of law, interpreting private letters or even solitary writing practices such as diaries, sheds light on the ways in which political language performed in public was appropriated, transformed, or rejected by individuals.[141] For non-pluralistic political systems, these source materials are often the only means of exploring the range and boundaries of what could be said, and of discovering what certain words, or other signs, would actually mean to political actors in situations of extreme power differentials. In this sense, the notion that the private is, or at least can always become, 'polit-ical' is part of this volume's conception of political history.

The study of political languages also involves much more than surveying the lexical side of language. All essays in this volume aim to study more than isolated words or concepts. The focus is extended to contexts produced by patterns of argument, narra-tions, or metaphors in other texts, but also to visual images, sounds, media constellations, and social practices in a variety of communicative situations. Instead of diachronically investigating the changing meanings of single or clustered keywords or concepts over a long time-span, the essays in this volume take a synchronic, or micro-diachronic, approach to communicative practices in

---

[140] The quotation is from Kämper's essay in this volume.

[141] On the other hand, real or faked private letters, e.g. 'last letters' from the front, could also be publicized for propaganda purposes. This practice was not limited to 'total-itarian' regimes, but was also used in democratic countries such as Britain. See Margaretta Jolly, 'Between Ourselves: The Letter as Propaganda', in Taithe and Thornton (eds.), *Propaganda*, 239–61.

specific historical settings. In an essay which supplements this introduction, Angelika Linke elaborates on this volume's methodological choices by presenting a systematic overview, informed by pragma-linguistics, on how best to analyse such communicative practices. Above all, she stresses that in order to grasp the 'meanings' of what has been said or written, it is not sufficient to look at the intentions behind an utterance. Rather, it is necessary to explore the range of what the hearers or readers of an utterance could possibly, or would actually, understand in a given situation. This situation-centred approach to the analysis of language use is shared by all contributors to the volume. With this common assumption as a starting point, the authors have developed their own research strategies, depending on the specificity of their chosen subject, the state of previous research, and their different disciplinary and national backgrounds. Even if Linke's categories and terminology are not strictly applied in each essay, her general advice concerning the embedding of individual speech acts in types of communicative practices is followed.

In methodological terms, then, this volume stands for an agent- and situation-centred approach to the historical study of political languages. At the same time, it decidedly abstains from proclaiming this as yet another 'turn' or 'paradigm shift'. The contributors have agreed that several theoretical framings should remain possible. If a common label is desirable at all, then 'historical semantics', understood in a broad sense as the historical study of the production of meaning through sign systems (language being only one of them), would be a reasonable choice. But empirical progress does not depend on terminological disputes. For the same reasons it would be misleading to claim that a conceptual history or keyword-based research programme is outdated in principle, or somehow inadequate when approaching the Short Twentieth Century. In fact, the opposite is true, at least if we take seriously Reinhart Koselleck's and Raymond Williams's claims that the changing meanings of concepts, or keywords, can only be elucidated by showing their interconnectedness and social embeddedness.

From this point of view the situation-centred approach practised in this volume constitutes a preliminary step towards an empirically sustainable history of concepts, or history of keywords, in the Age of Extremes. Unlike most conceptual history realized so far, such a new conceptual history of twentieth-century political terms can no longer proceed on the assumption that national languages, with their specific linguistic features and trajectories, form the single most important reservoir from which people's understandings and forms of expression are derived. Indeed, such a new conceptual history, still in the making, should be transnational from the outset. Although the demand to become transnational also applies to earlier periods, it seems particularly pertinent for the Age of Extremes because its conceptual contests have been dominated by competing ideologies that transcended borders to a new and unprecedented extent. That this history should also be comparative, synchronically and diachronically, is illustrated by the shared—and recurring—experiences of individuals and communities in the face of these ideologies.

Our historical enquiries into twentieth-century political languages may not prevent history's tendency to repeat itself. Yet, as historians we are obliged to our witnesses. Seeking to understand how they contended with, and were able to contest, boundaries of the speakable that were imposed upon them by oppressive rulers or, worse, their own routinized compliance, is the best we can do to pay tribute to their testimonies.

2
Politics as Linguistic Performance: Function and 'Magic' of Communicative Practices

ANGELIKA LINKE

I The Linguistic Construction of Reality

In his 1999 essay 'A Pragmatist View of Contemporary Analytic Philosophy', Richard Rorty pointedly expresses the central question of analytical philosophy as follows: 'What happens if we transform old philosophical questions about the relation of thought to reality into questions about the relation of language to reality?'[1]

The outcome of this re-evaluation of language not only in philosophy but also in other sciences is now called the 'linguistic turn'.[2] In the contemporary discussion in the humanities, the term is used in a generalized sense largely detached from philosophy.[3] The thesis of the power of language as both representing and generating reality stands out as one approach linked to the 'linguistic turn'.[4] In this socio-constructivist context, Humboldt's categoriza-

---

[1] Richard Rorty, 'A Pragmatist View of Contemporary Analytic Philosophy', in William Egginton and Mike Sandbothe (eds.), *The Pragmatic Turn in Philosophy: Contemporary Engagements between Analytic and Continental Thought* (New York, 2004), 131–44, at 139.

[2] Coined by Rorty's teacher Carl Gustav Hempel (see id., 'Reduction: Ontological and Linguistic Facets', in Sidney Morgenbesser et al. (eds.), *Philosophy, Science, and Method: Essays in Honor of Ernest Nagel* (New York, 1969), 179–99), this expression became popular when Richard Rorty used it as the title of a volume of essays. In this context, it refers to the importance and influence that philosophers and theoreticians of 'ordinary language philosophy' have exerted on twentieth-century philosophy.

[3] The fact that Rorty himself regarded the language analytical approach in philosophy as essentially outdated twenty-five years after its appearance (Richard M. Rorty, 'Twenty-five Years After', in id. (ed.), *The Linguistic Turn: Essays in Philosophical Method. With Two Retrospective Essays* (Chicago, 1992), 371–4, at 374) has been unable to stop an increasingly linguistic orientation in mainly the human and social sciences since the 1970s.

[4] German linguistics, strangely enough, has voiced an opinion neither on the theoretical concepts nor on the historical effectiveness of the 'linguistic turn', at least not explicitly. The essay by Antje Hornscheidt, 'Der "linguistic turn" aus der Sicht der Linguistik', in Bernd Henningsen and Stephan Michael Schröder (eds.), *Vom Ende der Humboldt-Kosmen: Konturen von Kulturwissenschaft* (Baden-Baden, 1997), 175–206, is an exception.

tion of linguistic signs as interpreting the world has definitely been
revivified.[5]

The new attention to the world's linguistic make-up and, from
there, to the linguistic make-up of scientific objects and data
within cultural studies is not directed at all linguistic levels or phenomena to the same extent: 'semantics' and 'symbolisms'[6] of linguistic elements are favoured objects of study, while narrative
patterns, structures, and textual genres are relatively neglected.
Thus it is above all the *lexical level* that historians have analysed, for
example, in French Lexicometrics, the history of concepts, historical semantics *à la* Koselleck, and works adopting Lakoff and
Johnson's analysis of metaphors and collective symbols.[7] In addition, linguistic entities such as texts and text sorts come to the fore
mostly at the secondary level of 'meta-history', that is, the analysis
focuses more on historiographical texts than on historical documents themselves, a scientific field that is fundamentally
influenced by the work of Hayden White. In all these approaches,
with regard to primary as well as secondary texts, the interest lies
mainly in language as a sign system through which our world
comes into being only at the moment when we make it 'readable'
through signs. This new understanding of language in cultural
studies can be tied to Ernst Cassirer's *Philosophy of Symbolic Forms*[8]
and its semiotic concept of language. Although Cassirer's work
(surprisingly) does not belong to the compulsory literature of reference in the discussion on the 'linguistic turn' within cultural

---

[5] See Peter Berger and Thomas Luckmann, *Die gesellschaftliche Konstruktion der Wirklichkeit:
Eine Theorie der Wissenssoziologie* (Frankfurt am Main, 1966, 1969).

[6] This is valid at least for the German discourse. These plural forms, which seem so
unusual to linguistic scholars, have become common in the language of neighbouring disciplines which are now more linguistically oriented because of the 'linguistic turn'. There
they enjoy an almost programmatic identity-constituting function. As far as I can see, the
plural form announces the variability and changeability of linguistic meaning and the significance of non-linguistic signs. Thus it might also signify a link between the (new) attention paid to language in cultural studies and a view that is both social-constructivist and
linguistic-relativist.

[7] Cf. George Lakoff and Mark Johnson, *Metaphors We Live By* (Chicago, 1980); George
Lakoff, *Moral Politics: How Liberals and Conservatives Think* (2nd edn. Chicago, 2002); Alan
Cienki, 'Bush's and Gore's Language and Gestures in the 2000 Presidential Debates: A
Test Case for Two Models of Metaphors', *Journal of Language and Politics*, 3/3 (2004), 409–
40, is an application of Lakoff's *Moral Politics* analysis to the presidential election campaign
between George W. Bush and Al Gore in 2000, which takes non-verbal aspects and the
visualization of metaphors into consideration.

[8] Ernst Cassirer, *The Philosophy of Symbolic Forms*, trans. Ralph Manheim, 3 vols. (8th
edn. New Haven, 1975).

studies, his rhetorically and theoretically outstanding definition of language as 'an entirely determinate formation, not exactly *of the world*, but rather *making for the world*',[9] focuses attention on linguistic processes of symbolization as constructions. Cassirer's definition of language could, therefore, be seen as the basic programmatic principle of this discussion.

II *The Performative Construction of Reality*

Approaches to performance theory in cultural studies,[10] which are now pursued under the label 'performative turn', do not present a contrast with the linguistic turn. Rather, under this umbrella term, they extend and dynamize the linguistic turn. It seems appropriate to discuss these approaches a little further since, to my knowledge, they have received only highly selective attention in historical and linguistic analyses of political language.[11] Performance-theoretical

---

[9] Ibid. i. 79–80. The definition refers to language and the other two systems of symbolization that Cassirer describes in his three-volume work on the 'symbolic forms', i.e. myth and art.

[10] Cf. e.g. Uwe Wirth, 'Der Performanzbegriff im Spannungsfeld von Illokution, Iteration und Indexikalität', in id. (ed.), *Performanz: Zwischen Sprachphilosophie und Kulturwissenschaften* (Frankfurt am Main, 2002), 9–62; Andrew Parker and Eve Kosofsky Sedgwick (eds.), *Performativity and Performance* (New York, 1995); Judith Butler, 'Burning Acts', ibid. 197–227.

[11] Furthermore, approaches influenced by aesthetics and/or theatre studies seem to dominate; see the anthology by Günter Berghaus (ed.), *Fascism and Theatre: Comparative Studies on the Aesthetics and Politics of Performance in Europe 1925–1945* (Providence, RI, 1996). The linguistic debate on the political use of language is dominated by linguistic discourse analysis, at least in the German-language context (see the works produced by the Düsseldorf School around Georg Stötzel and Martin Wengeler; for the particular form of 'critical discourse analysis' see the work by Ruth Wodak and her collaborators). Here, the interest is primarily in the vocabulary, concepts, topoi, and argument of political language. In addition, we find research which focuses on dialogic patterns in genres of political discourse; see the work by Armin Burkhardt, *Das Parlament und seine Sprache: Studien zu Theorie und Geschichte parlamentarischer Kommunikation* (Tübingen, 2003); id., *Zwischen Monolog und Dialog: Zur Theorie, Typologie und Geschichte des Zwischenrufs im deutschen Parlamentarismus* (Tübingen, 2004); some of the contributions to Jörg Kilian (ed.), *Sprache und Politik: Deutsch im demokratischen Staat* (Mannheim, 2005); still basic for German studies of political language is Walther Dieckmann, *Politische Sprache—Politische Kommunikation: Vorträge, Aufsätze, Entwürfe* (Heidelberg, 1981); and id., 'Wie redet man "zum Fenster hinaus"? Zur Realisierung des Adressatenbezugs in öffentlich-dialogischer Kommunikation am Beispiel eines Redebeitrags Brandts', in Wolfgang Sucharowski (ed.), *Gesprächsforschung im Vergleich: Analysen zur Bonner Runde nach der Hessenwahl 1982* (Tübingen, 1985), 54–76. Performative analyses still remain to be done. An exception is Joachim Scharloth, 'Ritualkritik und Rituale des Protests: Die Entdeckung des Performativen in der Studentenbewegung der 1960er Jahre', in Martin Klimke and Joachim Scharloth (eds.), *1968: Handbuch zur Kultur- und Mediengeschichte der Studentenbewegung* (Stuttgart, 2007), 75–87.

approaches focus less on language as a system of symbolization than on linguistic acts as a *dynamic activity* generating particular effects. Performative analysis of interaction is concerned less with the mediality of *language* than the transformational effect of *speaking*. The obvious potential of everyday life 'to bring about the fit between words and world'[12] can, of course, be understood as a profane version of the magic function of language,[13] which manifests itself in past practices such as magic spells, curses, and contemporary religious and legal contexts. The fundamental concept and the stimulating potential of performance theory both draw on two main lines of origin: John L. Austin's speech act theory and its development by John R. Searle, above all, as interpreted by Judith Butler; and the interactionist approaches in (mainly American) ethno-methodological and anthropological linguistics. Representatives of the latter direction are primarily Harold Garfinkel, Harvey Sacks, and Erving Goffman. Despite many differences in their main focus and views of the transformative potential of linguistic acts, these lines of enquiry converge in terms of their interests and theoretical basis. The central question is no longer one of linguistic reference, but of a performative and (inter)active construction of reality. In this context language plays a central part, but one that is no longer exclusive: para-verbal and non-verbal behaviour must also be taken into consideration. In so doing, the interacting partners step into the limelight on the theoretical stage. What language as such can do is no longer of interest; instead, attention focuses on *communicative practices*, which are understood as the 'place' of shaping, negotiating, questioning, and upsetting reality—a reality that also encompasses the acting agents and the communicative situation itself. Interaction consists not only of reciprocal activity such as staging and acting out the participants' social roles and their relationship to one another, but also of emphasizing selected aspects of the situative context by appropriate practices of contextualization.[14]

---

[12] John R. Searle, 'How Performatives Work', *Linguistics and Philosophy*, 12 (1989), 535–58, at 574, quoted in Ulrike Bohle and Ekkehard König, 'Zum Begriff des Performativen in der Sprachwissenschaft', in Erika Fischer-Lichte and Christoph Wulf (eds.), *Theorien des Performativen* (Berlin, 2001), 13–34, at 17.

[13] Cf. Toshihiko Izutsu, *Language and Magic: Studies in the Magical Function of Speech* (Tokyo, 1956).

[14] See Peter Auer, 'Introduction: John Gumperz' Approach to Contextualization', in id. and Aldo Di Luzio (eds.), *The Contextualization of Language* (Amsterdam, 1992), 1–38.

III 'Doing Being': The Performance of Identity

The expression 'doing being', a seemingly strange linguistic construction, enjoys expert status in Anglo-American conversation analysis. The term is based on the assumption that much of what we understand as an individual's *being*, that is, as a static property, turns out, when critically considered, to be a *doing*, that is, an activity and, in this sense, an achievement. Accordingly, the unusualness of the expression 'doing being' reflects a part of its meaning: a questioning of the obvious.

The action-oriented concept of 'doing x' (or also 'doing being x') implies that social roles, cultural identities, and their characteristics should not be understood as a stable individual 'property'. Instead, they should be seen as dynamic and unstable qualities positing demands (of the self and others) or expectations that must consistently be met anew through suitable performances. Seen in this way, even the normal, the obvious, and the unspectacular must be seen as an interactive achievement. Put differently: if humans are seen as social beings, there is no categorical difference between their 'being' and their 'doing'.

1. 'Doing Being Ordinary' (Harvey Sacks)

'On doing "being ordinary"', a posthumously published lecture by the American sociologist and ethno-methodologist Harvey Sacks, foregrounds this thesis:

Whatever you may think about what it is to be an ordinary person in the world, an initial shift is not to think of 'an ordinary person' as some person, but as somebody having as one's job, as one's constant preoccupation, doing 'being ordinary'. It is not that somebody *is* ordinary; it is perhaps that that is what one's business is, and it takes work, as any other business does. If you just extend the analogy of what you obviously think of as work—as whatever it is that takes analytic, intellectual, emotional energy—then you will be able to see that all sorts of nominalized things, for example, personal characteristics and the like, are jobs that are done, that took some kind of effort, training, and so on.[15]

---

[15] Harvey Sacks, 'On Doing "Being Ordinary"', in John Maxwell Atkinson and John Heritage (eds.), *Structures of Social Action: Studies in Conversation Analysis* (Cambridge, 1984), 413–29, at 414.

In order to make this definition more accessible, I cite the
example that Sacks uses to illustrate his basic thesis:

A core question is, how do people go about doing 'being an ordinary
person'? In the first instance, the answer is easy. Among the ways you go
about doing 'being an ordinary person' is to spend your time in usual
ways, having usual thoughts, usual interests, so that all you have to do to
be an ordinary person in the evening is to turn on the TV set. Now, the
trick is to see that it is not that it *happens* that you are doing what lots of
ordinary people are doing, but that you know that the way to do 'having
a usual evening', for anybody, is to do that. . . . (And some people, as a
matter of kicks, could say, 'let's do "being ordinary" tonight. We'll watch
TV, eat popcorn', etc. Something they know is being done at the same
time by millions of others around.)[16]

Social roles, cultural identities, and much of what we perceive as
a person's character are actually always tied to some (mostly interactive) *doing*. Identities are simultaneously produced and
confirmed in volatile communicative exchanges, in which they
might also change and adapt to new contexts.

The conceptualization of socio-cultural identities as the product
of the communicators' permanent performance is also a key
concept in the work of Harold Garfinkel[17] and Erving Goffman,[18]
who fruitfully pursued it, for example in the deconstruction of the
'naturalness' of gender identity.[19] Subsequently, the concept of
'doing x', which was more pointedly expressed in Judith Butler's
interpretation of Austin, gained great resonance and was further
explored in social science and linguistic gender studies.[20]

Helga Kotthoff, one of the scholars within German linguistics
who early picked up performance theory and made it productive
in her own work, defines the concept of 'doing' and 'doing being'
with regard to gender construction as follows: 'Anyone dealing with
"doing gender" wants to describe how people *performatively* identify

[16] Ibid. 415.
[17] Cf. Harold Garfinkel, *Studies in Ethnomethodology* (Englewood Cliffs, NJ, 1967); and id.,
'Remarks on Ethnomethodology', in John J. Gumperz and Dell H. Hymes (eds.), *Directions
in Sociolinguistics* (New York, 1972), 301–24.
[18] The basic texts are Erving Goffman, *Interaction Ritual: Essays on Face-to-Face Behavior*
(Garden City, NY, 1967); and id., *Frame Analysis: An Essay on the Organization of Experience*
(New York, 1974).
[19] Id., 'The Arrangement between the Sexes', *Theory and Society*, 4 (1977), 301–31.
[20] Cf. Candice West and Don H. Zimmerman, 'Doing Gender', *Gender and Society*, 1
(1987), 125–51; Helga Kotthoff, 'Was heißt eigentlich "doing gender"? Zu Interaktion und
Geschlecht', in Jirina van Leeuwen-Turnovcová et al. (eds.), *Gender-Forschung in der Slawistik*,
Wiener Slawistischer Almanach, Sonderband 55 (Vienna, 2002), 1–27.

themselves as male or female and through what strategies the cultural gender thus created is made relevant in everyday culture.'[21]

2. *Backgrounding and Foregrounding*

Helga Kotthoff emphasizes that not all interactive procedures of construing social and cultural identity have the same status. She differentiates between *foregrounding activities*, which are explicitly and consciously directed towards the staging of a social role or a particular identity, and activities which are performed in passing and therefore have the status of *background phenomena* but, despite this, have a crucial function in the construction of identity. Interacting partners are rarely conscious of such communicative activities.[22] In a functional perspective, they often do not seem relevant for the completion of the communicative task.

This differentiation is theoretically interesting and methodologically helpful. Hence, for 'doing gender', utterances which thematize 'common knowledge' of what tasks men or women are especially apt for, such as 'Let me do that, women are better at that', are examples of an explicit staging of gender. The fact that women perform many interactive activities with a smile, which men do less often, is, on the other hand, an example of a performative background phenomenon. Such background phenomena do not have the characteristics of an intentional activity; they are habitualized and are not interpreted as a conscious interactive achievement but as normal or 'natural' behaviour—by the actor himself/herself as well as by the addressee.

What Clifford Geertz demands of good ethnographical descriptions, namely, that they are 'microscopic' and 'thick',[23] is something that performance analysis should also be. Doing 'thick descriptions' of communicative practices is a methodological means of becoming aware of the systematics of background phenomena that are otherwise easily ignored.

3. *Actors, Co-Actors, and Addressees*

As the preceding discussion has made clear, performances are at least partly a communicative co-production. Social roles and

---

[21] Ibid. 1 (trans.), emphasis added.   [22] See ibid. 1.
[23] Clifford Geertz, *The Interpretation of Cultures: Selected Essays* (New York, 1973).

cultural identities are rarely constituted by the speaker alone, but must normally be brought forth, or at least ratified or supported, by all interlocutors *in cooperation*. And when Judith Butler emphasizes that 'the meaning of a performative act is to be found in [the] apparent coincidence of signifying and enacting',[24] this focus on the part of the actors must be widened to include that of the interacting partners. Only when signifying and enacting is complemented by understanding and co-acting is the performative effect fully achieved. This again presupposes a broad congruence between behavioural patterns and expectations of the co-actors and, as a condition for successful communication, a shared knowledge of social symbolics. This knowledge, which is culturally and historically conditioned and, accordingly, variable, is normally not explicit and the interlocutors do not have to be aware of it. Many of the discrepancies in intercultural or intergenerational communication that arise despite the interlocutors' goodwill can be traced back to infelicitous cooperations in the performative production of social roles because of a lack of shared knowledge. The analysis of performative acts therefore presupposes that critical attention is given not only to a 'sender's' staging performance but also to the interpretation and cooperation performed by the respective addressee(s).

In addition to the cognitive dimension of knowledge, the emotional level, which has frequently been discussed but rarely systematically investigated, probably plays a certain part. I make this point thinking of Paul Ricœur, who suggested it in a brief remark in his essay 'L'Écriture de l'histoire et la représentation du passé' (2000). He states that 'the creation of beliefs is not the theme of rhetoric only. It is the crossover of convincing and attracting.'[25] Whereas the term 'rhetoric' refers to the role of the speaker and thus his/her linguistic performance, the term 'attraction' refers to the role of the addressee and co-actor, on whose resonance the actor (speaker) depends. This emotional dimension of performative acts which Ricœur is talking about has so far largely been ignored in both performance theory and linguistic theory.[26] The

---

[24] Butler, 'Burning Acts', 198.

[25] 'Il apparaît alors que le faire-croire n'est pas la chasse gardée de la rhétorique. Il est le lieu d'entrecroisement du convaincre et du plaire.' Paul Ricœur, 'L'Écriture de l'histoire et la représentation du passé', *Annales: histoire, sciences sociales*, 4 (2000), 731–47, at 745 (trans.).

[26] Selective attempts to present the category theoretically and to make it productive in the analysis of political language have been made by e.g. Utz Maas, 'Konnotation', in

linguistic concept of 'connotation', which is suitable to account for the dimension of emotionality, at least at the lexical level, has so far been predominantly treated as the 'wastebasket of semantic analysis'.[27] However language, whether at the analytical level of words and phrases or at the level of communicative practices, must be considered a decisive factor in the way that emotions, attitudes, and values are collectively appropriated. Therefore emotional effects should also be included in the analysis of performative acts. Conceptions of the performative, which are more strongly oriented towards theatricality and its aesthetics, typically foreground self-referentiality.[28] The fact that both theatricality and aesthetics may contribute to the co-actors' 'attraction' and thus secure their part in the performative act is a theoretical point that should not be ignored.

IV *Performance(s) in Politics?*

The question of specific performative acts in the context of political communication can now be expressed with respect both to particular performative signatures used by individual exponents in the political arena, and complex systems of such signatures that distinguish political systems on the whole.

The 'manual' that Harvey Sacks recommends for the development of a performativity trained view of the world, 'to see that all sorts of nominalized things . . . are jobs that are done',[29] is helpful in both cases. Performance analyses and the questions they entail will neither open a radically new perspective on political communication nor will they give any completely new answers to the question of the function of 'Political Languages in the Age of Extremes'. However, an approach via performance theory can usefully (1) address existing questions more precisely, (2) complement existing investigative designs for the analysis of political communication, that is, for example, the theatricality of fascism

Franz Januschek (ed.), *Politische Sprachwissenschaft* (Opladen, 1985), 71–95; and Dieckmann, *Politische Sprache—Politische Kommunikation.*

[27] Utz Maas, 'Sprache im Nationalsozialismus: Analyse einer Rede eines Studentenfunktionärs', in Konrad Ehlich (ed.), *Sprache im Faschismus* (Frankfurt am Main, 1989), 162–97, at 168.

[28] Cf. Erika Fischer-Lichte, *Ästhetik des Performativen* (Frankfurt am Main, 2004).

[29] Sacks, 'On Doing "Being Ordinary"', 414.

proposed by Emilio Gentile,[30] and (3) increase the awareness of
the performative effects of linguistic acts in politics that are not
normally given foremost attention but precisely for that reason
might be all the more effective.

As mentioned earlier, so far not even linguistic research on
political language and communication has made any thorough
use of performance-theoretical approaches.[31] Konrad Ehlich's
innovative considerations on the use of political language in
National Socialism are an exception,[32] one which I shall discuss
briefly in what follows.

1. *Performative Signatures of Political Communication in National Socialism*

As one of the few linguists who deals extensively with the use of
language in fascism, Konrad Ehlich thematizes the level of speech
acts. In so doing, he carves out performative elements, without
using this terminology, that had a constitutive function in National
Socialism. What is at stake here is the speech act of 'promising',
that of 'commanding', and their specific interdependency—an
approach that can be further developed from the perspective of
performance analysis.

As Ehlich states, 'promising' is a speech act that was central to
fascist language practice,[33] and reappeared with striking frequency in various kinds of political performances and events.
According to Ehlich, the characteristic of the speech act of promising as a 'reference to a verbally anticipated future'[34] contributed
decisively to the success of National Socialism. However, given
that referring to the future is part of the verbal business of politics
in general,[35] and not only at times of uncertainty as was undoubtedly the case after 1928, the special effectiveness of Nazi acts of

---

[30] Emilio Gentile, 'The Theatre of Politics in Fascist Italy', in Günter Berghaus (ed.),
*Fascism and Theatre: Comparative Studies on the Aesthetics and Politics of Performance in Europe 1925–
1945* (Providence, RI, 1996), 72–93.

[31] Cf., however, Scharloth, 'Ritualkritik und Rituale des Protests', for an approach to
the forms of protest in the 1968 students' movement in Germany along the lines of performance theory.

[32] Konrad Ehlich (ed.), *Sprache im Faschismus* (Frankfurt am Main, 1989).

[33] See ibid. 23.   [34] Ibid. (trans.).

[35] As the felicity conditions for a promise presume that one only promises something
pleasant for the addressee, Ricœur's 'attraction' factor must be considered a systematic
element of this speech act.

promising does not seem to be satisfactorily explained by their reference to the future alone.[36]

What should be considered, therefore, might be less the speech act of promising as such but rather the overwhelming 'piling' of this particular kind of speech act in the context of public communication under National Socialism. What 'job'—*sensu* Sacks—was actually being done here? Before attempting an answer, one must consider, beyond Searle's 'felicity conditions', that when promising, a speaker not only announces what he/she is going to do, but *simultaneously* states that he/she has the means and the power to realize the thing promised. More technically formulated, it could be said that the speech act of promising *pragmatically presupposes* the necessary acting power of the speaker. And this means that in and with the (however theatrically supported) performance of promising, the relevant pragmatic presuppositions are performatively produced as well. Whoever makes a promise also claims to be in a particular position of power which, because of the promise's orientation towards the future, can only become falsified at a later point in time when the speaker can or cannot deliver what he/she has promised.

This argument is supported by Konrad Ehlich's observation that apart from 'promising', 'commanding' was the most salient speech act in the National Socialist speech act economy.[37] This is relevant to the extent that 'commanding', too, like 'promising', presupposes the speaker's *position of power*, in this case not towards the general social circumstances, but towards the addressee. Correspondingly, the agent of the future act to which the command refers is the recipient and not the speaker himself or herself.

The interaction of the 'central illocutionary types of promising and commanding'[38] in fascist political speech acts as described by Ehlich can therefore be analysed as a *doubling of the performance of power*. The speaker's superior position, systematically presupposed

---

[36] Nor is Ehlich's explanation of the particular credibility of National Socialist promises (that the addressees had 'not yet been disappointed by earlier promises') entirely convincing. Ehlich refers to the positive changes in the economy after 1933, which actually had no direct connection with fascist policies but were frequently experienced as a 'confirmation of precisely this credibility in the individual biography of many people'. Ehlich, *Sprache im Faschismus*, 23 (trans.).   [37] See ibid. 24.

[38] Ibid. (trans.). Ehlich sees this interaction primarily in that promising and persuasion help produce the 'preconditions for commanding'.

by promising but usually unnoticed, is reinforced and highlighted by the juxtaposition of promise and command: the saliency of the two speech acts in the performative economy of National Socialism thus appears to be an element of a particular 'doing being powerful'. And in this respect, the juxtaposition of promise and command can be understood as a *performative signature of fascism.*

2. *Performatives and Collective Identity*

Greetings and farewells are among the almost unnoticeable everyday performatives. Although quantitatively dominant in interactive everyday life, they rarely attract meta-communicative attention. In view of the level of social contacts, Erving Goffman describes them as 'access rituals', that is, as specific forms of 'supportive interchanges' which, as 'ritual brackets', separate states of 'increased access' from those of 'decreased access'. They mark a transition from one such state to the other.[39] Greetings create a rhythm in the stream of everyday interaction and in that sense have an 'auxiliary function'. At the same time they are independent performative acts whose formal spectrum stretches from the fleeting non-verbal toss of the head with which one greets a colleague in passing, to the complex and often highly ritualized greeting ceremonies in institutional contexts,[40] such as state visits whose central function is to produce or confirm social and cultural order. Greetings comprehend hierarchies of status or gender, configurations of social and emotional proximity or distance, modalities of communication such as formality and informality, etc. The practical variability of greeting acts is immense and correlates with the variability of the individuals' social relations and with the diverse socio-cultural identities of those taking part.

Yet in all communicative communities there are specific linguistic and gestural traditions and patterns of communication which to some extent restrict this variability at the individual level, in turn producing collectivity.[41] Hence greetings are cultural performances

---

[39] See Erving Goffman, *Relations in Public: Microstudies of the Public Order* (London, 1971), ch. 3, 62–94, esp. 79.

[40] See e.g. Adam Kendon, 'A Description of Some Human Greetings', in id., *Conducting Interaction: Patterns of Behavior in Focused Encounters* (Cambridge, 1990), 153–208, for a detailed description of the complex interplay between verbal and non-verbal practices in greeting ceremonies.

[41] Communicative communities differ in their more or less fixed greeting formulas.

par excellence: they serve the iterative generation of affiliation and of cultural and social orders. The history of (linguistic) greeting behaviour should therefore also be read as that of social and cultural change. Against this background, resistance on the part of the older generation or other social groups to 'new' greeting formulas—in German this currently applies to the upcoming greeting 'Hallo'—should be interpreted as resistance to changing socio-cultural orders. In these cases, the irritation is triggered not by the choice of words, but by the performance crystallized in it; the irritation is not a matter of language-worlds but of life-worlds.[42] Therefore a change in the use of linguistic greeting formulas displays long phases of competing linguistic habits.

From this perspective the introduction of the so-called 'Deutscher Gruss' (literally: German greeting; that is, the Hitler or Nazi salute, consisting of the verbal formula 'Heil Hitler' and/or the gesture of raising the right arm) by the German Nazi Party after 1926 and its general adoption by the German public after 1933 is a performative monstrosity. It is to the sociologist Tilman Allert's merit that he made this 'ghost of a twelve-year-long symbolic and spiritual masquerade of beginning and parting'[43] a topic of research. In his study, Allert explores and analyses the contexts and cognitive mechanisms that accompanied private and institutional forms of appropriation and approval of the 'Hitler salute'.[44] And despite the passage just quoted, which speaks of a linguistic and gestural 'masquerade' and thus *misses* the performative character of the act condensed in the Hitler salute, Allert's investigation is quintessentially performative. Neither the study's point of departure nor its framework explicitly subscribes to performance theory approaches. But by analysing in detail the potential of the Hitler

Examples are religious greetings ('Grüss Gott'), greetings typical of certain professions (such as 'Glück auf', used by German miners), military greetings, non-verbal greeting rituals in youth peer-groups, generational and/or socially marked forms of greeting, farewell kissing, etc.

[42] The quick dissemination of the German greeting formula 'Tschüss', which until the 1960s was reserved strictly for farewells between close friends, among strangers as well is, therefore, not only a historico-linguistic phenomenon, but also of socio-historical and cultural-historical pertinence. See Angelika Linke, 'Informalisierung? Ent-Distanzierung? Familiarisierung? Sprach(gebrauchs)wandel als Indikator soziokultureller Entwicklungen', *Der Deutschunterricht*, 52/3 (2000), 66–77. The same can be said of the generalization of the greeting form 'Hallo' earlier mentioned.

[43] Tilman Allert, *Der deutsche Gruss: Geschichte einer unheilvollen Geste* (Berlin, 2005), 21 (trans.).

[44] Ibid.

salute (consisting of a gesture and a linguistic act) to generate awareness and reality, Allert redirects the focus onto the performative power of the greeting as a medium of desired or enforced participation in the collective forming of a new societal order.

Allert's study shows how the communicative practice of the greeting can be understood as the place of the performative amalgamation of individual and collective identity and of public and private speech, thereby identifying the 'Hitler salute' as a constitutive element in the totalitarian society of National Socialism. The study thus demonstrates—even without the label—the productivity of the performative approach, especially for understanding the techniques of integrating individuals, citizens, and national subjects into political systems and for understanding the formation of a particular ordering of power.[45]

The two studies I have chosen here as examples deal with political communication under National Socialism as a political system, which is particularly characteristic of the 'Age of Extremes', and whose linguistic and performative signatures require further investigation. However, the performative construction of democratic systems is by no means less crucial as a topic of research.

One field of research that makes use of performance theoretical approaches in empirical studies and critically discusses and theoretically develops performance theory is (American) linguistic anthropology. Alessandro Duranti, who is one of its outstanding representatives, formulates the central concern of his work as to 'venture into the world of social action, where words are embedded in and constitutive of specific cultural activities such as telling a story, asking for a favor, greeting, showing respect, praying, giving directions, reading, insulting, praising, arguing in court, making a toast, or explaining a political agenda'.[46] As this quotation emphasizes, even the analysis of political communication should pay particular attention to the juxtaposition of unimportant and important, of ostentatious and elusive communicative practices, and their performative impact.

[45] The interactional and symbolic effects connected with the choice of the greeting formula 'Heil Hitler' and the corresponding gesture identified by Allert cannot be discussed in detail here. However, they represent one core issue of his study and offer many points of departure for further investigation based on linguistic performance theory.

[46] Alessandro Duranti, 'Linguistic Anthropology: History, Ideas, and Issues', in id., *Linguistic Anthropology: A Reader* (Malden, Mass., 2001), 1–38, at 1.

PART II

The Rise of the Dictators and the Semantics of Leadership

3

Fascistese: The Religious Dimensions of Political Language in Fascist Italy

EMILIO GENTILE

This paper will focus on the religious dimensions of fascist political language, which, for brevity, I will call *fascistese*. *Fascistese* is substantially made up of three dimensions: religious, military, and bureaucratic. However, the religious dimension was, in many ways, the predominant one in fascist rhetoric, being more closely linked to the fundamental structure of the political culture of the fascists. This culture was based on the supremacy of mythical thought and on the concept of politics as a total life experience, both in individual and collective terms. This is an extremely complex subject and can only be developed here in a very condensed form, by means of some general reflections, supported by examples, selected to represent the behavioural patterns that we may consider as constituting the essential characteristics of fascism, universally shared by all, or the majority of those who were fascist.[1]

The analysis of fascist political language has already been initiated within several research projects, but there are no in-depth studies in existence as yet. Up to now, the study of fascist political language has concentrated on the language used by Mussolini. There is no doubt that much of *fascistese* was the invention of the writer and orator Mussolini. He was an extremely able creator of neologisms and rhetorical formulas which were received and imitated in all fascist linguistic expression, from the highest fascist

---

[1] On fascist language see H. Ellwanger, *Sulla lingua di Mussolini* (Milan, 1941); M. T. Gentile, *Educazione linguistica e crisi della libertà* (Rome, 1966); E. Leso, 'Storia delle parole politiche: Fascista (Fascio, Fascismo)', *Lingua nostra*, 32/2 (1971), 54–60; id., 'Aspetti della lingua del fascismo: Prime linee e di una ricerca', in M. Gnerre, M. Medici, and R. Simone (eds.), *Storia linguistica dell'Italia nel Novecento* (Rome, 1973), 139–58; E. Leso, M. A. Cortellazzo, I. Paccagnella, and F. Foresti, *La lingua italiana e il fascismo* (Bologna, 1977); G. Fedel, 'Per uno studio del linguaggio di Mussolini', *Il politico*, 43/3 (1978), 467–95; A. Simonini, *Il linguaggio di Mussolini* (Milan, 1978); 'Parlare fascista', *Movimento operaio e socialista*, 7/1 (1984); G. Klein, *La politica linguistica del fascismo* (Bologna, 1986); E. Golino, *Parola di duce: il linguaggio totalitario del fascismo* (Milan, 1994).

party *Gerarca* to the lowest exponents of fascist power in the lowest grades of the hierarchy. In political circles within fascist Italy, *Mussolinese* as well as *fascistese* was usually spoken. However, having recognized Mussolini's vital contribution to fascist political language, it is important to clarify that *fascistese* does not correspond precisely to Mussolini's language. This is because fascist language was not just a creation of the *Duce*, but a much more complex phenomenon, which cannot be understood without first understanding the totalitarian nature of fascism and the significance of its religious dimensions.[2] These were not limited to the language, or to symbols, myths, rites, and monuments, but were present in all cultural, ideological, institutional, and behavioural aspects.

The historian Franco Venturi expressed this effectively in 1961 when he stated that 'the totalitarian regime was the kingdom of the word. Or rather, of the word together with the loudspeaker. To believe in the magic virtue of words and make use of the technical instruments which were becoming more commonly used in precisely that period, the radio, the rotary press, film, etc., without restraint or scruple [*sic*].' Fascist rhetoric, Venturi went on to clarify, however, was

an important element of the totalitarian State, not a feather that could be removed, as many good people of the period hoped and thought. It was not a mere whim of the regime. It was something far more important: the reduction to the limits of the absurd of the ideological currents from which fascism had originated. Contrary to solid fact, scientific coherence, and rational modern consciousness, ideological values, myth, and magical idealism had been discovered. All this was reduced to a firm and profound faith that words rule the world and that the changing of calendars, names, terms, and designations is enough to change years, men, concepts, and instruments.[3]

The totalitarian state, then, was the kingdom of the word. However, I think it would be a mistake to study this 'kingdom of the word' by analysing political language in terms of mystification,

---

[2] For the interpretation of fascism as totalitarianism and political religion according to the present writer's view, see Emilio Gentile, 'Fascism, Totalitarianism and Political Religion: Definitions and Critical Reflections on Criticism of an Interpretation', in Roger Griffin (ed.), *Fascism, Totalitarianism and Political Religion* (London, 2005), 32–81; Emilio Gentile, 'The Sacralization of Politics: Definitions, Interpretations and Reflections on the Question of Secular Religion and Totalitarianism', in Constantin Iordachi (ed.), *Comparative Fascist Studies: New Perspectives* (London, 2010), 257–89.

[3] Franco Venturi, 'Il regime fascista (II)', in *Trent'anni di storia italiana (1915–1945): lezioni con testimonianze presentate da Franco Antonicelli* (Turin, 1961), 183–97, at 186.

manipulation, and demagogy alone, because these aspects are not sufficient to allow an understanding of its fascist political language, and, above all, its religious dimensions. The interpretation of fascist rhetoric as an instrument of demagogic mystification is doubtless a valid one, but it is also, in a sense, banal, because it is in itself so obvious and corresponds so closely to the reality of historical fact as not to require many examples and arguments to be persuasive. The fascists themselves were entirely aware of the demagogic role of the word. They probably shared the conviction of Gabriele D'Annunzio, who stated that the 'science of words' was the only supreme science. Whoever knows this, declared the poet, knows all, because nothing exists if not by means of the word. There is nothing more useful than words. With these, man creates all, brings down all, and destroys all.

One prominent fascist ideologist, Antonino Pagliaro, the editor of *Dizionario di politica*, the political dictionary published by the fascist party in 1940, but also a renowned glottologist and scholar of Dante, stated that 'the value of language as a political factor is incomparably great'. And, he added, it was an indispensable propaganda tool:

Since the broadest realms of the population to be reached have no will nor opportunity to apply themselves to the particular knowledge of political doctrines and systems, and less still the opportunity and will to establish comparisons between the various systems and to weigh them up to then accept the useful or the most pleasing ones, the most effective propaganda is that which stimulates easily accessible ideas through their concise expression. There are words that have attained such a high level of meaning that just saying them is enough to evoke an ideal world and an entire political agenda . . . A politician's greatness also depends on the greatness of linguistic creation, that allows him to engrave an entire agenda of will and action upon the souls of the people with a word or a phrase.[4]

Consistently with these assumptions, fascism attributed a key role to the diffusion of *fascistese* for achieving a revolution which aimed to transform the Italian conscience, mind, and character. The totalitarian regime, obsessed by the project of regenerating the Italians, was also obsessed, for a while, with linguistic regeneration. It launched a campaign for the purification of the Italian

[4] A. Pagliaro, 'Lingua', in Partito nazionale fascista (ed.), *Dizionario di politica* (Rome, 1940), ii. 785–8.

language, and the abolition of words of foreign origin and the formal 'lei' form for 'you'. This was carried out as part of the fight for cultural reform, together with the anti-bourgeois campaign and the adoption of racist and anti-Semitic legislation. Giuseppe Bottai, speaking as Minister for National Education in November 1938, said: 'We insist on having a fascist school, fascist education, and a fascist teaching method to create the all-round fascist man.' He wanted children, 'at some point, to speak fascist just as naturally as they begin to babble the first words in their language at their mothers' bosom. This is the way for school to become one with politics.'[5]

The fascists theorized openly about the demagogic use of the word. *Fascistese* was largely a demagogic language of propaganda, consciously employed to influence, manipulate, and mystify the masses. As a consequence, the adoption of a demystifying approach to the study of fascist political language, as with any public language that attempts to influence people, is undoubtedly valuable. And as I have already said, it is the most commonly used approach by those studying fascist language. That said, there are other aspects of *fascistese* that cannot be satisfactorily explained using a demystifying approach. Nor can they be analysed using the categories of demagogy and manipulation alone.

At this point I should like to draw attention to an important aspect of fascism which, perhaps precisely because of its self-evidence, often escapes those who study fascist rhetoric. I refer, to be succinct, to the 'sincerity' of *fascistese*. Fascism made unscrupulous use of demagogy and mystification to attract the attention of, and to manipulate, the masses. However, if we stop to look at the contents of its political language, we must note that fascism never tried to mask its ideas and intentions.

The paradox of the fascist spell resides precisely in the 'sincerity' of its political language, and, above all, in the 'sincerity' of its religious dimensions. Indeed, with *fascistese* we find ourselves facing a frank and brutal declaration of aversion to freedom, and of scorn for equality, happiness, and peace as ideals; we find ourselves facing a political language that glorifies irrationality, the will to power of the elected minorities, the obedience of the masses, and the sacrifice of the individual for the greater good in terms of state and nation. It exalts all of these ideas in the name of a religious

---

[5] G. Bottai, *La carta della scuola* (Milan, 1939), 216.

concept of life. The fascists never proclaimed a will to defend freedom, critical thought, and rationality in the world. They said that reason counted for little in politics, where strength and consensus founded on myth and faith rule. Fascism never promised emancipation and freedom for mankind. Both before and after it gained power, fascism showed its aversion to the self-government of the masses, and it always declared openly that it considered the masses as material to be sculpted in order to achieve its political objectives of domination and power. And all of this was proclaimed publicly on the streets, formalized in doctrinal treatises, preached in schools, engraved on people's consciences, and stamped on the façades of houses and on the streets. The fact that all these convictions and intentions were expressed in predominantly religious language makes the aspect of fascist 'sincerity' an even more complex and important issue.

Faced with fascist 'sincerity', the demystifying approach clearly seems insufficient and can be misleading if it professes to explain everything by classifying it as demagogy, manipulation, and deception. This is particularly true of the religious dimensions of *fascistese*. At this point we find ourselves faced with the fundamental question which I intend to discuss. Why was fascist political language predominantly a religious language? Of course, in a country where the Church was a large and powerful institution, and in a society that was still, for the most part, traditional and traditionalist, demagogic propaganda addressed to a population that was still generally imbued with traditional religious beliefs could not do without a religious language that was easily understandable by the masses and, at the same time, bestowed the authoritative charisma of sacredness on the demagogue. However, in this case too, the demystifying interpretation responds only in part to the question of the religious dimension of *fascistese*, because this response is limited to the public and deliberately propagandistic area of fascist political language as a demagogic tool. The part of the question that remains unaddressed, however, is the most important because it relates to the role of fascist political language not as an *instrument of mystifying propaganda* of fascist demagogy, but as a *genuine form of expression* of fascist culture.

The question of the religious dimensions of *fascistese* does not relate to the language which the demagogue used to address the common people, to mystify and manipulate them. More importantly, it concerns the language in which one fascist addressed another, that is to say, the language through which fascism created and defined its own identity, interpreted and built on the reality in which to act and work on its principles, values, and aims. With this in mind, *fascistese* must be studied not as a language of *mystification*, but as a language of *mythification*, in the sense that it expresses fundamental values of a culture founded on the supremacy of mythical thought, as a basic category of interpretation of reality. Thus it is not a language that 'masks', but rather a language that 'reveals' the identity of a group that uses it to define itself, the meaning and purpose of its existence and actions.

In this sense, the question of the religious dimensions of *fascistese* cannot be examined except as part of the broader question of the omnipresence of the religious dimension in all its symbolic, ritual, and aesthetic manifestations, and in the behavioural, ideological, and institutional elements of fascism. At this point it is appropriate to note that the importance of the religious dimensions of fascism, manifested above all in its language and style, was recognized for the first time, and right from the start, by the same anti-fascists who were the first to guess at the true nature of fascism in terms of its totalitarian vocation. It is well known that the term 'totalitarian' was coined by the anti-fascists in the first few months after the 'march on Rome' to define the new system of government implemented by the fascist party in order to gain a monopoly of political power.

At the same time as the terms 'totalitarian' and 'totalitarianism' were invented and introduced into the political discourse, that is, from the beginning of 1923, the anti-fascists defined fascism as a political movement with religious pretensions because it conceived of its ideology as an irrefutable dogma, to which everyone had to subscribe. Terms such as 'lay religion' and 'political religion', although they had not yet been invented, came into use at that point to refer to fascism. What makes these early insights of anti-fascist culture regarding the nature of fascism particularly important for historical analysis is the fact that they were expressed before the fascist party had gained a monopoly of political power, when the *Duce* was still playing the role of a restorer of law and order and respecting the rules of the parliamentary regime, and the majority of both sympathizers and adversaries of fascism con-

sidered it a movement without an ideology and without auton-
omy, destined to dissolve within the space of a few months.

Developing these anti-fascist insights regarding the connection
and interdependency between the totalitarian dimension and the
religious dimension, I have come to an interpretation of fascism as
a totalitarian phenomenon of which the religious dimension is a
constituent, integral, and fundamental part.[6] From this perspective, the religious dimension of fascist political language is
analysed not in order to verify its instrumental and mystifying role
in line with fascist demagogic intentions—to which, I feel, little
can be added—but to evaluate its meaning and the functions in
defining the fascist identity and its totalitarian politics. In my interpretation fascist political language, apart from being a demagogic
tool, was the logical expression of its nature as a totalitarian movement. This was also the first and most consistent manifestation of
the political sacralization of the last century.

The sacralization of politics comes about every time any political entity, such as nation, state, race, class, or party, assumes the
characteristics of a sacred entity, that is to say, a supreme power
that is indisputable and intangible, and that becomes the object of
the faith, reverence, worship, loyalty, and dedication of citizens
to the point where they are prepared to sacrifice their own lives.
As such, it is at the centre of a string of beliefs, myths, values, commandments, rites, and symbols. Fascism was the first totalitarian
experiment of the twentieth century to display the fully developed
characteristics of the sacralization of politics, even though it was
not the first political movement to use a religious kind of language.
All the modern nationalisms are secular religions based on the
sacralization of the nation as a supreme entity to which its
members owe complete loyalty and dedication. In Italian nationalism, the religious dimensions of political language have been
present since the era of the Risorgimento, above all through the
political theology of the nation devised by Giuseppe Mazzini. But
the socialist left, despite the atheist and materialist ideology of
Marxism, also developed the religious dimensions of its political
language. In 1916, Antonio Gramsci, for example, declared that
socialism was the new religion that would have to destroy
Christianity and take its place in the consciousness of modern

---

[6] See Emilio Gentile, 'Fascism in Power: The Totalitarian Experiment', in Adrian
Lyttelton (ed.), *Liberal and Fascist Italy: 1900–1945* (Oxford, 2002), 139–74.

man.[7] Gramsci remained faithful to this idea, even during his years of imprisonment, in his reflections on the Communist Party as a Modern Prince who had to replace the divinity in our consciousness. When he was supporting the socialist party, Mussolini also maintained that socialism was not just a scientific concept, but had to become a 'faith': 'We want to believe in it, we must believe in it; humanity needs a creed.'[8]

The entire 'generation of 1914', to which the promoters and main protagonists of fascism belonged, actively aspired to create a foundation of lay religiousness in order to achieve the regeneration of the Italians. Gabriele D'Annunzio contributed a great deal to the making of a nationalist political language, inventing religious metaphors, symbols, and rites for the worship of the nation. Fascism drew on this heavily to furnish its symbolic universe, which for the most part was based on the experiences and the myths of the First World War. The war itself contributed to the sacralization of politics, providing new material with which to build a national religion, with the myths, rites, and symbols born in the trenches.[9]

All of the religious rhetoric of fascism was a reworking and adaptation to its own ideology of this tradition of lay religiousness, which was already widespread in Italian political culture before its birth. In the fascist press of the era and in the private writings of the fascists, such as letters and diaries, religious language predominates in the way in which they define their identity and the reasons behind their actions.

Fascistese was already imbued with religious rhetoric when the movement was made up of just a few hundred militant activists. In 1921, the official body of the fascist movement proclaimed: 'We have gone beyond the defenders of a generation which has long since left its historical reality behind and marches inexorably towards the future . . . We are the perfection of perfection . . . The Holy Eucharist of war formed us out of the same metal of generous sacrifices.'[10] During the Biennio Rosso (two red years), for example, the fascists compared themselves to 'missionaries of Christianity, lost in unexplored regions between savage idolatrous

---

[7] Antonio Gramsci, *Cronache torinesi 1913–1917*, ed. S. Caprioglio (Turin, 1980), 329.
[8] See Emilio Gentile, *The Origins of Fascist Ideology* (2005), 3–38.
[9] See id., *The Sacralization of Politics in Fascist Italy* (Cambridge, Mass., 1996).
[10] G. Leonardi, 'Noi siamo i superatori', *Il fascio*, 14 May 1921.

tribes'.[11] The violence which the *Squadrismo*, the fascist action squads, perpetrated against the proletariat was legitimized and exalted by a religious rhetoric that presented it as a redeeming crusade against the 'triumphant beast' of Bolshevism, in order to destroy those desecrating the homeland and restore religion to the nation.

For fascists, the foundations and essence of political militancy were always summed up as the principle of 'faith', a key word in fascist political language. The prototype of the new fascist man, as a believer and militant of a political religion, was defined once and for all in the fascist military regulations published at the beginning of October 1922:

The Fascist Militiaman serves Italy in purity; his spirit is pervaded by a profound mysticism, subject to an immutable faith, controlled by an inflexible will; he scorns opportunity and prudence, as he does baseness; sacrifice is the ultimate aim of his faith; he is convinced of the weight of his terrible apostleship, to save our great common mother and give her force and purity . . . Leader or follower, he obeys with humility and commands with force. In this voluntary militia, obedience is *blind, absolute, and respectful* to the peak of the hierarchy, to the Supreme Leader and the Leadership of the Party. The Fascist Militiaman has a morality all his own. Common morality, morality with a familiar face, political, social morality, prismatic, many-faceted, loosely linked, is of no use to the Fascist Militiaman. For him honor is, as it was for the knights of old, a law that seeks, without ever reaching its goal, the peak of a limitless perfection, even if he falls into error; it is all-powerful, absolutely just, even outside, and always superior to, written and formal law. Absolute honor is the law of discipline for the militiaman and is defended not only by the political organs but by the leaders of the hierarchy. The Fascist Militiaman refuses the impure, the unworthy, and the treacherous.[12]

After the fascist accession to power, the development of the religious dimensions of *fascistese* involved both symbolic and propaganda representation and theoretical elaboration. It should not be forgotten that the main promoters of the religious dimensions of *fascistese*, during the regime, were not party propagandists, but highly cultured intellectuals, such as Giovanni Gentile, who considered fascism a religion because it had 'the religious sentiment for which one takes life seriously . . . as worship given up by the

---

[11] R. Forti and G. Chedini, *L'avvento del fascismo: cronache ferraresi* (Ferrara, 1923), 90.

[12] Regulations of the Fascist Militia, 3 Oct. 1922, in Gentile, *Sacralization of Politics*, 19.

soul of the Nation'.[13] Some of these intellectuals were also fervent
Catholics, such as the first theorist of 'fascist mystique', Pietro
Misciattelli, a scholar of literature and medieval mysticism. In
1923 he defined fascism as 'a form of Catholic mysticism', maintaining that 'Catholic Truth and fascist Truth have come together
through mystic intuition'. He described the violence and intolerance of the fascist action squads as mystical, comparing it with the
violence of the 'mystic followers of Savonarola', who had fought
against pagan Florence, just as the fascists were fighting against
the Bolshevik deniers of the homeland, God, and the family.
Misciattelli concluded that 'there is a sublime violence within
every mystic movement'.[14]

The transformation of fascism into a political religion had been
accomplished by 1925, when its main arguments were laid out in
the organ of Italian fascists abroad:

The mystical element in Fascism is the chrism anointing its triumph.
Reason is incommunicable, so is feeling. Reasoning does not attract; it
convinces. Blood is stronger than syllogism. Science pretends to explain
the miracle, but in the eyes of the masses, the miracle remains, seduces,
and creates its own neophytes.

A century from now, history may tell us that after the war a Messiah
arose in Italy, who began speaking to fifty people and ended up evangel-
izing a million; that these first disciples then spread through Italy and
with their faith, devotion, and sacrifice conquered the hearts of the
masses; that their language was one in disuse, that it came from such a
remote time that it had been forgotten—they spoke of duty when others
spoke of rights, of discipline when all had abandoned themselves to
license, of family when individualism was triumphant, of property when
wealth had become anonymous, of a fatherland when hatred divided its
citizens and alien interests slipped through the frontiers, of religion when
all denied it from fear of the ultimate judge. But in the end they won:
because they returned good for evil; because they protected their very
enemies; because every day they accomplished miracles of love; because
every hour told tales of their humble heroism; because when men met
them, they became better men; because through their activity Italy
became more orderly, peaceful, prosperous, and great; because they had
a joyful song in their hearts, and in their eyes shone their sacrifices;
because they fell with a cry of faith, and for each man who fell, a
hundred sprang up; and because when the truth shines in every part,
not even an owl can gainsay it.

[13] Giovanni Gentile, *Fascismo e cultura* (Milan, 1928), 58.
[14] Pietro Misciattelli, 'La mistica del fascismo', *Critica fascista*, 15 July 1923.

This is how Fascism won: through its militia . . . The chalice of sacrifice is offered to the best, and we must drink of it. Then, as Christ said when he drank from the sponge soaked in vinegar, we can say, *Consummatum est.* Its sacrifice is the triumph of others. What matters a single individual? What counts is the race, the stock; its renewal is vital for the good of the fatherland and the world. The *Duce* has spoken . . . His command is our law—or, better yet, is the unfolding of our own law, that which is already within us. From every part of the world people look to Italy as a beacon to lead mankind to salvation . . . We are the princes, those who cast the die among the new legions of civilization.[15]

During the regime, the religious dimensions of fascist political language expanded and intensified so much as to give rise to growing fears on the part of the Catholic Church.[16] Soon after the signing of the agreement, the secretary of the fascist party, addressing young people, stated that they should 'believe in Fascism, in the *Duce*, in the Revolution, as one might believe in the Divinity'.[17] In 1930, Bottai stated that fascism was 'something rather more than a doctrine. It is a political and civic religion . . . it is the religion of Italy.'[18] In 1930 a school of fascist mystique was set up, and important intellectuals and artists of the regime taught at it. In 1932 the Young Fascists' Organization proclaimed: 'A good fascist is religious. We believe in a mystical Fascist because it is a mystique with its martyrs, its devotees, and humbles a whole people before an idea.'[19] In 1932 Mussolini decreed once and for all, in the official text of the fascist doctrine, published by the Italian Encyclopaedia: 'Fascism is a religious conception of life.'[20]

Consistently with this concept of politics, from 1926 on, fascism propagandized its ideology as a religious doctrine, condensing it in handbooks and catechisms. In 1938 the fascist party published an official catechism of the fascist religion addressed to young

---

[15] 'Santa milizia', *I fasci italiani all'estero*, 2 May 1925. Quoted from Gentile, *Sacralization of Politics*, 54–5.

[16] See Emilio Gentile, 'New Idols: Catholicism in the Face of Fascist Totalitarianism', *Journal of Modern Italian Studies*, 11/2 (2006), 143–70.

[17] *Il popolo d'Italia*, 29 Oct. 1926. Quoted from Gentile, *Sacralization of Politics*, 63.

[18] G. Botai, 'Il pensiero pensiero e l'azione di Giuseppe Mazzini', speech given in Genoa, 4 May 1930, reprinted in id., *Incontri* (Milan, 1943), 124. Quoted from Gentile, *Sacralization of Politics*, 73.

[19] Pietro Maria Bardi, 'Mostra della Rivoluzione Fascista', *Gioventù fascista*, 10 July 1932. Quoted from Gentile, *Sacralization of Politics*, 65.

[20] Benito Mussolini, *La dottrina del fascismo*, repr. in id., *Opera omnia*, 44 vols. (Florence, 1951–80), xxvi. 118. Quoted from Gentile, *Sacralization of Politics*, 59.

people. In a question and answer format, it intended to give fascists a 'simple guide, such as might be needed for the cultivation of the mind as for the relationships of daily life'.[21] *Critica fascista*, the most 'rational of the fascist reviews', considered this book to be a 'precious tool, to compare with those booklets of the "doctrine" that can go anywhere and through which it is possible to form and support much sincere faith', precisely because the fascist culture was a culture 'to be taught, just as the catechism is taught'. Bottai's review encouraged the distribution of this fascist catechism so that 'every generation should get used to considering it "the primer" of its faith'.[22]

The Church, as I have already mentioned, took fascist religious rhetoric very seriously, in the sense that it considered it not just as a propaganda device, but as an alarming manifestation of convictions deep-rooted in the fascist mentality, which the regime put into practice through its totalitarian politics. While it accepted compromises, the regime did not abandon its ambitions. In 1931, the Pope had energetically condemned, in an encyclical, the religiousness of fascism that idolized the state. During the second half of the 1930s, the Catholic press condemned the abuse of religious language to consecrate the nation, the state, and the race as earthly divinities. In 1939, in a secret address to the Lombard bishops, Cardinal Schuster, who had been an apologist of the regime during the war with Ethiopia, denounced the dangerous spread of the 'fascist religion': 'In contrast to the apostolic faith and Catholic Church of divine origin, we have then a fascist creed and a totalitarian State that, exactly like the Hegelian one, now claims divine attributes for itself. In religious terms, the Concordat has been stripped of its substance.'[23]

However, it is important to make clear that there were also Catholics who believed that fascism, precisely because it was a 'religious conception of life', could not dissociate itself from Catholicism. It could only find its religious foundations, they suggested, by recalling the Catholic tradition, just as this, in turn, recalled Roman traditions. As the review *Rassegna nazionale* stated in 1942, advocating the coming together of Catholicism and

[21] Partito nazionale fascista (ed.), *Il primo libro del fascista* (Rome, 1938), 7. Quoted from Gentile, *Sacralization of Politics*, 64.

[22] G. Bottai, 'Dogana', *Critica fascista*, 1 May 1939.

[23] See Gentile, 'Fascism in Power', 172.

fascism, Roman and Christian traditions provided the initial foundations of fascist doctrine. It thus attained its supreme value as a supernatural and divine ethic.[24]

The expansion of the religious dimensions of fascist language was also a consequence of the intensification of the totalitarian experiment in the last years of the fascist regime. This was characterized by an obsession with accelerating the revolution of mankind through racism, anti-Semitism, and a campaign for cultural reform, including the 'cleansing' of the Italian language of foreign influences. Similarly, from a theoretical standpoint, the ideologists of the regime stressed the irrationalist and mystical definition of the fascist identity, founded on myth. The *Dizionario di politica* affirmed that myth

expresses an interpretation of history or life, incites those men who believe in it to actions that are sometimes heroic or superhuman. In the name of an absolute that allows no doubt, in a language that is both accessible and imperious, and for as long as it goes on living, myth becomes a faith, a religion, and is capable of the boldest enterprises.[25]

The Second World War was naturally a time when the religious dimensions of fascism were accentuated. Fascism had never stopped considering war as the highest, most sublime moment of the individual's total dedication to the nation, through the sacrifice of human life. The experience of defeat itself, for those who did not abjure the belief in fascism after the fall of the regime, was interpreted as an opportunity to prove and strengthen one's own faith. The language of the social republic was imbued with religious rhetoric, but it is important to note that here, once again, we find ourselves facing not just a language of propaganda, but one that defines a political identity. I will limit myself to quoting just one example that is highly significant in itself. It is a written call, entitled 'Brothers in Mussolini', from one fascist to other fascists in August 1944. 'We', it concludes,

have our national and social agenda, and a living, human flag in the form of the *Duce*: around him we pull together, without doubts, without fears, Fascism is everything . . . and we are truly side by side, ready [to] sacrifice ourselves for others . . . Just as the first Christians felt, and

---

[24] See Emilio Gentile, *Politics as Religion*, trans. George Staunton (Princeton, 2006).

[25] C.[arlo] Curcio, 'Mito politico', in Partito nazionale fascista (ed.), *Dizionario di politica*, iii. 186.

indeed were, brothers in Christ, thus we must and can feel ourselves to be brothers in Mussolini. He is the only vertex where we can meet.[26]

The religious dimensions of fascist political language survived the fall of fascism. We still find religious dimensions of *fascistese* in the neo-fascist movement that in republican Italy gave life to the strongest neo-fascist party of the West, the descendants of which, having become post-fascists, today make up part of the coalition that governs Italy and, by number of votes, constitute a third of the Italian majority. To compare fascist language and neo-fascist language could offer new elements to reinforce the interpretation that I have put forward. In conclusion, it can be summarized as follows. From the start, the religious dimensions of political language had a fundamental role in fascism because it was through these that the fascists defined their political identity, through a concept of life and politics as the faith-based support of a myth, finding religious language to be the most congenial means of expressing it. Perhaps that is why fascists and neo-fascists have never been able to produce a critical explanation of the fascist experience through rational historical analysis, but have remained tied to apologist commemorations in mystical terms.

[26] Private collection (Emilio Gentile, Rome).

4

Visualizing Political Language in the Stalin Cult: The Georgian Art Exhibition at the Tretyakov Gallery

Judith Devlin

In November 1937, as part of the celebrations of the twentieth anniversary of the October Revolution, the Tretyakov Gallery in Moscow mounted an exhibition of Georgian art. The greater part of the display was devoted to a series of canvases illustrating the acclaimed new history primer mythologizing Stalin's early political career by Lavrenty Beria, First Secretary of the Transcaucasian Regional Committee of the Russian Communist Party, who would before long be promoted to head of the NKVD in Moscow. It was on Beria's orders that the show was initially organized in Tbilisi in 1935. Envisaged as an act of homage to Stalin, the exhibition was a great success with the critics and, as far as the visitors' book enables us to judge, with the public.[1]

Every professional artist and sculptor in Georgia was pressed into service and, by spring 1936, a feverish atmosphere had descended on Tbilisi. The anxiety which beset the artists was attributable to more than well-founded fear of their patron and the general context of the incipient Terror. They were embarked on a sensitive project—the depiction of the *vozhd'* (leader), whose image was carefully controlled by Stalin's private office. Furthermore, artists usually worked not from life but from approved photographs; in

I would like to express my thanks to the Tretyakov Gallery for kind permission to consult their archive for the preparation of this material.

[1] See e.g. the review 'Bol'shoi pochin' in *Tvorchestvo*, 1 (1938), 3–5. The show was hailed then and later for pioneering the modern (Stalinist) historical-revolutionary theme; see, for example, A. Mikhailov, 'Khudozhniki sovetskoi Gruzii', *Iskusstvo*, 1 (1947), 32. That Beria was directly involved in mounting the show emerges unambiguously from the acrimonious correspondence between the head of the Committee for Artistic Affairs, Platon Kerzhentsev, Agitprop, and Molotov's office. See Rossiiskii gosudarstvennyi arkhiv sotsial'no-politicheskoi istorii (RGASPI): fo. 82, op. 2, d. 952, ll. 54–62.

this case, however, there were almost no approved images to work from. Thus, rather than transcribe photographs, as did the leading court painter Isaac Brodsky, the Georgian artists were to work from Beria's book. Of necessity, this involved moving away from the established portraiture of the *vozhd'* in easel-painting. This generally presented Stalin as a static and isolated figure at the summit of power, austerely dressed in quasi-military brown tunic and boots: an authoritative figure engaged in intellectual work alone in his office or (in Gerasimov's favourite conceit) elevated above the crowd at the tribune addressing the Party Congress.

As was the case with the big shows in Moscow, the Georgians were given a series of scenes and themes from Beria's book to illustrate.[2] However, the exhibition was by no means a simple visual transcription of the text: the choice of subjects appears to have been inspired less by Beria's text (for he passed over most of them rapidly)[3] than by the desire, on the one hand, to stress the precocity of Stalin's espousal and leadership of Bolshevism, and on the other to escape the modest and controversial confines of Stalin's documented revolutionary career by dwelling on a period where the facts were conveniently shrouded in obscurity. The very insignificance of Stalin's early revolutionary career became an advantage, as it allowed the presentation of an inspiring leader whose charisma could be all the more vividly imagined in that fantasy was not constrained by inconvenient or unglamorous detail. Thus, despite the ostensible purpose of illustrating a history, the exhibition concocted an image of Stalin that owed more to imagination than to fact.

---

[2] See Y. Kriger, 'Istoriya bol'shevizma v zhivopisi', *Iskusstvo*, 1 (1938), 3–4. See, too, *Zarya vostoka*, 3 Oct. 1935, for a report on the initial viewing of the unfinished pictures and sketches, submitted for critical assessment and censorship. The idea of the exhibition is attributed to Beria.

[3] e.g. Beria affirms that Stalin and his friends did 'enormous revolutionary-propaganda and organizational work on creating the illegal social-democratic party organization; the members of the central party group conducted intensive revolutionary propaganda, each of them directed several workers' circles. Stalin alone had more than eight worker social-democratic groups in Tbilisi' in 1898, and he and his comrades, 'along with propaganda of the idea of social-democratic revolution directed strikes and the political struggle of the Tbilisi proletariat'. He enumerates various strikes, referring briefly to the May Day demonstrations in Tbilisi. L. Beria, *K voprosu ob istorii bol'shevistskoi partii* (1936), 21–2. Only on the heroism of the Batumi episode, which he knew to be especially dear to Stalin, did he enlarge, ibid. 23–7.

Iconographic Language of the Exhibition

Romantic realism and narrative were the typical solution adopted by the Georgian artists, and Stalin appeared as a romantic young rebel, instructing, converting, and inspiring his disciples.[4] The requisite image of the leader was established at the start of the exhibition (which proceeded, in Moscow, in chronological-bio-graphical order) with a much-reproduced painting of the young Stalin by Konstantin Gzelishvili. Criticized for its technical inep-titude, the painting was none the less praised for showing in the child a prefiguration of the future 'teacher and friend': the boy Stalin is reading a book, explaining every word to the little com-rades who surround him, listening with rapt attention to the 'future *vozhd*'.[5] A whole series of paintings reiterated this image, incidentally also dramatizing the text and its reading. Ivan Vepkhvadze's *Comrade Stalin with his Comrades-in-Arms* depicts an urgent young Stalin exhorting his companions, who listen to him thoughtfully.[6] Stalin's superiority to them is conveyed through a number of devices: he is standing, while all but one of his com-rades (a marginal figure in the dark background) are sitting in a circle around him; he is speaking, while they are listening; he appears to be interpreting a thick and meaty text (Marx, perhaps), while they are being instructed. The drama of the situation is accentuated by the lighting: the dark room is illuminated from below, bathing these key figures of the dawn of revolution in a halo of light. We do not see a lamp or candle, but we understand that the source of true (that is, political) illumination is Stalin, the revealer of truth. The painting, like an icon, points beyond what is seen with the naked eye to the unseen spiritual significance of the occasion and, like an icon, is transcendental in function. It

---

[4] The following discussion is based principally on the illustrations in *Vystavka proizvedenii zhivopisi, grafiki i skul'ptury gruzinskoi SSR: katalog* (Moscow, 1937); and B. Gogua (ed.), *Vystavka k istorii bol'shevistskikh organizatsii Gruzii i Zakavaz'ya: fotoreproduktsii* (Tbilisi, 1939).

[5] Gzelishvili's painting *Comrade Stalin in his Youth* is reproduced in *Vystavka proizvedenii zhivopisi*. Like many of the artists involved in the show, Gzelishvili, who was born in 1902, went on to have a successful career within the Soviet art establishment, becoming an Honoured Artist of Soviet Georgia. For brief biographical information on many of the participants in the show, see *Spravochnik chlenov i kandidatov v chleny soyuza khudozhnikov SSSR* (Moscow, 1966). For critical comments on this work, see Y. Kriger, 'Istoriya bol'shevizma v zhivopisi', *Iskusstvo*, 1 (1938), 9–10.

[6] Ivan Vepkhvadze (b. 1888) became a People's Artist of Georgia. This painting is reproduced in *Vystavka proizvedenii zhivopisi*.

suggests the existence of a higher truth and reality, which only Stalin can see and speak of.

Almost identical in conception was V. Krotkov's *Comrade Stalin: The Organizer of the First S.D. Workers' Circles in Tiflis (1898)*.[7] Here, Stalin's audience is composed of gnarled workers; they sit in a dark room around a table, hanging on the standing Stalin's words, imbibing from him the revolutionary faith. The workers' features are obscured by the prevailing gloom and their pose: some sit side-on or with their backs to the viewer, whose eye—like theirs— is drawn to the one illuminated figure, Stalin. Only one character is deemed worthy of our full attention. However, Stalin, although recognizable, is not fully realized as an individual: his pale, unmarked face expresses not so much character or temperament as an ideal of the romantic rebel. This treatment of the theme was clearly an agreed formal device, for it was rehearsed in most of the paintings of the young Stalin and his followers.[8] In these paintings, Stalin's pre-eminence is unchallenged: his dignity, authority, command of the situation, and wisdom ensure that he is surrounded by respectful and attentive crowds. The fact that they are implicitly his social inferiors (by dint of the fact that he belongs to the intelligentsia, while they are illiterate manual workers) serves, ostensibly, only to underscore his modesty, generosity of spirit, and benevolence. These paintings also indicate the appropriate stance for the whole country: like the obscure disciples of the paintings, the Soviet people were to listen, admire, contemplate, and follow in reverent awe the only person who commands speech, whose word alone was significant and truth-bearing. Stalin, in these paintings, appears as more than the young revolutionary propagandist. His teaching, it is implied, is more important than mere technical knowledge: it reveals higher truths, and discloses a better order and scheme of values. The idiom of these

---

[7] The reference in the title (abbreviated in the original) is to Social Democratic circles (i.e. to the study groups organized by Russia's first Marxist party, the Russian Social Democratic Workers' Party. The painting is reproduced in Gogua (ed.), *Vystavka*.

[8] In A. I. Gigolashvili's *Illegal Meeting Headed by Stalin at Khodzhevansky Cemetery in Tiflis (1898)* a dramatically lit Stalin is encircled by workers, listening to him in the dark: they are ignorant and he is enlightened. *Comrade Stalin at a May Day Meeting of Tiflis Workers (1900)*, by Maisashvili, puts Stalin in the central halo of light, instructing an attentive dark crowd around him; see *Vystavka* (1937) for illustration. The Adzhari peasants, who are listening to the dashing young central figure of Stalin in Kutateladze's painting, are gazing away from the viewer towards the teacher and their features are again obscured by their pose. See *Vystavka* (1937), for image.

paintings recalls religious iconography, with its use of chiaroscuro, its halo of light signifying exceptional virtue and merit. Even the grouping of the figures around Stalin is reminiscent of the way Christ was sometimes depicted with his disciples.[9]

Stalin, however, was not merely a prophet, as these paintings implied. They emphasized also the heroism of his revolutionary leadership, his sufferings, and self-sacrifice. Stalin the martyr was shown calm and dignified as he is arrested, walking unintimidated between the mounted soldiers in S. Maisashvili's *Arrest of Comrade Stalin in Batum (1902)*; K. Sanadze depicts him on the same occasion as standing resolutely in a halo of light, as his room is searched by the police. In S. Makashvili's *Comrade Stalin in Baku Prison in 1910*, Stalin leans defiantly out of his jail cell to shout to fellow prisoners below him to keep their chains, as they will be useful when they overthrow the tsar.[10] The painting of these themes, while implicitly referring to a religious sub-text of martyrdom, also exploited the idiom of the popular adventure story, which we know Stalin enjoyed in his youth. Moise Toidze depicted an implausibly heroic and handsome young Stalin, ineffectually restrained by two women, defending peasants from an evil, mounted landlord at the bottom left of the picture. Bagration depicted him defying the powers of State (present in the portrait on the wall) and Church as a schoolboy. Kutateladze, in one of the most often reproduced paintings from the exhibition, shows Stalin, as usual bathed in light while a dark crowd of striking workers follow him, marching resolutely forward into the left-wing future, defying watching sol-

[9] The use of chiaroscuro and the grouping of his disciples around the illuminated figure of Christ the teacher, miracle worker, or saviour was a common feature of religiously inspired art of the Counter-Reformation. It can be observed, for example in Claude Vignon's *Christ among the Doctors* (1623, Grenoble Museum), where an illuminated young Christ is surrounded by an attentive elderly audience. In *The Pilgrims of Emmaus*, by the Le Nain brothers (before 1640, the Louvre), Christ is seated on one side of a table in an austere room, holding the attention of those around him. Stalin's arrests are represented in several works in the exhibition and again their idiom—in their drama and lighting effects—recalls classical iconography. A more immediate source for these paintings was probably Repin, the great realist painter of the later nineteenth and early twentieth centuries. In particular, the series he devoted to the revolutionary populists and propagandists in the 1880s have much in common with Krotkov's painting: the composition and arrangement of the figures, the lighting, the centrality of the dynamic and Christ-like propagandist in Repin inform the style of several canvases in the Georgian exhibition.

[10] Both of these works are reproduced in Gogua (ed.), *Vystavka*. Another illustration of Stalin's indomitable spirit in prison is given in *Comrade Stalin Conversing with Political Prisoners in Kutaisi Prison (1903)*, reproduced in Gogua (ed.), *Vystavka*, which, as usual, depicts Stalin in a gloomy cell, instructing his attentive fellow prisoners.

diers.[11] This picture celebrated Stalin's leadership of the Batumi strike of 1902, to which the new Stalinist historiography attributed vast importance, as Beria was at pains to do in his history. Other famous pictures (showing Stalin leading the Baku strikes of 1908, displaying fiery oratory at Tsulukidze's funeral) used similar formal devices: surrounding Stalin with enthusiastic workers, elevating him above the crowd, and, where enemies are present, isolating them at the dark margins of the picture.[12] Critics approved of the fact that Stalin was depicted here not alone, as in the traditional portrait, but with the faithful, humble *narod* (people / *Volk*), whose devotion to him was made explicit.[13] This device helped to transform Stalin the individual (however important) of the conventional portrait into Stalin, the mythical revolutionary persona: his biography was no longer a matter of personal significance but—as the critical literature suggested—a heroic epic, involving not merely his own personal destiny or even that of the individuals who made up the crowds following him, but above all the fate of a country, a cause, humanity.[14]

Inevitably, when Stalin meets Lenin, it is as an equal (as, for example, in I. Vepkhvadze's account of their alleged encounter in Tammerfors in 1905, where only the use of lighting hints at Lenin's primacy).[15] In its peculiar perspective (even Lenin, who appeared in only three pictures, was overshadowed), cavalier treatment of the historical record, and dramatic handling of its

[11] Moisei Toidze, *Comrade Stalin Defends Kartalinski Peasants (1895)*; V. Bagration, *Comrade Stalin's Expulsion from Tiflis Seminary*, both works reproduced in Gogua (ed.), *Vystavka*; Apollon Kutateladze, *Comrade Stalin, the Leader of the Political Demonstration of Batum Workers (1902)*, reproduced in *Vystavka* (1937).

[12] I. Vepkhvadze, *Comrade Stalin Delivers a Speech at A. Tsulukidze's Funeral (1905)*; S. Nadareishvili, *Comrade Stalin Unmasks Mensheviks at a Meeting in Chiaturi (1905)*; V. Sidamon-Aristov, *Comrade Stalin at a Meeting of Baku Oil-Workers (1908)* (all reproduced in Gogua (ed.), *Vystavka*).

[13] Kriger, 'Istoriya bol'shevizma v zhivopisi', *Iskusstvo*, 1 (1938), 8–9.

[14] 'The introduction [to the exhibition] is done almost epically. We understand the first pictures as the beginning of a legend about the life of a national hero. Old Georgia. Ancient mountains. A stone fort, perched over the valley. A simple, poor house at the foot of the mountains. The house in Gori, where Iosef Vissarionovich Stalin was born.' Kriger, 'Istoriya bol'shevizma v zhivopisi', *Iskusstvo*, 1 (1938), 6. 'Inspired by the revolutionary biography of comrade Stalin and the history of the Transcaucasian organizations led by him, Georgian painters . . . have told their creative tale about our own beloved Stalin, his remarkable deeds, his work among the Bolshevik of the Caucasus. The best works . . . on this theme open new paths for Soviet history painting. . . . [They] have enormous political and artistic significance.' *Vystavka, katalog* (1937), 3.

[15] For illustration, see Gogua (ed.), *Vystavka*.

subject, the exhibition enshrined the myth of Stalin as a revolutionary Prometheus, whose heroic and daring exploits unfolded against the backdrop of the Caucasus—a landscape long established in Russian literary tradition as the locus of Romantic rebellion and Byronic adventure and drama. History, treated in this manner, shifted almost imperceptibly from the register of documentary prose to that of poetry and legend.[16]

Reception

This shift from the documentary to the poetic is precisely what the central authorities had been looking for in painting—and, indeed, in all the arts. This was the main thrust of the socialist realism that had been promulgated as the new aesthetic in 1934. As explained by Zhdanov at the first Congress of the Union of Soviet Writers in August 1934, writers (and artists) could not be content with the stylistic solutions of the past: the new socialist world required a correspondingly new aesthetic, a 'revolutionary romanticism' which would reveal 'our tomorrow' and the heroes of the new age.[17] The principal hero, it was hardly necessary to explain, was Stalin, and his preferences in the matter of his visual image were indicated in an article on portraiture of the leaders, in one of the leading art journals, by one L. Gutman. This suggested that the existing iconography of the *vozhdi* was inadequate to meet the recently promulgated requirements of socialist realism. The boundaries of portraits of the *vozhd'* had long outgrown the limitations of biographical exposition, but contemporary artists were unable to 'see the object of depiction beyond this or that historical fact'. Most limited themselves to the '"factographic" external appearance of the *vozhd'* and this or that historical-biographic fact connected with him'.[18] More, Gutman hoped, would follow the example of Petr Staronosev's 'graphic tale' of Lenin's biography, which was based not just on photographs, but on extensive historical research, interviews, and site studies. The socialist realist portraitist should 'overcome the "deathly-mirror" relationship to

---

[16] See also the comments by Kriger, 'Istoriya bol'shevizma v zhivopisi', *Iskusstvo*, 1 (1938), 6.

[17] *The Soviet Writers' Congress 1934* (London, 1977), 22.

[18] L. Gutman, 'O portretakh vozhdei', *Iskusstvo*, 1 (1935), 5–11. Further quotations are to be found here.

nature' and the desire for mere verisimilitude, and emulate those
few artists in whose portraits of the leaders 'we can find the historically faithful revelation of their inspirational (*ideinye*) depths'. The
desired '"dual vision" of nature—from within and without—presupposed in the artist the ability to explain the world, a phenomenon, man not in its static existence but in movement, in time'.
This amounted to a call to mythologize the leaders, to depict them
in a heroic inspirational vein, untrammelled by the inconsistencies
of biography and history.

Not surprisingly, in view of its timely response to these indications, the exhibition was a great success (though not with everyone: the visiting André Gide deplored it):[19] its transfer from Tbilisi
to Moscow and Leningrad in 1937–8 was a sure sign of this. Two
hundred thousand visitors, including groups of apparently enthusiastic workers (learning *kul'turnost'*), schoolchildren, soldiers, and
Party and Komsomol workers, it was claimed, had visited and
enjoyed it.[20] Photographers and film-makers sued for permission
to record it.[21] An elaborate, three-volume celebratory album of
the show was issued. Stalin, though he did not visit the exhibition,
kept a copy of this luxury work in his archive.[22] Several artists
made their careers thanks to the exhibition, for many copies of
the originals were commissioned, and they were frequently reproduced as illustrations to cult literature, especially before the war.[23]
This would not have been possible without the permission of
Stalin's office and, ultimately, Stalin's own agreement. Hung to
great acclaim, the exhibition thus put into circulation many
famous images of the young *vozhd'*.

It was greeted, in Moscow, as a new departure in the iconography of the *vozhd'*, and the entire cohort of professional artists in the
capital was assembled on 16 February 1938 to learn the lessons of
the exhibition. The clearest statement of the show's significance
was made, on this occasion, by the Party secretary of the
Tretyakov Gallery (who had maintained contact with Beria

[19] André Gide, *Retour de l'URSS* (Paris, 1936), 85.

[20] Rossiiskii gosudarstvenny arkhiv literatury i iskusstva (RGALI): fo. 2943, op. 1, ed.
khr., 172, ll. 3–5. The positive reception was reflected in the wall-papers of Moscow
factories, while the Gallery's visitors' book predictably reflected praise: Tretyakov Gallery
Archive, fo. 8.II (i), d. 770, d. 772.

[21] Tretyakov Gallery Archive, fo. 8.II, d. 693, ll. 111–13, 139, 153.

[22] Tretyakov Gallery Archive, fo. 8.II (i), d. 997–9; *Vystavka k istorii bol'shevistskoi
organizatsii v Gruzii* (Tbilisi, 1939) was another elaborate volume.

[23] Tretyakov Gallery Archive, fo. 8.II, d. 693, ll. 87–91; d. 993, l. 60.

throughout the preparations), Melikhadze. The celebrations of the twentieth anniversary of the Revolution had marked a turning point in all the arts, as artists had posed the problem of the *vozhdi* and the *narod*. Hitherto, artists' efforts to depict Lenin and Stalin had been less deep and significant than in the Georgian show. This was the first exhibition devoted to Stalin's revolutionary career; only now were artists mature enough to tackle Lenin's and Stalin's role in the revolutionary struggle and its significance. Lest there be any ambiguity, Melikhadze criticized two paintings for inadvertently consigning Stalin to the second plane and for not imposing the *vozhd'* on the viewer, while praising another for showing the *vozhd'* as close to the people and depicting 'the warmth, greatness and monumental form of Comrade Stalin'. The show was intended to create a precedent, and the country's leading artists should follow the Georgians' lead and prepare a big exhibition to Lenin and Stalin.[24] The leaders were now to become a major theme on which all artists should work. The catalogue's introductory essay stressed that the exhibition revealed the close relations between Stalin and the *narod*, and the masses' love of and faith in the *vozhd'*. This use of religious language was no accident but, as we have seen, corresponded to the iconographic solutions adopted by the painters. Henceforth, artists were to be urged to paint the *vozhd'* and especially his legendary or epic persona.

History and Biography as Sources

Judged not by the standards of Stalin's Soviet Union but by aesthetic criteria, the exhibition's allegedly new pictorial language was derivative rather than innovative. In reality, it embodied no properly painterly language, as shaped by form, plasticity, or colour: the language of iconography in this case was determined by a set text. As was the rule under Stalin (in posters, painting, and even film), the image was underpinned by an authoritative inscription, title, slogan, or text. This not only established its meaning, excluding the potential ambiguity or polyvalence of the image and proposing to the viewer the correct way of 'reading' it, but also pointed to a hierarchy in the means of expression. The text, with its explicit language, took precedence over other more

---

[24] RGALI: fo. 2943, op. 1, ed. khr., 172, ll. 3–15, 19.

fluid and thus dangerous forms. This scale of values was implicit in the idea of basing an art exhibition on a history text and of the movement towards narrative in the painting of the *vozhd'* in the mid-1930s. Hence the fact that the paintings were occasionally ugly or inept was a secondary consideration, so long as they offered an appropriate illustration of the assigned theme. The painting or image could ultimately be reduced to the text, establishing the priority of Word over Image.

What sort of texts formed the basis of the exhibition? Beria's history, *K voprosu ob istorii bol'shevistskikh organizatsii v Zakavkaz'i* (1935), was ostensibly the main source. It was a highly tendentious and distorted reading of history: the only figure of real distinction and merit to emerge from its pages, apart from those few who died early, was Stalin. Proceeding by assertion, selective quotation, and anathema, the work was closer to a catechism than to a work of history: each chapter closed with a series of summary theses to be memorized by the reader, lest any confusion had set in. In producing this work, Beria had seized upon the Party's and Stalin's perceived need for new Party (Stalinist) histories,[25] producing a more elaborate and formal version of the little tale of revolutionary heroism and Stalinist hagiography pioneered the previous year by the Abkhaz leader, Nestor Lakoba. The resulting work was opportune and became one of the classics of Stalinist historiography. That it found favour with Stalin is not in doubt: its publication in *Pravda* was approved by him and its speedy appearance and frequent reissuing in book form confirm this.[26] Despite its vocation of helping to establish the myth of Stalin as a

[25] As early as 1931 Stalin had indicated his hostility to academic history and the classic Marxist rejection of the role of great men in shaping it. These reservations had been formalized in a decree of 1934, which called for a new textbook of Party history that would identify 'important historical events [and] historical personages'. That Beria had been fully alive to the implications of these strictures and prescriptions is evident from his criticism of Georgian historians in the Tbilisi press. Stalin, *Sochineniya* (Moscow, 1951), xiii. 84–102; Robert V. Daniels (ed.), *A Documentary History of Communism in Russia* (Hanover, NH, 1993), 185–6, 193; Amy W. Knight, *Beria: Stalin's First Lieutenant* (Princeton, 1993), 57.

[26] L. Beria, 'K voprosu ob istorii bol'shevistskoi partii v Zakavkaz'i', *Zarya vostoka*, 24–5 (July 1935). Id., *K voprosu ob istorii bol'shevistskoi partii v Zakavkaz'i* (Moscow, 1936). For a critical discussion, see Bertram D. Wolfe, *Three Who Made a Revolution: A Biographical History* (Harmondsworth, 1966), 456–88. For Stalin's vetting, see RGASPI: fo. 558, op. 11, d. 704, ll. 10–14; 20–1; 340b–380b; d. 705 contains the amendments and additions Beria proposes to Stalin for the third Moscow edition of 1937. N. Rubin, *Lavrenty Beria: mif i realnost'* (Moscow, 1998), 76–7, asserts that Stalin made mainly stylistic changes to the manuscript before publication.

significant revolutionary leader and the equal of Lenin since his youth, this work was none the less couched in the formulaic language of Marxism–Leninism. In addition, it mimicked academic style, including abundant citations from 'sources', footnotes, and references to the works of the Great Men of Marxism, principally Lenin and Stalin. However, its stylistic formality, intended to make it pass muster as an official primer of Party history, precluded its having much popular appeal. Nor was its dry dogmatism a helpful source for the Georgian painters, or indeed akin to their dramatic and pathetic style.

Beria seems to have been anxious to show Stalin that Lakoba had no monopoly on works of popular Stalinist legend and hastened to use materials gathered for his official history to produce a volume of workers' tales obviously modelled on Lakoba's story *Stalin i Khashim* (1934). Lakoba's simple and stirring tale of Stalin's revolutionary cunning and daring, supposedly recounted by the colourful old Abkhaz peasant Khashim, was cast almost in the vein of an adventure story for children, but appealed to Stalin, who awarded Lakoba the Order of Lenin after its publication (although Lakoba and his family were to fall victim to the Purges).[27] Beria's workers' tales employed the same register and enjoyed much success. Supposedly a spontaneous response to Beria's July 1935 speech on the history of the Bolshevik party in the Caucasus, they were first printed in book form in Tbilisi in 1935 and subsequently as *Tales of Old Workers from the Caucasus about the Great Stalin*.[28] All of these works—the Party primer and the popular works of Stalinist hagiography and revolutionary folklore—furnished the texts on which the Georgian artists drew.

The old workers recounted stories of Stalin's revolutionary derring-do, likening his appearance, in the underground cells he organized, to an epiphany: a sudden revelation of truth, an

[27] *Stalin i Khashim: nekotorye epizody iz batumskogo podpolya* (Sukhumi, 1934). The book was reissued twice in Moscow in 1935, twice in 1936, and three times in 1938.

[28] First published in *Zarya vostoka*, 18 Sept., 24 Sept., 4 Oct., 5 Oct. 1935; they were published in book form in Tbilisi in 1935 and 1936 as *Velikii vozhd' i uchitel': rasskazy starykh rabochikh o rabote t. Stalina v Zakavkaz'i* (2nd edn. Tbilisi, 1936). Republished in a luxury edition in Tbilisi in 1937, they were reissued in Moscow as *Rasskazy starykh rabochikh Zakavkaz'ya o velikom vozhde* (Moscow, 1937), and frequently anthologized in children's literature and in works published for Stalin's (putative) sixtieth birthday in 1939. They were probably the result of Bedia's researches for Beria's history. Rubin affirms that he interviewed many veterans for it. See Rubin, *Beria*, 76.

inspiration of revolutionary energy. One old worker (P. G. Kuridze) describes the impact of Stalin's arrival in Batumi:

I was captivated by his speeches. At last we understood the secret of exploitation . . . How clearly, simply and convincingly comrade Soso spoke: in his words everything was revealed as though self-evident.[29]

Stalin's eloquence and message of worker liberation ensured, we are told, that he captured large audiences. Another disciple, Osman Gurgenidze, recalled his surprise when he saw that 'the whole room was packed with workers who, closely grouped around the young man, attentively listened to his words'. The hours passed quickly, according to Kuridze, and they spent nights sitting in a smoky room, 'holding our breath', listening to their 'fiery and wise . . . teacher'. The atmosphere and setting evoked by, among other things, Krotkov's picture of Stalin's workers' circles may readily be identified here. The melodrama of the paintings is present also in the workers' stories. Stalin's acolytes were taken, we are assured, by the conspiratorial atmosphere cultivated by Stalin, who used disguises and other ruses to deceive the tsarist police. His 'intelligence, courage and daring inspired us to go with him into the fight and to fight until victory'. Kuridze recalls Stalin's toast after a New Year gathering: 'Here's dawn! Soon the sun will rise. The sun will rise for us too!'[30]

Emotional and personal, simple and vivid, the tales were in a different stylistic register from Beria's dogmatic ideology primer. These heroic texts were clearly closer to the spirit of the paintings than Beria's dry references to Stalin's activities as a propagandist. From his arrival in Batumi, through his struggles in inspiring and leading the workers, his heroic defiance in jail, sufferings in prison, and clever deception of the tsarist authorities, Stalin appears not only as a prophet of revolution, but also as a martyr sacrificing himself for the oppressed people, who await their redemption after the 1917 Revolution. In addition, he was depicted in some respects like the hero of a folktale. He combines a daredevil spirit with cunning, directing underground revolutionary groups and publishing from his prison cell, assuming disguises, escaping from exile. The trickster is a no less familiar and popular character in the traditional tale than the prince, and folklorists have discerned

[29] *Rasskazy starykh rabochikh Zakavkaz'ya o velikom Staline* (Moscow, 1937), 95.
[30] *Rasskazy starykh rabochikh* (1937), 63, 65–6, 96–7.

in him a Bakhtinesque popular rebellion against the hierarchies of power. The Old Workers' Tales thus combined hagiographic elements with the popular narrative tradition of the folktale and adventure story. The exhibition, obeying the same stylistic impulse and recapitulating the same themes rather than, as its title suggested, illustrating history, thus assisted in the production of a myth of Stalin which obeyed the conventions of religious literature and art and folk narrative. In short, in the exhibition the faithful transcription of history and biography had been rejected in favour of the language of myth which was to become characteristic of the later cult.

The Language of Myth

Mythic language seems to have developed in the mid-1930s from earlier elements in the political culture in response to Stalin's known tastes and because it was opportune. Soviet mythologizing long pre-dated the flowering of Stalinist myth, but its earliest expressions had been modernist, and its official manifestations generally confined and shaped by Party convention and ideology. There were several registers of political language in Stalin's Russia. Official discourse was shaped by Marxism–Leninism, the ostensibly scientific exposition of the victorious ideology. Endlessly repeated and studied, this new political language was deployed in the leaders' ex cathedra speeches and pronouncements, in leading press articles, and the Party's academic works on such subjects as philosophy and history. On occasion Aesopian and impenetrable, long-winded and repetitive, infamous for its tedium, official language tended to function as a jargon or code, commanded only by the initiated and deployed by those empowered to speak on behalf of the Party. It was explicitly the language of power. This is not to say that attempts were not made to imitate or reproduce it by those outside the ruling circle, or that the regime was not anxious to inculcate it. Recognizing its limited appeal and communicative capacity, assiduous efforts were made to develop popular variants, principally by means of the propaganda machine.

Hence, alongside Party discourse, a more popular political language developed, officially sanctioned and encouraged, giving life to the abstractions, banalities, and occasional intricacies of official pronouncements. This language was deployed in a variety of media but the emphasis was on accessibility. Novels, songs, folklore, films, even works of popular history and biography were encouraged to adopt this idiom. Derived from elements of modernity (in form as well as symbolic content) and aspects of traditional culture, this language was generally more emotional, familiar, and simple than that of official discourse. It was the language not of Leninist theory (with its debts to philosophical and academic discourse) or even of that ideology in action (with its more vivid lexicon derived *inter alia* from religious anathema and war), but of 'living tradition', or of tradition transformed by modernity. Supposedly vernacular, spontaneous, national (that is, of the *narod*, in the Herderian sense), it was held to be the genuine product of the people, their act of homage to the regime and, above all, its leader. It was the language of myth, in the sense not only that it was reserved for the celebration of Soviet myths but also that it was characterized by a peculiar rhetoric, the quasi-popular, pseudo-traditional, emotional, and religious style deemed appropriate for the modern epic.

The toleration of the development of mythic language implies that official discourse was understood to be unable to fulfil all the regime's needs. These included more than the delivery of commands and the explanation of policy to cadres and the exhortation and instruction of the masses. Regime authority and legitimacy depended on genuine belief and enthusiasm, which required more elaborate rituals and energizing language than official discourse afforded. Stalin's attention to spectacle and entertainment indicates that he understood the need to present his message in a more palatable form. In addition, the language of myth, which crystallized around the cult of Stalin, enabled his colleagues to pay him more extravagant tributes than the Party's rituals and linguistic conventions normally allowed. For example, the Politburo's greetings to Stalin on his sixtieth birthday in December 1939, couched in official discourse, were highly rhetorical and ritualized, observing a typical pattern of development and using many of the same standard formulas. Invariable expressions of love and devotion (on behalf of the masses) were followed by more detailed rehearsals of his achievements, often in repetitive and even incantatory vein, and drawing on the same endlessly reiterated lexicon of Marxist–Leninist ideology. Vocabulary, sentence structure, and style followed a predictable, rigid model.[31] The mythic register allowed for more ingenuity. Beria, in particular, was quick to see its possibilities, pioneering tributes to Stalin in almost every medium: the *narod* in their folktales and legends, poets, artists, actors, and film-makers, in their transports of enthusiasm over the contemporary epic and its heroes, were expected to express themselves in the language of modern myth.

The most obvious example of the use of the language of myth is in Stalinist folklore. To this Beria also contributed, by ordering poets and folklorists to compose a volume of verse expressing the *narod*'s spontaneous love of the *vozhd'*. The context of this endeavour was a Central Committee decree of 1935 on the need to discover Soviet (as opposed to traditional) folklore. This, it was affirmed, was bound to exist as the people's consciousness must have been transformed thanks to the construction of socialism.[32] It was axiomatic that the *narod* would want to sing a chorus of praise to their new masters and heroes. As it happened there were ready collaborators, not necessarily motivated solely by opportunism.[33] The collection of appropriate examples started in Moscow province under the sponsorship of Kaganovich. Folklore scholars and writers of *belles lettres* were attached to the project to assist authentic folk bards in finding the right themes and terms of praise. Increasingly, folk-verse, song, and folktale were integrated into the literary canon, as the differences between high and popular culture were declared to be anachronistic in socialist society, while the new aesthetic of socialist realism affirmed the new literature to be popular in origin, content, and reception. The purpose was political: as with street festivals, the idea was to enact rituals of popular acclamation and thus establish a sense of regime legitimacy.

In Beria's volume of poetry and folk-verse, to which Pasternak contributed translations, the *vozhd'* appeared as a mountain eagle (a term applied by Stalin to Lenin in 1924),[34] the sun, a gardener

---

[31] See e.g. the offerings of Kaganovich, Khrushchev, and Beria in *Stalin: k shestidesyatiletiyu so dnya rozhdeniya* (Moscow, 1940).

[32] A. M. Astakhova et al., *Ocherki . . . russkogo tvorchestva sovetskoi epokhi* (Moscow, 1952), 190–2. E. A. Grin'ko (ed.), *Fol'klor v Rossii v dokumentakh sovetskogo perioda* (Moscow, 1994), 10–13; M. K. Azadovsky, 'Sovetskaya fol'loristika za 20 let', *Sovetskii fol'klor*, 6 (1939), 8–10.

[33] See T. G. Ivanova, 'O fol'klornoi i psevdofol'klornoi prirode sovetskogo eposa', in A. I. Poporkov, T. G. Ivanova, et al. (eds.), *Rukopisi, kotorikh ne bylo: Poddelki v oblasti slyavyanskogo fol'klora* (Moscow, 2002), 410–12.

[34] Stalin, *Sochineniya* (Moscow, 1947), vi. 52–4, speech to Kremlin *kursanty*, 28 Jan. 1924.

(Stalin fancied himself in this role and had a large library on this topic), Prometheus, and sundry Georgian epic heroes.[35] These conceits, supposedly exemplifying the people's penchant for metaphor and legend, its incapacity for abstract thought, and its love of tradition, were held to typify the language of the People, who, especially with the promulgation of Stalin's constitution, now appeared on stage in all their exotic and varied simplicity. In this, the little book resembled many others that appeared at this time celebrating not the legendary heroes (*bogatyry*) of the past, but the heroes of the contemporary epic, and first and foremost Stalin himself. To distinguish this new genre from the traditional heroic poems (*byliny*, with their connotation of the past, *byloe*) the term *noviny* (from *novyi*, new) was invented. In verse and tale, Stalin, Lenin and, to a lesser extent, other contemporary leaders appeared as wondrous heroes, transforming the world in magical ways—defeating evil, causing the land to flower, and the masses to sing and dance now that there were no miseries to bewail. For the famous northern folk-singer Maria Kriukova (who was tutored by the writer Viktorin Popov), Stalin was a miracle-worker who had transformed the country,[36] the falcon who had defeated the evil snake and wild animals of the White Army before taking over from Lenin and bringing happiness to the Soviet people. On visiting Moscow, she was moved to exclaim:

> The wise *vozhd'* started to beautify the country,
> He rebuilt everything anew.
> To the villages came strong *kolkhozy* (collective farms) . . .
> Fruit gardens began to flower,
> The people began to sing happy songs

[35] N. Mitsishivili et al., *Gruzinskie stikhi i pesni o Staline* (Tbilisi, 1937). After the 'disappearance' of Yashvili and Titian Tabidze in the purges, the book was re-edited (without their contributions) as N. Tikhonov (ed.), *Gruzinskie stikhi i pesni o Staline* (Leningrad, 1938). Pasternak's translations also disappeared.

[36] Stalin was also celebrated as a Father, whose authority and capacities were almost divine. For the moribund, possibly incapable, Kazakh bard Dzhambul, Stalin's fatherly voice on the radio, announcing the new constitution in November 1936, wakens the world:

> And how can I not sing, not play on the *dhombra*,
> And with my heart flying to the father of all the peoples,
> Not be delighted like a child!
> You first of the geniuses of all times—
> You gave all peoples the happy Law.

The constitution was given to the Soviet people by Stalin almost as God gave the Israelites the law of Moses. Dzhambul, 'Ya slishal Stalina', in id. and S. Stal'ski, *Stikhi i pesni o Lenine i Staline* (Novosibirsk, 1938), 16–17.

Small children became happy . . .
Under Mother-Moscow made of stone
Works an underground wonder-machine.
From all the world over people come
And wonder at the works of Stalin-light.[37]

The genre was traditional, the linguistic register direct, colourful, occasionally folkish and formulaic, and the symbols of modernity appeared as though refracted in the prism of a naive mind. Could the amazed peasant woman be expected to pronounce the word 'metro'? Marxist transformation was magic for the *narod*, whose consciousness, it must have been assumed, bore little trace of the inevitable enlightenment socialism was meant to bring: the new man and woman were different from the old only in their tireless jollity. Clearly, the text was gauged not, as the genre of folklore presupposed, for a traditional rural audience, but for an urban readership deluded by prejudice. It masqueraded as peasant speech but was, in fact, the product of an elaborate process of consultation and collaboration, in which it was typical of the language of Stalinist myth.

The language of myth corresponded to Stalin's own use of language in the famous speech in which he laid claim to the Leninist succession. In this highly ritualized declamation, which drew on religious language, Stalin swore on behalf of the Party and Soviet Communists to honour Lenin's testament (not that which had excoriated Stalin, but a new one, invented by Stalin). A cleverly constructed speech, it was built around a repetitive, formulaic oath, promising the dead Lenin that his instructions would be followed. The first of these incantations ran:

Departing from us, Comrade Lenin, you bequeathed us the task of holding high and keeping pure the great calling of being a member of the Party. We swear to you, Comrade Lenin, that we will fulfil with honour this your command.[38]

Honour, purity, fidelity, and faith were all central to this discipleship, as was a sort of communion of the elect, binding the living to the dead. This was in keeping with Stalin's insistence—despite Krupskaya and Trotsky—on embalming Lenin's body and pre-

[37] M. Kriukova, 'Slava Stalinu budet vechnaya: (russkaya bylina)', in N. P. Andreev (ed.), *Russkii fol'klor: khrestomatiya* (Moscow, 1938), 648–9.

[38] Stalin, *Sochineniya* (Moscow, 1947), vi. 46–51: speech to the second All-Union Congress of Soviets, 26 Jan. 1924.

serving it as a site of pilgrimage in the mausoleum on Red Square. Revolutionary Marxism, in this interpretation, was a faith which required a quasi-religious ritual and language to be communicated. That Stalin wished to be viewed through this prism is suggested by his handling of the cult as it developed (his encouragement of Lakoba and Beria, for instance) and by his acolytes' enthusiastic collaboration with him.

It was thus hardly fortuitous that Stalin's oath was to inspire paintings and famous films in the later years of the cult. Stalin loved film and attached great importance to it as a mass medium. For the twentieth anniversary of the Revolution in 1937, several attempts were made to mythologize revolutionary history, evoking Lenin and Stalin on stage and in film. Beria and the director whom he patronized, Mikhail Chiaureli, offered to these rites the film *Great Dawn* (1938), a celebration of Stalin's role in the October 1917 rising, which reportedly met with Stalin's approval.[39] Not all of these tributes were so successful: in November 1937, P. M. Kerzhentsev, Chairman of the Committee on the Arts, was severely criticized for allowing the figure of Stalin to be included as a character in Pogodin's play (the basis of Yutkevich's famous film) *Man with a Gun*, without the permission of the *vozhd'*.[40] Beria and Chiaureli guessed that the films and plays made to celebrate the anniversary of October, however much they distorted history to ascribe to Stalin a central role in these events and suppress Trotsky, were fundamentally uncongenial to the Boss, who wanted to escape the confines of 1917, where he was inevitably forced to play second fiddle to Lenin. They were too fact-bound and pedestrian for Stalin's tastes. Just as Gutman's article in 1934 had demanded the adoption of a more mythic style in portraiture of the *vozhd'*, Chiaureli, in 1939, called for more use of literature (as opposed to history, it was implied) in film, and more 'imagined' and personalized films about the *vozhd'*.

Klyatva (*The Oath*), on which Chiaureli was then working, reflected these priorities, he claimed, being more literary and

---

[39] It was sent to Stalin for vetting at the end of June 1938, but there is no record of Stalin's comments: RGASPI: fo. 558, op. 11, d. 159. However, Chiaureli is reported to have witnessed Stalin's first reaction to it, when he allegedly remarked: 'I didn't know I was so charming. Good!' V. A. Torchinov and A. M. Leontyuk, *Vokrug Stalin: Istoricho-biographicheskii spravochnik* (Sankt-Peterburgskii Gosudarstvennyi Universitet, SPB, 2000), 147 n. 1. It inspired imitative plays, according to Shmyrov, *Iskusstvo kino*, 8 (1989), 82.

[40] RGASPI: fo. 17, op. 120, d. 256, ll. 161–3.

pathetic, with fewer mass-heroic revolutionary scenes than was usual. Now, despite claims about the immortality of Lenin and the revolutionary zeal of the masses, the major actor was Stalin— the Lenin of today, inspiring the transformation of the *narod* and the country.[41] Amid the turmoil and dangers posed by internal enemies, pathetic scenes show Stalin walking in a blizzard and weeping by the snowy bench in Gorky where, we understand, he has spent many a happy summer hour with his old comrade Lenin, who has just expired. (The scene develops on the falsified photos of this 'friendship', which had collapsed in acrimony by early 1923.) Prostrate with grief, in this hour of peril, when internal enemies threaten the regime, Stalin must gather himself to inspirit the Soviet people. On Red Square (the hallowed ground where Lenin will be buried and symbol of the age-old Russian state, but not the actual historical location of Stalin's speech), Stalin appears, surrounded by the anxious and exotic masses, who depend on him. He pronounces his famous Oath, while the intertitles assure us that 'STALIN'S OATH HAS BECOME A SYMBOL OF THE FAITH OF THE WHOLE PEOPLE, THE PROGRAMME OF ITS LIFE.' The film reveals how Stalin's oath guides the simple Soviet people through all the dangers posed by internal enemies and external invasion to victory at Stalingrad and, it is implied, eventual victory in the Great Fatherland War.[42]

This portrait of Stalin, with its religious and romantic elements, is clearly reminiscent of the Georgian exhibition which had pioneered a new style and idiom in the portrayal of the *vozhd'* to accommodate the developing myth of Stalin. Chiaureli later commented on the difficulty of portraying Stalin in film, given his wisdom and world-historical significance. Although his eyes, gestures, handshakes, and words were those of a kindly and concerned, humane and modest man,

Involuntarily, you start to think that Stalin is more than a human being . . . None the less, he is distinguished from ordinary people even in external appearance . . . Subconsciously I was trying, as it were, to bring the

---

[41] M. Chiaureli, 'Zametki', in *Obrazy Lenina i Stalina v sovetskom kino* (Moscow, 1939), 48.

[42] P. Pavlenko and M. Chiaureli, 'Klyatva', in M. E. Chiaureli, *Izbranniye tsenarii kinofil'mov* (Moscow, 1950), 81–137. An early scenario of this film, emphasizing the Terror, was written as early as 1939–40 and vetted (and largely approved) by Stalin, who objected mainly to the lack of realism in the depiction of Party congresses. That Chiaureli went on to make the principal cult films about Stalin indicates that he and Beria had correctly divined the wishes of the *vozhd'*. RGASPI: fo. 558, op. 11, d.

figure of this great man 'down to earth', to translate the figure of the *vozhd'* into our customary, everyday conceptions. But at that very moment, I remembered the grandiose nature of his deeds and again felt that everything about him was unusual: his hands, eyes, smile . . . None of the portraits of Stalin can be seen as satisfactory. None of us artists has succeeded in transmitting . . . the hardly noticeable details which belong only to him, which make up the figure, which is simple but epic.[43]

Stalin was a superhuman being, whose human form was misleading: he did not fit mere historical time and space, but belonged to the epic sphere beyond ordinary human experience. The attempt to portray him in the language of everyday communication was thus doomed to failure. No actor could embody, no screenwriter provide adequate words, no director or painter capture the essence of this persona who overflowed the dimensions of commonplace humanity. It was, as Chiaureli pointed out, a hopeless attempt at translation. To speak of Stalin required not the language of everyday life, but a language commensurate with the figure, the language of higher spheres and significance, the language of myth.

By the time *The Oath* was released in 1946, Stalin the historical personage had already long been obscured by Stalin the legend, omnipresent as an iconic persona (in poster, painting, and film) while the graceless man of actuality hid from public scrutiny. Stalin had been transformed from the General Secretary of the Party, the first among equals, into a mythical figure, a sort of supra-historical persona, who transcended the constraints of historical circumstance and the limitations of individuality to become the Father of the Peoples, the embodiment of the Revolution, the State, and its inhabitants, and who could be spoken of in public only in the appropriate terms. If language was important to this transformation, then it follows that the language of Stalinism was distinct from that of other periods of Soviet history. It might be argued that it is the development of the mythic language characteristic of the Stalin cult, as an ostensibly popular trope on official discourse, which marks the originality of Stalinist discourse.

---

[43] Chiaureli, 'Voploshchenie obraza velikogo vozhdya', *Iskusstvo kino*, 1 (1947), 8.

PART III

Mind Your Words!
Policing Linguistic Boundaries
(1920s–1940s)

5

Revolutionary Selves: The Russian Intelligentsia from Old to New

IGAL HALFIN

To discover the self, to change the self—Russian revolutionaries took these as their most essential duties in 1917. The Bolsheviks looked inward, struggling to understand the meaning of their lives, their social roles, and the notions of justice and truth they wanted to live by. They spoke about freedom and equality, and counted on their own initiative, their own resourcefulness, to realize their ideals. Rather than reading the Bible or another sacred text they, like any other adherents of modernity, preferred to turn their gaze inward, counting on their own rationality, intellectual rigour, and inspiration. Bolshevik identity was malleable and shaped by inner labour, not assigned by law or any other convention. Tradition meant nothing: every citizen of the young Soviet republic was enjoined to break with the past, to work on himself or herself as a free agent. The Party perceived itself as a vehicle of emancipation precisely because it claimed to be a new type of political institution, one that was not coercive but expressive in nature. Official rhetoric emphasized initiative and enthusiasm, not fear and constraint.

The self is a relatively new object of historical enquiry.[1] Historians have in the past been inclined to view the human species as a given, explaining differences in terms of reactions to varying social, political, and cultural contexts. But recent research into how the self comes into being, how it articulates itself, and how it reflects upon itself suggests that the revolutionary transformation of subjectivity can be a fascinating agenda of research in

The research for this essay was financed by the Israeli Science Foundation, grant number 496–09.

[1] Luther H. Martin, Huck Gutman, and Patrick H. Hutton (eds.), *Technologies of the Self: A Seminar with Michel Foucault* (Amherst, Mass., 1988); Charles Taylor, *Sources of the Self: The Making of Modern Identity* (Cambridge, Mass., 1989).

its own right. No longer must we imagine a universal self putting on a range of disguises based on its environment; revolutionary language is not a façade, but one of the factors generating the self, helping the self assume its concrete outline.[2]

In the field of Soviet history, this new theoretical framework became available just as the Party archives were opened to serious research.[3] I was excited to be among the first Western scholars to work in the Leningrad Party archive in the early 1990s, with Lenin's portrait hanging behind me, and in front of me a discoloured patch of wall where Gorbachev's portrait had hung only weeks before. What struck me most were not the deceptions and manipulations the Party record revealed but the endless series of questionnaires, autobiographies, confessions, and letters in which individuals dared to speak about themselves, openly and in great detail. Suddenly I saw that the Bolsheviks' plan was far more ambitious than to consolidate power and search for spoils. They had set their sights on constructing a new man, a task they clearly took very seriously. The amount of paper—a very precious commodity at that time—they devoted to documenting the self attested to the seriousness of their purpose.

Nowhere is the work on the self more evident than in the records of the primary Party cells, the base of the Party's institutional edifice and the main source for the present study. In describing the struggle over the right to belong to the Party, protocols document the process through which new identities were constituted and elaborated. Few doubted that workers and peasants had to be promoted, that non-proletarians were undesirable, and that the brotherhood of the elect had to be constantly purified lest the bourgeoisie thwart the achievements of 1917. But how were identities to be determined? This was a contested issue and the transcripts convey the drama involved in grappling with it.

Every meeting of a primary Party cell was carefully recorded by a stenographer. The attentive reader of these protocols soon becomes familiar with the language Bolsheviks used in addressing each other and can trace fine shifts in terminology. The tran-

---

[2] N. Werth, *Être communiste en URSS sous Staline* (Paris, 1981).

[3] S. Fitzpatrick, 'Lives under Fire: Autobiographical Narratives and their Challenges in Stalin's Russia', in *De Russie et d'ailleurs. Feux croisés sur l'histoire: mélanges Marc Ferro* (Paris, 1995); C. Pennetier and B. Pudal (eds.), *Autobiographies, autocritiques, aveux dans le monde communiste* (Paris, 2002); B. Studer et al., *Parler de soi sous Staline: La Construction identitaire dans le communisme des années trente* (Paris, 2002).

scripts detail their self-fashioning, their perception of comrades and foes, their trustfulness, and their suspicion—readers may sometimes feel they are reading not Party documents but the field notes of an ethnologist.[4] Because they constitute rich materials for close, literary readings and anthropological investigations, the transcripts of the meetings of the Party cells constantly remind us, through their standardized language, their silences, and their evasions, of the effects of Bolshevik power on forming and expressing the new self.[5]

The Campaign against the Intelligentsia

In principle, every Soviet citizen could become a Party member. True, the Bolshevik Party was the party of the proletariat, but 'proletarian' was a way of thinking, not a socio-economic position one could not attain unless one was born into it. Every individual who assumed the proletarian perspective on life could become a member of the party of the proletariat (and inversely, workers who were children of workers were barred entrance if their consciousness was not ripe). This inclusiveness, provided the applicant embraced the Party wholeheartedly and sincerely, made Communism into a universalist creed, open to all.

The autobiographical statement by Korenevsky from the Smolensk Technological Institute, a navy officer who served during the First World War in the Baltic and the Black Sea fleets from 1921, can be examined from this angle. Korenevsky admitted that his background was scarcely proletarian and that he 'was not very much interested in politics before the Revolution'. But the year 1917 changed all that. 'I developed an interest in learning Party programmes and in April became a Bolshevik in my soul (*v dushe*) and, one might say, in my actions as well.' Mistaking the

---

[4] For the importance of historical studies of the poetics of self-fashioning see I. M. Lotman, 'The Poetics of Everyday Behavior in Eighteenth-Century Russian Culture', in Alexander D. Nakhimovsky and Alice Stone Nakhimovsky (eds.), *The Semiotics of Russian Cultural History: Essays* (Ithaca, NY, 1985), 74–81. For the poetics of the Stalinist rituals see A. Getty, '*Samokritika* Rituals in the Stalinist Central Committee, 1933–1938', *Russian Review*, 58 (1999), 49–51.

[5] Dominick LaCapra maintains that close reading of questions and answers may provide concrete understanding of the 'skewed reciprocity of speech' during public interrogations. Dominick LaCapra, 'The Cheese and the Worms: The Cosmos of a Sixteenth-Century Miller', in id., *History and Criticism* (Ithaca, NY, 1985), 45–69.

Bolshevik Party for a narrow class institution, Korenevsky was convinced Party doors were shut to him for ever.

What stood in my way to Party enrolment—or so I used to think—was my title as a former officer and the absence of comrades and comrades in arms who would be Bolshevik idealists (*ideinye bol'sheviki*). I looked around, searched my way, and, finally, in August 1919, found the right figure in the face of a military commander, Serpen', who convinced me that the Party welcomes any decent individual and that I would run into no grudge against me as a former officer.

His rejection anxiety alleviated, Korenevsky applied to the Party in 1920. 'Presently, I do all I can to help the toiling class', he assured his readers, 'although I have a major shortcoming—a total absence of rhetorical talents.'[6]

What was at stake in the Party admission rituals, first and foremost, was the malleability of the soul, its openness to the light. Korenevsky's imperfect class origins could be washed away. Politically, however, he had to be a *tabula rasa*; if he had ever manifested a formed consciousness, it had to be a Bolshevik one. Otherwise, the Party had to assume that he had once made a deliberate choice against it and conclude that this was not a naive but well-intending individual, but a conniving foe.

Judged from this perspective, the attitude towards applicants from the intelligentsia such as Korenevsky was ambivalent. On the one hand, the intelligentsia had a long-standing reputation as the class destined to bring light to the workers. The 'intelligentsia minority', its truly 'conscientious part', had proved its loyalty to the working class by joining the Party before the Revolution, when dedication to the proletarian cause had been very dangerous. 'When we deal with this segment of the intelligentsia', Party theoreticians stated, 'we are dealing with people whose loyalty to Communism is beyond doubt.'[7] On the other hand, the intelligentsia was suspect as a class traitor. During 1917, so the Bolshevik historians argued, this class was scared by the directness and violence of the revolutionary process. Terrified, it yoked itself to the defence of the old values—morality, self-restraint, and turning the other cheek. A wholesale excommunication of the intelligentsia as such was therefore uncalled for. The Tenth Party Congress

[6] Smolensky archive, reel collection, WKP 326, l. 26.
[7] 'Intelligentsiia v proshlom', 127.

ridiculed the Moscow electric plant for calling for a 'Party without the intelligentsia'.[8]

The Bolshevik leadership had always been dismissive of revolutionaries coming from the intelligentsia. From the early stages of his political career, Lenin believed that the intelligentsia was a pollutant, a group unfit for the new world. 'The preponderance of the radical intelligentsia in the ranks of Social Democracy cultivates opportunist psychology. . . . In their very nature, such people are incapable of formulating questions in a steadfast, direct manner. Like reptiles, they swerve between mutually exclusive points of view (*vietsia uzhom*), call their reservations "corrections" and "doubts", constantly profess their good intentions, innocent wishes, and so on.'[9] In 1919 Lenin wrote to Gorky: 'The petty intelligentsia (*intelligentiki*), those lackeys of capital, who deem themselves to be the brain of the nation but who in reality, are nothing but shit.'[10] Zinoviev translated this language into guidance to action. Following the assassination of Uritsky he urged workers to 'pick the intelligentsia from the street and lynch it'.[11]

Immediately after the end of the Civil War, preparations were made for a comprehensive cleansing of the intelligentsia from the Party.[12] 'Those who do not work with their hands, whose activity does not link them with the working class have no place in our ranks', stated the official press preparing the comprehensive Party purge of the autumn of 1921. 'Comrades, bear in mind that it is this uncompromising interpretation of membership requirements that distinguishes us from the Mensheviks.'[13] To be sure, a Bolshevik leader such as Rafail dubbed the propensity of some delegates to the Tenth Party Congress to see 'the origins of all our negatives in the intelligentsia that staffs the leading organs' as 'intelligentsia-cannibalism' (*intelligenstvoedstvo*). 'Turning the Party rudder in the correct direction', he assured his audience, 'we can easily digest all these tens of thousands of members of the intelligentsia

---

[8] *Desiatyi s''ezd RKP(b)*, 90.

[9] V. Lenin, *Polnoe sobranie sochinenii* (5th edn. Moscow, 1963–77), viii. 392–3.

[10] V. Shentalinskii, *Raby svobody: V literaturnykh arkhivakh KGB* (Moscow, 1995), 307.

[11] E. Stasova, *Stranitsy zhizni i bor'by* (Moscow, 1960), 105.

[12] *Pravda*, 28 Oct. 1921. Tsentral'nyi gosudarstvennyi arkhiv obshchestvennykh dvizhenii g. Moskvy (henceforth TsGAODM), fo. 64, op. 1, d. 78, l. 18. For the decision to embark on the purge, see *Pravda*, 30 June 1921; the national results of the purge are summarized ibid. 18 Dec. 1921.

[13] *Spravochnik partrabotnika*, no. 2 (Moscow, 1922), 77–8.

who entered our Party.'[14] Molotov spoke in two voices. 'We must
check the intelligentsia very carefully', he stated, but immediately
qualified himself: 'But we do need the intelligentsia.'[15]

Lenin, however, whose voice was more authoritative, urged the
Party to get rid of the old intelligentsia, described by him as a
bunch of 'the dishonest and the shaky, the bureaucrats and the
Mensheviks who had dyed their façade in new colours but who
remained just the same in the depth of their souls'.[16] Zinoviev
argued that 'even those members of the intelligentsia who
accepted the Revolution had in fact accepted only the New
Economic Policy'.[17] Indeed, the main question as the Party ideologues saw it was whether the intelligentsia would discard its
ancient robes and transform itself into 'new men' (*novye liudi*) or
'assimilate the psychology of our comrades'.[18] Speaking in 1920,
Kalinin recalled that before 1917 the Party had been able to
remould the old intelligentsia quite rapidly. 'When it joined the
Party the thin stratum made up of offspring of the bourgeoisie
could not introduce bourgeois habits into the proletarian milieu—
there were too few of them. Furthermore, underground activity,
the life of the Party itself, moved bourgeois offspring out of their
native milieu and placed them with the proletariat. Within two
or three years they acquired proletarian manners and, for all
intents and purposes, became proletarians.' But the Party could
no longer be so sure of its transformative capacities. 'While the
percentage of the offspring of the bourgeoisie who stream into our
Party has remained the same in relative terms, their absolute
numbers are much higher. . . . After they enter the Party they
tend to preserve their status and lifestyle. . . . This accounts for
the clash, evident everywhere, between the proletarian and petit
bourgeois Party newcomers. This clash does not necessarily
assume a political form: it may be expressed as a conflict between
two norms of behaviour typical of two different social groups.'[19]

The head of the Central Purge Commission, Sol'ts, translated
what Lenin and Kalinin said into practical language. He issued a

---

[14] *Desiatyi s"ezd RKP(b)*, 274.   [15] TsGAODM fo. 64, op. 1, d. 78, l. 18.
[16] J. Arch Getty, *Origins of the Great Purges: The Soviet Communist Party Reconsidered, 1933–
1938* (Cambridge, 1985), 46.
[17] G. Zinov'ev, 'Doklad na vserossiiskhom s"ezde nauchnykh rabotnikov 23-go noiabria
1923g.', in V. Soskin (ed.), *Sud'by russkoi intelligentsii: Materialy diskusii, 1923–25 gg.* (Novosibirsk,
1991), 137–8.
[18] *Deviataia konferentsiia RKP(b)* (Moscow, 1972), 144.   [19] Ibid. 168–9.

demand that 'the purge commissions pay special attention to the Party members from the intelligentsia'.[20] The working class was supposed to be the subject of the purge, the intelligentsia its object. Taking advantage of their privileges as judges, 'worker-purifiers' (*rabochii-chistil'shchiki*) said of the intelligentsia that 'it came to us by mistake; the Communist Party is not the intelligentsia's party'.[21] Whereas 'the working class was sent to battle by decades of exploitation', a Party spokesman explained, 'the intelligentsia could well have joined the Revolution purely out of a hope for promotion'.[22] Instructions given to localities reflected this sentiment: while the number of workers subjected to interrogation had to be cut to a minimum, 'the same yardstick could not be applied to the intelligentsia'. The Party had to know 'whether they had taken advantage of their bureaucratic position'.[23]

Shkiriatov reported that the purge commissions developed a special approach in dealing with members of the intelligentsia who clung to their old habits, particularly those who 'joined our Party in 1921, or 1920, or 1919, that is, after the October Revolution. . . . We not only double-checked to make sure that such a person was not a careerist, that he was a conscientious human being who works well in Soviet institutions and has the necessary theoretical preparation, but we also checked to make sure that his spirit was sufficiently Bolshevik and revolutionary.'[24] The official press recounted how, 'when workers come across a "specialist" their vigilance intensifies' and they ask one question after another.[25]

A feuilleton entitled 'The People's Judgment Day' threw the difference between the treatment of the intelligentsia and the working class during the purge into a sharp relief:

The chair of the meeting summons the first Party member—a worker-peasant—to the table. Two, three words and his autobiography is exhausted. Any derailments? None. 'Next!' An anxious Party functionary, a former chancery worker steps in. 'Your autobiography, comrade.' A long and boring story unfolds. One can see right away that this individual

[20] Thomas Henry Richard Rigby, *Communist Party Membership in the U.S.S.R., 1917–1967* (Princeton, 1968), 96–7; *Pravda*, 28 Oct. 1921.   [21] *Pravda*, 29 Nov. 1921.

[22] Ibid. 9 Oct. 1921.   [23] Ibid. 28 Oct. 1921.

[24] *Odinnadtsatyi s"ezd RKP(b)*, 373.

[25] In agricultural provinces such as Smolensk 23.8% of the purged were described as 'responsible workers'; 13.4% were Razdobreev-type 'specialists'. *Pravda*, 11 Oct. and 18 Dec. 1921; *Odinnadtsatyi s"ezd RKP(b)*, 746.

was never oppressed by capitalists, that this individual hovers somewhere up in the sky. 'Next!' A highly placed official wearing an intelligentsia face steps forward. Despite his higher education he had followed a wandering course without rudder or sail, had been with the Socialist Revolutionaries, with the Mensheviks, with the Bund. . . . As he tells his autobiography, this comrade seems like an actor. Gradually workers shake themselves up and expose the physiognomy of a bureaucrat.[26]

The message to the purge commissions was unequivocal—subject intelligentsia autobiographies to merciless examination: 'While mistakes committed by undeveloped proletarians may be forgiven, more should be expected from the knowledgeable.'[27]

The detailed minutes of the 1921 purge kept at the Smolensk Institute give a sense of what an intelligentsia identity meant to rank-and-file Bolsheviks and show that the baiting of the intelligentsia took place at the grass roots. The purge committee did its work in the presence of all the members of the cell as well as a number of 'extramural workers representing the Smolensk proletariat'. The meetings lasted for many hours—in one case from three in the afternoon to ten in the morning—as each member of the cell was called to centre stage to recount his autobiography aloud. Anyone present could comment on what he heard, advance derailments, and ask questions, while the Party's 'plenipotentiaries' (*upolnomochennye*)—Bolsheviks with underground experience and proletarian class origins delegated to the purge meetings by the county Party commissions—made their own enquiries.[28]

About every fourth Party member in the Institute belonged to the intelligentsia cohort that, as one would expect, suffered the brunt of the purge. Consider Mochelevkin's interrogation. Although this student claimed in his questionnaire that he was 'of peasant origins', a brief interrogation showed otherwise.

Q: You said your father was a land tiller. But did not the tsarist government prohibit Jews from working the land? Besides, did you not omit the fact that your mother used to run a shop?

---

[26] *Pravda*, 9 Oct. 1921. The Central Committee decreed that the following membership categories should be submitted to close scrutiny: (a) former members of other parties; (b) individuals who had once belonged to the bureaucratic apparatus of the tsarist regime or the Provisional Government; (c) employees.   [27] *Pravda*, 28 Oct. 1921.

[28] The plenipotentiaries could collect negative material against Communists independently of the cell. While it was the cell's vote that was binding, their assessments played a part when the cell's decisions were reviewed by the higher Party organs. *Pravda*, 9 Oct. 1921; N. Rodionova, *Gody napriazhennogo truda* (Moscow, 1963), 69.

A: My father had two *desiatinas* of land which he tilled himself. He also
worked at his brother's as a steward. In my mother's occupation I
had little interest.[29]

When Mochelevkin confessed that 'the February Revolution came
to me as a surprise; in the beginning, I was unable to orient
myself', an anonymous student recalled that he had been over-
heard to make such typically intelligentsia statements as: 'The toppling of Kerensky was premature and unnecessary.' Besides,
'when Mochelevkin delivered a speech at a political rally, soldiers
wanted to beat him up for some reason'—a bizarre inclination on
the part of a zealously pro-Bolshevik crowd, unless, of course, 'the
speaker objected to our withdrawal from the war'.

Undoubtedly the most intriguing remark on this case was made
when one of the detractors noted that 'Mochelevkin liked to kiss
ladies' hands'. Far from true working-class conduct, such behaviour 'was quite typical of the intelligentsia'. Ever on the alert for
the slightest physical clues, this physiognomist believed that
Mochelevkin's general demeanour, his grimaces, and the telltale
floridness of his gestures all betrayed an absence of proletarian
masculinity.

Mochelevkin's feminized portrait revealed the class–gender
nexus integral to the official discourse. Bolshevik poetics symbolically grafted the intelligentsia onto the traditional and deprecated
role of the female, assigning the active, masculine role to the proletariat. In this scheme, thinking itself became a feminine faculty
whereas acting was strictly masculine. 'Its feminine psyche',
Trotsky believed, 'the fact that it is trained to be contemplative,
impressionable, and sensitive, undercuts the intelligentsia's physical power.'[30] 'Obsequious' and 'weak' students of Mochelevkin's
ilk were allegedly effective in coaxing naive workers into turning
their bodily strength against themselves, which kept them from
demanding their rights. But now this strategy was unmasked, and
Mochelevkin was defenceless.

Another detractor brought Mochelevkin's intelligentsia identity
into particularly sharp focus when he called attention to the defendant's smoothness: 'Mochelevkin is eloquent about things that the
committee is not interested in, dodging what is really significant.'
As the following exchange suggests, he had not only shunned

[29] WKP 326, l. 16.
[30] Lev Trotskii, 'Ob intelligentsii', in *Sochineniia*, 21 vols. (Moscow, 1925–7), xx. 336.

physical labour, but had also lied in denying that others had done
household chores for him:

Q: Your autobiography states that your means were strained. But have
you not had servants?

A: No, my mother was the one who had servants, not I.

But apples could not have fallen that far from the tree. And
besides, Mochelevkin could not prove that he had distanced
himself from his family and had made true sacrifices for the
Revolution. Bereft of will and rotten to the core, he was purged by
an overwhelming majority.

Doubtless, the apogee of the purge was the interrogation of the
Institute's rector, Razdobreev, a quintessential intelligentsia
Bolshevik.[31] An older and better-educated Bolshevik, Razdobreev
had completed his formal training long before 1917. With the
coming of October he took the Red side and during the last stages
of the Civil War he had served as the military commissar of the
Smolensk Institute, a post he still occupied in 1921. Considering
his social physiognomy, his successful career in tsarist Russia, his
late admission to the Party (April 1920), and the fact that he 'had
been corrupted by long interaction with a petit bourgeois milieu',
Razdobreev's position was precarious.

The message the Central Committee sent regarding individuals
such as Razdobreev was somewhat contradictory: 'We have to be
particularly demanding toward Soviet employees and to the offspring of bourgeois intelligentsia', the Central Committee stated.
At the same time, it went without saying that 'each cell must find
enough wit and tact to retain the truly conscientious and loyal
people'.[32] Overall, the anxieties associated with the dramatic liberalization of economic policies tipped the balance in the direction of
exclusivism. 'The main target of the purge', Shkiriatov explained,
was not so much the 'crook who had wormed his way into our
Party . . . but even a conscientious individual, if he has nothing in
common with our Party. For when we take sharp turns—sometimes we have to swerve or make full reverse—such elements can
weaken us.'[33]

Razdobreev's interrogation took almost an entire night. The
bureau had done plenty of preparatory work on the case, solicit-

[31] WKP 326, ll. 1–7.
[32] *Izvestiia TsK RKP(b)*, no. 33, 39–40.   [33] *Odinnadtsatyi s"ezd RKP(b)*, 372.

ing and double-checking denunciations. As the process began, the rector responded to a list of questions presented to him in advance:

Q: Given that you are the son of a simple Cossack, how did you manage to pave your way to the tsarist Ministry of Transportation?

A: Through the recommendation of the railway management I was accepted by an institute run by the ministry on an academic fellowship.

Q: Where did you get the money that allowed you to study abroad?

A: When I lived abroad, I was broke. . . . Father borrowed 900 roubles [for me]. He barely came up with the money to repay the loan.

Having established that Razdobreev was a social upstart, the interrogation moved to enquire about the evolution of his political consciousness:

Q: You say that your feelings about the Party platform were for a long time unsettled, but not anymore? . . .

A: I did not want to join the Party earlier because Kolchak and Denikin were about to be defeated, so I hoped to avoid the impression that I had become a Bolshevik only because the Soviet power had the upper hand. But when the war with Poland began I did enrol.

Q: Was not the situation of the republic very sound in April [when you applied for Party membership]?

A: I insist that the republic was not safe then and that that was the reason for my enrolment.

Though Razdobreev claimed that he had lent a shoulder to the Reds at a moment of grave danger, his interrogators still suspected that he was motivated by his pursuit of a lucrative bureaucratic post.

Q: Having read Marx and Engels before, how could you waver for so long before joining the Party?

A: My interest in social issues goes back to 1905. I then participated in an anarchist circle. In the Institute I was doing scholarly work and met no one who could acquaint me with the Bolshevik programme. Yes, I read Marx. But my impression was that his ideas could be the basis for any socialist party, not just the Bolsheviks. I wanted to understand [the basic ideas of socialism], so I read Marx.

The purgers would focus on Razdobreev's interpretation of Marx, and he knew it was crucial to distinguish himself from the old intelligentsia, whose reading tended to be quite Menshevik.

Emphasizing that familiarity with Marxism did not automatically entail acquaintance with Bolshevism, Razdobreev conceded that his 1905 consciousness was perhaps moot. But he was careful to make it clear that he was definitely not distinctly Menshevik, or in any other way anti-Bolshevik.

Razdobreev's description of his past attitude as 'underdeveloped' left room for his personal growth in subsequent years. This, however, was not the only interpretation available. 'Razdobreev's belated enrolment in the Party calls for deep reflection', argued Zakharov, a member of the bureau. 'He must have been politically developed, since he had already read fathers of Marxism. Razdobreev joined the Party at a time when the Red Army had just achieved a great victory at the gates of Warsaw.'

If Razdobreev, along with the rest of the chauvinist, petit bourgeois intelligentsia, had joined the Party not because he was committed to the idea of the universal revolution but because of a belief that the new regime was about to replace 'national war' with 'class war', he may have stayed in the Bolshevik camp, according to his detractors, because he hoped that the New Economic Policy (NEP) would restore capitalist order. Had Razdobreev accepted Bolshevism in general, including its War Communist episode? Or was he perhaps simply attracted by NEP?

Q: Do you think the Party ever commits mistakes? Were the Bolsheviks right when they introduced *prodrazverstka* [tax proportional to the harvest imposed during the Civil War]?

A: It would not have been bad to introduce *prodnalog* [a pre-set agricultural tax that enabled peasants to keep most of their product, one of the key innovations of NEP] right away and skip over the *prodrazverstka*.[34] This is the only issue over which I had disagreements with Communists.

Q: What is your attitude toward specialists?

A: Specialists are indispensable everywhere, and in our republic particularly so. If I thought otherwise I would not have taken the position of a rector.

Q: Should specialists be financially supported?

A: Yes, we have to secure their livelihood.

Plenipotentiary: Listening to you one gains the impression that you base your sympathy for Communism on the NEP. But what if our economic policy changes?

[34] TaGAODM fo. 1673, op. 1, d. 48, l. 8; *Leninskii sbornik*, xxxv. 179.

A: It cannot change because it was meant to last for some years. If the Party sensibly and reasonably alters its policy, I think I will be able to comprehend such a step, come to terms with it, and endorse it. It is essentially temporary, but the NEP is necessary and appropriate right now. The Party ideal will have to be resurrected some time in the future. The dictatorship of the proletariat can wither away only gradually.

Citing Lenin to the effect that 'the NEP has to be embraced seriously, and for a long time', Razdobreev professed temperance. His enthusiasm for the NEP, however, was open to the objection that what might be desirable for the intelligentsia could be a step backwards for the proletariat. To prove that he was in all respects a Bolshevik, Razdobreev had to show that he was not one of the intelligentsia softies who harboured qualms regarding the use of force, for example, during the merciless suppression of the Kronstadt rebellion. This was especially important since the purgers had noticed that, despite his role as military commissar, Razdobreev had not participated during that crisis. He did not go to the military barracks when a military emergency was announced during the Kronstadt uprising because, he claimed, 'I was needed at my work place'.

As the flood of questions from the floor subsided, the bureau revealed the damaging material against Razdobreev that it had collected. Its affidavit included twenty-three complaints of minor misconduct and three more substantial denunciations including charges of embezzlement, high-handedness, and possession of a bourgeois proprietary instinct—all typical intelligentsia failings. It was asserted that Razdobreev had humiliated his subordinates. Razdobreev countered: 'I did not use the Institute's manpower for my personal needs. Nor is it in my character to desire to be called "master" (*barin*). The old nanny who calls me such is no longer young and cannot be untaught. There is no crime in that.' Other accusations alleged that Razdobreev had used the Institute's car 'as if it was his property', that he had constructed a fence around his summer house with the help of Red Army manpower, and that his maids had thrown away part of his meat ration muttering that 'even dogs would not eat it'. Here Razdobreev's response was brief and dismissive: 'In general, workers dislike Communists and administrators. But I did not teach my staff to say such things.'

But the charges were accumulating, and Razdobreev was beginning to look like a grandee. Another wave of allegations followed:

You could not possibly have produced a one-to-eighteen potato harvest when the average in this area is one-to-eight. While you and your collaborators get fat on the potatoes you embezzle, workers are starving on the Volga. What do you say to this? . . . And why does not everyone receive the same ration? Why should some be mighty and some be mice (*krali i karliki*)?

Razdobreev defended himself point by point: 'I see no crime in the land returning so much. Believe me, the Volga famine was much on my mind when I dug potatoes. Whether I will donate my potatoes for relief is as yet uncertain.'

Because Bolshevism did not distinguish between political and economic crimes—GPU, for example, regarded 'economic sabotage' and 'political sedition' as equally counter-revolutionary— the following diatribe, launched by a student named Grigorev, offered a unified model of Razdobreev's class and political outlook. 'The abnormal size of Razdobreev's harvest indicates where fertilizers were used and where they were not. . . . Potatoes were dug by Red Army soldiers; they had not contracted to do this work, but had been ordered to do it and were indignant at such exploitation. . . . Razdobreev says workers on the state farm do not approve of Communists. How could it be otherwise? Once they have seen the example set by a prominent Communist like him, they start thinking in a non-Communist way.' This was a damaging line of persecution. Using the language of class war Grigorev portrayed the rector as an enemy of the working class, precisely the type of element who sets workers against their own party. What else, if they see in the Bolshevik ranks arrogant exploiters who continue treating them as the dregs of society and believe that workers are too obtuse to see the tricks played on them? The remainder of the speech was a condemnation of the petit bourgeois possessiveness unfortunately brought back into favour by the NEP:

Razdobreev is a specialist to the bone, a sweet-talker who has wriggled out of trouble before and might succeed again today. I will not deny that as a specialist Razdobreev is priceless. But as a Communist he is good for nothing and has to be thrown out. The Party is not a shelter for specialists! I am not against providing specialists with an allowance, but this allowance is not a licence to 'take as much as you can'. Why should other trustworthy comrades of old standing suffer worse material conditions? The scion of a petit bourgeois family, Razdobreev has never been and will never become a part of the worker–peasant masses. Razdobreev adores the New Economic Policy and likes to say: 'This is mine.' He may be a worthy member of the petite bourgeoisie but he is not a worthy member of the Party.

Grigorev persevered, insisting that Razdobreev's intelligentsia instinct had led him to 'surround himself with cronies who took shelter behind him and wove themselves cosy nests. This is how the tiny little Mensheviks infiltrate our ranks.' The 'Menshevik bond' Grigorev was talking about did not have to be seen as a specific set of political convictions. Rather, it stemmed from the general 'physiognomy' of Razdobreev's company, 'which was sprightly, philistine, and exploiting'. Grigorev relied here on the Bolshevik press which advanced the notion of the 'good-for-nothing philistine intelligentsia which exists in every Party cell'.[35]

Even as the attacks became less concrete, they became more dramatic and, possibly, devastating. Grigorev squeezed Razdobreev into a coffin; Zakharov nailed it shut. 'His theoretical position was always in agreement with the Party, but in practical terms he was aloof and alienated himself from the grass roots, in no way had Razdobreev proved his loyalty to the Revolution.'

At this point, Ioffe, the first to speak in favour of the defendant after a long interval, interjected that ideological endorsement must be worth something: 'Razdobreev supports the Party platform, does he not? Believe me, an old Bolshevik; it is wrong to put on the same plane the work of a specialist and the work of an unskilled worker. Shepherd and specialist do not reap the same.' But Zakharov dismissed this attempt to defend the embattled rector:

I still insist that Razdobreev lacks a healthy, proletarian instinct because he was raised and now moves in a milieu which is alien to the proletariat and to our Party. Everything suggests that our Institute is not a Communist, but a White organization. Razdobreev neither enlisted in the special detachment, nor did he volunteer to participate in Saturday work (*Subbotniki*). To be sure, Razdobreev has pieces of paper to justify anything he does. This only further proves he is not a staunch

---

[35] *Pravda*, 12 Oct. and 30 Nov. 1921.

Communist, for had he been one he would have pleaded guilty and begged us for forgiveness.

Refraining from a head-on critique of the NEP, Bolshevik zealots limited themselves to showing that now that alien economic forces had been released it was all the more important to defend proletarian purity. If Razdobreev had to be tolerated as an administrator, there was no need to put up with him in the Party. 'I respect Razdobreev a great deal as a practical man', one of his detractors stated. 'It is impossible to exaggerate his contribution to the Institute since 1918. Yet, a Party tribunal is another matter. . . . He is a man of another camp and another set of convictions.'

The time had come for the moderates to attempt a rebuttal. Slesar' reminded the cell that Party specialists deserved special consideration: 'Razdobreev's peccadilloes are not grounds for expulsion. Razdobreev does not interact with the masses because his work has to be conducted in the office. . . . Our responsible workers do not and cannot live on a ration of the same size we live on. Everyone should receive not only "according to his needs" but also "according to his talents".' The combination of the egalitarian 'to everyone according to his needs' and the meritocratic 'to everyone according to his talents' betrayed contradictory feelings regarding the class meaning of the New Economic Policy. Apparently Slesar' had said the right thing, however contradictory, because Zakharov promptly backed down: 'I will summarize that Razdobreev is a bad Bolshevik but a good specialist. Our Party still needs him. In my view, we should not drum him out but expel him for a month with the right of re-admission subject to a probation period.' Another speaker proposed that 'since Razdobreev has never been on probation, he should be downgraded to Party candidate.' These compromises, however, were ruled out by the plenipotentiary on procedural grounds: 'Communists are reduced to the status of Party candidates only if they make unintentional mistakes and are able to improve their conduct. A rector of the Institute cannot be put into this category. Probation is not a "penalty battalion"!' If Razdobreev was to be retained, 'somebody had to touch on his political work in the Institute'.

This was the cue for Korolev, the Party secretary, to speak.

Had everyone had Razdobreev's discipline, things would have been excellent. Razdobreev came to all the meetings of the cell and regularly carried out the bureau's assignments. He reported on the Eighth Congress of Soviets, on the events in Kronstadt, and on the *prodnalog*. . . . His scholarly work explains why he has not done more politically. . . . The main charge against Razdobreev seems to be that 'his soul does not seem to be Communist'. The impressions of a few comrades, their idea of how things 'seem', is not sufficient grounds to have someone's political character assassinated. . . . We should not forget that in facing the present forum and having to justify himself in front of a hundred individuals, Razdobreev has already been sufficiently punished.

According to Korolev, the intelligentsia could not be measured by the same yardstick applied to workers. Razdobreev could not be a Bolshevik by instinct; but, and this was a no less important indication that his heart was in the right place, he was loyal and committed. Korolev's concluding speech saved the rector; only nine votes were cast for his expulsion.

In terms of the Bolshevik discourse, Razdobreev represented the upper intelligentsia, comprising old-time bureaucrats and specialists. But the intelligentsia could also appear in the shape of a 'declassed' mob; thrust into a disorienting class alignment, it might turn to the anarchism of the extreme left or, just as likely, to the Black Hundred sentiment of the extreme right. According to Party ideologues, impoverished intelligentsia swerved toward 'infantile radicalism', 'nihilism', and anarchism, that 'quintessential intelligentsia deviation'.[36]

Despite the crackdown on anarchism after the Kronstadt rebellion, the Party was lenient toward its ultras from the intelligentsia in the early 1920s, provided they distilled their radicalism into pure Bolshevism.[37] Though Rivkinson, one of Razdobreev's students, had a previous conviction for 'baiting Soviet employees', he was forgiven.[38] Of Podzniakov, to give another example, students said that 'in his youth he identified authority and upper classes with Jewishness'. Podzniakov's negative features, however, were 'impressed on him' by his petit bourgeois, intelligentsia milieu. 'Although Podzniakov had gone through a street school of anti-Semitism', his defenders explained, 'this mood is long since a mere ghost from his past.' In view of his 'exploits in defence of the Revolution', Podzniakov was retained.[39]

---

[36] *Pravda*, 28 Oct. and 30 Nov. 1921. Partiinyi arkhiv Tomskoi oblasti (henceforth PATO), fo. 1, op. 1, d. 981, l. 57.   [37] RGASPI fo. 613, op. 1, d. 6, l. 127.
[38] WKR 326, l. 16.   [39] WKR 326, ll. 9–10.

Redkov, on the other hand, who had seemed to be facing similar difficulties, was unanimously purged. In 1918 Redkov took part in the dispersal of Bel'ts' soviet by 'waving around a "Smith" revolver', a denunciation maintained. The accused tried to explain: 'When I heard that in Moscow and Petrograd power had collapsed I confronted the local soviets, in keeping with the slogan "To hell with all that constrains us!" . . . Since I believed that the Bolsheviks said one thing and did another I was anxious that the October Revolution might not fully realize its goals, that the commissar would simply replace the tsar as our new ruler. Now', Redkov assured the cell, 'I endorse the Bolshevik tactics. During the Kronstadt events I even got out my Nogan—I have liked revolvers since I was a child—thinking I would need it against the mutineers.' Having heard all that, the cell concluded that 'in all likelihood Redkov is not a real Bolshevik. A Kadet, a Menshevik or an anarchist'—what else could a declassed member of the intelligentsia be? —'he might turn his revolver against us at any moment.'[40]

Nikiforov, also from the Smolensk Technological Institute, was candid about his syndicalist past.[41] 'Before the October Revolution', his autobiography stated, 'destiny brought me to an anarchist circle where I became acquainted with the literature of this party. My soul and my mind felt at home there.' Nikiforov confessed that his anarchist pranks and daredevil feats were all tokens of childish exuberance:

Only a secondary school student, I already started quarrelling with my fellow pupils. I also rebelled against the administration, which brought down retaliation upon me. Since mine is a rambunctious character, I always pursued my goals openly and disregarded all obstacles. Direct and candid, I trusted the people I loved and rebelled against grandeur.

At this stage Nikiforov was full of impulsive creativity, not true revolutionary consciousness. Left alone during the war, 'unemployed and forced to take desperate measures to survive', he 'withdrew into himself'.

During the Revolution, Nikiforov embraced the revolutionary cause with all his heart. His autobiography makes it clear that resolute Bolshevik action left a deep impression on the protagonist:

---

[40] *Spravochnik partrabotnika*, no. 3 (Moscow, 1923), 105–8; WKP 326, ll. 9, 15–16.
[41] WKP 326, l. 17.

'When the October Revolution erupted, the whirlwind of events turned society upside down. The strong will of the Bolsheviks overcame the feeble will of Kerensky. The open and merciless struggle against the bourgeoisie made of me a Bolshevik supporter and, slightly familiar with the history of socialism as I was, I embraced Communism—the only way for humans to live together.'

This, however, did not mean that Nikiforov had fully converted. The autobiographer confessed to having thought that, 'if evaluated from the universal perspective, Communism is a temporary state of things' which would one day yield to anarchism. Little of that mattered in 1917. As far as Nikiforov was concerned, the distinction between anarchism and Bolshevism was purely academic.

Asked to expand on his autobiography, Nikiforov elaborated on his early political stand:

I did not like Kerensky because he talked too much. The Bolsheviks I respected but was scarcely familiar with their programme. While the history of socialism was known to me in broad outlines I knew nothing of the evolution of this party. I belonged to an anarchist-syndicalist group—'Communism is the shortest way toward anarchism', that was my argument. . . . Only later did I realize that Communism was unavoidable. I joined the Bolshevik Party because at the front, in the battle, specific party affiliation was secondary.

In July 1918 Nikiforov volunteered for the Red Army. Deployed to Smolensk during the last stage of the Civil War, he joined the Party in April 1920 and became the secretary of the military committee.

Nikiforov's confessors in the Smolensk Institute were in a quandary. On the one hand, the defendant had clearly been committed to the victory of the Reds in the Civil War; on the other, his lingering theoretical weaknesses could well be a dangerous vestige of anarchism. When he was quizzed as to why he had joined the Party, Nikiforov explained that 'I wanted to support the Bolsheviks in their struggle against capitalism, so that reaction would be eradicated. I realized that as far as political parties went, the Bolsheviks were the furthest to the left.' In principle, Nikiforov was against 'parties'; forced by political exigencies to choose one, he had made the correct choice. In a sense, the Communist Party was in his eyes not the absolute good but the least of all evils.

Nikiforov knew that his hesitation in accepting organizational discipline and a hierarchical chain of command could be held against him. Earlier in the year he had even clashed with the bureau: he had initially refused to submit an autobiography and escaped purge only by a hair. Now he stated that 'the Party is strong because of its discipline. Even if expelled, I will not abandon my convictions. A Party card does not prove that somebody is a Communist.' Again and again Nikiforov stated his hope that every-body would calm down and realize that he had weaned himself of anarchism. But he had gone too far in downplaying the signifi-cance of Party affiliation, one of the worst breaches of Party disci-pline a Bolshevik could imagine. A sympathetic listener described the defendant as 'a bitter proletarian . . . who has no problem throwing the truth in one's face, one in whom the spirit of "rebel-lion"—not "anarchy"—dwells'. 'Nikiforov is full of defiance', another speaker stated, 'but we should not blame him for this. True, he refused to work in student organizations, but this was because he thought they were bureaucratic.' Nikiforov was ulti-mately retained on the strength of the following argument: 'Take Razdobreev: undoubtedly a specialist, he carries the title of Communist. If we accept someone who is to the right of us, why should a person who is to the left of us have no place in our Party?'

The above proceedings bring to the surface many catchwords, nuances, and shades of meaning that were linked to the notion of the 'intelligentsia' in the official discourse.[42] Granting that some members of this class united with it body and soul, the Bolsheviks of the early 1920s maintained that, as a whole, the intelligentsia was the nemesis of the proletariat. Party members from the intel-ligentsia brought with them petit bourgeois economics (an exag-gerated enthusiasm for NEP or, inversely, a total incomprehension of its importance), petit bourgeois politics (rightist Menshevism or its close opposite, leftist anarchism), and petit bourgeois self-fashioning ('slyness', *lukavstvo*, and 'narcissism', *samovliubchivost'*). Tailored to fit a stock pattern of a class whose very essence was lies and dissimulation, intelligentsia Bolsheviks were described as indi-viduals who pretended they shared the Party's goals but who remained, in reality, 'spineless' (*bezkhrebetnye*) and 'without princi-

---

[42] The purge protocols from the Smolensk Technological Institute are all the more valuable if we take note of Kalinin's regret that 'for the most part minutes of Party meetings dedicated to the 1921 purge are not kept'. *Pravda*, 27 Oct. 1921.

ples' (*bezprintsipnye*). Believing that intelligentsia Bolsheviks were by and large sophists, obfuscators, and clerks, who turned every healthy impulse into abstract formulas, utopian blueprints, and much 'learned dust' (*mudrstvovanie*), the Party purists poured buckets of scorn upon this 'arid and cerebral cohort'.[43]

Restrictions on Intelligentsia Admissions

Soon after the 1921 purge the Party unfolded a complementary series of measures hampering intelligentsia admissions. The Eleventh Party Congress tightened the statutory screws that kept the intelligentsia out of the brotherhood of the elect. To become Party members, the intelligentsia had to prove they were 'experienced in public work and . . . well prepared to be an ideological auxiliary in the work of the proletarian masses'.[44] As non-proletarians, the intelligentsia had to find five recommenders and, in the rare cases that they were accepted, spend two years on probation as 'Party candidates'. As a result of the purge and admission restrictions the proportion of the Party made up of intelligentsia dropped by 3.6 per cent from 1921 to 1923. Following the Twelfth Party Congress's freeze on all intelligentsia promotions to full Party membership in 1923 (a provision that remained in force for over a year) the share of the intelligentsia in the Party fell even further.[45]

---

[43] For the intelligentsia's hatred of the 'intellectual, curious, and cerebral side of themselves' see Richard Stites, *Revolutionary Dreams: Utopian Vision and Experimental Life in the Russian Revolution* (New York, 1989), 72–3. The pervasiveness of the anti-intelligentsia sentiment during the 1921 purge was outstanding. Emilian Riutin, a Bolshevik Civil War hero, and a member of presidium of the Siberian Party committee, ran into trouble defending his Communist credentials. There were those who suspected that Riutin's education had supposedly moved him away from the ranks of the proletariat. Indeed, in one of the questionnaires, Riutin admitted his social position was that of a 'proletarian member of the intelligentsia' (by social origin he was a 'son of a middle-peasant'). During the meeting of the purge commission in Tomsk from 30 Nov. 1921 it was suggested that as 'Riutin belongs with the intelligentsia' his Party membership could not be ratified and the case had to be 'transferred to the Supreme Siberian Purge Commission'. A recommendation to the effect that 'Riutin has no bourgeois, philistine inclination' was a timely intervention in Riutin's defence and secured his possession of a Party card. B. Starkov, 'Tiazhkii put' prozreniia', in *M. Riutin: Na koleni ne vstanu* (Moscow, 1992), 4; Partiinyi arkhiv Novosibirskoi oblasti (henceforth PANO), fo. 1, op. 2, d. 478, ll. 235–8.

[44] PANO fo. 2, op. 1, d. 17, l. 233.

[45] Rigby, *Communist Party Membership*, 102–17; *KPSS v rezoliutsiiakh i resheniiakh* (Moscow, 1970), 452; Tsentral'nyi gosudarstvennyi arkhiv istoriko politicheskikh dokumentov (henceforth TsGA IPD), fo. 138, op. 1, d. 1g, l. 44.

This anti-intelligentsia campaign affected higher education
most directly. From September 1922 to February 1923, only four
applications were submitted to academic Party cells in the
Volodarsk district. (This can be compared with eighty-eight applications submitted in the factories during the same time.) During
the same period in Vasileostrovsk district, where most of
Petrograd's universities were located, only three Party applicants
from the intelligentsia became Party candidates (compared to
seventy-six workers and thirty-three peasants), and only three candidates belonging to this category were promoted to full Party
membership (compared to twenty-three workers and five peasants). It is highly likely that the eighty-two applications that were
not considered by the Party bureaux at all were put forward by
non-proletarians.[46]

In 1922 the Party cell of the Leningrad Engineering Institute
reported that 'we have received almost no student applications'.
No tears were shed, however. 'Most of our students come from
the intelligentsia anyway. There is no suitable material here.'[47]
While the number of applications rose during the following year,
the district committee instructed the cell to regard all these applicants as mental labourers. 'Though we have no formal grounds
to block the enrolment of the intelligentsia to the Party', the cell
candidly reported, 'we will take all possible measures to prevent
their admission.'[48]

If we consider the sheer volume of Party admissions, 'intelli-
gentsia-oriented' academic institutions compare poorly with the
technical, 'proletarian-oriented' institutes, to say nothing of the
workers' faculties.[49] A comparison between the Party cells at the
two main academic institutions in Tomsk, Tomsk State University
and Tomsk Technological Institute, suggests that the latter's cell
'attracted proletarian students', while the proletarianization of the
former left much to be desired.

Plagued by the 'preponderance' (*zasilie*) of the intelligentsia the
university fell out of favour with the Tomsk Party leadership.
During the 1923/4 academic year its Party cell was evenly divided
between proletarian and intelligentsia members (thirty-eight intel-

[46] *Sbornik Materialov Leningradskogo Komiteta RKP* (Petrograd, 1923), vi. 173, 201.
[47] TsGA IPD fo. 1085, op. 1, d. 10, l. 4.
[48] TsGA IPD fo. 1085, op. 1, d. 12, p. 65; d. 16, l. 15.
[49] PANO fo. 2, op. 1, d. 17, p. 233; d. 24, l. 318; PATO fo. 320, op. 1, d. 7, l. 29.

TABLE 5.1. *Social position of Bolsheviks enrolled in Tomsk academic institutions (1923)*

Social position	Tomsk Technological Institute	Tomsk State University
Intelligentsia	17 (35%)	26 (72%)
Workers and peasants	32 (65%)	10 (28%)

Source: GANO fo. 1053, op. 1, d. 682, l. 23.

ligentsia Party members and thirty-eight Party members from the working class and the peasantry).[50] But even this breakdown would not have been possible had it not been for the efforts of the local Party bureau.

Statisticians were, in fact, crucial in the constitution of the Bolshevik subject, thanks to their role in assigning class identity. The data lists at their disposal were divided among three categories: 'social origins' (*sotsial'noe proishozhdenie*), 'main profession' (*glavnaia professiia*), and 'social position' (*sotsial'noe polozhenie*). The last and the most significant category was supposed to be the result of combining the first two. How they were combined was effectively at the statistician's discretion. Determined to bestow acceptable class characteristics upon as many students as possible, statisticians became downright creative at times. 'Peasants' and 'workers' remained on their lists as such, even when the students in question assumed intelligentsia responsibilities: a 'hereditary worker' such as Galichanin remained a worker although he had served as a clerk on the state agricultural farm; the daughter of a peasant, such as comrade Derevianina, dodged the intelligentsia column despite the fact that she had been a primary school teacher. 'Peasants by social origin' such as Sleznev, Chernov, and Zolotorev also retained their proletarian status, though the Tomsk Party organization stipulated that medical assistants like them 'are no good in class terms and should be considered, strictly speaking, as employees'. When the university statistician conferred an intelligentsia social position it was usually the lesser of two evils. Baskovich and Khiletskaia, two 'merchant daughters', were thereby spared the ignominy of being thrust into the category of 'class aliens' and gained a modicum of Bolshevik class respectability. There were, however, instances when that was out of the question. A number of students had to be

[50] PATO fo. 115, op. 2, d. 3, ll. 6–16; d. 4, l. 41.

categorized as 'intelligentsia' despite their 'peasant' origins: comrade Zudilov became a mental labourer because of his 'clerical work', while Toletukhina and Kletkina were so categorized 'while teaching in school'. When the transition to intellectual labour took place before the student enrolled in the Party, his 'degeneration' could not be overlooked.[51]

Once the freeze on admission to university cells was abolished, the Technological Institute's Party cell grew by leaps and bounds. Admitting 'pure-blooded workers' into its ranks, it passed the 200 mark in 1925. 'Teeming with the intelligentsia', the university, by contrast, had to discourage students from applying to the Party: as a result, between March and June 1925, only seven applications were submitted and not all of them were accepted.[52] When a modest growth did occur in the 1925/6 winter trimester, much to the cell's chagrin, it further enlarged the intelligentsia cohort.

TABLE 5.2. *Social position of Bolsheviks at Tomsk State University (1925/6)*

Students' social position	Nov. 1925	Apr. 1926
Workers and peasants	33 (77%)	33 (60%)
Intelligentsia	10 (23%)	22 (40%)
Total	43 (100%)	55 (100%)

Source: Partiinyi arkhiv tomskoi oblasti, fo. 115, op. 2, d. 3, ll. 6–16; d. 4, l. 41; d. 7, l. 55; d. 8, ll. 26–35, 146.

Rather apologetically the cell's spokesman argued that class statistics 'are misleading' and that the 'bald intelligentsia figures give a false impression. In reality, at least every second intelligentsia student comes from a semi-proletarian family.' The local statistician continued doing all he could to improve students' class profile: while he counted only twenty-two students as non-proletarians, the cell's personal files contained nine 'chancery workers', nine 'medical assistants', three 'doctors', seven 'school teachers', one 'agricultural expert', and one 'Party functionary'—all excellent candidates for the intelligentsia column.[53]

Eager to act in concert with the statistician's agenda, students played down the intellectual component of their lives. Ostankin,

[51] GANO fo. 1053, op. 1, d. 589, l. 51; PATO fo. 320, op. 1, d. 19, ll. 126–7; PATO fo. 115, op. 2, d. 3, ll. 6–27.   [52] PANO fo. 2, op. 1, d. 963, l. 4.

[53] Only thirteen university Communists were 'workers' with real experience in production; ten other Communists were 'land tillers' (*khleboroby*). PATO fo. 115, op. 2, d. 8, l. 146.

a student at the Leningrad Agricultural Institute, stated in his autobiography that 'I was born to a worker family'. Further information suggested that he had spent most of his life working in clerical jobs and studying. In his defence, he emphasized that he had never acquired intelligentsia consciousness. The young Osankin wanted to follow in his father's footsteps and become an agricultural day labourer. Alas, local conditions dictated otherwise. Rather than disclose what had actually happened, the autobiographer produced a series of counterfactuals: he 'would have become' a worker, 'if not for the complete absence of factories in our vicinity. Thus the only alternative I had was either to remain at home or to study. Through no act of my own, I was later advanced from primary school to high school.'[54]

Suspicions aroused by the many telltale intelligentsia traits displayed by 'the unskilled worker Mal'kov', the bureau of the Tomsk Technological Institute grilled the student in 1925:[55]

Q: You say you have lived by the labours of your own hands since the age of 18 and yet your questionnaire states you 'have no profession'?
A: When I started working industry was weak, so I was employed in all kinds of jobs.
Q: Before you entered the Institute, what did you do?
A: I studied in a *Real Schule*.

Naiden knew that Ma'lkov's parents were artisans in the Altai, and that could mean that they were well off. 'Tell us what your parents are doing and what they own', he demanded. 'It is no good saying, how do I know, perhaps they have some stuff.' But Mal'kov insisted he could not add to what he had already written in his autobiography: 'It is difficult for me to state in a responsible way how my parents are. . . . I have had practically no contact with my father since 1921.'

The initial vote at the bureau was close: three for; zero against; five abstentions. The Party secretary was dissatisfied: 'that kind of a decision is worthless. It means going to the general meeting of the cell with practically no recommendation. Let's be determined. Accept him, yes or no?!' Further detail about the applicant's military service could elucidate his class physiognomy:

Q: What rank did you reach in Kolchak's army?
A: I was a private.

---

[54] TsGA IPD fo. 1085, op. 1, d. 23, l. 199.   [55] PATO fo. 17, op. 1, d. 747, l. 21.

Q: When were you drafted into the Red Army?

A: In Marinsk, in 1920. . . . I became an assistant to the communication officer.

'What kind of Red Army service is that if he sat in Tomsk and was in no battles?' Mal'gin exclaimed. This lack of commitment was typical of the intelligentsia. 'As far as I know', Zaikin commented, 'guys with education were officers in the White Army.' 'We need facts, not supposition', Borisov rebutted. But nothing could dispel Prikhod'ko's unease: 'only the privileged attended *Real Schulen* before the revolution. Something about Mal'kov is just not right.' 'Mal'kov's past is vague', Zaikin agreed. 'It is strange that he applies to the Party just before graduating. A speculator would behave in such a way. We should not attribute too much importance to his political erudition. When necessary the intelligentsia can master theory better than any of us.'

Popov called for more leniency: 'Remember that if we accept him we accept him not as a full Party member but as a candidate. It is up to us to make sure that Mal'kov will make a good expert. If we reject him we will demonstrate our attitude to such a category of persons.' The debate boiled down to the desirability of accepting the intelligentsia into the Party. Though this was a period of a favourable attitude towards the intelligentsia, the second vote produced exactly the same results as the first and Mal'kov's case remained pending.[56]

Knowledge could not be pursued for individual aims. Kolodin, a Leningrad student, was purged from the Party in the early 1920s because he was judged to be an 'individualist member of the intelligentsia'. The purge protocol stated that 'Kolodin strives only for personal knowledge and does nothing for the collective.'[57] But education was not inevitably construed as an anti-proletarian experience.[58] The 1923 autobiography of Tydman, born in Vitebsk to a family of railway employees and at the time of his application a student at the Leningrad Engineering Institute, forcefully argued that his studies had helped him to penetrate the meaning of class relations.[59]

Tydman, like Mal'kov, had attended a *Real Schule*, but his studies had somehow pointed his youthful consciousness in the right direction: 'I was converted to the revolutionary cause by the

[56] PATO fo. 17, op. 1, d. 747, p. 21.   [57] TsGAOR(L) fo. 2556, op. 1, d. 16, l. 84.

[58] TsGAODM fo. 67, op. 1, d. 97, l. 60b.   [59] TsGA IPD fo. 1085, op. 1, d. 24, l. 14.

October uprising of 1905, which became engraved in my memory. At that time, workers seized power for a short while in our small but revolutionary town.' Even university studies did not cloud Tydman's consciousness: 'In 1912 I entered the economics faculty of the Moscow Commercial Institute. There I attended lectures by almost the entire Social Democratic Central Committee: Manuilov (political economy); Novgorodtsev (philosophy and history of political theory); Kizevetter (Russian history); and Bulgakov (history of economic theory).' Believing that they had given him the basic tools of social analysis, the autobiographer presented his Kadet professors as Social Democrats! In any case, 'familiarity with the right literature and with Bolshevik students— who held several demonstrations and strikes—vaccinated me against a pure bourgeois ideology'.

All of this evidence of revolutionary activism was supposed to erase any suspicions that Tydman was a member of the old intelligentsia. A Red Army commissar, the autobiographer turned out to be a paragon of Bolshevik virtues: 'the NEP was the cause of bitter internal struggle and disenchantment to me. I found it very difficult to come to terms with this new atmosphere after I had been purified by the flames of War Communism. At the sight of thriving speculation and drunkenness I was as miserable as the dog who has to tolerate a cat right inside his doghouse.' Aware that the NEP was widely regarded as an attempt to reconcile the intelligentsia to Bolshevik power, and that identification with War Communism was characteristic of workers, Tydman was broadly hinting that he deserved to be classified as a proletarian.

The problem with Mal'kov and Tydman was that they were beneficiaries of the tsarist educational system. Their background could explain their not fully committed stance toward the Bolsheviks in recent years. If students with such backgrounds could only hope for consideration, Party applicants educated under the Soviet regime could, on occasion, actively oppose discrimination against the intelligentsia. Realizing that he had been grouped with non-proletarian applicants Trifonov, a student at Leningrad State University, was dismayed:

To my considerable surprise, I was facing a terrible dilemma: should I apply to the Party as a member of the intelligentsia or abstain from applying altogether. I reject the first option on principle and protest against the second as unfair. I feel compelled to declare that a policy that does not distinguish between the old, conservative intelligentsia and the new, toiling intelligentsia, is misbegotten down to its roots. Was the new intelligentsia not educated by the Soviet Power itself? . . . The very possibility of a comparison between me [and the old intelligentsia] is an insult to my spirit. Comrades, tell me what I have in common with members of the hereditary intelligentsia, who were educated in the old times![60]

To prove his point, Trifonov quoted from his autobiography: 'I attended high school in 1919–21, and served in the Red Army during that same period. Had it not been for the Revolution, I would not have seen the university any more than I see my own ears.' A 'peasant–proletarian' and by no means weak or effete, Trifonov felt that any talk about his degeneration 'is tantamount to a bad joke. I was sent to study not by mommy and daddy but straight from the plough!' His Party application, coinciding with a strong anti-intelligentsia bias, was flatly rejected (February 1924). Trifonov was instructed to start working in a factory and reapply later.

By and large, an intelligentsia background could be overlooked if one had accomplished meritorious deeds when political passions raged. Consider the brief interrogation of Cherniakov:

Q: When did your active political life begin?
A: I became a revolutionary in 1921 after my father was killed. I have been working in the Cheka ever since.

And a similar exchange with Trofimov, also from the mid-1920s:

Q: How was your political consciousness developed?
A: My father participated in the February uprising. I helped to distribute Bolshevik leaflets and arms. I am now applying to the Party merely in order to formalize my commitment to the Soviet Power.

Both of these intelligentsia students at Tomsk State University were accepted into the Party with honours as professional revolutionaries.[61]

In 1926–7 the status of the intelligentsia within the Party improved significantly. Re-christening it the 'toiling intelligentsia' (*trudiashchiesia intelligentsia*), class analysts put the intelligentsia on the same level as other 'labouring classes'.[62] According to the

[60] TsGA IPD fo. 984, op. 1, d. 188, ll. 143–4.
[61] PATO fo. 115, op. 2, d. 12, l. 62.   [62] Trinadtsatyi s"ezd RKP(b), 711.

August 1925 Central Committee circular, the 'intelligentsia' had been merged with the 'employees', a category that included 'administrators', 'professionals', and 'workers in culture and enlightenment'.[63] Furthermore, the henceforth mandatory category 'others', referring to declassed elements such as 'artisans', 'housekeepers', and 'students who had no profession before they entered the Party', assumed some of the worst connotations previously associated with the intelligentsia, although it was highly anomalous because it also subsumed 'professional revolutionaries'. No fewer than thirty-five delegates to the summer 1924 Thirteenth Party Congress, for example, were classified as 'others'.[64]

Fluctuations in the Leningrad State University's Party membership vividly display this short-lived tolerance of the intelligentsia. Depleted by a recent purge, the Leningrad State University Party cell numbered only 162 members in early 1925. However, during the 1925/6 academic year it tripled in size, largely because of the admission of 'employees' and 'others'; by 1927, the non-proletarian cohort comprised almost 40 per cent of the cell.

TABLE 5.3. *Social composition of the Leningrad State University Party organization in 1927*

	Party members	Party candidates	Komsomol members
Workers	190 (48.5%)	65 (37.4%)	394 (34.6%)
Peasants	51 (13.0%)	27 (15.5%)	365 (31.9%)
Employees	89 (22.7%)	55 (31.6%)	318 (27.9%)
Others	62 (15.8%)	27 (15.5%)	64 (5.6%)
Total	392 (100%)	174 (100%)	1,141 (100%)

Source: Tsentral'nyi gosudarstvennyi arkhiv istoriko politicheskikh dokumentov, fo. 984, op. 1, d. 148, l. 148.

So dire had the situation become that in order to keep the university's Party cells from being completely overrun by non-proletarians, the Vasilevsk Island District Committee (under whose jurisdiction the cell fell) refused to approve any more student mem-

[63] The pre-revolutionary mystique of the intelligentsia did not go away easily. Thus Nikolai Chaplin, head of the Komsomol in the 1920s, refused to put 'employee' as his social position, always preferring, 'member of the intelligentsia'. D. Poliakova, 'Poka serdtsa dlia chesti zhivy . . . ', in A. Afanas'ev, *Oni ne molchali* (Moscow, 1991), 358.

[64] TsGA IPD fo. 984, op. 1, d. 249, ll. 1–2, 5.

berships. This led to unhappiness in the 'enormous' local
Komsomol organization, which was the pool from which applicants were drawn, and after a general meeting of the university
Party organization, an appeal was made to the highest Party organs
'to reverse this decision'.[65] But the Leningrad authorities, eager to
protect the proletarian nature of the Leningrad Party organization,
insisted on the freeze. Eventually, a memorandum drafted by the
Leningrad Regional Party Committee on 7 December 1927 proposed guidelines that would ensure the induction of at least some
students into the Party: 'Aware of the Central Committee's stipu-
lation that the number of workers from the bench in the Party
should not fall below 50 per cent . . . we believe that students
should be enrolled solely in the third membership category.'[66] It is
remarkable that in order to enable at least some students to enrol
the apparatus was willing to endorse the assumption that academic
studies had a declassing effect (since this was the meaning of students' relegation to a non-productivist, third category of Party
membership).

As the 1920s drew to a close, battles over the class categoriza-
tion of student Bolsheviks were growing in intensity and sophistication. Statistics was a key area for administrative machinations.
Fearing 'finagling in classification', the statistical department at
the Central Committee instructed all Party organizations to
review the class affiliations of their membership in March 1928.[67]
As subsequent events in Tomsk make clear, however, this
command was thwarted and revisions in bookkeeping backfired.
Instead of unmasking the masquerading Party intelligentsia, the
commission that was working to implement the Central Committee's directive leaped at the opportunity further to improve
local students' identities.

---

[65] In 1927 about every fourth Leningrad student was enrolled in the Komsomol (1,542
out of 6,501). TsGA IPD fo. 6, op. 1, d. 224, l. 206. TsGA IPD fo. 984, op. 1, d. 244, l. 27;
fo. K-141, op. 1, d. 1a, l. 5.

[66] TsGA IPD fo. 984, op. 1, d. 120, l. 33; Komsomol members younger than 20 could
apply for Party membership only through the Komsomol district committee. TsGA IPD
fo. 138, op. 1, d. 1g, p. 17; *Spravochnik partiinogo rabotnika* (1923), iii. 124–5. On measures cur-
tailing admissions of Komsomol students into the Party see *Student revoliutsii*, 5 (1927), 21–
2; O. Dubatova and A. Tuliak, 'O rabote Komsomola v vuze', *Krasnoe studenchestvo*, 8
(1927–8), 38.

[67] Edward Hallet Carr and R. W. Davies, *Foundations of a Planned Economy, 1926–1929*
(London, 1971), i. 100–1; Rigby, *Communist Party Membership*, 163.

TABLE 5.4. *Alterations in the social positions of Tomsk students (1928)*
(cases in which students' social positions remained the same are not included in the table)

From	To	Technological Institute	State University Workers' Faculty
'other'	'student'	21	—
'other'	'employee'	19	—
'other'	'worker'	13	—
'employee'	'worker'	9	3
'other'	'peasant'	19	1
'worker'	'employee'	2	—
'employee'	'peasant'	2	1
'peasant'	'worker'	1	10
'employee'	student'	1	—
'peasant'	'employee'	—	1
'worker'	'peasant'	—	1

Source: PATO fo. 76, op. 1, d. 483, ll. 132–3; 138–42.

Very few workers or peasants were 'unmasked' as members of the intelligentsia; conversely, many who had been identified as 'employees' and 'others' saw a marked improvement in their status.

The flexibility built into the system allowed classes to be made and unmade after abrupt changes in Bolshevik policy. The social categorizations used by the Party apparatus were progressively refined: following the appearance of 'workers from the bench' and 'peasants from the plough' in 1923–4, the 'toiling intelligentsia' was called into existence a year later only to be amalgamated with 'employees'. Rather than an objective given, the intelligentsia appears to have been a flexible discursive artefact, made and unmade depending on the vagaries of Party politics. Admissions returns enable us not only to trace changes in the intelligentsia's numerical preponderance in Party cells, but also to examine the construction of the category itself. Indisputably, signals from the centre constantly elevated some social categories and lowered others. The fact that fluctuations in the status of the 'intelligentsia' emanated from policy shifts at the apex of the system, however, does not mean that class was not a question of discourse. In describing the discourse that classified and described

the 'intelligentsia', my point is not that the meaning of class categories was the result of a free exchange of opinion, but that the
centre never had—nor could it have had—full control over how
class vocabulary was used. The leaders of the local Party cells,
their statisticians, and the grass roots themselves had real latitude
in identifying who belonged to the intelligentsia and which intelligentsia students deserved Party admission.

Intelligentsia Conversions

The Party's increasing emphasis on identifying those with a proletarian spirit resulted in more attention being paid to story-telling
as the best means of determining class identity. This led to an
increased emphasis on the distinction between social origins and
social position, and, in many late 1920s documents, to the question
'What were your class origins?' being replaced by 'What sort of
milieu did you grow up in (*sreda gde vyros*)?'[68] Since 'formative
milieu' was much more amenable to narrativization than 'socio-
economic background', the element of self-fashioning in the creation of an intelligentsia subject grew in importance.

Offering a variety of strategies for the narrative presentation
of life experience, the autobiography allowed intelligentsia
Bolsheviks to inject a proletarian spirit into a non-proletarian
frame. Bolsheviks believed that typical members of the intelligentsia came from the urban petite bourgeoisie (*meshchanstvo*).
Their sins were usually committed close to the beginning of their
lives. Given that origins were impure, the corresponding life story
had to describe a fairly unilinear self-improvement, a steady and
uninterrupted movement towards universalist consciousness. It
was as if the sheer volume of their sins placed members of the
intelligentsia at a disadvantage by comparison with workers; any
further corruption of their souls would have made Party enrolment highly unlikely.

Thus the influences which formed the intelligentsia consciousness were usually presented as progressing from good to better.
In intelligentsia autobiographies, interaction with the proletarian
milieu and revolutionary activity drove protagonists towards the
comprehension of class relations, gradually relieving them of petit

---

[68] PATO fo. 76, op. 1 , d. 114.

bourgeois character traits. Alternatively, intelligentsia autobiographies could be composed according to the conversion crisis model, describing a story of miraculous transformation. But in these cases, a perdurable kernel of proletarian values, no matter how small and forgotten, was usually posited to make the eventual adoption of proletarian ideology slightly more likely.

Intelligentsia narrators of this sort tended to claim that deep within their souls a proletarian ember lay hidden, glowing beneath the cinders. Once blown into a flame, it kindled a conflagration that destroyed such intelligentsia vices as passivity, cowardice, opportunism, utilitarianism, and the tendency to make corrupt bargains with the enemies of the proletariat. In the 1930s the playwright Aleksandr Afinogenov described how he discovered his true revolutionary identity underneath his intelligentsia self: 'I set the knife to myself and took out not only my stomach but the heart as well. The self inside me died—and then a miracle happened. A new "self" revived . . . all the best that had ever been in me and had since vanished. Now it turns out that my positive features had not faded or evaporated, had not completely died, but laid down a foundation for a completely new me, tiny and weak as it may at first have been.'[69] Here the renunciation of the intelligentsia self was simultaneously the discovery of a lost proletarian identity.

The exact formula of the conversion was not so important; intelligentsia autobiographers paid much more attention to the phenomenological aspects of their conversion than worker or peasant autobiographers. Incessantly self-reflective, they documented every movement of their soul, revealed every inner spring of their intentions, and described every inch of their personal growth in cerebral terms. Cut off from active life, students who described themselves as members of the intelligentsia had to keep their narratives logical because rational deliberation and theoretical insight were the only impetuses accepted as forces that could convince them to embrace the Party.

Numerous Party applicants claimed to have refashioned themselves as members of the new intelligentsia. The autobiography of Kasintsev, a student at the Leningrad State University and a professional musician, is interesting in this regard.[70] Recapitulating those parts of intelligentsia autobiography that dealt with the

---

[69] Jochen Hellbeck, *Revolution on my Mind: Writing a Diary under Stalin* (Cambridge, Mass., 2006), 326. [70] TsGA IPD fo. 1085, op. 1, d. 26, ll. 142–3.

transformation of declassed urban dwellers into conscious proletarians, he made a powerful case for being able to contribute, not
necessarily as someone reborn into the working class, but as a
proud member of the new intelligentsia.

Kasintsev claimed he had come 'from a poor workers' milieu'.
His mother was a peasant, 'completely illiterate to this very day'.
His father, 'while still a barely literate urchin, was apprenticed to
a carpenter'. When he had witnessed the cruelty the exploiter
inflicted upon the exploited, Kasintsev's father became a champion
of the working class. 'He took the revolutionary nickname "Artar",
and made a red shirt from his favourite cloth.' The post-1905 reaction, however, soon deflated this radicalism and Kasintsev had to
admit that his father then crossed the lines and became a foreman.
In a word, the autobiographer's background was shoddy.

But not all was lost: rent into bourgeois and proletarian halves,
a petit bourgeois soul could evolve in a positive direction if circumstances were propitious. When Kasintsev begun his studies at
the Vladikavkaz high school, his wealthy classmates identified him
as their social opposite: 'I would constantly hear insults like
"muzhik", "paper boy", and so on thrown in my direction.' Long
years of experience in the struggle against Dinikin bands completed Kasintsev's conversion, 'and the experience left me devoted
heart and soul to the Soviet Power'.

But the autobiography's concluding part, where Kasintsev
comes close to speaking of the tutelage of the working class, is the
most interesting:

Advancing hand in hand with the people and fighting to defend their
interests, I wished for only one thing, to be an honest human being, a
friend and a servant of the Russian people. In 1922, an urge seized me
to become an engineer, for the good of the people. . . . I now write to
relieve and cleanse my soul, and my aim is to earn the trust of the
workers . . . and prove that we, the new generation of the intelligentsia,
do not strive to separate ourselves from the working class but on the contrary seek to be close to it, to be its friend. I look forward to a new way
of living, working hand in hand with the working class, so that no barriers will exist between us.

The use of 'we/them' suggests that the autobiographer distinguished himself, a member of the new intelligentsia, from the
working class proper. At the same time, the allusion to the fall of
all barriers between the workers and the intelligentsia attests to

Kasintsev's hope that in the classless future the gap between work and thought will at last disappear. 'Down with bureaucratism!' he inveighed. 'Let the engineer be distinguished from the worker by occupation alone, not by ideology. Once we have travelled a hard, thorny path, the day will come when the worker perceives the expert not as a softie (*beloruchka*) but as a friend.' When, in the passage cited at the beginning of this paragraph, Kasintsev switched to the present tense, this indicated that he was describing the contemporary, transitional period in which certain divisions between the working class and the intelligentsia were preserved. Shifting tenses yet again and adopting the future tense, the author replaced the division between 'me' (Kasintsev, a member of the intelligentsia) and 'them' (the working class) with the promise of a new 'we'—the unified revolutionary Subject. Since the tasks of the Party and the new intelligentsia were basically identical, namely, to enlighten workers and bring about the worker–intelligentsia synthesis, Kasintsev's place, the autobiography tacitly concluded, was with the Party.

No matter how bright and erudite, members of the intelligentsia always doubted their relevance. Knowledge was not a value in itself; detached from life it was obscurantist and irrelevant. Truth could not be assessed at a strictly theoretical level, though this was certainly important; it had to explain real events and make sense to the proletariat. That is why many intelligentsia autobiographies combine descriptions of intellectual discoveries with demonstrations that these discoveries were relevant to the struggle of the working class. Consider the case of Osinsky, a prominent Bolshevik Party leader and economist:

When I was about 14 years old I wrote my first article on religion and ethics. Although our circle evolved toward Marxism quite slowly it had a politically radical and materialist bent almost from the very beginning. . . . In the winter of 1904–5 our work in the *Gymnasium* took a political direction and we began putting out a daily newspaper, making presentations, and arranging discussions. Finally the time had come to decide our political orientation (*politicheski samoopredelit'sia*). For this purpose— and such behaviour is quite characteristic of the theoretical deviations that occurred over the course of our spiritual development—we decided to review, under the instruction of P. M. Lebedev, the history of the revolutionary movement in Russia.[71]

---

[71] Though his autobiographical narrative was quite contorted in this regard, Osinsky

Though overall he was moving along the correct trajectory, Osinsky was still suffering from his old intelligentsia habits. When he chose the Decembrists as the subject of his presentation he was overcome by a need to 'oppose strenuously everything "fashionable"'. Such an inclination to assert the originality of one's mind was—Osinsky now saw this clearly—'the psychological plague of the intelligentsia'. Since he had perceived Marxism as a fleeting intelligentsia fad the autobiographer had tried to give the Decembrist movement a non-Marxist interpretation, mainly out of spite. 'I set out on the road of baseless liberalism and this allowed Lebedev and Kerzhentsev to demolish my argument. Once I had carefully thought through the reasons for my "defeat" I arrived at the conclusion that old Marx knew what he was talking about.'

The intelligentsia's purely intellectual insight was not enough. Osinsky was not yet a consistent revolutionary thinker. It was not until the Revolution of 1905 that his Marxism was 'tangibly reinforced'. After the uprising had been put down Osinsky went to Germany to study political economy. He no longer tarried in unwholesome ideological byways: 'I divided my time between the study of Plekhanov and of Lenin.' Having finally joined theory to practice Osinsky returned to Russia and, in the autumn of 1907, 'deemed myself ready to become a conscious Party member'.[72]

The path to enlightenment, and the pitfalls the intelligentsia met along the way, feature prominently in the autobiography of Reisner, a major Soviet sociologist and psychologist. The beginning was modest: 'I received education in keeping with intelligentsia romanticism—that is, a jumble of unscientific ideas that doomed my young mind to years of slogging through an intellectual morass.' The remainder of Reisner's autobiography is an account of how he overcame this predicament. He began at an early age 'to seek for the path to humanity's salvation'. As he describes how he plunged into 'mysticism' and 'Tolstoyanism', then underwent the 'strong influence of Dostoevsky', his sarcasm

appears to have been an offspring of an old intelligentsia family. 'A son of a petty land owner in the Orlov province, my father . . . never possessed the princely title (so often ascribed to me without reason). Father had to commence his life working as a *Gymnasium* teacher. . . . But he was a man of radical convictions and high culture. Even at a time when he did not have a large income . . . foreign language tutors were hired for the children. Thus I have been fluent in German and French since childhood.'

[72] *Deiateli SSSR*, 570.

is quite evident. But soon enough he came to hate classicism and reject science—intellectual preoccupations relevant only to a pretentious, obscurantist, and totally detached intelligentsia—and the young graduate of the Petersburg *Gymnasium* went to study at Warsaw University. At that time, he said, 'I dreamed of dedicating myself to religion.'

A 'sharp break' in Reisner's evolution occurred when he came under the influence of Professor Blok. The father of the famous poet was 'a scholar who somehow managed to combine enormous erudition, materialist scepticism, and slavophilism. A sociologist-positivist in his premises, Blok was a Romantic in his conclusions.' Reisner absorbed his mentor's method but was not satisfied as to what implications he should draw from it. Confused, he went to Kiev to seek illumination from Evgeny Trubetskoi. 'A careful investigation of political schools', however, brought Reisner to the gloomy conclusion that 'contemporary science had come to a dead end and was unable to decide between two equally binding and logical systems of thought which were glaringly, irreconcilably antithetical. . . . Political science appeared to be an accumulation of equally binding "verities" (*pravdy*) and "truths" (*instiny*), each flatly contradicting the other.' Needless to say, a mystic such as Trubetskoi 'could not show a way out since he took one truth on faith and rejected all others'. It was then that Reisner was presented with the task to which he was to 'dedicate his theoretical and practical life—finding an objective law that would explain why various worldviews have come into existence and why they have to be mutually exclusive'.[73]

Reisner's conversion was piecemeal. Religion, for example, he spurned while a teacher at Tomsk University in the late 1890s; 'this was all to the good since mysticism was known to be the major obstacle on the path to enlightenment faced by Silver Age intelligentsia. His articles from that period exposed the purely political nature of the Russian Church and moral legislation.'[74] Ultimately Reisner managed to extricate himself from the remaining forms of scholastic thinking. While in Europe in 1903 he finally saw that Marxism alone was a science and that all other creeds were merely interest-driven beliefs. The serious materialist teaching focused not on the contradictions within human thought but

---

[73] Ibid. 623.   [74] Ibid. 624.

on the tensions at the base of society. 'Marxism was the only way to resolve these fundamental contradictions. The dialectical, contradictory character of political systems could not be explained in their own terms, only in terms of their social underpinnings. The secrets of the political realm could be unlocked only if one approached them in terms of the class interests for which they served as an ideological superstructure.'

As he approached that fundamental truth Reisner passed through the classic series of stages of the member of the intelligentsia on his way to the light, moving from the realm of ideas to the reality that explained it. But no theory, not even Marxism, could be fully absorbed without revolutionary practice. His legal expertise meant that his own revolutionary experience was the defence he mounted of German Social Democrats accused of crimes of state against the Russian tsar.[75] Once Reisner discovered the proletariat, this member of the intelligentsia found his true audience. Although the pre-revolutionary university auditoriums were full when Reisner lectured, his explanations of the social determination of human psychology fell on deaf ears. Only when he made his way to workers' auditoriums to disseminate scholarly socialist propaganda did his listeners seem attentive and receptive.[76]

Action, the property of the working class, and thought, the property of the intelligentsia, were expected to fuse in the New Man. In many a Bolshevik autobiography the marriage of a member of the intelligentsia to the proletariat was celebrated. The autobiography of Professor Shchepkin, a Kadet-turned-Bolshevik, included the following summary of the protagonist's conversion from member of the old intelligentsia to Bolshevik scholar: 'As social initiative is passed into the hands of the popular masses, higher education must be inspired by the life going on around it: theory must be subjected to practice. Contemplation, the child of detached cognition, must be replaced by an American type of pragmatism . . . a Will that pushes one to act.'[77]

One of the features that make the above autobiographies especially intriguing is how the new intelligentsia, even as it set about the task of inculcating the proletariat with Marxist theory, was, in the process, losing much of its own identity. For the 'purity' of the

---

[75] *Deiateli SSSR*, 624.   [76] Ibid. 626.   [77] Ibid. 775.

voice of the new intelligentsia depended, in the final analysis, on its ability to speak with the voice of the proletariat. By instilling a universalist consciousness in their working-class audiences, Osinsky and Reisner, themselves unequivocally offspring of the intelligentsia, came to identify with their protégés. To the extent that universalism was an intrinsically proletarian quality, those members of the revolutionary intelligentsia who acquired it through great mental labour somehow became proletarians. Of course, this dynamic worked both ways: with the obliteration of their exclusive identification with manual labour proletarians likewise lost their authentic self. As they became aware of their proletarian identity and grew to be conscious of their revolutionary duties, politically mature workers became, in a sense, members of the intelligentsia.

Clearly, universalist consciousness was the ultimate standard of Bolshevik identity, not class origins or occupation. And the new intelligentsia had plenty of this universalism. Lenin scolded those who tried to delegitimize its members on the grounds that they were petit bourgeois: 'If social origins are fetishized, workers, having been small landowners in the past, would have to be relegated to the petite bourgeoisie as well! Individuals distantly related to members of the intelligentsia were not barred from becoming "proletarians in spirit" (*proletarii dukhom*).' In the words of an anonymous Marxist pamphleteer, Marx, Engels, and Lenin, unhampered by their non-proletarian origins, 'were the best among the intelligentsia, capable of renouncing individualism, plumbing the depths of human suffering and sacrificing themselves for the proletariat'.[78]

What was expected from the new intelligentsia is clear from the assessment of the members belonging to this category by their superiors and inferiors. Consider the Communist University's personal evaluation of Terent'ev, composed in the spring of 1924 by the presidium of the Party cell in the Red Army unit to which he was briefly assigned as a propagandist:

During the period he spent in our division Terent'ev did not meet the expectations of someone sent by the Party. He arrived here not because he wanted to work with us but only because he was . . . eager to meet the upcoming German Revolution [as a member of a military staff]. As

[78] RGASPI fo. 17, op. 8, d. 396, l. 17.

a student of the Communist University, Comrade Terent'ev surely has sufficient theoretical education. Yet he does not want to pass on his knowledge to peasants or to the less developed Party members. For him, the Communist University is a place where one obtains a profession needed for one's personal happiness. . . . Here is Terent'ev's interpretation of the maxim, BEING DETERMINES CONSCIOUSNESS: first, make me a staff member, then develop expectations in my regard. Refusing to hang newspapers on the walls, to contribute to Lenin's corner, etc., he justifies himself by saying that this is something only political activists from the staff can be expected to do. Although Terent'ev attends Party meetings, lectures, and discussion groups regularly, he does not show proper initiative in agitating among the masses. Nor does this intemperate and undisciplined comrade care about personal conversations with comrades. His life style is secluded: 'I read and work on myself', he explains, 'so that I do not fall behind my fellow students.'[79]

This was a harsh condemnation: educated in Bolshevik institutions, Terent'ev was supposed to 'retain his ties with the masses', give generously of his ideological and political insights, and help to convert others to Communism. Instead, he treated the knowledge he received as private property—a telltale sign that this intelligentsia comrade was rapidly degenerating.[80]

Despite the very different historical context and the recent announcement that class struggle in the country had been terminated, expectations of the intelligentsia, now declared an 'intermediary layer' (*prosloika*) linking workers and peasants, did not change significantly in the 1930s. Kapustin, a young expert at the Leningrad Kirov plant who had just returned from university studies in England, was accused by fellow engineers of 'wrecking' in 1937, that is, his shop was not meeting its production norms. The following letter in his defence, jotted down with a pencil on an oily paper, was signed by twenty-eight workers operating different shifts. Wishing to save their boss, the signatories did not miss a single superlative that befitted a member of the new intelligentsia. The letter was addressed to Zal'tsman, the head of the turbine-producing shop and one of Kapustin's main detractors:

[79] TsGA IPD fo. 197, op. 1, d. 71, l. 17.

[80] Party officials maintained that cadres sent for higher education easily lost their proletarian attributes and turned into a cast of privileged specialists similar to the pre-revolutionary intelligentsia. 'Budushchee intelligentsii', in V. Soskin (ed.), *Sud'by russkoi intelligentsia: Materialy diskussii 1923–25gg.* (Novosibirsk, 1991), 16.

We consider Kapustin our best friend, our best boss. In his work, he never raises his voice, treats us as his equals, always greets us with a handshake. He gives exhaustive answers to all our questions, explains, shows, teaches. We always fully understand the orders coming from Iakov Fedorovich [Kapustin], a seasoned Party member who came from our ranks and who has the general sympathy of all the workers here. Under his leadership we became politically educated individuals. Every lunch break we would read newspapers and Iakov Fedorovich was our lecturer and general consultant very frequently. He had always known how to approach the worker with love, and we reciprocated and tried to execute his orders quickly and precisely. . . . Kapustin forged excellent production workers out of us, politically trustworthy people who work consciously.[81]

All the characteristics of the genre appear here: Kapustin came from the people, and remained in the people and of the people. While his studies put him in a position of authority, he did all he could to direct his workers so that one day they would close the remaining gap between manual and mental labour.

To be worthy of the Party, intelligentsia students had to show that they had overcome what were regarded as their most intrinsic traits—selfishness, highmindedness, and anti-social inclinations. This became all the more urgent when the applicant's intelligentsia individualism had taken a political form and had been expressed through identification with one of the anarchist currents that tried to outdo Bolsheviks in their radicalism. The autobiography of Buntar', a student at Leningrad State University, brought into sharp relief this connection between intelligentsia identity and unbridled sentiment.[82] Born in 1902 in a village called Iarunino, in Tver Province, the autobiographer had, despite his poor peasant origins, become an employee. 'The loss of class roots occurred very early in life', he confessed. The early death of his father and his mother's subsequent move to Petersburg, where she found employment as a servant, had had a declassing effect on the children: the autobiographer's youngest sister became a servant, and later a chambermaid, while the 1-year-old Buntar' was placed in a petit bourgeois primary school. Having abandoned agricultural work and failed to enter the capital's industrial labour force, Buntar' lost his social compass and embraced the

[81] V. I. Demidov and V. A. Kutuzov, *Leningradskoe delo* (Leningrad, 1990), 76–7.
[82] TsGA IPD fo. 984, op. 1, d. 126, ll. 66, 69.

dissolute pastimes of urban riffraff. 'After I graduated from school, a teacher with anarchist inclinations helped me enrol in college. I consumed some of the social democratic literature that filled her bookshelves.'

In 1915, the autobiographer came across a particularly impressive inflammatory leaflet which prompted him to join a local anarchist organization. In fact, the name 'Buntar'', which means 'rebel' in Russian, was clearly a pseudonym of the sort favoured by defiant anarchists. Buntar' played a major role in the almost mythical occupation of Durnovo's summer house and the capture of the palace of the Duke of Leikhtenberg—two major anarchist actions accomplished during that revolutionary year. He does not quite tell us how, but somehow Buntar' evolved from a wild and militant anarchist into a dedicated Bolshevik. During the Civil War many anarchists had decided to 'sell their swords' and side with the Reds.[83]

By 1920, the opinions of Buntar', too, had definitely 'drifted away from anarchism'. The Party cell of the Presnetsk region went so far as to 'enrol me in its ranks without any probation period'—a rare honour indeed that can be explained by the autobiographer's committed service in the ranks of the Red Army. But his past returned to haunt him and during the purge of 1921 he was expelled from the Party. The protocol of the proceedings of the Petersburg Control Commission, which oversaw his reinstatement request, indicates that 'Buntar''s purge was motivated by the sympathy he showed for the anarchist party before the February revolution'. Worse yet, Buntar' had reportedly refused to cooperate with the Cheka in suppressing anarchist organizations despite explicit orders to do so. 'Even now [June 1922], the supplicant is sympathetic to anarchist idealists (*anarkhisty ideinogo tolka*).'[84]

The matter of his expulsion obliged Buntar' to disclose to the Leningrad State University Party cell a set of highly revealing autobiographical reflections. Only toward the very end of his second autobiographical letter did he directly confront the accusation that he was an anarchist sympathizer: 'As far as my old views go, I renounced them a long time ago. Can anyone seriously believe that an anarchist would command Red Army battalions? . . . True, I did display a certain weakness in Tver when prominent anarchists were arrested. All I ask, however, is that the

---

[83] *Volna: Ezhemesiachnyi organ federatsii anarkho-kommunisticheskikh grupp*, 48 (1923), 38–9.
[84] TsGA IPD fo. 984, op. 1, d. 126, ll. 73–4.

Party use me without bringing pressure to bear on those parts of my constitution that remain weak.'

The remainder of his letter was dedicated to reflections on the role of the new intelligentsia in the Party, an issue that had a direct bearing on the autobiographer since he preferred academic studies to a military career:

> You refused to allow me to remain in the workers' Party, basing that decision . . . solely on the fact that I am not a 'worker' but a 'member of the intelligentsia'. The Party, you argued, draws its strength exclusively from workers from the bench. First, let me tell you that I by no means regard myself as a member of the intelligentsia in the full sense of the word. My course of university studies is not yet completed, so how can I be classified as a 'mental labourer'? Shouldn't you wait until I graduate and start actually working in a white-collar profession? Second, if I am purged from the Party and, following that, from the university, will I not have to work in a factory like any other worker? . . . In my view, this makes me not a 'mental labourer' but an 'educated unskilled worker' (*intelligentnyi chernorabochii*).

Had he been an old-fashioned member of the intelligentsia, Buntar' averred, he could have remained a chancery worker in the Red Army. The sole reason for his demobilization was a 'lack of desire to become a military specialist in times of peace'.

Next, Buntar' turned to the general meaning of the term 'intelligentsia': 'Setting aside for a moment the definition of a member of the intelligentsia which is based on one's relation to production, one has to admit that, from the point of view of proletarian ethics, mental development (*umstvennoe razvitie*) should be considered not a burden but, quite to the contrary, an asset. The workers' revolution cannot win until every single worker becomes sufficiently developed to be able to supervise the production process.' A wholesale attack on the intelligentsia and its spiritual values, Buntar' reminded the reader, had a name in the Bolshevik parlance—it was *makhaevshchina*, a syndicalist heresy condemned by the Party in every possible language.[85] According to Buntar', a workers' intelligentsia had to be built in order to secure proletarian victory in the struggle over minds:

> During the transitional period . . . the intelligentsia that thinks and feels with the Party is particularly valuable, especially when it comes from the

---

[85] On *makhaevshchina* as a pejorative term see L. Syrkin, 'Chto takoe makhaevshchina?', *Krasnaia letopis'*, 6 (1929) and 1 (1930).

lower echelons of society. It is not inferior but complementary to workers from the bench. . . . The Party has to be on the alert for the possible effects of economic hardship on the working class: when under duress, a worker may easily succumb to all kinds of deviations. At a moment of economic distress, only an imaginative enlightenment, and not some propaganda loaded with clichés, is capable of reanimating the workers and of forcing them to think as workers should think.

His underlying assumption was that each class had characteristic patterns of thought, but at times individual members of a class could be swayed by alien modes of thinking. Without assistance from the new intelligentsia, workers who were in trouble could succumb to petit bourgeois temptations. The autobiographer believed that only an alert and genuine revolutionary intelligentsia could unmask the false prophets who tried to lure the workers away from the right path:

A worker who is relatively poorly developed—and we should keep in mind that fully developed Bolshevik workers are still rare—is generally vulnerable to all sorts of criticism advanced by the seditious Mensheviks who worm their way into the factory. If that danger is to be staved off, the presence in the factory of intelligentsia with working-class roots is crucial. Saving the GPU plenty of effort, such intelligentsia can create the conditions for a widening of the freedom of speech without which it will be impossible to rekindle workers' political thought.

Since many workers were not yet conscious enough to have the upper hand in political debates with the Mensheviks, so the argument went, political freedoms had unfortunately to be suppressed. But this situation was bound to change with the growth of the true workers' intelligentsia.[86]

Almost imperceptibly, the autobiography of Buntar' metamorphosed into an extended apologia for the new intelligentsia. A vanguard of the proletariat, it alone could lead workers to a classless society. Buntar' was adamant that those who had purged him from the Party had inadvertently blasted the buds of the new intelligentsia: 'The Party cannot and does not rely solely on workers from the bench. Its anti-intelligentsia policies are aimed at only the worthless intelligentsia, the intelligentsia which is alien to the proletariat. To confuse me with that kind of intelligentsia . . . is to offend my pride. Insult is added to injury when I am

[86] TsGA IPD fo. 984, op. 1, d. 126, ll. 75–7.

identified with the hordes of individuals who grope for loopholes so as to worm their way into the Party. We seek not loopholes but legitimate ways to become Party members.' Pleading that he was not an old intelligentsia interloper but a member of the new intelligentsia that fully belonged to the Soviet political order, Buntar' sought to turn the weaknesses of intelligentsia identity into a source of strength. The conclusion of his autobiography—'in my view, the doors of the Party should be open to each and every member of the intelligentsia who thinks like a worker'—might have served as the motto of those who believed in the transcendence of class distinctions in Bolshevik society.

The autobiographies we have just examined might as easily be described as treatises in class theory. But this was entirely appropriate. One of the founding principles of the Bolshevik illiberal self was that society instilled in an individual his or her sense of identity. In presenting themselves, authors never limited their narrative to the contents of their private lives but, by dwelling at length and with considerable sophistication on the past and the present of the Party, elucidated their own place in the proletarian movement. Our autobiographers were well aware that after the Revolution the relationship between the intelligentsia and the working class had been reformulated from a relationship in which the intelligentsia played the guiding role to a class alliance under the guidance of the working class. Kasintsev, Reisner, and even Buntar', albeit a bit less enthusiastically, all acknowledged that in the pupil–teacher relationship, the two sides had switched positions. 'The intelligentsia has been adopted by the proletariat', Party spokesmen explained.[87] 'It is now the Party that sets the rules. The intelligentsia', Lunacharsky explained, 'is not the manager but the servant.'[88]

But Lunacharsky could also be cited by members of the intelligentsia who wanted to substantiate their claims for Party membership. When asked 'should we create a new intelligentsia? Can we not jump directly into a period devoid of intelligentsia?' Lunacharsky answered: 'We take the Dictatorship of the Proletariat seriously, though it is temporary, do we not? Why should we not treat the intelligentsia with equal seriousness, transient category

---

[87] 'Sotsial'naia fizionomiia intelligentsii', *Biulletini literatury i zhizni*, 1 (1924), 5.

[88] A. Lunacharskii, 'Intelligentsiia i ee mesto v sotsialisticheskom stroitel'stve', *Revoliutsiia i kul'tura*, 1 (1927), 25, 33–4.

though it is?'[89] Explaining that 'No form will be complete until the construction of Communism is complete', Lenin himself had warned that even a proletarian revolution could not eradicate the distinction between mental and manual labour right away: 'The antithesis between mental and physical labour . . . cannot on any account immediately be removed by the mere conversion of the means of production into public property, by the mere expropriation of capitalists.'[90]

The inclusiveness of the Bolshevik brotherhood ensured that alien social origins were never insuperable. The Soviet Constitution of 1918 established the category of the disenfranchised (*lishentsy*): formerly privileged estates and occupations such as nobles, merchants, and tsarist gendarmes were relegated to the ranks of the exploiters and deprived of citizens' rights.[91] Despite discrimination against these categories, the offspring of anti-social elements could claim a Party card if they were able to prove that they had severed ties with their parents. If youngsters demonstrated that their consciousness broke with the retrograde thinking of their parents, they could claim to become full participants in the Soviet social order. 'Our family fully degenerated (*razlozhilas'*)', Sashanova, a student at the Leningrad Communist University, stated in 1924. She had nothing to do with her father's business and had not been 'in touch with any of my relatives since 1917'.[92]

The most horrible class identities could be whitewashed. Even the son of a gendarme could become a Party member, as was the case with Galenchenko, who was accepted by the Smolensk Institute cell in May 1920. 'Already eleven years since my father left that occupation', Galenchenko explained. 'True, I get along with my father but this is so because he is a kind man with Tolstoyan convictions.' Pointing out that Galenchenko had been one of the first in the region to join the Bolsheviks, students concluded they 'should not brand Galenchenko because of what his father used to do'.[93] In principle, conversion was open to all.

[89] *Sud'by sovremennoi intelligentsii*, 45.

[90] 'Revoliutsiia i melkaia burzhuaznaia demokratiia: Rech' Lenina na sobranii otvet-stvennykh rabotnikov-kommunistov 27-go Noiabria 1918 goda', *Intelligentsiia i sovetskaia vlast'*, 18. Robert C. Tucker (ed.), *The Lenin Anthology* (New York, 1975), 379.

[91] Elise Kimerling, 'Civil Rights and Social Policy in Soviet Russia, 1918–1936', *Russian Review*, 41 (1982); Golfo Alexopoulos, *Stalin's Outcasts: Aliens, Citizens, and the Soviet State, 1926–1936* (Ithaca, NY, 2003).

[92] TsGA IPD fo. 197, op. 1, d. 115, l. 30.   [93] WKP 326, l. 211.

6

Faced with Death:
Gestapo Interrogations and Clemency Pleas in High Treason Trials by the National Socialist *Volksgerichtshof*

ISABEL RICHTER

Introduction: High Treason Trials as a Social Practice of Domination

To speak is to act. This basic insight of speech act theory[1] leaves wide open the question of what exactly we are doing when we speak. In interpreting the transcripts of Gestapo interrogations and clemency pleas in trials under the National Socialist regime, I am obviously dealing with speech and writing of a very specific kind. The actors in this communication—indeed, one can hardly imagine more different positions of power—were, on the one hand, Gestapo members, National Socialist judges, public prosecutors, and prison officers, and on the other, men and women from a wide variety of groups involved in resistance activities directed against the National Socialist regime. The title of my essay, 'Faced with Death', refers to communication in existential situations. The main question to be asked in this essay is: what forms of expression and ways of speaking were possible in such an extreme situation? Did the prisoners interrogated by the Gestapo, or writing clemency pleas, have any room for manoeuvre in choosing their words? And is it reasonable to assume that the words and arguments which appear in the transcripts come anywhere near an expression of the prisoners' subjectivity? Moving on from this close reading of trial documents, it will also have to be asked whether the way in which we deal with the history of resistance to National Socialism needs to be modified, and if so, how?

This essay draws on the transcripts of Gestapo interrogations and clemency pleas to be found in the files on high treason trials

---

[1] See John R. Searle, *Speech Acts: An Essay in the Philosophy of Language* (Cambridge, 1970).

held by the National Socialist People's Court (*Volksgerichtshof*).[2] A database documents a total of 6,543 files of *Volksgerichtshof* trials in the period from 1934, when the court was founded, to 1945. These files are archived in the Federal Archive (Bundesarchiv) in Berlin, and include documents of treason and high treason trials as well as of cases against those accused of demoralizing the troops (*Wehrkraftzersetzung*).[3] The post-war image of the *Volksgerichtshof* has long been shaped by its activities during the Second World War, and especially by the famous cases brought against members of the students' resistance group Weiße Rose, and against the noble or bourgeois leaders of the 20 July 1944 plot against Hitler. However, quite a different picture emerges when we look at the period before 1939. Before 1939 the vast majority of *Volksgerichtshof* trials were concerned with prosecuting organized left-wing opposition to the political system. Numerous cases were brought against activists, supporters, or sympathizers of the German Communist Party and the Social Democratic Party, but there were also trials against members of smaller parties such as the Socialist Workers' Party (SAP), the German Communist Party of Opposition (KPDO), or other small left-wing organizations, such as, for example, the International Socialist Fighting Alliance (ISK), various Trotskyist groups, or anarchist trade union groups.

A number of studies have dealt with the history of the *Volksgerichtshof*. Most have either examined the history of the institution,[4] or have concentrated only on the documents recording accusations and sentences, that is, documents which reflect the prosecutors' and judges' inhuman and often arbitrary practice.[5]

[2] The sources and ideas in this essay are drawn from my book on high treason trials as a social practice of domination under National Socialism viewed in terms of the history of everyday life and gender issues. See Isabel Richter, *Hochverratsprozesse als Herrschaftspraxis im Nationalsozialismus: Männer und Frauen vor dem Volksgerichthof 1934–1939* (Münster, 2001).

[3] See 'Akten des Oberreichsanwalts beim Volksgerichtshof', in the Berlin Bundesarchiv (henceforth BArch Berlin). For further information on the database file see Klaus Marxen, *Das Volk und sein Gerichtshof: Eine Studie zum nationalsozialistischen Volksgerichtshof* (Frankfurt am Main, 1994), 24; Holger Schlüter, *Die Urteilspraxis des nationalsozialistischen Volksgerichtshofs* (Berlin, 1995), 28; Edmund Lauf, *Der Volksgerichtshof und seine Beobachter: Bedingungen und Funktionen der Gerichtsberichterstattung im Nationalsozialismus* (Opladen, 1994), 20–1, 227–8; and Gabriele Erben and Ulf Rathje, *Die Abgeurteilten des Volksgerichtshofs: Datenbank aus dem Forschungsprojekt der Universität Münster, Institut für Kriminalwissenschaften* (Koblenz, 1997).

[4] Walter Wagner, *Der Volksgerichtshof im nationalsozialistischen Staat* (Stuttgart, 1974); Lothar Gruchmann, *Die Justiz im Dritten Reich 1933–1940: Anpassung und Unterwerfung in der Ära Gürtner* (Munich, 1988).

[5] See Marxen, *Das Volk und sein Gerichtshof*; Schlüter, *Die Urteilspraxis*; Lauf, *Der Volksgerichtshof*; and Jürgen Zarusky, 'Widerstand als Hochverrat 1933–1945: Eine Mikrofiche-

By contrast, I have assumed that the social practice of legal proceedings can only be understood if the whole of a case is examined, including the pre- and post-trial stages. For the period from 1934 to the beginning of the Second World War in 1939, there are 242 completely preserved files of high treason cases at the *Volksgerichtshof*. Of these, I have analysed fifty cases in detail.[6] The files allow insights into all stages of these cases—from the impulse initiating the proceedings, usually denunciation, to the arrest of the prisoner, the Gestapo interrogations, judicial preparatory examinations, preferral of charges, the trial in court, the judge's sentence, and the prisoner's clemency pleas. If we look at these proceedings as communicative practice, it soon becomes apparent that this is a sphere of action in which none of the actors, not even the judges and the Gestapo officers, could act as completely autonomous subjects. Rather, for all the actors involved, what they did and what they said in the proceedings was the result of earlier social processes in which, again, all actors involved had a certain amount of influence.

In this essay, two text types resulting from National Socialist judicial practice will be analysed in detail. One refers to an early stage, the other to a very late, post-trial stage, of proceedings. I will first look at Gestapo interrogation transcripts, in particular, at the way in which statements made by male or female prisoners concerning their motives for taking political action were recorded in these transcripts. I will then ask how judges reacted to the prisoners' statements concerning their motivation as transcribed by the Gestapo. Did what prisoners said, and how they expressed it, make any difference? Secondly, I will focus on petitions for clemency, and especially on the ways in which they can be read as autobiographical narratives. Again, the authorities' reactions to the clemency pleas will be commented upon.

Interrogation Transcripts as Sources in Contemporary History

It is only in the last fifteen years that historians of the Third Reich and post-war Germany have taken interrogation transcripts

---

Edition des Instituts für Zeitgeschichte in München', *Vierteljahreshefte für Zeitgeschichte*, 42/4 (1994), 671–6.

[6] This sample of fifty cases was established on the basis of a qualitative selection procedure which is explained in Richter, *Hochverratsprozesse als Herrschaftspraxis*, 19–23.

seriously as sources for the history of the period, and it is even
more rare that the textual structures and semantics used in these
sources have explicitly been studied. Good examples can be found
in the works by Reinhard Mann and Bernd A. Rusinek on everyday practices of resistance and repression in Düsseldorf and
Cologne respectively, and in studies by Insa Eschebach on trials
conducted in the GDR against former concentration camp
warders.[7] Historians of the early modern period have, in general,
produced more innovative methods for dealing with this kind of
source material. That historians of Nazi Germany have so far
largely neglected interrogation transcripts can certainly be attributed to the fact that they imagine that this type of source might
provide scant insights. These statements, made under extreme
pressure and transcribed by Gestapo officers, neither appear to
provide reliable information on facts, nor can they be trusted, or
so it seems, to reveal the 'real' thoughts of those interrogated.
However, although there can be no doubt about the basic
hermeneutic principle which must govern any work with these
sources, namely, that interrogation transcripts should primarily
be regarded as the interrogators' texts, they quite frequently
contain passages in which the suspects' voices and their hopes for
survival are clearly recognizable. I shall therefore start from the
assumption that, even under the often brutal conditions of interrogation, individual strategies of speaking were possible and can
be discerned in the documents.[8]

For example, for obvious reasons the suspects often attempted
to play down their importance in the resistance movement. Or,
conversely, they depicted themselves as very important members
of this movement, whether in order to survive the experience of

[7] Reinhard Mann, *Protest und Kontrolle im Dritten Reich: Nationalsozialistische Herrschaft im Alltag einer rheinischen Großstadt* (Frankfurt am Main, 1989); Bernd A. Rusinek, *Gesellschaft in der Katastrophe: Terror, Illegalität, Widerstand—Köln 1944/45* (Essen, 1989); Insa Eschebach, '"Ich bin unschuldig." Vernehmungsprotokolle als historische Quelle: Der Rostocker Ravensbrück-Prozeß 1966', *WerkstattGeschichte*, 4/12 (1995), 65–70.

[8] On the possibility of agency and strategies of non-dominant actors see Alf Lüdtke, introduction: 'Herrschaft als soziale Praxis', in id. (ed.), *Herrschaft als soziale Praxis: Historische und sozial-anthropologische Studien* (Göttingen, 1991), 9–66; Karin Hausen, 'Die Nicht-Einheit der Geschichte als historiographische Herausforderung: Zur historischen Relevanz und Anstößigkeit der Geschlechtergeschichte', in Hans Medick and Anne Charlotte Trepp (eds.), *Geschlechtergeschichte und Allgemeine Geschichte: Herausforderungen und Perspektiven* (Göttingen, 1998), 5–55; William Sewell, 'The Concept(s) of Culture', in Victoria Bonnell and Lynn Hunt (eds.), *Beyond the Cultural Turn: New Directions in the Study of Society and Culture* (Berkeley, 1999), 35–61, at 55ff.

being interrogated, to protect others, or to maintain their self-respect. Whatever their motives, there was clearly room for manoeuvre when prisoners had to choose *how* to tell what they had or had not done, thought, or said before they were arrested. The Gestapo officers, for their part, cannot reasonably be depicted as absolutely determined to establish the guilt of the suspects, regardless of what the prisoners said, or what the circumstances were. In many cases, it appears that the interrogators were trying to find out in detail how the suspects had been involved in the resistance networks, what their activities had been, and who their contacts were. Thus, even with regard to facts, but more so, of course, with regard to the mental maps of resistance movements in the Gestapo officers' minds, the interrogation transcripts are a valuable source. Their value consists in their police focus, that is, the keenness and seriousness displayed by the interrogators in reconstructing the background and the 'real' course of events. In this respect, Gestapo interrogation transcripts differ significantly from similar texts produced by interrogators in Stalinist Russia. Since public exposure of left-wing resistance groups was clearly not the purpose of *Volksgerichtshof* trials, it was less attractive for Gestapo officers than for their Stalinist counterparts simply to create fictions which would appear plausible in show trials.[9] Rather, it can be shown that the Gestapo often had a real interest in finding facts. Whether the 'facts' which the interrogators construed out of the prisoners' statements were indeed true or false is, of course, difficult to say. Reinhard Mann has rightly described Gestapo interrogations as 'forced communication' because of the physical violence and psychological duress to which the prisoners were subjected.[10] However, even if it is known that a statement was made under torture or abuse, one cannot necessarily conclude that it was in every respect false.

In the context of this essay, the question of how reliable the prisoners' statements are with respect to 'real' facts or feelings may safely remain unresolved because our (more modest) aim here is initially to establish the range of possible ways of speaking, arguing, and questioning used by both the suspects interrogated and the interrogators. The existence of a range of this sort, a linguistic room for manoeuvre, so to speak, is undeniable. The

---

[9] 'Schauprozessfähige Fiktionen' is a quotation from Zarusky, 'Widerstand als Hochverrat', 676. [10] Mann, *Protest und Kontrolle im Dritten Reich*, 97.

Gestapo transcripts are not stereotypical texts. In this they differ from the Stasi (GDR Ministry of State Security) transcripts of interrogations of former female concentration camp warders. In her analysis of these documents Insa Eschebach has drawn attention to the 'antifascist code' to be found there.[11] Similarly, although perhaps more surprisingly, Lutz Niethammer has pointed to the longevity of pronounced Nazi jargon, even within the SED, the ruling party of the GDR, and particularly among former Buchenwald prisoners who had held posts in the camp (*Funktionshäftlinge*).[12] There is no doubt that distinct National Socialist expressions can also be found in the written texts of the Gestapo interrogations. But there is no evidence of a consistent, stereotypical language code in the National Socialist transcripts which I have examined. Even if—as already mentioned—the sources are fundamentally interrogators' texts, they nevertheless contain self-interpretations by those being interrogated, referred to by Rusinek as 'scattered verbal fragments'.[13]

Fragments of Life Histories

In what follows I shall discuss statements, expressions, and verbal fragments in which interrogated suspects speak of the personal motives for their deeds. These fragments are too variable in their wording and content for it to be assumed that the Gestapo officers transcribed only what they wished to hear. A reading of this material, as transcribed by the Gestapo and the judges responsible for examining prisoners, shows three recurring patterns in the way in which the interrogated suspects explained their motives for political action. First, prisoners claimed to have acted out of love or friendship; secondly, they pointed to desperate economic and social circumstances; and thirdly they interpreted their actions as genuine expressions of political beliefs and made declarations of these beliefs.[14]

[11] See Eschebach, '"Ich bin unschuldig"', 67. Cf. also Ralph Jessen's remarks in this volume on the 'ritualization' of speech and writing in the GDR.

[12] See Lutz Niethammer (ed.), *Der 'gesäuberte' Antifaschismus: Die SED und die roten Kapos von Buchenwald* (Berlin, 1994), 147–8.

[13] Rusinek, *Gesellschaft in der Katastrophe*, 61. The German term is 'verbale Einsprengsel'.

[14] See also Isabel Richter, 'Entwürfe des Widerstehens: Männer und Frauen aus dem linken Widerstand in Verhören der Gestapo (1934–1939)', *WerkstattGeschichte*, 9/26 (2000), 47–70.

Female prisoners, in particular, irrespective of their social class or the circles in which they had moved, often described themselves and their actions as driven by emotional ties. For example, in a statement of October 1937, the painter Käthe Schuftan emphasized the emotional influence of her friend and lover. She was accused of being the SAP 'technician' responsible for distributing newspapers and fliers in the Berlin West district. Her wish to continue the work of her friend Ernst Eckstein, who was murdered in prison, is given in the transcript as her prime motive in working actively for the SAP. She regarded her subordinate activities as 'a legacy of her dead lover'. Apart from this, she claimed, she had never concerned herself with politics. She came, she said, from an apolitical family of academics and had been raised in a spirit of patriotism—'im vaterländischen Sinne'. It had most decidedly never been her aim to bring about any 'violent change in the constitution'.[15] Her actions appear here as those of a delicate aesthete, artist, and intellectual. The fact that she saw her tasks of continuing Eckstein's work as a political legacy, and of keeping his memory alive by following his political ideals, shows Käthe Schuftan as a woman in mourning for her lover. In this account she appears as the guardian of political utopias, and not as a politically active subject opposing Nazi 'normality' and policy. However, neither the judge nor the prosecution gave any credence to her version. They rejected her objection to an order for arrest because of the 'gravity of her offence'. In December 1934 the *Volksgerichtshof* sentenced her to two years' imprisonment for assisting in the preparation of acts of high treason.[16] The characterization of political work as an act of love was not limited to women's accounts of their motives. There were also men who tried to show that their actions in the resistance arose out of concrete situations of emotional and intellectual seduction.[17]

It was against the background of the 'misery of the masses', particularly in the early 1930s, that many political activists, both men and women, made statements in which they claimed that it had been the desperate social and financial situation which had

---

[15] BArch Berlin, ZC 10856, vi. Handakten des Oberreichsanwalts, 178. All translations from the German sources into English by Isabel Richter.

[16] Sentence, 1 Dec. 1934, Verfahren Köhler und Genossen, BArch Berlin, ZC 10856, i. 547–8.

[17] For further examples see Richter, *Hochverratsprozesse als Herrschaftspraxis*, 68–72.

ultimately driven them to participate in the resistance. In many cases this was accompanied by open declarations to the effect that they believed that the 'interests of the workers', and also of those out of work, were better represented by left-wing groups than by the National Socialists. For example, Karl Maier, a farm hand, stated in September 1935 that during his long spell of unemployment he had been won over by Communists at the Labour Exchange in Singen. When he went to collect his dole at the Labour Exchange and met Wilhelm Schwarz again, he had returned the Hitler salute, he said. The transcript of the statement quotes Maier's answer that the Communist Party was the natural home of every proletarian, because it worked to make sure 'that the worker gets his rights'.[18] In 1933 the two of them had agreed to go on a begging tour to Switzerland and not—as the Gestapo accused—to shuttle political refugees over the Swiss border in one of the regular Communist trips there. The Gestapo in Singen maintained their charge that he was a border courier. If he continued to refuse to confess they threatened to send him to the concentration camp in Kislau. The transcript shows an alteration in Maier's version: this time he claims to have been approached at a secret address by people known as the Schwarz family, who proposed that, as he was unemployed, he could earn a little money by guiding a stranger over the border.[19] The desperation of the financial situation also appears as a motive in the reports when, for instance, sick wives had to be cared for or debts paid.

The statements made by the worker Margarete Kellershohn attributed her actions to 'the destitution of the people'. In front of the examining magistrate at the district court in Essen she withdrew all statements she had made under duress to the Gestapo in Cologne in September 1933, and that were recorded there. In the magistrate's record of interrogation she explained her membership of the Communist Party as follows. She said she saw 'her economic interests best served there and where they helped with applications for support and similar things'.[20] Kellershohn's claim to be working for the Communist Party out of an interest in improving her economic situation did not, however, convince the magistrate who

[18] BArch Berlin, NJ 2823, 4.

[19] See Protokoll der Schutzpolizei, 6 Sept. 1935, and interrogation transcript Gestapo Konstanz, 15 Sept. 1935, BArch Berlin, ZC 11235, i.

[20] Interrogation transcript Landgericht Essen, 31 Jan. 1934, BArch Berlin, ZC 11445, i. 99.

interrogated her in Essen. He arranged for local police to gather information about her private life. Their reports spoke of her as 'an unmarried worker on piece-work with no children', and as having connections with the Communist Party. She was also known to be having 'intimate relations with leading Communists and had offered the police her services as a spy'.[21] When Kellershohn's sexual integrity was questioned in this way, the magistrate could no longer assume a clear political motive. He ordered an expert report of her mental state. In the examination of her intelligence this assessment observed 'favourable circumstances'.[22] Four weeks later she made a last confession which was recorded after 'quiet reflection and discussion with the magistrate'. In this she spoke of her action as stemming from 'inner conviction' and spoke of the 'rightness of the Communist idea'. She most certainly knew of the disadvantages which this version would create for her. In the eyes of the magistrate she was 'a speaker', 'an initiator', unusual for a woman—and the *Volksgerichtshof* sentenced her to two and half years in prison (*Zuchthaus*) even though 'the activities of the accused had not yet had any practical effect'.[23] Margarete Kellershohn's insistence highlights a level of significance that many surviving former prisoners and accused later pointed to in autobiographical texts. They emphasized the importance of attempts to maintain their self-respect in interrogations and court proceedings, even though they were well aware of the far-reaching negative consequences of this stance.

A third group of statements as recorded in the transcripts attributed acts of resistance to political conviction. The interrogated often linked their convictions with the hope of a political alternative to National Socialism. Statements such as the following, made by Frieda Franz, active in 1933 as a Communist Party instructor, were not uncommon: 'I acted from political conviction and was aware that I was carrying out illegal activities in working for the KP. But I cannot admit that my actions were treasonable.'[24] Often declarations of political beliefs—like this one by Frieda Franz—were accompanied by a firm declaration of belief in non-

[21] Report Ortspolizeibehörde Troisdorf for the examining magistrate of the Reichsgericht, 13 Jan. 1934, BArch Berlin, ZC 11445, i. 68.

[22] Forensic report in Essen by Dr Tudt, 21 Mar. 1934, BArch Berlin, ZC 11445, i. 211.

[23] Sentence, 12 July 1935, BArch Berlin, ZC 11445, i. 8.

[24] Interrogation transcript (Frieda Franz), Polizeipräsidium Breslau, 24 June 1933, BArch Berlin, ZC 8505, iv. 181.

violence. The transcript continues: 'It was clear to me that after it was banned, the Communist Party was a subversive movement. But as I was only involved in organizational activities to maintain what was left of the party, I do not believe that I committed treason. I did not call for a violent revolution, I did not propagate the use of political violence, nor did I prepare any armed uprising. While I admit that in my opinion the Soviet system is the best organization for workers, I did nothing to promote or bring about a change in the state constitution.'[25]

An attempt to bring about a violent change in the constitution was the precondition for a charge of conspiring to commit high treason. To proclaim non-violence can therefore without doubt be read as a strategy to avoid being accused on this count. The transcribed statements also show that often, political conviction was not a purely intellectual matter. In March of 1933 Werner Jurr, for instance, had worked in an office of the Berlin Rote Hilfe which had already been declared illegal. Here abuse and mass arrests of Communist Party members were documented, which—as he put it—'must wake up the public'. The 1934 transcript records expressions which appear stereotypical in his answer to the question as to why he had done this work in March 1933. There is talk of 'the liberation of the working class', and 'the conquest of political and economic power by the working class' as 'a final goal unattainable without violence'. But embedded in the hermetic density of these phrases there was also the answer to the question of his motives: he had always 'felt a Communist'.[26]

The Gestapo recorded these statements which were brought forward in the court proceedings at the *Volksgerichtshof*. As a rule, however, judges played down such motives by reference to instability of character in the accused, or to the achievements of National Socialism in building up the economy. Regardless of the particular political orientation of the men and women accused, they were classified as 'unwilling to learn', 'fanatical Communists', and 'agitators'.

---

[25] Ibid. 181.
[26] See transcript of the judicial preparatory examination, 6 Mar. 1934, BArch Berlin, ZC 8322, Sonderband 3, 302 and 323.

Clemency Pleas as Autobiographical Texts

For reasons similar to those that apply to interrogation transcripts, clemency pleas and the practice of granting clemency have rarely been considered by historians of contemporary Germany. Again, historians of early modern Europe have taken the lead in discovering the value of these texts as sources. In her wonderful book on pardon tales in sixteenth-century France, Natalie Zemon Davis was one of the first to deal with the narrative structures of these texts in particular.[27] In Germany, clemency pleas have been addressed in the context of historical research on 'ego documents'. This work is increasingly focused on relations between 'voluntary' and 'involuntary' autobiographical texts. In general, all sources in which people give information about themselves, whether of their own free will or under duress, are considered to be ego documents. They allow insights into the biography of a person who can only in some sense be considered the author.[28] This broadening of the definition introduces new aspects. On the one hand it tends to rank voluntary and forced autobiographical sources equally; on the other, there is a call for the meaning of the term 'ego document' to be extended beyond the confines of texts written explicitly with a view to giving an account of one's own life, and to include other documents with clear autobiographical dimensions, such as, for example, clemency pleas.

In the part of this volume devoted to 'policing linguistic boundaries' in an age of extremes, it seems particularly rewarding to read clemency pleas from prisoners in the Third Reich as autobiographical texts.[29] To what extent can the prisoners be considered the authors of these texts? What political, historical, and other events formed the framework within which these clemency pleas can be explained and interpreted? What strategies did the writers use to strengthen their case in the petitions? In the 50 high treason case files I have been able to examine in detail, there are 60

[27] Natalie Zemon Davis, *Fiction in the Archives: Pardon Tales and their Tellers in Sixteenth-Century France* (Stanford, Calif., 1987).

[28] See Winfried Schulze (ed.), *Ego-Dokumente: Annäherungen an den Menschen in der Geschichte* (Berlin, 1996), 7, 14, and 21.

[29] For details of clemency procedures and the institutional framework see Isabel Richter, 'Das Abseits als unsicherer Ort: Gnadengesuche politischer Gefangener im Nationalsozialismus als autobiographische Texte', *Österreichische Zeitschrift für Geschichtswissenschaft, Kultur und Geschichte*, 13/2 (2002), 57–83, at 60–2.

clemency pleas, 11 of which were written by female, 49 by male prisoners. The difference between the number of files and the number of clemency pleas is explained by the fact that several prisoners wrote more than one plea, while others did not write any at all.

In order to achieve the desired effect, that is, release from prison or, in the worst case, reversal of the death penalty, clemency pleas had to comply with certain expectations on the part of the addressees, in our case the Führer himself, or the authorities at the *Volksgerichtshof* to whom he had delegated his prerogative of giving mercy. Writers had to give plausible reasons why they should be pardoned. For prisoners, one way of doing so was to distance themselves from their former deeds and thoughts. In her study on narrative forms of clemency pleas in sixteenth-century France, Natalie Zemon Davis put it thus: 'Turning a terrible action into a story is a way to distance oneself from it, at worst a form of self-deception, at best a way to pardon the self.'[30] Such distancing is also apparent in the clemency pleas written by political prisoners under the Nazi regime, but what is pivotal in this specific form of autobiographical text is not in any way self-deception, self-searching, self-discovery, or self-pardoning. The central point here was to demonstrate a convincing alienation from the prisoner's previous life. At the same time it was a question of describing a credible future path. It is clear that, as a rule, the petitioners accompanied their attempts to distance themselves from the past with declarations of their intentions to prove themselves good citizens in future, and with concrete suggestions as to how they would reintegrate themselves into the *Volksgemeinschaft*— the community as defined by National Socialism.

The Communist Eva Lippold, sentenced by the *Volksgerichtshof,* made a clemency plea in 1942, after having spent eight years in prison. In her petition she spoke of changes in herself. She then pointed to her youth and immaturity at the time of her work for the KPD and the Rote Hilfe: 'Lucky is the person', she wrote, 'who can be so firm at 25 years of age that she need never experience how her world view turned out to be mistaken. I did not have this luck! My formative years fell in a period which was not of a kind to convey clearly to a young, immature person seeking her way what was right and what was wrong . . . I stammered

---

[30] Davis, *Fiction in the Archives*, 114.

something about my convictions in court which has cost me two further years of my life and stamped me as a fanatic.' The beginning of the Second World War, according to her account, deeply influenced the end of her search. She regretted that her prison sentence prevented her from taking part in, as she put it, significant events in world politics: 'Then came the war! To be shut out of society is hard, but to have to stand on the sidelines while world history is made out there and to have to answer the question "Where were you in the war?" with "In prison" seems to me a hard lot.'[31] Eva Lippold ended her petition with the promise that if granted an earlier release, she would care for her sick mother. Housework, care of the sick, raising children, and marriage were typical options for women to prove themselves valuable members of the *Volksgemeinschaft*.

Male prisoners, in contrast, spoke of taking an active part in the war, or working to play their part as breadwinners for their families. In his petition, Arthur Weisbrodt saw employment as a skilled worker as a convincing form of probation. His involvement with the Rote Hilfe in Berlin, he said, arose from his 'view of things' at that time, a view which had collapsed years ago. After his 'inner transformation', he wished to 'return to the *Volksgemeinschaft*', of which he unreservedly approved, in order to take part in the work of 'building up Germany'. He believed that as a skilled worker he 'would be able to do his duty in freedom'.[32] The way in which Weisbrodt's petition goes on points up the fact that clemency pleas sought different, and gender-specific, routes to lead a prisoner out of this exclusion from the *Volk*—out of the 'völkisches Abseits'. 'Now, since the war in 1939 has demanded such great efforts it has become intolerable for me to stand on the sidelines, excluded from the community of my people, a community I stand for unreservedly today. I beg the public prosecutor to grant me the chance to make amends for my past now and to submit this petition further with his approval.'[33]

In contrast to the focus of Arthur Weisbrodt's petition, it was not uncommon among male prisoners to underline their wish to become soldiers. In 10 out of 49 pleas, men applied for what was called, in administrative German, 'Wiederherstellung der

---

[31] Clemency plea, 29 Mar. 1942, BArch Berlin, ZC 7753, xx. 17ff. and ii. 322ff.
[32] Clemency plea, 1 Dec. 1940, BArch Berlin, ZC 7753, Gnadenheft, xviii. 26.
[33] Ibid.

Wehrwürdigkeit' (restitution of the right to bear arms). The background to the notion of *Wehrwürdigkeit*, that is, being worthy to bear arms, was the *Wehrgesetz* (military law) of 21 May 1935, according to which convicted men and political opponents of the National Socialist regime were not permitted to join the army.[34] Without any doubt, this was the normative perspective. But if we take the social practice of the *Bewährungsbataillone* (battalions of men on probation) into consideration, a different picture emerges. Since 1942 these battalions had accepted men sentenced in high treason trials. The expressed wish to take part in the war, therefore, does not come as a surprise. On the other hand, these clemency pleas do not necessarily prove a change in attitude, nor a Nazi conviction. It is much more likely that the male prisoners intended convincingly to demonstrate their will to be integrated into the *Volksgemeinschaft*. Ultimately, it is impossible to know whether prisoners really changed their minds. All we can do is analyse verbal strategies and patterns of argument.

To judge by the sample I have examined, the success rate of these strategies was moderate. In the sources that I examined Hitler did not make any use of his prerogative of mercy, which meant that the Clemency Office of the Public Prosecutor at the *Volksgerichtshof* (Gnadenstelle der Oberreichsanwaltschaft beim Volksgerichtshof) was the authority responsible for deciding what other offices should be consulted in a case of clemency. The staff of the various Gestapo headquarters, sometimes also the Berlin Central Gestapo, were regularly involved in the exercise of clemency after trials for high treason. But in many cases beyond these, the local police and the prison director were also consulted. If even *one* of these authorities voiced doubts as to whether a prisoner was worthy of clemency—that is, concerning his or her *Gnadenwürdigkeit*—the principal authority always turned down the plea for clemency. In my sample prisoners were refused clemency in 55 out of 60 cases. The prisoners were seen as being incapable of integration into society (*gemeinschaftsunfähig*), stubborn or unwilling to learn (*unbelehrbar*), or not open to reason (*uneinsichtig*).

---

[34] See § 13 Wehrgesetz, 21 May 1935 and Hans Peter Klausch, '"Erziehungsmänner" und "Wehrunwürdige": Die Sonder- und Bewährungseinheiten der Wehrmacht', in Norbert Haase and Gerhard Paul (eds.), *Die anderen Soldaten: Wehrkraftzersetzung, Gehorsamsverweigerung und Fahnenflucht im 2. Weltkrieg* (Frankfurt am Main, 1995), 66–82.

Conclusion

The exercise of power by authorities, if considered as a social practice, consists in promoting certain forms of behaviour and verbal expression which are deemed acceptable, and identifying forms of behaviour and expression which should be banned. It also consists in making certain interpretations of behaviour or expressions prevail over others. While this may be easy to understand in abstract terms, it is much more difficult in practice to assess the capacity of authorities to impose such rules of behaviour, expression, or interpretation when looking at concrete historical phenomena. This essay began by asking what the boundaries were of possible forms of expression and argument in the extreme situations experienced by prisoners of the National Socialist regime under interrogation by the Gestapo and writing clemency pleas from their prison cells. Clearly, as has been shown, prisoners anticipated the expectations of the interrogating Gestapo officers, the examining magistrates, the judges of the *Volksgerichtshof*, and the authorities responsible for exercising mercy. When justifying and motivating their actions before arrest, and when reconfiguring their life stories after being sentenced, prisoners frequently conformed to certain narrative patterns and patterns of argument which, they hoped, would at least serve the purpose of letting them off the hook. If we look at these identifiable patterns of evoking presumably reasonable motives and telling plausible life stories in isolation, it would seem that the National Socialist authorities were quite effective in exercising power over the prisoners' use of words.

On the other hand, my close reading of documents has shown a considerable variety of individual expressions in the interrogation transcripts and clemency pleas. Even if this variety appeared only in verbal fragments, scattered through the texts, these fragments are sufficient to indicate that prisoners did not always conform to the stereotyped National Socialist language which they perhaps assumed the Gestapo officers or judges wanted to hear. Moreover, the fact that these scattered verbal fragments of individual expression were recorded, sometimes faithfully, sometimes carelessly, in the interrogation transcripts also proves that the interrogating Gestapo members themselves did not, under any circumstances, 'make up' the prisoners' statements in order to

conform to the standard narrative of a left-wing activist's treasonable activities. Similarly, in the clemency pleas, although the prisoners clearly attuned their autobiographical narratives to the need
to make changes of mind appear plausible and future plans for
social integration realistic, it was the very requirement, known to
all prisoners, that they should present their willingness to be good
citizens in the National Socialist sense in a *convincing* form which
led prisoners to bring forward *real* details of their life stories.
Clemency pleas, therefore, cannot be regarded as presenting
entirely fictitious lives. Rather, fragments of individual life histories
and conformist National Socialist language were fitted together
to let the prisoners' reintegration into the *Volksgemeinschaft* appear
probable and plausible.

It is thus not possible to generalize in abstract terms about the
mixture of political conformity, the will to survive, hopes for a
minimal scope for action, and skilful and knowledgeable verbal
strategies exposed in clemency pleas and the prisoners' statements
during interrogation. It is not possible to draw a clear distinction
between immediate responses to the interrogators' expectations,
and clever anticipations of these expectations by the interrogated
suspects. No exact borderlines can be drawn between the strategic
exploitation of role models, self-interpretations, or artificial expressions of emotion by the prisoners on the one hand, and the 'real'
expression of experiences and fears on the other. What is clear,
though, is that even confronted with the most violent threats, even
when 'faced with death', prisoners had a certain, if minimal, scope
for verbal action which can be traced in these documents. This
minimal scope for action can be found in scattered fragments,
such as, for instance, open declarations of political beliefs in the
middle of a Gestapo interrogation. Such declarations may be
interpreted as reflecting a need to stabilize the prisoner's self by
showing allegiance to a real or imagined collective of resistance.
They may also be referred to as 'projects of resistance' ('Entwürfe
des Widerstehens'),[35] which served to shield the prisoner's inner
survival in a situation of extreme violence and repression.

However, it seems doubtful whether such scattered instances of
prisoners trying to preserve their own individual language should
be called a transgression of boundaries set by the regime, for in all
other, especially physical, respects, those interrogated by the

---

[35] Richter, 'Entwürfe des Widerstehens', 69–70.

Gestapo and sentenced by the *Volksgerichtshof* can well be described as having reached the limits. Many indications of brutal violence appear in the interrogation transcripts. The very real possibility that after the interrogation the prisoner might 'disappear' for ever, and the threat of a concentration camp sentence after imprisonment, demonstrate the life-and-death quality of the situations in which these scripts were written. During such communications, in which prisoners faced pain and the threat of death, their scope for action was, indeed, extremely limited. Here the historian, too, reaches a limit. We are repeatedly confronted with limits of interpretation when the experience of pain and imminent death has to be taken into account.

To apply historical analysis to thoughts and actions as they appear in the texts—even if, in the event, they were unsuccessful, or were, perhaps, morally dubious, or their originators became disheartened—seems to me to be particularly important in the study of the history of the resistance. For to orient historical narration purely by historical results and the so-called structures of history creates an impression of coherence which blanks out contradictory evidence and masks alternative views.

7

Policing Tonal Boundaries: Constructing the Nazi/German Enemy on the Wartime BBC

SIÂN NICHOLAS

I *Introduction*

To fix the enemy in the public mind as the embodiment of every-thing worth fighting against has always been an essential function of state propaganda in wartime. The co-opting of the mass media to project negative images of one's antagonists has been a key part of the war effort in the modern era, and the ways in which such images are constructed, received, adopted, and/or rejected by their audiences has been the subject of investigation by contemporary commentators and historians alike. But as important as the prop-aganda message is the cultural place of the medium used to project it. Propaganda messages entirely appropriate for one communica-tions medium, or one social, cultural, or class milieu, may not be appropriate in another. The success of any propaganda campaign depends ultimately on the 'fit' between message, medium, and audience.

This essay considers some of the ways in which the British con-structed images of the German enemy during the Second World War, specifically through the home broadcasting service of the British Broadcasting Corporation (BBC). In this task, British pro-pagandists were in some respects in a highly privileged position. Nazi Germany was self-evidently the aggressor, was ideologically anathema, and had been the aggressor barely a generation before, during the First World War. Opinion formers had access to a new and arguably more powerful medium of persuasion than in any previous conflict: a single monopoly broadcasting system that was nominally independent of government but over which govern-ment had potentially unlimited powers. Radio itself offered a new kind of power: the spoken word transformed, domesticized, and available to millions.

The use of language on the wartime BBC to discuss Germany, the Nazi regime, and the German people offers a case in which the vocabulary of discussion took on a particular resonance, whether in terms of its immediate emotional effect (such as imagery of 'gangsterdom', or the perennial fascination with perverted Nazi youth), or in its ideological and policy implications—specifically, the argument whether to use the terms 'Nazi' or 'German' to describe the enemy. However, the sometimes uneasy collaboration between official propagandists and broadcasting professionals in this period highlights how complex and contested the mobilization of language can be. Meanwhile, the use of language to create a particular stereotype, or series of stereotypes, of the enemy, is, of course, a powerful indicator of the self-image of the propagandists themselves: nothing, perhaps, says as much about British perceptions of themselves at this time as the ways in which they chose to characterize the Germans.[1]

However, to focus solely on the vocabulary of discussion would be to oversimplify the web of cultural negotiations required in transmitting and interpreting broadcast propaganda. Of at least as much importance is the 'tone' of propaganda: the voice behind the words (authoritative/familiar/satirical/sarcastic etc.), and the context in which it appears (a news broadcast/a 'serious' or 'light' talk/a comedy reference etc.). Policing *tonal* as well as linguistic boundaries was a highly significant element of the BBC's coverage of Germany and the Nazis, one that introduces both a number of important interpretative and methodological questions for the historian and a wider political dimension to the question of wartime propaganda policy. The following analysis has been guided by contemporary responses to both tone and language, as evidenced in listener research reports, newspaper reviews, and other contemporaneous comments. For while the style and content of BBC anti-German propaganda say much about both contemporary conceptions of broadcasting in British cultural life and attitudes among broadcasters to the radio audiences, contemporary *responses* to the tone of such broadcasts, particularly in comedic or satirical

---

[1] Throughout this discussion, the word 'propaganda' is used in its original neutral sense, as a description of rather than a judgement on the variety of means of persuasion employed. Similarly, my use of the word 'stereotype' derives from Walter Lippmann's original formulation as a method of simplification enabling people to classify and generalize. See Emer O'Sullivan, 'National Stereotypes as Literary Device', in Harald Husemann (ed.), *As Others See Us: Anglo-German Perceptions* (Frankfurt am Main, 1994), 81–9, at 82 n. 4.

references, expose not only some stark disagreements among propagandists themselves as to the most appropriate means of propagating their message, but some profound differences in class and cultural attitudes to the nature and role of propaganda in wartime Britain.

II *The Vocabulary of Discussion*

The BBC's importance as a medium of information and opinion in Britain during the Second World War is almost impossible to overestimate.[2] Its geographical reach across virtually the entire British Isles, its audience size, and, above all, its remarkable reputation for probity gained during the 1930s set it apart from almost every other national broadcasting service and meant that in wartime it assumed a uniquely prominent propaganda and informational role. If the BBC was well aware of its own likely importance in national life in wartime, the British government was equally well aware of the BBC's value as a wartime propaganda medium. No other single medium of communication reached virtually every household in Britain, rich or poor. No other medium offered such an intimately domestic setting, part of the very conversation of the home. No other medium offered such a variety of means of communicating propaganda messages. And no other medium was so vulnerable to government interference. During the late 1930s there had been serious discussion about how the BBC might be brought under government control in the event of war, discussions that persisted into the first months of war itself. Although government ministers were ultimately persuaded that overt control of the BBC would prove counter-productive (since it would undermine the very reputation for impartiality that was the BBC's greatest strength), the BBC's wartime 'settlement' with the newly reconstituted Ministry of Information (MOI) ensured that any independence was nominal. The MOI, for instance,

---

[2] For the history of the BBC between the wars, see especially Asa Briggs's magisterial *The Birth of Broadcasting* (London, 1961) and *The Golden Age of Wireless* (London, 1965); also Paddy Scannell and David Cardiff, *A Social History of British Broadcasting*, i. *1922–1939: Serving the Nation* (London, 1991); Mark Pegg, *Broadcasting and Society 1918–39* (London, 1983); and, for an influential contemporary viewpoint, Hilda Jennings and Winifred Gill, *Broadcasting in Everyday Life* (London, 1939). For the wartime BBC, see Asa Briggs, *The War of Words* (London, 1969), and Siân Nicholas, *The Echo of War: Home Front Broadcasting and the Wartime BBC 1939–45* (Manchester, 1996).

could censor any part of BBC output; could instruct the BBC to follow any specific propaganda line; could, ultimately, demand that the BBC broadcast anything it wanted.[3] But the terms of this settlement (which was widely, if unspecifically, understood by the listening public) also ensured that, while all wartime mass media were affected by censorship and official propaganda guidance, the BBC's output came under particular scrutiny from its own audience.

Examples of the monitoring of the BBC's use of language during the war reveal a propaganda machine highly sensitive to the political nuance of vocabulary. This might be in the use of specific words for simple emotive effect, such as using the word 'assailant' rather than 'assassin' to describe members of the French Resistance who killed collaborators, or avoiding the word 'executed' when referring to killings carried out by Germans on the grounds that this suggested a legal justification (the MOI suggested 'slaughtered' for single killings and 'massacred' for killings in quantity).[4] Broadcast references to world leaders held an obvious political significance: thus from mid-1940 (that is, once any hopes of a negotiated peace had vanished) the MOI suggested the BBC drop the traditional use of the courtesy titles 'Herr' and 'Signor' when referring to Hitler and Mussolini; in February 1942 BBC memoranda reminded broadcasters that Stalin preferred the prefix 'Monsieur' or 'Premier', and Chiang Kai-shek 'Generalissimo'; while by 1943 so bad were the relations between General de Gaulle and the other Allied leaders that Churchill himself briefed BBC Home News (as well as Fleet Street) that, as far as possible, de Gaulle should not be mentioned by name at all.[5] Meanwhile, the very words 'Allies' and 'Axis' had policy implications: the MOI and Political Warfare Executive alike objected to the use of the

---

[3] For details of this 'settlement' see Briggs, *Golden Age*, 625–53.

[4] Patrick Ryan, BBC Controller (News Co-ordination) (C(NC)) to Senior News Editor, 25 Apr. 1942, File R34/286, BBC Written Archive Centre, Caversham Park, Reading (hereafter BBC WAC); Bernard Sendall (at the instigation of Minister of Information Brendan Bracken) to Ryan, 20 July 1942, and reply 22 July, BBC WAC R28/121/3. In BBC internal correspondence, personnel were sometimes identified by name and sometimes by position. Where possible, I have identified both name and position on first reference in footnotes, and thereafter cited them as they appear on the document in question.

[5] Ian McLaine, *Ministry of Morale: Home Front Morale and the Ministry of Information in World War II* (London, 1979), 145; Sir Richard Maconachie, BBC Controller (Home) (CH) to Policy Scrutineers (Talks and Schools), 26 Feb. 1942, BBC WAC R34/275/1; A. P. Ryan's Papers, R28/19/2.

word 'Axis' and recommended the substitution of the looser term 'enemy' instead;[6] and even after the USA formally entered the war, the BBC was advised *not* specifically to describe the USA as one of the 'Allies' (it was, of course, an 'associated power'). Although the word 'allies' (uncapitalized) might be used colloquially, BBC policy scrutineers were advised that 'United Nations is a useful way out'.[7]

Beyond the immediately political lay a more ideologically loaded use of language. Thus, for instance, the BBC found itself during the war nervously policing the usage of the words 'English' and 'British', since the use of the former as a synonym for the latter, though conventional and even instinctive among most English people in Britain, was in wartime apparently raising hackles in Wales, Scotland, and Northern Ireland.[8] References to Empire were policed with similar care, the BBC tending to steer shy of overt 'imperial' propaganda, and, mindful of the sensitivities of colonial and, in particular, Dominion listeners, stressing partnership and responsible stewardship rather than power and influence. (As one internal memorandum tellingly laid bare: 'Don't use the adjective IMPERIAL at all. It is commonly used to mean three quite different things, and . . . creates both confusion and prejudice.'[9]) Meanwhile, the Soviet Union posed a particularly intractable ideological challenge for wartime broadcasters. In the early years of the war, with Soviet intentions unclear, the BBC was happy to follow MOI instructions to refer to the USSR infrequently and in neutral tone. But after Hitler's invasion of the Soviet Union in June 1941 the British government's switch to a propaganda policy that, while not pro-Soviet, was explicitly pro-*Russian* was both sudden (literally, overnight) and startlingly complete, the mood set by Churchill himself, whose BBC broadcast to

---

[6] Thomas Woodroffe (MOI) to W. P. Wessel (BBC), 23 Jan. 1943, BBC WAC R34/286. Objections to the use of the word 'Axis' go back at least to 1940.

[7] Foreign Advisor note to Basil Nicolls, BBC Controller of Programmes (CP), 3 Jan. 1942; CH to Policy Scrutineers (Talks and Schools), 26 Feb. 1942, BBC WAC R34/275/1.

[8] Lee (MOI) to Nicolls, 23 Oct. 1939, BBC WAC R28/121/1. The writer J. B. Priestley, in his celebrated *Postscript to the News* after Dunkirk (5 June 1940), famously sought to elide the two by saying, 'and when I say English I really mean British'. J. B. Priestley, *Postscripts* (London, 1940), 2–4, at 3. See also Nicholas, *Echo of War*, 228–40.

[9] BBC memorandum (n.p., n.d. [late 1942]), BBC WAC R34/350/1. For further details of BBC Empire policy during the war, see Siân Nicholas, 'Brushing up your Empire: Dominion and Empire Propaganda on the Wartime BBC 1939–45', *Journal of Imperial and Commonwealth History*, 31 (2003), 207–30.

the nation on the night after the invasion portrayed a valiant, pastoral Russia (*not* USSR) whose loyal sons were even now defending their motherland against the 'hideous onslaught' of the Nazi war machine.[10] Subsequent official policy, aimed at both the British people and the Soviet ambassador in London, Ivan Maisky, sought to create positive propaganda based on images of the Russian people, their history, traditions, and fighting spirit— and to say as little as possible about their politics. The BBC's most highly publicized gaffe, its failure to include the *Internationale* in the popular Sunday night music programme *National Anthems of the Allies*, prompted some contorted linguistic self-justification on the part of the BBC (namely, that the USSR was technically a co-belligerent rather than an Ally) and the Minister of Information at the time, Duff Cooper (namely, that to call the *Internationale* a national anthem was surely a contradiction in terms).[11] But elsewhere, BBC talks, features, and even drama wholeheartedly pursued the simple policy of portraying the best of 'Russia': considerable amounts of Tolstoy, Chekhov, and Shostakovich, lavish commemorations of the Sieges of Leningrad and Stalingrad, special broadcasts for Red Army Day, and celebrations for Stalin's birthday (though any positive references to the Russian Revolution itself were systematically deleted by censors). In consequence, the British people's approval of Russia during the war soared—as did their ignorance of the real political condition of the USSR.[12]

III *Germany in Wartime Broadcast Discussion*

Policing references to allies might be said to have had a dual function: boosting home morale, and smoothing Allied diplomatic relations. By contrast, propaganda constructions of the enemy could be seen as an essentially domestic matter, seeking primarily to foment and sustain among home audiences a particular view of the enemy

[10] Churchill broadcast of 22 June 1941, *The Listener*, 26 June 1941, 895–6.

[11] Duff Cooper to Anthony Eden, 12 July 1941, INF1/913, National Archives, Kew (hereafter NA).

[12] For a more detailed discussion of British wartime perceptions of the USSR, see McLaine, *Ministry of Morale*, ch. 7, *passim*; P. M. H. Bell, *John Bull and the Bear: British Public Opinion, Foreign Policy and the Soviet Union, 1941–1945* (London, 1990); Siân Nicholas, 'Partners now? Problems in the Portrayal of the USA and USSR on the Wartime BBC 1939–45', *Diplomacy and Statecraft*, 3 (1992), 243–71, at 244–55.

that would maximize resolve and commitment to the war effort. The projection of propaganda images of Germany might therefore have seemed relatively straightforward. Unfortunately for those charged with projecting such images, in particular the BBC, how to portray Germany, the German leadership, and the German people to the British people was, from the first, one of the most controversial propaganda debates of the entire war. For one thing, the conventional pejorative stereotypes of Germany were widely feared to be tainted by their association with First World War propaganda. For another, it was deemed a matter of considerable political and even strategic significance whether the principal focus of such propaganda should be the regime (the Nazis) or the people (the Germans).

The shadow of the First World War was a long one. Britain's anti-German propaganda effort of 1914–18 was, by the 1920s, no longer a source of national pride but in many quarters regarded with active shame, with some commentators challenging both the veracity and the morality of wartime atrocity propaganda, and others (most famously Harold Lasswell) using the British wartime propaganda experience to draw discouraging conclusions about the malleability of public opinion.[13] In the 1930s the BBC had steered clear of virtually any coverage of contemporary German politics, having been effectively warned off the subject by a Foreign Office wary of the Nazi regime's hypersensitivity to outside criticism;[14] it also banned the use of the word 'Hun' as

[13] See Arthur Ponsonby, *Falsehood in Wartime* (London, 1928); Harold Lasswell, *Propaganda Technique in the World War* (London, [1927] 1938). Alice Goldfarb Marquis relies heavily on Ponsonby in her 'Words as Weapons: Propaganda in Britain and Germany during the First World War', *Journal of Contemporary History*, 13 (1978), 467–98, but alternative accounts suggest that Ponsonby's own use of evidence should be treated with circumspection. See, for instance, Lindley Fraser, *Propaganda* (London, 1957), 34–5.

[14] The BBC's effective abandonment of serious news reporting from Nazi Germany in the 1930s is well documented, though ironically the move concerned Bartlett's broadcast of an allegedly sympathetic account of Germany's withdrawal from the Geneva Disarmament Conference in 1933, provoking representations from both Downing Street and the Foreign Office. From 1937, however, the BBC came under concerted government pressure to avoid antagonizing the Hitler regime. See Briggs, *Golden Age*, 146–7; Vernon Bartlett, *This is my Life* (London, 1937), 177; Scannell and Cardiff, *Serving the Nation*, 72–102. The BBC's quiescence on this issue contrasts with the widespread coverage of developments in Nazi Germany (generally critical in tone, though with some significant exceptions) in the popular press and current affairs publishing market. See Franklin Reid Gannon, *The British Press and Germany 1936–1939* (Oxford, 1971); Richard Cockett, *Twilight of Truth: Chamberlain, Appeasement and the Manipulation of the Press* (London, 1989); Benny Morris, *The Roots of Appeasement: The British Weekly Press and Nazi*

one of a number of derogatory references to foreign powers considered unacceptable for broadcast.[15] When war broke out, therefore (and in contrast to some elements of the popular press, which
adopted a tone more reminiscent of 1914), the BBC maintained
in its news and talks broadcasts the caution that was still charac-
terizing government policy. Thus, while it sought as a matter of
urgency to engage the listening public at last with the threat of
Nazi Germany, it carefully avoided a blanket reintroduction of
the old stereotypes, and sought to differentiate implicitly, if not
explicitly, between the Nazi leadership (bad) and the German
people (brainwashed, deluded, or otherwise misguided, but still
potentially the means by which the Nazis might be reined in or
even overthrown). The BBC's December 1939/January 1940 talks
series *The Voice of the Nazi*, a painstaking and authoritative investigation of the nature of Nazi propaganda technique, was therefore
careful to discuss Nazi propaganda aimed at the German people
themselves, as well as their external propaganda efforts such as
William Joyce's ('Lord Haw-Haw') already notorious broadcasts
on Radio Hamburg. A further talks series, *Under Nazi Rule* (from
February 1940), made the Nazis/Germans differentiation explicit
by focusing on physical rather than psychological oppression, by
detailing the ways in which the Nazi regime was destroying
German rights and civic structures, and by featuring personal testimonies of Germans who had been persecuted by, and subsequently fled, the Nazi regime. Meanwhile, a highly publicized
dramatized documentary series, *The Shadow of the Swastika*
(November/December 1939), a popular history of the Nazi movement that concentrated specifically on the rise of Hitler and the
Nazi Party, focused listeners' minds on Hitler himself as a
Messianic and hysterical demagogue.[16]

    With the accession of Churchill to the premiership, and the fall
of France, MOI policy explicitly changed. The German people
had had their chance to get rid of Hitler; now the whole of the
German nation was to be considered the enemy and the Nazis
simply their political face. Taking their lead in part from Lord

---

Germany During the 1930s (London, 1991); Dan Stone, *Responses to Nazism in Britain 1933–1939: Before War and Holocaust* (Basingstoke, 2003).

[15] See J. S. Macgregor, Empire Programme Director, to Empire Executive, 21 May 1937, BBC WAC R34/275/1.
[16] For further details of these and other series, see Nicholas, *Echo of War*, 150–5.

Vansittart's notorious best-seller of 1941, *Black Record* (itself based on a series of broadcasts made on the BBC Overseas Service in 1940), the MOI now to all practical intent adopted the 'Vansittartist' line that to draw distinctions between Germans and Nazis was specious (Foreign Office objections that such a policy would 'cement the German people behind their rulers' were over-ruled).[17] The BBC, like all other propaganda outlets, was required to make the new policy clear, a process that involved, among other measures, redrawing guidelines on the broadcast use of the term 'Nazi' to ensure that it was correctly applied to the Nazi Party and leadership, but no longer used as an adjective applied to inanimate enemy things such as armed forces, shipping, and so on; here, the term 'German' or 'enemy' should be used instead. (As a sop to the spoken word, however, latitude was permitted 'to avoid . . . wearisome repetition'.[18]) Kenneth Clark, Controller of Home Publicity at the Ministry of Information, described the new policy as 'The Same Old Hun'; BBC senior management took a marginally more subtle approach, calling it 'the MOI's "Jekyll and Hyde" scheme' (that is, that the Germans were Nazis *underneath*).[19]

Particular linguistic stereotypes of the Germans now reasserted themselves. Germans were portrayed in broadcasts as variously aggressive, brutal, intolerant, regimented, unimaginative, and humourless. It is, of course, an axiom of propaganda based on national identity that stereotypes of the 'other' are related to auto-stereotypes of oneself, and such identifications of the Germans were made in the context of an 'Englishness' (Britishness) explicitly defined as free, tolerant, phlegmatic, and resourceful.[20] Invoking such an imagology could provide reassurance in the darkest of moments, notably after the Dunkirk evacuation of 1940, when

---

[17] See Aaron Goldman, 'Germans and Nazis: the Controversy over "Vansittartism" in Britain during the Second World War', *Journal of Contemporary History*, 14 (1979), 155–91, at 162 and *passim*; also McLaine, *Ministry of Morale*, ch. 5, *passim*.

[18] There are repeated instructions from BBC senior management to all staff (including directives from the Directors-General) to this effect throughout the middle years of the war. See, e.g., John Watt, Director of Variety, to all producers, 28 Nov. 1942, BBC WAC R34/275/1.   [19] CH to Assistant CH, 24 June 1940, BBC WAC R51/397/4.

[20] See e.g. Angus Calder's typology of English versus German national character in his *The Myth of the Blitz* (London, 1991), whereby English (British) freedom, improvisation, volunteer spirit, friendliness, tolerance, timeless landscape, patience, calm, and thousand years of peace are matched against Germany's tyranny, calculation, drilling, brutality, persecution, mechanization, aggression, frenzy, and Thousand Year Reich dedicated to war. 'It will be seen that each promised characteristic of the Germans is (and has to be) opposed by a strong English opposite.' Calder, *Myth of the Blitz*, 196.

J. B. Priestley's BBC *Postscripts* turned military humiliation into salvation myth by crediting British grit, pluck, and improvisation with thwarting the ruthless but soulless efficiency of the Nazi war machine.[21] And certain specific images were highlighted to underline the general message.

For instance, the representation of German aggression as a form of 'gangsterism', a sinister dependence on mob brutality, was a constantly recurring feature of BBC talks propaganda that tied in neatly with wider ideas of both Germanness and Britishness. The Nazi leadership readily lent themselves to being depicted as a gangster cabal, while the theme of the thuggish and destructive Nazi could easily be expanded to embrace the entire German nation, in what was, in effect, a reprise of the old First World War stereotype of the brutish Hun. News talks highlighted the looting and extortion endemic in Nazi Germany, and the wanton German destruction of the greatest jewels of European civilization, while affirming the Allies' attempts to protect ancient buildings, works of art, and local populations. As the writer E. M. Forster put it in a talk broadcast in October 1940: 'The Germans don't hate culture, but they are doomed to oppose it because it's mixed up with thought and action, because it is mixed up with the individual.'[22]

A newer theme was that of German youth. Portrayals of Germany's younger generation, particular the Hitler Youth movement, traded on universal fears of 'lost' or changeling children (in this case children so morally corrupted that they were willing spies in their own homes, strangers to their parents, and potential betrayers of their families), and exerted a fascination on the British public and propagandists alike. German children were widely described as cruel, fanatical, and regimented; stories and plays depicted indoctrinated children betraying their parents to the authorities for such crimes as listening to London on the radio; and in one talks series the war was described as 'a battle for children's souls'. Meanwhile, several military commentators made a point of distinguishing between the relatively 'ordinary' older generation of German career soldiers and the depraved and fanatical new recruits.[23]

---

[21] Above all, his Dunkirk 'Postscript', 5 June 1940, Priestley, *Postscripts*, 2–4.

[22] *The Listener*, 10 Oct. 1940, 515–16.

[23] See e.g. talk by Enid Lockhart, *The Listener*, 10 Apr. 1941, 527–8; Zeta Gordon, *Boys in Uniform* (radio play); talk by the Revd Nathaniel Micklem in the series *A Christian Looks at the World*, *The Listener*, 14 Mar. 1940, 528–9; talk by 'A Royal Marine', *The Listener*, 13 Nov. 1941, 659.

And these two themes could be effectively linked. J. B. Priestley, for instance, described the 'gang spirit' as an adolescent impulse, the preserve of sadistic schoolboy bullies and their craven followers. Richard Crossman explained in the final edition of *Under Nazi Rule* how Hitler had fixed 'a whole generation of young people at the gangster stage . . . trained to accept the morals of a Chicago gangster as the standard of German civilisation'.[24]

It is worth noting how BBC broadcasts on these themes mirrored—but only up to a point—the propaganda efforts in other media. The analogy of the Nazi leadership with 'gangsterdom' was something explicitly referred to in, for instance, the wide range of anti-German 'sixpennies' and other popular literature published throughout the war years, whether the pocket-sized pamphlet *Fifty Facts about Hitler* (October 1939), which cast Hitler as 'the Chief Gangster', H. V. Morton's cautionary tale of a Nazi-occupied Britain, *I, James Blunt* (1942), in which former petty thieves rise to positions of abusive authority, modelling themselves on 'the tough guy in a gangster film', or Felix Gross's frankly sensationalist *Hitler's Girls, Guns and Gangsters* (1941).[25] One of the most chilling passages in *I, James Blunt* is where the narrator's 6-year-old granddaughter comes home from school proudly speaking German while his 5-year-old grandson relates how a schoolfriend betrayed his father to the teacher that day. But BBC propaganda tended to hold back from some of the more extreme explorations of these themes. Their coverage of the Hitler Youth, for instance, stopped well short of the explicit accusations of sadism and homosexuality (equated, inevitably, with sexual exploitation and perversion) that appeared in parts of the popular press, or in such 'true stories' as Hans Siemsen's *Hitler Youth* (1940).[26] And BBC Repertory Theatre actor Marius Goring's portrayal of Hitler as a dangerous hysteric in the BBC's *The Shadow of the Swastika*, widely praised at the time for its psychological acuity, was in fact a world away from the psychopathic, impotent, and sexually degenerate Hitler portrayed in contemporary psychology journals and (more graphically) in such popular wartime publications as former Nazi

---

[24] Priestley, *Postscripts*, 17; Richard Crossman, *The Listener*, 6 June 1940, 1092–3.

[25] *Fifty Facts about Hitler*, War Facts Press No. 1 (London, 1939); H. V. Morton, *I, James Blunt* (London, 1942), 50; Felix Gross, *Hitler's Girls, Guns and Gangsters* (London, 1941).

[26] Hans Siemsen, *Hitler Youth* (London, 1940). The popular Sunday newspaper *The News of the World* had earlier homed on the moral degeneracy of the Nazis, e.g. attributing the sadistic cruelty of the SS to 'mass sexual perversion' (*News of the World*, 5 Nov. 1939).

Otto Strasser's *Hitler and I* (1940) and *The Gangsters around Hitler* (1942).[27]

Why was this so? Unlike the press, where one chose a paper to read and could put it down at any point, or the cinema, where again one chose to go, to stay, and to watch, broadcasting was the 'guest in the home'. From its earliest days, the BBC had maintained a clear policy of broadcasting only what was acceptable to the mainstream of listeners, and of maintaining certain standards of taste and decorum. This was particularly evident in its news bulletins, where items of a potentially distressing nature had traditionally been carefully vetted before broadcast.[28] Broadcast propaganda in wartime thus had to negotiate the boundaries of taste far more carefully than any other mass medium. This caused problems when, as in the case of reporting German atrocities, the subject matter was inevitably harrowing. Over the summer of 1940, and again during 1941–2 the MOI sought to combat complacency by heavily promoting propaganda based on the threat of a German-occupied Britain (with H. V. Morton's *I, James Blunt* a key text in this campaign). The BBC followed this line with talks by German refugees and escaped British prisoners of war, with dramatized features (*Gestapo over Europe, Escape to Freedom, It Might Happen Here*), and drama (*They Call It Peace, The Machine That Disappeared*, Kenneth Clark and Graham Greene's *Gestapo in England*). In just one month over August/September 1942 the BBC managed to rack up twenty-one features and drama productions on the theme of 'If Hitler won the war'.[29]

However, with the First World War still a recent memory, 'atrocity propaganda', whether set in Germany, occupied Europe,

[27] Otto Strasser, *Hitler and I* (London, 1940) and *The Gangsters around Hitler* (London, 1942). Typical anecdotes included, variously, Hitler's alleged paedophile abuse of Elsa Hoffman, daughter of his personal photographer; his indecent propositioning—and probable involvement in the subsequent murder of—his own niece, Gely Raubahl; and his private film showings of the execution by beheading—on his personal orders—of two young and aristocratic German women for espionage. See also Samuel Igra, *Germany's National Vice* (London, 1945), 58. I am indebted to Gerald Hughes for this reference.

[28] See Scannell and Cardiff, *Serving the Nation*, ch. 3, *passim*. The 'mainstream' tended to be defined in elite terms: see D. L. LeMahieu, *A Culture for Democracy: Mass Communication and the Cultivated Mind in Britain between the Wars* (Oxford, 1988).

[29] In June 1940, the Ministry of Information Home Morale Publicists Committee first discussed 'how the meaning of a German victory might be brought home to the various sections of the population'. W. G. V. Vaughan to the Director-General, MOI, 22 June 1940, NA INF1/255. For Aug./Sept. 1942 snapshot of propaganda output see Ryan memorandum, 22 Sept. 1942, BBC WAC R34/686.

or Britain, was always controversial. While similar propaganda messages in other mass media met with generally positive audience responses—for instance, Humphrey Jennings's powerful and restrained *The Silent Village* (1943), which retold the Nazi elimination of the Czech village of Lidice as if it were set in a south Wales mining valley—broadcast talks and, especially, dramatized features on themes of German war crimes met with sustained listener resistance, and the BBC came to fear that, in the context of home listening, such topics served to depress the spirits rather than inspire resolve.[30] It is telling that the BBC's own dramatization of *I, James Blunt* (which they broadcast reluctantly at the behest of the MOI) ended with the narrator waking up to find it had all been a dream—in contrast to the book, where the story dramatically ends at the point where the narrator hears the knock of the Gestapo at his door. Even so, listeners still found the subject matter too depressing, and the changed ending simply annoying.[31] Meanwhile the BBC shrank from dramatizing the growing horror of the Nazi persecution of the Jews (fearing either complacency among the non-Jewish majority who might see themselves as less likely to become victims of Hitler, or a backlash among what some believed was a substantially anti-Semitic listening public), and confined such stories to news reports or to general accounts of Nazi atrocities across Germany and occupied Europe.[32]

It is arguable how effective the attempt to elide 'Nazi' and 'German' in the public mind actually was in practice. Certainly Churchill, for one, in his BBC broadcasts appears to have ignored BBC practice and used the words 'Nazi' and 'German' largely interchangeably, with a liberal scattering of 'Hun' for good measure.[33] And, while the 'Peace Aims' lobby persistently accused the BBC of 'Vansittartism', the Vansittartist lobby (and indeed

---

[30] See LR/897, 3 June 1942, BBC WAC R9/5/8, and Barnes to Maconachie, 29 Sept. 1942, BBC WAC R34/686.

[31] Graves to Radcliffe (MOI), 13 Apr. 1942, BBC WAC R19/527; LR/1010, 13 July 1942, R9/5/8.

[32] See e.g. BBC Programme Planning Minutes, Nos. 452 (11 Dec. 1942) and 461 (18 Dec. 1942), BBC WAC R28/88/2. For further discussion of official policy, see McLaine, *Ministry of Morale*, 155–8, 166–8; Tony Kushner, 'Different Worlds: British Perceptions of the Final Solution during the Second World War', in David Cesarani (ed.), *The Final Solution: Origins and Implementation* (London, 1994), 246–67.

[33] See e.g. Churchill's 22 June 1941 broadcast, which refers to 'German' armies/bombs/ troops/people, to 'Nazi' invasion/gangsters/violence/regime/war machine/leaders, and to 'Hun' raiders/soldiery/fighting machines. *The Listener*, 26 June 1941, 895–6.

Lord Vansittart himself) just as persistently accused the BBC of pulling its punches and insufficiently indicting the whole German people in the atrocities perpetuated in their name. In fact, though explicit forms of differentiation between German people and Nazi leadership largely disappeared from British airwaves, in practice, BBC talks and features tended still to stress 'Nazi' rather than 'German' iniquities. Meanwhile, propaganda imagery such as gangsterdom or youth indoctrination arguably tended to suggest 'Nazism' rather than 'Germanness'. The gangster elite and their petty henchmen preyed on the weak and helpless general population, in Germany as well as elsewhere. Emphasis on the peculiar horror of Nazified youth likewise cast the older generation as pitiable victims of their own children. Evidence about public opinion is equivocal: Mass-Observation, for instance, found a steady increase in the number of people professing 'no sympathy' for the German people, and wartime opinion polls confirmed that a significant proportion of the British population saw no practical distinction between Germans and Nazis. But even in February 1945 only 54 per cent of Mass-Observation respondents claimed to 'hate' Germans, and calls for retributive bombing of German civilians, for instance, seem to have been *least* vocal in cities that had suffered most from the Blitz.[34]

This equivocation, or ambiguity, of message may have stood the BBC in good stead towards the end of the war when the post-war settlement of Germany became the urgent new political topic, and the idea that the German people were re-educable, that is, not irredeemably tainted by their Nazi past, became politically important. Academics and political commentators discussed hopes for the re-education of Germany in BBC round-table discussions. The BBC's *War Report* correspondents in 1944/5 described a cowed and defeatist German people dissociated from their fanatical leadership. Even the BBC's reports from the death camps (notably Patrick Gordon Walker's harrowing talk *Belsen: Facts and Thoughts* on 27 May 1945) ended with pleas not to take revenge indiscriminately on all Germans—for, as the news reports made clear, there were Germans imprisoned in the camps too.[35]

[34] See Goldman, 'Germans and Nazis', 157; Tom Harrisson, *Living through the Blitz* (London, 1976), 316–21. For an account that stresses more heavily (and disapprovingly) the hostility felt towards Germans during the war, see Donald Cameron Watt, *Britain Looks to Germany: British Opinion and Policy towards Germany since 1945* (London, 1965), ch. 2, *passim*.

[35] See Nicholas, *Echo of War*, 161–3.

IV *Making Fun of the Germans? Questions of Tone and Style*

On the wartime BBC, policing language was reasonably straight-forward (memoranda, verbal and written instructions, censors, vigilant listening, etc.), if in practice laborious and of unclear effect. But how could censors, looking at the words on the page, police the tone of what were, of course, generally live, if scripted, broadcasts? The BBC's principal methods of anti-German broadcast propaganda tended to be talks and features or drama. Through talks the propaganda messages could appear reasoned and authoritative. Features and drama offered more emotive contexts, but generally within clear bounds. For BBC *comedy* (that is, the BBC Variety Department), however, the challenge was particularly intractable.

In the 1930s it was a fundamental tenet of BBC Variety policy that world leaders were never to be joked about. On the outbreak of war with Germany, this directive was withdrawn and the full weight of the BBC Variety Department thrown behind the propaganda war. Within the week comedian Tommy Handley could be heard on the new wartime BBC Home Service singing 'Who is this man who looks like Charlie Chaplin?'; shortly afterwards the BBC's greatest variety star, Arthur Askey, released an updated version of his popular novelty hit 'Run, Rabbit, Run', featuring the new verse 'Run, Adolf, run'.[36] On 6 October 1939 the BBC broadcast a 'pantomime' written by James Dyrenforth and Max Kester and closely based on Lewis Carroll's *Alice in Wonderland*, entitled *Adolf in Blunderland*, featuring Hitler as 'Little Adolf' (Alice), Goebbels as the 'Mad Flatterer' (Mad Hatter), Himmler as the 'March Into' (March Hare) and, as the 'Doormat' (Dormouse), the 'average German, He's asleep half the time . . . doped by propaganda', to apparently rapturous critical and audience reaction (it was repeated 'by popular demand' in February 1940).[37] Meanwhile, the BBC's new Variety show *It's That Man Again* introduced a comic German spy, Funf, who would periodically

---

[36] 'Run, Adolf, run, Adolf, run run run / Look what you've been gone and done done done / We will knock the stuffing out of you / Old fat-guts Goering and Goebbels too…' (etc.). Recording by Jack Hylton and his band, featuring Arthur Askey, held in the BBC sound archives, Broadcasting House, London. I am indebted to Christopher Stone for enabling me to hear this recording. See Dennis Gifford, *Run Adolf Run: The World War Two Fun Book* (London, 1975) for a slightly bowdlerized version.

[37] See James Dyrenforth and Max Kester, *Adolf in Blunderland* (London, 1939).

interrupt host Tommy Handley's telephone conversations with the lugubrious catchphrase 'This is Funf speaking', his distinctive muffled voice produced by actor Jack Train speaking into a glass.[38]

Within a very short period, however, BBC policy changed. As early as October 1939 Director of Variety John Watt announced a ban on further songs about Hitler,[39] and in January 1940 he prohibited jokes about Nazi leaders altogether. From internal BBC correspondence, is clear that this prohibition was not always policed with particular care: for instance, the BBC's Northern Ireland Director Melvin Dinwiddie complained to Controller of Programmes Basil Nicolls twice in two months in the spring of 1940 after hearing jokes that made reference to Goering's weight (in the first case, that owing to the fat shortage in Germany, Herman Goering had presented his stomach to the nation; in the second, that the Air Force had made a flight over Goering's paunch but had not had time to make the round trip).[40] But whatever the slips in practice, it was no longer considered good policy to make jokes about the Nazis. Policymakers felt that comedy belittled the threat, led audiences to discount the seriousness of the situation, and was in any case undignified. It set the wrong tone.

In other areas, too, the BBC's 'tone' was under attack. Suspicions that BBC newsreaders were introducing a sarcastic tone when reporting German war claims and official Nazi statements sparked accusations that the BBC was abandoning its traditional impartiality for cheap propaganda gains.[41] 'Gloating' was another accusation made against BBC announcers, first raised in July 1940 when the BBC Nine O'Clock News broadcast an eye-

[38] Funf appeared in the first series of *It's That Man Again* (*ITMA*) (Sept. 1939–Feb. 1940), was dropped for the 1940/1 series when a host of new characters were introduced, but returned during 1942. After a slow start *ITMA* became the emblematic BBC comedy show of the war years, with over 40% of the British listening public (fifteen million or more) regularly tuning in; its catchphrases became part of the popular vocabulary of wartime Britain. See *The ITMA Years* (London, 1974); Peter Black, *The Biggest Aspidistra in the World* (London, 1972), 110–20, and any number of popular histories of wartime Britain.

[39] See *Melody Maker*, 7 Oct. 1939.

[40] Melvin Dinwiddie, Northern Ireland Director, to CP, 19 Feb. 1940 and 27 Mar. 1940, and replies, 26 Feb. 1940 and 2 Apr. 1940, BBC WAC R34/275/1. Nicolls's first reply acknowledged that 'This is a sin, if only a venial one'; his second conceded defeat ('it looks as if we should give up struggling against Goering's paunch').

[41] John Snagge, Director of Programme Planning, to Miss Osborn, 7 Feb. 1941, BBC WAC R34/275/1. Tom Harrisson, *The Observer*, 5 Oct. 1942.

witness commentary by Charles Gardner of a dogfight over the Straits of Dover, the climax of which was his loud exultation as a Junkers 87 crashed into the sea. Although in this case public reaction was largely favourable (due to the sheer novelty of the broadcast as well as its exciting content), subsequent performances were generally discouraged. In January 1943 BBC Governor Violet Bonham Carter protested at the use in news bulletins of slang phrases such as 'this was not a bad haul' and 'a good kill' to describe enemy casualties; Director-General Sir Cecil Graves concurred, adding his own objection to the phrase 'German tanks were knocked out.'[42] As Allied bombing raids on Germany intensified over the summer of 1943, news bulletins were rigorously policed, with, for instance, the phrases 'good fires' and 'well bombed' specifically prohibited. In November 1943, sensitive to persistent accusations that the BBC was encouraging listeners to gloat over the raids on Hamburg, BBC Editor-in-Chief William Haley advised that bulletins play down as far as possible the Allied bombing of Berlin.[43]

But it was in talks rather than news that the problem of tone caused most controversy. Traditionally, BBC talks were authoritative in manner, reasoned in tone, and measured in cadence. The most popular Talks speaker on the early wartime BBC, J. B. Priestley, might conjure vivid images of 'thin-lipped and cold-eyed Nazi staff officers', 'half-crazy German youths', and Nazism itself as 'the most violent expression of the despair of the modern world', but his mellow Yorkshire tones softened the force of his words. Winston Churchill was more aggressive in manner and more flamboyant in language (the Nazi Party a 'seething mass of criminality and corruption', Hitler a 'monster of wickedness . . . [a] bloodthirsty guttersnipe'), with a way of pronouncing the word 'Nazis', emphasizing a long 'a' and rasping 'z', that conveyed a unique sense of both relish and disdain,[44] but much of his popularity lay in his very exceptionalism. When Churchill's first

[42] Lady Violet Bonham Carter to Sir Cecil Graves, BBC joint Director-General, 15 Jan. 1943; Graves to Patrick Ryan, Controller of News, 18 Jan. 1943, BBC WAC R34/286 ('I think this should either be "destroyed" or "put out of action"').

[43] CN to SNE, 24 June 1943; Assistant CN to Editor, Home News Bulletins, 30 Nov. 1943, BBC WAC R28/88/3.

[44] Churchill broadcasts 12 Nov. 1939 and 22 June 1941. Contemporary pronunciation of the word 'Nazi' varied, with the 'z' pronounced both hard ('Natzies') and soft ('Narzies'). Punning on the words 'Nazi' and 'nasty' was of course common throughout the war.

Minister of Information, Duff Cooper, tried something similar in a highly charged broadcast talk about the iniquities of Italian policy it split opinion, with MOI Home Intelligence reporting widespread approval among working-class listeners, but some Mass-Observation respondents describing Cooper as a 'lout'.[45] The most successful exponents of this more aggressive style of broadcasting were two American commentators, Dorothy Thompson and Quentin Reynolds, who made a number of broadcasts on both the BBC domestic and overseas services praising British resolve and attacking German perfidy. Reynolds, in particular, made a speciality of personal invective, above all, in two celebrated broadcasts of mid-1941, 'Are you listening, Dr Goebbels?' and 'Dear Mr Schicklgruber'. The directness of approach, the defiance of the message, and the contemptuous references to the Nazi leadership (Goebbels: 'your little Gabby man'; Goering: 'Slap Happy Herman'; and Hitler himself: 'Do you think for a moment that a man bearing the name of Winston Churchill will ever bend his knee to anyone named Schicklgruber?'), so very different from the typical BBC product, caused a public sensation.[46]

Yet this style did not easily translate to other speakers. Three weeks after Reynolds's 'letter' to Dr Goebbels, William Connor, the columnist 'Cassandra' of the *Daily Mirror*, made a broadcast attack on the author P. G. Wodehouse and his recent broadcasts on German radio. His talk, made at the personal invitation of Duff Cooper, and broadcast twice, on the BBC's Home and North American services, over the night of 15/16 July 1941, copied Reynolds in both style and tone: addressing Wodehouse directly, tearing into his past, his career, and his alleged collaboration with the enemy while under house arrest in Berlin. Wodehouse was an 'elderly playboy', carefully 'groomed for stardom' by Dr Goebbels,

---

[45] Calder, *Myth of the Blitz*, 123; Tom Harrisson, Mass-Observation Archive, University of Sussex (hereafter M-O A), File Report (FR) 122, 'Duff Cooper's broadcast', 18 May 1940.

[46] For full transcripts of Reynolds's broadcasts, see *The Listener*, 3 July 1941, 10–11 ('Are you listening, Dr Goebbels?') and 14 Aug. 1941, 227, 233 ('Dear Mr Schicklgruber'). Claims that Hitler's original surname was Schicklgruber were widespread in wartime Britain, and were used as a commonplace method of undercutting his demagogic persona. See e.g. Wyndham Lewis, *The Hitler Cult* (London, 1939), 76: 'It is generally conceded that with such a name as Schicklgruber Hitler would have been no trouble to anyone'; or Wickham Steed, *That Bad Man: A Tale for the Young of All Ages* (London, 1942), 2–3: 'If he had been called Schicklgruber you might never have heard of him because it isn't so easy . . . to shout Hail, Schicklgruber.'

pawning his honour 'for the price of a soft bed in a luxury hotel', and wilfully blind to the misery of the Blitz back home (Connor invoking the recent blitz on Dulwich, the London suburb where Wodehouse—or 'Mr Pelham Grenville Wodehouse', as Connor addressed him—had gone to school).[47] Unlike Reynolds's script, however, Connor's had caused consternation within the BBC senior management. Director of Talks George Barnes argued with MOI officials before the broadcast that such a talk was 'right out of key with anything that the BBC had done before', and that while such a broadcast would probably 'make the gallery shriek with pleasure', it would 'arouse distrust of the BBC as a medium for truth and fair comment, particularly among the professional classes'.[48] When Frederick Ogilvie and Sir Stephen Tallents, respectively the BBC's Director-General and Controller (Overseas), themselves read Connor's script prior to broadcast they took the unprecedented step of refusing to sanction it unless formally ordered to do so by the Minister, on the grounds that it was not only unsuitable but also actionable.[49] The order was duly sent and the broadcast went out on both services. It met with an immediate barrage of complaint. Newspaper editorials condemned it, an MP on the floor of the House of Commons described it at 'filthy', and a deluge of listeners' protests hit the BBC (166 letters, phone calls, and telegrams, of which 133 were critical).[50] Barnes's prediction about the probable outrage of the professional classes was almost exactly borne out, with complainants including a Fellow of the Royal Society, the President of the Library Association, and the Principal of Bedford College for Women.

P. G. Wodehouse was, of course, neither a Nazi nor a fifth columnist, but a hugely successful expatriate comic novelist, who had done more than almost any other writer to popularize an international stereotype of the British upper classes as affable and

[47] The BBC Written Archive Centre has a transcript of Connor's broadcast. See BBC WAC File R34/271. Briggs, *War of Words*, surprisingly makes no mention of this episode. Biographers of Wodehouse have covered it in some depth: for a particularly trenchant defence of his actions, see Iain Sproat, *Wodehouse at War* (London, 1981).

[48] George Barnes, Director of Talks (DT), memorandum, 12 July 1941, BBC WAC R34/271.

[49] See Frederick Ogilvie, BBC Director-General (DG) to CH and CO, 15 July 1941, BBC WAC R34/271.

[50] See filed press cuttings and BBC memorandum 'Cassandra on P. G. Wodehouse: Final Report', 24 July 1941, BBC WAC R34/271; also interjection by Captain Cobb, MP, *Hansard* (House of Commons, Fifth Series), vol. 373, no. 85, 580, 16 July 1941.

unworldly eccentrics. Such a sustained personal attack on him was widely considered to be an unacceptable extension of propaganda tactics normally reserved for high-ranking Nazis. The BBC's unusually forthright defence of its own position indicates its belief that in this propaganda exercise the MOI had gone too far. The Corporation issued an official statement the day after the broadcast confirming that it had gone out 'under the direction of the MOI',[51] followed by a tense meeting between the Minister and the BBC Board of Governors, after which the Chairman of the BBC, Sir Allan Powell, made the unprecedented threat that he would write to *The Times* to explain the BBC's position if the Ministry did not publicly acknowledge its part in the broadcast. Duff Cooper finally made a statement to the press that assumed all responsibility for the broadcast; it was one of his last acts as Minister of Information. The BBC Registry was instructed to keep duplicate files of all correspondence relating to the broadcast in a fire-proof location until after the war in case Wodehouse decided to sue for slander.[52]

Press and listener responses to the broadcast underline the BBC's concerns. An editorial in the *News Chronicle* called the broadcast 'one of the most vulgar pieces of propaganda ever heard in the English language', indeed, one that 'shamed the BBC'. Letters to *The Times* condemned the broadcast for aping the manner of Quentin Reynolds. Listeners writing in to the BBC accused the broadcast of 'senseless and vulgar vituperation' and 'deplorable bad taste'; of being a 'cheap and vulgar imitation of Mr Quentin Reynolds', and, repeatedly, of being 'not English', 'quite un-British', 'a disgrace to every British ideal of justice, decency and levelheadedness'. A personal letter from the writer Dorothy L. Sayers to Sir Stephen Tallents sums up the criticism: 'I have never heard anything like this from the BBC before; I hope I never shall again. *It was as ugly a thing as ever was made in Germany.*'[53] There were dissenters: the Irish writer Sean O'Casey, for instance, in a letter to the *Daily Telegraph*, considered it retributive justice on those who

[51] DG to Sir Cecil Graves, Deputy Director-General (DDG), 16 July 1941, BBC WAC R34/271.

[52] See DS to Jardine Brown (DAB), 17 July; DS to DDG 21 July, Miss Fuller to Registry Supervisor, 3 Sept. 1946, R34/271.

[53] Confidential memorandum, 'Cassandra's broadcast on P. G. Wodehouse', 13 Aug. 1941, Appendices K and L; Dorothy L. Sayers to Sir Stephen Tallents (my italics), 15 July 1941, BBC WAC R34/271.

in the inter-war years had banished James Joyce while honouring
Wodehouse ('English literature's performing flea'), and Hannen
Swaffer, writing in the *Daily Herald*, saw in it the lesson that if the
MOI had a free hand over propaganda, at least 'something might
happen'. In fact, despite the deluge of written complaints, a BBC
Listener Research report conducted after the broadcast concluded
that the 'predominant attitude of listeners . . . was one of approval,
indeed enthusiastic approval was more frequently met with than
criticism'.[54] But a broadcast that so inflamed the wrath of a vocal
minority could not be considered successful as propaganda. A
comment from the *Star* put it best: 'Pity the poor BBC. When it is
dignified it is denounced as anaemic. When it tries to be lively it is
accused of vulgarity.'[55]

The intractability—and unpredictability—of tone is perhaps
evident above all in an another example from the Variety
Department, this time over a popular song, Noel Coward's
inflammatory Vansittartist anthem 'Don't Let's Be Beastly to the
Germans', which debuted on the BBC two years almost to the
day after Connor's broadcast. By 1943 the BBC was rather tired
of the good/bad Germans debate, and tired, too, of the continued
attacks both from those who suggested they were too sympathetic
to the German people and those who implied they were not sympathetic enough. They were therefore less than thrilled at the
prospect of allowing the broadcast by Coward of a song that was
not only specifically designed as a rebuke to the 'Peace Aims'
lobby, but, since the lyrics were entirely sarcastic, was likely also
to offend less perceptive Vansittartists. Since banning anything by
Noel Coward would be bound to cause huge publicity (not least
from Coward himself), BBC senior management in this case privately voiced the *hope* that the MOI would step in to ban it on
their own authority; unfortunately, as a BBC internal memorandum mordantly noted, Coward had already given a private performance of the song to Churchill himself, who had
'appreciatively joined in the chorus'.[56] In the event, the BBC's
fears proved groundless. The broadcast went ahead with some
publicity, but there was, in the event, little controversy. However,
the popular photo-magazine *Picture Post*, which ran an illustrated

[54] *Daily Telegraph*, 18 July 1941; *Daily Herald*, 17 July 1941; BBC LR/311, BBC WAC,
R34/271.   [55] *Star*, 19 July 1941.
[56] Programme Organizer to DPP, 19 July 1943, BBC WAC R19/941/3.

feature on the broadcast, pointed out that Coward commenced
singing on the BBC Forces Programme just as J. B. Priestley on
the Home Service was winding up a talk about the SS training
school at Bad Tolz, in which he offered the thought that the
German people must also be considered victims of the SS: as the
magazine noted, 'Is this the BBC's way of "giving both sides"?'[57]

Was the BBC right in its flight from satirical anti-German propaganda? Certainly after the first few months of war policymakers
and programme-makers alike turned violently against comedic or
satiric references to the Nazis on the BBC, deeming them inap-
propriate, demeaning, and tending to minimize the danger the
Nazis posed. The priority instead was to harden up language, and
to emphasize in the simplest and most direct means possible the
dangers of the Nazi threat, therefore focusing on talks and features. Comedy references to the Nazi threat were mistrusted or
taken as evidence of weak, rather than strong, morale. Sarcasm
was widely felt to be more demeaning to the speaker than his
subject: it was underhand, not straight dealing, un-British.

Outside the walls of the BBC, however, comedy about the
Nazis persisted as a basic feature of wartime popular culture.
Popular songs of the war included 'What a Nice Lot of Nazis they
Are', 'A Very Little Nazi', 'Nasty Uncle Adolf', and even 'Hitler's
Lambeth Walk'. William Joyce, whose malign influence on ordinary British morale was so feared within government, appeared in
cartoons as a talking jackass, had the condition of his adenoids
questioned by a correspondent to *Picture Post*, and was the 'star'
of *Lord Haw Haw, the Humbug of Hamburg*, a West End revue star-
ring Max Miller. Cartoon Nazi leaders appeared on playing
cards, on dartboards, and at the bottom of ashtrays, in advertise-
ments for headache cures, or without their trousers in children's
comics.[58] A book version of the BBC's *Adolf in Blunderland* sold out
four editions in the three months after its publication in December
1939. Even the MOI eventually picked up on the idea that making
fun of the Nazis might have propaganda value, replacing their
scaremongering (and deeply unpopular) anti-careless talk poster
campaign 'Join the Silent Column' with Fougasse's 'Careless Talk
Costs Lives' campaign: tiny comic cartoon Hitlers and Goerings

---

[57] *Picture Post*, 7 Aug. 1943.
[58] For a wide range of Second World War ephemera, see Gifford, *Run, Adolf, Run*, and
Robert Opie, *The Wartime Scrapbook* (London, 1995), 4–5.

eavesdropping on people in phone boxes, on buses, from under tables, and behind sofas.[59] A double-page spread in *Picture Post* reproduced a sequence of stills from a German newsreel to mock Hitler's 'ridiculous' celebration (complete with arm-waving and private jig) on hearing of the French surrender.[60] Nowhere is this impulse to comedic anti-Nazi propaganda more evident than in the wartime British film industry. Despite the critical acclaim heaped on such thoughtful explorations of Anglo-German relations as Powell and Pressburger's *The Life and Death of Colonel Blimp* (1943), or such Gothic treatments of Nazi brutality as Cavalcanti's *Went the Day Well?* (1943), the most successful morale-boosting anti-Nazi film propaganda in Britain drew directly on popular comedy tradition: George Formby in *Let George Do It* (1940) as a ukulele-wielding accidental spy inadvertently cracking a Nazi code and fantasizing (in a full-blown dream sequence) of punching Hitler on the nose in the middle of a Nazi rally, or Will Hay in *The Goose Steps Out* (1942) instructing a class of trainee Nazi spies how to make a 'traditional English sign of respect' (in fact, the insult of a reverse V-sign) to their classroom portrait of Hitler.[61] And it remains the case that the most common popular epithet for the German enemy during the war was neither 'Nazi' nor 'Hun' but the far less emotionally loaded 'Jerry'.

One might argue that some light relief from the horrors of war was a psychological necessity: certainly, with German propaganda, as everyone knew, aggressive, heavy-handed, and based on fear, there was an important role for British propaganda that played on irreverence, humour, and popular appeal. But the BBC's decision to discourage this kind of propaganda, whether or not this was indeed the best use of the medium, represented a conscious demarcation of the cultural boundaries of the times. The

[59] McLaine, *Ministry of Morale*, 81–4. See also John D. Cantwell, *Images of War: British Posters 1939–45* (London, 1989). Fougasse's cartoon Hitlers were so popular that they migrated to other MOI poster campaigns, most strikingly the food economy campaign 'Waste the Food and Help the Hun'.

[60] *Picture Post*, 18 Jan. 1941.

[61] Richard Falcon, 'Images of Germany and Germans in British Film and Television Fictions: A Brief Chronological Overview', in Husemann (ed.), *As Others See Us*, 7–28, at 10–17; Anthony Aldgate and Jeffrey Richards, *Britain Can Take It: The British Cinema in the Second World War* (2nd edn. Edinburgh, 1994), ch. 4, *passim*. See, too, M-O A, FR/435, 'Let George Do It', Sept. 1940. Interestingly, Formby's dream punch receives the cheering approval of the surrounding stormtroopers, while Hay's class of young Nazis turns out to be a group of partisans in disguise.

role of the BBC was not, broadcasters believed, to split opinion, nor to force a division between the elite and the 'gallery'.

Tellingly, while broadcasters spent much of the war trying to teach the MOI (and other government departments) what propaganda was most suitable for what kinds of broadcast, it was ultimately the listeners themselves (as evidenced in the BBC's own extensive wartime listener research) who set the boundaries. BBC Listener Research made it clear that BBC news reports were generally considered no place for sarcasm or sardonic tone, but that Variety references to Nazis (if funny) were widely appreciated. However, the kind of universal appeal achieved by shows such as *ITMA* (which worked above all because it had something for everyone: clever word play, absurd situations, topical jokes, funny voices, and slapstick) was hard to replicate, in Variety or elsewhere. Talks, in particular, were a much more difficult propaganda challenge, highly likely to split listener opinion, very often on class lines. British listeners appear to have liked Churchill, Americans, or comedians to be rude about the Germans, but beyond that—as William Connor's Wodehouse broadcast demonstrated—it depended on the talk, the speaker, and the listener.

The most successful propaganda corresponds most closely to the preconceptions, prejudices, and/or expectations of its audience; but this correspondence needs to be measured in terms of both the propaganda message itself and its medium of communication. The British press, cinema, popular music establishment, and popular publishing industry had their own methods of engagement with their audiences and negotiated their audience expectations accordingly. The BBC had its own highly specific relationship with its audience, and while listeners regularly complained about the BBC's staidness and conservatism, this very conservatism of approach was fundamental to their respect for the BBC as an institution. Ultimately, the BBC's wartime projection of the Nazi/German enemy succeeded because it broadly met its listeners' expectations. It was in general reasonably balanced, unsensational, and informative about the Nazi regime and the responsibility of the German people for that regime. It avoided the kinds of prurience and sensationalism that were acceptable for popular newspapers or the publishing market, recognizing their unsuitability for a home and family listening environment. Occasional 'lapses of taste' might alienate some and enthuse others, but, kept within bounds, served to add variety while not upsetting expectations. The BBC's acknowledged success as a propaganda medium during the Second World War ultimately rested on the ways in which it was able to provide what British listeners expected of their BBC in wartime, and the broadcast construction of the enemy was no exception.

8

Keep Quiet ... But Tell!!
Political Language and the 'Alert Citizen'
in Second World War America

OLAF STIEGLITZ

In 1943 Professor Max J. Herzberg, editor of the scholarly journal *Word Study*, asked a number of eminent philologists to discuss the probable effects of the present war in their realm of interest. Herzberg asked his colleagues how the study of foreign languages was possibly being influenced by the war. He was curious to know if the war was creating new words or phrases in the USA; and he also wanted to know whether the tremendous increase of interest in science and mathematics was drawing students away from the study of languages. But there was another point on the questionnaire that focused on what Herzberg called 'Increased Linguistic Alertness'. He asked: 'Have people become more sensitive to words in this war of words? Are they more critical in their attitude?'[1]

Reactions to this point of enquiry were mixed. Some professors were convinced that Americans paid more attention to words and strove to interpret them more accurately because, as Herzberg stated, 'we realize that so much depends on what we do after we have listened'.[2] On the subject of propaganda and its range of implications for general language usage, Professor Lawrence H. Conrad concluded very optimistically: 'The total effect of the awakening has been good. It would be very difficult to fool the literate portions of the American public.'[3]

This essay aims to elaborate this final aspect of Herzberg's enquiries und its consequences for US political language during the Second World War. The concept of propaganda has been

---

[1] Max J. Herzberg, *The War and Language: A Symposium on the Effects of World War II upon the English Language, the Study of Foreign Tongues, and the Use of Words* (Springfield, Mass., 1943), 2. This booklet contains a synopsis written by Herzberg of the original papers returned in reply to the *Word Study* questionnaire.   [2] Ibid.
[3] Ibid. 4. Herzberg is here quoting from the questionnaire.

widely and usefully employed in historical research, most often within a critical frame of analysis, to demonstrate attempts by different governments to regulate and direct public opinion.[4] Yet, at least from the point of view articulated in recent post-structuralist theory, it has proved too inflexible for analysing the interrelated layers of transmission, perception, and reaction to announced threats and dangers. The notion of some 'official', government-authorized propaganda that produces a coherent blueprint to which the addressed mass audience might react as intended or anticipated does not fit into a multi-dimensional, de-centred idea of power as suggested, for example, by Michel Foucault, one which is becoming increasingly prominent in historical research.[5] Moreover, it still remains more or less unclear how propaganda actually influenced ordinary citizens, both in their daily speech and in their behaviour. Any analysis of the effects and outcomes of 'propaganda language' has to deal with a number of important aspects that structure discussions of politics and language: the role of the media and communication in general; the influences of symbolic and ritualized language; the relationship between a 'passive' audience and one considered to be actively engaged in adding new meaning to official statements; the questions of social and cultural inclusion versus exclusion, and of identifying loyal in-groups and enemy out-groups. These questions have arisen recently in studies dealing, for example, with the everyday history of National Socialist Germany, and they are even more important when dealing with Western-style democracies, in which those dictatorial aspects usually associated with 'true propaganda', such as, for example, one-party rule or complete control of the media, are

[4] The history of the term propaganda is elaborated in Wolfgang Schieder and Christof Dipper, 'Propaganda', in Otto Brunner et al. (eds.), *Geschichtliche Grundbegriffe: Historisches Lexikon zur politisch-sozialen Sprache in Deutschland*, 8 vols. (Stuttgart, 1984), v. 69–112. The literature on propaganda is abundant; see Robert Cole, *Propaganda in Twentieth Century War and Politics: An Annotated Bibliography* (Lanham, Md., 1996). The following were useful for this essay: Kevin Roberts, Frank Webster, and Michael Pickering, 'Propaganda, Information and Social Control', in Jeremy Hawthorne (ed.), *Propaganda, Persuasion and Polemic* (London, 1987), 1–18; Bertrand Taithe and Tim Thornton, 'Propaganda: A Misnomer of Rhetoric and Persuasion?', in eid. (eds.), *Propaganda: Political Rhetoric and Identity 1300–2000* (Stroud, 1999), 1–24; and Andreas Elter, *Die Kriegsverkäufer: Geschichte der US-Propaganda 1917–2005* (Frankfurt am Main, 2005).

[5] On Foucault's concept of power see esp. Colin Gordon (ed.), *Power/Knowledge: Selected Interviews and Other Writings 1972–1977* (New York, 1980). Foucault's influence on historiography is mapped out in Jürgen Martschukat (ed.), *Geschichte schreiben mit Foucault* (Frankfurt am Main, 2002).

missing. Is propaganda a useful term for the analysis of political languages in democracies? How influential are crises, moral panics, or wars in stimulating propaganda languages in such societies? And how might such a language actually work in a heterogeneous, pluralistic political culture?

The cited example from Professor Herzberg's *Word Study* is interesting here because some philologists' opinions on the effect of propaganda differed significantly from the optimistic assumptions quoted before. Professor Arthur G. Kennedy stated that he was 'not at all sure that people have become more sensitive to words, but I do believe that they are becoming more worried about them'. According to this expert, more and more vague and loose words were in the air at that time. The amount of certainty and assured meaning was decreasing.[6] At least in his opinion, it required some effort to interpret the patriotic language of the times.

This essay will demonstrate that US home front propaganda language during the Second World War not only produced interesting inconsistencies, but that it by and large rested on these conflicting options of interpretation. Despite this, I will argue that it was a highly effective language, for it successfully generated different kinds of subjects. By encouraging certain techniques of self-government, the 'alert citizen' came into existence on the American home front as a desired, active protagonist and character. But this subjection ultimately rested on another process which generated 'spies', 'saboteurs', 'traitors', and other deviants and enemies. Intentional language and techniques of self-governing and discipline served to stimulate and regulate desired behaviour on the home front; a behaviour that nevertheless rested more on discursive negotiation than on coherent, one-dimensional speech acts which might be described as propaganda.

I will develop my argument in three steps. The first part presents an overview of US war information policy aimed at the American public during this period, stressing both its reluctant beginnings and its de-centredness. Secondly, I shall briefly address questions of theory and methodology, outlining the ways in which I employ the ideas of Foucault, and, in particular, his concept of governmentality, to grasp the problems in question. The third and main part of the essay contains a two-stage argument. Using as

---

[6] Herzberg, *War and Language*, 4.

primary sources both internal material from war information
agencies, and pamphlets and posters designed by governmental
organizations and private companies to influence the public, I will
focus on how US propaganda attempted to act linguistically upon
the dangers of espionage and sabotage, and show how ideas of
watchfulness and alertness were activated in the political language.
I will then suggest, or, to be more precise, hint at, the actual consequences that this charged language might have produced in
word and deed.

I

When America entered the Second World War after a long and
heated debate between passionate isolationists and those who
favoured intervention, the Roosevelt administration increased its
efforts to generate popular support for the war.[7] While propaganda
was, historically, an important tool in the mobilization of war
efforts, a large majority of Americans were wary of this controversial technique. Many were suspicious of governmental pronouncements after they had observed the propaganda methods of the
European regimes during the 1930s. In addition, the Committee
on Public Information, or Creel Committee, the agency responsible for US First World War propaganda, had left a legacy of
heavy-handedness and deception.[8] To counteract these negative
associations, the government decided to de-emphasize propaganda
in the strict sense of the word, and to adopt instead what they
named a 'strategy of truth', that is, an attempt to disseminate information to the public while refraining from persuading or manip-
ulating directly. Instead, as Archibald MacLeish, the Pulitzer

---

[7] See Richard Steele, 'Roosevelt, the Media, and the Coming of the War, 1940–1941',
Journal of American History, 71 (1984), 69–92. A summary of these developments is presented
in Astrid M. Eckert, *Feindbilder im Wandel: Der Vergleich des Deutschland- und des Japanbildes in
den USA 1945 und 1946* (Münster, 1999), 32–41.

[8] On the debate on propaganda during the inter-war years see Erika G. King,
'Exposing the "Age of Lies": The Propaganda Menace as Portrayed in American
Magazines in the Aftermath of World War I', *Journal of American Culture*, 12 (1989), 35–40.
Basic information on US propaganda efforts during the Second World War is provided by
John Morton Blum, *V Was for Victory: Politics and American Culture during World War II* (New
York, 1976); and Alan M. Winkler, *The Politics of Propaganda: The Office of War Information,
1942–1945* (New Haven, 1978). See also Thomas Howell, 'The Writers' War Board: U.S.
Domestic Propaganda in World War II', *Historian*, 59 (1997), 795–813.

Prize-winning author and driving force behind such plans, argued, the 'government of a democracy, by virtue of its existence as a democratic government, has a very different function in relation to the making of opinion. It is the government's function to see to it that the people have the facts before them—the facts on which opinions can be formed.'[9]

For that purpose, on 13 June 1942 the President, Franklin D. Roosevelt, established the Office of War Information (OWI), headed by the well-known radio journalist Elmer Davis. Its main objective, as stated in the President's executive order, was to 'formulate and carry out, through the use of press, radio, motion picture, and other facilities, information programs designed to facilitate the development of an informed and intelligent understanding, at home and abroad, of the status and progress of the war effort and of the war policies, activities, and aims of the government'.[10] From its beginnings, OWI was confronted with an immense dilemma relating to the nature of wartime propaganda in a democratic society. While the agency wanted broadly to inform the public (which at that time, after Pearl Harbor, urgently demanded more and more detailed information on all aspects of the developing conflict), the military enforced severe restrictions on any matter concerning actual warfare.[11] Moreover, OWI was—for a number of reasons—set up as a rather weak organization. Roosevelt had carefully avoided creating another Creel Committee. OWI was not a central propaganda agency; it did not assemble the masterminds of public persuasion; and it was not able to formulate any coherent policy concerning war objectives. Rather, it was chiefly an organizational instrument that coordinated the information gathered and deployed by several other offices, both inside and outside the government. OWI had no authority if other agencies refused to cooperate, and the military, in particular, was extremely hesitant to share information with Davis's agency. Even the President himself, as historian Alan Winkler observed, was 'only mildly interested' in actually co-

---

[9] As quoted in Winkler, *Politics of Propaganda*, 12. On MacLeish and other interventionists, see Peter Buitenhuis, 'Prelude to War: The Interventionist Propaganda of Archibald MacLeish, Robert E. Sherwood, and John Steinbeck', *Canadian Review of American Studies*, 26 (1996), 1–30.

[10] Executive Order 9182, Consolidating Certain War Information Functions into an Office of War Information, 13 June 1942, *Federal Register*, 7/117 (1942), 4468–9.

[11] Eckert, *Feindbilder im Wandel*, 34–5.

operating with OWI.[12] Another reason for OWI's weakness was Congressional resistance. Outspoken leaders of the Republican Party regularly denounced the organization's information policy as promoting Roosevelt, the Democrats, and the New Deal. Thus despite its plans to become an agency of democratic war information, Davis's organization was mainly used to push the sale of war bonds and to finance the war.

While the government displayed reluctance in the matter of a coherent policy of war information, the fact that many privately funded organizations and business corporations also established units for promoting the war effort added to the de-centralized, and sometimes even contradictory, outlook of US propaganda.[13] Hollywood movies may serve as a case in point. Highly popular with the public, motion pictures offered an obvious opportunity and means of informing the people about the war, for each week approximately eighty million American men and women attended films. But while OWI's own Bureau of Motion Pictures produced films promoting America's official war goals as formulated in Roosevelt's famous Four Freedoms Speech of January 1941 or in the Atlantic Charter,[14] Hollywood itself cared neither about any larger war aims, nor about accepting far-reaching influence from Washington. Instead, ordinary Hollywood war productions featured brave and powerful American boys fighting cruel, ruthless, unscrupulous enemies. And in the case of the Japanese enemy, the depiction was thoroughly racialist.[15]

American broadcasting and the music industry provide many other examples. OWI raised the morale of Americans by elaborating guidelines for hopeful tunes and patriotic lyrics for songs to be programmed nationwide, but it failed in the long run. From

[12] As quoted in Winkler, *Politics of Propaganda*, 36.

[13] For a recent elaboration of this aspect, see Matthias Reiss, 'Kampf für den "American Way of Life": Kriegsziele in den amerikanischen Werbeanzeigen des Zweiten Weltkrieges', in Arbeitskreis Historische Bildforschung (ed.), *Der Krieg im Bild—Bilder vom Krieg: Hamburger Beiträge zur Historischen Bildforschung* (Frankfurt am Main, 2003), 77–103.

[14] Of these, director Frank Capra's series 'Why We Fight' is probably the best known; see David Culbert, '"Why We Fight": Social Engineering for a Democratic Society at War', in K. R. M. Short (ed.), *Film and Radio Propaganda in World War II* (London, 1983), 173–91.

[15] There is a large amount of literature on Hollywood's engagement in the war effort. See e.g. Jeanine Basinger, *The World War II Combat Film: Anatomy of a Genre* (New York, 1986), and Thomas Doherty, *Projections of War: Hollywood, American Culture, and World War II* (New York, 1993). The aspect of racism is emphasized by Thomas O. Kelly II, 'Race and Racism in the American World War II Film: The Negro, the Nazi, and the "Jap" in *Bataan* and *Sahara*', *Michigan Academician*, 24 (1992), 571–83.

the creative minds of freelance songwriters originated such immensely popular and memorable lines as 'You're a Sap, Mr. Jap', or 'To Be Specific, It's Our Pacific', that ran counter to all attempts to disseminate the 'strategy of truth' over the air.[16]

Another important development which characterized the landscape of US political language during the Second World War was its emphasis on the 'American Way of Life' as perhaps not the official, but probably most valuable, goal of the war effort. Although at that time 'sacrifice' was one of the most widely circulated words on the American home front, it merely meant, more or less, the ongoing postponement of any large-scale consumption.[17] For the majority of American citizens this war was fought 'on imagination alone'; and as historian Matthias Reiss points out, this situation gave American business in general, and advertising companies in particular, a good chance to promote the war effort as essentially a fight for white, middle-class ideals of 'freedom' and 'opportunity'.[18] This is important for two significant reasons. First, it stresses the role and very presence of non-governmental organizations in what constituted the political language of the time; institutions, moreover, which were often outspoken critics of the policies of the Democratic Roosevelt administration in general, and the economically interventionist New Deal in particular. Secondly, this perspective on promoting the 'American Way of Life' as a quasi-official war objective highlights the inner-directedness of this political language which, while it targeted foreign enemies, aimed to (re-)stabilize the coherence of the body politic at home.

Thus, all in all, any impression that US propaganda during the Second World War spoke with one voice and had an overall accepted idea about its role and objectives is misleading. From the viewpoint of the federal government, it was a programme started reluctantly, and it remained remarkably de-centred with the OWI in a coordinating role in which it had only modest success. Additionally, these governmental efforts were embedded in many and well-crafted private ones, which certainly shared

[16] Radio during the war is discussed in Gerd Horten, *Radio Goes to War: The Cultural Politics of Propaganda during World War II* (Berkeley, 2002); for the music industry see Kathleen E. R. Smith, *God Bless America: Tin Pan Alley Goes to War* (Lexington, Ky., 2003).

[17] See Mark H. Leff, 'The Politics of Sacrifice on the American Home Front in World War II', *Journal of American History*, 77 (1991), 1296–318.

[18] Reiss, 'Kampf für den "American Way of Life"'.

basic assumptions about how to guide the American public through the war years, but still underscored different aspects. It thus comes as no surprise that data provided by public opinion polls of that era indicate that a majority of Americans were not sure about the country's war objectives.[19]

II

How can this heterogeneous and pluralistic language of war information be analysed? One of the conceptual assumptions of this essay is that political languages at times of crisis, moral panic, or war are not just statements formulated by ruling elites, but that these official statements and announcements are embedded in a complex web of utterances and practices which contribute, in Foucauldian terms, to a dispositive of security. Drawing on the basics of Foucault's power/knowledge complex, on ideas of panopticism, and of normalization, I argue that this dispositive serves two basic purposes: first, it homogenizes and symbolically reproduces the social body; and, secondly, it establishes some combined techniques of power and of the self. Foucault elaborates on this interdependence of language, the self, and society in his theory of governmentality. In this web of language, institutions, and practices, people never act spontaneously or voluntarily in the common meaning of these words; they are part of a multi-layered, heterogeneous, and ever-changing field in which authority and ordinary citizens necessarily interact with historically changing arsenals of terms, signs, metaphors, and symbols. Many of these revolve around notions of visibility and strategies to translate images into words or meaning, and into practice. As I consider this aspect of visibility to be a core element of American political language during the Second World War, I shall elaborate on it further.

Governmentality studies emerged in the 1990s as a new approach in rethinking politics, the social, and power; making 'explicit a different relationship between governance and the subject as a way of drawing together the micro and macro analyses

[19] On opinion polls, see Richard Steele, 'American Popular Opinion and the War against Germany: The Issue of Negotiated Peace, 1942', *Journal of American History*, 65 (1978), 704–23.

of power'.[20] Governmentality refers to the arts and rationalities of governing, where the conduct of conduct is the key activity. It is an attempt to reformulate the relationship between the governor and the governed. Seen from Foucault's angle, this relationship does not depend entirely upon administrative machines, juridical institutions, or other apparatuses that are usually grouped under the rubric of the state. Rather, the conduct of conduct takes place at innumerable sites, through an array of techniques and programmes that are generally defined as cultural.[21] Governmentality as an analytic perspective defines the state's role as one of coordination. The importance of this coordinating function—its relative strength and effectiveness and its centripetal force—is historically variable.

Sociologist Mitchell Dean argues that the main effect of governmentality studies has been to substitute what he calls an analytics of government for a theory of the state.[22] What he suggests is that, first, questions concerning the analysis of culture are accorded a more significant role within an analytics of government than they are within theories of the state. Secondly, the place occupied by culture within such an analytics is a radically different one. Culture is conceived of as central to the operations and procedures through which governmental forms of power work. For me as a cultural historian, this concept thus enables me to 'bring the state back in' in a manner that still stresses the fundamental role of culture.

As Dean argues, and as anybody familiar with Foucault's oeuvre will recognize from some of his other texts, such an analytics of government pays particular regard to characteristic forms of visibility, and to ways of seeing and perceiving.[23] This understanding serves as my starting point for the analysis of patriotic

---

[20] Jack Z. Bratich, Jeremy Packer, and Cameron McCarthy, 'Governing the Present', in eid. (eds.), *Foucault, Cultural Studies, and Governmentality* (Albany, NY, 2003), 3–21. See also Graham Burchell, Colin Gordon, and Peter Miller (eds.), *The Foucault Effect: Studies in Governmentality* (Chicago, 1991), which also includes English translations of Foucault's few brief texts on governmentality.

[21] See Bratich, Packer, and McCarthy, 'Governing the Present', 4.

[22] See Mitchell Dean, *Governmentality: Power and Rule in Modern Society* (London, 1999).

[23] On the importance of notions of visibility in the texts of Foucault, see Gilles Deleuze, *Foucault* (Frankfurt am Main, 1992), 69–98. The increasing relevance of images both real and imagined in cultural history is underscored by Jens Jäger, *Photographie: Bilder der Neuzeit. Einführung in die historische Bildforschung* (Tübingen, 2000), 79–87. See also Gerhard Paul (ed.), *Visual History: Ein Studienbuch* (Göttingen, 2006).

language during the Second World War. I will draw a line of argument that links certain images—actual pictures and images of the mind—with distinctive ways of thinking about them and verbalizing them. Images and language, I will argue, go hand in glove in anticipating a field of possible, intended practices which lead to characteristic ways of forming subjects, persons, and actors. This way of arguing is, in many ways, linked to studies which deal with particular enemy images and their creation and dissemination.[24] But it differs from these approaches, which mostly use theories of sociology or political science as their starting points, by emphasizing the importance of discourse (in the sense of the word used by Foucault) for processes of othering. It thus analyses the emergence and stability of enemy images not as intended by certain actors, institutions, or groups, but as discursive effects originating from multiple sources.

In order to be more specific and approach the topic in question more closely, this essay will focus precisely on that hinge between language and acting which Professor Herzberg included in his questionnaire of 1943. I will demonstrate some contemporary notions of visibility during the Second World War, of seeing and recognizing the foreigner, the un-American, the spy, or the saboteur. The act of seeing is followed by a process of interpretation which translates images into language, a language which is simultaneously descriptive and a call for action, a language that underscores talking as much as it enforces quietness in order to reinforce the social body: 'Keep quiet . . . but tell!!' Taken together, words and images not only established characterizations of good and evil, but, in my view even more importantly, they also strengthened semantic patterns for structuring one's view of oneself and of others. Such verbal and pictorial patterns were part and parcel of panoptical strategies that produced enemy images in the first place. They were created not by some government, but by many different institutions, and by those employing languages of watchfulness in everyday practice. They served to create and confirm the 'alert citizen' in his or her subject status.

---

[24] Recent literature on enemy images is discussed in Eckert, *Feindbilder im Wandel*, 26–32; see also Ragnhild Fiebig-von Hase and Ursula Lehmkuhl (eds.), *Enemy Images in American History* (Providence, RI, 1997).

III

In spring 1941 a patriotic young American named Steve Rogers, shocked by what he believed was 'a wave of sabotage and treason', but too sickly and weak to qualify for army enlistment, volunteered for a dangerous scientific experiment. Injected with a strange liquid, Rogers underwent a startling transformation. Growing in height and mass, his muscles expanded and tightened to what was then generally considered to be masculine perfection. A new superhero was born, ready to fight the Axis: Captain America.[25] Six months before the Japanese navy attacked Pearl Harbor on 7 December 1941, and almost one year before Franklin Roosevelt established the OWI, American comic books had already gone to war—a war that was basically fought on the home front. Plate 8.1 is a panel from the first issue of the Captain America series, which was published by Marvel Comics from March 1941. The new fictional superhero's bold mission explicitly included his role as 'a powerful force in the battle against spies and saboteurs!' And, although, as a superhero, Captain America was beyond ordinary human capacity, his deeds served the educational function of a role model. Bucky, his young companion, displayed eager enthusiasm, and his wish to meet the 'Nation's No. 1 Spy Buster' was answered in a reassuring way: 'Maybe you can, Bucky . . . Maybe you can!' Comic book stories of Superman, Captain America, or some other superhero sold at a rate of more than 10 million copies per month, mostly to male teenagers and adolescents, many of them soon to fill the ranks of the military and to serve in all theatres of the war. This may indicate that US home front propaganda began early, without any government interference, and spread deeply into large sections of American society. Propaganda reached different American audiences through different channels and with rather different objectives. What might be called propaganda included highbrow intellectual deliberations, such as those of Archibald MacLeish and other lob-

---

[25] See Bradford W. Wright, *Comic Book Nation: The Transformation of Youth Culture in America* (Baltimore, 2001), 30. Joe Simon and Jack Kirby, who created *Captain America*, were young Jewish liberals who explained the role of their comics as deliberately political, because 'the opponents of the war were all quite well organized. We wanted to have our say too'; ibid. 36. See also Bruce Lenthall, 'Outside the Panel-Race in America's Popular Imagination: Comic Strips before and after World War II', *Journal of American Studies*, 32 (1998), 39–61.

bying public figures. But it also had a place in popular culture, offering aids to the interpretation of world politics, its consequences for everyday life in America, and, perhaps the most important aspect, how to respond to it in terms of actual behaviour. If you wanted to be like Captain America, watching out for spies was a good start!

In fact, by the time the USA entered the Second World War, a 'Fifth Column scare had deeply penetrated the nation's psyche', as historian Francis MacDonnell argues.[26] Although the actual incidents of German, Japanese, and Italian intelligence activities never amounted to much, and were easily detected and neutralized by the Federal Bureau of Investigation (FBI), from 1938 to 1942 frightening stories of Axis Trojan Horse activities, of hidden enemies conducting espionage, planning sabotage, and preparing the way for a hostile invasion, extended into the public at large. The mass media played an important part in creating the impression of the existence of a huge network of subversive agents, and for a while, 'next to sex scandals few stories were easier to sell than the Fifth Column'.[27] Indeed, the phrase 'Fifth Column', a new addition to the English language since the Spanish Civil War, served as an important catchphrase because it was able to gather together all the meanings associated with notions of war, siege, and invasion: foreign agents and domestic traitors, espionage and sabotage, deception and subversion. It was closely connected to totalitarianism in general, but was most strongly associated with National Socialist Germany. And the phrase worked particularly well in the social and historical context of the USA because it fell on fertile ground. Fitting perfectly into long-established concerns about the American republic being vulnerable to foreign conspiracies, it added to the established practice, in a country of immigrants, of linking the dangers of subversion to foreign faces.[28]

'Faces' is a well-chosen word from which to begin interpreting the relationship between images, language, and behaviour.

---

[26] Francis MacDonnell, *Insidious Foes: The Axis Fifth Column and the American Home Front* (New York, 1995), 3.   [27] Ibid. 6.

[28] The literature on this link between foreigner and subversion is large; standard references include John Higham, *Strangers in the Land: Patterns of American Nativism, 1860–1925* (New York, 1975; original publication 1963); David H. Bennett, *Party of Fear: From Nativist Movements to the New Right in American History* (Chapel Hill, NC, 1988); and the stimulating recent anthology edited by Nancy Lusigan Schultz, *Fear Itself: Enemies Real and Imagined in American Culture* (West Lafayette, Ind., 1999).

Stereotyped representations of enemy leaders' faces, especially those of Adolf Hitler, Benito Mussolini, and Hideki Tōjō, the Japanese prime minister during the Second World War, figured prominently in the arsenal of the visual language of US home front propaganda. Walt Disney's Academy Award-winning short film classic *Der Fuehrer's Face* (1943) might serve as an example, where Donald Duck living in Nazi Germany is forced to salute stereotyped picture portraits—a vivid image articulating simultaneously the amount of Nazi control and the possibility of making fun of it.[29] Much the same can be said of posters designed by private companies to be displayed on factory floors to stimulate a patriotic work ethic, also representing this popular form of ridiculing the enemy (see Plate 8.2). The stereotyped faces not only identified foreign political and military leaders, they also served as icons to characterize whole enemy nations. Although Germany might have been the more dangerous, Japan was certainly the more despised enemy. As opinion polls from the war years clearly show, President Roosevelt's Germany First Strategy did not stimulate any enthusiasm among the American public, whereas the reasons for fighting the Japanese seemed obvious.[30] In the months preceding the attack on Pearl Harbor, 'Americans [already] . . . had little trouble hating their [Asian] enemies.'[31] Racism against Asians had a long tradition, especially on the West Coast, but fears of a 'yellow peril' had usually been centred on the Chinese.[32] This changed remarkably during the 1930s and as a result of Japan's war in China. After Pearl Harbor, the image of that enemy was constructed with the intention of both ridiculing and dehumanizing: ridiculing by using the stereotyped 'all teeth and spectacles' face shown in an anti-loafing poster dating from 1942 (Plate 8.2), and dehumanizing by employing metaphors of pest control and annihilation. Like that in Plate 8.3, showing a pest called 'Louseous Japanicas' and published in a Marine Corps

[29] *Der Fuehrer's Face*, released by RKO Pictures in January 1943 and directed by Jack Kinney.

[30] An American citizen quoted in *Analysis of American Opinion on the War*, dated 10 Sept. 1942, stated: 'I can see why we are fighting the Japanese but I can't see why we are fighting the Germans.' Quoted in Steele, 'American Popular Opinion', 708.

[31] Blum, *V Was for Victory*, 45; see also Eckert, *Feindbilder im Wandel*, 54–66.

[32] See Ute Mehnert, *Deutschland, Amerika und die 'Gelbe Gefahr': Zur Karriere eines Schlagworts in der Großen Politik, 1905–1917* (Stuttgart, 1995). Additionally, see Robert MacDougall, 'Red, Brown and Yellow Perils: Images of the American Enemy in the 1940s and 1950s', *Journal of Popular Culture*, 32 (1999), 59–75.

magazine entitled *Leatherneck*, they were certainly meant to be humorous, but nevertheless culturally framed the events in Hiroshima and Nagasaki. In this last example, as in others that follow, it is the close link between the image of the all-teeth and hairy pest and the explaining, de-coding text in which it is embedded that opens the possible step-by-step relationship between seeing, interpreting, and acting on the enemy.

It should be noted that all the pictures mentioned which show Japanese were distributed not by OWI, but by private corporations or the US Marine Corps. And the same is true of another source which will bring me back to the home front and Trojan Horse dangers. To speak about the perceived Fifth Column threat and Japan is problematic from the start. The Japanese immigrant population in the USA was small (about 127,000 people, almost all of them on the West Coast) and of little or no political and economic importance. At most, it was of regional significance. These factors distinguished it significantly from both German and Italian immigrants, and certainly made it easier to implement the notorious internment policy. This involved taking almost the entire group of people of Japanese birth or ancestry from their homes in California, Oregon, or Washington and incarcerating them in so-called 'relocation centres'.[33] Moreover, and more importantly for my argument, they were not white. The construction of a racialized 'other' puts an interesting spin on perceived Fifth Column threats. *Time Magazine*, for example, worried about 'How to Tell Your Friends from the Japs', the title of an article published right after Pearl Harbor. It stated that the Japanese were hairier than the Chinese; 'the Chinese expression is likely to be more placid, kindly, open; the Japanese more . . . dogmatic, arrogant. . . . The Japanese are hesitant, nervous in conversation; laugh loudly at the wrong time. Japanese walk stiffly erect . . . Chinese more relaxed.'[34] Countering Fifth Column activities relied heavily on the correct identification of potential perpetrators, and articles like this provided guidelines for perception, interpre-

[33] On Japanese internment see Roger Daniels, *Prisoners without Trial: Japanese Americans in World War II* (New York, 1993). Franklin Roosevelt's personal role in the policy of internment is discussed in Greg Robinson, *By Order of the President: FDR and the Internment of Japanese Americans* (Cambridge, Mass., 2001).

[34] *Time Magazine*, 22 Dec. 1941, here quoted from Blum, *V Was for Victory*, 46. Please note the description here of the Japanese as hairier than the Chinese, which later allowed associations of hairy pests to be annihilated.

tation, and identification, and at least indirectly called for intervention.

But they were far from sufficient, because the idea of a Fifth Column additionally rests on collaboration, for whatever reasons, from within one's 'own' community. The need for correct identification was, therefore, not restricted to enemy aliens, but also applied to ordinary Americans. Plate 8.4 shows the back cover of an anonymous pamphlet presenting, in its upper right corner, the image of a white male, but this time without the identifiable features of a face. Instead, a large question mark, directly connected with the other two of the title 'Who is this man??', replaces the empty facial characteristics. Here, the text not only interprets the meaning of the image, but explains the danger originating in all-American-looking people and answers the question posed: 'Who is this man?? He is a Fifth Columnist!! Don't trust him!!'[35] Although this is a pre-war, anonymous print, it can easily be complemented by later examples. 'The least suspected persons are usually the most effective', reads a 1943 pamphlet by the US Office of Civilian Defense, and it also states that 'unscrupulous persons operating for pay, or those with grievances, or unthinking people, or normally good citizens misled by propaganda, blinded by greed, fear, or hope for reward, or occasionally even those whose positions shield them, are frequently the unsuspected perpetrators of sabotage'.[36]

Thus the act of identifying potential spies and saboteurs, guided simultaneously by established cultural stereotypes and recently constructed enemy images, was a highly complicated process. Other characteristic features of Fifth Columnists, such as their inside knowledge and expertise in disguise, made it even more complicated. J. Edgar Hoover, head of the FBI and in the early 1940s already *the* authoritative voice with regard to domestic dangers threatening the United States, was explicit on that point in a publication, published before Pearl Harbor by the National Foremen's Institute, addressing the alertness of the American worker: 'The skilled saboteur carries out his work with cleverness

[35] [Anonymous], *Hitler Doomed to Madness* (Greenwich, Conn., 1940). It is interesting to note that this image appeared in a liberal, pro-labour publication, thus demonstrating that it was not only the FBI or other more conservative organizations which disseminated the Fifth Column scare.

[36] US Office of Civilian Defense, *Sabotage and Preventive Measures* (Washington, 1943), 2.

and cunning.'[37] Traitors, spies, and saboteurs, his argument went
on, not only worked perfectly disguised in the dark, but were, furthermore, well-trained graduates of special schools, making them
experts in their fields of camouflage and deception. Hoover and
others drew two conclusions from this reasoning: first, the need
to maintain vigilance should not decrease, but increase with every
month that passed without an actual sabotage plot; and secondly,
that expert threats call for expert responses. It was at this point, of
course, that informing the FBI became essential. A poster distributed by OWI in cooperation with the FBI announced: 'The war
against spies and saboteurs demands the aid of every American.
When you see evidence of sabotage, notify the Federal Bureau of
Investigation at once. When you suspect the presence of enemy
agents, tell it to the FBI. Beware of those who spread enemy
propaganda! *Don't repeat vicious rumors or vicious whispers!* Tell it to
the FBI!'[38]

The text of this poster (which was also printed on matchbox
covers) contains all the important elements necessary for the
crucial process I am describing in general. It links images with
language and desired behaviour. 'Seeing evidence', 'suspecting
the presence' of the other, and 'telling it' to the authorities in
charge constituted the important, patriotic tasks of the alert
citizen. It created or reconfirmed 'every American' in his or her
position as a subject. But this text accomplished even more. It
addressed the complex web of language and utterances in which
these processes of perception, interpretation, and action were
embedded. Telling 'it' to the FBI was only one possible speech
act following the 'detection' and identification of the 'other'; it was
the intended, the 'successful' one. But it was accompanied by
rumours and whispers which endangered not only the intended
communication, but also the correctness of identification as such,
and, at a higher level, the reproduction of the social body.
Responsible, alert citizens were confronted with a serious and
difficult decision, one which nevertheless formed the core of their
civic duties, that is, the core of their being as a citizen: what to
tell and what to keep quiet about. The semantic field of espionage

[37] Hoover quoted in Harry Desmond Farren, *Sabotage: How to Guard against it* (New York,
1940), 22.
[38] Office of War Information, in collaboration with the Federal Bureau of Investigation,
the Office of Civilian Defense, and the Petroleum Administration for War, *Information
Program for the Prevention of Sabotage* (1943), 3; emphasis in original.

Plate 8.1 'Captain America Captures Spy Ring!' From the first issue of the Captain America series, Marvel Comics, March 1941. Reproduced by permission of Marvel Entertainment.

Plate 8.2 'Hang Around Girls, We Like It!' Poster designed for
Walter Kidde & Co. in 1942.
From the collections of the Division of Political History, National Museum of
American History, Smithsonian Institution.

Louseous Japanicas

The first serious outbreak of this lice epidemic was officially noted on December 7, 1941, at Honolulu, T. H. To the Marine Corps, especially trained in combating this type of pestilence, was assigned the gigantic task of extermination. Extensive experiments on Guadalcanal, Tarawa, and Saipan have shown that this louse inhabits coral atolls in the South Pacific, particularly pill boxes, palm trees, caves, swamps and jungles.

Flame throwers, mortars, grenades and bayonets have proven to be an effective remedy. But before a complete cure may be effected the origin of the plague, the breeding grounds around the Tokyo area, must be completely annihilated.

Plate 8.3 'Bugs Every Marine Should Know', by Sgt. Fred Lasswell, published in *Leatherneck* Magazine, March 1945.
Courtesy of *Leatherneck Magazine*.

WHO IS THIS MAN??

He **LOOKS** *like an American*
   He **DRESSES** *like an American*
     He **SPEAKS** *the same language as Americans*

But . . .

HE HATES American Democracy and maintains that it is doomed.

HE HATES Unions of working people because they are symbols of democracy in action.

HE SNEERS at the sacred liberties of the American people.

HE SPREADS religious hatreds among Protestants, Catholics and Jews to destroy our democratic unity.

HE PAYS lip service to the American Flag but his allegiance is to a foreign flag.

HE IMITATES his Nazi masters by using Anti-Semitism as a smokescreen for his betrayal of America.

HE AWAITS THE DAY WHEN A FOREIGN POWER "TAKES OVER" AMERICA AND "HEIL HITLER!" REPLACES "GOD BLESS AMERICA!"

Who Is This Man??
HE IS A FIFTH COLUMNIST !!
DON'T TRUST HIM!!

Plate 8.4 'Who is This Man??', back cover of an anonymous pamphlet, *Hitler Doomed to Madness* (Greenwich, Conn., 1940). Image courtesy of the Holocaust Center of Northern California, San Francisco, California.

Plate 8.5 'Wanted! For Murder' by Victor Keppler, 1944.
US National Archives and Record Administration, Still Picture Branch
(NWDNS–208–PMP–91).

Plate 8.6 '. . . Because Somebody Talked!' by Wesley, 1943. Printed
by the Government Printing Office for the US Office of
War Information.
US National Archives and Record Administration, Still Picture Branch
(NWDNS-44-PA-227A).

Plate 8.7 'The Sound that Kills', US Office of
War Information, 1942.
From the collections of the Division of Political History, National Museum of
American History, Smithsonian Institution.

and sabotage is structured by this dilemma which, following this logic, directly corresponded to the success of the war effort. This is demonstrated in other examples of posters and cartoons from OWI and other distributors.

Plate 8.5 takes up the 'wanted poster' motif also used in Plate 8.4. But the anonymous, unidentifiable white man is now, in this 1944 war poster, replaced by a woman, someone who could resemble the viewer's neighbour, sister, wife, or daughter. To present wrong behaviour on the home front, in this case, wrong speech, as murderous was the flip side of the same coin that demanded talk. It was the difficult and precarious task of the alert citizen to distinguish between these two closely related speech acts of talking and keeping silent. Failure resulted not only in loss of status as a citizen and transformation into a traitor; it meant becoming a murderer and a 'most wanted' person. Many posters distributed by OWI or other agencies during the war years created this link between leaking unnecessary information at home and large numbers of deaths overseas. Plate 8.6, distributed by OWI in 1944, is perhaps the best known, depicting a spaniel and a gold star symbolizing the loss of a loved one ' . . . because somebody talked'. Plate 8.7 actually takes the trouble to explain the relevance of correct speech acts and the whole network of communication to the public. The 'Sound that Kills' travels through the air from the well-meaning but careless all-American citizen to the unscrupulous Nazi spy, and, further, to the German submarine captain, who does not hesitate to kill the innocents on board the *Exeter*.

It is far more difficult to state in any detail how this language of seeing themselves and others, and of talking or not talking about others, stimulated accusatory practices or other forms of behaviour. But there are hints that indicate reactions which might be considered linked. Oral history sources compiled among groups of Italian and Japanese immigrants clearly indicate that suspicion increased and resulted in denunciations.[39] According to FBI sources, the public began to 'flood the government with reports of suspected cases of espionage' in the late 1930s.[40] The

---

[39] See e.g. Stephen Fox, *The Unknown Internment: An Oral History of the Relocation of Italian Americans during World War II* (Boston, 1990), 88–99. Cf. also Arthur A. Hanson (ed.), *Japanese American World War II Evacuation Oral History Project*, 5 vols. (Westport, Conn., 1991).

[40] MacDonnell, *Insidious Foes*, 8.

number of complaints received increased strikingly after the
United States entered the war, but seems to have decreased after
1942. Hoover's urge to maintain vigilance was obviously not convincing in a military situation which made invasion rather
unlikely. Moreover, many commentators now stressed different,
unwanted results of citizens reporting to the authorities. As OWI
warned in 1943: '*Cautions*: It is highly important to remember that
we do not want to stir up a wave of spy hysteria. . . . We do not want
people to get the erroneous idea that the country is filled with
saboteurs and one is probably lurking around each corner. To
create such an impression would bring to light thousands of
amateur detectives who would hinder the excellent work now
being accomplished by the government agents.'[41]

IV

As language expert Professor Kennedy remarked in *Word Study*,
US patriotic language deployed vague and loose words, with a
questionable degree of certainty and assured meaning. The reason
for this, as I have tried to show, was threefold. First, as a result of
historical experiences, conflicting interests, and political reasoning,
the government itself split its propaganda efforts between several
agencies. Secondly, semi-official and private bodies, institutions,
and businesses added other elements to that language which
stressed at least partially different contents and which, because of
its sheer quantity, almost dominated the propaganda arena. And
third, the language rested on images and metaphors which not
only allowed a range of meanings, but, in fact, deliberately played
with this ambiguity. Despite this, the patriotic language of the
Second World War years was highly effective because it was productive in the sense indicated by Foucault. It was a language
which created both the 'other' (the enemy and the un-American)
and the patriotic watchman (the 'alert citizen'). It was performative in the sense that it constituted citizenship not as a status of
having, but as a category of doing, thus corresponding to traditional elements of liberal political philosophy.

Foucault's concept of governmentality, on the one hand, served
as a valuable tool to understand a field of power relations and

---

[41] Information Program for the Prevention of Sabotage, 2; emphasis in original.

meanings difficult to survey, in which the state did not hold centre-stage but assumed a role as coordinator. On the other hand, however, it allowed a focus on culturally and linguistically produced meaning without ignoring or downplaying government policy, which tried to engineer predictable behaviour.

My method and findings raise questions regarding their place in a comparative framework for the analysis of politics and language. First, one is reminded that transfer and mutual learning are elements of comparative history: the way in which US officials and the wider public perceived European propaganda during the 1930s obviously influenced policies and reactions in America. Secondly, the concept of governmentality certainly rests on liberal forms of government and on a frame of 'modernity'. It raises questions about the degrees of consent and acceptance administrations need to be able to rely on 'governing at a distance'. And finally, this essay might be read in order to compare periods of war with periods of moral panic, for they might rest upon, or mobilize, similar sign systems. The construction of ridiculing and/or dehumanizing enemy images; semantic strategies of inclusion and exclusion; a linguistic mobilization of 'alert citizens': at that level, the Second World War pre-structured the use of the Cold War metaphor during the late 1940s and 1950s. Or, in the words of Francis MacDonnell, the 'Fifth Columnist of the early forties reemerged in popular cultural forms as the Communist spy of the fifties'.[42]

[42] MacDonnell, *Insidious Foes*, 8.

9

Telling the Truth: Counter-Discourses in Diaries under Totalitarian Regimes (Nazi Germany and Early GDR)

HEIDRUN KÄMPER

I *Introduction*

'To write is strictly forbidden, even so I do it. When I still was free and could write whenever and as much as I wanted, I often doubted the sense of this activity; now I consider it a huge personal relief. The written word benevolently isolates me from the naked experience of detention.'[1] Luise Rinser, German poet, noted this as a prisoner on remand in 1944. 'In the first place, it [diary-writing] is a means of concentrating my thoughts and energy on literature . . . A kind of self-protection.'[2] Nico Rost, Dutch prisoner in Dachau, sought to liberate himself from hell by writing a diary. The purpose was to maintain distance by putting the horror into words.

These short quotations from Luise Rinser and Nico Rost show what diary-writing can mean under totalitarian conditions. As texts of extreme privacy, diaries document the most intimate feelings, thoughts, and desires as well as the basic experiences of human existence. Written under totalitarian regimes, diaries can help their authors to overcome situations of life-threatening pressure. In this regard, diary-writing in custody may be seen as the prototype of 'diaristics' because nowhere else does writing take

---

[1] Luise Rinser, *Gefängnistagebuch* (Frankfurt, 1973), 17, entry for 22 Oct. 1944: 'Es ist streng verboten zu schreiben. Ich tue es trotzdem. Als ich noch frei war und schreiben konnte, wann und so oft ich wollte, habe ich oft am Sinn dieser Tätigkeit gezweifelt; jetzt halte ich es für eine große persönliche Wohltat. Das Wort schiebt sich gnädig isolierend zwischen mich und das nackte Erlebnis der Haft.' All translations in the text are my own; the original German is given in the footnotes.

[2] Nico Rost, *Goethe in Dachau: Ein Tagebuch*, ed. Wilfried F. Schoeller (Munich, 2001), 110: 'An erster Stelle ist es [Tagebuchschreiben] ein Mittel, um meine Gedanken und meine Energie auf die Literatur zu konzentrieren . . . Eine Art Selbstschutz.'

place in such an isolated situation—assuming, of course, that the diarist is not a member or supporter of the system.

For diarists who did not conform with the National Socialist regime, their diaries gave them a chance to speak the truth. For them, totalitarian regimes were predicated upon lying. Theodor Haecker, a member of the conservative German resistance and the intellectual father of the students' resistance group Weiße Rose, commented on the lies of the Nazis in his diary: 'How little truth human beings need for life—and how many lies! Nescis mi fili, quam multis mendiciis regitur mundus. [You do not know, my son, by how many lies the world is governed.]'[3] Haecker's next entry concerns the voices that transmit these lies: 'Their voices, my God, their voices! Their betrayal overwhelms me again and again. Most dreadful is their extinction. Sounding masks of human voices. . . . In the desert of a proud godforsakenness: death, plague, and lies.'[4] In this sense, the world created in diaries under totalitarianism can be regarded as a counter-world to lying. 'Telling the truth' is a leitmotiv of diary-writing under dictatorships. However, there are different motivations for writing. These can be reconstructed from the text because authors themselves often reflect on their own motives for noting down their experiences and perceptions. Diary-writers feel a strong responsibility to record the truth, irrespective of whether their impulses originate in individual feelings or external pressures.

Walter Tausk, a Jewish commercial traveller living in Breslau, kept a diary until 1940. In 1941 he was deported to Kowno, where all trace of him disappears. He was one of the observers of reality: 'More and more seeps out about this day [of the boycott of Jewish shops] and its consequences, and since all this is not allowed to be published in the newspapers, it shall herewith be preserved for posterity.'[5] Tausk was a highly self-conscious diarist, and the disastrous

---

[3] Theodor Haecker, *Tag- und Nachtbücher 1933–1945*, ed. Hinrich Siefken (Innsbruck, 1989), 50, entry for 20 Apr. 1940: 'Wie wenig Wahrheit braucht der Mensch zum Leben—und wieviel Lüge! Nescis mi fili, quam multis mendiciis regitur mundus.'

[4] Ibid. 'Ihre Stimmen, mein Gott, ihre Stimmen! Immer neu überwältigt mich ihr Verrat. Am furchtbarsten ist ihre Ausgestorbenheit. Tönende Masken menschlicher Stimmen . . . Tod, Pest, Lüge in der Wüste einer stolzen Gottverlassenheit!' 20 April 1940 was Hitler's 51st birthday, and Haecker was probably listening to the speeches broadcast on the radio on this occasion.

[5] Walter Tausk, *Breslauer Tagebuch 1933–1940*, afterword by Henryk M. Broder (Leipzig 1995), 47, entry for 14 Apr. 1933: 'Es sickert immer mehr durch von diesem Tage [des "Judenboykotts"] und seinen Folgen, und da das alles nicht in die Zeitungen kommen darf, soll es hiermit der Nachwelt überliefert werden.'

environment forced him, like other diarists under similar conditions, to escape into the inner monologue of his diary. 'I hope that many diaries from this time survive for posterity. Written unvarnished— so that subsequent generations can gain a clear picture of the enormous nonsense which we have witnessed: of the second German Middle Ages.'[6] Six months later, Tausk returned to the same point: 'The truth is unbelievably suppressed, individuals are spied upon, and their freedom limited. . . . It is damned dark in the "New Germany"', he noted, 'although scattered here and there . . . flames are glowing, and one of them is in this diary.'[7]

In addition to a strong commitment to telling the truth, common to all dissident diary-writers under National Socialism, they also shared the view that the practice of writing a diary was a kind of monologue. Ernst Jünger considered it the last possible form of conversation.[8] Other diarists, too, noted the existential relationship between the articulated word and memory. This also formed one of Walter Tausk's motives: 'Soon one will only be able to talk to oneself, and then the diary attains a high value: otherwise one forgets what one asked and answered oneself, and one forgets the questions which the times confronted one with—without giving an answer.'[9]

The counter-world of the diary may consist of worst-case scenarios. As contemporaries watched political developments carefully and critically, they formed views about what to expect and about what parts of the truth the regime was concealing. Prophecies are a characteristic of diary-writing under totalitarianism.[10] Entries

---

[6] Ibid. 65, entry for 25 June 1933: 'Hoffentlich kommen aus der Zeit viele Tagebücher auf die Nachwelt! Ungeschminkt geschrieben—damit andere Generationen ein klares Bild von dem Riesenunfug bekommen, den wir miterlebt haben: vom zweiten deutschen Mittelalter.'

[7] Ibid. 107, entry for 21 Jan. 1934: 'Die Wahrheit wird unglaublich unterdrückt, der einzelne ist bespitzelt und in seiner Freiheit eingeschränkt . . . Es ist verflucht finster in "Neu-Deutschland", und doch ist, hier und dort verstreut, etwas Licht . . . hier und dort glimmt irgendeine Flamme weiter—und eine davon ist dieses Tagebuch auch.'

[8] Ernst Jünger, *Strahlungen* (Tübingen, 1949), 8–9: 'das letzte mögliche Gespräch.'

[9] Tausk, *Breslauer Tagebuch*, 86, entry for 8 Aug. 1933: 'es ist bald soweit, daß man nur noch mit sich selber wird reden können, und da gewinnt ein Tagebuch großen Wert: man vergißt sonst, was man sich selbst gefragt und geantwortet hat und welche Fragen einem die Zeit vorlegte—ohne eine Antwort darauf zu geben.'

[10] Cf. Gustav René Hocke, *Europäische Tagebücher aus vier Jahrhunderten: Motive und Anthologie* (Frankfurt am Main, 1991), 196: 'das wahre politische Tagebuch läßt . . . nach einem Begriff von Henri Bergson, eine "offene", auf die Zukunft weisende "Moral" wirksam werden . . . Insofern können Erinnertes und Erlebtes immer wieder zu einer visionären Vorwegnahme von Zukünftigem führen.'

such as the following are typical: 'One sees the complete ruin and collapse of this "Third Reich", which inevitably rushes into its own catastrophe.' Or 'the Germans . . . will become the objects of the world's disgust'.[11] Prophecies such as these particularly affect readers when authors refer to well-founded presentiments of their own deaths. Walter Tausk foresaw himself as a 'little piece of life beaten to death in this wonderful Third Reich'.[12] Three weeks later he predicted the concentration camp scenario, which probably came true for him: 'Whenever I closed my eyes over these past few weeks, I saw a single image: a bare cell with smooth cement walls. I stood in it: a black cap . . . on my head, wearing a faded brownish-yellow prisoner's uniform, . . . the cloth with thin stripes, stout black military shoes on my feet. So one stands there, immobile.' Tausk was not sure whether this image was the symptom of a 'nervous disease' or evidence of 'second sight for things which might happen if one could not escape from hell'.[13]

It has been shown that the incidence of diary-writing in Germany and German-occupied Europe increased sharply between 1933 and 1945.[14] Provided that the authors were not part of the system, extreme experiences such as imprisonment (Rinser and Rost) or persecution and fear for one's life (Tausk) were typical motives for people to start recording experiences in a diary. Beyond such extreme situations the political system itself could compel contemporaries to write. Above all, diary-writing under totalitarianism was political. Even if a diary concerned only the most private subjects or was intended to be purely introspective, merely the fact that it was written in a dictatorship made it political.[15] Since totalitarian politics intruded into every sphere of life, there was no chance of escape. As a result, diarists included politics in their writing, if only

---

[11] Tausk, *Breslauer Tagebuch*, 207, entry for 24 June 1939: 'Man sieht den völligen Ruin und Zusammenbruch dieses "Dritten Reiches", das unausweichbar in seine Katastrophe rennt.' Haecker, *Tag- und Nachtbücher*, 28, entry for 13 Dec. 1939: 'Die Deutschen . . . werden der Abscheu der Welt.'

[12] Tausk, *Breslauer Tagebuch*, 195, entry for 20 Jan. 1939: 'als totgeschlagenes Stückchen Leben in diesem wundervollen Dritten Reich.'

[13] Ibid. 203–4, entry for 12 Feb. 1939: 'wenn man in diesen vergangenen Wochen zuweilen die Augen schloß, sah man immer nur ein Bild: eine kahle Zelle mit glatten Zementwänden. In ihr stand ich: eine schwarze Mütze . . . auf dem Kopf, eine verwaschene, braungelbe Sträflingsuniform an . . . der Stoff feingestreift, schwarze derbe Militärschuhe an den Füßen. So stand man da, unbeweglich. Nervenstörung? Zweites Gesicht für Dinge, die einem geschehen könnten, falls man nicht aus der Hölle käme?'

[14] Cf. Hocke, *Europäische Tagebücher*, 232; see also his list of European diarists between 1933 and 1945, ibid. 178.   [15] Ibid. 232–3.

to free themselves from the subject for the rest of the day: 'Each political entry in the diary demands willpower. But this allows me to get rid of politics for the rest of the day.'[16]

The loss of family members, friends, or property during the war was another reason for recording one's feelings. Hans Erich Nossack, for example, a writer and the heir to his father's firm in Hamburg, lost his financial existence in the big air raid on Hamburg of July 1943. He lost the family business, his manuscripts, and his diaries. Starting a new diary, Nossack thought about it as a 'loss of the past': 'Should it be granted me to grow to love this book with the same intensity that I hated the four or five preceding books—those that are lost, and whose loss I find so hard to bear, despite my hatred of them, that it sometimes threatens to pull me down with it—that would be good. Then, the complete loss of my past would be a mercy.'[17]

The heterogeneity of diaries prevents any classification, but there are similarities of function, subject matter, and circumstance of writing. Diaries are one of the most individual types of text, and they continued to be so under totalitarianism. Nevertheless, to some extent totalitarianism provides a unifying background. It is the political subject that engages the most diverse diary-writers. These conditions require that research on diaries must take into account the individuality of the diaries' authors as well as the external circumstances under which the texts are produced.

Diaries have their origin in the most intimate sphere of a human being's life—they belong to the text type of the self. Those who attempt to classify 'diaries' as a text type agree that they are a particular kind of monologue, a soliloquy.[18] In addition, diaries

---

[16] René Schickele, *Tagebücher 1918–1934*, 3 vols. (Cologne, 1953), iii. 1,110, entry for 8 May 1934: 'Jede politische Eintragung in das Tagebuch kostet mich Selbstüberwindung. Aber auf diese Weise werde ich die Politik für den Rest des Tages los.'

[17] Hans Erich Nossack, *Die Tagebücher 1943–1977*, ed. Gabriele Söhling, afterword by Norbert Miller, 3 vols. (Frankfurt am Main, 1979), i. 12, entry for 23 Feb. 1944: 'Sollte es mir noch vergönnt sein, daß ich dieses Buch so liebgewinne, wie ich die vier oder fünf vorhergehenden Bücher haßte, sie, die verlorengingen und deren Verlust mir so unbegreiflich schwer ist, trotz meines Hasses, so schwer, daß er mich manchmal mit hinabziehen will,—das wäre gut. Dann wäre der völlige Verlust meiner Vergangenheit eine Gnade.'

[18] Cf. Wladimir Admoni, *Die Tagebücher der Dichter in sprachlicher Sicht* (Mannheim, 1988), 15: 'Das Tagebuch dient einer sonderbaren, aber überaus wichtigen Kommunikationsart. Es dient namentlich der Kommunikation des Menschen mit sich selbst.' See also Hocke, *Europäische Tagebücher*; Herbert Kraft, '"Neue" Prosa von Kafka: Mit einer Theorie der Textsorte "Tagebuch"', *Seminar*, 19 (1983), 235–45; Helga Hipp, 'Zur formulativen Seite bei

written in dictatorships are inevitably political diaries. Political diaries, whose history begins at the end of the eighteenth century,[19] are characterized by the dominance of topical subjects.[20] Personal or individual reflections are correspondingly reduced.[21] This does not mean that the political diary loses its individual character. It remains a very personal type of text with regard to the language used in it.

In the following sections of this essay three diaries will be explored in greater detail. The diaries of Willi Graf and Ulrich von Hassell are two versions of dissident diaries written under Nazi totalitarianism. The diary of Victor Klemperer, on the other hand, was written under conditions of persecution and oppression. It was continued after 1945 during a period of adjustment to the new regime of the Soviet occupied zone and the early GDR.

II Diary-Writing under the Sign of Resistance: The Diaries of Willi Graf and Ulrich von Hassell

Although in general all diaries written under totalitarianism are political we can distinguish different degrees. Apart from official

Tagebucheintragungen: Anmerkungen zu Arbeits- und Lebensjournalen', *Neuphilologische Mitteilungen*, 89 (1988), 573–82; Kirsten Adamzik, *Textlinguistik: Eine Einführung* (Tübingen, 2004), 114; Wolfgang Heinemann and Dieter Viehweger, *Textlinguistik: Eine Einführung* (Tübingen 1991), 139 and 244.

[19] Cf. Hocke, *Europäische Tagebücher*, 164: 'After the "critical" diaries since the Renaissance, the beginning of the French Revolution saw the emergence of "protest" journals, that is, since the Romantic period. Their "protests", however, generally did not reach the public, but were written in worried seclusion and kept anxiously hidden' ('Nach den "kritischen" Diarien seit der Renaissance entstanden mit dem Beginn der Französischen Revolution, also seit der Romantik, die "Protest"-Journale, deren "Protest" jedoch meist nicht an die Öffentlichkeit drang, sondern in sorgender Verborgenheit geschrieben und in ängstlichem Versteck gehalten wurde').

[20] Ibid. 243: 'The "modern" political diary . . . is critical of current events. Ethical value-neutrality in the pseudo-Machiavellian sense is abandoned: self-criticism turns into moralistic criticism of current events ('Das "moderne" politische Tagebuch wird . . . ein zeitkritisches Tagebuch. Die ethische Wertneutralität im pseudo-macchiavellistischen Sinne wird aufgegeben: aus der Selbstkritik wird moralistische Zeitkritik').

[21] Ibid. 194: 'The political diary . . . [registers] political events or [describes] political individuals without introspection and with merely restrained personal views. . . . As a true diary that aims to be more than a calendar-based chronicle, the political diary too must be "revealing" more than merely descriptive' ('Das politische Tagebuch . . . [verzeichnet] ohne Introspektion mit lediglich gedämpften persönlichen Betrachtungen politische Ereignisse oder [schildert] politische Persönlichkeiten. . . . Als echtes Tagebuch, das mehr sein will als kalendarische Chronik, muß auch das politische Tagebuch mehr "enthüllen", als bloß beschreiben').

diaries such as, for example, those written by Hitler's Propaganda Minister Joseph Goebbels,[22] the most political diaries written under dictatorships are probably those by dissident authors.[23] The spectrum which diaries written under conditions of dictatorship can cover is illustrated by the diary of Willi Graf on the one hand and that of Ulrich von Hassell on the other. They can be seen as extremely different with regard to biographical conditions and functional implications—under the unifying sign of resistance.

Willi Graf was a member of the resistance movement Weiße Rose, a group of students who assembled in Munich in 1941, outraged by the cruel and brutal war.[24] Aiming to protest, and to enlighten and wake up their contemporaries, they distributed leaflets under the symbol of the white rose (the title of a novel by B. Traven, published in 1931). In summer 1942 Willi Graf, born in 1918, met the founder Hans Scholl, and Graf joined the group. He wrote and distributed leaflets and painted anti-fascist slogans on house walls. He was arrested on 15 February 1943, sentenced to death on 19 April, and executed on 12 October.

Ulrich von Hassell, born in 1881, was a civilian member of the bourgeois, national conservative resistance movement.[25] This movement was led by Carl Goerdeler, and its membership included, among others, Ludwig Beck, Johannes Popitz, Jens Jessen, Carl Langbehn, Wilhelm Leuschner, and Jakob Kaiser. They were all experienced men who saw themselves as a counter-elite to the National Socialist leaders. Members described themselves as the 'secret', the 'other', or the 'honourable Germany',

---

[22] Hocke, *Europäische Tagebücher*, 182, calls it the 'lemur diary' ('Lemuren-Tagebuch') of the 'downright existential denunciation type' ('geradezu existentiellen Denunzianten-Typus').

[23] In this respect the dissident diary is a first-rate political diary when it is 'true': 'The first-rate policial diary is . . . true only when it de-ideologizes history and alienates "diplomatic" secrets' ('Das politische Tagebuch von Rang ist . . . nur dann wahr, wenn in ihm Geschichte ent-ideologisiert wird, wenn "diplomatische" Geheimnisse entfremdet werden'), ibid. 195. Thus the political diary is characterized by 'the courage to reveal the entirety of one's own knowledge' ('Mut zur Preisgabe des gesamten eigenen Wissens'). This courage derives from an elementary recklessness. 'One single methodological quality is decisive if a policial diary is to attain historical value: fearless exposure' ('Eine einzige methodische Qualität ist entscheidend, wenn ein politisches Tagebuch historischen Rang erhalten soll: die Unerschrockenheit der Bloßlegung'), ibid. 194.

[24] See Wolfgang Benz and Walter H. Pehle, *Lexikon des deutschen Widerstandes* (Frankfurt am Main, 1994), 316–21.

[25] Members of this movement belonged to the university-educated upper classes, and some were employed by the regime. See Hans Mommsen, 'Bürgerlicher (nationalkonservativer) Widerstand', in Benz and Pehle, *Lexikon des deutschen Widerstandes*, 55–67.

the 'front of the clear-sighted', the 'good ones', the 'good-minded', or the 'band of brothers'.[26] Although they were a heterogeneous group in terms of biographical background, political objectives, and interests, they all shared one ambitious aim, namely, to overthrow the Nazi government.[27] Their plan was not a polished homogeneous strategy right from the start, but changed as the war progressed. At first they wanted merely to achieve a government reshuffle; the final objective, however, was to provoke a coup d'état by the army with their internal support, followed by the establishment of a caretaker government. Within this provisional government, von Hassell was intended to take the post of Foreign Secretary. Although after 1943 he was no longer part of the inner circle of conspirators, Hassell was arrested after the attempt to assassinate Hitler on 20 July 1944. Sentenced to death, he was executed on 8 September 1944.

Both Graf and Hassell wrote about their lives in the resistance—this was the single subject of each entry. They wrote in a style of camouflage and suggestion. Dissident diaries under totalitarianism comprise an archive of conspiratorial talks and conversations and the Graf and Hassell diaries are no exception.[28] We can therefore call the mode that links the diaries of the two writers a 'counter-world of talking'. This may be the dominant writing mode of dissidents under totalitarianism in general. Records of meetings and talks run right through the two diaries. From these records, we can reconstruct the genesis and development of the conspirators' groups and plans. Some examples: 'Conversation with Hans Scholl. I hope I will meet him more often.' This meeting on 13 June 1942 was probably not the first between Willi Graf and Hans Scholl, but it is the first diary entry in the context of the Weiße Rose's leafleting campaign of June and July 1942. Graf continued his diary entries as follows: 'We talk a lot', or 'We have stimulating conversations until late into the night, with inter-

---

[26] All these auto-designations are used in Hassell's diary. Ulrich von Hassell, *Die Hassell-Tagebücher 1938–1944: Aufzeichnungen vom Anderen Deutschland*, ed. Friedrich Freiherr Hiller von Gaertringen with the assistance of Klaus Peter Reiss (3rd rev. edn. Berlin, 1989).

[27] In this respect Hassell's diaries reflect the attitudes and mentality of the dissident German upper class towards the Nazi regime. See Hans Mommsen, 'Geleitwort', in *Hassell-Tagebücher*, 11–18, at 12.

[28] Diaries written under totalitarianism provide a historically valuable archive which can complement the theory of totalitarianism by the addition of the aspects of privacy and resistance. Beyond their importance as documents they have a supra-individual or mental value as manifestations of humanism.

esting results', or 'The conversation is very fruitful, almost touching on matters of principle.' On 17 December 1942, Graf noted: 'Very interesting conversation with Huber.' It is believed that the subject of this conversation was the drawing up of leaflets and Professor Kurt Huber's contribution. At the beginning of 1943 the group started a new leafleting campaign and acts of resistance such as painting anti-fascist slogans on house walls. The preparation of these actions can be reconstructed from an increasing number of entries such as these: 'In the morning I am with Bollinger again for a good conversation', or 'Later we stay in the studio as guests for a long time and talk a lot, almost too much', or 'The conversation is lively and principled.'[29]

From the beginning similar records of conspiratorial meetings, talks, and conversations characterize the diary of Ulrich von Hassell. However, it contains a more differentiated lexical register since Hassell, an administrator, also used the jargon of his profession. Thus while Graf more or less confined himself to terms such as 'conversation' and 'talk', Hassell also used 'meeting' and 'discussion'. A few examples: 'Conversation with B[ruckmann] and Professor A. v. M[üller] concerning what one could do to express disgust at these methods'; 'A long, historical-philosophical conversation with Kehr'; 'We agreed on further meetings in Berlin'; 'Detailed, very objective and frank discussion'; 'Countless meetings in Berlin'; 'discussions at every opportunity'.[30] Such insinuations about conspiratorial communication continue right through Hassell's diary until the end.

[29] Willi Graf, *Briefe und Aufzeichnungen*, ed. Anneliese Knoop-Graf and Inge Jens, introd. Walter Jens (Frankfurt am Main, 1994), 37, entry for 13 June 1942: 'Gespräch mit Hans Scholl. Hoffentlich komme ich öfter mit ihm zusammen'; ibid. 43, entry for 21 July 1942: 'wir sprechen viel'; ibid. 48, entry for 23 Oct. 1942: 'Bis spät in die Nacht unterhalten wir uns sehr anregend und mit interessantem Ergebnis'; ibid. 85, entry for 5 Dec. 1942: 'Das Gespräch ist sehr ergiebig, fast grundsätzlich'; ibid. 88, entry for 17 Dec. 1942: 'Sehr interessantes Gespräch mit Huber'; ibid. 93, entry for 1 Jan. 1943: 'Vormittags bin ich wieder bei Bollinger zu einem guten Gespräch'; ibid. 96, 8 Jan. 1943: 'Später sitzen wir noch lange im Atelier als Gäste und reden viel, fast zu viel'; ibid. 96, 9 Jan. 1943: 'Das Gespräch ist lebendig und grundsätzlich.'

[30] *Hassell-Tagebücher*, 64, entry for 27 Nov. 1938: 'Unterhaltung mit B[ruckmann] und Professor A. v. M[üller], was man tun könnte, um den Abscheu gegen diese Methoden zum Ausdruck zu bringen'; ibid. 78, entry for 30 Jan. 1939: 'Mit Kehr langes historisch-philosophisches Gespräch'; ibid. 129, entry for 11 Oct. 1939: 'Wir verabredeten weitere Besprechungen in Berlin'; ibid. 133, entry for 22 Oct. 1939: 'Eingehende, sehr sachliche und offene Aussprache'; ibid. 348–9, entry for 14 Feb. 1943: 'In Berlin zahllose Besprechungen'; ibid. 366, entry for 9 June 1943: 'bei jeder Gelegenheit Aussprachen.'

'Talking', 'telling of', 'telling about', 'speaking to', 'speaking about', 'confirming', 'conversation', 'talk'—if there is one typical linguistic feature common to all dissident diaries, it is the frequent occurrence of designations such as these for communicative acts. Since communication is vitally important in constituting the status of dissident, confirming it to oneself and like-minded people, reflecting on it, planning campaigns, and, in brief, making conspiratorial dissent possible at all, it is obvious that communication is a central subject of dissident diary-writing. By contrast, the communicative acts of the regime's leading figures are the opposite of the 'democratic' communicative forms of talk and conversation. In line with the *Führerprinzip*, orders, instructions, propaganda slogans, and speeches are versions of authoritarian communication. Even what is called 'conversation', such as Hitler's 'table talks' ('Tischgespräche'), are the public monologues of a leader who does not allow the expression of other opinions.[31]

While the diaries of Graf and von Hassell are thus similar in their common focus on conspiratorial 'conversation', they can also be considered representative examples of different forms of resistance, and the different functions of diary-writing in Nazi Germany.

1. *Willi Graf: Economy of Concealment*

The phrase 'economy of concealment' perhaps best describes Graf's diary. This characteristic feature comprises verbal strategies of cover, suggestion, and coding. Graf's diary never exposes the Weiße Rose plan. With very few exceptions, such as 'Hans Scholl', Graf never explicitly mentioned names or details of the subjects and plans he was dealing with. For example, in order to avoid names, he made cryptic notes such as the following: 'In the early afternoon, I make an important visit; I get a quick response, and fundamentally we are in agreement'; or 'We talk a lot, and some good ideas are born.'[32] Graf kept secret who he visited on the 'important visit',[33] and the identity of 'we' was not revealed.

---

[31] See a number of entries in Albert Speer, *Spandauer Tagebücher* (Frankfurt am Main, Berlin, 1994).

[32] Graf, *Briefe und Aufzeichnungen*, 93, entry for 31 Dec. 1942: 'Am frühen Nachmittag mache ich einen wichtigen Besuch, sehr rasch finde ich Widerhall und grundsätzlich sind wir uns einig'; ibid. 96, entry for 11 Jan. 1943: 'Wir reden viel und mancher gute Gedanke wird geboren.'

[33] The identity of this interlocutor could not be ascertained by the editors of Graf's diary, cf. ibid. 304.

Graf also used this avoidance strategy when referring to conversations and their subjects: 'Discussions about the structure; some ideas are new to me', or 'A visit to Fr., with whom some important things are to be discussed', or 'We start with a discussion whose main topic was our situation.'[34] 'Structure', 'important things', 'our situation'—such empty phrases were meant to disguise reality. They read like code words. In this respect, an entry such as 'I was late to bed that night'[35] demonstrates the highest level of coding—it is quite certain that this refers to the distribution of leaflets in the city of Munich that night.[36]

Code words. When Graf referred to subversive acts of resistance, he used two terms, 'plan' and 'work', which were typical of his private political language. In respect of the specific action—preparing the leafleting campaign—Graf noted: 'Visit Hans; I am still there in the evening; we really start work; the rock is beginning to move.'[37] It is assumed that on this day the group began to duplicate the leaflets and planned the distribution. This was the last Weiße Rose campaign at the University of Munich in February.[38] Further examples of the use of 'plan' and 'work' are: 'I am spending a great deal of time occupied with the plan', 'We worked hard today for some hours', and 'To fencing, a meal—roll call. At noon visited Hans. Did some writing during the

---

[34] Ibid. 84, entry for 2 Dec. 1942: 'Gespräche über den Aufbau, manche Gedanken sind mir neu'; ibid. 84, entry for 4 Dec. 1942: 'Besuch bei Fr., mit dem einige wichtige Dinge zu besprechen sind'; ibid. 95, entry for 7 Jan. 1943: 'Wir beginnen mit einem Gespräch, in dessen Mittelpunkt unsere Situation stand.'

[35] Ibid. 102, entry for 28 Jan. 1943: 'Die Nacht sieht mich spät im Bett.'

[36] The editors' commentary (ibid. 318) discusses Graf's interrogation about this entry: 'This entry, which undoubtedly refers to the distribution of leaflets in Munich's city centre, concurs with the time given by WG [Willi Graf] in his interrogation on 26 February 1943, in which, given the volume of evidence, he describes in detail his part in the distribution campaign. Similarly, the report sent by the Director of Public Prosecutions Munich I to the Reich Justice Minister on 5 February 1943 quite clearly refers to this campaign: "In the last few days, about 1,300 anti-Nazi, pro-democracy, and pro-federalism leaflets have been found on the streets of Munich' ('Dieser Eintrag, der sich mit Sicherheit auf die Verteilung der flugblätter im Stadtkern Münchens bezieht, deckt sich mit WGs [Willi Grafs] Zeitangabe im Verhör am 26.2.1943, bei dem er angesichts der Beweislast seinen Anteil an der "Streu-Aktion" genau beschreibt. Auch die Meldung des Oberstaatsanwalts München I an den Reichsjustizminister vom 5.2.1943: "In den letzten Tagen wurden etwa 1300 flug-blätter antinationalsozialistischen Inhalts mit demokratisch-föderalistischer Tendenz auf den Straßen der Stadt gefunden", verweist eindeutig auf diese Aktion').

[37] Ibid. 99, entry for 13 Jan. 1943: 'Besuch bei Hans, auch am Abend bin ich noch dort, wir beginnen wirklich mit der Arbeit, der Stein kommt ins Rollen.' There is no doubt that the phrase 'der Stein kommt ins Rollen' refers to the production of the fifth leaflet, see editors' commentary, ibid. 309.   [38] Cf. ibid.

evening. Work.'[39] 'Work'—during the night of 8 February 1943 the group posted freedom slogans on buildings.[40]

Private terms. Another feature of Graf's language was his frequent use of the word 'sensible', especially in combination with terms such as 'conversations', 'discussions', and 'secret understandings'. A few examples: 'From time to time, a sensible conversation develops', or 'This afternoon quite sensible things are said; we understand each other', or 'a sensible discussion until late into the night', or 'After the meal, we have quite sensible conversations about our situation.'[41] 'Sensible conversation' had a special meaning in the context of dissident writing. Here it meant speaking disapprovingly about National Socialism and the war with a like-minded person.

To sum up a few observations concerning the style of Willi Graf's diary, 'economy of concealment' means to talk about subversive actions in the style of camouflage and suggestion, or by using special 'code words' such as 'work' and 'plan', or private terms such as 'sensible conversation'.[42] These characteristics refer

[39] Ibid. 102, entry for 28 Jan. 1943: 'Viel Zeit geht damit vorbei, daß ich mich mit dem Plan beschäftige'; ibid.: 'Heute arbeiten wir einige Stunden angestrengt'; ibid. 106, entry for 8 Feb. 1943: 'Zum Fechten, Essen—Appell. Am Mittag Besuch bei Hans. Am Abend einiges geschrieben. Die Arbeit.'

[40] Cf. editors' commentary, ibid. 322: 'The painting of freedom slogans on buildings in the centre of Munich during the night from 8 to 9 February. In the interrogation of 26 February 1943 WG [Willi Graf] denied taking part in this campaign. But given the "existing points of reference" he had to admit his participation on 2 March 1943' ('Das Anbringen von Freiheitsparolen an Gebäuden in der Münchener Innenstadt während der Nacht vom 8./9. Februar. WG [Willi Graf] bestritt im Verhör vom 26.2.1943, bei dieser Aktion mitgemacht zu haben. Aufgrund "vorhandener Anhaltspunkte" mußte er aber am 2.3.1943 seine Teilnahme eingestehen').

[41] Ibid. 72, entry for 3 Nov. 1942: 'Ab und zu kommt es zu einem vernünftigen Gespräch'; ibid. 92, entry for 30 Dec. 1942: 'An diesem Nachmittag werden recht vernünftige Sätze gesagt, wir verstehen uns'; ibid. 93, entry for 1 Jan. 1943: 'wir sprechen ein vernünftiges Stück bis weit in die Nacht hinein'; ibid. 103, entry for 30 Jan. 1943: 'Nach dem Essen kommen wir zu ganz vernünftigen Gesprächen über unsere Situation.'

[42] The use of code words and private terms is a crucial feature of diary-writing under totalitarianism in general. As life under totalitarian regimes is by definition life in a community, diarists, unless completely in agreement with the dominant ideology or utterly reckless, have to hide their individuality. Cf. Hocke, *Europäische Tagebücher*, 189–90: 'at times of an enforced "sense of community", a purely ideological notion of community which evades specific social demands in the age of industrialization or, like Communism, makes them absolute, the force of the individual personality is in every case reduced, or human beings are forced to live a "hidden" life of their own' ('In jedem Fall . . . wird der Mensch als Ich-Person in Epochen eines aufgezwungenen "Gemeinschaftssinns", einer rein ideologischen Gemeinschaftsvorstellung, die den konkreten sozialen Forderungen im Zeitalter der Industrialisierung ausweicht oder sie—wie der Kommunismus—verabsolutiert, in seiner Persönlichkeitskraft reduziert und zu einem "versteckten" Eigenleben gezwungen'). This 'hidden life of their own' takes place in the diary.

to the function which diary-writing had for Graf. Apart from the fact that diarists felt independent when facing their blank pages,[43] it may be supposed that diary-writing helped them in a special way. They used their diaries as intimate friends to whom moving and dangerous experiences could be confided, as Anne Frank, for example, told her secrets to her diary 'Kitty'.[44] However, unlike Hassell, Graf did not use his notes with the intention of gathering, keeping, and mediating contemporary history for future readers. For him, it was something individual and personal that helped him to bear the enormous pressure of dissident life under Nazi totalitarianism. In this respect, Graf's diary does not display the attributes of text known as 'self-description' ('Selbstdarstellung').[45] It seems that this function, a sign of real privacy, has less relevance under totalitarianism when the diarists live the highly political life of resistance members.

2. Ulrich von Hassell: Generosity of Explanation

'Generosity of explanation' is an appropriate description of the style of Ulrich von Hassell's diary. While Graf only hinted at the Weiße Rose campaign and its activities, von Hassell gave detailed descriptions of the emergence of his own and his friends' dissident thoughts, of the rise and fall of their expectations, and, finally, of their project to overthrow Hitler's government, although he did not imagine an organized and structured project.[46] Other important subjects of Hassell's diary are the group's members and, especially, their different intentions and ideas. Faithfully recording these thoughts and facts in his diary, Hassell used what we may call the itemizing language of a chronicler.

Exposing the conspiracy. Hassell started to write his diary in February 1938 when he was dismissed from his post as German ambassador in Rome. Even before that date he had made no systematic attempt to hide his critical attitude, and he referred to it

[43] 'Vor seinen weißen Blättern fühlt sich der Tagebuchschreiber unabhängig, auch wenn er Angst haben mag vor seinen wölfischen Mitmenschen. Seine Eigenmacht an Kritik wird bald zu einem vitalen Ereignis.' Ibid. 197.

[44] Ibid. 184 n. 2.

[45] See E. U. Große, *Text und Kommunikation: Eine linguistische Einführung in die Funktionen der Texte* (Stuttgart, 1976), 30ff.

[46] It is obvious that the rush of events often did not permit a thoroughly reflected arrangement of entries.

more openly in his diary.[47] During his lifetime he was accused of being too imprudent in his utterances.[48] Indeed, Hassell's dissidence is expressed clearly in almost every entry,[49] for example, when he comments on *Reichskristallnacht*: 'I write under the oppressive impression of the malicious pursuit of the Jews after Rath's murder.'[50] At this period, in the autumn of 1938, the conservative resistance met for the first time,[51] and a few weeks after the November pogrom, Hassell was convinced of the need to take action. In 1939 he seemed to be ready: 'The entire situation leads me to the conclusion that it is high time to put on the brakes. My visitor was of the same opinion.'[52] The following pages of the diary reveal the history of the conservative resistance movement from the perspective of one of its most prominent members. It had a widespread and heterogeneous membership, and so had different ideas about how to subvert Hitler's regime and bring about a post-Nazi Germany. It maintained temporary connections with other movements, such as, for example, the Kreisauer Kreis. In his open style Hassell recorded, for example, the beginnings of this connection: 'I was always concerned that we had too little contact with younger groups. This desire has now been fulfilled, but it has also revealed great new difficulties. First I had a long conversation with Saler [Trott], in which he passionately advocated avoiding any semblance of "reaction", "gentleman's club", and militarism, internally and externally . . . Afterwards I met the clever, cultured Blum [Yorck] . . . With him, I continued the conversation with Geißler [Popitz]. Finally a few days ago . . . I went to him again. I found Hellmann [Moltke], Saler [Trott], and

---

[47] Von Hassell had been appointed German ambassador in Rome in 1932. Trying to influence Hitler's foreign policy from the start, he shared the illusion typical of many of Hitler's conservative allies, politicians such as Papen and Schacht, who unsuccessfully tried to steer him and later used this as a defence. See Mommsen, 'Geleitwort', in *Hassell-Tagebücher*, 11–18, at 12.   [48] See *Hassell-Tagebücher*, 28.

[49] Hassell tried to protect himself and his circle by constantly sending his diaries to Switzerland; alternatively, he hid them in his house, or buried them in the garden (see *Hassell-Tagebücher*, 28).

[50] Ibid. 62, entry for 25 Nov. 1938: 'Ich schreibe unter dem schwer lastenden Eindruck der niederträchtigen Judenverfolgung nach der Ermordung vom Raths.' The entry for this date also provides one of numerous proofs that Hassell's resistance to the Nazi regime had religious motivation. His aim was a return to Christian morality and a constitutional state.

[51] See Hans Mommsen, 'Bürgerlicher (nationalkonservativer) Widerstand', 57.

[52] *Hassell-Tagebücher*, 126, entry for 11 Oct. 1939: 'Die ganze Lage führt mich zu dem Schlusse, daß es hohe Zeit wird, den hinabrollenden Wagen zu bremsen. Derselben Ansicht war mein Besucher.'

Burger [Guttenberg] there, and all four (leader Saler [Trott]) worked on me with passion.'[53] This entry is typical of Hassell's habit of making no secret of his own oppositional attitudes or the actions of the resistance movement.

Code-naming. When Hassell mentioned the group's members, he often assessed their reliability. For example: 'In the event of something happening, Terboven is someone of whom much can be expected'; or 'he [Stülpnagel] makes an excellent impression; not particularly important, but intelligent, clear-sighted, a good Prussian officer-type character'; or 'Zollerntal [Stauffenberg], whom I recently met at Nordmann's [Jessen's] and who made an excellent impression on me'.[54] From a linguistic point of view the entries referring to leading figures of the movement are interesting because Hassell vacillates between extreme carelessness and utmost caution in his use of personal names. Thus in 1939 he sometimes speaks of Goerdeler or Beck as 'my visitor' or 'my friend', while only a few pages later he openly names them: 'At noon I met Goerdeler. He has revised his rather wild plans.'[55] From about 1940 onwards, Hassell apparently tried to be more consistent in giving code names to the group's members. However, some of these are extremely easy to decode since they play on the semantic components of German family names. Thus Goerdeler is Pfaff (ibid. 210); Oster is Hase (ibid. 210); Witzleben is Scherz (ibid. 293); Gerstenmaier is Roggenmüller (ibid. 347);

---

[53] Ibid. 289, entry for 21 Dec. 1941: 'Ich hatte immer etwas das Bedenken, daß wir zu wenig Kontakt mit jüngeren Kreisen hätten. Dieser Wunsch ist jetzt erfüllt worden; grade dabei haben sich nun neue große Schwierigkeiten gezeigt. Zuerst hatte ich ein langes Gespräch mit Saler [Trott], bei dem er leidenschaftlich dafür focht, nach innen und außen jeden Anstrich von "Reaktion", "Herrenclub", Militarismus zu vermeiden . . . Danach traf ich mit dem klugen, feingebildeten Blum [Yorck] zusammen . . . Mit ihm zusammen setzte ich das Gespräch bei Geißler [Popitz] fort. Schließlich ging ich vor einigen Tagen . . . noch einmal zu ihm, wo ich Hellmann [Moltke], Saler [Trott] und Burger [Guttenberg] fand und von allen vieren mit wilder Passion (Anführer Saler [Trott]) bearbeitet wurde.' As in this entry, Hassell often presents himself as a man of integration. This may be one reason for the lack of clear focus in his diary. Hassel's attention goes in many directions, and he tries to absorb and preserve every little detail of the resistance group and its history, thus losing sight of the bigger picture (see also below, n. 60).

[54] Ibid. 352, entry for 6 Mar. 1943: 'Terboven, von dem im Fall eines Falles allerhand zu erwarten ist'; ibid. 372, entry for 4 July 1943: '[Stülpnagel] der einen ausgezeichneten Eindruck macht: nicht überragend bedeutend, aber klug, klarblickend, guter Typ preußischer Offizier'; ibid. 418, entry for 7 Feb. 1944: 'Zollerntal [Stauffenberg], den ich neulich bei Nordmann [Jessen] kennenlernte und der mir einen ausgezeichneten Eindruck machte.'

[55] Ibid. 126–7; 132, entry for 22 Oct. 1939: 'Mittags traf ich mich mit Goerdeler. Er hat seine etwas wilden Pläne revidiert.'

Falkenhausen is Adlerheim (ibid. 345); and Stauffenberg is
Zollerntal (ibid. 410). Moreover, Hassell was inconsistent in his
rather half-hearted attempts at disguise. Sometimes he simply
forgot to use the code names; sometimes he used the first letter as
an abbreviation; sometimes he invented different code names for
the same person. Thus Langbehn was called Streitfuß (ibid. 340)
or Kurzfuß (ibid. 346); Schulenburg was referred to as Lehrberg
(ibid. 347), Sholslott (ibid. 348), or Castelloscuola (ibid. 358).[56] This
technique of absent-minded code-naming was Hassell's only
attempt to conceal the group's identity; in all other respects he
used an open style.

Bookkeeping of intentions and concepts. From the beginning, Hassell
was particularly open when he felt the need to comment on different intentions and concepts within the conservative resistance
groups. This became even more apparent after the defeat of the
German army at Stalingrad and the failure of the Russian campaign. In 1943–4 Hassell arranged his diary as if he were the
accountant of the German resistance movement. The following
examples are typical entries recording conflicts about strategies
and leadership within the group: 'Nordmann [Jessen] recently had
a violent argument with Hase [Oster], who accused him of pre-
tending that his dreams were reality'; or 'Geißler [Popitz] is
anxious about Pfaff's [Goerdeler] "parliamentary" methods. I also
think that Pfaff is too much a man of outdated methods'; or
'There are strong conflicts within the inner circle because Geibel's
[Beck] leadership has so far been too weak . . . Adlerheim
[Falkenhausen] is often rejected'; or 'let down by all those in
whom one had placed one's hope.'[57] Thus, in his diary, Hassell
kept account of names, individuals, talents and abilities, and plans
and projects. The ultimate aim of all these activities, the coup
d'état against Hitler, it is true, was only alluded to in vague terms

---

[56] Hassell coded the names not only of his friends, but also of his main enemy, Hitler,
who was called by his original surname, Schicklgruber, or Schickert (ibid. 285), or Inge
(ibid. 410).

[57] Ibid. 356, entry for 28 Mar. 1943: 'Nordmann [Jessen], der neulich in heftigen
Konflikt mit Hase [Oster] geriet, der ihm vorwarf, Wunschträume als Realitäten aus-
gegeben zu haben'; ibid. 415, entry for 27 Dec. 1943: 'Geißler [Popitz] ist besorgt wegen
Pfaffs [Goerdelers] 'parlamentarischen' Methoden. . . . Auch mir ist Pfaff zu sehr Mann
der alten Methoden'; ibid. 345–6, entry for 22 Jan. 1943: 'Im inneren Kreise starke
Gegensätze bei bisher allzu schwacher Führung durch Geibel [Beck]. . . . Adlerheim
[Falkenhausen] wird vielfach abgelehnt'; ibid. 360, entry for 20 Apr. 1943: 'Alle, auf die
man gehofft hatte, versagen.'

such as 'in case of something happening', or 'the central point'.
Sometimes, too, Hassell used metaphorical language similar to
that of Willi Graf, for example, when he spoke of 'putting the
brakes on the moving vehicle'.[58] The main reason, however, why
Hassell resorted to indefinite terms or metaphors when writing
about the coup d'état was not to conceal clear-cut plans, but the
indecisiveness and disagreement within the group itself about how
to achieve Hitler's downfall. This applied especially to the main
point of disagreement, namely, whether it was necessary to assassinate Hitler. The following seemingly cryptic entry reflects this
dilemma: 'Pfaff [Goerdeler] once again returned to the question
of whether it was possible to carry out the change without the
elimination of Inge [Hitler]; Geibel [Beck] did not want to go in
that direction. Nor did I.'[59] Apart from these vague references to
the ultimate goal and how to achieve it, however, Hassell's writing
style was more often the opposite. His diary provides concrete
information about the group, its ideas, and activities, and can
therefore be used today as an archive of the 20 July group and its
history.

Comparing Hassell's diary with Graf's helps to account for the
different motives for writing a diary which, in turn, led to differences of wording and style. Concerning the motives, I suggest that
Hassell, unlike Graf, did not use his diary to compensate for the
pressure of his dangerous activities. We should be aware of the different circumstances in which Hassell was active. He had to deal
with a relatively widespread group of people and with complex
ideas, and he and his circle also had the problem of how to translate their divergent plans into reality. Therefore Hassell, as an
experienced politician, used his diary mainly to focus his ideas and
reflect on people and plans. Since the diary's function for Hassell
was to gain a general idea of the complex resistance group and its
intentions, he turned to the language of accounting, bookkeeping,
and faithful explanation which has just been described.[60] In addi-

[58] Ibid. 'im Falle eines Falles'; ibid. 'Kernpunkt'; ibid. 'den hinabrollenden Wagen
bremsen.'

[59] Ibid. 410, entry for 5 Dec. 1943: 'Pfaff [Goerdeler] kam . . . wieder auf die Frage
zurück, ob es nicht doch möglich wäre, den Wechsel durchzuführen, ohne daß Inge
[Hitler] ausgefallen wäre; Geibel [Beck] wollte da nicht heran. Ich auch nicht.'

[60] A surviving member of the 'other Germany', Rudolf Pechel, assessed the value of
the published diary and its author as follows: 'Hassell's diaries . . . have documentary value,
even if a superfluity of detail prevents the bigger picture of the resistance and the intellectual forces active in it from emerging clearly. They reveal Hassell's noble personality, but

tion, Hassell was well aware of his role as a witness of contemporary history. He knew that as a historical agent, he was about to write—and thus make—history. Thus the idea that he was recording the history of the 'other Germany' for future historians and generations may have been a further strong motive for Hassell to reveal as much as possible, and cover up as little as necessary.

III *Diary-Writing under the Sign of Persecution and Adjustment: The Diary of Victor Klemperer*

These two examples of dissident diaries will now be supplemented by discussion of the diary of an author who was persecuted during the Nazi period and had to come to terms with the subsequent totalitarian regimes. Victor Klemperer wrote under three different political regimes: Nazi totalitarianism; Soviet occupation; and socialist rule in the GDR. Of course, the subjects and style of Klemperer's diary depend on each of these external conditions, although the thread of his linguistic observations runs throughout his diary for more than thirty years.[61]

Chronicler of the catastrophe 1933–1945. In 1933 Victor Klemperer continued his long-standing habit of keeping a diary. He wrote his diary as a scholar of language and literature, in 1933 as before. Looking at Klemperer's intentions, we notice that they change with the increasing intensity of the regime's influence on his life. Initially Klemperer refused to be a historian: 'I am not writing a contemporary history here',[62] he noted after the first three weeks of the National Socialist government. He preferred to write as he

also his limits' ('Die . . . Tagebuchblätter Hassells . . . haben dokumentarischen Wert, wenn auch eine Überfülle von Details die große Linie des Widerstandes und die in ihm lebendigen geistigen Kräfte nicht klar zum Ausdruck kommen läßt. Sie zeigen Hassells noble Persönlichkeit, aber auch seine Grenzen'). Rudolf Pechel, *Deutscher Widerstand* (Erlenbach, 1947), 227–8. Pechel, incidentally, was not sure whether Hassell was a member of the 'other Germany' at all, given that he remained ambassador in Rome, even in SA uniform, until his violent dismissal by Hitler. While it is certain that Hassell was a member of the 'fighting Germany' in his final years—'history will decide whether he belonged to the "other Germany"' ('über seine Zugehörigkeit zum "andern Deutschland" wird die Geschichtsschreibung entscheiden'), ibid. 257–8.

[61] See Heidrun Kämper, 'Das Sprach- und Kulturkonzept Victor Klemperers', in Karl-Heinz Siehr (ed.), *Victor Klemperers Werk: Texte und Materialien für Lehrer* (Berlin, 2001), 53–69.

[62] Victor Klemperer, *Ich will Zeugnis ablegen bis zum letzten: Tagebücher 1933–1945*, ed. Walter Nowojski with the assistance of Hadwig Klemperer, 2 vols. (Berlin, 1995), i. 6, entry for 21 Feb. 1933: 'Ich schreibe hier nicht Zeitgeschichte.'

had always done, that is, collecting notes for an autobiographical work which he called 'Curriculum Vitae'. As time went by, his notion that he was capable of maintaining a distance from the outside political world proved to be an illusion. Klemperer's efforts to exclude external political events were not successful, and with the onset of discrimination and suppression he became more ambitious. National Socialist politics, and the language of politics, increasingly became his main diary subjects. In 1934 he was dismissed from his post as Professor of Romance Literatures at Dresden university, and in 1935 he noted: 'The baiting of Jews has become so excessive. We expect to be murdered here in the near future.'[63] In 1940 he and his wife Eva had to give up their home and were committed to a *Judenhaus*. 'I should gladly like to write the cultural history of the present disaster',[64] was Klemperer's final objective in 1942. In fact, what he became was the cultural chronicler of the catastrophe from 1933 to 1945 under the sign of persecution, although he did not devote much space to expressing a fear of death. What is dominant is the will to report precisely what he observed around him in his daily life, as represented by the following entry: 'For the first time today, news of the deaths of two women in the concentration camp. . . . Both were . . . transported to Auschwitz, which seems to be a fast-working slaughter house.'[65] One of Klemperer's main reasons for writing a diary was, it seems, to maintain a distance from cruelty and inhumanity in order to retain his capacity to report. We recognize his strong will to resist Nazism as well as his awareness as someone who feels responsible for preserving history for posterity. Thus Klemperer's diary is not only a manifestation of 'inner emigration'. Above all, it is also a diary of critical observation and contemporary comment. His diary is a political chronicle. It documents the politicization of everyday life at the time of the Nazi dictatorship.

The precondition for this type of diary is, of course, that the subjects are not coded. We can underline this point by comparing

[63] Ibid. i. 212, entry for 11 Aug. 1935: 'Die Judenhetze ist so maßlos geworden. . . . Wir rechnen damit, hier nächstens totgeschlagen zu werden.'
[64] Ibid. ii. 12, entry for 17 Jan. 1942: 'Ich möchte auch gar zu gern der Kulturgeschichtsschreiber der gegenwärtigen Katastrophe werden.'
[65] Ibid. ii. 259, entry for 14 Oct. 1942: 'Heute zum ersten Mal die Todesnachricht zweier Frauen aus dem KZ. . . . Beide wurden . . . nach Auschwitz transportiert, das ein schnell arbeitendes Schlachthaus zu sein scheint.'

Klemperer's diary with the two conspiratorial diaries by Graf and
Hassell. Since Klemperer's diary is not conspiratorial, all forms
of conspiratorial language are missing; he neither hides nor codes
what he describes. His language is the overt language of description. This is the reason for a peculiarity of diary-writing under
totalitarianism—the need to hide the diary.[66] In contrast to
Hassell, who recorded neither a fear of discovery nor the places in
which he hid his diary, Klemperer often felt anxious about being
discovered, and he recorded this feeling.[67] Nevertheless, he continued, protecting himself either by hiding pages of his diary in a
book,[68] or by sending the written pages to a friend, which placed
his wife Eva's life in danger every time she took a new bundle of
sheets away from home.[69] As hiding is a characteristic of diary-
writing under totalitarianism, so the difficulty of retrieval is also
typical. Klemperer seriously doubted that he would ever re-
cover his manuscripts: 'Since we arrived here [in Falkenstein/
Vogtland], my chances of surviving have probably risen to about
50 per cent. However, my manuscripts in Pirna, which include . . .
all my work and diaries, I give a chance of 10 per cent at most.'[70]

---

[66] See Hocke, *Europäische Tagebücher*, 162ff. and 185.

[67] Ibid. ii. 19, entry for 8 Feb. 1942: 'The fear that my writing could take me to the concentration camp. The feeling of a duty to write; it is my life's task, my profession. The
feeling of *vanitas vantitatum*, of the worthlessness of my writing. In the end, I continue to
write the diary, the Curriculum' ('Die Angst, meine Schreiberei könnte mich ins
Konzentrationslager bringen. Das Gefühl der Pflicht zu schreiben, es ist meine Lebens-
aufgabe, mein Beruf. Das Gefühl der Vanitas vanitatum, des Unwertes meiner Schreiberei.
Zum Schluß schreibe ich doch weiter, am Tagebuch, am Curriculum').

[68] Ibid. ii. 42, entry for 8 Mar. 1942: 'Now this diary page into the encyclopedia. . . .
Putting it into Ziegler . . . I came across . . . the word "liberal"' ('Jetzt . . . dieses
Tagebuchblatt ins Lexikon . . . Wie ich das Blatt . . . in den Ziegler lege . . . stieß ich . . .
auf das Wort liberalistisch').

[69] Ibid. ii. 260–1, entry for 23 Oct. 1942: 'Tomorrow Eva wants to go to Pirna again
. . . a number of things have to be taken out of harm's way—. . . above all my manuscripts
of course.—Is it right that I burden Eva with this? In an emergency it would undoubtedly
cost her life as well as mine. Today people die for less important things' ('Morgen will Eva
wieder einmal nach Pirna . . . einiges ist in Sicherheit zu bringen —. . . vor allem natürlich
meine Manuskripte.—Ist es recht, daß ich Eva damit belaste? Es würde im Notfall fraglos
ihr Leben genauso kosten wie meines. Man stirbt jetzt um geringerer Sachen willen').
These doubts and twinges of remorse are not strong enough, however, for him to halt the
dangerous undertaking. The dangers it poses becomes apparent when Eva is late: 'Eva
not back yet, and the feeling of fear begins to increase. One says to oneself "It has always
turned out alright", but one also says to oneself that it does not always have to' ('Eva noch
nicht zurück, und das Angstgefühl beginnt zu steigen. Man sagt sich "Es ist noch immer
jut jegangen", aber man sagt sich auch, es muß nicht immer gut gehen'). 27 Sept. 1944;
ibid. ii. 596.

[70] Ibid. ii. 691, entry for 7 Mar. 1945: 'Seit wir hier [Falkenstein im Vogtland] angekom-

Yet, 'Yesterday in the afternoon our surviving belongings from Pirna arrived here. They had their special angels. . . . Above all, the manuscripts have been preserved.'[71]

Victor Klemperer's diary is a testimony not only to contemporary history but also to language and everyday communication under totalitarianism. The most outstanding aspect is, of course, Klemperer's linguistic observations of the totalitarian regime. In chronological order he calls it 'language of the Third Reich', 'new language', 'language tertii imperii', and 'Lingua tertii imperii', until the name is finally found: 'LTI (nice learned abbreviation for Lingua tertii imperii, to be used in future).'[72] These linguistic records are concerned not only with the lexical aspects of the language of Nazism (such as reflections on 'charakterlich', 'fanatisch', 'kämpferisch', 'Gleichschaltung', and so on), but beyond this, and related to the subject of this essay, 'telling the truth'. Klemperer's diaries develop a strategy of revelation that provide evidence of the Nazis' systematic lies: 'The *Anzeiger* carries an article about the harvest, which glosses over indications of the direst need. "Worst fears" have not been realized, it suggests, but we must be very economical.'[73]

Coming to an arrangement 1945–1949. From 1945 to 1949, Klemperer wrote his diary while living under the Soviet military government and German Communist administration. Klemperer had already dealt with Communism in 1933, and in November of the same year he placed Communism and National Socialism into one and the same context: 'both are materialistic and lead to

men, dürften meine Chancen des Überlebens einigermaßen auf 50 Prozent gestiegen sein. Meinen Manuskripten in Pirna aber, die . . . alle Arbeit und alle Tagebücher umfassen, gebe ich höchstens 10 Prozent Chance.'

[71] Victor Klemperer, *So sitze ich denn zwischen allen Stühlen: Tagebücher 1945–1959*, ed. Walter Nowojski with the assistance of Christian Löser, 2 vols. (Berlin, 1999), i. 38–9, entry for 4 July 1945: 'Gestern nachm. kamen die überlebenden Sachen aus Pirna. Sie haben ihre besonderen Engel gehabt . . . Vor allem: die Mss. [Manuskripte] sind erhalten.'

[72] Klemperer, *Ich will Zeugnis ablegen*, i. 622, entry Zelle 898, 23 June–1 July 1941: 'Sprache des 3. Reichs', 'neue Sprache', 'Sprache tertii imperii', 'Lingua tertii imperii', 'LTI'.

[73] Ibid. ii. 211, entry for 18 Aug. 1942: 'Der "Anzeiger" . . . bringt einen Artikel über die Ernte, der unter den nettesten Schönfärbungen krasse Not hervorstehen läßt. "Die schlimmsten Befürchtungen" seien nicht in Erfüllung gegangen, immerhin müsse sehr sparsam gewirtschaftet werden.' For further aspects see Heidrun Kämper, 'Zeitgeschichte—Sprachgeschichte: Gedanken bei der Lektüre des Tagebuchs eines Philologen. Über die Ausgaben von Victor Klemperers Tagebuch 1933–1945', *Zeitschrift für Germanistische Linguistik*, 24 (1996), 328–41.

slavery.'[74] He was convinced of this, and, six weeks later, commented on the new party affiliations of his friends. One had become a National Socialist; the other a Communist. Klemperer saw both conversions as resulting in a loss of 'human dignity'.[75]

In 1945, dealing with Communism became an urgent concern for Klemperer as he himself now lived under Communist rule. Of course, he realized that the reality of Communism was the opposite of the pseudo-reality conveyed by the radio: 'Hardship, administrative chaos, daily violence, arbitrary acts by individual commanders, and official cases of plundering—all this shows that the reality is completely different from what is broadcast on the radio.'[76] During the initial post-war months, Klemperer intended to regain his professorship. He expressed, therefore, not only criticism but also an affinity with Communism. This created a typical state in which Klemperer fell between all stools: 'For myself, I am in a constant dilemma. I would like to be part of the extreme left wing of the KPD [German Communist Party]; I would like to be for Russia. But on the other hand: it is liberty that I mean.'[77] Klemperer felt that there was a true incompatibility between Communism and liberty, and he was therefore under intense pressure. In order to regain his professorship, he had to become a member of the German Communist Party. On the other hand, the Communist version of life without freedom made him hesitate: 'Am I a coward if I do not join . . . ; am I a coward if I do? Are my only reasons for joining egoistical? No! If I have to join a party, then this one is the lesser evil. It alone really presses for the radical elimination of the Nazis. But it is a new bondage in place of the old. However, this cannot be avoided at the moment.—But perhaps I am personally backing the wrong horse?'[78] 'Am I', 'are

[74] Klemperer, *Ich will Zeugnis ablegen*, i. 69, entry for 14 Nov. 1933: 'beide sind sie materialistisch und führen in Sklaverei.'

[75] Ibid. ii. 75, entry for 31 Dec. 1933: 'Beide sind . . . nicht einer politischen Partei beigetreten, sondern ihrer Menschenwürde verlustig gegangen.'

[76] Klemperer, *So sitze ich denn*, i. 138, entry for 8 Nov. 1945: 'uns wird hier doch durch Not, Verwaltungschaos, tägliche Ausschreitungen, Willkürakte einzelner Kommandanten, amtliche Plünderungen andauernd demonstriert, daß faktisch die Dinge ganz anders als im Radio beschaffen sind.'

[77] Ibid. i. 68, entry for 8 Aug. 1945: 'Für meine Person bin ich in stetigem Dilemma. Ich möchte an den linkesten Flügel der KPD, ich möchte für Rußland sein. Und andererseits: Freiheit, die ich meine.'

[78] Ibid. i. 146, entry for 20 Nov. 1945: 'Bin ich feige, wenn ich nicht eintrete . . . ; bin ich feige, wenn ich eintrete? Habe ich zum Eintritt ausschließlich egoistische Gründe? Nein! Wenn ich schon in eine Partei muß, dann ist diese das kleinste Übel . . . Sie allein

my', 'but', 'however', and 'but perhaps'—this is the language of someone trying to find a positive attitude towards problematic totalitarian appearances. Although torn by extreme doubts, finally, on 23 November 1945, Klemperer joined the German Communist Party. Nevertheless, his relations with the Communist Party remained reserved and critical. This is shown especially by the attention which he paid to the linguistic parallels between Communism and National Socialism: 'I must begin to pay systematic attention to the language of the Fourth Reich. It sometimes seems to me that it differs from that of the Third Reich less, for instance, than the Saxon spoken in Dresden differs from that spoken in Leipzig,'[79] he noted as early as June 1945.

The extent of his conversion is illustrated, for example, by his preparations for the publication of the linguistic notes which he had made during the Nazi period. The book is well known under the title *LTI: Aus dem Notizbuch eines Philologen*. In this respect, Klemperer's diary is a very specific case of what has been called 'diary-writing as work-in-progress'.[80] This refers to the reflections on the genesis of a work in diary entries. The work-in-progress of *LTI* is a case of adjusted historical writing. This means that there is a discrepancy between the diary version of LTI and the published version of *LTI*. This discrepancy, of course, was caused by the totalitarian government under which Klemperer lived as well as by his personal aims. Accommodation with the regime was the precondition for him to be able to publish and regain his professorship. The published version of *LTI* was shaped by deliberation and alignment with the new rulers, and this increased the value of the diary from which it was developed. The diary preserved the language of Nazism recorded immediately and directly and without the filter of deliberation.[81]

Public supporter—private dissident: 1949–1959. From 1949 to his death in 1960 Klemperer wrote his diary under socialist rule in

---

drängt wirklich auf radikale Ausschaltung der Nazis. Aber sie setzt neue Unfreiheit an die Stelle der alten! Aber das ist im Augenblick nicht zu vermeiden.—Aber vielleicht setze ich persönlich auf das falsche Pferd?'

[79] Ibid. i. 26, entry for 25 June 1945: 'Ich muß allmählich anfangen, systematisch auf die Sprache des vierten Reiches zu achten. Sie scheint mir manchmal weniger von der des dritten unterschieden als etwa das Dresdener Sächsische vom Leipziger.'

[80] 'Diaristik als "Werkgeschichte"'. Hocke, *Europäische Tagebücher*, 336ff.

[81] See Heidrun Kämper, 'Sprachgeschichte—Zeitgeschichte: Die Tagebücher Victor Klemperers', *Deutsche Sprache*, 1 (2000), 25–41.

the GDR, while leading the double life of a public supporter and private dissident. As a public supporter, Klemperer was a candidate for the *Volkskammer* elections and, indeed, he was elected in 1950. In 1952 he was awarded the National Prize Third Grade for Art and Literature, something he had long coveted. Although Klemperer was a professed citizen of the GDR, as we see, he maintained a distance. 'Where is the truth?'[82] he asked in 1950. His habitual feelings of insecurity and doubt also motivated his diary-writing in the GDR. At the end of his life, Klemperer was irreconcilable with the *Arbeiter- und Bauernstaat*, the state of workers and peasants, as the GDR was known, and saw only continuity and parallels between Nazi and GDR totalitarianism. This inner distance towards the regime, which did not prevent him from belonging to the political class with pride, enabled him to continue his diary-writing.

Klemperer reflected upon the linguistic continuity between the two totalitarian systems. He described LQI (language of the Fourth Reich) as a version of LTI. As under the Nazi regime, he used his diary to record the linguistic traces of the new reality. Klemperer's diary continued to be a chronicle of contemporary politics, and especially its language. Germany was divided in 1949, and this was preceded linguistically when German territory was divided into zones of occupation. Thus even before 1949 Klemperer noted down the terms typically used in a socialist planned economy and working world ('Kombinat', 'Aktivisten', 'Werktätige'); he registered the main terms of dialectic materialism ('Monopolkapitalismus', 'dialektisch', 'positiv'); and an implicit lack of understanding was expressed in the terse comment 'it used to be called "Collegium"', referring to the socialist term 'Kollektiv'.[83]

Beyond this, Klemperer's diary has a special contemporary history quality. From November 1945 he described the Cold War from the Eastern perspective in linguistic terms. 'The West'/'Der Westen' and 'over there'/'drüben' were the significant terms. There were also entries commenting on Western influence, for example, 'penetrating from the West: nuclear-biological-chemical weapons',[84] and linguistic techniques of suggestion in the Eastern

---

[82] Klemperer, *So sitze ich denn*, ii. 39: 'Wo ist Wahrheit?'

[83] Ibid. i. 404, entry for 4 July 1947: 'früher nannte man das Collegium.'

[84] Ibid. ii. 457, entry for 30–1 Oct. 1954: 'vom Westen eindringend: ABC-Waffen.'

language of propaganda: 'Incarceration—languishing: politicized and desensitized. Every politically unsound person in the Bonn republic is arrested and condemned, incarcerated, and languishes. In the same situation here: justly sentenced to prison, etc. Thus elevated language in the service of politics.'[85] Up to 1959 Klemperer constantly made such observations on the East–West division of Germany and its linguistic ramifications.[86]

In conclusion, Klemperer's diary style is the result of a typically German constellation. He wrote first in a state of persecution, then of arrangement, and finally while leading a double life. In view of these different conditions, Klemperer's diaries are an example of the continuity of private language as a version of political language under changing political circumstances. In Klemperer's case, this element of continuity was the attention he paid to linguistic phenomena in two different totalitarian systems. His awareness of language use was the factor that outlasted these changes. It was the 'balancing pole' which allowed him to withstand the challenges of the Age of Extremes.

IV *Conclusion*

We have examined three diaries written under the National Socialist and the Communist regimes. The only common trait that could be observed was the importance accorded by the authors to the subject of 'conversation' and, correspondingly, a high frequency of use of designations for communicative acts. Independently of this, the three diaries are typical of three different types of political language.

As a representative of the youth resistance movement, Willi Graf practised highly elaborated concealing strategies in his diary. He gave neither names nor details, and made extensive use of code words and private terms. These linguistic techniques corre-

---

[85] Ibid. ii. 741, entry for 20 Mar. 1959: 'Einkerkern—schmachten: politisiert u. abgestumpft: jeder politisch Mißliebige, im Bonner Staat verhaftet u. verurteilt, ist eingekerkert, schmachtet. In gleichem Fall hier: zur gerechten Strafe verurteilt, in Zuchthaus etc. Die gehobene Sprache also im Dienst des Politischen.'

[86] For this see Heidrun Kämper, 'LQI—Sprache des Vierten Reichs: Victor Klemperers Erkundungen zum Nachkriegsdeutsch', in Armin Burkhardt and Dieter Cherubim (eds.), *Sprache im Leben der Zeit: Beiträge zur Theorie, Analyse und Kritik der deutschen Sprache in Vergangenheit und Gegenwart. Helmut Henne zum 65. Geburtstag* (Tübingen, 2001), 175–94.

sponded to the diary's function as a repository of private thoughts and feelings. Graf's diary is the testimony of a morally outraged contemporary who could not stand crime and injustice and who acted in accordance with his age and social position as a student.

As a member of the bourgeois, (national-)conservative resistance movement, Ulrich von Hassell had a semi-developed sense of the conspiratorial necessity for concealment. His diary is the testimony of someone who had a strongly developed awareness of his role as a historical agent, whose achievements were part of the better German history, and who therefore used linguistic strategies that revealed as much as possible and covered up as little as necessary.

As one of the few German Jews who survived the Nazi era thanks to his 'privileged' status, Victor Klemperer was the diarist with the least elaborated concealing strategies and with the most highly developed awareness of the conditions of everyday life under totalitarianism. This awareness made him an archivist of the linguistic manifestations of totalitarianism. As such, Klemperer had the self-confidence to see himself not so much as a victim but as a contemporary who was bound to bear witness.

Despite these differences all three diaries are manifestations of dissidence. All three authors, each in his own way, asserted their individuality under totalitarianism and thus defied the regimes' attempts to impose conformity. With respect to the definition of political language, it has become clear that even the apparently most private linguistic expression is a political speech act. We can therefore conclude that political language is used not only by politicians to transmit their political objectives to various audiences, nor only by those who support a particular political orientation.[87] Rather, political language is every kind of linguistic act

---

[87] See Peter von Polenz, *Deutsche Sprachgeschichte vom Spätmittelalter bis zur Gegenwart*, iii. *19. und 20. Jahrhundert* (Berlin, 1991), 548: 'Political language refers not only to propaganda and "manipulation" of "below" by "above", but also to the linguistic behaviour of the masses which support a particular political direction on the basis of linguistic and political predispositions and expectations' ('Unter politischem Sprachgebrauch ist nicht nur Propaganda und "Manipulation" von "oben" nach "unten" zu verstehen, sondern auch das Sprachverhalten der eine politische Richtung mittragenden Massen aufgrund sprachlicher und politischer Prädispositionen und Erwartungen'). Linguistic research examines official political language under the headings of 'language of agitation', 'propaganda', 'persuasion', and 'semantic struggles'. For political language see Wolfgang Bergsdorf, *Politik und Sprache* (Munich, 1978); Walther Dieckmann, *Politische Sprache, politische Kommunikation: Vorträge, Aufsätze, Entwürfe* (Heidelberg, 1981); Josef Klein (ed.), *Politische Semantik:*

that applies to political realities. Hence, as an aspect of the history of political languages, the study of diaries can help to delineate the limits of totalitarian influence and to describe linguistic counter-discourses to totalitarian language.

Bedeutungsanalytische und sprachkritische Beiträge zur politischen Sprachverwendung (Opladen,1989); Gerhard Strauß, *Der politische Wortschatz: Zur Kommunikations- und Textsortenspezifik* (Tübingen 1985).

PART IV

The Growth of Linguistic Awareness
in the Cold War Era

10

The Unknown and the Familiar Enemy: The Semantics of Anti-Communism in the USA and Germany, 1945–1975

THOMAS MERGEL

In January 1947, the American magazine *Life* issued an illustrated report on French Communists. The text accompanying the pictures revealed a certain amazement because the report included photographs not only of the relevant politicians, but also of the party headquarters. Above all, it gave an account of a meeting of a Communist cell. So much publicity? The magazine called the report 'a pictorial scoop' and emphasized the difference between Europe and America: 'This could not possibly have been taken in the U.S., where Communists usually work in secrecy, or in the Soviet Union, where they select their own type of publicity. But the French party, now standing halfway between the two positions, is eager to look like a democratic party and thus induce the voters to put it into power.'[1]

The amazement of *Life* points to differences in the organizational forms of Communism in Europe and America, and also to different perceptions of what Communism was. In the USA the movement was a secretive phenomenon; in Europe it shamelessly appeared in public. In the USA it consisted of faceless men and women, whereas European Communists appeared in public, and had faces and names. Although *Life* did not have the slightest doubt that the French party was as dictatorial as its Soviet role model, it was still surprised that the French Communists behaved like a normal political party. In the eyes of an American magazine, this could only be tactics and camouflage. As I shall argue in this essay, taking the examples of America and Germany, these differences were the expression of nationally different anti-Communisms. Moreover, distinct images of the enemy not only

---

[1] 'French Communists', *Life*, 13 Jan. 1947, 49.

mirrored specific experiences with Communism, but also reflected normative ideas of what one's *own* society should be like.

After the Second World War the 'anti-Communist consensus' formed the basis of political culture in both the USA and Germany.[2] Opinion polls in both countries left little doubt that Communism was a political option only for a marginal minority. The degree of rejection in Germany is revealed by the fact that in the late 1940s a large majority of Germans, given the choice, would have preferred National Socialism to Communism.[3] This was not an option in the USA. But in 1949, more than two-thirds of those interviewed wanted membership of the Communist Party to be prohibited by law.[4] Thus the refusal was consensual. However, the semantics of anti-Communism were quite different in the two countries under consideration, and this points to different views of the enemy, different functions of Communism, and even to different ideas of what Communism ultimately was.[5]

In the USA as in Germany, Bolshevism had, after 1917, provoked panic reactions and created images which deeply permeated

[2] In my terminology, therefore, anti-Communism does not mean a pathological and undemocratic attitude which is necessarily reactionary because it rejects the humanitarian and progressive message of (utopian) Communism. A political-moralistic evaluation of this sort, long widely shared, viewed the pathologies of the lunatic fringe as the true face of anti-Communism. For analytical purposes it is not helpful. Instead, anti-Communism will here be understood as a political attitude that identifies (real) Communism as the antipode of one's own society and thus attempts to influence one's own society. This definition enables a far wider range of attitudes, and it abstains from a normative assessment of political attitudes. Cf. 'Antikommunismus', in Hanno Drechsler et al. (eds.), *Lexikon der Politik* (10th edn. Munich, 2003).

[3] Patrick Major, *The Death of the KPD: Communism and Anti-Communism in West Germany, 1945–1956* (Oxford, 1997), 272; the rates of approval for Communism fell from 35% (Nov. 1945) to 2% (Feb. 1949), while National Socialism was approved by 19% in 1945 and 43% in 1949.

[4] George H. Gallup, *The Gallup Poll: Public Opinion 1935–1971*, 3 vols. (New York, 1972), ii. *1949–1958*, 873. For the anti-Communist consensus during the 1950s, see Michael Heale, *American Anticommunism: Combating the Enemy Within* (Baltimore, 1990), 167–90.

[5] For German anti-Communism see, in addition to Major, *Death of the KPD*, Klaus Körner, *'Die rote Gefahr': Antikommunistische Propaganda in der Bundesrepublik 1950–2000* (Hamburg, 2003), emphasizing the lunatic fringe; Alexander von Brünneck, *Politische Justiz gegen Kommunisten in der Bundesrepublik Deutschland 1949–1968* (Frankfurt, 1978); and most recently Till Kössler, *Abschied von der Revolution: Kommunisten und Gesellschaft in Westdeutschland 1945–1968* (Düsseldorf, 2005). For the USA, where the debate is highly politicized and shaped by a policy of coming to terms with the past, see Richard Gid Powers, *Not without Honor: The History of American Anticommunism* (New Haven, 1995) (conservative); and Ellen Schrecker, *'Many Are the Crimes': McCarthyism in America* (Princeton, 1998), who stresses the pathological dimension. For a discussion of this debate see Thomas Mergel, '"The Enemy in our Midst": Antikommunismus und Amerikanismus in der Ära McCarthy', *Zeitschrift für Geschichtswissenschaft*, 51 (2003), 237–57.

the political imaginations of both countries. In the USA the Communists came from the outside and were thus viewed as aliens; 90 per cent of the members of the Communist Party of the USA (CPUSA) were immigrants. But it was not only this that gave rise to the idea that Communism was something un-American. This idea also grew out of a religious-political tradition which tended to see Communism as an antithesis to religion. In Germany, by contrast, after 1918 Communism had grown into a powerful mass movement with solid roots in the labour movement. Although in Germany Communism was linked to another old tradition, that of the 'other', namely, 'Asiatic' Russia, it was a highly visible phenomenon associated more with the masses than with obscurity.

These perceptions outlasted 1945, but were changed by new experiences with Communism. After the Second World War it was revealed that Stalin had used the intense cooperation of the war years to build up a dense network of spies in the USA. It was not until the Soviet Union came to an end that his success in this endeavour became apparent.[6] Yet since the late 1940s Americans had been angst-ridden that Soviet agents could be part of the US government's inner circle. This experience shaped a widely shared notion that Communists did their work of infiltration in obscurity or underground. By contrast, in Germany after 1945 Communism was, if not a popular movement, at least something familiar. It was closer than ever before, now being associated with the other part of Germany. Moreover, Communism was also closely linked with violence. In the light of the new experience of West German democracy, which also pushed forward a process of political secularization, Communism was perceived as a political religion to be confronted with rationality and democratic belief.

These are the opposite poles of the two political cultures: contrasting ideas of Communism which were also shared by those who considered themselves to be moderates. I do not claim that there was a clear distinction between German and American perceptions. Especially in the realm of ideological conflict, international transfers of ideas and languages were frequent. An outstanding example of these transfers is the Congress for Cultural Freedom and its liberal anti-Communism.[7] In 1950 this interna-

---

[6] Allen Weinstein and Alexander Vassiliev, *The Haunted Wood: Soviet Espionage in America—the Stalin Era* (New York, 2000).

[7] Peter Coleman, *The Liberal Conspiracy: The Congress for Cultural Freedom and the Struggle for*

tional movement united intellectuals from different countries, including many renegades who were considered to speak about Communism with a different kind of authority from those who had never personally experienced it. The Congress for Cultural Freedom promoted a determinedly 'Westernized' concept of anti-Communism. It focused on individual freedom, was doubtful about religious arguments against Communism, and decidedly critical of authoritarian and restorative trends in society. This earned the Congress the dubious honour of coming under scrutiny by the American Communist-hunter Joseph McCarthy. As an international network, the Congress understood its anti-Communism as self-enlightenment, so to speak, and to this extent it was an elitist organization. But the ideas of the Congress for Cultural Freedom also found a response in Berlin's Social Democratic circles around Ernst Reuter and Willy Brandt.[8] However, this organization is not the focus of the following analysis because its influence was limited. Instead, I shall refer to serious newspapers and magazines with a wide circulation in order to identify everyday semantics which were neither limited to the lunatic anti-Communist fringe nor to the intellectual elites. In particular, I shall refer to the US magazines *Life*, *Newsweek*, and *Time Magazine*. In Germany, where magazines of this style were new and less widespread (with the notable exception of the 'German *Time Magazine*', *Der Spiegel*), newspapers such as the *Süddeutsche Zeitung* and the *Frankfurter Allgemeine Zeitung* form the basis of my analysis. These media used language which they did not consider to be propaganda; rather they claimed that it was sober and rational. I shall argue that these semantics constituted nationally different discourses of anti-Communism. Thus, beyond the undoubted similarities, I shall concentrate on the differences.

The period under scrutiny here is mainly the 1950s and 1960s: my analysis begins after the Second World War and ends with the movement of 1968, the Vietnam War, and the Prague Spring. Within this period, a change from an 'old' to a 'new' anti-Communism can be perceived, and this change reflects the fact

---

the *Mind of Post-War Europe* (New York, 1989); Giles Scott-Smith, *The Politics of Apolitical Culture: The Congress for Cultural Freedom, the CIA, and Post-War American Hegemony* (London, 2002). For the German perspective see Michael Hochgeschwender, *Freiheit in der Offensive? Der Kongreß für kulturelle Freiheit und die Deutschen* (Munich, 1998).

[8] Peter Merseburger, *Willy Brandt 1913–1992: Visionär und Realist* (Stuttgart, 2002), 292.

that new types of Communists were coming to the fore. Above all, the change in global politics, with new policies of détente and the USA's reorientation away from Europe and towards Asia from the late 1960s, made for a shift of perspective, with the result that Communism was now regarded more under the aspect of world politics than as an ideological competitor. Behind this new attitude there also lay a growing sense of security, which, coupled with a new feeling of self-confidence, no longer took Communism seriously as an ideological factor. Along with these changes, American and German semantics converged over time, although the languages that construed enmities still remained largely different.

The following analysis will concentrate on three areas. First it will look at the historical modes of self-description implied by the terms 'Americanism' and 'National Socialism'. Secondly, it will examine the different ways of using religious languages and referring to religious ideas. And thirdly, the modes of describing Communists, their bodies, characters, and attributes will be discussed.

I *Americanism and National Socialism as Historical Imprints*

The name of the House of Representatives committee which dealt with Communist activities was programmatic: House Un-American Activities Committee (HUAC). Americans perceived Communism as a deeply un-American idea.[9] Samuel Huntington has explained the rationale behind this. America, he suggests, considers itself a nation which is not legitimized by descent or tradition, but constitutes itself in a deliberate political act. To be a member of the American nation involved an explicit commitment: to become an American meant to avow to a certain way of living. Hence this affiliation could also be abandoned again.[10] To be 'un-American' therefore meant turning away from central doctrines of the American conception of self and thus standing outside the community. To the Republican Senator Joseph McCarthy, who had

---

[9] For this line of argument see Mergel, '"The Enemy in our Midst"'.

[10] Samuel P. Huntington, *American Politics: The Promise of Disharmony* (2nd edn. Cambridge, Mass., 1982), 25. Cf. Hartmut Wasser, 'Die Rolle der Ideologie in den Vereinigten Staaten: "Amerikanismus" als geistig-politisches Fundament der transatlantischen Gesellschaft', in id. (ed.), *USA: Wirtschaft—Gesellschaft—Politik* (3rd edn. Opladen, 1996), 35–56.

spearheaded a campaign against Communism in America since 1950 which took on hysterical features and seriously put into question the civic self-conception of the USA, the Communists, whom he suspected of having infiltrated the State Department, were worse than Judas with the thirty pieces of silver: to betray America was worse than to betray Jesus Christ.[11] *Life* magazine was more tolerant when it conceded: 'Un-American activities are not necessarily criminal.'[12] Yet it was precisely this concession which laid bare the general assumption; even for a moderate magazine like *Life*, un-American activities bore the scent of crime.

Americanism was based on the conviction of a nation being chosen in a very religious sense, and with this came a far-reaching promise of equality and happiness. It could be argued that Communism was a structurally similar utopia, and was in competition with Americanism. They shared the idea of being chosen, and a political vision which had a specific geographical basis, America, 'God's own country', on the one hand, and the USSR as Communism's Promised Land on the other. Both held out promises of equality, albeit different ones: in the USA for those who could make it on their own; under Communism for all proletarians. Furthermore, Communism and Americanism alike offered the chance of belonging to this chosen people as a matter of individual choice. This was different from National Socialism, in which the circle of those who could belong to the *Volksgemeinschaft* was confined to the 'Aryan' race. The purpose of rituals such as saluting the American flag (which became mandatory from 1943 onwards), the 'pledge of allegiance', and the oath to the American constitution was to demonstrate and confirm a free decision in favour of America; acts like these could demonstrate one's belonging.[13] Communism had similar rituals: ritualistic self-criticism; the deployment of proletarian workers; and the singing of the *Internationale*.[14] Americanism, like Communism, was driven by the constant fear of

[11] '[W]e are not dealing with spies who get thirty pieces of silver to steal the blueprints of a new weapon. We are dealing with a far more sinister type of activity because it permits the enemy to guide and shape our policy.' Joseph McCarthy, speech given in Wheeling, West Virginia, 9 Feb. 1950, printed in Ellen Schrecker, *The Age of McCarthyism: A Brief History with Documents* (Boston, 1994), 212.

[12] 'Red-Hunting', *Life*, 3 Mar. 1947, 32.

[13] Richard M. Fried, *The Russians Are Coming! The Russians Are Coming! Pageantry and Patriotism in Cold-War America* (New York, 1998), 11ff.

[14] Cf. Christel Lane, *The Rites of Rulers: Ritual in Industrial Society—the Soviet Case* (Cambridge, 1981).

an internal enemy, of spies, or unknown fellow travellers of the enemy within one's own society.[15] Stalin, like Joseph McCarthy, used the populist instrument of the show trial to combat this fear.

Americanism was characterized by a very corporal understanding of the nation, and this corporality was applied to the enemy. Communism was constructed semantically as something alien, more like a bug, germ, or disease than a social movement or group of people. In the words of the Democratic politician Adlai Stevenson, Communism was 'worse than cancer, tuberculosis, and heart disease combined'.[16] It infiltrated American society, infected the American corpus, and 'crept into the U.S. labor movement'.[17] It was a piece of dirt, a contamination which weakened America from within. That is why the chairman of the HUAC, Thomas Parnell, saw it as his task to make America 'as pure as possible'.[18] J. Edgar Hoover, director of the FBI and one of the most influential theoreticians of anti-Communism, used metaphors of viruses, disease, and infection when speaking about Communism. 'It reveals a condition akin to disease that spreads like an epidemic and like an epidemic a quarantine is necessary to keep it from infecting the Nation.'[19] In parallel to the emerging culture of science fiction movies, Communists were described as aliens from outer space who crept into the heads and bodies of humans. Similarly non-human features were attributed when Communists were depicted as robots who turned other people into aboulic robots as well.[20] *Life* described the German Communist and spy Gerhart Eisler as 'almost a different species of mankind'.[21]

These linguistic strategies, which made Communism something alien by describing it in terms of metaphors drawn from the realm of machinery or hygiene, dehumanized Communists. It was therefore not self-evident that Communists should be granted human and civil rights. From a contemporary German point of view, it was striking that democracy came to an end when Communists

---

[15] Jörg Baberowski shows this lucidly for the Caucasus in *Der Feind ist überall: Stalinismus im Kaukasus* (Stuttgart, 2002). For the USA see Schrecker, *'Many Are the Crimes'*, 119–200.

[16] Quoted in Schrecker, *'Many Are the Crimes'*, 144.

[17] 'How They Run a Union', *Life*, 17 Mar. 1947, 34.

[18] Eric Bentley, *Thirty Years of Treason: Excerpts from Hearings before the House Committee on Un-American Activities, 1938–1968* (New York, 1971), 147.

[19] J. Edgar Hoover, Testimony before HUAC, 26 Mar. 1947, reprinted in Schrecker, *Age of McCarthyism*, 114–20, at 120.

[20] Examples in Schrecker, *'Many Are the Crimes'*, 135.

[21] 'The Career of Gerhart Eisler as a Comintern Agent', *Life*, 17 Feb. 1947, 99.

were involved. A poll held by the National Opinion Research
Center in 1963 revealed that 63 per cent of those interviewed were
in favour of denying Communists the right to give speeches in
public. A total of 77 per cent wanted Communists to be deprived
of their nationality, and 61 per cent wanted Communists to be
imprisoned.[22] No wonder that Communists were not eligible for
an angler's licence in New York State; nor is it surprising that
some cities fined Communists just for being in town.[23]

In German society, by contrast, Communism was something
familiar. To turn it into something 'other' or 'alien' in the way
that Americans did was not possible, as Communism had been a
mass movement prior to 1933. Moreover, on the other side of the
Iron Curtain, German Communists were in power, and many
Germans had personal relations with those 'yonder'. To be sure,
there were also radical anti-Communists in Germany, who sub-
scribed to McCarthyist techniques.[24] The mainstream press,
however, considered the treatment of Communism a litmus test of
democratic culture. Thus it was unusual to employ language
which described Communism as something fundamentally alien.
Though the reference to American languages of anti-Communism
was omnipresent, it was used more as an instrument of delimitation than as a familiar mode of description. One example is the
ban on the German Communist Party (KPD) in 1956, which was
accompanied by an immediate promise on the part of politicians
and the media that there would be no such thing as a 'witch
hunt'.[25] Another front page article in the reputable *Süddeutsche
Zeitung* only superficially echoed McCarthy's language. Under the
headline 'A New Bacillus' it discussed the expected struggle for
words, which was already apparent in the semantic strategies used
by Communist organizations to revalue the meaning of words
such as 'freedom' or 'democracy'. Yet the article was a struggle
for words in and of itself because it expressed fears that anti-
Communism in the American style would discredit all those who
took their citizenship seriously by inducing subservience and fear

[22] Eugen Kogon et al., *Anatomie des Antikommunismus* (Olten, 1970), 98.
[23] Examples in Mergel, '"The Enemy in our Midst"'; Heale, *American Anticommunism*.
[24] For the Volksbund für Frieden und Freiheit (People's League for Peace and
Freedom), an organization led by a former member of Goebbels's staff, Eberhard Taubert,
see Körner, *'Die rote Gefahr'*, 21–3.
[25] This was the German Minister of the Interior's word: 'Keine Hexenjagd, verspricht
Schröder', *Süddeutsche Zeitung*, 18–19 Aug. 1956.

of political deviation: 'McCarthy, who has long been done for in the USA, both morally and politically, threatens to make a nuisance of himself in our country too.'[26] This, then, was the new bacillus. It was McCarthyism itself and the oppression of tolerance which came with it. The journalist Ernst Müller-Meiningen, who also used the words 'witch hunt', wrote about his worry that 'moved by fear of Communism and Bolshevism, to which we have finally proven ourselves to be largely immune, we might once again opt for conformism and fascism, that is, for ideologies which, in the wake of the economic miracle and rearmament, have more appeal than some might believe. Perhaps democracy will succumb again.'[27] The German public perceived the McCarthyist language of hygiene as a sign of the American neurosis. Semantic strategies like the ones just quoted from the *Süddeutsche Zeitung* subversively undermined this language.

This was particularly important since for the German public the struggle against Communism had the immediate appeal of an education in democracy. In the USA democracy was not a matter of concern, whereas in Germany the media and politicians were not so sure about the democratic convictions of their fellow citizens. Communism, therefore, could not be a reason for depriving citizens of their civil rights; instead, the upholding of democratic rights was seen as a test of German democracy. This became very clear in the Rosenberg case.[28] Julius and Ethel Rosenberg, a couple from New York, were sentenced to death in 1951 for nuclear espionage for the Soviet Union. Since then the Rosenbergs had been on death row. An international campaign, joined even by the Pope, demanded an act of mercy because the couple had two young children and there were emotional scruples about capital punishment for women. While the American public, in the fever of McCarthyist agitation, called for execution and denounced all dissenting votes as Communist, the *Süddeutsche Zeitung* sided with those demanding they be pardoned, albeit aware that the Rosenbergs were professed Communists. However, the most remarkable feature of this article was its date, namely 18 June 1953. It appeared on the front page, the very page that was dominated by reports of the uprising in East Berlin the previous day. This position meant that the article could

---

[26] 'Ein neuer Bazillus', *Süddeutsche Zeitung*, 1–2 Sept. 1956.
[27] Ernst Müller-Meiningen, 'Vor Hexenjagd wird gewarnt', *Süddeutsche Zeitung*, 18–19 Aug. 1956.   [28] Weinstein and Vassiliev, *The Haunted Wood*.

be read as a commentary on the differences between the rule of
law and a dictatorial regime: 'Under the rule of law even the most
dangerous criminal may not be treated in such an inhumane way',
that is, sentenced to death and executed.[29]

While the need for purity of the nation led to prosecutions for
deviation in the USA, diametrically opposed motives guided the
treatment of Communism and Communists in Germany. The
starting point was Germany's historical experience of National
Socialism, which was an open or hidden point of reference in all
these discussions. As early as 1930 the Social Democratic politician
Kurt Schumacher had called Communists mere 'red-varnished
Nazis',[30] and since then this parallel had been employed across
party lines. It was used often in the 1950s, and even more frequently during the 1960s. The rudimentary totalitarianism theory
implied in Schumacher's formula did not so much play down
National Socialism as function as a metaphor for dangerousness.
When the Christian Democratic Union (CDU) accused the Social
Democrats of using 'Nazi methods' during the election campaign
of 1953,[31] or when, in 1957, the Social Democratic Party (SPD)
warned against giving Adenauer twelve years in power (like
Hitler),[32] it was not an ideological affinity that was at stake.
Rather it was a violent political style which was called 'National
Socialist'. Hence the foreign policy of the GDR and the USSR
were also subjected to this comparison, and even more so when
military actions were involved. The *Frankfurter Allgemeine Zeitung*
compared the Soviet occupation of Prague to Hitler's invasion of
Czechoslovakia, and in the same article the commentator called
Walter Ulbricht 'a veritable epigone of Hitler who is now letting
German soldiers invade the neighbouring country under the pro-
tection of its big brother'.[33] The language which *Spiegel* used to
describe de-Stalinization was similarly used for the Nazi past:
'With Khrushchev the entire society of the Soviet Union feels
mercilessly ensnared in a fate which was brought upon Russia by
the demonic titan Stalin.'[34]

---

[29] 'Das Streiflicht', *Süddeutsche Zeitung*, 18 June 1953.
[30] Kurt Schumacher, *Reden, Schriften, Korrespondenzen*, ed. Willy Albrecht (Bonn, 1985), 64.
[31] Volker Hetterich, *Von Adenauer zu Schröder: Der Kampf um Stimmen* (Opladen, 2000), 270.
[32] Ibid. 273.
[33] 'Panzer statt Politik', *Frankfurter Allgemeine Zeitung*, 22 Aug. 1968; a number of letters
to the editor also expressed this opinion. See ibid. 30 and 31 Aug. 1968.
[34] 'Heimkehrer: Wer klopft an die Tür?', *Spiegel*, 28 Mar. 1956, 27.

In a way, the Nazi comparison was employed to express a rejection of coercive regimes in general. Russian imperialism suggested obvious comparisons. Thus the *Süddeutsche Zeitung* could compare the Russian invasion of Hungary in 1956 to the tsarist occupation of 1849.[35] The function of these comparisons was to suggest that democracy is non-violent, while dictatorship is brutal. This reflected public opinion quite precisely, as an opinion poll of 1955, displayed in graphic form in *Spiegel*, made clear. Almost two-thirds of those interviewed associated Communism with notions such as 'war and fire', 'world enemy no. 1', 'flight', 'angst and terror', and 'rape', while ideological concepts such as 'government by the workers' or 'nationalization' were marginal.[36] On the other hand, democracy stood for doing things without violence and having confidence in rational discourse. On the first anniversary of the 1953 East German uprising, the CDU deputy Böhm insisted on this point. The events of 16 and 17 June, he said, had proved the power of the non-violent word of truth. 'Only with dedication to these ideas can we achieve unity and overcome terror and its weaknesses.'[37]

Americanism and German references to National Socialism thus placed Communism in relation to their own respective histories. In the USA the language of hygiene expressed a fear that the 'other' would contaminate their utopia, as they were so similar. By emphasizing violence, German semantics condemned the Nazi past and, at the same time, neutralized it in a specific way. After all, it was not violence as such which had made National Socialism so special. To emphasize violence thus achieved both a valid self-description of the Bonn republic and an interpretation of National Socialism which ousted it from the history of German democracy.

One can speculate as to why the language of hygiene was not successful in Germany, which also had a certain tradition of describing enemies. The language of anti-Semitism referred to Jews as bugs or germs, as a disease or infection, and this usage can be traced back far into nineteenth-century Germany.[38] The

---

[35] 'Die Erhebung gegen Moskau', *Süddeutsche Zeitung*, 25 Oct. 1956.
[36] 'Ost-Arbeit—den Brüdern helfen', *Spiegel*, 29 June 1955, 10.
[37] 'Feiern zur Erinnerung an den Volksaufstand vom 17. Juni', *Süddeutsche Zeitung*, 18 June 1954.
[38] Sarah Jansen, *Schädlinge: Geschichte eines wissenschaftlichen und politischen Konstrukts 1840–1920* (Frankfurt, 2003).

description of 'Jewish' Bolshevism was also in this tradition,[39] and
the Soviet semantics of parasites was similarly used to characterize
social or political deviance.[40] Yet this tradition has obviously
been discontinued. If this language was used in relation to
Communism, then it happened contra-intuitively. With reference
to the Soviet suppression of the Prague Spring, the editor of *Spiegel*
wrote: 'It is not only the Communists of this quarantine strip who
pay for Russia's cordon sanitaire, being destined to protect Russia
from infection.'[41] For Rudolf Augstein, the contagious virus was
not Communism, as for J. Edgar Hoover; rather, it was Western
democracy and Western freedom. In other words, the Soviets
were afraid of freedom in the same hysterical way that the
Americans feared Communism. It could be argued that by distancing itself from American usage, the German discourse wanted
to jettison the anti-Semitic tradition of the language of hygiene.
To refuse to talk in this way was to demonstrate that democratic
anti-Communism was of a different kind from Nazi anti-
Communism. Even when negating it, the language of German
anti-Communism remained tied to the past.

II *Communism and Anti-Communism as Religious Phenomena*

Reiner Prätorius has recently reminded us of the profoundly religious aspect of the Americans' perception of themselves as a 'chosen
people'.[42] Communism, too, involves the idea of being chosen, and
American anti-Communists had to deal with these two types of
being selected. They identified the difference as lying in America's
moral commitment, which was based on biblical commandments,
whereas for Communists, all moral limits were said to be subordi-
nated to the imperatives of class struggle. J. Edgar Hoover, one of
the masterminds of anti-Communism, formulated this difference in
the following way:

There is a vast difference between Americanism and Communism. One
teaches morality; the other, expediency. One follows up the Law of God;

---

[39] Alexander Bein, '"Der jüdische Parasit": Bemerkungen zur Semantik der
Judenfrage', *Vierteljahreshefte zur Zeitgeschichte*, 13 (1965), 121–49.
[40] Paul Hagenloh, '"Socially Harmful Elements" and the Great Terror', in Sheila
Fitzpatrick (ed.), *Stalinism: New Directions* (London, 2000), 286–308.
[41] Rudolf Augstein, 'Breschnews Tränen', *Spiegel*, 35 (1968), 20.
[42] Rainer Prätorius, *In God We Trust: Religion und Politik in den USA* (Munich, 2003).

the other, no law. One is founded upon spiritual values; the other is complete secularism. One is characterized by deep religious conviction; the other, by ruthless, atheistic materialism. The Communist world is a world of walls, searchlights, and guards—a prison for the heart, mind, and soul.[43]

Thus America had ideals; Communism did not. The success of the latter was, in biblical terms, the success of false prophets. Therefore American magazines and newspapers called Lenin 'the Communist deity',[44] and Stalin 'a false god'[45] with followers 'who had professed to worship him',[46] yet a god who was still mortal and thus shared 'the common fate of all men'.[47] Anyone who wanted to be a good Communist had to renounce their old religion and turn away from their family, such as was the case with the spy Julius Rosenberg. Descended from an Eastern Jewish immigrant family on New York's Lower East Side, he 'rejected the Jewish faith of his parents (a sore blow to Julius' father, a garment worker who yearned for his son to be a rabbi)'.[48] For *Newsweek*, this secularizing drift of Communism was proved by an interview with a young man from the GDR who did not even know to which denomination he belonged.[49]

This struggle between good and evil was eternal, so to speak. After all, the devil does not switch sides. According to *Time Magazine*'s commentary on Stalin's death, the dictator had established 'a religion of evil', one 'that threatened every country and every people, every truth and every faith. . . . He repealed truth and denied God. . . . But he was just another human animal.'[50] The use of this semantic tradition was by no means restricted to the Cold War of the 1950s; it remained amazingly alive throughout the following decades. Ronald Reagan's famous speech on the 'evil empire' (1983) employed the same discursive strategies. In the USA this speech did not cause as much of a sensation as it did in Europe since its language was well known and well established

---

[43] Address given at the American Legion Convention, Las Vegas, Nevada, 9 Oct. 1962, and printed in J. Edgar Hoover, *On Communism* (New York, 1969), 152.

[44] 'The Real Story . . . the Kremlin's Secrets', *Newsweek*, 26 Mar. 1956, 24.

[45] 'False God Dies, Crisis is Born', *Life* (International Edition), 6 Apr. 1953, 8.

[46] 'The Real Story', *Newsweek*, 26 Mar. 1956, 24.

[47] 'Death in the Kremlin', *Time*, 16 Mar. 1953, 29.

[48] 'Espionage', *Time*, 29 June 1953, 7–10, at 9–10.

[49] 'This Is What a Red-Indoctrinated Youth Thinks', *Newsweek*, 16 Apr. 1956, 22.

[50] 'Death in the Kremlin', *Time*, 16 Mar. 1953, 29.

there.[51] Reagan gave this speech to the Annual Convention of the National Association of Evangelicals in Orlando, Florida, meaning he was among friends. His subject was morality in politics and the religious foundation of American society. Reagan quoted William Penn: 'If we will not be governed by God, we will be governed by Tyrants', and he dedicated a large section of his speech to the internal moral problems of American society, such as premarital sex and abortion. Reagan insisted that there was sin in the world, and that America had its share. Yet the country had demonstrated its ability to overcome sin—and at this point in his speech the Soviet leaders abruptly entered the scene, for they had declared that they accepted only one morality, namely the one that leads to world revolution. This was Hoover's old argument about the instrumental morality of class struggle. According to Reagan, Marxism–Leninism was the second oldest faith, identical to the one that proclaimed: 'Ye shall be as gods.' He insisted that it was a mistake to ignore the aggressive impulses of the 'evil empire'; the Western world could not simply 'remove from the struggle between right and wrong and good and evil'. And, indeed, he ended with the words of the prophet Isaiah: 'He giveth power to the faint; and to them that have no might he increased strength; . . . and they shall mount with wings as eagles.' Reagan's religious motivation was not just a front. Even though he packaged himself as a radical of the religious revival, he spoke in the context of a long tradition of American self-perceptions.

This religiously charged language appeared quite strange to German anti-Communists, and some may have become suspicious when hearing such emphasis because it was not long ago that German leaders had used quasi-religious language to justify the German mission. Instead, German politicians and journalists developed a deliberately sober and rational language to describe Communism and the conflict with it. Religious metaphors were used in Germany as well, however, for the other side. It was the Communists who were the faithful. From this perspective Communism was perceived as a political religion which exhibited all the typical attributes: a promise of salvation, albeit a secular one; the total organization of all the faithful; high priests and possibly a pope; and an inherently violent attitude to heretics and apostates.

---

[51] For the following quotations see Ronald Reagan, *Speaking my Mind: Selected Speeches* (New York, 1989), 168–80.

The difference from the American discourse was obvious. There, America's religion was considered to be the true one, whereas Communism was considered a false religion, a lie. In contrast to this understanding, which saw the conflict between Good and Evil as something eternal, German anti-Communism viewed Communism as an aspect of political modernity, a sacralization of social goods. The reward for going through the 'purgatory of the dictatorship of the proletariat' was to be the 'paradise of the class-less society'.[52] Not the Antichrist, but the great dogmatic world religions had to serve as cases for comparison. Thus Stalin appeared as 'prophet and caliph of the infallible gospel' to the metaphor-laden *Spiegel*,[53] which tried to juggle the different notions of orthodoxy that were associated equally with Islam and Catholicism.

Again, the peculiarity of the discourse can better be understood by asking what kind of semantic strategies did *not* work. In Germany, simply confronting Western Christendom with oriental or even Slavic paganism did not work, despite occasional efforts to do so. The attempt to use the 1,000-year memory of the battle of Lechfeld to invoke a Christian *Abendland* is one example. On the Lechfeld, a lowland area close to Augsburg in Bavaria, Bishop Ulrich had defeated the Hungarians in 955, thus preventing them from invading the heartlands of the Holy Roman Empire. In 1955 the dramaturgy and semantics of this memory were used as a metaphor for the battle against Communism.[54] The German Secretary for Foreign Affairs, Heinrich von Brentano, elaborated the comparison: 'The similarity is frightening. At that time pagan nomad bands from the East stood before the gates of the Occident, before the gates of this town where we are right now. Perdition and doom menaced. Today again, the masses from the East are standing not much further away from this town.' However, readers of *Spiegel* strongly objected to this attempt to present the struggle against Communism as a battle of Christendom against paganism. In a letter to the editor, a certain Dr Hinrichs polemically pointed out that the leader of the 'pagan' Hungarians was, in fact, a baptized Christian.[55]

[52] 'Der Chruschtschewismus', *Spiegel*, 29 Feb. 1956, 34.
[53] 'Stalin oder die Technik der Macht', *Spiegel*, 18 Mar. 1953, 26.
[54] The following quotations are from 'Abendland: Die missionäre Monarchie', *Spiegel*, 10 Aug. 1955, 12–14.
[55] *Spiegel*, 24 Aug. 1955, 5–6. More critical letters to the editor in *Spiegel*, 31 Aug. 1955, 4–5.

Unlike in the USA, religious metaphors describing one's own society as 'good' did not go down well at all in Germany. Admittedly, the idea of a Christian *Abendland* focused a great deal of energy and language against Communism in the early 1950s.[56] But there is reason to believe that the *Abendland* movement was already running out of steam in the late 1950s because the semantic opposition of Christendom and paganism did not convince the Germans. It had not worked before 1945 either. Even the language of National Socialism did not succeed in labelling Bolshevism as pagan. It is a strong indication of the degree of secularization in Germany that this term was no longer effective when identifying an enemy as malicious. In Germany, paganism was no longer terrifying. This was certainly not the case in the USA, where anti-Communism successfully dwelt on religious metaphors because the Christian imprint on society was much more profound. Descriptions such as these confirmed the everyday understanding of common Americans.

These different perceptions of Communism—as the evil empire on the American side; as a political religion on the German side—had important consequences for the issue of whether Communism was perceived as capable of undergoing substantial change. In brief, in Germany it was believed that change was possible, at least in principle, through the kind of critical self-enlightenment represented by the Czech president, Alexander Dubček. In the USA, Communism was perceived to be as unreformable as Satan himself; just like the devil, Communism had to be defeated and eliminated. Thus semantics left a limited range of options when it came to assessing political settings and processes. This is illustrated by Khrushchev's sensational speech at the twentieth convention of the Soviet Communist Party in 1956, which condemned Stalin and Stalinism. In the eyes of François Furet this speech was 'perhaps the most spectacular text for a historian of the Communist idea throughout the entire twentieth century'.[57] The sensation it caused is comparable only to that precipitated by an event such as the Hitler–Stalin pact because the relentless accusation it expressed came not from an anti-Communist or renegade,

---

[56] See Axel Schildt, *Moderne Zeiten: Freizeit, Massenmedien und 'Zeitgeist' in der Bundesrepublik der 50er Jahre* (Hamburg, 1995), 333–5.

[57] François Furet, *Das Ende der Illusion: Der Kommunismus im 20. Jahrhundert* (Munich, 1996), 559.

but from the very heart of the system itself. Moreover, it was articulated by people who had undoubtedly participated in the
system.[58] For the West German press these events gave rise to a
vague hope that Soviet Communism could be reformed. *Spiegel*
saw 'without doubt the beginning of a new phase in Soviet politics', one which it called 'Khrushchevism'. The magazine predicted a period of loosening control and the return to some kind
of downright biblical 'original Bolshevism' which would renounce
the cult of personality (the 'Stalin heresy') and instead reintroduce
Lenin's concept of the collective. In terms of foreign policy, *Spiegel*
regarded any such development as a danger, for it could mean
the abandonment of Stalin's 'Socialism within one country' and
the adoption of a strategy of keeping up with Western capitalism.[59] Indeed, *Spiegel* emphasized the plurality of the Eastern
bloc,[60] and made ironic references to the quandaries of old
Stalinists in the GDR who were now desperately trying to lead
the younger generation, which had enjoyed a thoroughly Stalinist
education, on to new paths.[61]

Things were quite different in the USA. The American press
remained openly sceptical as to whether the renunciation of
Stalinism was sincere. *Newsweek* looked behind 'Russia's mask' and
called de-Stalinization 'a trap for neutral and disarmament-hungry
nations. Anti-Stalinism will be used to chip away the West's unity
and convince uncommitted nations of Russia's new "reasonable-
ness".'[62] In short: 'Tactics are altered. That's all.'[63] The term
'Khrushchevism' was also used in the USA, but with a completely
different meaning, that is, as a mask for Stalinism continuing under
a different name.[64] *Newsweek* even published a column on 'What
Has Not Changed in Russia', focusing on the suppression of the
satellite countries, the military power of the Red Army, and the
Iron Curtain.[65] This view would seem justified only a few months

[58] For the motives and presumptive strategy behind this see Manfred Hildermeier,
Geschichte der Sowjetunion 1917–1991: Entstehung und Niedergang des ersten sozialistischen Staates
(Munich, 1998), 762–4.   [59] 'Der Chruschtschewismus', *Spiegel*, 29 Feb. 1956, 34–9.
[60] 'Ostblock: Die Totenfeier', *Spiegel*, 18 Apr. 1956, 26–7.
[61] Examples: 'Generationsproblem: Die Ideale der Jugend', *Spiegel*, 11 Apr. 1956, 31–2;
'SED: Viel lustiger als man glaubt', *Spiegel*, 18 Apr. 1956, 17–19; 'Stalin-Kult: Abbau in
Wellen', *Spiegel*, 25 Apr. 1956, 22–3.
[62] 'Behind Russia's Mask', *Newsweek*, 2 Apr. 1956, 25.
[63] 'Worldwide Significance of Anti-Stalinism—the Q's and A's', *Newsweek*, 2 Apr. 1956, 26.
[64] 'The Real Story . . . The Kremlin's Secrets', *Newsweek*, 26 Mar. 1956, 25.
[65] 'What Has Not Changed in Russia', *Newsweek*, 2 Apr. 1956, 27.

later, when Soviet tanks bloodily put down the Hungarian rebellion. Events in Hungary appeared to support the Stalinist philosophy, according to which the Communist empire could be held together only by sheer oppression.[66] Communists had different faces; yet Communism always stayed basically the same. It was particularly the twentieth party convention in conjunction with the Hungarian rebellion which demonstrated to the Americans that Communism would not change.

III *What makes a Communist a Communist?*
Character, Body, and Lifestyle

Religious metaphors, associations with violence, views of the masses, and historical comparisons were the frames that shaped what one actually *saw* when facing a Communist, and, conversely, defined the attributes by which a Communist could be identified. Indeed, the two different conceptions of Communism led to completely discriminatory images of Communists as people.

For Americans, to call someone a 'Communist' defined all the other qualities of the individual because Communists had dedicated themselves completely to one idea. They were part of a conspiracy, and therefore they lied and deceived; they were able to put their wives, children, and fatherland last, or even, ultimately, to betray them. During the 1950s, much furore was caused by reports of Communists who had led double lives unnoticed by their wives, or who had abandoned their families in order to go underground.[67] The word 'Communist', therefore, described not merely an ideological orientation, but an entire lifestyle. 'Communist' was code for a mask which hid the specific features of a person or of national diversities. Hence it is not surprising that in the 1950s *Time Magazine* periodically ran a column entitled simply 'Communists'. In it news was bandied principally about Eastern bloc countries, but Fidel Castro and anti-colonial movements in Africa were also mentioned as soon as they were identified as Communist. In this column, Ulbricht or Malenkov did not appear as East German or Russian, but merely as Communist politicians.

[66] 'You can be sure of this: The Kremlin's Stalinists are saying "We told you so"', 'The Kremlin's Weakness, the Red Army's Strength', *Newsweek*, 5 Jan. 1956, 19.
[67] Schrecker, *'Many Are the Crimes'*, 146–7.

Ironically, it was precisely this sort of labelling that made well-informed and experienced politicians distinguish between 'Communists' and 'Russians'. In his memoirs Richard Nixon, deeply entrenched in the Cold War, described Communists as 'masters of bluff' who were 'taught to be conspirators virtually from birth'. But he drew one crucial distinction: 'As Russians, they are very hospitable hosts; they are generous, strong, and courageous; above all, they are proud of their Russian background and extraordinarily sensitive to personal put-downs or affronts. As Soviet communists, they lie, cheat, take advantage, bluff, and constantly maneuver—trying always to win by any means necessary to achieve their goal.'[68] 'Communist' was the description of their ideological character, whereas 'Russian' referred to a national imprint.

Surprisingly, and in stark contrast to the USA, the word 'Communist' did not feature prominently in Germany until the 1960s, whether in utterances by politicians, newspaper articles, or letters to the editor. When it appeared, the word was used almost exclusively for the Communists in Germany. It was rarely used in front page articles concerning the East German rebellion of June 1953, or in descriptions of everyday reality in the Eastern bloc, or in analyses of the competition between world powers. Rather, the enemies were called 'Russians', 'Soviets', or, with reference to the location of the East German government, 'Pankow'. Semantically, the ideology which was so important for the Americans to describe the enemy vanished almost completely behind a nationalizing, even ethnicizing depiction of Communism. In German discourse Communism was described not by ideological features, but much more in terms of attributes such as violence, constraint, or anti-Western attitudes. Whereas *Time Magazine* talked about the 'Communist empire',[69] German newspapers talked about the Soviet sphere of control, or simply the Eastern bloc. This was the only occasion when the language of the *Abendland* worked, but not in a religious sense. To sum up, in American perceptions, Russians or Chinese were essentially Communists, whereas in German eyes Communism was essentially Russian, that is, 'Asiatic'. It was defined as 'other' not in a religious sense, but in an ethnicized discourse, most graphically in a CDU election

[68] Richard Nixon, *The Memoirs of Richard Nixon* (New York, 1978), 292.
[69] 'Hungary', *Time*, 5 Nov. 1956, 30.

poster of 1953, which carried the (anti-Social Democratic) message that 'all paths of Marxism lead to Moscow', and showed an Asian-looking Red Army soldier lurking on the horizon.

This language was derived from the National Socialist armoury.[70] It survived and was renewed in the post-war discourse because it could be linked with a concept of Europe which conveyed connotations of *Abendland* rhetoric but without its explicitly religious dimension. Rather, it referred to (Western and Central) Europe as the place of civilization. Thus the Hungarian rebellion of 1956 served as proof that 'this proud and knightly people' was part of Europe.[71] 'The Hungarians are Europeans just like us. In recent days the thousands who have died as martyrs have borne impressive testimony to this.'[72] It made sense, therefore, to stress the violence of Communism: it was 'Asiatic' violence. After all, the different constructions of otherness could, in ideal-typical terms, be distinguished as such. For Americans, Communism was paganism, a false religion. For Germans, it was a different race—to be more precise, a lower race. For Americans it represented a danger arising from the inside, unrecognized, while Germans were afraid of an invasion of subhumans.

These notions were reflected in physical descriptions of Communists. In Germany there was an older picture which interfered with the newer one. Still prevalent, although in retreat, was a semantics which had dominated descriptions of Bolsheviks since 1917. This was the language of the proletarian, the corporal, and the masses. Communists were imagined as the many; after the First World War they had been depicted as the 'red flood'.[73] But this language was losing ground, since, with the Sovietization of Eastern Europe, the 'masses' were associated with fundamentally different things. Now these masses had fallen prey to their enemies, the Communist functionaries. The functionaries were ideologically inflexible, even ossified. At the same time they were so disciplined as to abandon every independent thought. 'To do nothing more than just be amazed when established values are thrown overboard seems to us to be rather disciplined behaviour and a good start for the necessary ideological re-education.' This

---

[70] Pierre Ayçoberry, 'Der Bolschewik', in Étienne François and Hagen Schulze (eds.), *Deutsche Erinnerungsorte* (Munich, 2001), 455–68, who overstates the unbrokenness of this line of tradition.   [71] Adolf Zopf, letter to the editor, *Süddeutsche Zeitung*, 3 Nov. 1956.

[72] 'Warum helft Ihr uns nicht?', *Süddeutsche Zeitung*, 29 Oct. 1956.

[73] For this discourse see Klaus Theweleit, *Männerphantasien*, 2 vols. (Reinbek, 1980).

was how a critical voice in the *Süddeutsche Zeitung* assessed the astonished yet guarded reaction of GDR journalists to Nikita Khrushchev's surprising invitation to Chancellor Adenauer to visit Moscow in June 1955.[74]

Along with this assessment of the functionaries, the masses acquired a more positive colouring, since they were the ones who stood up against Communist rule. Thus the revolts in Hungary in 1956 and East Germany in 1953 were called an 'outburst of fury of the disappointed masses'.[75] With this change of setting, the masses attained individual features. They were seen as honest workers with names and a family background, as 'good guys' who resisted Communist levelling. 'The powerful East Berlin demonstrations of workers this week and their violent suppression have shown quite plainly to the world that the alleged "dictatorship of the proletariat" in a territory controlled by Communists is strongly rejected precisely by the labouring masses and, if the opportunity arises, meets open resistance.'[76] Moreover, the rising masses had emancipated themselves from the oppressive functionaries: 'So often they had to march, in East Berlin. But now things are different. No bored faces, no standardized patterns, no banners, no papier mâché heads of "beloved labour leaders", no marching music, no lockstep.'[77] Those who demonstrated their rights in this way were, so to speak, middle-class masses, self-confident citizens. In return, the former attributes of the masses were attached to the functionaries, who were now depicted as being uneducated, bad-mannered, and proletarian in their attitudes. Physical descriptions showed functionaries to be the real proletarians. They were excessive drinkers, talked much too loudly, and most were overweight.[78]

In the USA the exact opposite could be observed. Here Communists had always had been few in number. The CPUSA had never numbered more than 50,000 members and, above all, most workers had never been attracted by the movement. Thus, semantically, Communists were portrayed as barely visible,

[74] 'Das Streiflicht', *Süddeutsche Zeitung*, 11–12 June 1955.

[75] 'Die Erhebung gegen Moskau', *Süddeutsche Zeitung*, 25 Oct. 1956.

[76] 'Wenn die Menge auf die Barrikaden steigt', *Süddeutsche Zeitung*, 19 June 1953.

[77] 'Wir haben lange genug rot gesehen . . . ', *Süddeutsche Zeitung*, 18 June 1953.

[78] Like 'chubby little Khrushchev' ('Der Chruschtschewismus', *Spiegel*, 29 Feb. 1956, 34), or Hermann Axen, 'a small, corpulent man' ('Stalin-Kult: wir alle machen Fehler', *Spiegel*, 28 Mar. 1956, 23). Descriptions of drinking rituals: 'Kanzler-Besuch: Lesen Sie Karl Marx', *Spiegel*, 21 Sept. 1955, 11; 'Kommunisten: Amputierte auf den Straßen' (on German Communists binge drinking), *Spiegel*, 4 Oct. 1956, 5.

inconspicuous members of the urban middle classes, with a clear
anti-intellectual bias. 'The pudgy little Austrian-German looked
like a secondhand bookseller or perhaps a secondrate insurance
man. Baldish and bespectacled, only 5 feet 5 inches tall, with an
owlishly genial face, he seemed strangely miscast in his role of
alleged boss of U.S. Communists.' This is how *Life* described the
professional revolutionary and Communist spy Gerhart Eisler,
brother of the German composer Hanns Eisler and the former
Communist icon Ruth Fischer.[79] Julius Rosenberg was described
as 'a mousy little engineer'.[80] Even the buildings of the Communist
world were grey.[81] In American eyes Communists were anything
but violent and bibulous proletarians. Rather, they looked like
everybody else, hidden within the middle class, and exactly this
made them so dangerous. 'They always sneak around', was how a
Wisconsin citizen replied to the question of how he imagined
Communists.[82] For J. Edgar Hoover, Communists were dangerous
because they were so few in number. If they were numerous, they
could not hide from the public so easily.[83] Joseph McCarthy added
a clear anti-elitist tone. When speaking for the first time about his
list of alleged agents in the US government, he pointed to 'the bright
young men who are born with silver spoons in their mouth',[84] that
is, the sons of wealthy families who had been at Harvard or Yale
and were now implementing Franklin D. Roosevelt's New Deal.
American imaginations assumed Communists to be members of the
middle if not upper class; they were well educated and fitted perfectly into American society and its cities, which they took to like a
duck to water.

These were men without qualities and, moreover, without emotions. 'There was no animation in the cold clear eyes behind the
rimless bifocals. . . . Among his relentless, cold-blooded fellow
plotters, Walter Ulbricht stood out as the iciest of them all, for he
had no trace of sentiment or warmth.'[85] Soviet functionaries were
similarly inconspicuous, but this contrasted sharply with the personality cult around Stalin, whose death caused a succession

[79] 'The Career of Gerhart Eisler as a Comintern Agent', *Life*, 17 Feb. 1947, 99.

[80] 'Espionage', *Time*, 29 June 53, 7.

[81] 'Cold War (East Berlin)', *Time*, 22 June 1953, 27.

[82] Cedric Belfrage, *American Inquisition 1945–1960* (New York, 1973), 195.

[83] J. Edgar Hoover, *Masters of Deceit* (New York, 1958), 134.

[84] Joseph McCarthy, speech given in Wheeling, West Virginia, 9 Feb. 1950, printed in
Schrecker, *Age of McCarthyism*, 211.   [85] 'Berlin: The Wall', *Time*, 25 Aug. 1961, 21–2.

problem of a special kind: 'A pale-faced politician in a badly cut lounge suit who has been kept in the shade by a god all his lifetime cannot assume the attributes of a deity overnight. The people have to be educated to see a god where there was only a professional party boss.'[86] Men without qualities do not have it in themselves to become godlike.

While they were proletarians in German political discourse, Communists were regarded in America as ordinary people living in ordinary environments—yet in secret they were very different. Language reflected the fact that there were few Communists in the USA, and that only about 10 per cent of Americans knew anybody who they believed to be a Communist.[87] In Germany, Communism was a well-known, even familiar, phenomenon, despite all the stigma attached to it. Only twenty years earlier, one out of six Germans had voted Communist. For the new Germany of the economic miracle, which longed for a levelled middle-class society, proletarian features were a memory of past times. It was no coincidence that semantically the roughneck Communist functionaries were described in terms similar to those which, only shortly before, had been used for the National Socialists.

IV *The 1960s and the 1970s: A New Communism*

During the 1960s, the anti-Communist discourse of enmity waned temporarily in Germany, only to receive a new boost with the rise of the student movement. The students nourished the almost forgotten language of the threatening masses again. But it was a new kind of Communism which, like the Czech reform movement, raised the question of whether this Communism was the same as the old Stalinist Communism had been. Similar questions arose with regard to the Vietnam War and the diplomatic rapprochement with China. Still, the categories were similar. The Germans talked about the masses (whether good or bad), 'Asiatic' features, and National Socialism. In the USA, by contrast, people talked about inconspicuous middle-class behaviour and agents. Yet it now became a matter of debate whether these categories still applied, and if so, to whom.

[86] 'False God Dies, Crisis is Born', *Life* (International Edition), 6 Apr. 1953, 8.
[87] Schrecker, *'Many Are the Crimes'*, 141–2.

'A Red Guard ran riot in the city streets, a . . . student mob',[88] was how the conservative newspaper *Die Welt* described a demonstration in Berlin early in 1967. *Spiegel* published a photograph of student leader Rudi Dutschke on its front page, and readers interpreted this image as representing an 'Asiatic', even brutish, figure: 'When I want to see something like this I go to the zoo.'[89] Others sent in photomontages of the picture, graphically underlining this interpretation.[90] The animal imagery, which was nothing but a radicalization of the topos Asiatic equals subhuman, attained some prominence when, during the election campaign of 1969, the leader of the Bavarian Christian Social Union (CSU), Franz Josef Strauß, said in public: 'These people behave like animals and the laws made for human beings cannot apply to them.'[91] But all this was controversial now. If anybody supported this sort of language, an opponent always appeared to contest such labelling. Just as the National Socialist past caused strife on both sides, readers argued about whether Dutschke's face really was brutish or 'infinitely more human than the mugs of our average citizens'.[92]

One change was striking: it became customary to treat the matter satirically. This could work both ways and was often ambiguous. When Hitler was described as the APO—the extra-parliamentary opposition—of the 1920s, it was unclear whether this comparison was intended to offend the left-wing extra-parliamentary student movement of the 1960s, or to rehabilitate the National Socialists. Ironic references to Nazi propaganda language could be understood as equating conservative world views with those of the Nazis—or were students to be seen as victims like the Jews? 'An end must be put to the demoralizing and state-subverting attitude of world studentry [*Weltstudententum*, by analogy with 'world Jewry']! We need a student-free Germany!'[93] The historical comparison with National Socialism was omnipresent, but in contrast to the 1950s there was constant debate about how to interpret such comparisons. The satirical treatment added another element of ambivalence by ridiculing the traditional language of propaganda.

---

[88] *Die Welt*, quoted in *Spiegel*, 7 (1967), 39.
[89] Dr Alphonse Schwarz, letter to the editor, *Spiegel*, 1 (1968), 8.   [90] Ibid.
[91] Telegram to the Bavarian Minister-President Alfons Goppel, 18 July 1969, *Spiegel*, 28 July 1969.   [92] Franz Niemrod, letter to the editor, *Spiegel*, 18 (1968), 8–9.
[93] Jan Grother, letter to the editor, *Spiegel*, 11 (1968), 9.

With the student movement, Communism re-entered the heart of German society. It aroused the same fears and provoked images similar to those from after the Second World War. However, voices were now increasingly to be heard which considered a humane Communism possible. The different outlooks and political self-descriptions of the student activists made people surmise that there were different kinds of Communists. This change was paralleled by growing legitimization problems on the part of anti-Communism itself. The left-wing APO movement developed the strategy of anti-anti-Communism and attacked anti-Communists for being anti-democratic themselves. Increasingly, anti-Communism appeared dull and illiberal; thus the term could now become an accusation in itself.

According to the media under scrutiny, the movement of 1968 was generally not perceived as being Communist in the USA. In the public debate there was almost no reference to Communism, even when Europe was at stake. Instead there was much talk about bad conditions for students or authoritarian attitudes in society. German and French students were sympathetically described as 'young radicals' or 'young revolutionaries', but even when they shouted 'Ho-Ho-Ho-Chi-Minh', they were not called Communists. This term was reserved for the GDR regime which, in the eyes of *Time Magazine*, still 'posed a potentially greater peril to the city [of West Berlin] than even the hotheaded students'.[94] The French May movement of 1968 was perceived as a civil protest movement against the old president, Charles de Gaulle, not as a radical revolutionary movement. 'The convulsion was part carnival, part anarchist spree, increasingly spurred on by Communists—but, more than anything, it was a spontaneous spark of national temper.'[95] There is reason to assume that the emphatically public character and expressive self-presentation of the movement of 1968 did not match the idea of Communists 'sneaking around'. Because of their overt character, the 1968 generation could not be Communists in American eyes.

The same impression is conveyed by American assessments of the Prague Spring and the ensuing occupation of Czechoslovakia by the Warsaw Pact armies. American media took note that Dubček was a Communist, albeit a reformist one. And this meant,

---

[94] 'West Berlin: Ignoble Emulation', *Time*, 19 Apr. 1968, 35–6.
[95] 'France enragée: The Spreading Revolt', *Time*, 24 May 1968, 32.

in American eyes, that he was not considering a thorough systemic overhaul. Rather, 'the Czechoslovak people got quite out of hand',[96] and this could explain the Prague Spring: it was a riot of the people against the Communists. The reports delivered romantic pictures of the Vltava with dreamy young people and metaphors of spring ('Czechoslovakia sprang to life'). It was not Communism that had reformed itself in the Prague Spring; rather it was the people who had taken advantage of freedom, gained their own momentum, and tried to get rid of Communism. Thus, ultimately, the actors of the Prague Spring were not really Communists, apart from the men around Dubček who were more driven than driving. However, the Prague Spring, for the first time, suggested that there was a chance of reforming Eastern Communism. It seemed that Dubček had allies in the Kremlin, and that therefore there must be people with similar ideas in Moscow, too. The uninspired Leonid Brezhnev, however, threatened by this 'infection of ideas in the remaining satellites and in the Soviet Union', was driven only by anxieties for his own power. He had to cope with these young reformers, who could not even be named by *Life*, but who were dynamic and future-oriented, whereas Brezhnev and his ilk were depicted as 'mediocre, frightened, divided, totally lacking the sense of direction, the decisiveness, and the drive, which Khrushchev brought to the problems of his day'.[97]

In Germany, the concept of Communism as a political religion proved valid again with the advent of Communist reform movements. At times like these, Moscow turned semantically into Rome, not tolerating any deviation from the dogma. Equally, political reformers such as Dubček were compared to the religious reformer Jan Hus, who took up not only the religious but also the national cause of the Czechs.[98] The occupation of Czechoslovakia became an 'account of the Passion',[99] and consequently Walter Ulbricht was called a 'Judas' because he had supported the Soviet invasion with help and advice.[100] The Kremlin was seen as an assembly of old men just like the Vatican—after all, the widely criticized encyclical letter *Humanae Vitae*, which condemned birth

---

[96] 'The Kremlin has its Dubčeks too', *Life*, 16 Sept. 1968, 21.   [97] Ibid. 23.

[98] 'Tschechoslowakei: Teure Genossen', *Spiegel*, 30 (1968), 61–2.

[99] 'Tschechoslowakei: Potschemu?', *Spiegel*, 35 (1968), 21.

[100] C. Steinberg, letter to the editor, *Spiegel*, 36 (1968), 8.

control, had been issued only one month before the occupation of Czechoslovakia. Like the Pope, the old men in Russia wanted to enforce their true faith by any means: 'Zealots who practise their socialist ardour by means of violation.'[101] Accordingly, the young Czechs were associated with the early Christian apostles. In this imagery, Communism was still conceived of as a political religion, but there was room for a reformation with a new gospel:

The challengers remained Communists, just as Luther had remained a Christian when leaving the bosom of the only true Church. They remained Communists in a way the world had not seen before: Communists who put an end to the corrupt dictatorship of their own party . . . Communists who opened the jails, freed the abased, and rehabilitated the oppressed [one is tempted to add: who made the blind see and the lame walk] . . . Communists who proclaimed the freedom of the press. As the anti-Christ traumatized the pious during the Middle Ages, so the New Communism in Prague traumatized the faithful of the Soviet empire. Prague became a 'counter revolution'. Moscow tried everything to eliminate the heresy and to lead the apostates back on to the right track—in vain.[102]

To describe Dubček as Luther could, in a German news magazine, also imply a glimpse of hope for the GDR: Luther was a German, after all. Thus, to recapitulate, Communism was a political religion, and the new Communists/Protestants were even more part of German society than the older ones had been.

For Americans, the decisive encounter with Communists during the 1960s was the Vietnam War. At first glance, this experience seemed to change American views of the enemy profoundly.[103] As it seemed, these were Communists who were overwhelmingly rural, non-white, non-intellectual, and spoke a language incomprehensible to Americans. On closer inspection, however, the semantics used here strongly resembled the older ones. The Vietcong were invisible and hid amongst the Vietnamese peasants and in the jungle, just as, during the 1950s, the common man or the grey functionary had hidden amongst

---

[101] Gerhard Kummer, letter to the editor, *Frankfurter Allgemeine Zeitung*, 30 Aug. 1968.

[102] 'Tschechoslowakei: Teure Genossen', *Spiegel*, 30 (1968), 56–8.

[103] See Katherine Kinney, *Friendly Fire: American Images of the Vietnam War* (Oxford, 2000); Fabian Hilfrich, '"Nation" and "Democracy": Representations of the American Self in the Debates on American Imperialism (1898–1900) and on the Vietnam War (1964–1968)' (Ph.D. thesis, Free University of Berlin, 2000); Marc Frey, *Geschichte des Vietnamkriegs: Die Tragödie in Asien und das Ende des amerikanischen Traums* (Munich, 1998).

the urban middle class. Consequently, they were also called 'infil-trators',[104] who simply hid out when facing combat,[105] and built underground tunnels so that there was always the danger of a 'Communist presence below'. When chasing them one would surely find 'North Vietnamese trenches and bunkers . . . but hardly a trace of opposition'.[106] In Vietnam, Communists could be identified by the very fact that they were almost invisible. Therefore, in contrast to German political language, the American media always employed a semantics well aware that 'Vietcong' was just an abbreviation of 'the Vietnam Communists'. Thus the traditional picture was confirmed, but also changed, by the fact that these Communists were not middle-class intellectuals, but belonged to another race, came from the countryside, and did not have much in common with Western civilization. In American discourse, too, the ethnicizing undertones of the German image of Communism became apparent. The discovery that the 'other' *looks* different would now become a constant feature of views of the enemy in the USA.

V *Final Considerations*

From the late 1960s the landscape of world politics changed rapidly. The politics of détente, the American–Chinese rap-prochement, and the proxy wars in the Third World brought about a shift of perspective which fostered a view of Communism as a world-political movement rather than as ideological compe-tition. At first glance this did not change much in relation to the images of Communism. Certainly the reform movements in Prague and Paris enabled new perceptions, and some conver-gence between German and American perceptions can be regis-tered. But these changes could not mask the older national patterns of perceptions. There was a lasting civil-religious tradition of the 'empire of evil' in America. The image of the fanatic who dedicates his entire life to a sinister idea, tries to avoid attention, and vanishes among the masses displays all the characteristics of a conspirator. This view remained alive throughout the Vietnam

---

104 'Czechoslovakia and Viet Nam', *Time*, 9 Aug. 1968, 24.
105 'The War', *Time*, 19 Apr. 1968, 25–6.
106 'How the Battle for Khe San was Won', *Time*, 19 Apr. 1968, 30.

War. However, the idea of a middle-class intellectual, the 'secondhand bookseller' as the enemy in the midst of one's own society, receded in favour of a more ethnicized image, as was the tradition in Germany. Here the picture of Communism had long been tied to images of the masses. But the Sovietization of Eastern Europe gave the masses a better image because they obviously resisted the functionaries. The idea of an ethnic Communist came under fire with the student movement, although many metaphors of animals and 'Asiatics' were still current. Instead, the image of the Communist gained an anti-intellectual and generational aspect in Germany. In contrast to the Kremlin rulers, the students were young. But essential elements of the older picture remained stable, such as that of the mob which occupies the streets.

Certainly these national distinctions are to some extent exaggerated. It was possible to describe Communism as 'diabolical' in Germany too. And on the other side of the Atlantic people were, of course, quite aware that the rebellions in Eastern Germany, Hungary, and Czechoslovakia were national uprisings as well, and that therefore the usurpers were not merely Communists, but Russians first. In Germany as in the USA there was talk of 'Khrushchevism'—even if this meant two different things. Communists were criminalized in Germany too, and they were denied civil rights not only in the USA.[107] Yet visible differences in the quality media show that distinct images of the 'other' were still effective. These images were to a large degree the product of different national political cultures. The secularizing language of Germany, like the religious semantics of the USA, related Communism directly to their own society in each case. Their own society was to be identified in the mirror of the enemy. There were different social centres of gravity when it came to describing Communism: the proletariat in Germany; the middle class in the USA. Yet both had a similar concern with industrial mass society and the class at its heart. In Germany industrial mass society was thought of as proletarian, whereas in the USA the same term gave rise to images of a suburban middle class. Both carried specific threats. In Germany proletarian Communists were believed to occupy the streets noisily and violently, whereas in the USA they

---

[107] Kössler, *Abschied von der Revolution*, 269ff.; Alexander von Brünneck, *Politische Justiz gegen Kommunisten in der Bundesrepublik Deutschland 1949–1968* (Frankfurt, 1978); Major, *Death of the KPD*, 257–93.

were considered to be in hiding, be it in the tropical jungle or, as before, in the urban jungle.

11

Semantic Strategies of Inclusion and Exclusion in the German Democratic Republic (1949-1989)

RALPH JESSEN

I *Introduction*

In the German Democratic Republic, as in all dictatorships, political jokes flourished. Today, the websites of GDR nostalgics still display lovingly cultivated collections of this extinct variant of German humour. A curious visitor to such websites would certainly find one of the best-known GDR jokes, typically cast as a rhetorical question: 'Question: the Russians used to be our "friends", after that our "brothers and sisters". Why? Answer: you can't choose your brothers and sisters.'

This fictitious dialogue brings us directly to the subject of this essay. The joke deals with the content as well as the form of rhetorical strategies of inclusion and exclusion endemic in the GDR. It alludes to official metaphors which defined affiliation—in this case, the country's membership in the socialist bloc. At the same time, it veils the compulsory character of this affiliation. Indirectly, it also indicates the integrative and exclusive impact which the canonized terminology had on the people of the GDR: only those who adopted the current phrases were considered to be good GDR citizens. Those who refused to do so excluded themselves. Moreover, the joke demonstrates the limits of the imposition of a particular language by politically motivated pressure. The point of the joke quoted above is, of course, to show that voluntary action is a central criterion for defining one's friends. Many GDR citizens used to have a rather negative image of 'the Russians' and had profound mental reservations about the official ideology of friendship. By joking about the official semantics of friendship and brotherliness they expressed their distance from the propaganda and thus demonstrated the limits of its effectiveness.[1]

This essay discusses the ways in which the official propaganda of the GDR's ruling Socialist Unity Party, the SED, defined relations of inclusion and exclusion. Recent debates on cultural history have emphasized the importance of inclusion and exclusion processes and the distinction between 'own' and 'other' in concepts of collective identity. Internal integration by way of delimitation towards the outside world is a classical pattern for establishing coherence and concepts of solidarity within 'communities'.[2] This is true for social classes and religious communities as well as for inhabitants of different city quarters, but recently it has, above all, been related to the development of ethnic and national concepts of membership. Since Benedict Anderson described nations as 'imagined communities', the process of establishing, propagating, and transferring collective self-images and counter-images of the 'self' and the 'other' has been considered to be constitutive for national communities.[3]

What concepts of inclusion and exclusion were conveyed by the GDR's official propaganda? What kind of communities did it define? What was the relationship between concepts of inclusion and the legitimacy of power? And how did the *form* of official and public communication influence definitions of affiliation and difference? In dealing with these questions I will focus on the Walter Ulbricht era, that is, the first two decades of the GDR's existence, while the peculiarities of the 1970s and 1980s will be touched upon only briefly. There is, however, no doubt that the SED's basic problems of legitimacy, which its policies of inclusion were intended to overcome, remained the same during the forty years of the GDR's existence. Enduring problems of legitimacy were created by the division of Germany, the reinterpretation of the

[1] Jan C. Behrends, 'Sowjetische "Freunde" und fremde "Russen": Deutsch–Sowjetische Freundschaft zwischen Ideologie und Alltag (1949–1990)', in id., Thomas Lindenberger, and Patrice G. Poutrus (eds.), *Fremde und Fremd-Sein in der DDR: Zu historischen Ursachen der Fremdenfeindlichkeit in Ostdeutschland* (Berlin, 2003), 75–98. For general comments on the categories of kinship and friendship see Peter Schuster et al., 'Freundschaft und Verwandtschaft als Gegenstand interdisziplinärer Forschung: Einleitung zum Themenschwerpunkt', *sozialer sinn: Zeitschrift für hermeneutische Sozialforschung*, 1 (2003), 3–20.

[2] See Jan Assmann, *Das kulturelle Gedächtnis: Schrift, Erinnerung und politische Identität in frühen Hochkulturen* (Munich, 1992), 145–7.

[3] Benedict Anderson, *Imagined Communities: Reflections on the Origins and Spread of Nationalism* (2nd edn. London, 1991).

formerly hostile Soviet Union as a country of friends and brothers, the relationship with the National Socialist past, and the forced restructuring of East German society. All these challenges made it necessary basically to redefine the borderlines between citizens and outcasts at various levels. Only if the SED succeeded in conveying a credible interpretation of these circumstances to the population of the GDR, one which would serve as a focal point for a proper 'GDR identity', could the party hope to minimize its chronic deficit of legitimacy.

This essay will deal with two aspects of these problems. First, it will explore a set of typical propaganda strategies and their alleged impact on patterns of inclusion and exclusion in East German society. I will interpret these semantic strategies as constituent parts of a master narrative which invented the GDR as an imagined community. Four recurrent strategies will be highlighted. (1) The *temporalization* of concepts of inclusion and exclusion integrated the GDR and its citizens into a specific narrative of history and future. (2) A strategy of *territorialization* defined inclusion with regard to spatial categories, and these, in turn, were enriched with political qualities. (3) Strategies of *scandalization* were employed to identify and stigmatize political enemies. (4) A rhetoric of *homogenization* was used to characterize East German society as a fundamentally harmonious society. In the second part of the essay I will turn to the specific *forms* and structures of public communication in the GDR. In particular, I shall discuss how the extreme standardization and ritualization of official political language in the GDR helped to sustain, or disrupt, the aforementioned processes of inclusion and exclusion.

II *Four Semantic Strategies*

1. *Temporalization*

One of the SED's first propaganda devices constituted the GDR as an integral whole by placing its population in a specific relation to past experiences and expectations of the future. It is this strategy which, adapting a term coined by Reinhart Koselleck, I propose to call the 'temporalization' of belonging.[4] Even if this

---

[4] See Reinhart Koselleck, *Futures Past: On the Semantics of Historical Time* (Cambridge, Mass., 1985), esp. the essay '"Space of Experience" and "Horizon of Expectation": Two

message was, in principle, directed towards all GDR citizens, its main addressee was GDR youth as 'heir' to the past and representative of the future. The message was spread not only by propaganda, but also through the official historiography which established itself from the late 1940s onwards.[5]

The offer of 'temporal' identification was based mainly on two arguments: one distinguishing between 'good' and 'bad' strands in the German past; the other directing attention towards a future Communist utopia. With regard to the German past, SED propaganda and historiography put forward the concept of two competing paths in German history, one of which—the path of reaction—had resulted in imperialism and fascism as the ultimate stages of the capitalist order, while the other—the path of progress—had led to the founding of the GDR. The GDR gained its particular legitimacy within the second, 'progressive' strand of German history as the apogee of an 'anti-fascist' recent past. The Communist definition of 'fascism' had been canonized in the 1930s by the Comintern, the Moscow-led Communist International, and since then capitalist class interests and the anti-Communist blindness of the Weimar elites had been held exclusively responsible for National Socialism. As the power of these groups had been irrevocably broken in the GDR, the anti-fascist foundation myth assigned a status of collective innocence to the majority of the East German people.[6] The counterpart to this

Historical Categories', ibid. 267–88. Cf. also Lucian Hölscher, *Weltgericht oder Revolution: Protestantische und sozialistische Zukunftsvorstellungen im deutschen Kaiserreich* (Stuttgart, 1989). This book deals with similar processes of identity construction by strategies of temporalization.

[5] Recent surveys of GDR historiography: George G. Iggers et al. (eds.), *Die DDR-Geschichtswissenschaft als Forschungsproblem*, Historische Zeitschrift, NS 27 (1998); Joachim Käppner, *Erstarrte Geschichte: Faschismus und Holocaust im Spiegel der Geschichtswissenschaft und Geschichtspropaganda der DDR* (Hamburg, 1999); Martin Sabrow, *Das Diktat des Konsenses: Geschichtswissenschaft in der DDR 1949–1969* (Munich, 2001); id. (ed.), *Verwaltete Vergangenheit: Geschichtskultur und Herrschaftslegitimation in der DDR*, Geschichtswissenschaft und Geschichtskultur im 20. Jahrhundert, 1 (Leipzig, 1997); id. (ed.), *Geschichte als Herrschaftsdiskurs: Der Umgang mit der Vergangenheit in der DDR* (Cologne, 2000).

[6] For this aspect see Manfred Agethen et al. (eds.), *Der missbrauchte Antifaschismus: DDR-Staatsdoktrin und Lebenslüge der deutschen Linken* (Freiburg, 2002); Christiane Brenner, 'Die mythische Qualität des Antifaschismus: Ein Geschichtsmythos und seine Wirkungsgeschichte', in Clemens Friedrich and Birgit Menzel (eds.), *Osteuropa im Umbruch: Alte und neue Mythen* (Frankfurt am Main, 1994), 169–82; Antonia Grunenberg, *Antifaschismus—ein deutscher Mythos* (Reinbek bei Hamburg, 1993); Michael Lemke, 'Instrumentalisierter Antifaschismus und SED-Kampagnenpolitik im deutschen Sonderkonflikt 1960–1968', in Jürgen Danyel (ed.), *Die geteilte Vergangenheit: Zum Umgang mit Nationalsozialismus und Widerstand in beiden deutschen Staaten* (Berlin, 1995), 61–86; Jeffrey Herf, *Zweierlei Erinnerung: Die NS-Vergangenheit im geteilten*

narrative of the past was the projection of a future in which the East German population and, above all, its youth were depicted as those who would realize a Communist utopia. The propaganda of the 1950s in particular constantly evoked new variants of eschatological expectations. A few typical catchphrases may serve as an illustration: 'Socialism and Communism—the future of mankind'; 'Risen from the ruins and turned towards the future'; 'Country of freedom, happiness, justice'; 'Our youth has a great and wonderful goal. Nobody is allowed to exclude themselves . . . Everybody belongs to the big socialist family.'[7] The official narratives of the past and the future thus defined the population of the GDR as a community of destiny and expectation.

One remarkable fact concerning these intertwined narratives of the past and the future is that they defined inclusion and exclusion not by particularist assumptions, but by universalist ones. The narrative of anti-fascism explicitly located the causes of National Socialism in the universal tendencies of capitalist and imperialist power, not in the supposed peculiarities of German history.[8] This justified the dictatorship of the Communist Party as the radical anti-capitalist alternative and relieved East Germany's population from its responsibility for the past, as long as it followed the path of Communism. The attractiveness of this interpretation hinged on the fact that all responsibility for the Nazi past was shifted onto a clearly defined social group which, after socialism had taken root in the GDR, would be found only in West Germany. The universalist vision of Communism connected the East Germans with the transnational camp of progress and with the future of mankind in general, while 'imperialism' was depicted as producing a society without a future.

Even if the SED's narratives of the past and the future followed a teleological conception of history, the related concept of inclusion was not restricted to mere passive membership, but

---

Deutschland (Berlin, 1998); Ulrich Herbert and Olaf Groehler, *Zweierlei Bewältigung: Vier Beiträge über den Umgang mit der NS-Vergangenheit in beiden deutschen Staaten* (Hamburg, 1992).

[7] All quotations from the book *Weltall Erde Mensch: Ein Sammelwerk zur Entwicklungsgeschichte von Natur und Gesellschaft* (8th edn. Berlin, 1959), 387, 400, and 408. During the 1950s and 1960s every East German teenager received this propaganda book when attending the *Jugendweihe* ceremony at the age of 14 or 15.

[8] Cf. Rainer M. Lepsius, 'Das Erbe des Nationalsozialismus und die politische Kultur der Nachfolgestaaten des "Großdeutschen Reiches"', in Max Haller et al. (eds.), *Kultur und Gesellschaft: Verhandlungen des 24. Deutschen Soziologentages* (Frankfurt, 1989), 247–64.

connected with constant appeals for active participation. The gloomy doctrines of the past were regarded as 'heritage' and 'legacy', and the alluring Communist future as a 'mission' to be carried out by all members of the socialist society. For the GDR citizens, membership in the socialist community of destiny and expectation was not available free of charge. The price was loyalty and collaboration.

2. *Territorialization*

In the years of the GDR's foundation and consolidation, the nation-state was still the dominant concept of collective inclusion. The model of the nation-state was widely accepted by the whole German population, in West as well as East Germany. This implied a double challenge for the SED's politics of identity. On the one hand, the model of a national community contradicted the concept that the GDR and its citizens should be part of a universal community of Communist values which reached beyond all national borders. On the other hand, it was obvious that the power of the SED extended only to a relatively small part of the German nation. With reference to Charles Maier's reflections on territoriality, it is plausible to point out that, in the case of the GDR, the territorial area of political rule (decision space) was not congruent with the area of belonging (identity space).[9]

Since territoriality conveys stable relations of inclusion only when decision space and identity space are congruent, political propaganda had to attempt to reconcile this contradiction. Roughly speaking, two phases of these efforts can be distinguished. During the 1950s, in the first decade after the foundation of the GDR, the SED entered into an aggressive competition on the question of which of the two German states was the 'true' representative of the German nation. The SED's propaganda tried to use the identification resource of the nation to legitimize the GDR. The official language policy put this into effect by using the attribute 'national' in an inflationary way. The label 'nation' was applied to all kinds of organizations, events, and campaigns:

---

[9] 'Territory . . . assures a stable sense of community only when "identity space"—the unit that provides the geography of allegiance—is congruent with "decision space"—the turf that seems to assure physical, economic, and cultural security.' Charles S. Maier, 'Consigning the Twentieth Century to History: Alternative Narratives for the Modern Era', *American Historical Review*, 105 (2000), 807–31, at 816.

National People's Army, National Reconstruction Organization, National Front, National Culture—the list of examples could easily be extended. At the same time, the national rhetoric was connected to a selective concept of national history that only accepted the so-called 'good', revolutionary, progressive, or humanistic traditions of German history as truly 'national' properties. In this way, it was possible to combine inclusive criteria which were universalist as well as particularist (national).

In spite of this reinvention of German national history,[10] the semantics of the nation still referred to 'the whole of Germany' in the East and the West. The area of national rhetoric included friend and enemy, own and 'other'. In this constellation, exclusion and inclusion could only be achieved by excluding the 'others' from the imagined collective of the nation. It is not by chance that images of the enemy were sharp as long as the SED leaders adhered to the concept of a unitary nation in this cold civil war. The 'Adenauer gang' in Bonn was repeatedly reproached with national 'betrayal', 'splitting the nation', 'mental Marshallization',[11] and collaborating with the 'Anglo-American imperialists'.[12]

The GDR's claim to represent the whole of the German people was at no time very credible, although Socialist Party leader Ulbricht used the concept of a unitary German nation even after the construction of the Berlin Wall in 1961. To reconcile the GDR identity and the traditional concept of national identity by re-inventing national history and stigmatizing the political enemies in the West as enemies of the nation had, of course, been attempted and failed long before. It was not until the mid-1970s that Ulbricht's successor, Erich Honecker, drew conclusions from this failure and gave up the concept of a unitary German nation. Instead, the GDR was now presented as its own nation, as opposed to the Federal Republic as a nation. From one day to the next, all references to 'Germany' as a whole were banned from public language.[13] The German Television Channel became the Television of the GDR and the East German 'national' anthem

---

[10] Aleida Assmann and Ute Frevert, *Geschichtsvergessenheit. Geschichtsversessenheit: Vom Umgang mit deutschen Vergangenheiten nach 1945* (Stuttgart, 1999), 175.

[11] Referring to the famous Marshall Plan, i.e. the European Recovery Programme.

[12] Examples can be found in Assmann and Frevert, *Geschichtsvergessenheit. Geschichtsversessenheit*, 178–9.

[13] Cf. Barbara Marzahn, *Der Deutschlandbegriff der DDR: Dargestellt vornehmlich an der Sprache des NEUEN DEUTSCHLAND* (Düsseldorf, 1979).

with its reference to 'Germany, united fatherland' was no longer
sung. East German linguists even went so far as to argue that the
German language had split into two distinct national languages.[14]
From the aspect of semantic inclusion and exclusion strategies,
the identification areas of state and nation were finally unified,
and the congruence of decision space and identity space (Maier)
was restored. The fact that this offer of identification failed to
reach the hearts of the East German people is a different story.

3. Scandalization

The distinction between own and 'alien', alongside that between
'good' and 'bad', constituted a third variation of the official East
German linguistic policy of inclusion. East German society was
to be praised as a 'good' society by stigmatizing and excluding
internal and external enemies as morally inferior, or even criminal. To this end, the SED leadership frequently used the propaganda device of the enacted scandal.[15] The peculiarity of political
scandals is that the infringement of rules by political actors is
made a public issue and thus evokes a storm of indignation from
the general public. Mass media play a key role in this context.
Political scandals deal with the moral order of a society. In some
respects, they are embodiments of the 'moral economy' of a
society, if we may adapt E. P. Thompson's famous concept.[16] The
scandal highlights the stock of values which is considered to be

[14] See Wolf Oschlies, *Würgende und wirkende Wörter: Deutschsprechen in der DDR* (Berlin,
1989); Horst Dieter Schlosser, *Die deutsche Sprache in der DDR zwischen Stalinismus und
Demokratie: Historische, politische und kommunikative Bedingungen* (Cologne, 1990); Manfred W.
Hellmann, 'Zwei Gesellschaften—zwei Sprachkulturen? Acht Thesen zur öffentlichen
Sprache in der Bundesrepublik Deutschland und in der Deutschen Demokratischen
Republik', *Forum für interdisziplinäre Forschung*, 2 (1989), 27–38; Peter Christian Ludz, 'Zum
Begriff der "Nation" in der Sicht der SED: Wandlungen und politische Bedeutung', *DA*
(1972), 17–27; Dirk Bauer, *Das sprachliche Ost–West-Problem: Untersuchungen zur Sprache und
Sprachwissenschaft in Deutschland seit 1945* (Frankfurt, 1993); Gerhard Nauman and Eckhard
Trümpler, *Der Flop mit der DDR-Nation 1971: Zwischen Abschied von der Idee der Konföderation und
Illusion von der Herausbildung einer sozialistischen deutschen Nation* (Berlin, 1991).
[15] Categories for the analysis of scandals in general are provided by Rolf Ebbighausen
and Sighard Neckel (eds.), *Anatomie des politischen Skandals* (Frankfurt, 1989); Dirk Käsler et
al., *Der politische Skandal: Zur symbolischen und dramaturgischen Qualität von Politik* (Opladen, 1991);
Sighard Neckel, 'Macht und Legitimation im politischen Skandal', *Vorgänge: Zeitschrift für
Bürgerrechte und Gesellschaftspolitik*, 6 (1988), 38–48; Dietrich Thränhardt, 'Scandals, Changing
Norms and Agenda Setting in German Politics', *Journal of Social Science*, 30/2 (1991), 13–32.
[16] E. P. Thompson, 'The Moral Economy of the English Crowd in the Eighteenth
Century', *Past and Present*, 50 (1971), 76–136.

valid in a society. 'The ritual of scandal and the punishment of the responsible people provides social systems with instruments of self-legitimacy and purification.'[17] At the same time, it excludes those who have infringed the system of values promoted.

It is obvious that within the politically controlled media of the GDR, an independent scandalization of the political ruling class from the bottom up was unthinkable. Instead, we find the opposite: the production of the scandalous from above as a method of public inclusion or exclusion. The enacted scandal was an important method used by the SED leadership to give its policy moral legitimacy and to stigmatize its enemies. The scandal policy of the SED was also a moral policy. By marking the enemy as morally inferior and criminal, the country's own population was presented as the community of the good.[18]

The propaganda history of the GDR in the 1950s and 1960s supplies many examples of this kind of moral policy. At the show trials of the early 1950s the pattern of the enacted scandal was greatly in evidence. In 1950, for example, some managers were given a show trial of this sort. Characteristically, it took place in a theatre building and was followed by 1,200 spectators every day. The defendants were accused of having transferred money from a formerly private company to the West and thus having damaged 'national property'. Basically, its purpose was to criminalize practices which were 'normal' in a private economy and morally to exclude the actors. For this purpose, the court and the controlled media mobilized the whole rhetoric of scandal and moral indignation. 'Unmasked—the story of an uncovered fraud', we read in a booklet on the 'robber trust', whose 'spiderweb' spread over the whole of Germany. The defendants were 'agents' of 'inferior character', 'corrupt subjects', 'corrupt saboteurs', and 'notorious criminals' who had hatched a 'conspiracy' against 'national property'. First they had to learn how 'to behave like good humans in a democratic state'.[19] In the courtroom, there was no talk of Marx and Lenin, but the private economy was described as a scandalous offence against law and morality.

[17] Andrei S. Markovits and Mark Silverstein, 'Macht und Verfahren: Die Geburt des politischen Skandals aus der Widersprüchlichkeit liberaler Demokratien', in Ebbighausen and Neckel (eds.), *Anatomie des politischen Skandals*, 151–70, at 154 (my translation).

[18] Cf. the essays in Martin Sabrow (ed.), *Skandal und Diktatur: Formen öffentlicher Empörung im NS-Staat und in der DDR* (Göttingen, 2004).

[19] *Entlarvt—Die Geschichte eines aufgedeckten Riesenbetruges* (Berlin, n.d. [1950]).

In the propaganda battles against the Federal Republic, instrumentalized scandals also played a prominent role. The SED scandal policymakers went to great lengths to prove that the top of West German society was infiltrated by Nazis. In this way, it was possible to keep up the anti-fascist legitimacy myth of their own regime and, at the same time, to denounce their Western competitor. The SED's West Commission launched a campaign against Hans Globke, one of the top officials in the administration of the West German Chancellor, Konrad Adenauer, denouncing Globke's Nazi involvement. This campaign lasted a number of years until a show trial was held in 1963, in his absence. A similar case was the campaign against the West German Federal President, Heinrich Lübke, who was accused of having participated in the construction of Nazi concentration camps. Among other things, faked documents were used to give plausibility to a story without any real basis.[20]

The importance of the scandal itself in these cases and the unimportance of actually persecuting Nazi delinquents is revealed by the fact that the GDR media obsessively denounced the West German federal government for not bringing to trial the murderers of Communist leader Ernst Thälmann, who had been executed at Buchenwald concentration camp in the summer of 1944. In reality, only the GDR state security police knew of the prime suspect's whereabouts in West Germany, but they did not inform the West German authorities. Fostering the scandal of Western courts which were unwilling to prosecute was much more important than prosecuting Thälmann's murderers.[21] More examples could be cited. The decisive point was to disqualify the political enemy by the semantics of moralization and criminalization and indirectly to portray the majority of GDR citizens as a collective of 'proper' citizens.[22]

4. Homogenization

By employing strategies of temporalization, territorialization, and moralization through enacted scandals the SED propaganda

---

[20] Jutta Illichmann, *Die DDR und die Juden: Die deutschlandpolitische Instrumentalisierung von Juden und Judentum durch die Partei- und Staatsführung der SBZ/DDR von 1945 bis 1990* (Frankfurt, 1997), 176–83.

[21] Falco Werkentin, *Politische Strafjustiz in der Ära Ulbricht* (Berlin, 1995), 215–34.

[22] Marie-Luise Frein-Plischke, *Wortschatz Bundesrepublik-DDR: Semantische Untersuchungen anhand von Personalkollektiva* (Düsseldorf, 1987).

machine of the 1950s and 1960s set out to create the fiction of a
purified society. 'Enemies' were embodiments of the past or the
outside world. While 'others' were externalized, East German
society itself was made the object of an inclusive rhetoric whose
most spectacular feature was the image of a conflict-free society.
Although internal 'enemies' were made the subject of public
attacks even after the construction of the Berlin Wall, on the
whole, the party's self-description presented a picture of social
harmony—the fourth aspect of East German inclusion rhetoric
which must be taken into account here.

One of the most frequently used inclusive terms was the word
'people' (*Volk*) that saturated the public language in innumerable
combinations from People's Army to People's Elections.[23] The
long and highly ambivalent history of the word 'people' and its
political connotations, and ultimately its inflationary use by the
National Socialists, did not prevent the SED from using this
diffuse label as a general phrase of inclusion. Its blurred positive
connotations in particular were appropriate for addressing the
people of the GDR as a whole in an emotional way and to define
them as a homogeneous unit.[24] One reason why the word 'people'
was especially suited for use as a generalized code of inclusion is
that in the German language, as in many other European languages, it can have two different connotations. On the one hand,
'people' means the citizens and bearers of the nation as a whole;
this is a definition which, traditionally, is to be found more on the
right side of the political spectrum. On the other hand, the
'people' can also be identified with 'the masses', the lower classes
or the (hard) working part of the population; this definition, of
course, was more suitable for left-wing propaganda purposes. In
the public language of the SED, these two meanings increasingly
came to coincide. If the intention was to describe the 'progressive
movements of the people' in history, the lower classes were
addressed. In the socialist society of the GDR, however, the
'people' included all parts of society.[25]

---

[23] Examples in Herbert Bartholmes, *Das Wort 'Volk' im Sprachgebrauch der SED*
(Düsseldorf, 1964); id., '"Volk" als Bestimmungswort in Zusammensetzungen im
Sprachgebrauch der Sozialistischen Einheitspartei Deutschlands', in *Das Aueler Protokoll:
Deutsche Sprache im Spannungsfeld zwischen West und Ost* (Düsseldorf, 1964), 40–57.

[24] Hans Heinrich Reich, *Sprache und Politik: Untersuchungen zu Wortschatz und Wortwahl des
offiziellen Sprachgebrauchs in der DDR* (Munich, 1968), 220.

[25] Bartholmes, '"Volk" als Bestimmungswort', 40–2.

In addition to making excessive use of the obviously unifying force of the word 'people', SED propagandists also managed to impress an integrative sense onto the whole vocabulary of 'class', despite its original connotations of antagonism. Thus, even when lexicographical references were made to the Marxist–Leninist terminology of 'class', notions of harmony prevailed. The 'working class', the 'class of farmers', the 'intelligentsia', and all other 'working classes' were depicted as maintaining 'relations of mutual help and co-operation in all areas of social life'.[26] The semantics of integration and inclusion were omnipresent, for example, in the continuous conjuring-up of 'unity', 'friendship', and brotherhood.[27] Moreover, the idea of social groups 'getting closer' to each other and entering 'alliances' reflects this rhetoric of community, as do various slogans, such as the exhortation that the attitude of the socialist citizen should change 'from me to we'. 'Join in, let's rule together,' the SED called out to the citizens of the GDR, and in his later years Ulbricht spoke of the 'socialist community of humans', a phrase which totally abandoned the notion of a socially stratified society.[28]

The brutal reality of dictatorial rule was thus wrapped up in a semantics of community which no longer had any legitimate words to designate conflict, a clash of interests, competition, or inequality. Even when this fiction of community finally collapsed in 1989, both sides remained strangely committed to this GDR language of community. While the head of the Stasi, the Minister of State Security, Erich Mielke, was stammering his most famous sentence, 'But you know that I love you all,' in the East German parliament, the People's Chamber, the demonstrators on the streets were crying out: 'We are the people!'[29]

---

[26] Entry: 'Klasse, soziale', in *Wörterbuch der marxistisch-leninistischen Soziologie* (Berlin, 1983), 343.

[27] See Herbert Bartholmes, *Bruder, Bürger, Freund, Genosse und andere Wörter der sozialistischen Terminologie: Wortgeschichtliche Beiträge* (Göteborg, 1970).

[28] Schlosser, *Die deutsche Sprache in der DDR*, 16.

[29] Armin Mitter and Stefan Wolle (eds.), *Ich liebe euch doch alle! Befehle und Lageberichte des MfS* (Berlin, 1990); Hartmut Zwahr, *Ende einer Selbstzerstörung: Leipzig und die Revolution in der DDR* (Göttingen, 1993); Christian Bergmann, *Die Sprache der Stasi: Ein Beitrag zur Sprachkritik* (Göttingen, 1999).

III *The Effects of Forms and Structures of Public Communication in the GDR*

The preceding sections have discussed the characteristic features of the GDR's official language with regard to semantic content. I have identified and explained the key concepts, narratives, rhetorical devices, and patterns of argument used by SED politicians, historians, and propagandists who proclaimed the GDR's internal unity and tried to define its external enemies. In this section I shall briefly examine the *formal* side of official communication in the GDR and explain its inclusionary and exclusionary effects.[30]

The political language of the GDR, whether spoken or written, whether appearing openly in the mass media or hidden in internal reports and files, was characterized by a number of stylistic, grammatical, and symbolic features. First, the dominant ideology was present in all contexts of communication, not only in public discourse, but also in internal administrative correspondence. Ideological language was an integral part of the way in which the SED regime administered itself. Beyond this, anybody who has ever dealt with East German history knows that the standard political language of the GDR had a number of stylistic peculiarities.[31] Thus, for example, the passive voice was widely used, and almost every piece of political writing used phrases such as 'objective development' or 'further completion'. These stylistic features served to confer upon every political decision or social process the dignity of fulfilling the 'laws of history' without identifying responsible individual or collective actors. Another element typical of East German official language was its high level of formalization. Newspaper articles usually named all the titles and functions of state officials, and internal reports always had the same structure. Sometimes researchers in East German archive files feel that they are reading highly formalized medieval documents. Not individual style, a personal way of writing, or individual rhetoric, but adaptation and subordination were rewarded. Even oral contributions

---

[30] Cf. Ralph Jessen, 'Diktatorische Herrschaft als kommunikative Praxis: Überlegungen zum Zusammenhang von "Bürokratie" und Sprachnormierung in der DDR-Geschichte', in Alf Lüdtke and Peter Becker (eds.), *Akten. Eingaben. Schaufenster: Die DDR und ihre Texte. Erkundungen zu Herrschaft und Alltag* (Berlin, 1997), 57–75.

[31] For a more thorough investigation of these see Steffen Pappert, *Politische Sprachspiele in der DDR: Kommunikative Entdifferenzierungsprozesse und ihre Auswirkungen auf den öffentlichen Sprachgebrauch* (Frankfurt, 2003).

to discussions at public events were in most cases prepared in writing. Official communication in the GDR has been compared with the notorious *Plattenbauten*, residential buildings assembled out of huge, prefabricated building blocks. In the same way, official communication was ready-made, consisting of prefabricated elements which were put together.[32] If speakers or writers deviated too far from such given wording, they were suspected of 'subjectivism', 'voluntarism', or 'spontaneity'.

All in all, public language in the GDR had a strong tendency towards ritualization, which again has important implications for the issue of inclusion and exclusion.[33] Language rituals in general are characterized by features such as repetition, stylization, and formalization. These typically occur in situations of public communication when speakers or writers adopt given roles and use strongly standardized language. Religious liturgies or the awarding of academic honours are good examples. Even a superficial comparison of these ritual occurrences with the political language of the GDR is sufficient to show that the thesis of its ritual character is quite plausible.

The consequences of such strongly ritualized communication, both for the actors immediately involved and for the wider problem of inclusion and exclusion, were highly ambivalent. From the perspective of the ruling party, linguistic rituals had three main positive functions. First, they conveyed values. Political values were an integral part of the public language. Thus the desired interpretation of the world and the targets of the ruling ideology were always present. Secondly, ritual practices guaranteed order and security. The given form, the identical or only slightly varied course taken, and the repetition symbolized control, order, and the successful execution of power. And thirdly, the ritual language contributed to integration. It forced all those who

---

[32] Cf. Corinna Fricke, 'Überlegungen zu einem Neuansatz der gesellschaftswissenschaftlichen Linguistik, ihre Aufgaben und Quellen', *Osnabrücker Beiträge zur Sprachtheorie*, 43 (1990), 141–60.

[33] Ulla Fix, 'Rituelle Kommunikation im öffentlichen Sprachgebrauch der DDR und ihre Begleitumstände: Möglichkeiten und Grenzen der selbstbestimmten und mitbestimmenden Kommunikation in der DDR', in Gotthard Lerchner (ed.), *Sprachgebrauch im Wandel: Anmerkungen zur Kommunikationskultur in der DDR vor und nach der Wende* (Frankfurt, 1992), 3–99; Elisabeth Rauch, *Sprachrituale in institutionellen und institutionalisierten Text- und Gesprächssorten* (Frankfurt, 1992); Sally F. Moore and Barbara G. Myerhoff (eds.), *Secular Ritual* (Assen, 1977); Iwar Werlen, *Ritual und Sprache: Zum Verhältnis von Sprechen und Handeln in Ritualen* (Tübingen, 1984).

participated in public communication to speak in a given way, thereby dissociating them from other speakers. In certain respects, then, the official language of the GDR was an in-group language which was characterized by a specific vocabulary, given structures of argument, and identifiable rules as to what could and could not be said. All those who used or accepted this firmly established terminology thereby expressed a willingness for subordination. Thus regardless of the semantic content of spoken or written texts, the extremely ritualized *forms* of language use themselves achieved inclusion or exclusion. Only those who used the official code were part of the company; anyone who refused linguistic gestures of conformity in the relevant communicative situations was quickly labelled an outsider and possibly subjected to sanctions. The official language was one of the most generalized symbols of inclusion in the GDR.

However, this was only one way to view the formal aspects of communication in the GDR. In fact, the totalitarian shaping of language had obvious limits. The first one was its restricted social reach. It hardly penetrated the verbal communication of everyday life, least of all conversations in private circles. Although the SED leadership tried to restrain dialects and youth slang, its language policy remained unsuccessful in this respect. Certainly all GDR citizens were perfectly capable of switching codes between the official language and everyday German.

A second, related limit resulted from the ritualization of language itself. As in all rituals, the formalization of language may become a value in itself. Compliance with language rules may become a merely outward obligation which gives little evidence of the true inner attitude of speakers. The fixed forms and obligatory rules of linguistic ritualization reduced insecurity in an environment which could arbitrarily be manipulated by the ruling party. Already at school, GDR citizens learned that verbal adaptation was rewarded and indispensable for their future professional careers. It is likely that the celebration of ritual gestures of conformity was among the everyday routine of East Germans, whether we call it pragmatic adaptation or opportunism. For the ruling party, this was a dilemma that it could not escape. On the one hand, it was not willing to abolish the instrument of a hegemonic linguistic code. On the other, it did not know whether official observance was honest conviction or mere conformity.

IV *Conclusion*

This essay set out to differentiate four semantic strategies which, taken together, helped to sustain the propaganda master narrative of the GDR as a distinct, progressive, and harmonious political entity. It also considered the integrative as well as disruptive effects of an extremely ritualized public language. Identity-forming narratives are intended to hold people together and to dissociate them from the outside world. Of all the twentieth-century dictatorships, the GDR probably had the greatest difficulty in defining the rules of belonging, of inclusion and exclusion. East Germany was not only the experimental field of a new social order and a new form of dictatorship. The country was, at the same time, a successor state of the Third Reich, a Soviet-occupied territory, and a part of the German nation. This created new borders defining inclusion and exclusion, whereby the regime's requirements for dissociation and the inclusion sentiments of the population could hardly ever be made to coincide.

I shall conclude this essay by looking briefly at the long-term impact of the GDR's official language. If we look back to the dramatic events of 1989—the breakdown of the SED dictatorship and German unification—it seems obvious that the SED's ideological messages had no lasting effect on the East German people's concepts of belonging. The SED's anti-fascist foundation myth was apparently a 'one generation phenomenon'. Above all, it played an important role for the young intellectuals of the reconstruction generation who were looking for orientation after the horrors of National Socialism. For the next generation, those born in the GDR with no personal experience of Nazi dictatorship, the integrative power of the anti-fascist narrative quickly faded. In the same way, the Communist narrative of progress dramatically lost its appeal when Ulbricht's policy of modernization and technological optimism failed in the 1960s. In the 1970s and 1980s, most GDR citizens paid only lip service to the vision of socialist modernity and its promised supremacy over the West. The invention of the 'GDR nation' in the Honecker era was similarly unsuccessful. At no point was it able seriously to compete with the traditional ethnically and linguistically defined concept of the nation-state. In the end, the decision space of the dictatorship and the identity space of the East German population were never really congruent.

The lack of cohesive force of these narratives was long covered up, and compensated for, by the GDR's language policy. Particularly because the party could not be sure of the inclusive power of its ideological narratives, it put great emphasis on compliance with ritual gestures of approval. Beginning with his investigations of East German historiography, Martin Sabrow has described the GDR as a 'dictatorship of consensus',[34] in which the ruling party expended a great deal of energy to create at least the *impression* of voluntary compliance. The official language was undoubtedly one of the most important means of implementing this policy of consensus.

Whether, and if so, to what extent, the official 'moral policy' and the corresponding rhetoric of equality, justice, and social harmony have had a lasting impact on the East German people's concepts of inclusion and exclusion is more difficult to assess. My thesis is that in this respect the official semantics of inclusion and exclusion met with a greater response. The moral stigmatization of enemies, for example, appealed to pre-political standards of 'good' and 'bad', and the rhetorical criminalization of the 'others' took advantage of one of the most popular definitions of 'in' and 'out'. The potential of the semantics of justice and homogeneity for identification was probably greater still. It may well be no accident that precisely these ideals provided a point around which attempts to create a kind of delayed GDR identity crystallized during the 1990s. Indignation about the 'injustice' of a liberal society and nostalgic longing for a society in which the 'little people' had their place can be interpreted in this way. Similarly, the East German phenomenon of widespread xenophobia, in a society with a relatively small percentage of foreigners, must be seen against the background of an ideal of homogeneity which did not acknowledge plurality and difference. In this way the official semantics of inclusion and exclusion probably contributed to the establishment of East German concepts of inclusion, but this was of no benefit to the legitimacy and stability of the GDR dictatorship.

[34] Sabrow, *Das Diktat des Konsenses.*

12

War over Words:
The Search for a Public Language
in West Germany

MARTIN H. GEYER

The quip, attributed to the satirist Karl Kraus in the 1920s, that nothing divided Germans and Austrians more than their common language still seemed pertinent fifty years later. By that time, in the 1970s, however, the divisions ran through Germany itself and had acquired a definite political dimension. Politically motivated differences in the use of terms sprang up not just between the official languages of East and West Germany, but increasingly within West Germany itself. West German observers evaluating the impact of the 1968 student rebellion and the ensuing transformation of political culture expressed concerns that the German language was about to disintegrate into distinct social, political, and academic idioms. Particular attention was paid to the language used by the political left and the new 'alternative' social movements. Conservative critics feared that leftist theoretical jargon was not only infiltrating academic discourse and public life as a whole but also transforming them fundamentally.[1] These debates were not limited to West Germany. In the United States, best-selling authors such as William Saffire and Edwin Newman expressed unease about the apparent disrespect for 'proper' English and the erosion of fundamental values which they believed went along with it. It became common to argue that the decline of the moral and political order was accelerated by a new language pioneered by the 'counterculture', the media, and advertising—at

I should like to thank Willibald Steinmetz very much for his many suggestions and comments. I am no less heavily indebted to Angela Davies (GHIL) and Dona Geyer for improving my English.

[1] For a summary see Peter von Polenz, *Deutsche Sprachgeschichte vom Spätmittelalter bis zur Gegenwart*, 3 vols. (Berlin, 1991–9), iii. *19. und 20. Jahrhundert* (1999); Jürgen Schiewe, *Die Macht der Sprache: Eine Geschichte der Sprachkritik von der Antike bis zur Gegenwart* (Munich, 1998), ch. 7.

the expense of what Richard Nixon called the 'silent majority' who had no public voice.[2]

The idea that the fabric of society and the state are closely linked to conventions or rules of speech is an age-old theme, not unlike the idea that individuals and groups wilfully or unconsciously 'manipulate' our world view by using and abusing certain political or social terms.[3] Such criticism has existed since the French Revolution. It received a new impetus from the official and non-official uses of language under National Socialism and Communist Russia. Most influential was George Orwell's depiction of 'Newspeak' in the appendix to his novel *1984*, in which he expressed the possibilities of 'thought-control' by way of a manipulated language. Orwell's exposure of 'Newspeak' could be read as a critique not only of totalitarianism but also, more generally, of the excesses of the mass media and modern commercial culture and their pernicious effects on the polity. Twisting the language—for example, by arguing that 'war' was 'peace'—amounted to more than just twisting the truth; it changed people's minds to such an extent that they began to act differently.[4]

Language, looked at in this way, becomes the battleground for the hearts and minds of the people, in advertising as much as in politics. A similar perspective can be found in the following quotation:

Language, dear friends, is not only a means of communication. As the conflict with the Left demonstrates, it is also an important means of strategy. What is occurring in our country today is a new type of revolution. It is the revolution of society by way of language. To overturn the order of the state it is no longer necessary to occupy the citadels of state power. Today, revolutions take place differently. Instead of public buildings terms are being occupied (*werden die Begriffe besetzt*)—terms by which the state governs, terms with which we describe our state order, our rights and duties, and our institutions. The modern revolution fills them with meanings which make it impossible for us to describe a free society and

---

[2] William Safire, *The New Language of Politics: A Dictionary of Catchwords, Slogans and Political Usage* (New York, 1972); Edwin Newman, *Strictly Speaking: Will America be the Death of English* (Indianapolis, 1974); For a survey see Birgit Meseck, *Studien zur konservativ-restaurativen Sprachkritik in Amerika* (Frankfurt am Main, 1987).

[3] For a very broad survey see Schiewe, *Macht der Sprache*.

[4] Appendix: The Principles of Newspeak, in George Orwell, *1984* (1st edn. 1949; New York, 2003), 309–23; John W. Young, *Totalitarian Language: Orwell's Newspeak and its Nazi and Communist Antecedents* (Charlottesville, Va., 1991).

to live in this society . . . [This revolution] occupies terms and thus the information of a free society.[5]

It is clear that this quotation is not taken from a leftist advocate of the German-American philosopher Herbert Marcuse or from a follower of Antonio Gramsci. Rather, these are the words of someone who was critical of the left—not in an academic journal or an Oxford university seminar, but at a political party conference, namely, that of the German Christian Democratic Union (CDU) in 1973, a platform which also ensured that the message would be transmitted to a larger public audience. The speaker was neither a backbencher nor a party esoteric, but a legal scholar, former manager of the Henkel Corporation, and previous rector of the University of Bochum, Kurt Biedenkopf, who had been appointed secretary general of the CDU earlier that year by the new party chairman and opposition leader, Helmut Kohl.[6]

In this essay I will use this passage from Kurt Biedenkopf's speech to explore the peculiar historical junctures in the early 1970s that led to an increased awareness of the malleability of language among intellectuals and politicians in post-war West Germany. The CDU secretary general's speech in 1973 was indeed an interesting turning point in this process. In a first step I will discuss how and why Biedenkopf's few sentences at the CDU party conference were transformed into a coherent essay entitled 'Politics and Language', published in 1975.[7] Although not intellectually brilliant, this essay bore the signature of many authors and, in fact, might be understood as a political meta-text that not only offered a narrative of German history in terms of an evolution of language after National Socialism, but at the same time energetically pushed the idea that West German conservatives should follow the example set by the left and actively 'occupy', or rather 're-occupy', key political terms and thus public language. This venture was intended to be part of a proclaimed

---

[5] Christlich-Demokratische Union Deutschlands (CDU), *22. Bundesparteitag der Christlich-Demokratischen Union Deutschlands: Niederschrift. Hamburg, 18.–20. November 1973* (Bonn, 1973), 58.

[6] Wolfgang Jäger, 'Die Innenpolitik der sozial-liberalen Koalition 1969–1974', in id. and Werner Link (eds.), *Republik im Wandel 1969–1974* (Stuttgart, 1986), 15–160, at 102–7; Peter Köpf, *Der Querdenker Kurt Biedenkopf* (Frankfurt am Main, 1999), 89–128.

[7] Kurt H. Biedenkopf, 'Politik und Sprache', in Bernhard Vogel (ed.), *Neue Bildungspolitik: Plädoyer für ein realistisches Konzept* (Berlin, 1975), 21–32 (this version is quoted); a shorter version is reprinted in Hans Jürgen Heringer (ed.), *Holzfeuer im hölzernen Ofen: Aufsätze zur politischen Sprachkritik* (Tübingen, 1982), 189–97.

Tendenzwende—a suggestive term which was successfully coined in the mid-1970s by intellectuals close to the CDU in order to describe, and bring about, a fundamental shift in West German politics and culture towards conservative ideas.[8] Moving backwards in time from the 1970s, the second part of this essay explores the links between the ideas of the 1970s on 'occupying' political terms and earlier attempts at language criticism in the Federal Republic. Almost all of these attempts, beginning in 1945, revolved around the question of how to deal with the remnants of Nazi words, terms, and phrases in politics and everyday life. The focus will be on one specific aspect of this debate, namely, on the notion of the 'theft' of words. This notion frequently came up in the context of arguments directed as much against those who argued for a purification of the German language from Nazism as against those on the left who supposedly 'unhinged' terms and words from their 'true' meanings. The student movement transformed and radicalized this earlier language critique. At the same time, many critical observers developed their own critique of the language of the left. The final part of this essay will deal with certain aspects of the new conservative *prise de parole* of the 1970s and 1980, including one that pertains to the issue of 'historical correctness'.

All of these debates have inspired much discussion among German linguists.[9] Historians, interestingly enough, have rarely been involved. In part this has to do with the fact that, also in Germany, the focus has been on the socio-political 'languages' or discourses of the early modern period. Peculiar to Germany is an infatuation with individual terms or concepts (*Begriffe*), and, as far as linguists and public intellectuals are concerned, an almost obsessive fixation on totalitarianism, which provided the key to

---

[8] Hermann Glaser, 'Die Mitte und rechts davon: Bemerkungen zur Tendenzwende in der Bundesrepublik', *Aus Politik und Zeitgeschichte*, 42 (1974), 14–36; Clemens Graf von Podewils, *Tendenzwende? Zur geistigen Situation der Bundesrepublik* (Stuttgart, 1975); Axel Schildt, '"Die Kräfte der Gegenreform sind auf breiter Front angetreten": Zur konservativen Tendenzwende in den Siebzigerjahren', *Archiv für Sozialgeschichte*, 44 (2004), 449–78.

[9] See esp. Manfred Behrens, Walther Dieckmann, and Erich Kehl, 'Politik als Sprachkampf', in Heringer (ed.), *Holzfeuer im hölzernen Ofen*, 216–65; Georg Stötzel, 'Semantische Kämpfe im öffentlichen Sprachgebrauch', in Gerhard Stickel (ed.), *Deutsche Gegenwartssprache: Tendenzen und Perspektiven* (Berlin, 1990), 45–65; Josef Klein, 'Kann man "Begriffe besetzen"? Zur linguistischen Differenzierung einer plakativen politischen Metapher', in Frank Liedtke, Martin Wengeler, and Karin Böke (eds.), *Begriffe besetzen: Strategien des Sprachgebrauchs in der Politik* (Opladen, 1991), 44–79.

understanding language. German historians, foremost among them the early practitioners of *Begriffsgeschichte*, left discussions of twentieth-century political terms to the linguists and concentrated instead on conceptual changes in earlier periods, the *Sattelzeit*.[10] Thus this essay may also be seen as exploring some specificities of the 'linguistic turn', and not just in Germany. Of particular interest in this respect is the double bind that informs many of these studies, resulting from the confrontation with totalitarian languages on the one hand, and more recent political language struggles on the other. For the heightened interest in the political uses and misuses of language brought about a deluge of academic literature on the topic of language, politics, and social movements. This essay also intends to contribute to exploring the ways in which German historiography is rooted in its own particular *Zeitgeschichte*.[11]

'Occupying Terms'

When Kurt Biedenkopf addressed the issue of political language at the CDU party conference in 1973, he expressed concerns that had been preoccupying many people, not just conservatives, for some time. In fact, his remarks can be understood as the starting signal in an effective rally against the Social–Liberal coalition government and the political left in general. At the time, the CDU and its Bavarian sister party, the Christian Social Union (CSU), were still licking the wounds inflicted on them in the 1972 national elections. The Christian Democrats' attempts to topple Willy Brandt's new *Ostpolitik* had failed, as had the motion of no-confidence against Chancellor Brandt in the Bundestag. The CDU/CSU had not only lost the elections of 1972, but the Social–Liberal coalition under Chancellor Willy Brandt had found remarkable support among the traditionally conservative Catholic electorate. Moreover, the party itself was torn apart by internal strife. The Bavarian CSU, led by Franz Josef Strauß, was threatening to leave the parliamentary group it constituted with the

---

[10] See the introduction to this volume by Willibald Steinmetz.

[11] See also Martin H. Geyer, 'Im Schatten der NS-Zeit: Zeitgeschichte als Paradigma einer (bundes-)republikanischen Geschichtswissenschaft', in Alexander Nützenadel and Wolfgang Schieder (eds.), *Zeitgeschichte als Problem: Nationale Traditionen und Perspektiven der Forschung in Europa* (Göttingen, 2004), 25–53.

CDU. In this situation, the need for new impulses in political strategy was urgent. Kurt Biedenkopf was among the key figures who tried to redirect the CDU's attention towards new and politically more rewarding issues. Shortly before he was elected secretary general, he had criticized his party in an article published in the weekly newspaper *Die Zeit*.[12] As the influence of the established churches waned, he argued, the CDU was losing contact with the working classes. The influence of 'groups within the CDU oriented towards business and capital' had increased at the cost of groups representing employee interests. More dangerously still, he claimed, 'relations between the CDU and intellectual and cultural groups' were on the 'defensive'. How could the party communicate its aims to the public at large? How could the party, which had just elected Helmut Kohl as its chairman, promote itself and gain a new profile? In the speech he gave at the party conference as the new secretary general, Biedenkopf made this necessary reorientation of the CDU his central point. In particular he emphasized social policy and other issues that he felt were interconnected 'with the changes that are taking place so strikingly in our times'. Above all, however, the political success of the party, he argued, depended on whether it was possible 'to find and practise a language that is our own'; otherwise the party would remain 'speechless'.[13] To speak up, to raise one's voice, was the prerequisite not only for being heard, but also for acting politically.

At the heart of Biedenkopf's reflective yet defensive speech was the feeling that the Social Democratic Party (SPD) and the coalition government had a programme that appealed to the public through a string of attractive terms such as 'inner reform', 'peace politics', 'détente', 'humanization of labour', and 'quality of life'. Slightly more controversial than this high-grade vocabulary was perhaps the slogan at the centre of Willy Brandt's bold governmental programme of 1969: the notion that Germans should 'dare more democracy', expand 'liberty' and 'social justice', and thus bring about what Jürgen Habermas later called West Germany's *Fundamentalliberalisierung* (fundamental liberalization).[14] Brandt's

---

[12] Kurt Biedenkopf, 'Eine Strategie für die Opposition', partially reprinted in Jäger, 'Die Innenpolitik', 103.   [13] Ibid.; CDU, *22. Bundesparteitag*, 61.

[14] Jürgen Habermas, 'Der Marsch durch die Institutionen hat auch die CDU erreicht', *Frankfurter Rundschau*, 11 Mar. 1988, quoted in Ulrich Herbert, 'Liberalisierung als Lernprozess: Die Bundesrepublik in der deutschen Geschichte—eine Skizze', in id. (ed.), *Wandlungsprozesse in Westdeutschland: Belastung, Integration, Liberalisierung* (Göttingen, 2002), 7–49.

agenda thrived on the idea that the times favoured the reformers; their optimism was supported by strong economic growth and, more importantly perhaps, by the belief that growth could be sustained by economic policies. This language of 'reform' was in tune with similar trends throughout Western Europe and the United States. With respect to American 'new politics', William Saffire wrote that '*participatory democracy, power to the people, and reordering priorities* bestrode the stage, with *quality of life* in the wings'. But the columnist also noted: 'Linguistically, the past four years have been enlivened by a counterattack of the political right.'[15]

For the politician Biedenkopf, 'occupying terms' was a matter of recapturing political territory lost to the opponent. He was neither the first nor the only contemporary to take notice of the Social Democrats' peculiar semantics of 'reform' and 'progress'. Starting in 1969 this theme was widely discussed in newspaper columns, often in an ironic tone. One of the main contributors to this debate was the political scientist Hans Maier, who served as Bavarian Minister for Education and Culture from 1970 to 1986. In various lectures on the topic 'Current Trends in Political Language', which were published und republished, first in newspapers and by 1975 also in the form of an essay, Maier had presented an astute criticism of the language of the German New Left. A student of Eric Voegelin and an expert on political religions, Maier had gained a good deal of practical experience both in dealing with unruly students at the University of Munich, where he taught, and in handling rebellious church members whom he faced before becoming head of the lay organization of German Catholics in 1976. He claimed that the language of the left not only prevented political dialogue, but even exhibited some of the essential characteristics of totalitarian languages.[16] Maier's arguments had sparked

---

[15] Safire, *The New Language of Politics*, p. xv.

[16] His various lectures were reprinted as 'Die Sprache der Neuen Linken: Die gegenwärtige politisch-semantische Doppelstrategie', *Frankfurter Allgemeine Zeitung*, 13 July 1972; 'Aktuelle Tendenzen der politischen Sprache', *Bayernkurier*, 21 Oct. 1972, partly reprinted in Bernhard Gebauer (ed.), *Material zum Thema Politik und Sprache*, with contributions by Josef Klein, Mathias Schmitz, Wulf Schönbohm, and Wilhelm Schwarz (Bonn, 1973), 77; Hans Maier, 'Können Begriffe die Gesellschaft verändern?', in Gerd-Klaus Kaltenbrunner (ed.), *Sprache und Herrschaft: Die umfunktionierten Wörter* (Munich, 1975), 55–68; Hans Maier, *Sprache und Politik: Essay über aktuelle Tendenzen—Briefdialog mit Heinrich Böll* (Zurich, 1977), 9–28 (this edition is quoted in this essay); id., 'Aktuelle Tendenzen der politischen Sprache', in Wolfgang Bergsdorf (ed.), *Wörter als Waffen: Sprache als Mittel der Politik* (Stuttgart, 1979); Heringer (ed.), *Holzfeuer im hölzernen Ofen*, 179–88.

a major debate in conservative circles, and some of his ideas found their way into a lengthy, coherent, but stylistically not exactly elegant text entitled 'Politics and Language', which was published under Biedenkopf's name in 1975.[17] In fact, this essay combined Biedenkopf's remarks on 're-capturing terms' from the Social Democrats with some of Maier's earlier and more specific reflections on the language of the New Left. In addition to Maier and Biedenkopf, the essay had several other authors. Among them were the members of a special task force on semantics (Arbeitsgruppe Semantik). The initiative for forming this task force came from a group of younger party officials, among them Wolfgang Dettling, head of the Grundsatzabteilung of the CDU, a section of the party whose ambition was to introduce scientific expertise into politics from public opinion polling to linguistics. Officially the group was headed by the linguist Hans Messelken, Professor of German Language Didactics at the Pädagogische Hochschule in Cologne.[18] But most outspoken were Gerhard Mahler and especially Wolfgang Bergsdorf, who at the time headed Helmut Kohl's office. Although Mahler was originally more active in unravelling the language of the Social Democrats and their chancellors, Willy Brandt and Helmut Schmidt, it was Bergsdorf who, in the end, built his career on this issue with a long list of edited volumes and other publications, including his Bonn habilitation thesis, published as *Herrschaft und Sprache*. Under Chancellor Kohl, Bergsdorf later became director of the German Federal Press Office (Bundespresseamt).[19]

The Arbeitsgruppe Semantik did not stop at analysing the polit-

[17] Biedenkopf, 'Politik und Sprache'.

[18] For short surveys see Behrens, Dieckmann, and Kehl, 'Politik als Sprachkampf', 222–6; Anja Kruke, *Demoskopie in der Bundesrepublik Deutschland: Meinungsforschung, Parteien und Medien 1949–1990* (Düsseldorf, 2007), 57–8. At least in public Hans Messelken did not play an important part; nor did his work in empirical linguistics lend itself to sweeping generalizations. See Hans Messelken, *Empirische Sprachdidaktik* (Heidelberg, 1971). For his work within the group framework, see id., 'Fragen eines lesenden Bürgers zur Sprachstrategie der SPD', in Karl Ermert (ed.), *Politische Sprache: Maßstäbe ihrer Bewertung. Tagung vom 9.–11. November 1979*, Loccumer Protokolle 20/1979 (Rehburg-Loccum, 1979), 80–146.

[19] Gerhard Mahler, 'Politik und Sprache', *Sonde*, 9 (1975), 34–8; id., 'Die Sprache des Bundeskanzlers', *Sonde*, 9 (1976), 72–6; Wolfgang Bergsdorf, 'Die sanfte Gewalt: Sprache—Denken—Politik', *Aus Politik und Zeitgeschichte*, 24 (1977), 39–47; id., *Politik und Sprache* (Munich, 1978); id. (ed.), *Wörter als Waffen*, 7–14; id., *Herrschaft und Sprache: Studie zur politischen Terminologie der Bundesrepublik Deutschland* (Pfullingen, 1983); id., 'Zur Entwicklung der Sprache der amtlichen Politik in der Bundesrepublik Deutschland', in Liedtke, Wengeler, and Böke (eds.), *Begriffe besetzen*, 19–43.

ical language of their opponent. Turning their attention to the next general election in 1976, members of the group deliberated on how the CDU should formulate its own political statements in the party programme and organize its semantic counter-offensive. Maier's and Biedenkopf's initial ideas served as a reference point not only for the group but also for a more widespread debate among conservative intellectuals. In fact, between 1974 and 1977 a considerable number of journalists, politicians, and scholars contributed articles to newspapers, journals, and volumes of collected essays on the topic of 'Language and Politics', or as one author called it, 'red semantics'.[20] Most of the earlier articles started from a rather narrow repertoire of ideas which, as the debate went on, were pondered, enlarged, and critically reviewed, and in some respects also adopted by linguistic scholars. Some arguments also found their way into academic publications.[21] Here we see the formation of a scholarly discourse which converged on several important points.

First, one feature of that discourse was a specific narrative of post-war developments in West German (political) language. This narrative basically revolved around the argument that a totalitarian language had successfully been replaced by a democratic one in the Federal Republic. Even trends in ordinary, non-political language had contributed to what could be called a new politics of consensus in post-war West Germany.[22] This included a decline in the use of regional dialects and sociolects in favour of High German, which was interpreted as a sign of an evolution towards

---

[20] See the volumes edited by Bergsdorf (n. 19). The essays in Kaltenbrunner (ed.), *Sprache und Herrschaft*, some of which are reprints, were widely quoted. Also Heinrich Dietz, 'Rote Semantik', ibid. 20–43. Examples of how this topic was taken up by political education are ibid. 65–74; D. Bauer, 'Begriffe gegen Inhalte: Zur semantischen Akrobatik der CDU', *Neue Gesellschaft*, 7 (1975), 564–6 (critical); Iring Fetscher and Horst Eberhart Richter (eds.), *Worte machen keine Politik: Beiträge zu einem Kampf um politische Begriffe* (Reinbek, 1976); Martin Greiffenhagen (ed.), *Kampf um Wörter? Politische Begriffe im Meinungsstreit* (Munich, 1980); Ermert (ed.), *Politische Sprache*; and id. (ed.), *Wissenschaft, Sprache, Gesellschaft: Über Kommunikationsprobleme zwischen Wissenschaft und Öffentlichkeit und Wege zu deren Überwindung, Tagung vom 18.–20. März 1982*, Loccumer Protokolle 6/1982, (Rehburg-Loccum, 1982).

[21] For academic treatments see esp. Heringer (ed.), *Holzfeuer im hölzernen Ofen*; Hugo Steger, 'Sprache im Wandel', in Wolfgang Benz (ed.), *Die Bundesrepublik Deutschland*, 3 vols. (Göttingen, 1983), iii. *Kultur*, 15–46; Stötzel, 'Semantische Kämpfe'; Erich Straßner, *Ideologie —Sprache—Politik: Grundfragen ihres Zusammenhangs* (Tübingen, 1987); Georg Stötzel and Martin Wengeler (eds.), *Kontroverse Begriffe: Geschichte des öffentlichen Sprachgebrauchs in der Bundesrepublik Deutschland* (Berlin, 1995); Klein, 'Kann man "Begriffe besetzen"'.

[22] This differentiation was introduced later by Bergsdorf, *Herrschaft und Sprache*, 63–124; Steger, 'Sprache im Wandel'.

a more egalitarian society.[23] The old language of class society and class conflict, still dominant in the late 1940s and early 1950s, had been transformed into a new language of industrial 'social partnership' and the 'social market economy' which, it was argued, had also been embraced by the Social Democrats and trade unions during the Adenauer era. 'Language as a mirror of social evolution duplicated what had happened in the state, the economy, and society', wrote Biedenkopf, and he went on to assert that in the Adenauer era 'political language was open to alternatives without letting political antagonism become irreconcilable hostility'. This, he continued, was not least an achievement of the CDU, 'which had been acting creatively not just in political matters, but also in its use of language' by advocating, for example, the 'social market economy' and 'European integration'.[24]

The sociologist Helmut Schelsky had already anticipated this line of argument in the 1950s, when he claimed that social homogenization in West Germany had reached a stage which made it possible to describe it as a *nivellierte Mittelstandsgesellschaft*, a society in which class antagonisms had been progressively evened out to the level of a broadening middle class. In the 1970s, Schelsky was an outspoken advocate of the idea of reconquering lost ground in the field of political language. His highly polemical work entitled 'The Work is Done by Others: Class War and the Priesthood of the Intellectuals' (*Die Arbeit tun die anderen: Klassenkampf und Priesterherrschaft der Intellektuellen*, 1975) included a long chapter in which he presented the many ways in which (leftist) intellectuals were believed to have manipulated and politically instrumentalized public language for their sinister purposes. Schelsky juxtaposed this with the political language of the earlier, happier days of the Federal Republic, which he thought had created a *Schicksalsgemeinschaft*, a community of fate that was based not just on common experiences, but on a common language.[25]

---

[23] The replacement of dialects by High German and the revival of dialects in the 1970s is an important social phenomenon that has as yet received little historical treatment. The media played an important part here. See von Polenz, *Deutsche Sprachgeschichte*, iii. *19. und 20. Jahrhundert*, ch. 6.12.

[24] Biedenkopf, 'Politik und Sprache', 21; likewise Maier, *Sprache und Politik*, 9–11; see also Steger, 'Sprache im Wandel', 15–16.

[25] The book develops a conservative and pessimistic dystopia that almost turns upside down Daniel Bell's altogether optimistic ideas on the coming post-industrial 'knowledge society', in which language was to play an important role as a 'means of production' of the new information society. Helmut Schelsky, *Die Arbeit tun die anderen: Klassenkampf und*

Hans Maier took much the same line, although he was some-what more critical. He pointed to the numerous 'odd abuses in everyday language' and to the manifold tendencies to 'conceal' (*verschleiern*) social reality in the German language after 1945. But he also saw this tendency to conceal things as having a 'human-izing' effect on the language. The function of language, he claimed, was not just 'analytical exposure'; rather, 'one should keep in mind that human culture began with Adam and Eve's fig leaf and that naked truth, although much-praised nowadays, was—to quote [the Austrian writer Franz] Werfel—"the whore of the barbarian"'.[26] When Maier spoke of 'efforts to conceal' in post-war West Germany, he himself was using coded language, for he did not dare to explain openly what Germans had chiefly attempted to conceal in these years, namely, National Socialism and the Holocaust.[27]

Secondly, from a linguistic point of view the conservative narra-tives about German public language in the 1970s were all built on a more or less simple understanding of language, according to which an unequivocal relationship could be established between (political) terms and the 'real' phenomena they designated. In addi-tion, these authors asserted that terms such as 'liberty', 'democ-racy', 'representation', and the 'social state' were clearly defined by law and in the Federal Republic's constitution, the Basic Law (*Grundgesetz*). It was therefore easy, in principle, to find the 'true' meaning of terms. A crude statement of this doctrine would read thus: 'Words exist to name things. They express what is. And if they succeed in this, they tell the truth.'[28] At the 1973 CDU party conference, Biedenkopf expressed this thought when he com-mended the 'clear language' of Chancellor Adenauer (who, by the way, was not renowned as an excellent speaker and certainly no

---

Priesterherrschaft der Intellektuellen (Cologne, 1975), 237. See also a shortened version entitled 'Macht durch Sprache', *Deutsche Zeitung*, 12 Apr. 1974, reprinted in Kaltenbrunner (ed.), *Sprache und Herrschaft*, 176–8; Bergsdorf (ed.), *Wörter als Waffen*.

[26] Maier, *Sprache und Politik*, 11.

[27] Literature on the 'culture of shame' after 1945: Raphael Gross, 'Relegating Nazism to the Past: Expressions of German Guilt in 1945 and Beyond', *German History*, 25 (2007), 219–38; Heidrun Kämper, *Der Schulddiskurs in der frühen Nachkriegszeit: Ein Beitrag zur Geschichte des sprachlichen Umbruchs nach 1945* (Berlin, 2005); ead., *Opfer—Täter—Nichttäter: Ein Wörterbuch zum Schulddiskurs 1945–1955* (Berlin, 2007).

[28] Helmut Kuhn, 'Despotie der Wörter: Wie man mit der Sprache die Freiheit über-wältigen kann', in Kaltenbrunner (ed.), *Sprache und Herrschaft*, 11–17, at 11; see also e.g. Heinrich Dietz, 'Rote Semantik'.

slave to High German).[29] Adenauer, the CDU delegates were told, exhibited no need to conceal his intentions behind 'a veil of nice words'; he had nothing to 'hide' and did not need intellectuals as 'administrators of political language'. On the contrary, he upset intellectuals because he made his points without having recourse to them as 'translators'.[30] Thus Biedenkopf's argument again revolved around the ideas of authenticity and disguise—with respect both to language itself and to those who used it.

Thirdly, the crucial rupture in the evolution of post-war German language came, so the conservatives' narrative went on, with the student revolt and the emergence of the New Left in the 1960s. The students and their leftist seducers and emulators, it was claimed, had caused the present-day Babylonian confusion of terms which brought the Adenauer consensus to an end, politically as well as semantically. By 'occupying' political terms and twisting their 'true' meaning, they had dominated and radically transformed public language and, along with it, perceptions of reality. In the essay derived from his speech at the party conference, Biedenkopf directed a side swipe against the media, who, in his view, had also been captured by these 'modern revolutionaries'.[31] This contention was yet another blow levelled by the CDU intellectuals against the media in an escalating conflict which was led most vehemently by, among others, Helmut Schelsky, Elisabeth Noelle-Neumann, influential director of the Allensbach Institute für Meinungsforschung (an important public opinion research institute), and Karl Steinbuch, a renowned expert in cybernetics and computer sciences who also spoke out against the New Left's 'clever technique of non-violent revolution'.[32] Similarly, the spearhead of German conservatism, Klaus-Gerd Kaltenbrunner, argued that the dissemination of information and

[29] Heinz Kühn, 'Konrad Adenauer und Kurt Schumacher als politische Redner', in Bernd Rebe, Klaus Lompe, and Rudolf von Thadden (eds.), *Idee und Pragmatik in der politischen Entscheidung: Alfred Kubel zum 75. Geburtstag* (Bonn, 1984), 81–93.

[30] CDU, *22. Bundesparteitag*, 62.   [31] Ibid. 22.

[32] Karl Steinbuch, *Kurskorrektur* (Stuttgart-Degerloch, 1973), 82; see also id., *Maßlos informiert: Die Enteignung des Denkens* (Munich, 1978); for the reception of Steinbuch see also Maier, *Sprache und Politik*, 27. Elisabeth Noelle-Neumann, 'Die Schweigespirale: Über die Entstehung der öffentlichen Meinung', in Ernst Forsthoff and Reinhard Hörstel (eds.), *Standorte im Zeitstrom: Festschrift für Arnold Gehlen zum 70. Geburtstag am 29. Januar 1974* (Frankfurt am Main, 1974), 299–330. She did not publish the much discussed book with the same title until 1980. She follows up on the American debate on the 'silent majority' with the argument that the perception of *Mehrheitsmeinungen*, the opinions of the majority as they are shaped by the mass media, determines the articulation of opinions by the majority of common people.

access to the machinery of public opinion-making had become the means by which highly developed technological societies could be ruled most effectively.[33]

Fourthly, the entire conservative discussion of public language in Germany had a twofold thrust from the start. One was a pragmatic attempt to cope with the apparent success of the Social–Liberal coalition at the expense of the Christian Democrats; the other was a more far-reaching critique of the left in general, one that dramatized personal and ideological contacts between the Social Democrats and the radical left and laid the responsibility for whatever went wrong in Germany on the student movement and youth rebellion of the late 1960s and early 1970s. The second line of reasoning became more pronounced as the left's extreme fringes turned to terrorism. Hints of this kind of reasoning were present in Biedenkopf's articles and speeches, but Hans Maier was far more explicit on this point. Again, he supported his arguments with a few astute linguistic observations. In the public utterances of the left he discovered a mechanism of escalation that started with a 'purist overstretching of terms' resulting in 'disillusion' with existing reality and 'destruction of that which was originally meant by the term'. The next step was to charge the term with a new, 'eschatological' or 'utopian' meaning (as had happened in earlier political religions), whereby the term would hold out great hopes for the future. The final point was reached when paramilitary vocabulary was used to indicate that the time was ripe to realize such hopes—the sooner the better. The polemical twist in Maier's argument, one that was more implicit than explicit, was to associate closely the Social Democrats' language of reform and their belief in the feasibility of progress (*Machbarkeitsglaube*) with the language of New Left Marxism. Its advocates, Maier argued in several different contexts, had learned a great deal in this respect from the self-proclaimed 'revolutionary' right of the Weimar Republic.[34] Other conservative polemicists were more direct in drawing such comparisons: 'in 1933 and 1967 an ideological belief forced its way, and in both cases the revolution in the real world was preceded by a revolution in language.'[35]

[33] Gerd-Klaus Kaltenbrunner, 'Schöpferischer Konservatismus und konservative Aktion heute', in id. (ed.), *Konservatismus International* (Stuttgart, 1973), 255–74, at 261; see also id. (ed.), *Die Macht der Meinungsmacher* (Munich, 1976).

[34] Maier, *Sprache und Politik*, 15, 27.

[35] Kuhn, 'Despotie der Wörter', 17; similarly Dietz, 'Rote Semantik'.

Again, the premise of this argument was that the 'ongoing revolution' de-coupled terms from their 'true meaning' and reality. In
Maier's words, it was an 'alienation of political language from the
norms and terms of our political order as laid down in constitu-
tions and legal procedures'.[36] Like many other conservatives at
the time, Biedenkopf and Maier, in almost identical words,
bemoaned the 'triumphal march of an all-encompassing concept
of society' ('Siegeszug des total gewordenen Gesellschaftsbegriffs'),
regretting that 'society' had replaced 'the state' as the central reference point for political theorizing and practical politics.
Similarly, they noted, terms such as 'freedom' and 'democracy'
also underwent a fundamental shift in meaning when, for
example, 'democracy' in the language of the left was said to have
become a 'polemical concept against any attempt to consolidate
the status quo by legal and parliamentary means', or when 'concepts designating an existing order' (*Ordnungsbegriffe*) were transformed into 'concepts promising a new state of things'
(*Verheißungen*), as had been the case in the late Weimar Republic.[37]

The strange thing in all this reasoning was that Maier,
Biedenkopf, Schelsky, and most of their intellectual followers still
insisted, despite their at times shrewd dissections of past and
present political struggles about the meaning of terms, that at
some stage in history these terms had acquired their 'true'
meaning and that, somehow, it might be possible to re-establish
and re-stabilize these true meanings by strategic linguistic acts.
Thus Schelsky argued that in the nineteenth century and the first
half of the twentieth, public language had kept its 'constant form,
that is: a common understanding of meanings and ideas', whereas
today this form had been lost (implying that it should and could
be regained).[38] His claim that the meanings of terms had
remained undisputed right into the middle of the twentieth
century (including the National Socialist regime!) was not only
somewhat odd, but also incompatible with the narrative of those

---

[36] Maier, *Sprache und Politik*, 12–14; Biedenkopf, 'Politik und Sprache', 22. Thus Helmut
Kuhn argued that it 'makes a difference whether I say "Third Reich" or "New Society".
But in the structure of an ideological profession of faith, both statements have the same
value.' Kuhn, 'Despotie der Wörter', 17.

[37] Maier, *Sprache und Politik*, 13; Biedenkopf, 'Politik und Sprache', 22.

[38] Schelsky, *Die Arbeit tun die anderen*, 236. For a classic account of ideologies quite contrary to this view see Karl Mannheim, *Ideologie und Utopie* (1st edn. 1929; Frankfurt am Main,
1985).

who argued that 'the radicals of today pick up the work of destruction begun by the National Socialists'.[39] Such differences in chronology, however, were less important than the common belief of most critics that the distortions inflicted on political language by the left could, ultimately, be put right and semantic stability restored.

Even at the time, many saw this latter argument as somewhat naive. The philosopher Hermann Lübbe sympathized with the conservative language critics, yet he was very clear-cut and detached in his outlook on what could reasonably be expected of any attempt to recapture terms from one's political opponent. Among the conservative analysts of political language, Lübbe was the only one who accepted straight away that a state of constant struggle about the meaning of terms, not stability, was the normal case in history. Consequently, he told his fellow conservatives, the best result that linguistic strategists of any political party could hope for was a temporary advantage in their power to impress upon the public what they believed were the 'proper' meanings of terms.[40] More neutral academics in the field of linguistics were even more sceptical. In their opinion, the whole idea that terms could be 'occupied' and their true meaning defined was not much more than a badly chosen metaphor, and any attempt to put it into practice was, they believed, doomed to failure.[41]

These theoretical reflections had their own logic; they mattered little in daily political life. Within the intellectual circles around the CDU in the mid-1970s, more pragmatic positions centring on the idea of 'occupying terms' prevailed. Party members had to be committed to a common language; moreover, the persuasiveness of terms and slogans had to be established on a trial-and-error basis. Most of all, success proved the viability of an argument or a strategy, and many looked to advertising and the marketplace for analogies with their own case and that of their opponents. If companies were able to attach certain attractive images (and along with such images: ideas) to their products and thus manipulate

---

[39] Kuhn, 'Despotie der Wörter', 17.

[40] Hermann Lübbe, 'Das Problem der Sprache', in Hans-Georg Gadamer (ed.), *Das Problem der Sprache* (Munich, 1967), 351–71.

[41] See e.g. Steger, 'Sprache im Wandel'; Erich Straßner, '1968 und die sprachlichen Folgen', in Dieter Emig, Christoph Hüttig, and Lutz Raphael (eds.), *Sprache und Politische Kultur in der Demokratie: Hans Gerd Schumann zum Gedenken* (Frankfurt am Main, 1992), 241–60; Klein, 'Kann man "Begriffe besetzen"'.

customers into buying these products (and the ideas attached to them), should it not be possible to achieve similar results in politics? In the early 1970s, the classic German skin cream Nivea, which had traditionally been marketed in an old-fashioned blue tin, was losing ground to Creme 21 (marketed by Henkel), which was packaged in a bright orange tin and advertised in body-oriented, slightly erotic commercials. Could its success be attributed to the actual nature of the product, or to the images (and ideas) transported by the colour orange, namely, 'modernity'? How was it possible to fabricate the image of a product or to 'capture' an attractive image from another product? Self-confident advertisers boasted of their ability to make consumers buy almost any article.[42] To one of the members of the CDU task force on semantics, the public image of the party was slightly 'greasy' (*pomadig*).[43] An analogy between advertising strategies and politics could thus easily be drawn, even though in the eyes of advocates of principled positions, this was tantamount to a trivialization of politics on both sides of the political fence.

Instead of analogies with peaceful competition in the marketplace, many conservative intellectuals in the mid-1970s still preferred to use metaphors of war when suggesting what should be done. The sociologist Schelsky went as far as to borrow directly from Carl Schmitt's definition of sovereignty. For Carl Schmitt, the sovereign was he (definitely not she) who defined the state of emergency. Schelsky declared: 'Souverän ist, wer den Sachverhalt definiert' (the sovereign is he who defines the facts). As a more practical piece of advice, he added that 'empty formulas' were especially apt for those who wished to dominate: 'Leerformeln sind immer Herrschaftsformeln.'[44] For others, too, there was no alternative but to take the bull by the horns and reduce the problem to a simple question of power. 'Who interprets society?', the philosopher Günter Rohrmoser asked.[45] In the end, this

---

[42] For a detailed analysis see Rainer Gries, *Produkte als Medien: Kulturgeschichte der Produktkommunikation in der Bundesrepublik und der DDR* (Leipzig, 2003), 453–560; Wolfgang Fritz Haug, *Kritik der Warenästhetik* (Frankfurt am Main, 1971) is important for the contemporary debate.

[43] 'Bestimmte Zeichen', *Der Spiegel*, no. 32, 5 Aug. 1974, 48.

[44] Helmut Schelsky, 'Macht durch Sprache', 176, 177. This article was originally published as 'Macht und Sprache: Wer eine neue Politik durchsetzen will, braucht neue Worte', *Deutsche Zeitung*, 12 Apr. 1974.

[45] Günter Rohrmoser, *Revolution—unser Schicksal?* (Stuttgart, 1974), 48.

advice amounted to nothing other than 'to capture' one's opponents' terms and adopt what appeared to be their methods of 'linguistic warfare'. No doubt this says a great deal about the confrontational political culture of the 1970s, and not only in West Germany.

'Word Theft' and Post-1945 Criticism of German Public Language

One of Biedenkopf's key arguments in the period 1973 to 1975 was that the left was committing 'language robbery' or 'word theft'. The SPD, he maintained, was attempting 'systematically to establish "language barriers" that blocked the CDU's communication with the people'. The exclusion of individuals and groups from the chance to participate in society was a broadly discussed theme at the time; after all, the political, economic, and social inclusion of groups who had formerly been disadvantaged was a favoured topic in the Social Democratic programme.[46] Biedenkopf now turned the accusation of practising exclusion against the SPD itself, albeit with a specific twist. In usurping certain highly valued political key terms for its own exclusive use, the SPD, according to Biedenkopf, not only made the opposing party appear as if it had no positive agenda of its own but, what was more, left it literally 'speechless' because it could no longer express its thoughts without constantly adopting the SPD's vocabulary and the ideas transported with it.[47] As if to illustrate this dilemma faced by the CDU, Biedenkopf demanded 'equal opportunities' (*Chancengleichheit*)—which was precisely one of those highly valued key terms 'occupied' by the SPD. Biedenkopf thus involuntarily demonstrated how difficult it was to introduce alternative terms, such as *Chancengerechtigkeit* ('fair distribution of opportunities'), the term officially recommended by the CDU to replace the more egalitarian-sounding *Chancengleichheit*.[48]

In Germany, the accusation of 'language robbery' and the underlying sentiment of being silenced and shut off from public

---

[46] Bernhard Badura, *Sprachbarrieren: Zur Soziologie der Kommunikation* (2nd edn. Stuttgart, 1973). [47] Biedenkopf, 'Politik und Sprache', 28.
[48] Ibid. 29; for usage of the term 'Chancengerechtigkeit' see e.g. Bernhard Vogel, 'Kurskorrektur für die Schulpolitik', in id. (ed.), *Neue Bildungspolitik*, 91–118, at 96–7; Silke Hahn, 'Zwischen Re-education und zweiter Bildungsreform: Die Sprache der Bildungspolitik in der öffentlichen Diskussion', in Stötzel and Wengeler (eds.), *Kontroverse Begriffe*, 163–209, at 180–1.

debate is part of another, older tradition that goes back at least
to 1945. It is linked to debates which dealt with continuities of
National Socialist language in post-war Germany and were conducted under the general heading of 'language criticism'
(*Sprachkritik*). *Sprachkritik* exhibited many facets in Germany. As in
other countries, it was concerned with grammatically incorrect or
improper usage of language and words. More important than
these aspects, however, was the critique of what later became
known as 'politically incorrect' speech, in particular, the use of
Nazi vocabulary or words and phrases that had acquired specific
'inhumane' meanings during the years of National Socialist rule in
Germany. *Sprachkritik* in this sense was a political act. It was, as
the linguist Jürgen Heringer put it, 'a continuation of politics by
better means'.[49] *Sprachkritik*, in the eyes of its practitioners, played
an essential part in the process of denazification and democratization after 1945.

Eradicating Nazi language from any public debate was one
point on the agenda; finding and establishing a new public and
more 'civil' language was the other. Immediately after 1945, the
eradication of the old vocabulary and the establishment of a new
one were closely linked to programmes of 'denazification' and 're-
education' in both Western and Eastern occupation zones.[50] In
the months and years immediately following the war, censorship of
language became a highly controversial issue and was subtly
inscribed into German political culture. It is not surprising to see
that sensitivity to the improper use of language was spread
unevenly in post-war society. Those who had been treated as 'outsiders' by the *Volksgemeinschaft* were more prone to see semantic
continuity than those who had been 'insiders', irrespective of
whether they had been Nazi enthusiasts or hangers-on. American
press officers were shocked to realize that Nazi words, phrases, and
stereotypes had survived military defeat and were still being used,
mechanically and unscrupulously. For example, immediately after

---

[49] For an overview of German *Sprachkritik* see Hans Jürgen Heringer, 'Sprachkritik—die
Fortsetzung der Politik mit besseren Mitteln', in id. (ed.), *Holzfeuer im hölzernen Ofen*.

[50] Georg Stötzel, 'Die frühe Nachkriegszeit', in id. and Wengeler (eds.), *Kontroverse Begriffe*,
19–34; id., 'Der Nazi-Komplex', ibid. 355–82; Konrad Ehlich, '"... LTI, LQI, ..."': Von
der Unschuld der Sprache und der Schuld der Sprechenden', in Heidrun Kämper and
Hartmut Schmidt (eds.), *Das 20. Jahrhundert: Sprachgeschichte—Zeitgeschichte* (Berlin, 1998),
275–303, at 280; Jürgen Schiewe, 'Wege der Sprachkritik nach 1945', in Martin Wengeler
(ed.), *Deutsche Sprachgeschichte nach 1945: Diskurs- und kulturgeschichtliche Perspektiven. Beiträge einer
Tagung anlässlich der Emeritierung Georg Stötzels* (Hildesheim, 2003), 125–38.

the war, a city official in Munich declared that the devastation of the Jewish cemetery in that city was a 'problem for which an *Endlösung* (final solution) had to be found'.

The same feeling was shared by many contemporaries. The newly founded political and cultural magazines of the immediate post-war period were full of articles proposing a 'new language' (odd as both the arguments and the language were).[51] It was in this atmosphere that, after 1945, Dolf Sternberger, Gerhard Storz, and Wilhelm Süskind published a series of articles in the journal *Die Wandlung* under the heading 'Wörterbuch des Unmenschen' (Dictionary of the Non-Human). At a glance, they argued, words such as *Auftrag* (mission), *Betreuung* (taking care of), *tragbar/untragbar* (acceptable/unacceptable), or *Raum* (space) seemed altogether harmless. During the Third Reich, however, these words had been stripped of their earlier innocence. They were now tainted and imbued with Nazi ideology to a degree which, in their view, made it impossible to use them as innocent words any longer. When in 1957 the three authors collected their earlier articles in a book, they saw no reason for optimism about the progress made in purifying the German language of such tainted words. On the contrary, they wrote, 'no pure and new, no more decent and flexible, no more friendly language has developed; to the present day the ordinary, nay the dominant way of using our German language still relies on these remnants [of Nazi language]'.[52]

A similar point was made by the famous contemporary observer of the *Lingua Tertii Imperii* (Language of the Third Reich, LTI), Victor Klemperer, a professor of Romance literature who had been chased out of office by the Nazis because of his 'non-Aryan' descent, but survived the regime thanks to his marriage with a Christian woman. 'Words', Klemperer wrote in an often quoted line, are like 'tiny doses of arsenic; they are swallowed inadvertently, they don't appear to have any effect, but after a while, the

---

[51] Urs Widmer, *1945 oder die 'Neue Sprache': Studien zur Prosa der 'Jungen Generation'* (Düsseldorf, 1966); see also Martin H. Geyer, 'Am Anfang war . . . die Niederlage: Die Anfänge der bundesdeutschen Moderne nach 1945', in Inka Mülder-Bach and Eckhard Schumacher (eds.), *Am Anfang war. . . : Ursprungsfiguren und Anfangskonstruktionen der Moderne* (Munich, 2008), 279–306.

[52] Dolf Sternberger, Gerhard Storz, and Wilhelm E. Süskind (eds.), *Aus dem Wörterbuch des Unmenschen: Neue erweiterte Ausgabe mit Zeugnissen des Streits über die Sprachkritik* (Hamburg, 1957), 10; see also Manfred Gawlina, 'Dolf Sternberger 1907–1989', in Wilhelm Blum and Michael Rupp, *Politische Philosophen* (Munich, 1997), 269–307; Schiewe, *Macht der Sprache*, 227–34.

poisonous effect is indeed there.'[53] Klemperer recorded in great
detail the ways in which Nazi language worked its way into everyday social relations during the regime, and how it was perpetuated
after the defeat. This continuity, Klemperer noted with dismay,
was not only happening in the West, but also in the Eastern occupation zone under its officially 'anti-fascist' rulers. Klemperer, who
had become a member of the Communist Party after the war, was
struck by the similarities between 'Nazi and Bolshevik language' in
East Germany.[54]

Both Sternberger and Klemperer presented a strong case for
purging the German language of what they considered Nazi terminology and speech. If this were not done, ran the argument,
the National Socialist uses of language—and with it, National
Socialism—would be catapulted from the past back into the
present. The LTI vocabulary needed to be buried in a 'mass
grave', argued Klemperer with the help of rather macabre
imagery.[55] Purging the tainted terms from language use was said
to be the prerequisite for purging Nazi ideology and *Weltan-
schauung* from society as a whole. 'The depravity of a language is
the depravity of a people,' Sternberger said.[56] Where the argument was pressed to the extreme, it was even suggested that the
German language was so badly infested with Nazi terms and
phraseology that it could hardly any longer be used in a sensible
way. Even those who wished to give the German language a new
lease of life after 1945 often fell into the trap of using the very language they criticized.[57]

Klemperer's and Sternberger's calls to purge German vocabulary did not go uncriticized. In the early years after the war, unre-
pentant German nationalists and conservatives saw such demands
as just another aspect of the ill-advised attempts to re-educate,
censor, and preach to the defeated German people. More important and intellectually more challenging were the objections raised

[53] Victor Klemperer, *LTI: Notizbuch eines Philologen* (1st edn. Berlin, 1947; Halle, 1957), 21;
Dirk Deissler, 'The Nazis May Almost be Said to have "Invented" a New German
Language: Der anglo-amerikanische Diskurs über nationalsozialistischen Sprachgebrauch
im Zweiten Weltkrieg und in der Besatzungszeit', in Wengeler (ed.), *Deutsche Sprachgeschichte
nach 1945*, 319–37.
[54] Ehlich, 'LTI, LQI', 287–8; Schiewe, *Macht der Sprache*, 209–27.
[55] Klemperer, *LTI*.
[56] Dolf Sternberger, 'Gute Sprache und böse Sprache: Zehn Thesen', *Neue Rundschau*
(1963), 403–14, at 412.
[57] Many examples can be found in Widmer, *1945 oder die 'Neue Sprache'*.

against Sternberger (less so against Klemperer) by academic linguists beginning in the early 1960s. Sternberger's style of *Sprachkritik* was denounced by them as mere 'feuilleton', 'a pastime for amateurs', and a type of moralizing. Armed with arguments drawn from modern structuralist linguistics, critics such as the young Peter von Polenz argued that words did not simply reflect reality; rather, the meaning of terms constituted itself and changed continuously while they were being used. According to Polenz, Sternberger's idea that ordinary German words such as *Auftrag*, *Betreuung*, or *Raum* were forever contaminated just because the Nazis had used them in a particular way was erroneous. However, words such as *Untermensch* or *Zinsknechtschaft*, which had been coined by the National Socialists or were so closely associated with their ideology that no one could be mistaken about their meaning, were a different matter.[58] It is interesting that Polenz also emphasized the necessity to defend the 'common folk' against the arrogance of intellectual critics such as the writer and essayist Hans Magnus Enzensberger. Enzensberger had mocked the use of 'inhumane' Nazi language by people 'sitting in German commuter trains' using stock phrases and expressions such as 'bis zur Vergasung etwas tun' ('doing something to the point of being "gassed"', that is, to the utmost).[59] Basing his argument on the findings of linguistic structuralism, Polenz rejected Sternberger's belief that certain 'words necessarily contained' recollections of National Socialism. Therefore it would be wrong to accuse 'ordinary language-users, workers "in commuter trains" of being guilty of failing memories or cynicism'.[60]

Taking the same line, Konrad Ehlich has argued more recently that the authors of the 'Wörterbuch des Unmenschen' had made 'language itself into an actor'. By doing so, he said, they made use of a conception of language that had also informed Goebbels's propaganda; theirs was a conception of language 'that fatally resembled the one which they were about to criticize from good

[58] Hans Jürgen Heringer, 'Der Streit um die Sprachkritik: Dialog mit Peter von Polenz im Februar 1981', in id. (ed.), *Holzfeuer im hölzernen Ofen*, 161–75, at 165; Peter von Polenz, 'Sprachkritik und Sprachwissenschaft', *Neue Rundschau*, 74 (1963), 391–403.

[59] Thus Polenz looking back to the debate in the early 1960s, repeating his own position. Polenz, 'Sprachkritik und Sprachwissenschaft'; Heringer, 'Der Streit um die Sprachkritik', 165–6.

[60] Ibid. One might draw parallels with structuralist interpretations of the Nazi regime such as Nicolas Berg, *Der Holocaust und die westdeutschen Historiker: Erforschung und Erinnerung* (Göttingen, 2003).

motives and the best intentions'. Ehlich maintains that their form of *Sprachkritik* demonstrates better than anything else what he suspects to be their 'naive' understanding of Nazi ideology, in particular, their confusion of language with 'reality'.[61] It is noteworthy that many linguists were critical of the political controversy initiated by the CDU for very similar reasons. For some of them, the conservative language campaign smacked of old-style *Sprachkritik*; for others, the CDU critics were wrong because they made a simple equation between words and the world, and implied that the latter could be transformed solely by exchanging the former.

From a historical point of view, however, it is hard to overlook that those authors in the 1950s and 1960s who criticized the continuation of Nazi language were indeed contributing to *some* changes in German public language, though perhaps not always in the way they had intended. The use of language mattered; recasting the political and cultural life of post-war Germany was a matter of finding a new language. What might, in any case, be attributed to the efforts of the practitioners of *Sprachkritik* of whatever political persuasion is a growing sensitivity among the German public to the fact that words can 'do' certain things (harm other people, for example), even if the speaker does not intend to do so—in other words, a sensitivity to what nowadays is called (mostly with negative connotations) 'political correctness'. To be sure, it is far from easy to demonstrate exactly how *Sprachkritik* contributed to linguistic change,[62] especially if we cling to the somewhat narrow models of linguistic structuralism. Yet it is impossible to deny that from the early 1960s on almost all sectors of West German society were far from a consensus on language; instead, Germany was immersed in fierce controversies about the 'proper' or 'improper' use of words and terms to describe the past, present, and future. West Germany's modernism thrived on these efforts, as the debates in the fine arts, music, the aesthetics of everyday life, and various academic fields, including history, show. More often than not, these controversies merged with social and political movements that attacked the proverbial 'stuffiness' of the Adenauer era and engaged in new forms of political and social expression. Equally important was the fact that a broad spectrum of intellectuals closely observed

---

[61] Ehlich, 'LTI, LQI', 287.   [62] Schiewe, 'Wege der Sprachkritik', 134.

the use of language and speech, and expressed their concerns in critical reviews of culture, language, and morality.[63] Linguistic continuities were closely monitored, regardless of where they were found, whether in connection with new debates over 'degenerate art', the so-called *Spiegel* affair of the early 1960s, or German history, to name just a few examples.[64]

Public sensitivity to the use of terms in West Germany increased considerably starting in the late 1950s. In some respects, this sensitivity was stimulated by critical impulses from abroad, but it also had roots in a long-standing German academic discussion on the history of concepts. Sparked by debates on Germany's recent past in the early decades of the Federal Republic, concepts and their meanings became the object of critical revisions whose history can be traced back to the age of the Enlightenment or other, less progressive, traditions.[65] One example is Theodor W. Adorno's polemical work *Jargon der Eigentlichkeit: Zur deutschen Ideologie* (1964), in which he attacked Martin Heidegger's irrational and pseudo-individualistic language of *Erhabenheit* (grandeur) laced with that of existentialism. For Adorno, Heidegger's jargon was prototypical of that of many other post-war German philosophers or would-be philosophers. Adorno claimed that it was not only blind to the realities of war and, worse, to the extermination of the Jews, but was, in its entirety, the successor of Nazi language.[66]

Almost obsessively, all reflection on language began or ended with National Socialism. As Peter von Polenz noted, it reached the point where people were soon unable to distinguish between outright 'Nazi language' and ordinary 'language used in the Third Reich', between the real vocabulary of the 'Dictionary of the Non-Human', and the *Jargon der Eigentlichkeit*, between 'the everyday language of a bureaucratized world' and 'the frozen language'.[67]

---

[63] Rainer Wimmer, 'Überlegungen zu den Aufgaben und Methoden einer linguistisch begründeten Sprachkritik', in Heringer (ed.), *Holzfeuer im hölzernen Ofen*, 290–313, at 290; Steger, 'Sprache im Wandel', 17.   [64] Stötzel, 'Der Nazi-Komplex', 358–9.

[65] In my essay 'Im Schatten der NS-Zeit' I suggest that conceptual history was all about redefining national history after the 'catastrophe' of 1945; for the obsession with *Begriffsgeschichte* see also Hans Ulrich Gumbrecht, *Dimensionen und Grenzen der Begriffsgeschichte* (Munich, 2006).

[66] Theodor W. Adorno, *Jargon der Eigentlichkeit: Zur deutschen Ideologie* (1st edn. 1964; 6th edn. Frankfurt am Main, 1971).

[67] Peter von Polenz, 'Sprachkritik und Sprachnormenkritik', in Heringer (ed.), *Holzfeuer im hölzernen Ofen*, 70–93, at 82; in addition to the above-mentioned books by Sternberger and Klemperer, the references pertain to Adorno, *Jargon der Eigentlichkeit*; Karl Korn, *Sprache*

While there was consensus that 'real' Nazi vocabulary and those euphemisms with which they had designated their extermination policies, such as *Sonderbehandlung* (special treatment), should disappear, this consensus ended when critics such as Sternberger or Adorno depicted continuities. If Sternberger was right, and ordinary German words such as *echt* (pure) or *Anliegen* (concern) were tainted with National Socialist ideology, where could the enquiry stop? Was it possible to use the German language? Was there not a long linguistic continuity encompassing all aspects of life, reaching back at least into the nineteenth century, leading to conformism, fascism, and war? If one started to think along these lines, the 'Wörterbuch des Unmenschen' needed to be considerably expanded—thus ran the argument, also of Peter von Polenz. It should then certainly include such terms as 'Ehre, Treue, Pflicht, Opfer und Schicksal' (honour, loyalty, duty, sacrifice, and fate); it should include archaisms such as 'das deutsche Schwert' (the German sword), and collective singular forms such as 'der deutsche Soldat', 'der Deutsche', 'der Jude', and 'der Russe' (*the* German soldier, *the* German, *the* Jew, *the* Russian).[68] It is noteworthy that Polenz wrote this in 1973, the same year in which German conservatives lamented having lost 'their' language and claimed that they did not even dare to use the word 'conservative' anymore.[69]

The almost obsessive treatment of concepts and key terms in the German language can be seen in other areas. There may be no explicit references between these expressions of fear at the imminent loss of German words for everyday use and the academic enterprise of *Begriffsgeschichte* (history of concepts) launched at about the same time by Reinhart Koselleck and his colleagues (the first volume of the dictionary *Geschichtliche Grundbegriffe* appeared in 1972). Yet this huge academic enterprise by Koselleck and others thrived on the belief of West German historians that it was necessary to clarify the meanings of contested terms. Historicization of German key political and social terms and their meanings was the main purpose of that enterprise, although the focus of the dictionary was, in general, on the period of transition (*Sattelzeit*) between the late eighteenth and the early nineteenth

---

in einer verwalteten Welt (Freiburg, 1958); and Friedrich Handt, *Deutsch, gefrorene Sprache in einem gefrorenen Land* (Berlin, 1964).

[68] Polenz, 'Sprachkritik und Sprachnormenkritik', 82–3.
[69] Schelsky, *Die Arbeit tun die anderen*, 248.

centuries.[70] Despite this different chronological focus, however, it was certainly no comfort to conservatives, who were looking for some sort of stable world view anchored in traditional concepts, to see that no such concepts existed without an ever-changing and ever-contested history behind them.

The Year 1968, or the Great Delusion of Language

In his polemic against left-wing intellectuals in 1975, Helmut Schelsky identified yet another form of 'word theft'. He claimed that the new academic generation was robbing 'anal speech' from the 'average guy on the street'.[71] With the advent of 'dirty speech', we can discern a characteristic type of spoken language: provocative political slogans mingled with ordinary language and violent imagery directed against objects and people. This kind of 'dirty speech' and, a few years later, 'kaputte Sprachen' (wrecked languages) used by the *Spontis* were disturbing phenomena, regardless of whether they were interpreted as outgrowths of a fundamental shift in values, evidence of the emergence of new youth cultures bereft of bourgeois virtues, or the breeding ground of anarchism and violence.[72] The estrangement from established norms of speech and formalities of writing can be seen as the mere tip of the iceberg, a sign not only of a fundamental estrangement from bourgeois values but also of conventions of speech in the post-war period. The jargons of the various strands of Marxism, including that of the Frankfurt School, psychoanalysis, feminism, environmentalism, and the social sciences in general permeated public

---

[70] See the introduction to this volume by Willibald Steinmetz; Reinhart Koselleck and Christoph Dipper, 'Reinhart Koselleck im Gespräch mit Christoph Dipper: Begriffsgeschichte, Sozialgeschichte, begriffene Geschichte', *Neue politische Literatur*, 43 (1998), 187–205; Gumbrecht, *Dimensionen und Grenzen*.

[71] Schelsky, *Die Arbeit tun die anderen*, 248.

[72] There are many descriptions of the various ideological strands and characteristics of the language of the left: Wolfgang Kraushaar, 'Denkmodelle der 68er-Bewegung', *Aus Politik und Zeitgeschichte*, 22/3 (2001), 14–27; Siegfried Jäger, 'Linke Wörter: Einige Bemerkungen zur Sprache der APO', *Muttersprache: Vierteljahresschrift für deutsche Sprache*, 80 (1970), 85–106; Andreas von Weiss, *Schlagwörter der Neuen Linken: Die Agitation der Sozialrevolutionäre* (Munich, 1974); Straßner, '1968 und die sprachlichen Folgen'; Matthis Dienstag, 'Provinz aus dem Kopf: Neue Nachrichten über die Metropolen-Spontis', in Peter Brückner and Wolfgang Kraushaar (eds.), *Autonomie oder Getto? Kontroversen über die Alternativbewegung* (Frankfurt am Main, 1978), 148–86; Herbert Stubenrauch, '"Scheiße, irgendwie blick ich da halt nicht mehr so durch . . .": Eine philologische Miniatur über die Sprache der Sponti-Linken', *PÄD.extra*, 3 (1978), 44–7.

happenings and university seminars. This was tantamount to creating new hybrid forms of language, some of which became practically incomprehensible to outsiders; it was not just conservatives who felt shut off from public and academic discourse and relegated to the position of observers. More disconcerting was the fact that by the mid-1970s a general denunciation of almost everything was all that was left of the critical questioning of terms that had helped to drive the student movement a decade earlier. This was the environment in which the new conservative language critique originated.

This development took place with almost breathtaking speed, starting with the emergence of the student movement. The earlier language criticism became more radical, and some of the earlier practitioners of *Sprachkritik*, such as Sternberger, were estranged if not silenced.[73] The student movement was obsessed with the legacies and continuities of Nazism or 'fascism', as it now became common to say. For the radical critics there was no topic in contemporary society that was not related to this past. A seemingly endless contestation and denunciation of terms occurred in a new setting that featured a highly performative way of speaking and writing and, most surprisingly for contemporaries, a *prise de parole* (M. Certeau) by way of 'sit-ins', 'go-ins', street theatre performances, and similar events. The fact that the act of speaking is a form of social and communicative action was certainly not a new theoretical finding, but it was no accident that this idea attracted a great deal of attention under these particular circumstances.[74]

The student movement did not speak about language in the abstract, but criticized individual uses of speech by politicians,

---

[73] See von Polenz's observation with respect to Sternberger who taught at the University of Heidelberg; Heringer, 'Der Streit um die Sprachkritik', 164.

[74] Michel de Certeau, *La Prise de parole: Pour une nouvelle culture* (Paris, 1968); Hermann Lübbe, 'Sein und Heißen: Bedeutungsgeschichte als politisches Sprachhandlungsfeld', in Reinhart Koselleck (ed.), *Historische Semantik und Begriffsgeschichte* (Stuttgart, 1978), 334–57; on *Sprechhandlungen* (speech acts), which otherwise play a minor part in *Geschichtliche Grundbegriffe*, see Reinhart Koselleck, 'Sozialgeschichte und Begriffsgeschichte', in Wolfgang Schieder and Volker Sellin (eds.), *Sozialgeschichte in Deutschland: Entwicklungen und Perspektiven im internationalen Zusammenhang*, 4 vols. (Göttingen, 1986–7), i. *Die Sozialgeschichte innerhalb der Geschichtswissenschaft* (1986), 89–109, at 94; Josef Kopperschmidt, 'Der politische Kampf ums Heißen', in Oswald Panagl (ed.), *Fahnenwörter der Politik* (Vienna, 1998), 151–68; Josef Kopperschmidt, '1968 oder "die Lust am Reden": Über die revolutionären Folgen einer Scheinrevolution', *Muttersprache: Vierteljahresschrift für deutsche Sprache*, 110 (2000), 1–12; Straßner, '1968 und die sprachlichen Folgen'; Martin Wengeler, '"1968" als sprachgeschichtliche Zäsur', in Stötzel and Wengeler (eds.), *Kontroverse Begriffe*, 383–404.

industrialists, and professors, past and present. This may be seen, for example, in Wolfgang Fritz Haug's often cited work *Der hilflose Antifaschismus* (1967), which in many respects reformulated ideas found in Adorno's *Jargon der Eigentlichkeit*. In this work Haug, who was also the editor of the leftist journal *Das Argument*, offered a close reading of the language used by German university professors in the mid-1960s when they undertook to lecture on National Socialism, often in response to student demand. Haug's main point was that these academics seemed absolutely 'helpless' when searching for an adequate new language in which to speak on the topic. He ridiculed these professors, who had pursued their careers during the Third Reich and had sometimes been actively involved in the Nazi system, and now tried to come to terms with it using language that strikingly resembled the language they had been using at the celebrations of the Nazi regime itself. For example, when they spoke of the 'Blutzeugen der Weißen Rose' they were using a term which the Nazis had reserved for their own 'martyrs' (*Blutzeuge*) of the Hitler putsch of 1923 in order to express their respect for the sacrifices of the resistance movement Weiße Rose.[75] Another object of Haug's scorn was the jargon of German *Innerlichkeit* (introspection) in general and, in particular, the emotional proximity of tone between expressions of enthusiasm (*for* Nazism) before 1945 and expressions of outrage (*against* Nazism) in the 1960s: 'The contemptuous still have much to learn. Their "no" and their expressions of outrage are still very close to their "yes" to fascism.' And he added a quotation from Eric Voegelin, who was making the same point: '"That is atrocious"—that is what those who then said: "That is wonderful" can say today.'[76]

Adorno and Haug were often emulated by left-wing students who wanted to target Establishment figures by criticizing their language. The man most revered by the students and most abhorred by the conservatives was Herbert Marcuse. The German-American philosopher became a guru of the student movement, perhaps in no small measure because of his role as an outspoken anti-Nazi and ersatz father figure for this generation. His intellectual roots were to be found in the ideological and

---

[75] Wolfgang Fritz Haug, *Der hilflose Antifaschismus: Zur Kritik der Vorlesungsreihen über Wissenschaft und Nationalsozialismus an den deutschen Universitäten* (Frankfurt am Main, 1967), 17–24. [76] Ibid. 24.

conflictual inter-war period (not unlike those of Carl Schmitt). Marcuse's biography as a victim of fascism placed him in a position to help bridge the gap dividing the American and European left. For Marcuse, too, language criticism was an essential part of his general critique of society. Arguing that the 'dominant language was but the language of the dominating classes', he maintained that language was the most 'subtle form of oppression'. If, however, language was nothing but the armour of the Establishment, then this very language had to be challenged; words needed to be liberated and newly appropriated in an effort to create a new consciousness: 'When the radical opposition develops its own language, it is protesting spontaneously and unconsciously against one of the most effective "secret weapons" of domination and defamation. The ruling language of law and order, declared valid by the courts and the police, is not only the *voice* of oppression, it is also the *act* of oppression. Language not only defines and condemns the enemy, it creates him as well.' Therefore revolution, in order to be effective, had to extend to language by appropriating it and turning it against the ruling class. It should not come as a surprise that Marcuse's words were picked up by conservative critics.[77]

Marcuse's ideas fitted well with the rebelling students' belief that consciousness could be changed and authorities rocked by unconventional actions and, in particular, verbal attacks. His ideas were also a good reflection of a much broader contemporary preoccupation with questioning everything and everyone in order to 'contribute to the emancipation of our society' or to expose 'manipulation through political speech . . . or through advertising', a preoccupation that also pervaded linguistics and other academic disciplines at the time.[78] Even the German Catholic Church was hit by this unruly attitude of questioning. A group of 'leftist pious' followers attending the 1968 Catholic Convention in Essen successfully introduced a resolution stating that Catholics

[77] Clemens Albrecht, Günter C. Behrmann, Michael Bock, Harald Homann, and Friedrich H. Tenbruck, *Die intellektuelle Gründung der Bundesrepublik: Eine Wirkungsgeschichte der Frankfurter Schule* (Frankfurt, 1999), esp. ch. 11; Herbert Marcuse, *Versuch über die Befreiung* (Frankfurt, 1969), 22, 110. There are many references to this book; see e.g. Wengeler, '"1968" als sprachgeschichtliche Zäsur', 387–8; and Bergsdorf, *Politik und Sprache*, 237–8; for a good analysis also of other texts by Marcuse, see Kopperschmidt, '1968 oder "die Lust am Reden"', 4–7.

[78] Franz Januscheck, *Sprache als Objekt: 'Sprechhandlungen' in Werbung, Kunst und Linguistik* (Kronberg im Taunus, 1976), 6–7.

could not accept the 'demand for obedience with regard to the papal decision on the question of methods of contraception' and that the Pope needed to submit his doctrine to 'a fundamental revision'.[79] For the above-mentioned Catholic Hans Maier, these were the kinds of incidents that prompted his observations on the 'purist overstretching' of terms and the destruction of the existing order after the use of such terms.[80]

Another worrying aspect of linguistic change, also noted at the time by observers on the left, was changes in the discourse of violence. Expressions such as 'destroy that which destroys you' ('macht kaputt was Euch kaputt macht') and 'violence against objects' ('Gewalt gegen Sachen') were widely used, thus implying that this was a kind of legitimate violence. By the early 1970s, a mixture of radicalized speech and action could be experienced in many different places: in university classrooms, where it caused frustration and shock among an entire generation of professors; in the house-squatting movement in urban centres, where it caused bitter skirmishes and hostile confrontations with local police; in radical factory cells, where it disconcerted management and conservative unions alike; and, not least, in the embrace of violence by a segment of the protest movement, where it caused increasingly vicious acts of terrorism.[81] The language of violence which accompanied all these actions soon led to splits within the movements of the left,[82] and this was picked up by their conservative critics who, like Maier, were quick to draw parallels between the polemical writings of the terrorist Red Army Faction (Rote Armee Fraktion) and the way in which writers such as Ernst Jünger had praised violence in the years before National Socialism. In a public exchange with the writer Heinrich Böll in 1974, Maier referred not only to the murders committed by the Rote Armee Fraktion, but also to the suicides of some of his

[79] Christoph Kleßmann, *Zwei Staaten, eine Nation: Deutsche Geschichte 1955–1970* (Bonn, 1997), 284.   [80] Maier, *Sprache und Politik*, 20.

[81] For a good survey and different aspects, see the essays in *Archiv für Sozialgeschichte*, 44 (2004); Wolfgang Kraushaar, *Die RAF und der linke Terrorismus*, 2 vols. (Hamburg 2006).

[82] The critical account by the editor of the magazine *konkret* and former husband of Ulrike Meinhof is not necessarily reliable, but very informative: 'Everything that the Baader-Meinhof group translated into blood reality, not shying away from claiming human victims, had already been foreshadowed trivially somewhere in a flyer or underground newspaper produced in a Kreuzberg backyard.' Klaus Rainer Röhl, *Fünf Finger sind keine Faust: Eine Abrechnung* (1st edn. 1974; repr. Munich, 1998), 228; see also Wolfgang Kraushaar, *Die Bombe im Jüdischen Gemeindehaus* (Hamburg, 2005).

friends and colleagues who had been verbally attacked.[83] The
marked increase in terrorist violence gave the public debate on
language in the mid-1970s its acidity, the more so as 'violence
against objects' increasingly turned into 'violence against people'.
The climax came in the autumn of 1977 when an anonymous
student at Göttingen University, calling himself 'Mescalero', wrote
in a leaflet of his 'klammheimliche Freude' (secret joy) at the
murder of Attorney General Siegfried Buback that year. Cynically
he expressed his regret that 'this face [Buback's] need no longer
appear in the small red-and-black album of criminals . . . that we
will publish after the revolution'. The author also included a few
passages in which he expressed a more critical view of the use of
violence ('Our path to socialism or, if you prefer, to anarchy,
should not be paved with corpses'), but these passages paled by
comparison with the overall cynical tone.[84]

Early on, it was not just conservative observers who noted the
delusions of some members of the student movement that
stemmed from its own language. As early as 1969, Jürgen
Habermas accused radicals of exhibiting signs of 'leftist fascism',
and confusing linguistic and symbolic actions with reality. It was
a sign of insanity, said Habermas, to interpret the act of occupying
a university as a real seizure of power, analogous to the storming
of the Bastille, as some student leaders did.[85] Habermas compared
the new activism to that of 1848 utopian socialism, and that of
Georges Sorel and Benito Mussolini, whose origins both lay in the
left. There can be no doubt that the analogy with National
Socialism and the linguistic delusions that befell Germans during
the Third Reich played an important part, if only implicitly, in
these debates and within the left itself. The older generation of
the Frankfurt School was quite outspoken in this respect; for Max
Horkheimer, the anti-Americanism of the German student movement fulfilled 'more or less the function of anti-Semitism'.[86]

If Habermas and Horkheimer dwelled on the illusions and

[83] This correspondence with Böll is reprinted in Maier, *Sprache und Politik*, 29–43, at 38.

[84] 'Buback: Ein Nachruf', reprinted in Utz Maas, *Sprachpolitik und politische Sprachwissenschaft: Sieben Studien* (Göttingen, 1989), 305–9, at 305, 308.

[85] Jürgen Habermas, 'Die Scheinrevolution und ihre Kinder: Sechs Thesen über
Taktik, Ziele und Situationsanalysen der oppositionellen Jugend', *Frankfurter Rundschau*, 5
June 1968, reprinted in id. (ed.), *Protestbewegung und Hochschulreform* (Frankfurt am Main,
1969), 188–201.

[86] Max Horkheimer, *Gesammelte Schriften*, xiv. 444, quoted in Albrecht, Behrmann, Bock,
Homann, and Tenbruck, *Die intellektuelle Gründung*, 324.

delusions of radical language, conservatives were infatuated with the issue of power, much like Marcuse. 'Ist das Reich der Vorstellung erst revolutioniert, so hält die Wirklichkeit nicht mehr stand' (once the realm of imagination has been revolutionized, reality cannot hold out for long): these are the words not of Marcuse, but of Hegel, as quoted by Kurt Biedenkopf.[87] Even more curious (and verging on the tautological) is the invocation of the 'power of language' by Wolfgang Bergsdorf:

The role of key terms in history demonstrates that the power-holders and the power-seekers are equally interested in using language for their own political purposes. Thus language becomes a factor of power because the powerful and those who want to become powerful consider language as a factor of power. The language of politics becomes a language of power. Whoever is powerful tries to prescribe the 'right' usage of words. Only those who have powerful positions are powerful. People who are capable of enforcing the content and the use of words also possess power.[88]

This passage was not meant as a satire on Marcuse; just the opposite. It illustrates yet again how obsessively some conservatives chose to adopt the notion that terms could be 'occupied' and 'reoccupied' from the New Left.[89]

At an academic level, the problem raised by the experience of the 'power of language' in the late 1960s led to more far-reaching theoretical debates, and not just in Germany. 'Symbolic power is the power to create things with words', argued Pierre Bourdieu and, with explicit reference to E. P. Thompson's *The Making of the English Working Class*, he added that in order to change the world, all social groups have to attempt to '"make" and remake the world'. Although this sounds like the standard fare of the linguistic turn in the social sciences, Bourdieu also stressed the power of the

---

[87] Biedenkopf, 'Politik und Sprache', 23; see also Kopperschmidt, '1968 oder "die Lust am Reden"', 6.

[88] Wolfgang Bergsdorf, 'Einführung', in id. (ed.), *Wörter als Waffen*, 7–14, at 10.

[89] Thus in 1992, the linguist Erich Straßner, not an advocate of the political left, came to the conclusion when looking back at the work of the CDU task force on semantics in the 1970s that it had accepted 'the principle which had already been used by the National Socialists before 1933 against other parties', namely, 'to adopt the catchwords and keywords of the SPD, to twist them semantically and integrate them into the ideological and political context of their own party'. Ironically, in order to make this point, Straßner quoted almost verbatim the earlier accusations directed by Maier and Biedenkopf against the New Left's adoption of National Socialist strategies. See Straßner, '1968 und die sprachlichen Folgen', 250.

'objective world', the construction of which stood in a dialectical relationship with language: 'only if the concepts of a new language are true, that is, conform to things, can the new language create a new description of things.'[90] Yet, who was to define what was 'true' and what not?

The Conservative prise de parole

In 1979, a decade after Jürgen Habermas had accused the rebellious students of 'leftist fascism', he found himself again expressing his incredulity, this time at the conservatives who seemed to share some of the naive ideas on the power of language that had once been harboured by some within the New Left.[91] Again, politicians who wanted to win the next election did not much care about Habermas's theoretical subtleties. Closer to their concerns was Hermann Lübbe's advice that only in 'de-politicized semantic spaces' such as an Oxford college or a university seminar on philosophy was it possible to observe the Aristotelian rule that disputes about words were futile. In the political space, Lübbe said, 'the person who gives in is not always the more intelligent', for he/she 'leaves to the political opponent a monopoly on defining the purposes for which the disputed words become catchwords'.[92] This was more to the taste of Biedenkopf and his followers when they set out to update the CDU's agenda and recapture the political initiative.

In hindsight, it is obvious that they were quite effective in this respect, partly because the Zeitgeist was on their side from the mid-1970s on (but what, after all, is the Zeitgeist if it does not find its expression?). Although the shift in political power and the

---

[90] Pierre Bourdieu, 'Sozialer Raum und symbolische Macht (1986)', in id., *Rede und Antwort* (Frankfurt am Main, 1992), 135–54, at 152–3. These reflections are part of a larger debate in the social sciences that cannot be dealt with here, see e.g. Jürgen Habermas, *Zur Logik der Sozialwissenschaften: Materialien* (Frankfurt am Main, 1970), esp. 290–308; Claus Mueller, *The Politics of Communication: A Study in the Political Sociology of Language, Socialization, and Legitimation* (New York, 1973), published in German as *Politik und Kommunikation* (Munich, 1975).

[91] Jürgen Habermas, 'Einleitung', in id. (ed.), *Stichworte zur 'Geistigen Situation der Zeit'*, 2 vols. (Frankfurt am Main, 1979), i. *Nation und Republik*, 7–35, at 21; see also Kopperschmidt, '1968 oder "die Lust am Reden"', 10.

[92] Hermann Lübbe, 'Der Streit um Worte: Sprache und Politik (1967)', in Heringer (ed.), *Holzfeuer im hölzernen Ofen*, 48–69, at 66, 67; a shortened version is reprinted in Kaltenbrunner (ed.), *Sprache und Herrschaft*, 87–112.

'geistig-moralische Wende' (intellectual-moral turn) as proclaimed by Helmut Kohl did not come until 1982, several factors worked in favour of a conservative counterattack. The most notable of these were the aftershocks of the oil crisis, the widespread disillusionment among the left after the downfall of Chancellor Brandt in 1974, the ensuing pragmatic politics of the new chancellor, Helmut Schmidt, and, not to be forgotten, the excesses of terrorism. These events lent plausibility to conservative talk of a *Tendenzwende*, which then became a self-fulfilling prophecy. In retrospect, it is difficult to distinguish between cause and effect when considering, on the one hand, the changing economic parameters that evolved with recession, unemployment, and the ensuing disillusionment with 'reform euphoria', and, on the other, the new conservative discourses on the end of social reform policies and the limits of the achievable in politics generally. This narrative of the course of change, including the critique of 'reform euphoria' and a fading 'belief in achievability' (*Machbarkeitsglaube*), is now firmly established in historical literature.[93]

The conservative *prise de parole* was pursued at many levels. By 1974, confidence had already been restored in the strength and direction of the party because 'equal opportunities in semantics' had been achieved through the 'occupation of key political terms' in important policy fields.[94] By 1977, when Biedenkopf and Helmut Kohl parted ways in a far from cordial manner, the former secretary general could pat himself on the back in the conviction that the party had, after all, 're-conquered the intellectual and political leadership of the country'.[95] Indeed, the years between 1974 and 1977 marked a high point in the acerbic political war over words. Hardly an issue existed for which the CDU did not develop its own alternative term: a New Social Question was invented, implying that the opponent had only an Old Social Question in mind, associated with organized corporate interests

---

[93] On Chancellor Willy Brandt's 'utopian vocabulary' that foundered on reality, see Bergsdorf, *Herrschaft und Sprache*, 243–52; for the end of 'reform euphoria' see e.g. Gabriele Metzler, *Konzeptionen politischen Handelns von Adenauer bis Brandt: Politische Planung in der pluralistischen Gesellschaft* (Paderborn, 2005).

[94] Mahler, 'Politik und Sprache', 38; see also Behrens, Dieckmann, and Kehl, 'Politik als Sprachkampf', 229.

[95] Report as secretary general to the 1977 party conference, see Christlich-Demokratische Union Deutschlands (CDU), *25. Bundesparteitag der Christlich-Demokratischen Union Deutschlands: Niederschrift. Düsseldorf 7.– 9. März 1977* (Bonn, 1977), 57; others had proposed this much earlier see e.g. Mahler, 'Politik und Sprache', 38.

working at the expense of families and the individualized poor. As already mentioned, the SPD's favourite term *Chancengleichheit* became *Chancengerechtigkeit* for the CDU. Other high-grade terms, such as 'liberty', 'solidarity', and 'justice', which the SPD reaffirmed as their 'basic values' in their 1975 party programme, were adopted and redefined by the CDU in the context of their efforts to modernize their own party programme.[96] In the eyes of the German conservatives, these attempts to redefine political terms were a means of stabilizing and controlling social change. They acted in the belief that the polity needed concepts which were shared by all and expressed a certain order (*Ordnungsbegriffe*) to establish its identity. The necessity of these shared concepts was underlined by pointing to the failure of the Weimar Republic, which had lacked a 'community of democrats' in the face of totalitarian attacks.[97]

However, it should not be overlooked that an integrative and consensual strategy had its limits. The war over words required large war chests—funds to subsidize conferences, magazines, authors, and books. By the early 1980s, frequent scandals over illegal contributions to the big parties almost broke many politicians and discredited the lofty rhetoric of many others. In addition, from 1973 on, the Bavarian minister president and CSU party leader, Franz-Josef Strauß, heaped scorn on the CDU reformers. Instead of the slow strategy of 'occupying' key themes of the Social–Liberal coalition, he advocated outright confrontation.[98] For the 1976 federal election campaign he recommended the slogan 'freedom or socialism', which was meant not only to suggest an irreconcilable opposition between liberty and the SPD's 'democratic socialism', but also identified the SPD's goals with the policies of the East German Communists. The CDU reformers reluctantly accepted this slogan, but only after replacing the word 'or' with 'instead of' in the belief that 'freedom instead of socialism' sounded less harsh. Many observers still thought the

---

[96] For a good overview of the war over words, see esp. Stötzel and Wengeler (eds.), *Kontroverse Begriffe*; for a more detailed account of the programmatic debates, see Martin H. Geyer, 'Rahmenbedingungen: Unsicherheit als Normalität', in id. (ed.), *Geschichte der Sozialpolitik in Deutschland seit 1945*, vi. *Die Bundesrepublik 1974 bis 1982: Der Sozialstaat im Zeichen wirtschaftlicher Rezession* (Baden-Baden, 2008), 1–107, at 23–38.

[97] Bergsdorf, *Herrschaft und Sprache*, 15, 266–72.

[98] Geyer, 'Rahmenbedingungen', 39–41; Behrens, Dieckmann, and Kehl, 'Politik als Sprachkampf', 231–7.

slogan in either version was too crude and polarizing. Helmut Schelsky had already warned at the CSU party conference in 1973 that voters would no longer be duped into identifying the Social Democrats with a planned economy and the nationalization of businesses. Instead, the sociologist proposed that the Social Democrats should be identified with a term taken from the 'Wörterbuch des Unmenschen', namely, *Betreuung*, that is, tutelage not by the Nazi state, but by the modern welfare state, and that the CDU/CSU should choose *Selbständigkeit* (self-reliance, independence) as the opposite term to characterize their own policy.[99]

There can be no doubt, however, that ultimately the slogan 'freedom or/instead of socialism' fitted quite well into the general strategy of 'occupying terms'. Support for the slogan came from the CDU in the federal state of Baden-Württemberg, where it had worked well in earlier state elections. The party was also advised to adopt the slogan by an advertising agency contracted to manage its election campaigns. Lastly, it had been recommended by Elisabeth Noelle-Neumann. On the basis of surveys conducted by the public opinion research institute she headed, Noelle-Neumann emphasized that there was overwhelming support for the concept of 'liberty' in the population at large, whereas 'socialism', regardless of shade, was widely discredited.[100]

With respect to the ongoing 'war over words', the conservative election slogan of 1976 had another interesting dimension. It had considerable resonance among the right-wing fringes of the CDU and CSU and found even greater favour among the radical right outside the established party system. The well-known leftist publicist Bert Engelmann actually argued that the origins of this slogan were to be found in Josef Goebbels's propaganda campaign 'freedom or Bolshevism', dating from the end of the Second World War. Engelmann also tried to prove the existence of a conspiracy of former SS men and old propagandists who had found

---

[99] Helmut Schelsky, 'Die Selbständigen und die Betreuten', *Frankfurter Rundschau*, 2 Oct. 1973 and 4 Oct. 1973, quoted in Behrens, Dieckmann, and Kehl, 'Politik als Sprachkampf', 234–5.

[100] See Bergsdorf's summary, based on the institute's polls: Bergsdorf, *Politik und Sprache*, 107–12. There is no doubt that if the conservatives had gained more votes than the Social–Liberal coalition in the election, many would have prided themselves on this victory, not least because of the slogan 'Freiheit oder/statt Sozialismus'. Instead there was much soul-searching as to what went wrong, and why and how this polarizing campaign might have contributed to their failure.

a new political home on the right-wing fringes of the CDU/CSU. These people, he wrote, were preparing the basis for a political change in Bonn at whatever cost.[101] Although evidence for such a conspiracy was extremely thin, there are indications that the general idea of 'occupying terms' found much favour among those who, as young men, had supported the 'conservative revolution' of the early 1930s and were now approaching retirement age.[102]

One biographer and admirer of these men was Armin Mohler, a Swiss German who liked to see himself as the self-styled intellectual of a 'new' political right. Mohler kept in close touch with one of the figureheads of the French New Right, Alain de Benoist, who advocated a 'cultural revolution' which Mohler attempted to make popular in Germany.[103] Benoist was not only an avid reader of German right-wing literature of the inter-war period, but also suggested that the European right should learn from the Italian Marxist Gramsci's concept of 'cultural hegemony'. Language thus rose to a strategic pre-eminence, and by the late 1970s articles were appearing in the German right-wing press ridiculing the German left for having neither read nor understood Gramsci. By and large, this claim was probably true (in fact, Gramsci was not mentioned in the earlier conservative debate), although it is doubtful that many of these authors of the right had themselves read any more than what they picked up in the emerging right-wing discourse. This intellectually armed political right had many axes to grind: socialism, multiculturalism, feminism, universal human rights, détente, the politics of consensus of the established big parties, and the supposed lack of backbone among many conservatives, to name just some of the more important issues.[104] The one that most inflamed Mohler and his kind in Germany was the way historians and politicians handled the Nazi

---

[101] Bernt Engelmann, *Schwarzbuch: Strauß, Kohl & Co* (Cologne, 1976), 21–38. Engelmann also tried to argue against Biedenkopf who, through his second wife, supposedly had contacts with groups of former SS men. He identified the former CDU Bundestag deputy Artur Mierbach as the inventor of the slogan.

[102] See Claus Leggewie, 'Kulturelle Hegemonie: Gramsci und die Folgen', *Leviathan*, 15 (1987), 285–304; Armin Pfahl-Traughber, *Konservative Revolution und Neue Rechte: Rechtsextremistische Intellektuelle gegen den demokratischen Verfassungsstaat* (Opladen, 1998), 35–8.

[103] Armin Mohler, *Die Konservative Revolution in Deutschland 1918–1932*, 2 vols. (3rd edn. Darmstadt, 1989); id., *Das Gespräch: Über Linke, Rechte und Langweiler* (Dresden, 2001).

[104] Ibid. 31–6; for similar references to Gramsci by the far right in the United States, see Benedetto Fontana, 'Power and Democracy: Gramsci and Hegemony in America', in Joseph Francese (ed.), *Perspectives on Gramsci: Politics, Culture and Social Theory* (London, 2009), 80–96.

past, summed up in the word *Vergangenheitsbewältigung* (coming to terms with the past), which Mohler used as the title of a book he wrote in 1969 and which was republished with some success in 1980.[105]

Mohler's attack was straightforward. It dealt not only with the supposed misrepresentation of German history by historians who dwelt on the issue of German 'guilt' with respect to the rise of Hitler and particularly the Holocaust—we should remember that the latter was also becoming a new focus in historiography at the time. Wherever these right-wing extremists looked, they saw a self-imposed 'language of guilt' that seemed to dominate the political culture of the Federal Republic. In their opinion, there was a long tradition of 'intellectuals' committing 'language theft' and creating a high moral ground with which to impose their own world view. According to Mohler and his coterie, these intellectuals spoke a language that was foreign to the majority of the population. It was a few more years before a new term, namely 'political correctness', was injected into the German language. This was immediately jumped upon by the New Right, which denounced 'historical correctness' as a specific German version of 'political correctness'.[106]

The 'war over words' was not over when the CDU recaptured power in 1982. More than in the 1970s, however, semantic warfare returned to the question that had originally dominated it in the earlier decades of the Federal Republic: how to deal with the German past. Important landmarks within this ongoing debate were the visit by Chancellor Helmut Kohl and President Ronald Reagan to the military cemetery in Bitburg, the remarkable speech by Federal President Richard von Weizäcker in which he asserted, although with many caveats, that the year 1945 should be viewed as one not of German 'defeat', but of 'liberation', and the *Historikerstreit* of 1987. The leitmotiv of the 1970s war over words, the idea of 'occupying terms', was present in all these struggles. During the *Historikerstreit*, a prominent participant, the historian Michael Stürmer, was reported to have said something which

---

[105] Armin Mohler, *Vergangenheitsbewältigung* (Krefeld, 1980).

[106] For an overview see Jens Kapitzky, *Sprachkritik und Political Correctness in der Bundesrepublik* (Aachen, 2000); Caroline Mayer, *Öffentlicher Sprachgebrauch und Political Correctness: Eine Analyse sprachreflexiver Argumente im politischen Wortstreit* (Hamburg, 2002). Several authors in this debate were old '68ers' who put their language critique to new political uses.

recalled the words used by Biedenkopf in 1973: 'In a land without history, the future belongs to those who create memory, define terms, and interpret the past.'[107]

[107] Michael Stürmer, 'Geschichte in einem geschichtslosen Land', *Frankfurter Allgemeine Zeitung*, 25 Apr. 1986, quoted in Jürgen Habermas, 'Eine Art Schadensabwicklung: Die apologetischen Tendenzen in der deutschen Zeitgeschichtsschreibung', in Rudolf Augstein (ed.), *Historikerstreit: Die Dokumentation der Kontroverse um die Einzigartigkeit der nationalsozialistischen Judenvernichtung* (Munich, 1987), 62–7, at 62.

13

The Return of Language: Radicalism and the British Historians 1960–1990

GARETH STEDMAN JONES

It is common knowledge that the twentieth century witnessed fundamental changes in philosophical and scientific conceptions of the significance of language. Modern linguistics dated from Saussure's ground-breaking *Cours de linguistique générale* of 1916. In analytical philosophy, the early twentieth-century arguments of Russell and Moore suggested that the best route to a theory of the mind was through a description of our linguistic powers. In his later works, which began to be published in the 1950s, Wittgenstein argued that language is a rule-governed activity analogous to a game which is context-dependent and related to purpose. In the 1960s in the philosophy of linguistics, Noam Chomsky suggested a rationalist rather than empiricist approach to the theory of innate ideas. According to his notion of a universal grammar, human beings possess a language faculty specially equipped to acquire natural human languages. In anthropology, psychoanalysis, and literary criticism, initially in the 1960s under the banner of structuralism, focus upon language led to the assumption that discourses and cultural forms of every kind—even that of the unconscious—were best understood by analogy with language treated as a synchronic system of sound and sense.

All these claims and insights have pointed to the idea that forms of linguistic representation constitute the furthest point that philosophy can reach in its quest for knowledge and truth. There are no facts outside language and no reality other than that which presents itself under some linguistic description.

Not surprisingly, in every area of the humanities, this new-found focus upon language produced lively debate. But nowhere did it produce more passionate protest and intense disagreement than in history in the 1980s and 1990s in a battle over the so-called 'linguistic turn'.[1] This battle did not affect all history by any means. It engaged foremost that form of social history, and the cultural criticism associated with it, which had become prevalent in mid-twentieth-century Britain and was associated with the work of Raymond Williams and Edward Thompson. It was a form of history particularly close to contemporary political preoccupations.[2]

This approach had first attracted wide attention in the aftermath of the crisis of Communism of 1956. However different the particular points of emphasis found within the writings of Thompson and Williams, both were closely associated with the formation of a 'New Left', a movement defined by its rejection both of the mechanical Marxism which it associated with Stalinism, and of the social democratic compromise of the 1950s put forward by Crosland, Gaitskell, and other would-be modernizers in the British Labour Party.

This double rejection helps to explain the otherwise seemingly idiosyncratic founding project of the original New Left: to affirm and restate, from within an indigenous tradition, the centrality of a Marxist notion of class experience as the defining feature of English history and English culture during the nineteenth and twentieth centuries.

Heightened attention to language among historians did not actually begin with the 1980s polemics over the linguistic turn. In intellectual history, a new approach insisting upon the common concerns which linked history with the social sciences and philosophy had developed in the 1960s. Inspired by Wittgenstein's conception of a language game and Austin's theory of the speech act, intellectual historians proposed a novel and contentious set of methodological procedures which henceforth should underpin the study of the relationship between text and context in the construction of the history of political thought. But this innovation had made little impact upon the social historians and cultural critics

---

[1] For a brief account of the controversy, see D. Feldman, 'Class', in Peter Burke (ed.), *History and Historians in the Twentieth Century* (Oxford, 2002), 180–206.

[2] For some account of the emergence and particular characteristics of social history in Britain in the thirty years after the Second World War, see Gareth Stedman Jones, 'Anglo-Marxism, Neo-Marxism and the Discursive Approach to History', in Alf Lüdtke (ed.), *Was bleibt von marxistischen Perspektiven in der Geschichtsforschung?* (Göttingen, 1997), 149–209; see also Lin Chun, *The British New Left* (Edinburgh, 1993); and Dennis L. Dworkin, *Cultural Marxism in Postwar Britain: History, the New Left, and the Origins of Cultural Studies* (Durham, NC, 1997).

who had been inspired by Thompson and Williams. They remained suspicious of what they referred to as 'Oxford philosophy' which they had associated with parochialism and political complacency; and their suspicions were reinforced by the battle between the new intellectual history and C. B. MacPherson's Marxist interpretation of Hobbes and Locke in his *Political Theory of Possessive Individualism.*[3]

The potential conflict between social and intellectual history did not lead to confrontation at that stage, since the paths of these two branches of history rarely crossed. For all their strictures upon 'the great books' approach to the history of ideas, the majority of intellectual historians continued to concentrate upon the interpretation of canonical works of high theory. Conversely, much of the energy of social and cultural historians was devoted not to the recovery of the illocutionary force attending particular utterances, but rather to the reconstitution of the messages supposedly conveyed in non-verbal forms of action (ritual, play, etc.). Thus, while intellectual history cleaved towards analytical philosophy, game theory, and theoretical sociology, social and cultural history increasingly aligned itself with anthropology and literary studies.

But sooner or later, a clash was unavoidable. Social and cultural historians modified, but never wholly abandoned, the fundamental tenets of a theory of ideology which they had inherited from classical Marxism, a theory in which conscious intention was explicitly assigned a subordinate and derivative role. This was implicit in Edward Thompson's 'social being', or Raymond Williams's 'structure of feeling', as starting points in the understanding of agency or the role of 'social movements'. The main point at issue would be the insistence by the followers of Thompson and Williams upon the centrality of class as the structuring experience underlying thought and action.[4]

The pre- or extra-discursive primacy accorded to 'social being' could, of course, be found within an English Marxist tradition of history and cultural criticism dating back to the inter-war years. But the claim to authority made by Thompson and Williams rested upon something deeper and more powerful than a standardized

[3] Crawford Brough Macpherson, *The Political Theory of Possessive Individualism: Hobbes to Locke* (Oxford, 1962).
[4] See Raphael Samuel, 'British Marxist Historians 1880–1980: Part One', *New Left Review*, 120 (Mar.–Apr. 1980), 21–96.

Marxism. It drew upon an older, and allegedly indigenous, cultural tradition, of which Marxism was arguably one of the offshoots. This was, for Thompson, the legacy of Blake, the Romantic poets, and William Morris; for Raymond Williams, the tradition described in *Culture and Society* which began with Thomas Carlyle.[5]

The notion of class remained the basic point of connection between Marxism and this culturalist approach to history, and this helps to explain the vehemence of arguments about the linguistic turn. The passion aroused, therefore, must be related not simply to the growing disarray of Marxism in the 1980s, but also, and perhaps more fundamentally, to the precipitate disappearance of an enduring and recognizable landscape of class relations apparently stretching back to Disraeli's 'two nations' in the 1840s. An examination of the cultural assumptions shaping that landscape also helps to explain why arguments about language rather than other forms of criticism should have played such a central role in undermining the presuppositions of the culturalist approach.

No one was more formative in shaping that tradition than Thomas Carlyle (1795–1881). Without Carlyle, there would have been no 'condition of England question' in the 1840s, nor would the cultural criticism embedded in Victorian, Edwardian, or even Georgian literature have looked remotely similar. Carlyle's impact upon British thought in the nineteenth century was enormous, whether directly, or through intermediaries like Dickens, Disraeli, Charles Kingsley, George Eliot, John Ruskin, or William Morris. According to George Eliot, writing in 1855, 'it is an idle question to ask whether his books will be read a century hence: if they were all burnt as the grandest of Suttees on his funeral pile, it would be only like cutting down an oak after its acorns have sown a forest. For there is hardly a superior or active mind of this generation that has not been modified by Carlyle's writings; there has hardly been an English book written for the last ten or twelve years that would not have been different if Carlyle had not lived.'[6]

But Carlyle's prime sources of inspiration were not 'indigenous'. They were German, in particular the proto-Romanticism of *Sturm und Drang*, especially that of Goethe and Herder, and the

---

[5] See Edward P. Thompson, *William Morris: From Romantic to Revolutionary* (London, 1955); id., *Witness against the Beast* (London, 1993); Raymond Williams, *Culture and Society 1780–1950* (London, 1958).

[6] 'G. Eliot, an unsigned review, *Leader*, 27 Oct 1855, vi, pp. 1034–5', cited in Jules Paul Seigel (ed.), *Thomas Carlyle: The Critical Heritage* (London 1971), 409–10.

first generation of German Romantics, especially Jean Paul Richter. But in order to explain the distinctive sources and emphases of the Carlylean tradition and its twentieth-century legacy, it is first necessary to discuss the intellectual inheritance to which it was opposed.

When this is done, it will become easier to explain the centrality of issues of language in the constitution of the Carlylean tradition. For the main targets singled out for special attack by Carlyle were the principal ancestors of the semiotic approach inaugurated by Saussure: Locke, Condillac, and the *Idéologues*. Locke had challenged the habitual belief in the identity of words and things, 'as if the name carried with it the knowledge of the species and of the essence of it'.[7] He stressed that words were about ideas and not about things. Locke was attacking the seventeenth-century 'Adamic' view in which languages contained elements of an originally perfect language created by Adam when he named the animals and plants in the Garden of Eden. In other words, the relation between signifier and signified was not arbitrary. In contrast to Locke's idea that human languages were human and conventional, the 'Adamic' view—to some extent taken up again in early nineteenth-century Romanticism—conceived them as divine or natural. Locke's views were elaborated in the Abbé Condillac's *Essai sur l'origine des connaissances humaines* of 1746. Condillac's work was developed in differing directions by Rousseau, Maupertuis, Herder, and most controversially, during the years of the French Revolution, by the *Idéologues*, as part of their secular and materialist philosophy.[8]

Carlyle forcefully rejected Locke and Condillac as progenitors of an approach which had generated the atheism and materialism of the 'shallow' and faithless eighteenth century, culminating in the French Revolution and the work of the *Idéologues*. Like so

---

[7] This passage from Locke's *Essay on Human Understanding* is cited and discussed in Hans Aarsleff, *From Locke to Saussure: Essays on the Study of Language and Intellectual History* (Minneapolis, 1982), 24–6.

[8] On the 'Adamic' position, see Aarsleff, *From Locke to Saussure*, 19. On Condillac's development of Locke's position, see Aarsleff, 'The Tradition of Condillac', in id., *From Locke to Saussure*, 120–46. The controversiality of the *Idéologues* was contained first of all in the name they gave to themselves. The theory of 'idéologie' was in many respects an elaboration of the approach first set out in Condillac. But unlike Condillac, who was a Catholic priest, the position of the *Idéologues* was self-proclaimedly materialist. The term 'idéologie' was chosen to emphasize an idea of a theory which unified body and mind, while removing any reference to the 'psyche', the immaterial and, for Christians, immortal 'soul'.

many writing in the aftermath of the Revolution, Carlyle mistakenly believed that Locke and Condillac had considered that the senses alone were 'enough to account for the richest intellectual and emotional experiences of man'. It was this approach which had been responsible for the decline of metaphysics. In France, metaphysics had disappeared in a country which had once had its Pascals and Malebranches. Now with 'Dr Cabanis', a leader of the *Idéologues*, the French believed that, 'as the liver secretes bile, so does the brain secrete thought'. In England ever since Locke there had been no metaphysics, merely 'a genetic history of what we see in the mind'. Locke's whole doctrine was also 'mechanical, in its aims and origin, in its method and results'.[9] Locke himself, Carlyle conceded, was a 'religious man', but he had 'paved the way for banishing religion from the world'.[10]

In some ways, Carlyle's impact upon Victorian thought can be likened to that of his German predecessor, and another of his heroes, Georg Hamann. Hamann's rejection of the rationalism of the *Aufklärung* (Enlightenment) came as the result of a nervous breakdown followed by a dramatic recovery of his Lutheran faith. The friend, and Königsberg neighbour, commissioned, unsuccessfully, to save him for the Enlightenment was Immanuel Kant.[11] Carlyle's rejection of the 'shallow' eighteenth century was also the result of a spiritual crisis which ended in the building of a new post-Christian faith. The friend who thereafter helped him most towards the composition of his new and decidedly non-rationalist history of the French Revolution was John Stuart Mill, the standard-bearer—not always wholehearted, it is true—of precisely the philosophical radicalism which Carlyle considered most responsible for the degradation of the age. Carlyle, Hamann, Herder, and *Sturm und Drang* all rejected the separation of reason from other faculties, the head from the heart, body from mind. From the beginning, this position had also involved a general distrust of reason's pretensions, a disbelief in the politics of perfectibility, and a dislike of abstract

[9] Thomas Carlyle, 'Signs of the Times', *Edinburgh Review* (1829); id., *Selected Writings*, ed. Alan Shelston (Harmondsworth, 1971), 68–9.

[10] Thomas Carlyle, 'Goethe', in *Critical and Miscellaneous Essays*, 5 vols. (New York, 1899), i. 215. See also Hans Aarsleff, 'Locke's Reputation in Nineteenth Century England', in id., *From Locke to Saussure*, 120–45.

[11] On Hamann's spiritual crisis and his relations with Kant and Herder, see Frederick C. Beiser, *The Fate of Reason: German Philosophy from Kant to Fichte* (Cambridge, Mass., 1987), chs. 1 and 5.

universalism: a stance much reinforced by the events of the French Revolution. Instead, Carlyle's aesthetic, like that of Hamann, was built upon a taste for the concrete, for the particular, for the immediacy of image, for the infinite significance of the smallest event as a symbol or emblem of the truth. Like Hamann, Carlyle now believed God to be a poet rather than a mathematician, and the universe to be one vast enciphered symbol of divine presence.

In some of his writings, Hamann resurrected a fully-fledged 'Adamic' view of language: 'every appearance of language was a word—the sign, image and pledge of a new secret and inexpressible communion of divine energies and ideas. Everything that man at first heard, saw and touched with his hands was a living word.'[12] Carlyle could not go quite this far. Symbols he believed to be of human origin. They therefore withered and decayed in the course of time and had periodically to be renewed; and this was the task of poets and prophets.[13] Nevertheless, it was through symbols that mankind was connected to eternity. All visible things were emblems; it was not merely language, but the world itself which was metaphoric. Similarly, in his conception of words, Carlyle implicitly rejects the arbitrariness of signification. While Horne Tooke, a follower of Locke, traced all words back to sensible perceptions as grounds for opposing any notion of the divine origin of language and as support for rational and sceptical philosophy, Carlyle used the same materials as occasions for wonder and mystic speculation on divine hieroglyphs. 'All visible things are emblems; what thou seest is not there on its own account; strictly taken, is not there at all: matter exists only spiritually, and to represent some idea and body it forth.'[14]

---

[12] J. G. Hamann, *Samtliche Werke: Historisch-Kritische Ausgabe*, ed. Josef Nadler (Vienna, 1948–57), xi. 76, cited in Beiser, *Fate of Reason*, 139. Carlyle sometimes wrote in similar terms. 'The name is the earliest Garment you wrap round the Earth-visiting ME; to which it thenceforth cleaves, more tenaciously . . . than the very skin. And now from without, what mystic influences does it not send inwards, even to the centre . . . Not only all common Speech, but Science, Poetry itself is no other, if thou consider it, than a right *Naming*. Adam's first task was giving names to natural appearances: what is ours still but a continuation of the same?' T. Carlyle, *Sartor Resartus* (1831) (London, 1870), 53.

[13] Carlyle, *Sartor Resartus*, 137–8. On Carlyle's conception of the ironic potential of symbols, see Catherine Gallagher, *The Industrial Reformation of English Fiction: Social Discourse and Narrative Form 1832–1867* (Chicago, 1985), 195–6.

[14] Carlyle, *Sartor Resartus*, 43; See also Georg Bernhard Tennyson, *Sartor called Resartus: The Genesis, Structure and Style of Thomas Carlyle's First Major Work* (Princeton, 1965), 262 and 268. Or, as John Holloway put it: 'Carlyle does not wish to be thought of as explicitly allotting his own senses to . . . words, but as discovering what really they mean already, what

Carlyle was also deeply indebted to Herder's historicism, his cultural relativism, and his freedom of speculation about man and nature. These had been crucial to the resolution of the religious crisis Carlyle had experienced between 1814 and 1822. In *Sartor Resartus* (1831), the garments in which each civilization clothed itself—its language, its mythology, its religion, its literature, its culture—were incommensurable and incomparable; they could only be judged in their own terms as particular expressions of the infinite creativity of Herder's *Humanität*; truth, as he jotted down from Herder in one of his notebooks 'immer wird, nie ist'. Truth is always in the process of coming to be, it is never completed.[15]

But to this, Carlyle also added a darker and more ominous note, not to be found in the Goethean or Herderian original. For if, as Goethe had said, 'all genuine things are what they ought to be', it also followed that all false things were and deserved to be swept away. Thus in addition to Scripture seen as divine poetry, and Nature conceived in *Sartor Resartus* as God's 'second Bible', Carlyle renewed the idea of history as a sacred drama. From Jean Paul Richter, another of his German mentors, he adopted the notion of history as 'the third Bible', as 'that divine book of Revelation, whereof a chapter is completed from epoch to epoch'. It was this thought that inspired his vision of the French Revolution as a great and terrible process of divine purgation.[16]

Carlyle's *French Revolution* (1837) was arguably the first of a new type of history in which a collective entity, the French People, was conceived as the active protagonist of the historical process. This, again, could not have happened but for Carlyle's intimate acquaintance with the aesthetic and religious theories of *Sturm und Drang* and German Romanticism. Back in the 1820s, Mill had perceived that the novelty of the Revolution lay in the part played by the whole people and therefore that its understanding required insight into popular enthusiasm. But Mill could never have written Carlyle's book.[17]

their existing present use both depends upon, and perhaps conceals.' John Holloway, *The Victorian Sage: Studies in Argument* (London, 1953), cited in Aarsleff, *From Locke to Saussure*, 37.

[15] On Carlyle's indebtedness to Herder, see Ruth apRoberts, *The Ancient Dialect: Thomas Carlyle and Comparative Religion* (Berkeley, 1988), 15–17.

[16] On Carlyle's idea of history as a 'third Bible', see John D. Rosenberg, *Carlyle and the Burden of History* (Oxford, 1985), 9–10.

[17] See Hedva Ben-Israel, *English Historians on the French Revolution* (Cambridge, 1968), 58–9.

Carlyle believed that history was 'the sole Poetry possible' in the disbelieving modern world; the grandest of fictions faded before 'the smallest historical *fact*'; history was 'an inarticulate Bible; and in a dim manner reveals the Divine Appearances in this lower world'.[18] The historian was the successor to the epic poet; that was why Carlyle prepared for his writing of *The French Revolution* by reading the *Iliad*, Dante, and Milton and why, like the ancient bards and Hebrew prophets, he composed his history in a state of semi-trance.[19] It was this belief that history was a form of bardic poetry, and thus a narrative of 'facts, facts, no theory' without the distance that enabled reflection or abstraction, that made Carlyle's history so novel and powerful.[20]

The French Revolution evokes a peculiarly gruesome and disturbing vision of revolution as a war between rich and poor born out of the loss of faith and habit. It was disturbing because, unlike Disraeli's picture of the two nations whose ancient feud could notionally be removed by the marriage between Sybil and Egremont, Carlyle's picture was drawn from a notion of the conflicting forces which reside within the self. The primitive, the instinctual, the murderous *is not* reassuringly projected onto another class or race, but remains in a state of suppressed yet smouldering rebellion within each self.[21] The vision of revolution found in the book is inspired by the uprising of the Titans against the Olympians, by Lucifer's rebellion, or by a picture of primeval Holocaust. Carlyle wasted few pages on the constitution-making of successive assemblies. For him the Revolution was 'sansculottism', 'the open violent rebellion, and victory of disimprisoned anarchy against corrupt worn out authority'.[22]

English historians have not generally understood how important Carlyle's *French Revolution* was in fuelling a literature of social fear in the 1830s and 1840s. They have been even less aware how

---

[18] Thomas Carlyle, 'Goethe', in *Collected Works*, xxviii. 45, 53–4.

[19] See Rosenberg, *Carlyle and the Burden of History*, 16–17.

[20] 'Men believe in Bibles and disbelieve in them: but of all Bibles the frightfullest to disbelieve in is this "Bible of Universal History" . . . It was not true that the Past had "no God's Reason in it".' 'Men will again be taught this. Their acted History will then again be a Heroism; their written History, what once it was, an Epic. Nay, forever it is either such, or else it virtually is—Nothing.' Thomas Carlyle, *Past and Present* (1843) (London, 1870), 258.

[21] 'every man . . . holds confined within him *mad*-man'. Once 'the thin Earth-rind' of Habit is broken, 'instead of a green flowery world there is a waste wild-weltering chaos'. Thomas Carlyle, *The French Revolution* (1837) (Oxford, 1989), 40.   [22] Ibid. 221.

important was Carlyle's German proto-Romantic inheritance in shaping the peculiar definition which he gave to the social question and its resolution. Two aspects of his approach which affected the culturalist tradition of Thompson and Williams should be briefly mentioned: first, his definition of the social realm and its attendant downgrading of the political; and secondly, the role which he assigned to 'the people', the 'sansculottes', or the 'working classes' in his providential conception of history.

On the first point, no commentator could miss Carlyle's hostility to democracy.[23] What has attracted less attention has been the subordinate and, in some sense, degraded position he assigned to the political as such. In *Past and Present* he despised political reform as a mere tinkering with machinery. Fundamentally, his distrust was similar to that of Hamann or Herder and related to the vanity of the pretensions of reason when it aspired to legislate in abstraction from any social embodiment. Hamann had protested against Kant that reason could not be 'pure', that is, it could not claim any right to existence as a disembodied entity. In Carlyle, this scepticism appeared clearly in a definition of what would later be called ideology. 'Man's philosophies are usually the supplement of his practice; some ornamental logic varnish, some outer skin of articulate intelligence with which he strives to render his dumb instinctive doings presentable when they are done.'[24] The 'true law code and constitution of society' was unwritten and rested upon 'its system of habits', 'the only Code, though an Unwritten one, which it can no wise disobey'.[25] Political discourse in *Sartor* is a mere 'wrappage' of civilization.

What Carlyle pitted against Benthamite or mechanical conceptions of society was Herder's idea of culture. Society was a living tissue, an organism, held together by what *Sartor* described as 'organic filaments'—language and custom, the living landscape, dress, climate, and a shared past.[26] Man is spirit, he wears clothes; this is a visible emblem of the bonds that tie him to other men. It is 'in society that man first feels what he is; first becomes what he can be'. This is why Carlyle was so alarmed by the fear that in

[23] 'Democracy, which means despair of finding any Heroes to govern you, and contented putting up with the want of them—alas, thou too, *mein Lieber*, seest well how close it is of kin to *Atheism* and other sad *Isms*: he who discovers no God whatever, how shall he discover Heroes, the visible Temples of God?' Carlyle, *Past and Present*, 238.

[24] Ibid. 217.   [25] Carlyle, *French Revolution*, 40.

[26] Carlyle, *Sartor Resartus*, bk. 3, ch. 8.

the England of his time, persons were held together by nothing except 'the cash nexus'.

The second point through which Carlyle's approach, and the German inheritance that inspired it, shaped the subsequent culturalist tradition was through the role he assigned to the *sansculottes, the people* or the working classes. What is most noticeable here is that while the main protagonists of Carlyle's social and historical dramas make sounds and create a noise, they do not speak. Carlyle describes the French people whose grievances were met by Louis XV's gallows as 'a dumb generation; their voice only an inarticulate cry'.[27] By the time Carlyle gets to the Assembly of Notables, the people were ceasing to be dumb, but had not quite achieved true utterance. The people 'speaks through pamphlets, or at least bays and growls behind them, in unison—increasing wonderfully their volume of sound'.[28] At the siege of the Bastille, once again the people achieves sound, maybe even speech, but not thought: 'Great is the combined voice of men; the utterance of their instincts, which are truer than their thoughts.'[29] Although at certain points in the narrative the people appear to be on the point of breaking into articulate speech, they never actually do so.

In the case of the English working classes, the inarticulacy becomes threatening and deafening. Carlyle first introduces them in *Chartism* by bemoaning a lack of understanding among the upper classes of 'what it is that the under-classes intrinsically mean; a clear interpretation of the thought which at heart torments these wild inarticulate souls, struggling there with inarticulate uproar, like dumb creatures in pain, unable to speak what is in them. Something they do mean; some true thing withal, in the centre of their confused hearts—for they are hearts created by heaven too.'[30] As for the supposed demands of the Chartists, the demands of the Charter, Carlyle comments: 'what is the meaning of the five points, if we will understand them? What are all popular commotions and maddest bellowings, from Peterloo to the Place de la Grève itself? Bellowings, *in*articulate cries as of a dumb creature in rage and pain.' But, Carlyle goes on, 'to the ear of wisdom they are inarticulate prayers: Guide me; Govern me. I am mad and miserable and cannot guide myself.'[31] It is not

---

[27] Carlyle, *French Revolution*, bk. ii, ch. ii, p. 37.   [28] Ibid. bk. 4, ch. i, p. 122.
[29] Ibid. bk. 5, ch. 6, p. 202.
[30] Thomas Carlyle, *Chartism* (London, 1870), ch. i, p. 6.   [31] Ibid. ch. 6, p. 33.

simply the underclasses who cannot speak their meaning,
however—who can only act it. It is also the English who are
praised as a dumb race. 'Not the least admirable quality of Bull is
. . . of remaining insensible to logic.' Long after the logical argument is settled, for instance the repeal of the Corn Laws, (John)
Bull will see whether nothing else *illogical*, not yet spoken, not yet
able to be spoken, do not lie in the business, as there so often
does.[32]

At a more metaphysical level, this emphasis upon silence and
inarticulacy touched the core of Carlyle's vision of history and
reality. 'The cloudy-browed thick-soled opaque Practicality, with
no logic utterance, in silence mainly, with here and there a low
grunt or growl, has in him what transcends all logic-utterance: a
congruity with the unuttered.' On the other hand, 'the Speakable,
which lies atop, as a superficial film, or outer skin, is his or is not
his; but the doable which reaches down to the world's center, you
find him there.'[33] Or, as he stated elsewhere, 'Speech is time,
Silence is eternity'. Speech is related to the visible universe. But
the poet, 'the seer penetrates the visible universe to reach the
invisible, but truly real universe, of which the visible is indeed the
garment or symbol'.[34]

It is at this point—that of the silence or inarticulacy of the
people, the English, the oppressed, the working classes—that the
affinity between German proto-Romanticism and the subsequent
Marxian tradition appears at its clearest. In 1844, the young
Frederick Engels wrote an enthusiastic review of Carlyle's *Past and
Present* for the *Deutsche-französische Jahrbücher*, edited in Paris by Karl
Marx and Arnold Ruge. Carlyle's book, according to Engels, was
the only work in England to show 'traces of a human point of
view'. Discounting a few phrases which 'derived from Carlyle's particular standpoint, we must allow the truth of all he says'. Engels
agreed that the evils from which England suffered were social not
political, and that democracy would only be a 'transitional stage',
whether, as Carlyle thought, on the way to true aristocracy, or, as
Engels thought, to 'real human freedom'.[35] Engels also agreed with
Carlyle about the religious roots of the social crisis. 'We too are

---

[32] Carlyle, *Past and Present*, bk. III, ch. 5, p. 197.
[33] Ibid. 194–5.   [34] Carlyle, *Sartor Resartus*, 133–4.
[35] Frederick Engels, 'The Condition of England: *Past and Present* by Thomas Carlyle,
London 1843', in *Karl Marx Frederick Engels Collected Works* (hereafter *MECW*), iii (London,
1975–), 444, 450, 455, and 464.

concerned with combating the lack of principle, the inner empti-
ness, the spiritual deadness, the untruthfulness of the age . . . We
want to put an end to atheism, as Carlyle portrays it, by giving back
to man the substance he has lost through religion.'[36] Finally, Engels
agreed with Carlyle about 'the revelation of history'. Carlyle's position represented the first step towards the position of Marx's and
Ruge's journal. The disagreement, as Engels saw it, was between
Carlyle's 'pantheism', which Engels likened to that of Strauss or
the early Schelling, and Feuerbachian humanism, the position
espoused at that moment by Engels and Marx.[37]

This review of *Past and Present* was followed a year and a half
later by Engels' celebrated account of *The Condition of the Working
Class in England* (1844). In that book, the basic stance remained that
of Feuerbachian Communism, but now conceived as the outcome
of a revolution, 'in comparison with which the French Revolution
and the year 1794 will prove to have been child's play'.[38] The text
resonates with Carlylean references. Engels was impressed not
merely by Carlyle's denunciation of a society in which all forms of
connection have been reduced to that of 'the cash nexus'. Like
others of Carlyle's admirers in the 1840s and 1850s, Engels was fas-
cinated by the highlighting of violence as the primitive vehicle of
the struggle between what he called the 'upper' and 'under' classes,
or what Engels called the proletariat and the bourgeoisie. Thus the
first stage of the existential choice between enslaved animality and
rebellion, as the expression of humanity, was crime, whether
against person or property. Similarly, Marx, like Engels eagerly
adopted Carlyle's analogy between the violent justice allegedly
meted out to blacklegs by the Glasgow cotton spinners and the
vengeance once wreaked upon high-living miscreants by the old
Fehmgericht of medieval Germany.[39]

But the greatest affinity between Engels' position and that of
Carlyle is suggested not by a presence, but an absence. Despite
the wealth of descriptive detail about the condition of the proletarians in town and country and about the history of the emergence of the proletarian class, no proletarian was offered a
speaking part throughout the whole book. As in Carlyle, so here

[36] Ibid. 463.　　　　　　　　　　　　　　　　[37] Ibid. 460–1.
[38] Frederick Engels, 'The Condition of the Working-Class in England', *MECW*, iv. 323.
[39] See Carlyle, *Chartism*, ch. 5, p. 26; Frederick Engels and Karl Marx, 'Speech at the Anniversary of the *People's Paper*' (delivered in London, 14 Apr. 1856), *MECW*, xxiv. 656.

speech was only a masquerade. What mattered was action.[40] As Goethe—a hero both for Carlyle and for Engels—had stated: 'Erst war die Tat' (first came the deed). Marx and Engels had written only a few months before, 'it is not a question of what this or that proletarian, or even the whole proletariat, at the moment *regards* as its aim. It is a question of *what the proletariat is* and what in accordance with this *being*, it will historically be compelled to do.'[41]

Marx absorbed from German proto-Romanticism a pronounced scepticism about the role of subjective reason and individual intention in history. The rationality of history inhered not in the individual agents who composed it, but in the process as a whole. For Carlyle, history possessed a redemptive and purgative function because it was made into a manifestation of divine justice. Marxism postulated that history possessed a teleological goal, unconsciously powered by a class struggle which hastened the onward march of the forces of production. In both cases, these were processes which took place behind the backs of historical agents. They were only decipherable by the seer or the philosopher. History itself, as Hegel once claimed, advanced through its bad side—through wars and destruction, through violence and unreasoning passions, through the obscure and subterranean movements of aversion and desire. If, therefore, there was a relationship between individual activity and the movement of history, speech or rational discourse was not its medium. This is why for those still close to the Marxist tradition, like Gyatry Spivak, it is still by no means self-evident that 'the subaltern' can 'speak'.[42]

It was also a crucial precondition, both of Marx's theory and of the subsequent English culturalist tradition, that Carlyle had changed the representation of the working classes. They were henceforth no longer just the volatile city crowd, the playthings of demagogy, the reincarnation of the Roman mob, or the oppressed and childlike equivalents of West Indian slaves. They had been made into the powerful sphinx-like symbol of the age. In place of the passive, dependent, and predominantly feminine image of pauper apprentices, indentured children, and white

---

[40] 'What *is* this Infinite of Things itself, which men name Universe, but an Action, a sum-total of Actions and Activities?' Carlyle, *French Revolution*, 407–8.

[41] Karl Marx and Frederick Engels, 'The Holy Family', *MECW*, iv. 37.

[42] Gyatry C. Spivak, 'Can the Subaltern Speak?', in Cary Nelson and Lawrence Grossberg (eds.), *Marxism and the Interpretation of Culture* (Chicago, 1988), 271–313.

slaves, Carlyle substituted a more sullen, angry, and threatening picture of the resentment, confusion, and choleric temper of grown men. The looming and swelling presence of the working classes now portended something—a warning to the governors of the need to rule, a still barely moving yet faintly stirring Enceladus, who might suddenly arise from the fiery deep, as he already had in France, toppling the flimsy superstructures of Anglo-Saxon civilization in his wake.[43]

A Carlylean respect for the slumbering Enceladus set the tone of British culture for at least a century after his unveiling of 'the condition of England question'. To Carlyle's call for leadership and guidance of the working classes was added Arnold's demand that industrial Britain and the slums of great cities be brought 'sweetness and light'. As a counterpoint to the prosaic utilitarianism of mass primary education, university extension, workers' education, and a range of institutions from the People's Palace to Ruskin College, Oxford, strove to bridge the gulf between the 'two nations'.[44] In the case of Thompson and Williams, active engagement with this tradition was intensified both by their years of experience of extra-mural adult education, but also by the impact made upon them of the teaching and cultural criticism of F. R. Leavis, an avowed disciple of Arnold.[45]

In comparison with the periods which came before and after, the years between the 1870s and 1950s were also a period of extraordinary social stability. The first World War produced the enfranchisement of women, the emergence of labour, mass unemployment in the old staple industries, and the end of the gold standard. But the basic trends in British society continued to be those first established around the 1870s. The prevailing demographic pattern and its attendant family values, involving clearly demarcated sex and generation roles and low rates of illegitimacy or divorce, were those established in the 1870s. There was also a more or less continuous decline in the crime rate through to the 1960s.

European observers were impressed by what they called the 'social peace' which reigned in Britain's industrial heartlands.

---

[43] Carlyle frequently uses the image of Enceladus to evoke the working classes. See, e.g., Carlyle, *Chartism*, ch. 9, p. 54.

[44] See Lawrence Goldman, *Dons and Workers: Oxford and Adult Education since 1850* (Oxford, 1995).   [45] See F. Mulhern, *The Moment of Scrutiny* (London, 1981).

Industrial relations were stabilized by the legislation of Gladstone and Disraeli and a legal framework according a privileged position to trade unions which was not fundamentally altered until the premiership of Mrs Thatcher in the 1980s. Even exceptional periods of industrial conflict, such as that which had led to the General Strike in 1926, were conducted in a strikingly restrained and orderly way. As A. J. P. Taylor remarked of the British working classes, 'they were loyal to their unions and their leaders, as they had been loyal during the war to their country and to their generals. They went once more into the trenches, without enthusiasm and with little hope.'[46]

The dominant trends in Britain during this period were the growth of a global market in food resulting in a cheap breakfast table, the crisis and decline of old staple industries (but well away from the South-East), the depopulation of the countryside, and the retreat of the landed classes. These developments were accompanied by the continuous expansion of the urban and suburban populations, the growth of great retail chains, of holiday resorts, of 'the servantless house', and of increasingly homogeneous patterns of mass culture and mass leisure. Two world wars reinforced, but did not alter, the direction of change. Britain did not experience fascism or foreign occupation. Its industries were not dismantled or destroyed. There was no disruption in the functioning of British political institutions. Both the strengths and the weaknesses of the culturalist form of the Anglo-Marxist attitude towards history derived from the insularity of its development. Like the larger political culture of which it was a part, Anglo-Marxism had been untroubled by wartime defeat, by the collapse of the state, by the reality of revolution, or the consolidation of a one-party state.

But the flourishing of the culturalist version of Anglo-Marxism occurred just when the social structure and cultural values it presupposed were beginning to disintegrate—and political change was soon to follow. Socially, 'the working-class' life which culturalist Anglo-Marxism took as its starting point was already becoming a sentimental memory evoked in such works as Richard Hoggart's *Uses of Literacy*.[47] Politically, even within the New Left, a younger generation had emerged which was not the product of

[46] A. J. P. Taylor, *English History 1914–1945* (Oxford, 1964), 245.
[47] Richard Hoggart, *The Uses of Literacy* (London, 1957).

the struggle against fascism, of the Popular Front, or of the Second World War, but of the post-imperial and non-Communist radicalism of the years after 1956. It was a group interested in continental philosophical traditions, in the novel use of concepts, and in making a break with the inherited verities of Anglo-Saxon culture, whether of right or left; and it raised comparative questions hitherto virtually absent from English radical historiography. Unspoken assumptions about England's status, clothed in Marxist terminology, but inherited from a Romantic and Protestant past, were subjected to unsentimental scrutiny. In 1965, Edward Thompson led the Anglo-Marxist riposte in a famous essay called 'The Peculiarities of the English'. It signalled a growing divide between the 'old' and 'new' New Left.[48]

Outside the New Left, culturalist Anglo-Marxism, now with the Marxists of the 'new' New Left, was equally threatened by the growth of movements, beginning with the Women's Liberation Movement, whose preoccupations were no longer comprehensible within a framework of 'class'. Furthermore, as older forms of deference and submission came under pressure, the unacceptable face of working-class life became more visible. In Northern Ireland, student radicals began to protest against the gerrymandered Protestant state. On the mainland, battles around racism came into the open following the notorious 'rivers of blood' speech by Enoch Powell and the march of solidly white proletarian meat-porters in his support.

Thompson's 1978 polemic against Althusser in *The Poverty of Theory* was the last of the cultural-political battles, still stuck in the years before 1956.[49] It highlighted the parochialism of a stance which was unprepared to take any account of the theoretical challenge represented by the new work in the 1960s of Lévi-Strauss, Barthes, Althusser, and Lacan. These authors presupposed a more explicit theoretical engagement with the status of language and discourse in history, and in some cases pointed beyond a Marxian paradigm altogether.

As the 1970s drew to a close, the battle about 'theory' still rumbled on, culminating in a large and bad-tempered History Workshop Conference held in Oxford in 1979. Nothing ends neatly, but this Conference more or less brought these debates to

---

[48] See E. P. Thompson, 'The Peculiarities of the English', in id., *The Poverty of Theory and Other Essays* (London, 1978), 35–92. [49] Ibid. 193–399.

a conclusion. Thereafter, the pressure of external events pushed such discussion to the sidelines. The year 1979 was the first of Mrs Thatcher's government, followed soon after by the triumph of Ronald Reagan in the United States and a renewal of the Cold War antagonisms. Domestically, Mrs Thatcher's government launched an uncompromising counter-offensive against all the gains made by organized labour in the 1960s and 1970s. This provoked the disastrous miner's strike of 1984 and the disintegration of the politics of organized labour as it had developed during the previous hundred years.

By the late 1970s, for others, too, the time for these battles between history and 'theory' had all but passed. The May events of 1968 had created the real parting of the ways. Thereafter, politically, the French theorists became increasingly volatile. Foucault called for a prisoners' revolt. The future 'new philosopher' Andre Glucksmann, then still in his Maoist phase, called for 'resistance' against a new 'occupation' of France. Althusser's writings zigzagged between a crude agitprop Leninism and a rudderless liberalism. In Britain also, the 1968 events had produced a recrudescence of Marxist groupings, intent on direct action or revolutionary organization, and seemingly oblivious of the gathering Thatcherite conservative reaction.

Yet the 1970s also saw the emergence of more positive reasons for redefining the content and direction of historiographical debate. The growth of the Women's Movement, accompanied by the crystallization of a feminist perspective on history, created growing interest in forms of experience which could not be adequately recounted in the categories employed by Anglo-Marxist social history or New Left theory. It raised increasing doubts about the explanatory value of class and the historical narrative built upon it. Furthermore, while feminism raised uncomfortable questions about who was included within particular historical narratives and upon what terms, literary theorists, starting with Hayden White in California, began to raise questions about the tropes underlying the construction of historical narrative, and to dramatize history as a form of literary artifice.[50] The usefulness of such questioning was underlined by the local findings of social and labour historians themselves who, without any settled inten-

---

[50] See Hayden White, *Tropics of Discourse: Essays in Cultural Criticism* (Baltimore, 1978); id., *Metahistory: Six Critiques* (Middletown, Conn., 1980).

tion to do so, cleared away or undermined one after another of the cherished milestones of a heroic Popular Front history of the people.

The introduction of a semiotic approach into the reading of post-eighteenth-century British history was not therefore an isolated or extraneous development. It formed part of a larger shift in British culture and politics, a small sign that, politically and culturally, Britain was finally getting beyond its once so powerful Victorian and Carlylean critical inheritance.

14

Suppression of the Nazi Past, Coded Languages, and Discourses of Silence: Applying the Discourse-Historical Approach to Post-War Anti-Semitism in Austria

RUTH WODAK

I *Setting the Agenda*

In this essay I discuss some aspects of the revival/continuance of Austrian anti-Semitism since 1945. First, a short summary of the history of post-war anti-Semitism in Austria is necessary in order to allow a contextualization of specific utterances from the Vienna election campaign of 2001 which will be analysed in detail below. Secondly, I will elaborate the Discourse-Historical Approach (DHA) which should allow readers to follow and understand the in-depth discourse analysis of specific utterances by Jörg Haider, the former leader of the Austrian Freedom Party (FPÖ), during the 2001 election campaign. Finally, the question of whether we are dealing with 'new–old' anti-Semitism in Europe or just 'more of the same' will be raised. This topic is constantly

I am very grateful to the Leverhulme Trust which awarded me a Leverhulme Visiting Professorship at UEA, Norwich, in the spring term of 2004. This made it possible to elaborate this essay which is based on previous and ongoing research on anti-Semitic discourses. Thus I draw on research published in Ruth Wodak, J. Pelikan, P. Nowak, et al., *'Wir sind alle unschuldige Täter!': Diskurshistorische Studien zum Nachkriegsantisemitismus* (Frankfurt am Main, 1990); M. Reisigl and Ruth Wodak, *Discourse and Discrimination* (London, 2001); Ruth Wodak and M. Reisigl, '". . . wenn einer Ariel heist . . . ": Ein linguistisches Gutachten zur politischen Funktionalisierung antisemitischer Ressentiments in Österreich', in A. Pelinka and Ruth Wodak (eds.), *'Dreck am Stecken': Politik der Ausgrenzung* (Vienna, 2002), 134–72; and Ruth Wodak, 'Discourses of Silence: Anti-Semitic Discourse in Post-War Austria', in L. Thiesmeyer (ed.) *Discourse and Silencing* (Amsterdam, 2004), 179–210. I am also grateful for discussions with András Kovács, Alexander Pollak, Rudolf de Cillia, Richard Mitten, Lynn Thiesmeyer, and Anton Pelinka on the emergence of a 'new–old' anti-Semitism in Europe, and their comments on this essay. Of course, the final version of this essay is my sole responsibility.

debated in the media and by politicians in relation to the events of 11 September 2001, the war in Iraq, and the current crisis in the Middle East.

The research presented here was undertaken at the Department of Applied Linguistics at the University of Vienna in the context of a number of interdisciplinary projects (involving linguists, historians, psychologists, and political scientists).[1] The strategies and linguistic realizations of anti-Semitic discourse, the *discourse of justification*, are presented in this essay taking the notion of 'syncretic anti-Semitism' as a point of departure.[2] This concept suggests that the traditional boundaries between a racist, ethnic, or Catholic anti-Semitism are no longer valid; instead, anti-Semitic stereotypes are produced and functionalized whenever a political context seems suitable. In all of these studies, the theoretical framework of the DHA was applied (see below). This implies problem-oriented, interdisciplinary research while focusing on verbal and non-verbal expressions of meaning in context, that is, discourse.[3] The DHA was developed in the course of our first research project on anti-Semitic discourse, which investigated the so-called Waldheim Affair of 1986. The data came from the media (TV, news broadcasts, newspapers, and journals) on the one hand and speeches by politicians and everyday conversations on the street on the other.[4] Thus different strata of the Austrian public sphere were studied.

[1] e.g. Wodak, Pelikan, Nowak, et al., *'Wir sind alle unschuldige Täter!'*; Ruth Wodak, F. Menz, Richard Mitten, and F. Stern, *Die Sprachen der Vergangenheiten* (Frankfurt am Main, 1994); B. Matouschek, Ruth Wodak, and F. Januschek, *Notwendige Maßnahmen gegen Fremde?* (Vienna, 1995); Ruth Wodak, R. de Cillia, M. Reisigl, and K. Liebhart, *The Discursive Construction of National Identity* (Edinburgh, 1999; 2nd rev. edn. 2009); Martin Reisigl and Ruth Wodak, *Discourse and Discrimination: Rhetorics of Racism and Antisemitism* (London, 2001); Ruth Wodak, 'The Discourse-Historical Approach', in ead. and M. Meyer (eds.), *Methods of Critical Discourse Analysis* (London, 2001), 63–95; Ruth Wodak, 'Freund- und Feindbilder: Diffamierung politischer Gegner oder berechtigte und notwendige Kritik?', in R. Möhring (ed.) *Österreich allein zuhause: Politik, Medien und Justiz nach der politischen Wende* (Frankfurt am Main, 2001), 124–44; Ruth Wodak and A. Pelinka (eds.), *The Haider Phenomenon in Austria* (New Brunswick, NJ, 2002); Pelinka and Wodak (eds.), *'Dreck am Stecken'*; Wodak and Reisigl, '. . . wenn einer Ariel heist . . . '; and Wodak, 'Discourses of Silence'.

[2] Richard Mitten, *The Politics of Antisemitic Prejudice: The Waldheim Phenomenon in Austria* (Boulder, Colo., 1992).

[3] N. Fairclough and Ruth Wodak, 'Critical Discourse Analysis', in T. A. van Dijk (ed.), *Discourse as Social Interaction* (London, 1997), 258–84.

[4] Ruth Wodak, 'Der Ton macht die Musik', *Werkstattblätter*, 4 (1991), 16–22; ead., 'Turning the Tables: Anti-Semitic Discourse in Post-War Austria', *Discourse and Society*, 2/1 (1991), 65–84; ead. and B. Matouschek, 'We are Dealing with People Whose Origins One Can Clearly Tell by Looking: Critical Discourse Analysis and the Study of Neo-Racism in Contemporary Austria', *Discourse and Society*, 4/2 (1993), 225–48.

When necessary and available, data from opinion polls was also analysed and integrated into our research.[5]

II *Anti-Semitism in Austria after 1945*

1. *General Perspectives*

At the 'zero hour' of 1945, the Second Austrian Republic's main concern, in contrast to Germany, was whether Austria's ruling elite could and would do ideological, constitutional, and political justice to the various demands it faced, demands that frequently arose out of opposing values, and if so, how.[6] The result was the construction of a self-image in which the 'Jewish question' was not so much denied as concealed. As result, there was 'silence'. A number of critical studies attribute this lack of public debate (in comparison to Germany) about the 'Jewish question' to the remains of anti-Semitic hostility among the political elites.[7] However, if we consider the conditions (such as occupation, reservoir of anti-Semitic prejudices from the first Austrian Republic, and commitment to becoming a 'Western democracy') under which a new collective or public memory was to be constituted, one can hardly be surprised by the outcome. In the end, the 'Jewish question' took a subordinate place in Austria's official public memory of the Nazi period. Ultimately, this new policy, as described in detail by Richard Mitten,[8] resulted in the creation of a new community of 'victims' in which the Jews occupied an insignificant place: they were just victims like everyone else, and

[5] Richard Mitten, 'Anti-Semitism in Austria', *Anti-Semitism World Report* (London, 1995), 10–19; Ruth Wodak, 'The Genesis of Racist Discourse in Austria since 1989', in C. R. Caldas-Coulthard and M. Coulthard (eds.), *Texts and Practices: Readings in Critical Discourse Analysis* (London, 1996), 107–28.

[6] Richard Mitten, 'Zur "Judenfrage" im Nachkriegsösterreich: Die Last der Erinnerung und die Aktualisierung der Erinnerung', Project Report, Ministry of Science and Education (Vienna, 1997).

[7] Robert Knight (ed.), '"Ich bin dafür, die Sache in die Länge zu ziehen"', in *Die Wortprotokolle der österreichischen Bundesregierung von 1945–1952 über die Entschädigung der Juden* (Frankfurt, 1988); O. Rathkolb, 'Die Wiedererrichtung des Auswärtigen Dienstes nach 1945', Project Report, Ministry of Science and Education (Vienna, 1988); R. Wagnleitner (ed.), *Understanding Austria* (Salzburg, 1984).

[8] Mitten, 'Zur "Judenfrage" im Nachkriegsösterreich'; id., 'Guilt and Responsibility in Germany and Austria', paper presented to the Conference 'Dilemmas of East Central Europe: Nationalism, Totalitarianism, and the Search for Identity. A Symposium Honoring István Déak', Columbia University, 24–5 Mar. 2000.

Nazi policy concerning the Jews was minimized or concealed. This silence was first broken by the Waldheim Affair of 1986 and the commemorative year of 1988.[9] Since the beginning of the 1990s Austrian politicians have been debating the question of Austrian responsibility,[10] and the two exhibitions of 1995 and 2001 about the crimes of the German *Wehrmacht* have further contributed to the lifting of the taboo.[11]

Austria became a democratic state in 1918 (first Republic), and had to survive the change from a large multi-ethnic and multi-cultural monarchy to a small state. Between 1938 and 1945, Austria was occupied by the Nazis and became part of the Third Reich. Since 1945, Austria has undergone many political and sociological changes: occupation by the Allied forces until 1955, the signing of the State Treaty in 1955, attaining the status of neutrality although clearly retaining a pro-Western orientation, and the creation of a social welfare society on the Swedish model. A major qualitative change occurred in 1989–90 when the so-called Iron Curtain fell and new immigrants from the former Eastern Communist countries crossed Austria's borders. In 1994 politics in Austria were dominated by two events, both of which represented major breaks with the post-war era. In June, Austrians voted by an overwhelming 66.4 per cent majority to join the European Union (EU). By October, however, the reigning euphoria among the governing parties, the Social Democratic Party (SPÖ) and the People's Party (ÖVP), over the EU referendum had turned into the opposite, to despair as they contemplated the implications of their disastrous general election results.[12] Both parties suffered massive losses, primarily to the populist Freedom Party (FPÖ), a party similar to Le Pen's party in France. Although they formed a new coalition government, the SPÖ and the ÖVP no longer possessed the two-thirds majority necessary to pass constitutional laws in parliament.

The election on 3 October 1999 finally brought the FPÖ 27 per

---

[9] Wodak, Pelikan, Nowak, et al., *'Wir sind alle unschuldige Täter!'*; Wodak, Menz, Mitten, and Stern, *Die Sprachen der Vergangenheiten.*

[10] Wodak, de Cillia, Reisigl, and Liebhart, *The Discursive Construction of National Identity.*

[11] Hannes Heer, Walter Manoschek, Alexander Pollak, and Ruth Wodak (eds.), *'Wie Geschichte gemacht wird': Erinnerungen an Wehrmacht und Zweiten Weltkrieg* (Vienna, 2003), published in English as *The Discursive Construction of History: Remembering the German Wehrmacht's War of Extermination* (Basingstoke, 2008).

[12] András Kovács and Ruth Wodak, *Nato, Neutrality and National Identity: The Case of Austria and Hungary* (Vienna, 2003).

cent of the vote. The coalition broke down, and a new one between the ÖVP and the FPÖ was formed on 4 February 2000. This was followed by an immediate reaction on the part of the fourteen other member states of the European Union,[13] and 'sanctions' against the Austrian government were established which led to a new nationalistic wave in Austria. An exit strategy for the EU fourteen was created by the so-called 'report of the three wise men', which established that Austria was still a democratic country like all other Western states. Under this international pressure, restitution towards slave labour and Jewish survivors was resolved in January 2001.

2. A New Anti-Semitism in Austria?

The year 1945 undoubtedly also represented a qualitative break in the history of anti-Semitism in Austria. All discriminatory measures against Jews introduced by the Nazis were rescinded, and the open profession of anti-Semitic beliefs lost its previous normative legitimacy. It would be wrong, however, to assume that these measures necessarily eroded the long tradition of anti-Semitic prejudice in the Austrian population. There are both historical and theoretical arguments that strongly suggest a continuity rather than discontinuity in anti-Semitic prejudice in Austria.

The collapse of the Third Reich forced many, in Austria as well as in Germany, to confront the extent of the Nazis' crimes. Doubts, guilt feelings, and the need to justify or rationalize one's behaviour encouraged the development of strategies for 'coming to terms with this past'. The facts of the persecution were frequently mitigated, while the victims of Nazi persecution were—again—made into the causes of present woes.

Moreover, Austria's officially recognized status as the first victim of Hitlerite aggression provided many Austrians with an important argument to deflect any responsibility that went beyond the commission of individual crimes. The search for a new identity emphasized Austrian distinctiveness, which at the same time became a negation of all ties with the Nazi (that is to say, German) past. This, in turn, reinforced a specific definition of insiders and outsiders, of 'us' and 'them', of 'the others' at all levels of discourse.

[13] See Michael Kopeinig and Christoph Kotanko, *Eine europäische Affäre* (Vienna, 2000).

Anti-Semitism in post-war Austria must therefore be viewed chiefly in relation to the various ways of dealing with alleged or real guilt, with alleged or actual accusations about the Nazi past. Discursive remedies may be found not only in the large, traditional reservoir of anti-Semitic prejudice and in a general discourse of collective experiences and attitudes, but in several new argumentative topoi[14] as well. The forms of expression chosen vary significantly: they may be manifest or latent, explicit, or indirect. But each and every one appears to be embedded in a discourse of justification.[15]

In this context, therefore, 'silence' relates to at least three different issues: first, the coding of anti-Semitic beliefs through insinuations, analogies, and other implicit and vague pragmatic devices; secondly, the silence of large sections of the elites when anti-Semitism is instrumentalized for political reasons;[16] and thirdly, the explicit denial through justification discourses that prejudiced utterances could be identified as such accompanied by vehement counter-attacks against the elites, media, intellectuals, and laypeople.[17] The new wave of anti-Semitism was basically triggered by public debates on restitution, which was finally decided upon, more than fifty years after the Shoah, by the new government at the beginning of 2001. Specifically, the topos of 'we are all victims' became common usage; many did not, and still do not, understand that it depends on who was a victim why, where, and under what circumstances.

3. The Waldheim Affair

The Waldheim Affair is the term conventionally applied to the controversy surrounding the disclosure of the previously unknown past of Kurt Waldheim, former Secretary General of the United Nations, which started during his campaign for the Austrian

[14] For the definition of argumentative 'topoi', see Reisigl and Wodak, *Discourse and Discrimination*, 69ff. Briefly put, a topos functions like a warrant in a condensed argument without making the evidence ('datum') explicit, thus relying on common-sense and shared knowledge of the participants of the interaction.

[15] Wodak, Pelikan, Nowak, et al., *'Wir sind alle unschuldige Täter!'*; Mitten, *The Politics of Antisemitic Prejudice*.

[16] See Wodak, 'Discourses of Silence'.

[17] See also S. Rosenberger, 'Kritik und Meinungsfreiheit als Regierungsprivilegien', in R. Möhring (ed.), *'Österreich allein zuhause': Politik, Medien und Justiz nach der politischen Wende* (Frankfurt am Main, 2001).

presidency in 1986. The affair not only focused international attention on Waldheim personally, but also raised broader questions relating to the history of anti-Semitism in Austria. It also drew attention to the alleged Nazi pasts of prominent politicians, officials, and prominent scholars in other countries as well as to the attitudes and policies of Allied and other nations which knowingly accepted and protected former Nazis. Moreover, employing a coded idiom more appropriate to 'post-Auschwitz' political debate, the Waldheim camp (the ÖVP, which had nominated him) helped to construct an enemy-picture (*Feindbild*) of Jews. This served both to deflect criticism of Waldheim's credibility and to explain the international 'campaign' against him. The central assumption of this *Feindbild* was that Waldheim (=Austria) was under attack from an 'international Jewish conspiracy (coded as *das Ausland*)'.[18]

The relatively uneventful early phase of the election campaign ended abruptly in March 1986, when the Austrian weekly *Profil* published documents revealing details of Waldheim's unknown past during the Second World War. *Profil*'s disclosures were followed on 4 March by almost identical revelations by the World Jewish Congress (WJC) and the *New York Times*. Waldheim had always denied any affiliation with Nazis of any kind, and had claimed in his memoirs that his military service had ended in the winter of 1941–2, when he was wounded on the Eastern Front. The evidence made public by *Profil*, the WJC, and the *New York Times* suggested the contrary: Waldheim had been a member of the Nazi Student Union and he had also belonged to a mounted unit of the *Sturmabteilung*, or SA, while attending the Consular Academy in Vienna between 1937 and 1939. Other documents revealed that Waldheim had served in the Balkans after March 1942 in Army Group E, commanded by Alexander Löhr; this Army Group was known for its involvement in the deportation of Jews from Greece and for the savagery of its military operations against Yugoslav partisans. Hence the official and international 'history' of Waldheim up to that point was seen to have silenced the actual anti-Semitism of his acts. These assumed a wider significance when it was realized that the actor had become the

---

[18] *Ausland* is used as an insinuation for 'Jews living outside of Austria', and implies the meaning of 'international Jewish conspiracy'. For details see Mitten, *The Politics of Antisemitic Prejudice*.

Secretary General of the United Nations. This old silencing and denial then produced a new silencing to justify the original silencing of an officially disapproved past.

For his part, Waldheim first denied any membership in any Nazi organization and claimed to have known nothing about the deportation of the Jews of Thessaloniki. The general strategy of the Waldheim camp was to brand any disclosures as a 'defamation campaign', an international conspiracy by the foreign press and the Jews (*im Ausland*). Waldheim, meanwhile, stated that he had simply forgotten to mention such minor events in his life because his injury had been the major caesura at that time. In the course of the election campaign, the WJC became the major object of abuse, and the political invective directed against it by the politicians of the ÖVP helped to promote and legitimize anti-Semitic prejudice in public discourse to an extent unseen since 1945. Waldheim also attempted to identify his own fate with that of his generation and country by claiming that he, like thousands of other Austrians, had merely been doing his 'duty' (*Pflichterfüllung*) under Nazi Germany. This appeal gained a positive response from many Austrian voters of his generation, but also from younger generations (such as from some children of the *Wehrmacht* soldiers). Waldheim finally won the second round of the elections on 6 June 1986 with 53.9 per cent of the vote.

However, contrary to Waldheim's expectations, interest in the unanswered questions about his past did not disappear after the election.[19] Waldheim received no official invitation from any country in Western Europe, and some official visitors even avoided travelling to Vienna because they did not want to call on him. In April 1987, the US Department of Justice announced that it was placing Waldheim on the so-called 'watch list', thus reinforcing his pariah status.[20] More broadly conceived, the Waldheim Affair symbolizes the post-war unwillingness or inability adequately to confront the implications of Nazi crimes.

---

[19] Wodak, Menz, Mitten, and Stern, *Die Sprachen der Vergangenheiten*.
[20] For more details see ibid.

III. *Critical Discourse Analysis and the Discourse-Historical Approach*

1. *Text and Context*

Like other approaches to discourse analysis, critical discourse analysis (henceforth CDA) analyses instances of social interaction that take a (partially) linguistic form.[21] CDA sees discourse—language use in speech and writing—as a form of 'social practice'. To describe discourse as social practice implies a dialectical relationship between a particular discursive event and the situation(s), institution(s), and social structure(s) that frame it: the discursive event is shaped by them, but it also shapes them. That is, discourse is socially constitutive as well as socially conditioned; it constitutes situations, objects of knowledge, and the social identities of, and relationships between, people and groups of people. Since discourse is so socially consequential, it gives rise to important issues of power.[22]

Discursive practices may have major ideological effects; that is, they can help produce and reproduce unequal power relations (between, for instance, social classes, women and men, and ethnic/cultural majorities and minorities) through the—frequently implicit and latent—ways in which they represent things and position people. CDA aims to make these opaque and latent aspects of discourse more visible.

The distinctive feature of the DHA is its attempt to integrate all available background information systematically into the analysis and interpretation of the many layers of a text. Relating individual utterances to the context in which they were made, in this case, to the historical events that were being written or talked about, is crucial in decoding the discourses of racism and anti-Semitism, for example, during the above-mentioned Waldheim Affair. Otherwise, current metaphors and allusions referring to 'the past', Nazism, and anti-Semitism would remain incomprehensible.

It is important to emphasize that 'anti-Semitic language behaviour' may, though not necessarily, imply explicitly held and/or

---

[21] Fairclough and Wodak, 'Critical Discourse Analysis'; Ruth Wodak and M. Meyer, *Methods of Critical Discourse Analysis* (London, 2001); R. Wodak, 'Critical Discourse Analysis', in C. Seale, G. Gobo, J. F. Gubrium, and D. Silverman (eds.), *Qualitative Research Practice* (London, 2004), 197–213; Reisigl and Wodak, *Discourse and Discrimination*.

[22] See Fairclough and Wodak, 'Critical Discourse Analysis' for an extensive discussion.

articulated hostility towards Jews, but it does imply the presence of prejudicial assumptions about the Jews as a group. For example, the slogan 'Kill Jews' painted on the Sigmund Freud monument in Vienna (1988) clearly does contain an explicit, though anonymous, imperative call for the most hostile of actions against Jews. On the other hand, a Jewish joke, which can have various meanings depending on such things as the setting, the participants, and the function of the utterance, also forms part of what we termed 'anti-Semitic language behaviour', but only in circumstances where the joke expresses anti-Jewish prejudices.

Thus, analysing the *context of an utterance* is indispensable in determining whether that utterance expresses anti-Semitic prejudice or not. Which anti-Semitic contents are expressed depends, among other things, on the setting (public, private, or media), the formality of the situation, the participants, the topic, and the presence or absence of Jews. Anti-Semitic language behaviour, moreover, covers a wide range of speech acts, from explicit remarks or appeals for action to mere allusions. Anti-Semitic language behaviour includes all levels of language, from text or discourse to the individual word, or even sounds, for example, the Yiddish intonation of certain words or phrases (in specific contexts, as mentioned above). Official disapproval or prohibition of anti-Semitic discourse, the attempt to suppress it in all contexts, is an important factor which presents a further important layer in deconstructing the specifically Austrian context. It influences both the coded style of its current expression and the meta-discursive issues of reproduction of discourse and the effectiveness or ineffectiveness of silencing and denial in general.[23]

To illustrate this context-dependent approach, I list some of the many layers of discourse we investigated in the study of the Waldheim Affair:

- There were *Wehrmacht* documents concerning the war in the Balkans in general, as well as documents relating specifically to Waldheim's activities there.
- There were also statements and interviews with other *Wehrmacht* veterans who had served with Waldheim.

[23] See Ruth Wodak, 'Blaming and Denying', in Keith Brown (ed.), *Encyclopedia of Language and Linguistics*, 14 vols. (2nd edn. Amsterdam, 2006); Ruth Wodak, 'Pragmatics and Critical Discourse Analysis: A Cross-Disciplinary Inquiry', *Pragmatics and Cognition*, 15/1 (2007), 203–25.

- One step removed from these was research by historians on the Balkan war in general, and on Waldheim's wartime role in particular.
- At another level again, there was the reporting in Austrian newspapers on the Balkan war, on Waldheim's past, and on the historical research on war and Waldheim's role.
- There were newspaper reports on Waldheim's own explanation of his past; on the other hand, there was the reporting of all these previously mentioned aspects in foreign newspapers, especially the *New York Times*.
- Simultaneously, the press releases and documents of the World Jewish Congress provided an autonomous informational and discursive source.
- finally, in addition to these, there were statements by, and interviews with, politicians as well as the *vox populi* on all these topics.

Though sometimes tedious and very time consuming, such an approach allows the varying perceptions, selections, and distortions of information to be recorded. As a result, we were able to trace in detail the constitution of an anti-Semitic enemy-picture of 'the others' as it emerged in public discourse in Austria in 1986.

Although the specific linguistic methods applied were dependent on the genre (for example, story, newspapers, conversation), all data was analysed along three dimensions: the anti-Semitic contents expressed; the discursive strategies employed; and the linguistic realizations at all levels of language.

2. *Contents: Anti-Semitic Stereotypes*

With the exception of those dealing with sexuality, virtually every imaginable prejudice against Jews appears in our data. In the following only a few of those are elaborated that appeared most frequently from 1986 to 2001; I also indicate the contexts in which they were most often expressed.

The first group is subsumed under the category 'Christian Anti-Semitism'. According to this prejudice, Jews are regarded as murderers of Christ, and/or as traitors. The character of 'Judas' provides everlasting 'proof' of the unreliability and lack of credibility of Jews. In 1986, Christian anti-Semitic motifs were found most frequently in newspapers and in the semi-public realm.

Although the stereotype of the 'dishonest', 'dishonourable', or the 'tricky Jew' originated in Judas' betrayal of Christ, corollary to this are the economic stereotypes that date from the Middle Ages. Jews were forced into certain occupations, such as lending money, principally because they were excluded from most others. The clichés about the Jewish commercial spirit as well as the suspicion that Jews did business dishonourably in principle were both employed in varying ways from 1986 to 2001.

The most pervasive anti-Jewish cliché, however, was and is that of the 'international Jewish conspiracy'. The Jews, so it is said, dominate or control the international press, the banks, political power, and capital, and they amass awesome power against their foes. In the Waldheim election rhetoric, the term 'campaign' became virtually synonymous with an international Jewish conspiracy against Waldheim and/or Austria.

Yet another prejudice is that Jews are 'more privileged than others'. Although such a belief was traditionally identified with the belief that all Jews were rich, this particular cliché has taken on additional significance since the Holocaust. Those Jews who 'emigrated' and thereby escaped a far worse fate, so the argument goes, especially the many 'rich ones', had no reason to complain: nothing had happened to them anyway.

As mentioned above, the collapse of the Third Reich in 1945 gave rise to a number of additional reasons for fearing the anger of the 'vengeful Jew'. One was fear of the discovery of war crimes and the persecution and conviction of war criminals. Another was fear that stolen (so-called 'Aryanized') property could be demanded back. Finally, there was fear that the former refugees would want to return to their homeland. Not only might they want their property back, or take legal action against their former persecutors, but they might 'take over' certain professions or reclaim their previous jobs and positions.

As a whole, the discourse about the 'Waldheim Affair' 'spread' to different fields of political action, involving many different genres and different discourse topics.[24] (See Fig. 14.1. *facing page*.)

---

[24] Reisigl and Wodak, *Discourse and Discrimination*.

FIG. 14.1. *The discourse about the Waldheim Affair*

Source: Martin Reisigl and Ruth Wodak, *Discourse and Discrimination: The Rhetoric of Racism and Antisemitism* (London, 2001), 100. Reproduced by permission of Routledge.

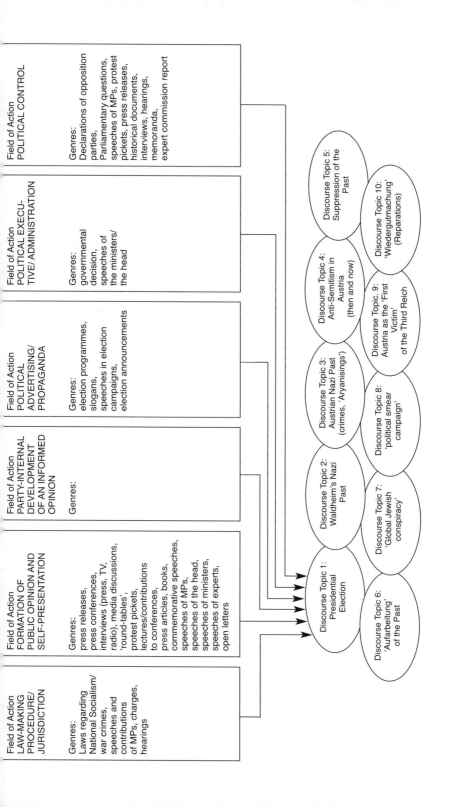

Field of Action LAW-MAKING PROCEDURE/ JURISDICTION	Field of Action FORMATION OF PUBLIC OPINION AND SELF-PRESENTATION	Field of Action PARTY-INTERNAL DEVELOPMENT OF AN INFORMED OPINION	Field of Action POLITICAL ADVERTISING/ PROPAGANDA	Field of Action POLITICAL EXECU-TIVE/ADMINISTRATION	Field of Action POLITICAL CONTROL
Genres: Laws regarding National Socialism/ war crimes, speeches and contributions of MPs, charges, hearings	Genres: press releases, press conferences, interviews (press, TV, radio), media discussions, 'round-tables', protest pickets, lectures/contributions to conferences, press articles, books, commemorative speeches, speeches of MPs, speeches of the head, speeches of ministers, speeches of experts, open letters	Genres:	Genres: election programmes, slogans, speeches in election campaigns, election announcements	Genres: governmental decision, speeches of the ministers/ the head	Genres: Declarations of opposition parties, Parliamentary questions, speeches of MPs, protest pickets, press releases, historical documents, interviews, hearings, memoranda, expert commission report

Discourse Topic 1: Presidential Election

Discourse Topic 2: Waldheim's Nazi Past

Discourse Topic 3: Austrian Nazi Past (crimes, 'Aryanisings')

Discourse Topic 4: Anti-Semitism in Austria (then and now)

Discourse Topic 5: Suppression of the Past

Discourse Topic 6: 'Aufarbeitung' of the Past

Discourse Topic 7: 'Global Jewish conspiracy'

Discourse Topic 8: 'political smear campaign'

Discourse Topic 9: Austria as the 'First Victim' of the Third Reich

Discourse Topic 10: 'Wiedergutmachung' (Reparations)

IV *Case Study: The 2001 Election Campaign in Vienna*

1. *The Broader Context*

In spring 2001, during the mayoral election campaign for the city
of Vienna, which has a SPÖ majority, the FPÖ and its former
leader, Jörg Haider, began a campaign which again stimulated
anti-Semitic beliefs and prejudices.[25] Old stereotypes were used
as political weapons. This campaign was characterized by vehement attacks on the president of the Jewish Community, Ariel
Muzicant. The campaign came as no surprise. Restitution negotiations had just come to an end, and the new government had
decided to pay back some of the 'Aryanized' monies and goods
to Jewish victims. This time, the 'play' with insinuations or allusions did not work as well as in 1986. The FPÖ lost at this
election, mostly because the Mayor of Vienna, Michael Häupl,
explicitly opposed the anti-Semitic ideologies expressed. The political debate was extremely revealing: it centred on the issues of
'freedom of opinion' and 'possible criticism of Jews'. These new
strategies can be seen as part of the above-described justification
discourse. The *topos* of *criticism* has been taken up elsewhere as
well.[26] Recent studies have illustrated that these discourses have
spread out across other European nation-states ('Haider effect',
'Haiderization of Europe'; see below).[27]

Here, I focus on the following three utterances by Jörg Haider,
made during the election campaign of 2001 (see Appendix 14.1 for
the entire debate during the 2001 election campaign).

Haider, 21 Feb. 2001, opening of the election campaign:

'Mr Häupl has an election strategist: he's called Greenberg [loud laughter in the hall]. He had him flown in from the East Coast. My friends,
you have a choice: you can vote for Spin Doctor Greenberg from the
East Coast, or for the Heart of Vienna!'

('Der Häupl hat einen Wahlkampfstrategen, der heißt Greenberg
[loud laughter in the hall]. Den hat er sich von der Ostküste einfliegen
lassen! Liebe Freunde, ihr habt die Wahl, zwischen Spindoctor
Greenberg von der Ostküste, oder dem Wienerherz zu entscheiden!')

---

[25] See R. Möhring (ed.), *'Österreich allein zuhause': Politik, Medien und Justiz nach der politischen
Wende* (Frankfurt am Main, 2001); S. Rosenberger, 'Kritik und Meinungsfreiheit als
Regierungsprivilegien', in Möhring (ed.), *'Österreich allein zuhause'*.

[26] Wodak, 'Pragmatics and Critical Discourse Analysis'.

[27] Pelinka and Wodak (eds.), *'Dreck am Stecken'*; and Wodak and Pelinka (eds.), *The Haider
Phenomenon*.

'We don't need any proclamations from the East Coast. Now we've had enough. Now we're concerned with another part of our history, reparations to those driven from their homes.'

('Wir brauchen keine Zurufe von der Ostküste. Jetzt ist es einmal genug. Jetzt geht es um einen anderen Teil der Geschichte, die Wiedergutmachung für die Heimatvertriebenen.')

Haider, 28 Feb. 2001, Ash Wednesday Speech:

'Mr Muzicant: What I don't understand is how someone called Ariel can have so much dirty linen . . . I do not understand this at all, but I mean . . . he will certainly comment this tomorrow, right?. . . But, I am not timid in these matters.'

('Der Herr Muzicant: I versteh überhaupt net, wie ana, der Ariel haßt, so viel Dreck am Steckn haben kann . . . des versteh i überhaupt net, aber i man . . . das wird er schon morgen kommentieren, nicht . . . aber ich bin da nicht sehr schreckhaft, in diesen Fragen.')

In order to be able to understand, analyse, and explain such utterances systematically, I draw on the DHA, presented above. The linguistic analysis of these utterances in the Austrian multi-layered context thus has to draw on, *inter alia*:

- historical analysis of anti-Semitism and its verbal expressions (i.e. 'coded language').
- socio-cognitive analysis of collective memories and frames guiding the acquisition of specific knowledge to be able to understand the 'coded language'.
- socio-political analysis of the election campaign, the ongoing debates, and the political parties taking part; these two dimensions form the broader context.
- genre theory; the functions of political speeches (persuasive strategies; positive self-presentation/negative other-presentation; populist rhetoric, etc.).
- the setting, speakers, etc. of the concrete utterances; this is the narrower context.
- the co-text of each utterance.
- and finally, verbal expressions have to be analysed in terms of linguistic pragmatic/grammatical approaches (presuppositions; insinuations; implications; etc., as characteristics of the specific 'coded anti-Semitism').

These devices are embedded in discursive macro-strategies of positive self-presentation and negative other-presentation as

defined in the DHA.[28] Such strategies employ various other linguistic features, rhetorical tropes, and patterns of argument/legit-
imization.[29] Moreover, we have to situate this election campaign
in other discourses about foreigners, Jews, minorities, and mar-
ginalized groups in Austria and Europe in order to be able to
grasp the interdiscursivity, intertextuality, and re-contextualization
of certain topoi and arguments in the wider context. In this essay,
it is impossible to analyse the entire election campaign in detail.[30]
In what follows, I will highlight the essential recurrent anti-Semitic
topics, topoi, stereotypes, and the linguistic devices used in the
speech given in Ried on 28 February 2001.

2. Relevant Linguistic Notions

As 'allusions' (insinuations) are of central importance in the case
we are concerned with, they should be defined in more detail:
through allusions one can suggest negative associations without
being held responsible for them. Ultimately the associations are
only suggested. The listeners must make them in the act of reception.[31] Allusions thus depend on shared knowledge. The person
who alludes to something counts on resonance, that is, on the pre-
paredness of the recipients consciously to associate the facts that
are alluded to.

In the area of politics, those making allusions may have the
intention, and achieve the result, of devaluing political opponents,
without accepting responsibility for what is implicitly said. In the
case of allusions, what is not pronounced creates a kind of secrecy,
and familiarity suggests something like: 'we all know what is
meant.' The world of allusion thus exists in a kind of 'repertoire
of collective knowledge'. Allusions frequently rely on topoi and
linguistic patterns already in play and with a clear meaning
content,[32] or on topoi which point to well-established and perhaps
even anti-Semitic stereotypes (such as 'Jewish speculators and
crooks').[33]

[28] Martin Reisigl and Ruth Wodak, 'The Discourse-Historical Approach', in Ruth
Wodak and Michael Meyer (eds.), *Methods of CDA* (2nd rev. edn. London, 2009).

[29] See Reisigl and Wodak, *Discourse and Discrimination*, ch. 2.

[30] See Wodak and M. Reisigl, '. . . wenn einer Ariel heist . . . '

[31] R. Wodak and R. de Cillia, *Sprache und Antisemitismus*, Mitteilungen 4 (Vienna, 1988),
10.

[32] See the notion of 'East Coast'; for discussion Mitten, *The Politics of Antisemitic Prejudice*.

[33] Wodak and de Cillia, *Sprache und Antisemitismus*, 15.

In accusing Ariel Muzicant, Jörg Haider frequently made allusions. By using this kind of discourse strategy, he (and others) implied certain presuppositions, which many people saw as 'common sense beliefs' or 'shared truth'. This is, of course, not a new linguistic strategy in prejudiced discourse. Allusions, as mentioned above, enable politicians and other speakers to deny the possible meaning attributed to the allusion and refer to the beliefs of the readers or listeners projected onto the utterance.

The concept of presuppositions is central to linguistic pragmatics. The analysis of presuppositions within speech act theory makes it possible to make explicit the implicit assumptions and intertextual relations that underlie text production.[34]

Many linguistic phenomena have been related to presuppositions. Here I shall follow the survey given in Yule, which concentrates on six types (see Table 14.1).

TABLE 14.1. *Types of presupposition*

Type	Example	Presupposition
existential	The X	• X exists.
factive	I regret having done that	• I did it.
non-factive	He claimed to be a teacher	• He was not a teacher.
lexical	She managed to escape	• She attempted to escape.
structural	Who is coming?	• Someone is coming.
counter-factual	If I were not ill	• I am ill.

Source: George Yule, *Oxford Introduction to Language Studies: Pragmatics* (Oxford, 1996), ch. 4. Reproduced by permission of Oxford University Press.

In the case of anti-Semitic allusions, at least since 1945, no enclosed ideological edifice of anti-Semitism is completely addressed and spelled out. Rather, an amalgam of ideological tenets is invoked by linguistic 'clues and traces' in order to relate to a particular set of beliefs and a 'discourse space'—irrespective of where the 'roots' of this 'discourse space' may lead.

Finally, I would like to consider the term 'word play'. In his infamous remark during the election campaign, Haider made a word play on 'Ariel', Muzicant's first name. This was then relativized as a 'joke', as 'irony', and so on, in the sense of 'why not have a bit of fun during the carnival'?

---

[34] D. Schiffrin, *Approaches to Discourse* (Oxford, 1994); Wodak, 'Pragmatics and Critical Discourse Analysis'; ead., *The Discourse of Politics in Action* (Basingstoke, 2009).

Word play ('play on words')' refers to playful use of words, the
humorous effect of which depends particularly on the ambiguity
of the words used or on the identical or similar pronunciation of
two related words with different meanings: a funny or silly word.

3. Discourse Strands

The topic of compensation in relation to the criminalization of
Muzicant was triggered at the New Year's meeting on 22 January
2001 (see Appendix 14.1). There it was claimed that Muzicant had
piled up debts and that the compensation would partly serve his
own interest (that of paying off debts). These first utterances imply
many presuppositions: first, that Muzicant had actually made
criminal moves, exploiting the interests of the survivors for himself
and his business. Secondly, a chain of anti-Semitic insinuations is
triggered off by further presuppositions: Jews are rich, are busi-
nessmen, etc. At the same time, compensation is, in general terms,
devalued as not a very important 'problem'. This topic is pursued
at the start of the election campaign, when there is an attack on
the 'East Coast', and the apparent influence of the 'East Coast'
(this is related both to the Mayor of Vienna, Michael Häupl, and
to the SPÖ, as well as to the compensation negotiations). The use
of the insinuation 'East Coast' goes back at least as far as the
Waldheim Affair of 1986 (see above). The latent meaning implies
that the SPÖ is dependent on these 'powerful Jews'; thus the
'World Conspiracy stereotype' is presupposed. Moreover, in this
speech the extermination of the Jews and the matter of compensation are explicitly set against the expelled Sudeten Germans (a
well-known argument of both the FPÖ and Haider). In the Ried
statement that has been closely analysed elsewhere the criminalization of Muzicant is pursued in the form of an allusion ('dirty
linen'). However, its vagueness is removed and clarified in the following statements. On 8 March 2001 there are further suggestions
of Muzicant's criminal activity, and this is continued in the *News*
interview of 14 March 2001 (see Appendix 14.1).

This entire discourse strand serves to present Dr Ariel Muzicant
as a criminal, in order to focus on his role in the compensation
negotiations. Ultimately, however, what also seems important is to
devalue the compensation of Jewish victims of the Holocaust and
to set it against the expulsion of the Sudeten Germans.

The second discourse strand concerns the sub-division of Austrian citizens into those with a 'true Viennese heart', and those who allow themselves to be influenced by the 'East Coast'. In the 2 April 2001 issue of *Profil*, Peter Sichrovsky himself, general secretary of the FPÖ, provides this interpretation and thereby contradicts Haider's defence of 16 March 2001 that 'East Coast' is a 'purely geographical description'.

Stanley Greenberg, adviser to the Mayor of Vienna, Dr Michael Häupl, is presented as, among other things, a Jew who is employed by the SPÖ as a spin doctor. The characterization of a person primarily as a 'Jew' serves exclusively to arouse anti-Semitic attitudes, because this characteristic is irrelevant for Greenberg's work. Jews are therefore contrasted with 'real' Austrians. The topos of the 'real Austrian' is not new. This attribution was already used in the 1970s when Bruno Kreisky, later Chancellor of Austria, a Social Democrat and of Jewish origin, campaigned against the People's Party. The use of 'real Austrians' appeared again in the election campaign 1999 (Haider was and is a 'real' Austrian) and alludes to the fallacious argument that Jews or Austrians of other ethnic origins are not 'on the same level', even if they have Austrian citizenship. The Austrianness (or citizenship) of Austrian Jews is thereby implicitly denied. This exclusion is also extended to Muzicant, who is described as having been an 'immigrant'; as a 'guest' in a host country, it is suggested that he ought to behave (*Zeit im Bild*, 2, 16 March 2001). In this way, Haider is introducing a racial concept: citizenship is not enough to be a 'real' citizen. These utterances, therefore, presuppose racist attitudes. At the same time he emphasizes the Nazi era: emigration, immigration, and re-immigration of Jews are viewed as a 'voluntary' decision and not as determined by the Holocaust. Finally, Haider presupposes that Jews should actually be grateful to Austria, the country from which they had had to flee in order not to be deported and murdered (and where their entire property was Aryanized).

On the basis of criticism by opposition politicians, the media, and politicians and scholars from abroad, a discourse of justification and legitimization began. The attacks on Jews, like Greenberg and Muzicant, now had to be given a 'real' foundation in Haider's perception and discourse, or they had to be simultaneously played down.

On the one hand, therefore, the insinuations are described as 'criticism' and thereby shifted on to a rationally factual level. The relevant topos is: 'why can't one criticize Jews?' The underlying argument for the 'criticism' is as follows: Muzicant has denigrated Austria, is a 'denouncer' who has 'declared war on a democratically elected government'. Muzicant, therefore, is 'not a good Austrian'. On the other hand, the anti-Semitic stereotype of the 'traitor' is alluded to, the 'betrayer of the fatherland'. The presupposition runs: anyone who is not satisfied with the government and who voices criticism is a 'traitor' and 'not a good Austrian'. This means that the government is equated with the state and that there is no longer room for plurality of opinion, unless, of course, one criticizes such 'traitors', for Haider does claim this freedom of opinion for himself and defends himself against the 'left-wing thought-police' (*Zeit im Bild*, 16 March 2001, and *Presse Kommentar*, 17 March 2001). The stereotype of 'traitor', which at that time embraced all critics of the government in Austria and also elsewhere, presupposes, in the case of Muzicant—and in the context of an anti-Semitic discourse—the additional meaning of the Christian anti-Semitic stereotype of 'traitor' (it is 'not acceptable to denigrate one's own country': Muzicant displays an 'anti-Austrian mentality', 22 March 2001).

The fourth discourse strand is concerned with Muzicant's 'motives': on the one hand, to pay off the debts that he has accumulated in an apparently criminal fashion; on the other, he is 'filled with hatred', 'vengeful' ('he refuses to give his signature'), and 'greedy for recognition' ('the applause of the enemies of Austria [was] apparently more important'). This alludes to another familiar anti-Semitic stereotype: the 'vengeful Jew' (where the Old Testament is often—inaccurately—quoted: 'an eye for an eye, a tooth for a tooth').

V 'New–Old' Anti-Semitism in Austria and Europe?

These examples demonstrate the extent to which Jörg Haider has used and spread anti-Jewish stereotypes since the FPÖ's New Year meeting in 2001. The linking of the Vienna election campaign with restitution becomes obvious. The defamation of Ariel Muzicant, and, thereby, the whole of the Jewish community and the Austrian Jews, did not, in fact, bring any electoral gain in the Vienna election, but discourses take on a life of their own.

Anti-Semitic rhetoric has also gained new dimensions: through the redefinition of 'abuse' and 'insult' as 'legitimate criticism', anti-Semitic clichés have become acceptable. Many people reiterate Haider's explanations and legitimizations. As in 1986, during the Waldheim affair, the familiar *Iudeus ex machina* strategy was again introduced: scapegoats are ideal for constructing enemy-images and thereby reinforcing the ego of the in-group.

After Auschwitz, as T. W. Adorno already noted, nothing has remained the same and nothing should remain the same.[35] Adorno labelled anti-Semitism as the 'archetypical prejudice', the 'Jew as the archetypical other'. Whenever a scapegoat is needed, 'Jews' are functionalized as scapegoats.

Exclusionary rhetoric has been re-contextualized and projected onto many other minorities in recent years in Europe—Roma and Sinti, foreigners from the former Eastern bloc after 1989, and Turks and Muslims. Nowadays, however, we can observe a re-emergence of explicit anti-Semitic rhetoric in several EU countries; old stereotypes which had been kept in the realm of latency (coded) for a long time are uttered explicitly again. The triggers for such a re-emergence differ from country to country because of past and present policies, political goals, and functions.

Moreover, we notice an abundance of analogies and comparisons between the past and the present in the media and in political and everyday discourses.[36] Comparisons are drawn between the Holocaust and 'Holocaust-farms', meaning chickens which are kept in very small cages; or between the extermination policies of the Nazis and the politics of the Israeli government (which is frequently generalized to 'Israelis' or 'Jews' worldwide). Such comparisons serve to deny guilt in the sense that 'all of them are doing or did terrible things, thus nobody is worse than "the Jews"'.[37]

---

[35] T. W. Adorno, *Studien zum autoritären Charakter* (Frankfurt am Main, 1973; 1st pub. 1950).

[36] See Ruth Wodak and Gertraud Auer-Boreo (eds.), *Memory and Justice* (Vienna, 2009).

[37] See e.g. Stephen Byers, 'Anti-Semitism is a Virus and it Mutates', *Guardian*, 15 Mar. 2004, who states: 'Of course, criticism of Israel's policy is not, of itself, anti-Semitic. But it can become so when it involves applying double standards, holds all Jews responsible for the actions of the Israeli government or reveals a demonisation of Jews . . . If Chinese restaurants in London were firebombed by angry mobs, would it be right to withhold sym-

In an interesting and controversial article, András Kovács claims that the existing, unofficial but recognized, post-war contract between Jews and non-Jews in Europe after 1945 has been de-legitimized:

In place of the unwritten contract between the European Jews and the European states, which came into being after the Second World War, a gap yawns today. For the Jews, there is a question about what constitutes their place in Europe if they do not see themselves as a collective in their religious community, and if they have doubts about whether Europe will accept them as they define themselves. Beyond this, not insignificant forces are active in the most diverse positions of the political spectrum, whose interests are not served if something new takes the place of the contract which has lost its validity, and the Jews feel at home in Europe . . . If we look soberly at the situation today, then it must seem most likely that a new 'contract' will not come about in response to political pressures, for these work against it. It will require a courageous decision on the part of Jewish and non-Jewish public figures and politicians in Europe . . . for harmony to be restored between Europe and its Jews.[38]

Taking the arguments of Kovács even further, the post-war taboo on anti-Semitism has, in my view, changed and been lifted; one of the most important functions seems to be getting rid of alleged or subjective/collective guilt. Former victims (of the Shoah) have turned into perpetrators; historical contexts are conflated and de-historicized. Specifically, six elements can be detected which might explain these developments.

(a) The conflict in the Middle East leads to a new rhetoric equating Israeli with Nazi politics ('if they are doing this, then we do not have to feel guilty anymore'). European Jews are made responsible for whatever is happening in Israel. This implies an anti-Semitic fallacious argument: if one Jew is said to have done something 'bad', this is attributed to all Jews—they are now 'all bad'; the feature is generalized.

pathy for the victims until they condemned China for its policies in Tibet?' (p. 12). The debate in the *New York Review of Books*, ongoing since September 2003 (see Tony Judt's much acknowledged and also refuted article and the following letters to the editor), points to a heated discussion in the USA and also to a rift between more liberal and more conservative Jewish Americans; see also Eva Schweitzer, 'Die Angst wächst in Manhattan', *Die Zeit*, 8 Jan. 2004, p. 42.

[38] A. Kovács, 'The Latency of Anti-Semitic Prejudice', in P. A. Chilton and Ruth Wodak (eds.), *New Agenda in Critical Discourse Analysis* (Amsterdam, 2007), 273–4.

(b) *Realpolitik* in Western European countries supports the new Muslim communities because they represent future voters. Conflicts on asylum laws and migration policies are apparent; the integration of multi-cultural communities has rarely succeeded. In France and Belgium, for example, these phenomena have led to a transformation of the position of right and left. The left support Arab and Muslim refugees and sometimes merge anti-Israeli politics with anti-Jewish beliefs, whereas the right proposes strict anti-immigration policies and thus seemingly supports the Jewish population.

(c) The restitution to Jews of 'Aryanized' monies and belongings in Austria, Switzerland, and Germany has resulted in new stereotypes: 'The emigrants are rich anyway, the victims are all dead'; 'Why should "our tax money" be given to them?'; 'They exploit the Shoah'; and so forth. Committees composed of historians, lawyers, and other experts have explored and investigated these issues in detail.

(d) The two *Wehrmacht* exhibitions 1995 and 2001 have challenged the German and Austrian post-war consensus that a small group around Hitler, comprising the SS and SD, was guilty, but certainly not the millions of soldiers in the *Wehrmacht*.[39] Discourses of justification have re-emerged and have led to a victim–perpetrator reversal.

(e) EU enlargement has triggered a comeback of right-wing populist parties in Hungary, Bulgaria, and Romania, frequently discriminating against Roma minorities and employing blatant anti-Semitic rhetoric. These debates relate to the complex problem of coping with the Nazi and Communist pasts in Europe.[40]

(f) Such controversies (as illustrated above) lead to a new rhetoric: one should finally be allowed to criticize 'bad Jews'. The fallacious (straw-man) argument continues: 'Immediately, if criticism is made explicit, one is labelled anti-Semitic.' Of course, this sometimes occurs because some people do not distinguish between anti-Zionism, criticism of the policies of the Israeli

---

[39] For details see Heer, Manoschek, Pollak, and Wodak (eds.), *The Discursive Construction of History*. See also the debates triggered by Jan T. Gross, *Neighbors: The Destruction of the Jewish Community in Jedwabne, Poland* (Princeton, 2001).

[40] Adorno, *Studien zum autoritären Charakter*.

government, and anti-Semitism. A differentiated, rational debate is thus unfortunately rendered impossible.

We are thus confronted with a very mixed bag of motives, arguments, stereotypes, and policies. The past is related in an irrational way to the present and functionalized for many different political aims. We detect both 'de-historicization' and de-contextualization/re-contextual-ization. Such discourses have been reinforced by anti-American sentiments and the conflict in the Middle East.

Jews have a long tradition as scapegoats, and apparently still lend themselves to this role: anti-Semitism without Jews and without anti-Semites. Bunzl and Marin identified this tendency almost thirty years ago.[41] In fact, what the case study illustrates in the specific Austrian context can be experienced in a similar way in a much larger European context. Political calculation still clearly finds a wide measure of support for irrational claims and prejudices under the cloak of 'criticism'.

Appendix 14.1

Quotations from Vienna election campaign, 2001: Jörg Haider verbatim (chronologically from 21 Jan. to 22 Mar. 2001)

Report in *Der Standard*, 22 Jan. 2001, on the FPÖ's New Year Meeting of 21 Jan. 2001:

'We have other problems than constantly negotiating about how we ought to carry out the reparations', said Haider. 'Some time there has to be an end.'

('Wir haben andere Probleme, als ständig zu verhandeln, wie wir Wiedergutmachung zu leisten haben', sprach Haider, 'einmal muss Schluss sein.')

'Mr Muzicant will be satisfied only when the debt of 600 million Schillings that he has run up in Vienna has been paid for him.'

('Der Herr Muzicant ist erst zufrieden, bis man ihm auch jene 600 Millionen Schilling Schulden bezahlt, die von ihm in Wien angehäuft worden sind.')

---

[41] J. Bunzl and B. Marin, *Antisemitismus in Österreich* (Innsbruck, 1983).

Haider on 21 Feb. 2001 at the opening of the electoral campaign in Oberlaa:

'Mr Häupl has an election strategist: he's called Greenberg [loud laughter in the hall]. He had him flown in from the East Coast. My friends, you have a choice: you can vote for Spin Doctor Greenberg from the East Coast, or for the Heart of Vienna!'

('Der Häupl hat einen Wahlkampfstrategen, der heisst Greenberg [loud laughter in the hall]. Den hat er sich von der Ostküste einfliegen lassen! Liebe Freunde, ihr habt die Wahl, zwischen Spindoctor Greenberg von der Ostküste, oder dem Wienerherz zu entscheiden!')

'We don't need any proclamations from the East Coast. Now we've had enough. Now we're concerned with another part of our history, reparations to those driven from their homes.'

('Wir brauchen keine Zurufe von der Ostküste. Jetzt ist es einmal genug. Jetzt geht es um einen anderen Teil der Geschichte, die Wiedergutmachung für die Heimatvertriebenen.')

Haider on 28 Feb. 2001, Ash Wednesday Speech:

'Mr Muzicant: What I don't understand is how someone called Ariel can have so much dirty linen . . . I do not understand this at all, but I mean . . . he will certainly comment this tomorrow, right? . . . But, I am not timid in these matters.'

('Der Herr Muzicant: I versteh überhaupt net, wie ana, der Ariel haßt, so viel Dreck am Steckn haben kann . . . des versteh i überhaupt net, aber i man . . . das wird er schon morgen kommentieren, nicht . . . aber ich bin da nicht sehr schreckhaft, in diesen Fragen.')

Haider, in a campaign speech on 8 Mar. 2001 in the Gösser brewery:

'Someone [Muzicant] who, together with the Vienna City Council, and because of his good contacts there as an estate agent and speculator, carries out rebuilding projects in protected areas, where no one else gets permission—that is something that's not right.'

('Jemand [Muzicant], der im Verbund mit der Wiener Stadtregierung und aufgrund seiner guten Kontakte dorthin als Immobilienmakler und -spekulant hier in Schutzgebieten

Sanierungen durchführt, wo kein anderer eine Bewilligung bekommt, dann ist das etwas, was nicht in Ordnung ist.')

Haider interview in *News*, 14 Mar. 2001:

'In my Ash Wednesday speech I referred to his [Muzicant's] role concerning Austria during the EU sanctions. I have kept back a few more things.'

('Ich habe bei meiner Aschermittwochsrede auf seine [Muzicants] Rolle gegenüber Österreich während der EU-Sanktionen Bezug genommen. Da behalte ich mir noch ein paar Dinge vor.')

'In addition he has made explicit use of his political connections to benefit his business affairs.'

('Dazu kommt, dass er seine politischen Beziehungen durchaus ausnützt, um geschäftlich seine Dinge unter Dach und Fach zu bringen.')

'And then he and the religious community have debts of around 600 million Schillings and in Washington he stabbed Austria in the back.'

('Und dann noch, dass er mit der Kultusgemeinde rund 600 Millionen Schilling Schulden hat und Österreich in Washington in den Rücken gefallen ist.')

'I really do not see why the taxpayer should cough up a single Schilling because of Mr Muzicant's sloppy business-dealings.'

('Ich sehe wirklich nicht ein, warum der Steuerzahler für die schlampige Wirtschaft des Herrn Muzicant nur einen Schilling berappen soll.')

'And in the end his business connections will have to be exposed.'

('Und schließlich wird man seine Geschäftsverbindungen durchleuchten müssen.')

'He [Muzicant] is the personification of irreconcilability and therefore has relatively little place in the spectrum of the forces of democracy.'

('Das [Muzicant] ist ein Mensch, der die personifizierte Unversöhnlichkeit ist und daher im Spektrum der demokratischen Kräfte relativ wenig Platz hat.')

Haider, 16 Mar. 2001, *Zeit im Bild*, 2.

'In a difficult period for this country', Muzicant 'proved not to be
a good Austrian.' Abroad, he behaved as if his Jewish co-citizens
were endangered again, and denounced the country.

(Muzicant 'hat sich in einer schwierigen Phase nicht als guter
Österreicher erwiesen.' Er habe im Ausland so getan, als ob die
jüdischen Mitbürger wieder gefährdet seien und habe das Land
schlecht gemacht.)

H: 'It was a light-hearted word play. That, I think, is absolutely
acceptable in politics. The deeper background, however, should
not be hushed up. And that is simply the criticism of Mr Muzicant
who has not behaved like an Austrian during a difficult phase for
the Republic.'

(H: Es war ein scherzhaftes Wortspiel. Das glaube ich, ist in der
Politik absolut zulässig. Der tiefere Hintergrund soll aber nicht
verheimlicht werden. Und der ist einfach die Kritik am Herrn
Muzicant, der in einer schwierigen Phase der Republik sich
nicht als guter Österreicher erwiesen hat.)

H: 'So, you know, thank God, that we live in a democracy where
there are no thought-police of politically correct people to prescribe what we are allowed to say. The East Coast is a geographical expression, and that's where the political centre is in America.
Everyone knows that, and that's where Greenberg comes from,
and he is to advise Mr Häupl.'

(H: Also, Sie wissen, dass wir Gott sei Dank in einer Demokratie
leben, in der es keine Gedankenpolizisten der politisch korrekten
Gutmenschen gibt, die uns vorschreiben, was wir noch for-
mulieren dürfen. Die Ostküste ist eine geographische
Bezeichnung, und dort liegt das politische Zentrum in Amerika.
Das weiß jedermann und von dort kommt der Greenberg, der
den Herrn Häupl beraten soll.)

'What I want to ensure in Austria is simply that people can
express their opinion freely. And that there is no ban on thinking.
When the government was being formed I also signed a preamble
in which we recognize that we reject every form of racism and
anti-Semitism. And those people will have to look very hard to
find anything negative in what I said. Because I have already told

you: someone like Mr Muzicant who, firstly, is always trying to
get rid of the FPÖ, and then has given this country a bad name,
demonstrably run it down—he was one of the "chief denouncers"
of Austrians and Austria in the course of forming the government.
He will have to put up with criticism. That is simply the most
essential thing in a democracy, and if he can't cope with that, he's
worth nothing to a democracy.'

(H: Was ich in Österreich gewährleisten will, ist einfach, dass
die Menschen eine freie Meinung äußern dürfen. Und dass es
keine Denkverbote gibt. Ich habe anlässlich der Regierungsbildung auch eine Präambel mitunterschrieben, in der wir
uns dazu bekennen, dass wir jede Form von Rassismus und
Antisemitismus ablehnen. Und es werden sich jene sehr anstren-
gen müssen, in der Äußerung von mir jetzt wiederum etwas
Negatives zu finden. Denn ich habe es Ihnen schon vorhin
gesagt: jemand, wie der Herr Muzicant, der ständig den
Versuch macht, erstens amal die FPÖ herabzusetzen, dann
dieses Land schlecht gemacht hat, nachweisbar schlecht
gemacht hat, er gehört zu den Obervernaderern der Öster-
reicher/Österreichs im Zuge der Regierungsbildung. Der muss
sich eine Kritik gefallen lassen. Das ist ja einfach in einer
Demokratie das Notwendigste und wenn er das nicht aushält,
dann taugt er nicht für eine Demokratie.)

Haider, comment in *Presse*, 17 Mar. 2001:

'I will not allow them to prevent me from criticizing a representative of a religious community, when he declares war on a democratically elected government.'

('Ich lasse mir nicht verbieten, einen Repräsentanten einer
Religionsgemeinschaft zu kritisieren, wenn dieser einer demo-
kratisch gewählten Regierung den Krieg erklärt.')

'Dr Ariel Muzicant was one of those most responsible for the
intolerable witch-hunt against our country after the formation of
the FPÖ–ÖVP coalition.'

('Dr Ariel Muzicant war einer der Hauptverantwortlichen für
die unerträgliche Hetze gegen unser Land nach Bildung der
FPÖ/ÖVP-Koalition.')

'He has given interviews to foreign newspapers in which he passes
judgement on Austria with incomprehensible rage and anger.'

('Er hat ausländischen Zeitungen Interviews gegeben, in denen er mit unverständlicher Wut und Zorn über Österreich urteilte.')

'He is cited as a witness in hate-mail against Austria from the World Jewish Congress.'

('Er wird in Hassbriefen des World Jewish Congress gegen Österreich als Zeuge zitiert.')

'He refuses to give his signature to an agreement which would finally make it possible to achieve just compensation for the victims of the Nazi period.'

('Er verweigerte seine Unterschrift auf einer Vereinbarung, die endlich den Opfern der NS-Zeit eine gerechte Entschädigung ermöglicht.')

'[Dr Muzicant] is not ashamed of writing off as "indecent" and insulting the majority of the people who gave him and his family a home when they were immigrants.'

('[Herr Dr. Muzicant] schämt sich nicht, die Mehrheit eines Volkes, das ihm und seiner Familie als Einwanderer eine Heimat gab, als "unanständig" abzuqualifizieren und zu beleidigen.')

'For Mr Muzicant the applause of the enemies of Austria was more important.'

('Herrn Muzicant war der Applaus der Österreich-Feinde wichtiger.')

Haider, 22 Mar. 2001 (reported in *Der Standard*, 23 Mar. 2001):

It is 'unacceptable to denigrate one's own country'. . . . It is precisely this, according to Haider, that Ariel Muzicant, the president of the Jewish religious community, has done, thereby showing an 'attitude hostile to Austria'.

(Es sei 'unstatthaft, das eigene Land schlecht zu machen'. . . . Ebendies, so Haider, habe der Präsident der israelitischen Kultusgemeinde, Ariel Muzicant, getan und so 'österreichfeindliche Gesinnung' demonstriert.)

Notes on Contributors

JUDITH DEVLIN is Senior Lecturer in Modern History at University College, Dublin. She took her Ph.D. at Oxford and has worked at the Irish Department of Foreign Affairs, the École Nationale d'Administration, and the Embassy of Ireland in Moscow. Her publications include *The Rise of the Russian Democrats: The Causes and Consequences of the Elite Revolution* (1995) and *Slavophiles and Commissars: Enemies of Democracy in Modern Russia* (1999). She has co-edited *Religion and Rebellion* (1997) and *European Encounters* (2003).

EMILIO GENTILE is Professor of History at the University La Sapienza in Rome and a distinguished expert in the history of Italian fascism, antifascism, nationalism, and the comparative history of political religions in the twentieth century. His numerous publications in English include *The Sacralization of Politics in Fascist Italy* (1996); *The Struggle for Modernity, Nationalism, Futurism and Fascism* (2003); *The Origins of Fascist Ideology* (2005); *Politics as Religion* (2006); *God's Democracy: American Civil Religion after September 11* (2008); and *La Grande Italia: The Myth of the Nation in the Twentieth Century* (2009).

MARTIN H. GEYER is Professor of Modern and Contemporary History at the University of Munich. His current research concerns notions of time and modernity in twentieth-century Germany. He is the author of *Verkehrte Welt: Revolution, Inflation und Moderne* (1998) and has co-edited *The Mechanics of Internationalism in the Nineteenth Century: Culture, Society, and Politics from the 1840s to the First World War* (2001) and *Two Cultures of Rights: Germany and the United States* (2002). His most recent edited book, *Die Bundesrepublik 1974 bis 1982: Der Sozialstaat im Zeichen wirtschaftlicher Rezession* (2008), is a thorough exploration of the crisis of the German welfare state in the 1970s and 1980s.

IGAL HALFIN is Associate Professor of History at Tel Aviv University and Head of the Cummings Center for the Study of Russia and the Former Soviet Union. He has held several

Fellowships at Columbia University where he also took his Ph.D. He is editor of *Language and Revolution: The Making of Modern Political Identity* (2002), and his most important publications are *From Darkness to Light: Class, Consciousness and Salvation in Revolutionary Russia* (2000); *Terror in my Soul: Communist Autobiographies on Trial* (2003); and *Intimate Enemies: Demonizing the Bolshevik Opposition, 1918–1928* (2007).

RALPH JESSEN is Professor of Modern History at the University of Cologne. He has worked on the history of police and policing in nineteenth- and twentieth-century Germany and the history of the German Democratic Republic. He is the author of *Polizei im Industrierevier: Modernisierung und Herrschaftspraxis im westfälischen Ruhrgebiet 1848–1914* (1991) and *Akademische Elite und kommunistische Diktatur: Die ostdeutsche Hochschullehrerschaft in der Ulbricht-Ära* (1999). With Richard Bessel he has edited *Die Grenzen der Diktatur: Staat und Gesellschaft in der DDR* (1996), and he has co-edited a number of other volumes, most recently *Zivilgesellschaft als Geschichte: Studien zum 19. und 20. Jahrhundert* (2004) and *Wissenschaft und Universitäten im geteilten Deutschland der 1960er Jahre* (2005).

GARETH STEDMAN JONES is Professor of Political Thought at Cambridge University. A Fellow of King's College, Cambridge, he is also a Director of the Centre for History and Economics. Professor Stedman Jones has written widely on nineteenth and twentieth-century European political thought. His publications include *Outcast London* (1971); *Languages of Class* (1983); an edition of Charles Fourier, *Theory of the Four Movements* (1995); a new edition of Karl Marx and Friedrich Engels, *The Communist Manifesto* (2002); and *An End to Poverty: A Historical Debate* (2005).

HEIDRUN KÄMPER is a Fellow of the Institut für deutsche Sprache, Mannheim, and Associate Professor in Linguistics and History of the German Language at the University of Mannheim. She has worked extensively on lexicography and political language in Nazi Germany and post-war Germany, and is co-editor and co-author of the *Deutsches Wörterbuch* (founded by Hermann Paul) and the *Deutsches Fremdwörterbuch*. She is the author of *Lieder von 1848: Politische Sprache einer literarischen Gattung* (1989), and has co-edited *Das 20. Jahrhundert: Sprachgeschichte—Zeitgeschichte* (1998) and

Sprache—Kognition—Kultur (2008). Her most important recent publications are *Der Schulddiskurs in der frühen Nachkriegszeit* (2005) and *Opfer—Täter—Nichttäter: Ein Wörterbuch zum Schulddiskurs 1945–1955* (2007).

ANGELIKA LINKE is Professor of German Linguistics at the University of Zurich and permanent Guest Professor in the Department of Language and Culture at the University of Linköping (Sweden). She has been visiting professor at several continental European universities and at Washington University in St Louis, and spent the academic year 2009/10 as a Fellow at the Wissenschaftskolleg zu Berlin. She is the author of *Sprachkultur und Bürgertum: Zur Mentalitätsgeschichte des 19. Jahrhunderts* (1996) and has co-edited several volumes on the history of language use, historical discourse analysis, and cultural semiotics of the body in the modern period, most recently *Attraktion und Abwehr: Die Amerikanisierung der Alltagskultur in Europa* (2006); *Der Zürcher Sommer 1968: Zwischen Krawall, Utopie und Bürgersinn* (2008); and *Oberfläche und Performanz: Untersuchungen zur Sprache als dynamischer Gestalt* (2009).

THOMAS MERGEL is Professor of Twentieth-Century European History at the Humboldt University Berlin. He has been professor at the University of Basle and has held visiting professorships at the University of Chicago and Charles University Prague. He is the author of *Parlamentarische Kultur in der Weimarer Republik* (2002); *Grossbritannien 1945–2000* (2005); and *Propaganda nach Hitler: Eine Kulturgeschichte des Wahlkampfs in der Bundesrepublik 1949–1990* (2010). He has also co-edited several volumes of essays, most recently *European Political History, 1870–1913* (2007). He is currently preparing a book on the comparative history of election campaigns.

SIÂN NICHOLAS is Senior Lecturer in Modern British History and Co-Director of the Centre for Media History at Aberystwyth University, and a Fellow of the Royal Historical Society. Her research interests are in the history of mass media, the British experience of the Second World War, and the Americanization of British culture. She is the author of *The Echo of War: Home Front Propaganda and the Wartime BBC* (1996), and has published widely on aspects of broadcasting and British national identity in the first half of the twentieth century. Her most recent publication is (co-ed. with Tom O'Malley and Kevin Williams) *Reconstructing the Past: History in the Mass Media, 1890–2005* (2008).

ISABEL RICHTER is Visiting Professor at the University of Bochum. Her Berlin Ph.D. on the National Socialist People's Court was published as *Hochverratsprozesse als Herrschaftspraxis im Nationalsozialismus: Männer und Frauen vor dem Volksgerichtshof 1934–1939* (2001). Her research interests are in gender history, body history, and historical anthropology in the modern period. She has just completed a book on fantasies of death in the modern age which will be published in spring 2011.

WILLIBALD STEINMETZ is Professor of Modern and Contemporary Political History at the University of Bielefeld and head of the collaborative research centre The Political as Communicative Space in History at Bielefeld. He was a Fellow of the German Historical Institute London and of the Freiburg Institute for Advanced Studies. He is the author of *Das Sagbare und das Machbare* (1993) and *Begegnungen vor Gericht: Eine Sozial- und Kulturgeschichte des englischen Arbeitsrechts* (2002), and editor of *Private Law and Social Inequality in the Industrial Age: Comparing Legal Cultures in Britain, France, Germany, and the United States* (2000) and *'Politik': Situationen eines Wortgebrauchs im Europa der Neuzeit* (2007).

OLAF STIEGLITZ is currently Visiting Professor at Erfurt University and has held fellowships and visiting professorships at Florida State University and the University of Münster. His research interests are in the history of masculinities and the social and cultural history of the twentieth-century USA. His Hamburg Ph.D. was published as *'100 percent American Boys': Disziplinierungsdiskurse und Ideologie im Civilian Conservation Corps, 1933–1942* (1999). He has co-edited and co-authored several volumes on the history of masculinities, most recently (with J. Martschukat) *Geschichte der Männlichkeiten* (2008), and a comparative volume on practices of denunciation. He is preparing a book on the cultural history of informing in the USA.

RUTH WODAK has been Distinguished Professor of Discourse Studies at Lancaster University since 2004. She remains affiliated to the University of Vienna, where she was Professor of Applied

Linguistics. With her colleagues in Vienna she elaborated the 'Discourse-Historical Approach in CDA', which is interdisciplinary and problem-oriented and analyses changes in discursive practices over time and in various genres. She is co-editor of the journals *Critical Discourse Studies, Discourse and Society,* and *Journal of Language and Politics,* and has co-authored, amongst other books, *The Discursive Construction of National Identities* (1999; 2nd rev. edn. 2009); *Discourse and Discrimination* (2001); *Critical Discourse Analysis: Theory and Interdisciplinarity* (2003; 2nd rev. edn. 2007); *The Politics of Exclusion: Debating Migration in Austria* (2008); *Qualitative Discourse Analysis in the Social Sciences* (2008); and *Migration, Identity, and Belonging* (2008). Her most recent monograph is *The Discourse of Politics in Action: Politics as Usual* (2009).

Index

Abendland 259–60, 263–4
Abkhazians 92–3
abortion 258
academic, scholar 7, 10, 20, 71, 157, 182, 295, 301–3, 314, 317, 319–21, 347–8, 357, 369
accusation 15, 18, 118–19, 143–4, 146, 152, 158–60, 181–2, 184–5, 189, 211, 260, 269, 283, 324, 356
Adenauer, Konrad 254, 265, 281, 284, 302–4, 314
administrator 117, 120, 133, 203, 283, 287, 304
Adorno, Theodor W. 23, 315–16, 319, 371
adventure tale 39, 87, 89, 93, 95
advertising 201, 293, 307–8, 320, 327, 363
aesthetics 61, 74, 89, 91, 97, 157, 337
Afinogenov, Aleksandr 137
Africa 262
Age of Extremes 3, 5–8, 13, 20, 25, 30–2, 37, 41, 44, 49–50, 66, 161, 239, 260
aggression, aggressiveness 169, 177–8, 185–6, 191, 258, 321–2, 355
Air Force 184
Allert, Tilman 65–6
Allies/Axis 172–4, 178, 185, 205–6, 354, 357
allusion 356, 359, 364, 366–70
Altai 129
Althusser, Louis 347–8
ambassador 174, 227
ambiguity 39, 41, 91, 182, 212, 268, 285, 368
America (USA) 21, 34, 38, 41–3, 142, 173, 195–213, 245–74, 281, 293, 299, 319–20, 348, 373
    way of life 24, 201, 249
Americanism 249–51, 255–6
anarchism, anarchist 115, 121–4, 145–6, 152, 269, 317, 322, 339
Anderson, Benedict 276
anthropology 36, 66, 331, 333

anti-Americanism 322, 374
anti-Bolshevism 116, 256
anti-colonialism 262
anti-Communism 11, 42, 245–74, 278
anti-fascism 15, 74–5, 156, 221, 223, 278–9, 284, 290, 312, 319
anti-intellectualism 266, 273, 302
anti-Semitism 7, 15, 21–2, 25, 36, 42–3, 72, 81, 121, 181, 255–6, 322, 351–3, 355–74, 377–8
anti-Zionism 373
archives 90, 106, 152, 222, 284, 287
Aristotle 324
Arnold, Matthew 345
artist 79, 83–5, 89–91, 93, 97, 102, 157
Aryan/non-Aryan 250, 311
Aryanization 362–4, 369, 373
Asia, Asian, Asiatic 43, 207, 247, 249, 263–4, 267–8, 273
Askey, Arthur 183
assailant/assassin 172
Atlantic Charter 200
atrocity propaganda 33, 175, 180–2
Augsburg 259
Augstein, Rudolf 256
Auschwitz 10, 23, 233, 357, 371
Austin, John L. 56, 58, 332
Austria, Austrians 11, 24, 36, 42, 266, 293, 303, 351–79
Austrian Freedom Party (FPÖ) 351, 354–5, 364, 368–9
Austrian People's Party (ÖVP) 354–5, 357–8, 378
authority 86, 96, 110, 121, 145, 170, 179, 185, 189, 199, 202, 248, 320, 333, 339
autobiography, memoir 8, 13, 20–5, 44–5, 106–7, 111–12, 114, 122–4, 129–32, 136–42, 145–9, 153, 159, 161–3, 166, 233, 263
Axis *see* Allies

bacteriology 28, 42–3, 251–3, 255–6
Bad Tölz 190
Baden-Württemberg 327

Baeck, Leo 22
Bagration,V. 87
Bakhtin, Mikhail 95
Baku 87–8
Balkans 357, 360–1
Baltic Sea 107
Barns, George 187
Barthes, Roland 347
Bastille 322, 341
Batumi 87–8, 94
Bavaria 24, 259, 268, 297, 299, 326
BBC 33–4, 38, 169–93
Beck, Ludwig 221, 229–31
Begriffsgeschichte see history of concepts
Belgium 373
Belsen 182
Benoist, Alain de 328
Bentham, Jeremy 340
Berdichev (Ukraine) 14
Bergsdorf, Wolfgang 300, 323
Beria, Lavrenty 83–4, 88, 90, 92–4, 97,
    100
Berlin 14, 152, 157, 160, 163–4, 185–6,
    223, 248, 253, 265, 269
Berlin Wall 43, 281, 284
Bible, biblical figures 22, 42, 77–9, 105,
    250, 256–8, 270–1, 303–4, 335,
    338–9, 361–2, 370
Biedenkopf, Kurt 295, 297–306, 309,
    323–5, 330
Bitburg 329
Black Sea 107
Blake, William 334
Blitz 182, 187
blood 78, 128, 347
Blum, Léon 33
Bochum 295
body 99, 113, 124, 185, 205–9, 249,
    264–8, 336
    collective 43, 47, 201–2, 204, 210,
        251, 340
    language 19, 31, 85–6, 101–2, 113,
        145, 186, 191, 208
Böll, Heinrich 321
Bolshevism, Bolsheviks 18, 38, 44–5,
    49, 77–8, 84, 93, 105–9, 111–25,
    127, 131–2, 134–6, 142–50, 246, 253,
    256, 260–1, 264, 312, 327
bombing 182, 185, 219
Bonn 239, 255, 281, 300, 328
border 33, 51, 158, 354

Bottai, Giuseppe 72, 79–80
Bourdieu, Pierre 323
bourgeoisie, bourgeois 20, 72, 106, 110,
    114, 117, 123, 131, 138, 152, 221,
    240, 317, 343
boycott 216
Brandt, Willy 30, 248, 297–8, 300, 325
Brentano, Heinrich von 259
Breslau 216
Brezhnev, Leonid 270
Britain 8–10, 32–6, 169–93, 281, 331–49
British empire 173
Brodsky, Isaac 84
brotherhood 81–2, 106, 125, 150, 222,
    275–7, 286
brutality 43, 177–8, 191, 255
Buback, Siegfried 322
Buchenwald 156, 284
Bukharin, Nicolai 17
Bulgaria 373
Bull, John 342
Bunzl, John 374
bureaucracy, bureaucrat 18, 20, 69,
    110–12, 115, 121, 124–5, 128, 139,
    315
Bush, George W. 41
Butler, Judith 56, 58, 60

California 208, 348
Cambridge 8
camouflage 48–9, 209–10, 222, 224–6,
    230–1, 233–4, 239–40, 245, 263
capital 109, 145, 298, 362
capitalism, capitalist 29, 112, 116, 123,
    150, 238, 261, 278–9
Carlyle, Thomas 35, 334–45
Carrol, Lewis 183
cartoon 38–9, 190, 211
Cassirer, Ernst 54–5
Castro, Fidel 262
catchword, catchphrase 48, 124, 184,
    206, 279, 324, 326–7
catechism 79–80, 92
Catholic Church, Catholics 73, 78–80,
    259, 270–1, 297, 299, 320–1, 352
Caucasus 89, 93
Cavalcanti, Alberto 191
Celan, Paul 23
censorship 5, 15–16, 172–4, 177, 180,
    183–4, 187–9, 192, 310, 312
Certeau, Michel de 318

Chaplin, Charlie 183
character 16, 58, 71, 86, 117, 121–2,
  137, 160, 197, 229, 235, 249, 262–3,
  283
charisma 40–1, 73, 84
Charter 77 28
Chartists 341
chauvinism, chauvinist 116
Cheka 132, 146
Chekhov, Anton 174
Chiang Kai-shek 172
Chiaureli, Mikhail 100–2
children 14, 20–3, 25, 33, 40, 72, 85, 90,
  93, 99, 107, 145, 159, 163, 178, 182,
  190, 253, 262, 344
China, Chinese 207–8, 263, 267, 272
Chomsky, Noam 331
Christian Democrats 35
  Germany (CDU/CSU) 254–5,
    263–4, 268, 295–309, 314, 324–30
Christianity, Christians 41–2, 75–6,
  81–2, 259–60, 271, 311, 336, 361,
  370
Christianstadt (camp) 23
church 298
Churchill, Winston 172–3, 176, 181,
  185, 189, 192
citizen 3–5, 15, 19, 26, 28, 40, 66, 75,
  106, 196, 201–2, 209, 212, 238, 265,
  268, 275, 277–8, 280, 284–6,
  289–90, 369, 377
  figure of 38, 105, 150, 162, 166, 197,
    204, 210–11, 212–13
citizens' education 34, 204–5, 253
citizens' movements 28–9, 265
citizenship 249, 252, 276, 369
civil rights 7, 251, 253, 273
civil society 28–9
civil war 20, 281
  Russian 109, 114, 116, 123, 146
  Spanish 206
civilian 24, 47, 182
civilian defence 209
civilization 29, 79, 178–9, 264, 272, 338,
  340, 345
Clark, Kenneth 177, 180
class 9, 31, 35–6, 44–5, 75, 108, 112–13,
  118, 120–2, 129–30, 138–9, 143–5,
  148–50, 157, 169, 171, 187–8, 192,
  276, 278, 302, 320, 332–4, 339,
  341–3, 359

language of 124, 127–8, 132–6, 266,
  286, 320, 347
class interest 142, 286, 298, 325
class struggle, class war 10, 116, 118,
  256, 258, 286, 302, 339, 343–4
classicism 141
classless society 259
cleansing 109, 138
  see also purity
clemency plea 151, 153, 161–6, 253
code name 48, 228–30
code switching 289
code word 225–6, 239
coded language 7, 208, 303, 351, 356–7,
  359–60, 365, 371
Cold War 29, 34–5, 41–3, 213, 238, 257,
  263, 272, 281, 348
collaboration, collaborator 15, 172,
  186–7, 209, 280–1
Cologne 154, 158, 300
comedy 38, 170, 183–5, 190–2
comics 190, 205
communicative practices 3, 16–19,
  21–2, 25, 30, 48–50, 58–62, 153,
  202, 204, 210–11, 217, 224, 239,
  287–8, 318
  definition of 56
  face-to-face 4, 49
  non-verbal 17, 19, 31, 56, 64, 333,
    352
  ostentatious/elusive 66
  ritualized 19, 27–9, 44–6, 64–5, 97,
    99–100, 196, 250, 264, 283, 288–91
  violence in 155, 161, 166–7, 321–2
Communism, Communists 7, 10–11,
  42–3, 45–6, 48, 76, 123, 150, 213,
  239, 245, 248–9, 252–4, 256–9,
  262–5, 267, 269–73, 278–80, 294,
  326, 332, 343, 347, 354, 373
Comintern 278
  France (PCF) 152, 245
  Germany (KPD) 152, 158–60, 162,
    235–7, 251–2
  Germany (KPDO) 152
  Soviet Union 83, 99, 107–8, 111,
    116–21, 123–4, 131, 143–4, 260–2
  USA (CPUSA) 246–7, 250–1, 265–6
  Vietnam 271–2
community 6, 9, 33, 37, 42–4, 65–6, 99,
  162–3, 249, 276–7, 280–1, 286, 302,
  326, 353, 364, 371–3, 376, 378–9

comparison, analogy 7–8, 16, 22, 24–5,
    29–31, 39, 42–3, 46, 51, 71, 76, 78,
    81–2, 109, 126, 132, 136, 155–6, 213,
    235–6, 245–8, 250, 254, 256,
    259–60, 262–3, 267, 270–1, 273,
    288, 305, 307–8, 311–12, 321–2,
    326, 338, 345, 352, 356, 371
  with National Socialism 16, 237–8,
    254–5, 267–8, 322, 371–2
competition 286, 308
  between German states 278–80, 284
  between world powers 263
  ideological 36–7, 249–50, 272
complacency 181, 333
concentration camp 16, 21–4, 26, 154,
    156, 158, 167, 182, 215, 218, 233,
    284
Concordat (Italy) 80
Condillac, Étienne Bonnot de 335–6
confession 106, 113, 123, 145, 158–9
Congress for Cultural Freedom 247–8
Connor, William 186–7, 189, 192
connotation 61, 133, 206, 285–6
Conrad, Lawrence H. 195
consciousness 9, 76, 107–8, 114–16, 122,
    129–32, 136, 138, 140, 143–5, 148,
    150
consensus 73, 246, 373
conservatism, conservatives 36, 132,
    192, 216, 221, 228, 230, 240, 268,
    293, 295–7, 300–1, 303–8, 312, 314,
    316–22, 324–8, 348
conspiracy 15, 94, 152, 160, 206, 222–4,
    227, 234, 240, 262–3, 272–3, 283,
    327–8, 357–8, 362–3, 368
constitution 7, 98, 157, 160, 306,
    339–40, 353–4
  American 250
  German of 1949 303
  Soviet of 1918 150
consumption 201, 307–8
containment 42
content analysis 34
contested concepts/terms 5, 8–9, 13,
    25–6, 28–31, 51, 124, 127–8, 133,
    135–6, 147, 170, 172–7, 181–2, 185,
    198, 238, 252, 261, 263, 268–70,
    278, 280–1, 285–6, 293–321,
    323–30, 371
conversation 17–18, 46, 144, 171, 184,
    208, 217, 222–6, 228, 239, 289, 352

  analysis of 57, 361
conversion 85, 123, 136–9, 141–2, 144,
    150, 163, 236–7
Cooper, Duff 174, 186, 188
corruption 114, 136–7, 178, 185, 271,
    283, 339
Cossacks 115
counter-discourse 21, 23, 25, 28–9, 48,
    215, 241
counter-revolution 118, 271
courtesy 172
Coward, Noel 189–90
crime 117–18, 142, 178–9, 181, 185, 240,
    250, 254, 273, 282–4, 291, 321–2,
    343, 345, 354–5, 358, 362–3, 368,
    370
crisis 5, 11–13, 117, 137, 197, 202, 325,
    332, 336, 338, 342–3, 352
Critical Discourse Analysis 36, 359
criticism 11, 15, 23–4, 27, 91, 148, 175,
    187–9, 191, 201, 227–8, 293–4, 296,
    299, 301–2, 307, 310–16, 318–20,
    331, 334, 357, 364, 369–70, 373–4,
    377–8
Crosland, Anthony 332
Crossman, Richard 179
crusade 77
cultural change 65, 293
cultural criticism 332–4, 345
cultural studies 8, 54–5
culture 9, 18, 58–9, 80, 133, 170, 178,
    203, 208, 294, 296, 299, 303,
    314–15, 328, 332, 334, 338, 340–1,
    344–5, 347, 349
  high/popular 38–9, 95, 97, 102, 174,
    179–80, 183, 189–92, 200–1, 205–6,
    213, 317, 346
culture wars 41
cybernetics 304
Czechoslovakia 26–9, 45, 181, 254, 260,
    267, 269–73

Dachau 215
Daladier, Édouard 33
D'Annunzio, Gabriele 71, 76
Dante Alighieri 71, 339
Davis, Elmer 199–200
Davis, Natalie Zemon 161–2
Dean, Mitchell 203
death penalty/sentence 48, 162, 167,
    221, 253–4, 284

Decembrists 140
decency 188
defamation 358, 371
defeat 40, 81, 176, 191, 230, 310, 312, 329, 346
defeatism 182
degeneration 128, 132, 144, 150, 179, 315
demagogy 71–3, 176, 344
democracy, democrats 7, 9, 29, 34, 42–3, 196–7, 199–200, 224, 245, 247, 251–3, 255, 269, 283, 298–9, 301, 303, 306, 326, 340, 342, 353–5, 376–8
Democratic Party (USA) 200–1, 251
democratization 11, 310
denunciation 16–18, 26, 48, 115, 117, 122, 153, 210–12, 318, 370, 377–9
destiny 122, 279–80
see also fate
détente 249, 272, 298, 328
Dettling, Wolfgang 300
Devlin, Judith 38–9
devotion 78–9, 88, 96
dialect 289, 301
dialectics 5, 27, 142, 238, 324
diary 13, 48–9, 76, 215–41
Dickens, Charles 334
dictatorship 5, 7, 39–40, 196–7, 216, 220–1, 233, 245, 253, 255, 271, 279, 286, 290–1
   of the proletariat 117, 149, 259, 265, 275
dictionary 9–10, 12–13, 71, 79, 81, 311, 313, 315–16, 327
difference 6, 25, 276, 291
dignity 7, 27, 86–7, 236
Dinwiddie, Melvin 184
diplomacy 174, 357–8
discipline 77–8, 120, 124, 144, 197, 264
discourse 6, 96, 121, 135–6, 204, 296, 331, 333, 340, 347, 352, 355–6, 358, 360, 362–5, 367–71, 373–4
discourse analysis 34, 37, 351–2, 359–60, 365–6
   see also Critical Discourse Analysis
discrimination 131, 150, 233, 262, 355, 373
Disney, Walt 207
displaced persons 10
Disraeli, Benjamin 334, 339, 346

dissident 5, 28, 45, 48, 217, 220–2, 224, 226–9, 232, 237–8, 240
   see also opposition
dissimulation, concealment 26, 48–9, 72, 74, 94, 124, 209–10, 217, 224–6, 239–40, 263, 266, 303–4, 353–4
distrust 18, 27, 29, 187
dog 117, 131, 185, 211
'doing being' 57–9
Donald Duck 207
Dostoyevsky, Fyodor 140
doubt 16, 81, 109, 139, 164, 236–8, 355, 372
drama 174, 176, 180–1, 183
dream 17, 181, 191, 230
Dresden 233, 237
drink 17, 131
Dubček, Alexander 260, 269–71
Duce 70, 74, 79, 81
Duranti, Alessandro 66
Düsseldorf 154
Dutschke, Rudi 268
duty 78, 105, 143, 163, 210, 294, 316, 358
Dyrenforth, James 183

East, Eastern bloc 27–9, 238–9, 259, 261–4, 269–71, 273, 275, 354, 371
East Coast (USA) 364–5, 368–9, 375, 377
economic miracle 253, 267
economy 41, 114, 118, 120, 124, 131, 139, 148, 156, 158, 160, 208, 235, 238, 283, 299, 302, 307–8, 325, 327, 362
   see also New Economic Policy
education 10, 21–2, 72–3, 80, 85, 90, 112, 114–15, 121–2, 126, 129–32, 138–42, 144–7, 162, 177–9, 205, 261, 266, 299, 345
efficiency 178
ego-document 13, 161
   see also autobiography, diary, letters
Ehlich, Konrad 62–3, 313–14
Ehrenburg, Ilya 15
Eisler, Gerhart 251, 266
Eisler, Hanns 266
election, election campaign 36, 238, 254, 263–4, 268, 285, 297, 301, 324, 326–7, 351, 354, 356–8, 363–71, 374–5, 378

Eliot, George (Mary Anne Evans) 334
emancipation 25, 41, 105, 320
emergency 117, 308
emigration 362, 369
emotion 16, 19, 22, 39, 57, 60–1, 64, 94,
    96, 156–7, 166, 170, 172, 182–3, 191,
    253, 266, 269–71, 285–6, 319, 322,
    334, 336, 341, 344–5, 370, 379
empiricism 331
employee 114, 121, 127, 130, 133, 135,
    145, 298
Endlösung 311
enemy 78, 173, 186, 196–7, 201, 281,
    284–5, 287, 291, 320, 370, 379
  depiction of 6, 37–9, 42–3, 88,
    169–70, 174–9, 182, 185, 190–3,
    200, 204, 207–9, 212–13, 251,
    255–6, 259–60, 263–7, 277, 282,
    357, 361, 371
  internal 101, 118, 206, 209–11, 251,
    264, 273, 282–3
  of the proletariat 137
  perception of 107, 245–7, 249, 255,
    271–3
  tricks of 34, 118, 206, 362
Engelmann, Bert 327
Engels, Friedrich 115, 143, 342–4
engineer 138–9, 144, 266
England 144, 323, 332–4, 336, 339–49
  see also Britain
Enlightenment 11–12, 315, 336
enthusiasm 22, 90, 96–7, 105, 117, 124,
    149, 189, 205, 207, 319, 338
environmentalism 29, 317
Enzensberger, Hans Magnus 313
equality 72, 105, 120, 145, 250, 291, 302,
    309, 326
Eschebach, Insa 154, 156
Essen 158–9, 320
Ethiopia 80
ethnology 59, 107
euphemism 24, 27, 302, 316, 369
Europe 10, 24, 41, 46, 141, 161, 178,
    180–1, 198, 213, 218, 245, 249, 257,
    264, 269, 299, 320, 345, 351, 358,
    364, 366, 372–4
European Union (EU) 302, 354–5, 371,
    373, 376
Evangelicals 258
exclusion *see* inclusion
existentialism 315

experience 51, 69, 76, 112, 175, 227, 277,
    299, 302, 332–3, 338, 345–6, 348
  collective 33, 356
  with Communism 245, 247–8
  of defeat 81, 346
  formation of 35
  human 102, 215, 336
  of National Socialism 254–5, 290
  personal 3, 8–14, 19, 22, 24–5, 30–1,
    130, 136, 138, 154–5, 162, 166–7,
    216, 218
  revolutionary 142
  of war 12, 76, 131, 191, 201, 219,
    271–2, 315
expert 128, 130, 139, 144, 159, 209–10,
    363, 373
  see also specialist
exploitation 94, 111, 118, 138, 179
Extraparliamentary Opposition (APO)
    35, 268–9

façade 106, 110
factory 126, 129, 132, 144, 147–8, 207,
    321
facts 84, 89, 100, 155, 179, 182, 199,
    227, 308, 331, 339, 355, 366
fairness 187
faith 73, 75–8, 80–1, 86, 91, 99–101,
    141, 257–8, 271, 335–6, 338
Falkenhausen, Alexander von 230
Falkenstein 234
family 10, 14–16, 20–2, 40, 47, 78,
    112–15, 119, 128–30, 132, 138, 145,
    150, 157, 163, 178–9, 192, 219, 257,
    262, 265–6, 326, 345, 379
family narrative 39–41, 44, 99, 102,
    275–7, 279
famine 118
fanaticism, fanatic 160, 163, 178, 182,
    235, 272
fascism, fascists 7, 21, 26, 30, 41, 61–2,
    71, 74–7, 81, 253, 278, 316, 318–20,
    322, 324, 346–7
  language of 39–41, 46, 63, 69–82
fate 14, 17–18, 24, 88, 254, 257, 302,
    316, 358, 362
fatherland/motherland 15, 78–9, 101,
    174, 262, 282, 370
fear 18–19, 26, 78–9, 81, 83, 105, 178,
    209, 233–4, 247, 250–3, 255–6,
    269–70, 273–4, 339–41, 345, 362

Federal Bureau of Investigation (FBI) 206, 209–11, 251
feminism 21, 317, 328, 348
Feuerbach, Ludwig 343
fiction 13, 16, 155, 166, 205, 275, 286, 339
fidelity 99
fifth column 187, 206, 208–9, 213
film 16, 22, 39, 70, 90–1, 96–7, 100–2, 179–80, 191–2, 199–200, 207, 251
Fischer, Ruth 266
Florence 78
folklore 39, 93–7, 99
forgiveness 112, 120–1
formality/informality 64, 72, 360
Formby, George 191
Forster, Edward Morgan 178
Foucault, Michel 36–7, 196–7, 202–4, 212, 348
France 33–4, 40, 161–2, 172, 176, 245, 269, 328, 335–6, 338, 341, 345, 348, 354, 373
Franco, Francisco 46
Frank, Anne 227
Frankfurt School 317, 322
Freeden, Michael 36
freedom 105, 163, 177, 180, 201, 226, 236, 247–8, 256, 270, 279, 294–5, 326–7, 342
    aversion to 72–3
    meaning of 252, 306
    of opinion 364, 370, 377
    and power 28
    of the press 17–18, 271
    of speculation 338
    of speech 7, 17–18, 22, 37, 148, 377
    suppression of 148, 217
Freud, Sigmund 360
friendship 17–18, 101, 139, 145, 156, 219, 275–7, 281, 286
Führer 47, 162, 207
functionaries 3, 111–12, 128, 264–7, 271, 273
Furet, François 260
future
    references to 62–4, 76, 87, 89, 117, 162, 166, 232–3, 330
    visions of 11, 27, 44, 138–9, 270, 277–9, 290–1, 305–6

Gaitskell, Hugh 332

gangster 170, 178–80, 182
gardening 42–3, 97–8
Gardner, Charles 185
Garfinkel, Harold 56, 58
gas chambers 16, 20, 22, 313
Gaulle, Charles de 40, 172, 269
Geertz, Clifford 59
gender relations 20–2, 31, 39–40, 58–9, 64, 113, 157, 163, 211, 344–5, 347–8, 359
generation 8–10, 36, 60, 65, 76, 80, 138, 169, 178–9, 182, 217, 232, 261, 269–70, 273, 290, 317, 319, 321–2, 334–5, 341, 345–6, 358
genocide 20
    see also Holocaust
Gentile, Emilio 39–40, 62
Gentile, Giovanni 77
Georgia (Soviet Republic) 83–5, 91, 98, 101
Gerasimov, Mikhail 84
German Democratic Republic (GDR) 27, 43–5, 48–9, 154, 156, 232, 237–9, 247, 253–5, 257, 261–3, 265, 269, 271, 273, 275–91, 293, 312, 326
Germany, Germans 10, 12, 17, 22, 24, 32–4, 38, 44, 140, 142–3, 208, 215–41, 258, 266, 276, 280, 290, 293, 310, 312, 316, 336, 343, 353, 355, 373
    Federal Republic 35, 42–4, 161, 239, 245–74, 279–80, 284, 293–330
    National Socialist Germany 38, 46–8, 65, 151–67, 169–93, 196, 206–7, 215–35, 239, 290, 354–5, 358, 362
    Soviet occupation zone 48–9, 220, 232, 235–7, 290, 310, 312
    see also Weimar Republic
Gerstenmaier, Eugen 229
Gestapo 16, 48–9, 151, 153, 155–6, 158, 160, 164–7, 180–1
gesture 19, 65–6, 100, 113, 289, 291
Geyer, Martin 35
ghetto 14, 20, 22
Gide, André 90
Gladstone, William Ewart 346
Glasgow 343
Globke, Hans 284
Glucksmann, André 348

God, god 42, 78–9, 216, 250, 256–8, 267, 337–8
Goebbels, Josef 33, 47, 183, 186, 221, 313, 327
Goerdeler, Karl Friedrich 221, 229–31
Goering, Hermann 184, 186, 190
Goethe, Johann Wolfgang 22, 334, 338, 344
Goffman, Erving 56, 58, 64
Gorbachev, Mikhail 30, 106
Gorky (city) 101
Gorky, Maxim 19, 109
Göttingen 24, 322
governance 202
government 5, 33–4, 82, 112, 169, 171, 173, 176, 190, 192, 195, 197–9, 201, 203–5, 212–13, 222, 227, 247, 255, 266, 284, 297–8, 300, 348, 354–5, 363–4, 370–1, 373, 377–8
governmentality 37, 197, 202–3, 212–13
GPU 118, 148
Graf, Willi 220–7, 231, 234, 239–40
Gramsci, Antonio 25, 75–6, 295, 328
grass roots 112, 119, 136
Gravers, Cecil Georg 185
Greece 357–8
Greenberg, Stanley Bernard 364, 369, 377
Greene, Graham 180
greetings 64–6, 96, 145
Gross, Felix 179
Grossman, Vasily 14–20, 31
guilt 17, 25, 155, 313, 329, 355–6, 371–3
Gulag 16, 26
Gurgenidze, Osman 94
Gutman, L. 89, 100
Guttenberg, Karl Ludwig Freiherr zu 229
Gzelishvili, Konstantin 85

Habermas, Jürgen 298, 322, 324
habit 11, 21, 23–4, 45, 59, 65, 110–11, 140, 229, 232, 265, 340
Haecker, Theodor 216
Haider, Jörg 351, 364–5, 367–71, 374–9
Haley, William 185
Halfin, Igal 38, 44–5, 49
Hamann, Johann Georg 336–7, 340
Hamburg 176, 185, 219
Handley, Tommy 183–4
happiness 72, 144, 250, 279

harmony 44, 285–6, 290–1, 372
Harvard 266
harvest 116, 118, 235
Hassel, Ulrich von 220–4, 227–32, 234, 240
hatred 78, 178, 182, 207, 219, 370, 379
Haug, Wolfgang Fritz 319
Häupl, Michael 364, 368–9, 375
Havel, Václav 26–31, 44–5
Hay, Will 191
Hegel, Georg Wilhelm Friedrich 323, 344
hegemony 26, 328
Heidegger, Martin 315
Heidelberg 11
Herder, Johann Gottfried 96, 334–5, 338, 340
Heringer, Jürgen 310
heroism 15, 78, 81, 87–90, 92, 94, 97–8, 101, 205
Herzberg, Max J. 195, 197, 204
hierarchy 64, 70, 77, 86, 95, 124
high treason 48, 151–3, 157, 160–1, 164
Himmler, Heinrich 183
Hiroshima 208
historical semantics 6, 8–9, 12–13, 31, 50, 54, 154
historicism 338
historiography 54, 88–90, 92–3, 96, 100, 106, 108, 139, 196, 276, 278, 297, 325, 328–30, 331–4, 339–40, 347–9, 361
history 131, 174, 232, 357
    appeals to 78, 254–5, 259, 262, 268, 365
    illustrations of 84, 92, 95
    laws of 287
    and legend 39, 88–9, 93, 98, 100–2
    visions of 11–12, 35–6, 44, 80–1, 123, 277–81, 290–1, 295, 306–7, 325, 332, 338–45, 349, 372–3, 375
    writing of 60, 232–3, 339
history of concepts 10, 12–13, 35, 49–51, 54, 296–7, 315–16
history of ideas/intellectual history 6, 36, 332–3
Hitler, Adolf 10, 34, 38–9, 42, 46, 65, 152, 164, 172–3, 176, 179, 181, 183–6, 190–1, 207, 222, 224, 230–1, 254, 268, 319, 329, 355, 373
    see also Schicklgruber

Hitler salute ('Heil Hitler') 65–6, 158, 207
Hitler–Stalin pact 260
Hitler Youth 178–9
Hobbes, Thomas 333
Hobsbawm, Eric 3, 11
Ho-Chi-Minh 269
Hoggart, Herbert Richard 346
Hollywood 200
Holocaust/Shoah 13–15, 23–4, 43, 47, 181–2, 303, 315–16, 329, 339, 356, 362, 368–9, 371–3
Holy Roman Empire 259
home 33, 38, 171, 180–1, 192, 233
Honecker, Erich 44, 281, 290
honour 77, 99, 146, 187, 221, 316, 361–2
Hoover, Edgar J. 209–10, 212, 251, 256, 258, 266
hope 23, 30, 111, 124, 139, 154, 159, 166, 182, 189, 209, 217, 230, 271, 305, 346
Horkheimer, Max 322
horror 181–2, 191, 215
House Un-American Activities Committee (HUAC) 249–51
housework 114, 163
Huber, Kurt 223
human rights 251, 328
humanism 343
humanity, mankind 27, 73, 76, 79, 81, 88, 140, 251, 279, 337–8
Humboldt, Wilhelm von 53–4
humiliation 117, 178
humour 38, 177, 183–4, 190–2, 207–8, 275, 360, 367–8
Hun 175–8, 181, 191
Hungary, Hungarians 255, 259, 262, 264–5, 273, 373
Huntington, Samuel 249
Hus, Jan 270
hygiene 42–3, 47, 251, 253, 255–6

iconography 87, 89–91
idealism, idealists 108, 146, 257
identity 57–60, 64, 66, 134, 150
  Bolshevik 105, 143, 149
  collective 44, 276–8, 280, 282, 290–1, 326, 359, 372
  creation of 58–9, 106, 127, 280
  determination of 136

fascist 74–6, 81–2
of intelligentsia 112–13, 137, 142–3, 145, 149
national 177, 355
personal 24
proletarian 143
revolutionary 137
ideologue 38, 110, 121, 335
ideology 10–11, 21–2, 25–6, 30, 37, 43–4, 46–7, 51, 70, 74–6, 79, 81, 94–6, 125, 131, 137, 139–40, 142, 144, 169–70, 173, 247, 249, 253–5, 262–4, 272, 275, 287–8, 290, 305, 311, 313–14, 316, 359, 364, 367
  definition of 36, 339
  theory of 333
ignorance 174
image 31, 38–43, 83–5, 90–1, 169–70, 174, 177–8, 182, 185, 204, 206–7, 212, 218, 246–7, 264, 266, 269–73, 275, 307–8, 317, 337
  relation to text 39, 84–5, 87–8, 91–4, 207–10, 245
  see also visual image
immigrant 206, 208, 211, 247, 257, 354, 369, 371, 373, 379
impartiality 171, 184
imperialism 173, 278–9, 281
improvisation 178
inclusion/exclusion 6, 21, 37, 42–4, 107–10, 114, 118–21, 124, 130, 132, 134, 143, 146–7, 150, 162–4, 166, 196, 213, 275–7, 279–83, 285–91, 309–10, 318, 348, 355, 362, 369, 371–2
individualism 78, 124, 130, 143, 145, 249–50, 288, 315, 326–7, 333
individuality 102, 165–7, 178, 219, 240, 287
industry 9, 129, 345–6
infection 43, 251, 255–6, 270
infiltration 247, 250–1, 272, 284, 293
informality see formality
information 18, 33, 158, 171, 177, 185, 192, 197–200, 202, 211, 295, 304–5, 361
inner emigration 233
innocence 278, 311
  see also guilt
instinct 117, 119, 121, 173, 339, 341

intellectuals 3, 6, 8, 14, 26, 31, 77–9,
  157, 205, 248, 265, 272–3, 290,
  295–6, 298, 301–2, 304–8, 313–15,
  317, 319, 328–9, 356
intelligentsia 38, 45, 86, 107–14, 116–17,
  119, 121–2, 124–45, 147–9, 286
  old/new 110, 115, 131–2, 137–40,
  142–4, 147–9
  petty 109
interaction 6, 13, 49, 56, 60, 63–4, 136,
  358
Internationale (anthem) 250
interrogation 16, 18, 45, 48–9, 111–20,
  123–4, 129–30, 132, 151, 153–61,
  165–7
intertextuality 366
intolerance 78, 177
invasion 173–4, 206, 212, 254–5, 259,
  262, 264, 269–71
invective 186, 358, 371, 376–7
Iraq 352
Iron Curtain 252, 261, 354
irrationality 72, 81, 374
Islam 259
  see also Muslims
isolationism 198
Israel 371–4
Italy, Italians 39, 41, 46, 69–82, 186,
  206, 208, 211, 328

Japan, Japanese 38, 43, 200–1, 206–8,
  211
jargon 95, 156, 293, 315, 317–19
Jenning, Humphrey 181
Jessen, Jens 221, 229–30
Jessen, Ralph 43–5
Jews 11, 14–15, 21–2, 24, 42, 47, 112,
  121, 181, 216, 228, 233, 240, 255–7,
  268, 311, 315–16, 353–79
Johnson, Mark 54
Jones, Gareth Stedman 35–6
journalist 14, 28, 199, 253, 258, 265, 301
Joyce, James 189
Joyce, William ('Lord Haw-Haw') 176,
  190
judge 38, 151–3, 156–7, 160, 165
Jünger, Ernst 217, 321
justice 105, 188, 279, 291, 298, 326, 353

Kaganovich, Lazar M. 97
Kaiser, Jakob 221

Kalinin, Mikhail Ivanovich 110, 124
Kaltenbrunner, Klaus-Gerd 304
Kämper, Heidrun 48–9
Kant, Immanuel 336, 340
Kazakhstan 10
Kazan 15, 17–18
Kennedy, Arthur G. 197, 212
Kerensky, Alexander Fyodorovich 113,
  123
Kerzhentsev, Platon Mikhailovich 100
Kester, Max 183
KGB 15
Khrushchev, Nikita Sergeyevich 16,
  254, 260, 265, 270, 273
Kiev 141
Kingsley, Charles 334
Kislau (camp) 158
Klemperer, Eva 233–4
Klemperer, Victor 48–9, 220, 232–40,
  311–13
Klüger, Ruth 20–5, 30–1
knowledge 28, 59–60, 71, 86, 130, 139,
  144, 202, 331, 335, 359, 365–6
Kohl, Helmut 295, 298, 300, 325, 329
Komsomol 90, 134
Königsberg 336
Koselleck, Reinhart 10–13, 19, 31, 35,
  50, 54, 277, 316
Kotthoff, Helga 58–9
Kovács, András 372
Kowno 216
Kraus, Karl 293
Kreisau Circle 228
Kreisky, Bruno 369
Kriukova, Maria 98
Kronstadt (Russia) 117, 121–2
Krotkov, V. A. 86, 94
Krupskaya, Nadezhda 99
kulak 43
kul'turnost' 90
Kuridze, P. G. 94
Kutateladze, Apollon K. 87

labour
  forced 355
  humanization of 298
  inner 105
  physical/mental 114, 129, 143, 145,
  147, 150
  see also work
labour exchange 158

labour movement 247, 251, 345, 348
Labour Party 10, 332
Lacan, Jacques 347
Lakoba, Nestor 92–3, 100
Lakoff, George 54
landowner 87, 143
Langbehn, Carl 221, 230
language 4, 38, 50, 53–5, 102, 271, 282,
    285, 293, 337, 340, 347
  academic study of 3, 6–13, 19, 30–2,
    34–8, 46, 49–51, 53–6, 61–2, 72,
    151, 153–4, 161, 167, 195–7, 202–4,
    212–13, 235, 237–9, 282, 296–7,
    299–303, 305, 310–20, 323–4, 331,
    335, 351–2, 359–61, 363, 365–6
  administrative 163–4, 287, 315–16
  and anti-Semitism 6, 15, 22, 255–6,
    322, 351–79
  of class war 118, 133, 286, 320
  control of 5, 17–20, 46–9, 83, 95,
    136, 153, 155, 161, 165–7, 170–7,
    180–1, 183–5, 187–92, 196, 215, 217,
    275–6, 280–3, 288–9, 291, 294–5,
    329, 362, 370, 377
  conventional 24, 26–7, 46, 59, 64–5,
    96–7, 173, 271–2, 294, 317, 335
  of everyday life 13, 46, 64, 102, 196,
    233, 235, 238, 296, 301, 303,
    311–17, 352
  as game 331–3
  official/popular 43, 95–7, 102, 124,
    147, 184–5, 196, 201–2, 275–7,
    279–80, 289–91, 329
  philosophical views on 53, 335–7
  private 22, 24, 46–9, 166, 215, 225–6,
    239–40, 285, 289
  and power 3, 5, 15, 17, 20–1, 25–6,
    28–30, 46, 49, 53, 62–4, 71, 95, 107,
    151, 155, 165–7, 169–70, 196, 202–3,
    238–9, 275–6, 288–9, 294, 300,
    308, 320, 323–4, 359
  purification of 71–2, 81, 296, 311–12
  and reality 27, 35, 53–6, 74, 212,
    302–6, 313–14, 322–4, 331, 333,
    335, 347
  religious 22, 39–42, 56, 69–82, 87,
    91, 95–6, 99–100, 245, 248–9,
    258–62, 271–3
  revolutionary 106, 305, 320, 323
  semiotic concept of 4–5, 335, 349

shifting usages 8–9, 12, 106–7, 305–6,
    321
spoken/written 4, 9, 33, 46–7, 70,
    151, 153–4, 156, 165–7, 169, 177,
    183, 187, 215, 217, 287–9, 317, 359
standardized 93, 96–7, 107, 156,
    165–6, 275, 277, 287–8
strategic uses 3, 6, 23, 26, 28–9,
    37–8, 42, 44–5, 48, 135–8, 154–5,
    160–2, 164–6, 170, 175, 204, 213,
    224–5, 239–40, 252–3, 257, 259,
    275, 277, 280–7, 294, 297–302,
    304–10, 314–16, 320, 323, 326–8,
    352, 355–8, 360–1, 364–71
Lasswell, Harold 175
law, legislation 72, 77, 79, 105, 141, 164,
    203, 245, 257, 268, 283, 303, 306,
    340, 346, 363, 373
  of God 256
  and order 74, 320
  rule of 254
leader, leadership 39–40, 74, 77, 83–5,
    87, 89, 93, 96, 109, 145, 172, 175–6,
    178–9, 182–3, 185–6, 207, 221, 224,
    230, 258, 266–7, 281–3, 295, 325–6,
    345–6, 351
leaflet 17, 221–3, 322
Leavis, Frank Raymond 345
Lechfeld (battle) 259
left/right 5, 10, 29, 32, 75, 121, 123–4,
    152, 155, 158, 166, 268–9, 285,
    293–7, 299, 302, 305–7, 317,
    319–22, 324–5, 327–9, 347, 370, 373
legal proceedings 48–9, 151–4, 157–60,
    162, 166–7, 283–4, 320, 362–3
Leipzig 237
Lenin, Vladimir I. 88–9, 91, 93,
    97–101, 106, 109–10, 117, 140,
    143–4, 150, 257, 261, 283
Leningrad 90, 126, 129–31, 133–4, 137,
    144–6, 150, 174
Leninism 93, 95–6, 258, 286, 348
Le Pen, Jean-Marie 354
letters 13, 15, 19, 20, 47, 49, 76, 106,
    144, 146–7, 187–9, 259, 263
Leuschner, Wilhelm 221
Lévi-Strauss, Claude 347
liberalism, liberals 5, 7, 11, 20, 36, 140,
    212–13, 247–8, 291, 297, 305, 326,
    348
liberalization 16, 114, 298

liberation 329
liberty 236, 298, 303, 326–7
  see also freedom
Lidice (Czechoslovakia) 181
lies 114, 124, 216, 235, 259, 262–3
life 101, 136, 142, 270
  concept of 72–3, 79–81
  perspective on 107
  quality of 298–9
lifestyle 110, 144, 262
life-world 65
light, enlightenment 85–8, 99, 108, 133,
  142, 148, 248, 260, 345
linguistic turn 12, 36, 53–5, 297, 323,
  332, 334
linguistics 12, 34, 36, 50, 55–60, 66,
  282, 296–7, 300–1, 303, 307, 310–
  14, 320, 331, 352, 359–61, 365–7
Linke, Angelika 50
literacy 138, 195, 346
literature 13, 15–16, 18, 20, 22–3, 27–8,
  78, 88–9, 95, 97, 100, 146, 179–80,
  189, 215, 232–3, 238, 294, 311, 328,
  331, 333–4, 338, 348
Locke, John 333, 335–7
logic 78, 137, 141, 340, 342
Löhr, Alexander 357
London 174, 178, 187
Louis XV 341
love 16, 20, 78, 91, 96–7, 145, 156–7,
  286
Lower Saxony 11
loyalty 40, 75, 108, 114, 119, 121, 174,
  196, 280, 316, 346
Lübbe, Hermann 307, 324
Lübke, Heinrich 284
Lubyanka 18, 20
Lunacharsky, Anatoly Vasilyevich 149–
  50
Luther, Martin 271, 336
luxury 187

McCarthy, Joseph 42, 248–9, 251–3, 266
MacDonnell, Francis 206, 213
MacLeish, Archibald 198, 205
MacPherson, Crawford Brough 333
magic words 27, 29–31, 56, 70, 99, 287
Mahler, Gerhard 300
Maier, Charles 280, 282
Maier, Hans 299–301, 303, 305–6, 321
Maisashvili, S. D. 87

Maisky, Ivan 174
Makashvili, Sh. K. 87
Malebranche, Nicolas 336
Malenkov, Georgy M. 262
manipulation 71–3, 106, 198, 289, 293,
  302, 307–8, 320
Mann, Reinhard 154–5
Maoism 348
Marcuse, Herbert 29, 295, 319–20, 323
Marin, Bernd 374
martyr 39, 79, 87, 94, 264, 319
Marshall Plan 281
Marx, Karl 115, 140, 143, 283, 342–4
Marxism 35–6, 75, 93, 95–6, 100, 116,
  139–43, 258, 264, 286, 305, 317,
  328, 332–4, 342, 344, 346–8
masculinity 113, 205
mask/unmask 65, 72, 74, 99, 113,
  134–5, 148, 216, 261–2, 283, 344
massacre 172, 181
masses 9, 32–3, 72–3, 78, 87–8, 91, 96,
  98, 101, 113, 119–20, 125, 142, 144,
  157, 245, 252, 259, 262, 264–5, 267,
  272–3, 285, 345–6
mass media 4, 32–3, 38–40, 43, 49, 70,
  96, 100, 169, 171–2, 179–81, 190–3,
  196, 199, 206, 248, 252–3, 268–9,
  272–3, 282–4, 287, 293–4, 304, 352,
  356, 360, 363, 369, 371
Mass Observation 182, 186
master 117
materialism 26, 75, 139, 141, 235, 257,
  335
mathematics 195, 337
Maupertuis, Pierre Louis 335
mausoleum 100
Mazzini, Giuseppe 75
meaning 7, 38, 49–50, 60, 71, 91, 130,
  209, 226, 303, 313, 341–2, 352, 360,
  366–8, 370
  changes in 3, 13, 202, 206, 212–13,
  297, 314–17
  contested 8–9, 28, 31, 120, 124,
  135–6, 147, 196–7, 252, 261, 285,
  296, 303–6, 310–11
Melikhadze, E. S. 91
memory 21, 23–4, 82, 131, 157, 217, 259,
  267, 313, 329–30, 346, 353, 365
Menshevism, Mensheviks 109–10, 112,
  115–16, 119, 122, 124, 148
Mergel, Thomas 41–3

Messelken, Hans 300

metaphor 22–3, 31, 39–40, 42–3, 47, 49, 54, 76, 97–8, 109, 137, 185, 202, 207, 212–13, 231, 251, 254, 258–60, 262, 264, 270, 273, 275, 279, 283, 307–8, 337, 359

Middle Ages 78, 217, 271, 343, 362

middle class 201, 265–7, 272–3, 302

Middle East 352, 372–4

Mielke, Erich 286

milieu 110, 119, 121, 136, 138, 169

militarism 228

military service 8, 10, 14, 47, 107, 114, 117, 123, 129–30, 132, 143, 146–7, 163–4, 178, 205, 357–8, 360

militia 77–8

Mill, John Stuart 336, 338

Miller, Max 190

Milton, John 339

minister, ministry 33, 72, 115, 171, 174–7, 180–1, 186–90, 192, 207, 221, 250, 259, 299, 358, 363

minority, minorities 6–7, 18, 25, 72, 108, 181, 245, 359, 366, 371, 373

miracle 98–9, 137

Misciatelli, Pietro 78

misogyny 21, 25

Mitten, Richard 353

mob 121, 178, 268, 273, 344

modernity, modernism 12, 75–6, 95–6, 99, 105, 169, 185, 213, 259, 290, 294, 308, 314, 326, 332

Mohler, Armin 328–9

Moltke, Helmuth James Graf von 228

monarchy 354

money 115, 158, 283, 341, 343, 345, 362, 364, 368, 370, 373–6

monument 70, 91, 100, 178, 360

Moore, George Edward 331

moral panic 197, 202, 213, 246

morale 174, 190–1, 200

morality 77, 108, 179, 256, 258, 282–4, 291, 313, 315, 317, 325, 329

Morris, William 334

Morton, Henry Vollam 179

Moscow 14, 17–18, 38–9, 83–5, 90, 97–101, 109, 122, 131, 264–5, 270–1, 273, 278

Müller-Meiningen, Ernst 253

multiculturalism 328, 354, 373

Munich 221, 225, 299, 311

murder 14–15, 18–19, 43, 47, 109, 157, 211, 228, 233, 284, 321–2, 360–1, 369

music 38, 96–8, 137, 174, 183–4, 189–92, 200–1, 250, 265, 314

Muslims 41, 371, 373

Mussolini, Benito 39–41, 46, 69–70, 76, 79, 81–2, 172, 207, 322

Muzicant, Ariel 364–71, 374–9

mysticism 77–8, 141, 337

myth 39, 69–70, 73–6, 81–3, 88–90, 92, 95–7, 99–102, 146, 178, 278, 284, 290, 338

Nagasaki 208

narcissism 124

narod (people) 88, 91, 96–7, 99, 101

nation 33, 72, 75–8, 80–1, 171, 174–5, 178, 184, 205–6, 249–51, 254, 263, 273, 276, 280–2, 285, 290, 334, 339, 345

national anthem 174, 281–2

national flag 250

nationalism 11, 75–6, 270, 273, 312, 355 methodological 51

nationalization 255, 327

National Socialism, National Socialists 7, 26, 42, 151, 153, 157–60, 162, 164–6, 169–70, 216, 221, 226, 235–9, 245, 249–50, 254–5, 268, 277–9, 284, 295, 303, 318–19, 321–2, 328–9, 353–9, 363, 369, 371–3, 379 depictions of 38–9, 43–4, 206–7 language of/in 22, 35, 42–3, 46–9, 62–6, 156, 166, 196, 235, 237, 260, 264, 268, 285, 294, 296, 306–7, 310–16, 319

National Socialist Party (NSDAP) 65, 176–7, 185

National Socialist People's Court 48, 152–3, 155, 157, 159–60, 162, 164–5, 167

navy 107, 205, 208

neo-fascists 82

neologism 69, 313

Netherlands 215

neutrality 173, 261, 354

New Deal 200–1, 266

New Economic Policy 110, 114, 116–20, 124, 131

New Left 29, 299–300, 304–5, 323–4, 332, 346–8
new man 72, 77, 99, 106, 110, 137, 142
New Right 328–9
New Social Question 325
New York 24, 252–3, 257
news 38, 170, 172, 176, 178, 180–2, 184–5, 191–2, 352
newspapers, magazines 6, 17, 19, 43, 78, 139, 144–5, 157, 170, 172, 187, 216, 235, 263, 287, 299, 301, 326, 352, 357, 361, 379
 Das Argument 319
 Critica fascista 80
 Daily Herald 189
 Daily Mirror 186
 Daily Telegraph 188–9
 Frankfurter Allgemeine 248, 254
 Kraznaya Zvezda 14
 Leatherneck 208
 Life 245, 248, 250–1, 266, 270
 News Chronicle 188
 Newsweek 248, 257, 261
 New York Times 357, 361
 Picture Post 189–91
 Pravda 15, 92
 Presse 378–9
 Profil 357, 369
 Rassegna nazionale 80
 Der Spiegel 248, 254–6, 259, 261, 268, 271, 315
 Der Standard 374–6, 379
 Star 189
 Der Stürmer 22
 Süddeutsche Zeitung 248, 252–3, 255, 265
 Time Magazine 208, 248, 257, 262–3, 269
 The Times 188
 Die Wandlung 311
 Die Welt 268
 Die Zeit 298
Nicholas, Siân 34, 38
Nicolls, Basil 184
Niethammer, Lutz 156
nihilism 121
'9/11' 41, 352
'1968' 26, 248, 268–9, 293, 305, 317, 348
Nixon, Richard 263, 294
NKVD 83

noble 150, 152
Noelle-Neumann, Elisabeth 304, 327
non-governmental organizations 34, 201, 212, 247–8
normality, normalization 37, 157, 202, 283
Northern Ireland 173, 347
Nossack, Hans Erich 219
nostalgia 44, 275, 346

oath 99–102, 250
obedience 72, 77, 321
obscurantism 139, 141
O'Casey, Sean 188
Office of War Information (OWI) 199–201, 208, 210–12
officer 107–8, 130, 229
Ogilvie, Frederick 187
opportunism 19, 25–6, 77, 97, 109, 111, 137, 166, 236, 289
opportunity 25–6, 81, 201, 309, 325–6
opposition 7, 15, 25, 28–9, 35, 48, 152, 164, 272, 309, 320, 363, 369
oral history 211
order 64–6, 294, 306, 326
Oregon 208
Orlando (Florida) 258
Orlov 140
Orwell, George 294
Oster, Hans 229–30
Ostpolitik 30, 297
othering, the 'other' 6, 43, 204, 208, 210, 212, 247, 252, 263–4, 272–3, 276, 281–2, 291, 355, 361, 365, 371
Oxford 295, 324, 333, 345, 347

Pacific Ocean 201
Pagiaro, Antonio 71
painting 38–9, 83–9, 91–2, 94, 100–2, 106
pamphlet 179, 198, 209, 341
pantomime 183
Paris 272, 342
parliament 49, 74, 187, 200, 249, 286, 297, 306, 341, 354, 363
Parnell, Thomas 251
particularism 279, 281, 325–6, 338
partisans 47, 357
partnership 173
Pascal, Blaise 336

past 60, 143, 149, 267, 340
  break with 105, 116, 146, 150, 162,
    182, 254–5, 278–80, 355
  commemoration of 82, 146, 353–4
  coming to terms with 23–4, 256,
    313–16, 318–19, 328–30, 353,
    355–8, 363, 372–3
  contests about 21, 44, 186, 268,
    277–8, 284–5, 306, 358, 374
  loss of 219
  personal deeds in 17–19, 48, 121–2,
    130, 132, 155–6, 162, 319, 357–8,
    361
  references to 359, 371
  suppression of 24, 255, 303, 353,
    357–8, 360, 363, 372
Pasternak, Boris 16, 97
patriotism 157, 197, 200, 203–5, 207,
  210, 212
peace 30, 72, 147, 172, 180–1, 189, 294,
  298, 345
Pearl Harbor 199, 205, 207–9
peasant 87, 93, 99, 106, 111–12, 116,
  119, 126–9, 132–3, 135, 137–8, 144–
  5, 238, 271, 286
Penn, William 258
people 35, 47, 71, 94, 96, 98, 111, 138,
  145, 158, 163, 199, 285–6, 291, 299,
  309, 340–1, 349
  American 42, 250, 256
  Czechoslovak 270
  English/British 173–5, 342
  French 338, 341
  of GDR 44, 275, 278–9, 282, 286,
    290–1
  German 170, 175–7, 182, 189–90,
    192, 280–1, 312
  Hungarian 264
  Italian 79
  Russian 18, 39, 174
  Soviet 86, 101
perestroika 30
perfidy 186
performance 3–4, 19, 26, 49, 97, 212,
  250, 282–3, 318, 323, 341–2
  theory 55–66
  of power 63–4
perversion 170, 179
pest control 43, 207–8
Pétain, Philippe 40
Peterloo 341

petit bourgeois 110, 114, 116, 118–19,
  121, 124, 136–8, 143, 145, 148
Petrograd 122, 126, 145–6
philology 195, 197, 232, 237
philosophy 13, 53–4, 95–6, 131, 212,
  307, 315, 319, 324, 331–3, 335–7,
  340, 342, 344, 347–8
phlegma 177
photograph 83–4, 89–90, 189–90, 245,
  268
  falsified 101
physiognomy 112–14, 119, 129, 206–9,
  266
pilgrimage 100
Pirna 234–5
playboy 186
Plekhanov, Georgi Valentinovich 140
pluralism 197, 202, 291, 370
Pocock, J. G. A. 36
poem 21–3, 25, 97–9
poet 71, 97, 141, 215, 334, 337, 339, 342
Pogodin, Nikolai Fyodorovich 100
pogrom 228
Poland 28, 115
Polenz, Peter von 313, 315–16
police 87, 94, 155, 159, 164, 284, 320,
  370, 377
political activism 26, 28, 76–9, 144,
  151–3, 156–7, 159–60, 221, 223,
  267–9, 273, 322–3, 348
political conformity 18–19, 26, 48, 166,
  238–40, 253, 275, 287–9, 291, 316
political conviction 10, 72–3, 80, 118,
  120, 123–4, 150, 156, 159–60,
  163–4, 166, 289, 332
political correctness 15, 45, 177, 296,
  310, 314, 329, 370, 377
political culture 197, 245, 247, 252, 273,
  293, 309–10, 314, 329, 346
political decision 4–5, 270, 280, 282,
  287, 290, 363, 372
political economy 131, 140
political institution 7, 105, 111, 294, 346
political legitimacy 5, 28, 39, 96–7, 143,
  276–8, 280, 283–4, 291, 321, 355
political rally 113, 191, 268, 297
political religion 40–2, 74–7, 79, 247,
  250, 258, 260, 270–1, 299, 305
political party 29, 35, 46, 71, 74–7, 82,
  95, 105, 108, 123, 152, 176, 196,
  306–7, 346, 354, 373

political party (*cont.*):
 archives 106–7
 congress 84, 108–9, 121, 125, 133,
  260, 262, 295, 297–8, 303–4, 327
 finances of 326
 headquarters 245
 historiography 92–3
 membership 10, 38, 44–5, 99,
  106–11, 114–16, 118–21, 123–37,
  139–40, 145–50, 158–9, 236–7,
  245–7, 265, 312
 organization 4, 38, 69–70, 79, 83, 90,
  106–7, 119, 124, 126, 133–6, 143–4,
  146, 158–60, 245, 266–7, 295,
  297–8, 300–1, 357–8
 policy 5, 18–19, 45, 116–17, 135, 148,
  276, 279–81, 283–4, 287, 291, 298,
  301, 307, 309, 324–8, 363
 programme 107, 115, 119, 122–3, 298,
  301, 309, 326–7
 purge 38, 44–5, 49, 93, 109–15,
  117–18, 120–2, 124–5, 129–30, 133,
  146–8
 ritual 38, 65, 96, 99–100, 108, 288
political science 36, 141, 204, 299–300,
 352
political space/sphere 41, 61, 324
political system/regime 49, 61–2, 74,
 149, 152, 196–7, 199, 238–40
 comparisons between 7, 16, 30, 46,
  71, 253–5
 dialectical character of 142
 performative construction of 66
 stability of 5, 26–30, 45–6, 96–7, 101,
  176–7, 260–1, 269–70, 276–7,
  283–4, 287–9, 291, 326, 345–6
political work 28, 120–1, 125, 139,
 157–8, 162, 225–6
politics, the political 4–5, 13, 26, 28, 36,
 61–2, 124, 142, 162, 175, 202,
 218–20, 239–41, 261, 280, 291,
 294–7, 299–301, 310, 323, 325, 349,
 354, 362, 366
 definitions of 28, 41, 49, 69, 79, 82,
  309
 downgrading of 340, 342
 interest in 107, 157, 163, 233
 reason in 73, 261
 sacralization of 75–6, 259
 and school 72
 trivialization of 308

Pope 80, 253, 270–1, 320
Popitz, Johannes 221, 228, 230
Popov, Viktorin 98
popular front 33, 347–8
popularity 185, 189, 200–1
populism 251, 354, 364–5, 373
Portugal 46
positivism 141
poster 38, 91, 102, 190, 198, 207,
 210–11, 264
posterity 216–17, 232–3
postmodernism 6
post-structuralism 196
post-totalitarianism 26, 29–30
Powell, George Allan 188, 191
Powell, John Enoch 347
power 73, 106–7, 115, 131–2, 138, 160,
 165, 169, 196, 202–3, 212, 261, 276,
 278, 308, 322, 359, 362, 368
pragmatism 142, 325
Prague 254, 272
Prague Spring 26–8, 248, 256, 269–70
Prätorius, Reiner 256
prejudice 173, 192, 353, 356, 358,
 360–1, 364, 367, 371
press 39, 70, 76, 80, 95, 109, 111, 119,
 176, 179–80, 192, 199, 252, 261,
 300, 310, 328, 358, 362–3
 see also newspapers
Pressburger, Emeric 191
pride 148, 175, 238, 263–4
Priestley, J. B. 178–9, 190
prisoner 18, 25–6, 38, 48–9, 76, 87, 94,
 151, 153, 155, 157–9, 161–3, 165–6,
 215, 239, 252, 271, 348
 in camps 22–3, 156, 182, 208, 215, 218
 of war 10–11, 17, 180
private/public 19–20, 26, 36, 40, 46–9,
 65–6, 76, 144, 149, 198, 200–2, 208,
 212, 218, 233, 237–40, 262, 283,
 289, 360
private life, privacy 159, 215, 227, 289
privilege 111, 130, 150, 362
production 144–5, 147, 150
profession 127, 129, 133, 144, 147, 170,
 187, 289, 362
progress 12, 278–9, 290, 299, 305, 315
proletarian, proletariat 77, 106–7, 110,
 112–13, 117, 119–20, 124–8, 130–4,
 136–9, 142–3, 147–9, 158, 250, 264,
 266–7, 273, 343–4, 347

Prometheus 89, 98
promise 29–30, 48, 62–4, 73, 99, 139, 163, 250, 252, 258, 305–6
propaganda 3, 17, 32–5, 38–41, 43–4, 46–9, 71–3, 77, 79–81, 95, 142–3, 148, 169–84, 188–93, 195–201, 205, 207, 209–10, 212–13, 239, 248, 276, 279–80, 282, 284, 286–7, 290, 313, 327, 363
property 78, 117–18, 144, 150, 219, 283, 333, 343, 362, 369, 373
prophecy 217–18, 325
prophet 87, 94, 148, 257–9, 337, 339
prosecutor 38, 151–2, 157, 163–4
protest 49, 187, 221, 265, 269, 320–1, 331
Protestantism 271, 336, 347
psyche 113
psychoanalysis 317, 331
psychology 109–10, 140, 142, 159, 179, 191, 352
psychotherapy 24
public/audience 4, 28, 32, 35, 38, 42, 71, 73, 83, 86, 94, 99, 102, 160, 171–4, 176, 178, 181, 183–9, 195–200, 205, 213, 253, 295, 298, 307, 314, 352, 361, 366–7
public exposure 155, 320, 376
public opinion 33–4, 169–71, 175, 182, 192–3, 196, 199, 202, 207, 246, 252, 255, 268–9, 282, 300, 304–5, 327, 353, 361, 363, 370
publicity 189, 245
purity/dirt 47, 77, 99, 106, 109, 111, 120–1, 125, 128, 131, 136, 142–3, 251, 254, 283, 285, 317, 365, 375

questionnaire 18–19, 106, 112, 115, 129, 195, 204

radicalism 121, 138–9, 145, 258, 269, 306–7, 318, 320–3, 336, 347
radio 33–4, 38–40, 70, 169–93, 199–200, 236, 352, 363
race, racism 36, 43, 72, 75, 79–81, 200, 207–8, 250, 264, 272, 339, 347, 352, 359, 369, 377–8
rage 22, 319, 341, 379
railway 115, 130, 313
rape 255
Rath, Ernst vom 228

rationalism 331, 336–7
rationality, reason 29, 73, 78, 105, 137, 183, 185, 247–8, 255, 258, 261, 340, 344
reaction 123, 138, 228, 278, 348
Reagan, Ronald 41, 257–8, 329, 348
Realpolitik 373
rebellion 89, 95, 117, 121–2, 124, 146, 273, 339
Red Army 10, 14, 17, 47, 116–18, 123, 130–2, 143, 146–7, 174, 261, 264
Red Army Faction (RAF) 321
Red Square 100–1
Reds/Whites 115, 119, 146
re-education 11, 182, 253, 264, 310, 312
reflexivity, awareness 3, 25, 31, 137, 195, 197, 239–40, 252, 295, 298, 310, 314–15, 320, 332
reform 12, 30, 72, 81, 260–1, 267, 269–70, 272, 298–9, 305, 325–6, 340
refugee 158, 176, 180, 362, 373
regeneration 71, 76
Reiss, Matthias 201
relativism 338
religion 22, 39–42, 56, 74–8, 80–1, 139, 141, 245, 250, 256–9, 264, 335–6, 338–9, 342–3, 347
renegade 248, 260, 271–2
repression 5, 15, 154, 166, 262, 265, 271, 320
Republicans (USA) 200, 249
resistance 21–2, 48, 151–2, 154–5, 157–9, 166–7, 172, 216, 220–1, 223–4, 227–31, 233, 239–40, 265, 319, 348
respect 66, 120, 192
restitution, reparation 355–6, 363–5, 368, 370, 374–5, 379
restoration 248
Reuter, Ernst 248
revenge 42, 182, 362, 370
revolution 71, 79, 85, 88–9, 91, 93–4, 109, 139–40, 142–3, 147–9, 160, 269, 294, 304–6, 322–3, 339, 343, 346, 348
  acceleration of 81
  conservative 328
  cultural 328
  defence of 121
  of 1848 322

revolution (*cont.*):
  era of 12
  French of 1789–93 40, 294, 322,
    335–9, 343
  of 1989 27, 29, 290
  Russian of 1905 130–1, 138, 140
  Russian of February 1917 113, 132,
    146
  Russian of October 1917 44, 83–4,
    91, 94, 100–2, 105–8, 110–11, 114,
    119, 121–3, 130, 132, 149, 174
  universal 116, 258
Reynolds, Quentin 186–8
rhetoric 60, 108, 275, 326, 362, 365–6,
  370, 372–3
  binary 6
  classical 31
  of difference 6
  fascist 69–72
  of inclusion 285–6
  of moral indignation 283
  official 105, 113, 201–2, 279–81,
    287–8, 291
  religious 6, 41–2, 76–7, 80–1, 96,
    99–100, 258, 264
Richter, Isabel 38, 48
Richter, Jean Paul 338
Ricœur, Paul 60
rights 23–4, 26, 78, 113, 150, 158, 164,
  176, 252–3, 265, 294
Rinser, Luise 215, 218
riot 268–70
Risorgimento 75
ritual 70, 96–7, 99–100, 250, 333
  of communication 5, 18–19, 26–9,
    31, 44–6, 64–5, 277, 288–91
  religious 22, 74–6, 99–100, 288
robots 251
Rogers, Steve 205
Rohrmoser, Günter 308
Roma, Sinti 371, 373
Romania 373
romanticism 39, 85–6, 89, 140–1
  English 334, 347
  German 334–5, 338, 340, 342, 344
  revolutionary 89, 101, 270
Rome 74, 227, 270
  ancient 80–1
Roosevelt, Franklin D. 33, 198–9,
  200–1, 205, 207, 266
Rorty, Richard 53

Rosenberg, Ethel 253
Rosenberg, Julius 253, 257, 266
Rost, Nico 215, 218
Rote Hilfe 160, 162–3
Rousseau, Jean-Jacques 335
Ruge, Arnold 342–3, 345
rumour 210
Rusinek, Bernd A. 154
Ruskin, John 334
Russel, Bertrand 331
Russia 14–16, 19, 38–40, 101, 105, 114,
  138–42, 155, 173–4, 236, 247, 254–6,
  261–3, 271, 273, 275, 294, 316
  see also Soviet Union
Russian Orthodox Church 39, 87, 141

SA 357
sabotage, saboteur 118, 197–8, 204–6,
  209–12, 283
Sabrow, Martin 291
Sacks, Harvey 56–8, 61, 63
sacrifice 11, 72, 75–9, 81, 87, 94, 114,
  143, 201, 316, 319
sadism 179
Saffire, William 293, 299
Salazar, Antonio de Oliveira 46
salvation 39, 79, 140, 178, 258
Sanadze, Korneli 87
sanctions 355, 376
sarcasm 38, 140, 170, 184, 189–90, 192
satire 38–9, 170, 190, 268, 293, 323
Sattelzeit 12, 297, 316–17
Saussure, Ferdinand de 331, 335
Savonarola, Girolamo 78
Sayers, Dorothy 188
scandal 44, 206, 277, 282–4, 326, 352,
  354, 356–60, 362–3
scapegoat 18, 371, 374
scepticism 11, 30, 141, 337, 340, 344
Schelling, Friedrich Wilhelm Joseph
  343
Schelsky, Helmut 302, 304, 306, 308,
  317, 327
Schicklgruber 186
Schiller, Friedrich 21–2
Schmidt, Helmut 300, 325
Schmitt, Carl 11, 308, 320
Scholl, Hans 221–2, 224–5
school *see* education
Schulenburg, Friedrich Werner Graf
  von der 230

Index

Schumacher, Kurt 254
Schuster, Alfredo Ildefonso 80
science 53–4, 78, 140–1, 195, 205
  of words 71
science fiction 251
Scotland 173
Searle, John R. 56, 63
secrecy 3, 48, 221, 245, 265–7, 366
  see also conspiracy
secularization, secularism 41–2, 247,
  257, 260, 273, 335–6, 339
security 202, 249, 288–9
sedition 118, 148
self 339
  conception of 19–20, 37–8, 44–5, 48,
    106, 149, 249–50, 258
  construction of 105–7, 124, 136–7,
    143, 156, 162, 166, 197, 219
  image of 170, 204, 227, 276, 353, 363
  preserving of 49
  research on 105–6
selfishness 145
self-criticism 19, 28, 250
self-deception 162
self-government 197, 202–3
self-improvement 136
self-justification 174, 355–8, 364,
  369–70, 373
self-pardoning 162
self-protection 215
self-respect 155, 159
self-restraint 108
sensationalism 179, 186, 192
seriousness 184
servant 114, 117, 145, 149
sex, sexuality 21, 159, 179, 206, 258,
  345, 361
shame 19, 33, 175
Shkiriatov, Matvei Fedorovich 111, 114
Shostakovich, Dmitri D. 174
show trial 155, 251, 283–4
Sichrovsky, Peter 369
siege 174, 206, 341
Siemsen, Hans 179
silence, silencing 15, 17, 19, 24–5, 31,
  47, 107, 204, 210–11, 309–10, 318,
  341–2, 353–4, 356–8, 360
silent majority 294
sin 258
sincerity 72–3
Singen 158

situation 5, 8, 13, 16–18, 23, 30–1, 45,
  49–50, 56, 85–6, 151, 154, 157–8,
  165–7, 215–16, 218, 226, 288–9,
  352, 359–61, 363, 365–6
Skinner, Quentin 36
slander 187
slang 185, 289
slave 344–5
slavophilism 141
Smolensk 107, 112, 114, 122–4, 150
Social Democrats 35, 109, 131, 142, 146,
  152, 332
  Austria (SPÖ) 354, 364, 368–9
  Germany (SPD) 152, 248, 254, 264,
    297–300, 302, 305, 309, 326–7
social history 35, 332–3, 340, 348–9
social market economy 302
social movements 29, 247–8, 251,
  272–3, 293, 297, 314, 317, 321, 333,
  347–8
socialism, socialists 27, 36, 44, 48, 75–6,
  97, 99, 115, 123, 142, 152, 232,
  237–8, 261, 271, 275, 279–80, 290,
  322, 326–8
Socialist Realism 16, 18, 89, 97
Socialist Revolutionaries 112
Socialist Unity Party (SED) 154, 156,
  276–87, 289–90, 312, 326
Socialist Workers' Party (SAP) 152, 157
society 9, 73, 97, 118, 123, 127, 131, 142,
  148–50, 163–4, 202, 205, 245, 248,
  251–2, 254, 258, 260, 266–7, 269,
  271, 273, 277, 279, 282–6, 291,
  294–5, 302, 305–6, 308–9, 312, 320,
  334, 340, 343, 346
sociology 65, 140–1, 203–4, 302, 308,
  317, 323–4, 327, 333
soldier 24, 47, 87–8, 90, 113, 118, 163–4,
  178, 200, 254, 264, 316, 358, 373
solidarity 276, 326
soliloquy 217, 219
sophist 125
Sorel, Georges 322
soul 40, 71, 78, 107–8, 110, 121–2, 124,
  136–8, 178, 257, 341
sovereignty 308
Soviet system 160
Soviet Union 5, 27, 40, 43–6, 83–102,
  105–50, 173–4, 245, 247, 250,
  253–4, 256, 258, 261–2, 270–1, 277
  see also Russia

soviets 122
space, territoriality 42, 277, 280, 282, 290, 311, 313
Spain 46, 206
specialist 111, 116, 118–21, 124, 147
speech act 28, 38, 50, 56, 62–4, 151, 195, 197, 210–11, 224, 239–40, 314, 318, 321–3, 332–3, 359–60, 367
spirit 18, 77, 111, 124, 132, 136, 143, 147, 174, 178, 181, 336, 340, 343, 362
Spivak, Gayatri Chakravorty 344
spy, espionage 159, 178, 183–4, 191, 197–8, 204–6, 209–13, 217, 247, 251, 253, 257, 266
Squadrismo 77–8
SS 16, 23, 190, 327–8, 373
Stalin, Joseph 15–17, 19, 38–40, 45, 83–102, 172, 174, 247, 251, 254, 257, 259, 260–1, 266
Stalingrad 10, 15, 18, 101, 174, 230
Stalinism 14–16, 26, 40, 43, 45, 88, 92, 95, 99, 102, 155, 254, 260–2, 267, 332
Staronosev, Petr 89
Stasi (GDR State security) 156, 284, 286
state 72, 75, 87, 102, 142, 169, 213, 280, 282, 290, 293–4, 302–3, 306, 346–7, 354–5, 370, 372
  apparatus 5, 18, 203
  Hegelian notion of 80
  idolization of 80
  theory of 203
state visit 64, 265, 329, 358
statistics 45, 127–8, 134–6
status 110
Steinbuch, Karl 304
stenography 106
stereotype 21, 25, 31, 36, 42–3, 170, 175, 177–8, 187, 207–9, 263, 310, 352, 361–2, 364, 366, 368, 370, 373–4
Sternberger, Dolf 311–13, 316, 318
Stevenson, Adlai 251
Stieglitz, Olaf 37–8
stigmatization 7–8, 138, 267, 277, 281–3, 291
story-telling 25, 44–5, 66, 136–7, 155, 161–2, 165–6, 179, 206
Storz, Gerhard 311
Strasser, Otto 180
Strauss, David Friedrich 343

Strauß, Franz Josef 268, 297, 326
strike 87–8, 131, 346, 348
structuralism 313–14, 331
structures/agency 35, 50, 333, 344
structures/semantics 9, 12, 31, 50, 167, 359
students
  America (USA) 195
  France 269
  Germany 216, 221, 240, 267–9, 273, 293, 296, 299, 304–5, 318–20, 322, 324, 357
  Northern Ireland 347
  Soviet Union 112–13, 115, 118, 121–2, 124, 126–37, 144–5, 147, 150, 152
Stülpnagel, Carl Heinrich von 229
Sturm und Drang 334, 336, 338
Stürmer, Michael 329
subjectivity 105–6, 139, 151, 197, 202, 204, 210
submarine 211
subordinate 117
subversion 5, 206, 225–6, 228
Sudeten Germans 368
suicide 321–2
survival 3, 23, 45, 154–5, 165–6
Süskind, Wilhelm 311
suspicion 107, 115, 131, 155, 209–11, 250, 333, 362
Superman 205
Swaffer, Hannen 189
swastika 176, 179
Sweden 354
Switzerland, Swiss 158, 328, 373
symbol 5, 23, 31, 39, 44, 54–5, 60, 70, 74–7, 99, 101, 113, 191, 202, 219, 287, 289, 337, 342, 344
symbolic action 28–9, 40, 65, 322–3
sympathy 116, 146, 152, 182, 189
syndicalism, syndicalist 122–3, 147

taboo 17, 21, 39, 354, 372
tact 114
Tallents, Stephen George 187–8
Tammerfors 88
Tartars 18
taste 180, 188, 192–3, 337
Tausk, Walter 216–18
tax 116, 373, 376
Taylor, Alan John Percival 346
Tbilisi 83, 86, 90, 93

technology 29, 107, 290, 304–5
telegram 187
telephone 19, 184, 187, 191
television 4, 58, 281, 352, 363, 369–70, 377–8
terror 16, 18, 26, 37, 43, 45, 83, 255
terrorism 305, 321–2, 325
Thälmann, Ernst 284
Thatcher, Margaret 36, 346, 348
theatre 22–3, 27, 100–1, 179, 283, 318
theatricality 61–3, 96, 283
theory/practice 25–6, 31–2, 35, 37, 96, 119, 123, 125, 130, 137, 139–42, 144, 306, 318, 321, 324, 339–40, 347–8
Theresienstadt 22
Thessaloniki 358
Third World 272
Thompson, Dorothy 186
Thompson, E. P. 35–6, 282, 323, 332–4, 340, 345, 347
toast (speech act) 17, 66, 94
Toidze, Moise 87
Tōjō, Hideki 207
tolerance 133, 177, 253
Tolstoy, Leo 140, 150, 174
Tomsk 125–30, 132, 134–5, 141, 230
tone, sound 17, 31, 170, 176, 183–6, 189, 192, 360, 368
  see also voice
Tooke, John Horne 337
topos 356, 364, 366, 369–70
torture 18, 155
totalitarianism 7, 11, 26, 33, 66, 70–1, 75, 80–1, 206, 215–20, 222, 227, 232, 234–5, 237–41, 289, 294, 296–7, 299, 301, 326
  term coined by anti-fascists 74
  theory 254
trade unions 152, 302, 321, 346
tradition 10, 35–6, 39–41, 73, 80–1, 89, 96, 105, 113, 174, 207, 245, 247, 249, 255–8, 268, 272–3, 281, 290, 310, 332–5, 340–2, 344–5, 347, 349, 355–6, 361–2, 374
traditionalism 73, 96–9
Train, Jack 184
translation 102, 109–10, 204, 304
Traven, B. 221
treason, traitor 37, 42, 108, 152, 159–60, 166, 197, 205–6, 210–11, 250, 270, 281, 361, 370

Treblinka 14
Trotsky, Leo 17, 99–100, 113
Trotskyists 152
Trott zu Solz, Friedrich Adam Freiherr von 228–9
Trubetskoi, Evgeny 141
truth 29, 78, 85–6, 93, 105, 124, 139, 141–2, 155, 187, 198, 201, 215–17, 235, 238, 255, 257, 259, 289, 294, 303–4, 324, 331, 337–8, 341–3, 367
tsar, tsarist regime 87, 94, 112, 114–15, 122, 131, 142, 150, 255
Tsulukidze, Alexander 88
Turks 371
Tver 145–6

Uhland, Ludwig 21
Ukraine 14, 20
Ulbricht, Walter 43, 254, 262, 266, 270, 276, 281, 286, 290
Ulrich of Augsburg 259
underground activity 93–4, 110, 112, 157–60, 247, 262, 271–2
unemployment 122, 158, 325
United Nations 173, 356–8
universalism 107, 143, 279–81, 328, 331, 336–7
university 8, 10–11, 126–8, 131–4, 137, 141–7, 150, 225, 233, 266, 295, 299–300, 318–19, 321–2, 324, 345, 352
Uritsky, Moisei Solomonovich 109
utilitarianism 137
utopianism 11–12, 124, 157, 250, 255, 278–9, 305, 322

Vansittart, Robert Gilbert 176–7, 181–2, 189
Vatican 270
Venturi, Franco 70
Vepkhvadze, Ivan 85, 88
victim 24, 38, 93, 181–2, 190, 240, 268, 320, 353–6, 363–4, 368, 372–3, 379
victimization 6–7
victory 32, 94, 100, 116, 123, 147, 180, 191, 339
Vienna 21, 24, 351–2, 357–8, 360, 364–71, 374–5, 384–5
Vietcong 271–2
Vietnam 248, 267, 271–3
vigilance 111, 183, 198, 204–6, 209–12

violence 5, 10, 14, 30, 37, 43, 77–8, 108–9, 117, 155, 157–60, 166–7, 185, 233, 236, 247, 254–5, 258, 262–6, 273, 317, 321–2, 339, 343
virtue 131, 317
visual image 4–6, 38–9, 49, 83–9, 190–1, 202–4, 207–11, 245, 264, 268, 354, 373
Vitebsk 130
Voegelin, Eric 299, 319
voice 18–19, 38, 143, 145, 154, 184, 192, 216, 294, 298, 320, 341
  see also tone
Volga 118
Volk (people) 163
Volksgemeinschaft 48, 162–4, 166, 250, 310
Volodarsk 126
vozhd' (leader) 83, 85, 89–92, 97, 100–2
vulgarity 188–9

Waldheim, Kurt 352, 354, 356–62, 368, 371
Wales 10, 173, 181
Walker, Patrick Gordon 182
war 12, 96, 115–16, 131, 163–4, 195, 197, 200, 219, 255, 271–2, 294, 315–16, 339, 344, 346
  First World War 32–3, 76, 107, 113, 122, 169, 175, 178, 180, 198, 345
  in Iraq 352
  Italian–Ethiopian 80
  memories of 21, 180
  in politics 308–9, 325–7, 329, 378
  Second World War 8, 10, 13–15, 34, 38, 43, 48, 81, 101, 152–3, 163, 169–84, 190–3, 195, 197–9, 201–2, 204–7, 212–13, 221, 245, 247–8, 269, 327, 347, 354, 360–1, 372
  Vietnam war 248, 267, 271–3
  see also Cold War
Warsaw 116, 141
Warsaw Pact 269
Washington, DC 200, 376
Washington (state) 208
we/them 43, 138–9, 286, 355
Wehrmacht 10, 354, 358, 360, 373
Weimar Republic 278, 305–6, 326
Weiße Rose 152, 216, 221–2, 224–5, 227, 319

Weizäcker, Richard von 329
welfare state 327, 354
Werfel, Franz 303
West, Western 11, 16, 28–9, 33–4, 42, 196, 238, 248, 256, 258–9, 261, 272, 281, 353–5
whisper 3, 18, 23, 210
White, Hayden 54, 348
White Army 98, 130
will 71, 77, 123, 142, 161, 164, 166, 219, 233
Williams, Raymond 8–10, 13, 19, 31, 35–6, 50, 332–4, 340, 345
Winkler, Alan 199
Wisconsin 266
witch hunt 252–3, 378
Wittgenstein, Ludwig 7, 331–2
Witzleben, Erwin von 299
Wodak, Ruth 7, 36, 42
Wodehouse, Pelham Grenville 186–9, 192
word play 367–8, 377
World Jewish Congress (WJC) 357–8, 361, 379
world politics 163, 206, 249, 272
work 16, 57, 84, 109, 112–13, 115, 117–21, 124–5, 128, 132, 139, 144–5, 147, 163, 207, 225–6, 238, 302
work camp 23
workers, working class 10, 36, 43, 45, 86–8, 90, 93–5, 106–9, 111–13, 117–21, 126–32, 134–5, 137–9, 142–5, 147–9, 158–60, 163, 186, 209, 238, 250, 257, 265, 286, 298, 313, 323, 340–7

xenophobia 291

Yale 266
'yellow peril' 207
Yiddish 360
youth 20–1, 79–80, 87, 121, 139, 162, 170, 178–9, 182, 185, 205, 239, 269, 273, 278–9, 289–90, 305, 317
Yugoslavia 357
Yule, George 367
Yutkevich, Sergei I. 100

Zhdanov, Andrei 89
Zinoviev, Grigory 109–10